INTELLIGENT INFORMATION PROCESSING II

IFIP – The International Federation for Information Processing

IFIP was founded in 1960 under the auspices of UNESCO, following the First World Computer Congress held in Paris the previous year. An umbrella organization for societies working in information processing, IFIP's aim is two-fold: to support information processing within its member countries and to encourage technology transfer to developing nations. As its mission statement clearly states,

> *IFIP's mission is to be the leading, truly international, apolitical organization which encourages and assists in the development, exploitation and application of information technology for the benefit of all people.*

IFIP is a non-profitmaking organization, run almost solely by 2500 volunteers. It operates through a number of technical committees, which organize events and publications. IFIP's events range from an international congress to local seminars, but the most important are:

- The IFIP World Computer Congress, held every second year;
- Open conferences;
- Working conferences.

The flagship event is the IFIP World Computer Congress, at which both invited and contributed papers are presented. Contributed papers are rigorously refereed and the rejection rate is high.

As with the Congress, participation in the open conferences is open to all and papers may be invited or submitted. Again, submitted papers are stringently refereed.

The working conferences are structured differently. They are usually run by a working group and attendance is small and by invitation only. Their purpose is to create an atmosphere conducive to innovation and development. Refereeing is less rigorous and papers are subjected to extensive group discussion.

Publications arising from IFIP events vary. The papers presented at the IFIP World Computer Congress and at open conferences are published as conference proceedings, while the results of the working conferences are often published as collections of selected and edited papers.

Any national society whose primary activity is in information may apply to become a full member of IFIP, although full membership is restricted to one society per country. Full members are entitled to vote at the annual General Assembly, National societies preferring a less committed involvement may apply for associate or corresponding membership. Associate members enjoy the same benefits as full members, but without voting rights. Corresponding members are not represented in IFIP bodies. Affiliated membership is open to non-national societies, and individual and honorary membership schemes are also offered.

INTELLIGENT INFORMATION PROCESSING II
IFIP TC12/WG12.3 International Conference on Intelligent Information Processing (IIP2004) October 21-23, 2004, Beijing, China

Edited by

Zhongzhi Shi and Qing He
Key Laboratory of Intelligent Information Processing,Institute of Computing Technology, Chinese Academy of Sciences

 Springer

Editors: Zhonzhi Shi and Qing He
Institue of Computing TechnologyKey
Laboratory of Int. Infor. Process.
Chinese Academy of Sciences
Beijing 100080, China

email: shizz@ics.ict.ac.cn; heq@ics.ict.ac.cn

A C.I.P. Catalogue record for this book is available
from the Library of Congress.

Shi, Zhongzhi
    Intelligent Information Processing II, edited by Shi, Zhongzhi and He, Qing

ISBN 1-4899-8798-3   ISBN 0-387-23152-8 (eBook) Printed on acid-free paper.

9 8 7 6 5 4 3 2 1   SPIN 11323952 (HC) / 11324034 (eBK)

springeronline.com

Contents

Welcome Address

Dear Colleagues,

The International Conference on Intelligent Information Processing is opening. On behalf of the organizers, we welcome all scientists and practitioners who are interested in Intelligent Information Processing around the world participate in this event. The world is quickly stepping into the Information Age successfully on one hand, as well as problematically on the other hand. It is well recognized nowadays that Intelligent Information Processing provides the key to the Information Age. Intelligent Information Processing supports the most advanced productive tools that are said to be able to change human life and the world itself. However, experiences of recent years also clearly show that there is no way a lead straight into the Information Age. Rather, people become aware of more and more questions about Intelligent Information Processing. The conference provides a forum for engineers and scientists in academia, university and industry to present their latest research findings in all aspects of Intelligent Information Processing.

As scientists, professors, engineers, entrepreneurs, or government officials all over the world, we have the responsibility to understand the truth and explore an effective way to a better life in the Information Age. This is the motivation of IIP2004.

B. Neuman
J. Kephart
S. Doshita
Conference Chairmen of the IIP2004

Greetings from Chairs' of Program Committee

Dear colleagues and friends:

First of all, we would like to extend to you our warmest welcome and sincere greetings on behalf of the Technical Program Committee of the International Conference on Intelligent Information Processing, ICIIP04-Beijing.

This is the second International Conference on Intelligent Information Processing. We received over 270 papers, of which 66 papers are included in this program. We are grateful for the dedicated work of both the authors and the referees, and we hope these proceedings will continue to bear fruit over the years to come. Papers were submitted and reviewed by several referees.

A conference such as this cannot succeed without help from many individuals who contributed their valuable time and expertise. We want to express our sincere gratitude to the program committee members and referees, who invested many hours for reviews and deliberations. They provided detailed and constructive review reports that will significantly improve the papers included in the program.

We are very grateful to have the sponsorship of the following organizations: IFIP TC12/WG12.3, The China Computer Federation and Chinese Association of Artificial Intelligence

We hope all of you enjoy this diverse and interesting program.

Zhongzhi Shi
Institute of Computing Technology,
Chinese Academy of Sciences

The Organizations of the Conference

General Chairs

B. Neumann (Germany)　　J. Kephart(USA)　　S. Doshita(Japan)

Program Chairs

Z. Shi (China)　　A. Aamodt (Norway)　　V.Honavar (USA)

PC Committee

N. Bredeche (France)

Z. Bubnicki(Poland)

P. Chen (USA)

H. Chi (China)

E. Durfee (USA)

B. Faltings (Switzerland)

T. Finin (USA)

I. Futo (Hungary)

N. Gibbins (UK)

F. Giunchiglia (Italy)

V. Gorodetski (Russia)

J. Hendler (USA)

T. Ishida (Japan)

D. Leake (USA)

J. Lee (Korea)

D. Lin (Canada)

J. Liu (Hong Kong)

R. Lu (China)

R. Meersman (Belgium)

H. Motoda (Japan)

M. Musen (USA)

G. Osipov (Russia)

M. Sasikumar (India)

Y. Shi（USA）

R. Studer (Germany)

R. Sun (USA)

M. Stumptner (Australia)

K. Wang (Canada)

B. Wah (USA)

S. Willmott (Spain)

X. Yao (UK)

J. Yang(Korea)

P. Yu (USA)

Eric Yu (Canada)

C. Zhang (Australia)

N. Zhang (Hong Kong)

Y. Zhong (China)

Z. Zhou (China)

Refereers List

N. Bredeche (France)
Z. Bubnicki(Poland)
P. Chen (USA)
H. Chi (China)
E. Durfee (USA)
B. Faltings (Switzerland)
T. Finin (USA)
I. Futo (Hungary)
N. Gibbins (UK)
F. Giunchiglia (Italy)
V. Gorodetski (Russia)
J. Hendler (USA)
T. Ishida (Japan)
D. Leake (USA)
J. Lee (Korea)
D. Lin (Canada)
J. Liu (Hong Kong)
R. Lu (China)
R. Meersman (Belgium)

H. Motoda (Japan)
M. Musen (USA)
G. Osipov (Russia)
M. Sasikumar (India)
Y. Shi（USA）
R. Studer (Germany)
R. Sun (USA)
M. Stumptner (Australia)
K. Wang (Canada)
B. Wah (USA)
S. Willmott (Spain)
X. Yao (UK)
J. Yang(Korea)
P. Yu (USA)
Eric Yu (Canada)
C. Zhang (Australia)
N. Zhang (Hong Kong)
Y. Zhong (China)
Z. Zhou (China)

Keynote Speech

Keynote Speaker: Ian Horrocks

Title: Reasoning with Expressive Description Logics: Logical Foundations for the Semantic Web

Abstract: Description Logics (DLs) are a family of logic based Knowledge Representation formalisms descended from semantic networks and KL-ONE. They are distinguished by having formal (model theoretic) semantics, and by the provision of (sound and complete) inference services, with several highly optimised implementations now being available. DLs have a wide range of applications, but are perhaps best know as ontology languages (they provide the basis for recent "Semantic Web" ontology languages such as OIL, DAML+OIL and OWL). In this talk I will give a brief history of DLs and of DL applications, in particular their application in the context of the Semantic Web. If time permits, I will then give an overview of the reasoning techniques that are employed by state of the art DL implementations, and which enable them to be effective in realistic applications, in spite of the high worst case complexity of their basic inference problems. Finally, I will point out some interesting areas for future research, in particular those related to the Semantic Web application area.

Biography: Ian Horrocks is a Professor of Computer Science at the University of Manchester. His FaCT system revolutionised the design of Description Logic systems, redefining the notion of tractability for DLs and establishing a new standard for DL implementations. He is a member of both the Joint EU/US Committee on Agent Markup Languages and the W3C

Web Ontology Language working group, and was heavily involved in the development of the OIL, DAML+OIL and OWL ontology languages. He has published widely in leading journals and conferences, winning the best paper prize at KR'98. He is/was a member of the programme/editorial committees of numerous international conferences, workshops and journals, was the program chair of the 2002 International Semantic Web Conference and the Semantic Web track chair for the 2003 World Wide Web Conference.

Invited Speech

Invited Speaker: Toru Ishida
Department of Social Informatics,
Kyoto University Yoshida-Honmachi,
Kyoto 606-8501,
Japan
TEL 81 75 753 4821 FAX 81 75 753 4820
E-mail ishida@i.kyoto-u.ac.jp
WWW http://www.lab7.kuis.kyoto-u.ac.jp/~ishida/

Title: Mega-Navigation: Multi-Agent Navigation for Millions

Abstract: In this talk, I will propose a new digital city application, called mega navigation, that covers millions of people or vehicles with GPS. We apply multiagent technology to realize mega navigation such as wide-area traffic control, crisis management in metropolitan areas, and large-scale event navigation. We implement the mega navigation platform by combining Q and Caribbean: Q is a scenario description language for socially situated agents, and Caribbean is a mega-scale agent server. We use a new system design method called society-centered design to develop complex applications that are to be embedded into human society. In this method, we first conduct simulations consisting of a million software agents. We then perform participatory simulations, where some of the agents are replaced by real humans. We then move to the real city, and conduct augmented experiments, where real-world participants are augmented by socially situated agents.

Biography: Toru Ishida is a full professor of Kyoto University, from 1993, a research professor of NTT Communication Science Laboratories from 1998, a visiting professor of Shanghai Jiao Tong University from 2002, and IEEE fellow from 2002. I was a guest professor at Institut fuer Informatik, Technische Universitaet Muenchen in 1996, an invited professor at Le Laboratoire d'Informatique de Paris 6, Pierre et Marie Curie in 2000 and 2003, and a visiting professor at Institute for Advanced Computer Studies, University of Maryland in 2002. I have been working on autonomous agents and multiagent systems for more than twenty years. My research contribution can be classified into the three categories: production systems, multiagent search, and community computing. In production systems, I first proposed parallel rule firing, distributed rule firing and introduced organizational self-design for adapting to environmental changes. In multiagent search, I worked on realtime path finding problems and distributed constraint satisfaction problems, the two major search problems in AI. For path finding problems, I extended realtime search to be capable to utilize and improve previous experiments, and to adapt to the dynamically changing goals. In community computing, I proposed a concept of communityware to support the process of organizing diverse and amorphous groups of people, while groupware mainly addressed the collaborative work of already-organized people. My team developed mobile assistants and tried out them at international conference ICMAS96 with 100 PDAs with wireless phones. We also worked on a 3D interaction space called FreeWalk/Q, and applied it to Digital City Kyoto. I published three LNCS proceedings and created a network among digital cities. I have been working for conferences on autonomous agents and multiagent systems including MACC/JAWS (Japanese Workshop), PRIMA (Asia/Pacific Workshop), ICMAS / AAMAS (International Conference). I was a program co-chair of the second ICMAS and a general co-chair of the first AAMAS. I am an associate editor of Journal on Autonomous Agents and Multi-Agent Systems (Kluwer) and a co-editor-in-chief of Journal on Web Semantics (Elsevier).

Invited Speaker: Jung-Jin Yang
Professor Dr. Jung-Jin Yang
School of Computer Science and Information Engineering
The Catholic University of Korea
43-1 YeockGok-dong WonMi-gu
Bucheon-si Kyunggi-do, Seoul Korea
Email: jungjin@catholic.ac.kr

Fax: +82 2 2164 4377
Phone: +82 2 2164 4777

Title: Semantic Search Agent System Applying Semantic Web Techniques

Abstract: Semantic analysis occurs both during the collection and classification phases and at the final stage of users search. When users submit a query, the Semantic Search Agent understands the meaning of the request according to their work context, finds relevant documents, and searches on a pre-qualified corpus. In order to infer and extract relevant information by weaving through heterogeneous databases with different schema and terminologies, the standardized way of integrating heterogeneous data is necessary. The obtained results also need be of the highest relevance for the information obtained is in effect right away. The talk describes OnSSA (Ontology-based Semantic Search Agent). It aims to develop a distributed agent-based architecture of semantic search and communication using community-specific ontologies and to equip ontologies with an inference layer grounded in W3C standards. The community-specific ontologies of OnSSA in this talk are in medicine.

Biography: Dr. Jung-Jin Yang is an assistant professor in the School of Computer Science and Information Engineering at the Catholic University of Korea. Currently, she is a head of the Division of Information System Engineering, and its research group is for Intelligent Distributed Information System – IDIS Lab. Her research group cooperates on regular basis with the company of 4HumanTech in Seoul Korea, that is a bio-informatics company. Her main research interests are in Intelligent Autonomous Agents and Multi-Agent System, Information Retrieval, Machine Learning, Ontological Engineering and User Modeling. In particular, her research is more focused in both learning and building user models to understand users better and modeling and building autonomous interface agents to provide continuous and unobstructive assists to users. As relevant research, her dissertation is directly related to the automated induction of user models bridging theory and practice. The knowledge acquisition about users is achieved through individual human-computer interactions gathered from real data in order to predict and assess user behaviors. She's been involved in a research project developing a case-based planning and execution system that is designed to work under conditions of limited computational resources and an incomplete domain theory. Later, She's participated in a project with a research team working on large scale, multi-agent, and distributed mission planning and execution employing intelligent user interfaces, hybrid reasoning and mobile agent technology with Prof. Eugene Santos Jr. at the University of

Connecticut supported by AFIT (Air Force Office for Scientific Research) 2000-2001. As recent research of hers, the study of Semantic Web applicability in bio-informatics systems and the development of the agent system within the Semantic Web was directed in order to produce and exchange useful bio-medical information by dealing with heterogeneous representations and storing schema of bio-related data. The work, which she worked as PI, was supported by Korean Science and Engineering Foundation, KISTEP 2002-2004.

Invited Speaker: Honghua Dai
Daekin University, Australia

Title: Software Warehouse and Software Mining: The Impact of Data Mining to Software Engineering

Abstract: Automating Software Engineering is the dream of software Engineers for decades. To make this dream to come to true, data mining can play an important role. Our recent research has shown that to increase the productivity and to reduce the cost of software development, it is essential to have an effective and efficient mechanism to store, manage and utilize existing software resources, and thus to automate software analysis, testing, evaluation and to make use of existing software for new problems. This paper firstly provides a brief overview of traditional data mining followed by a presentation on data mining in broader sense. Secondly, it presents the idea and the technology of software warehouse as an innovative approach in managing software resources using the idea of data warehouse where software assets are systematically accumulated, deposited, retrieved, packaged, managed and utilized driven by data mining and OLAP technologies. Thirdly, we presented the concepts and technology and their applications of data mining and data matrix including software warehouse to software engineering. The perspectives of the role of software warehouse and software mining in modern software development are addressed. We expect that the results will lead to a streamlined high efficient software development process and enhance the productivity in response to modern challenges of the design and development of software applications.

Biography: Dr Honghua Dai joined the School of Information Technology at Deakin University in Australia at the start of 1999. Prior to that Honghua was on the faculty of the University of New England. Before that, he was a research fellow in Monash University worked in the Minimum Message Length Principle Research Group. From 1983 to 1989, Dr Dai was a scientist in the Institute of Atmosphere Physics, Academia Sinica. Dr. Honghua Dai is the leader of the Data Mining and Machine Learning group at Deakin University. His research interests include Data Mining and Machine Learning, Minimum Message Length principle, Knowledge based systems and e-Systems, Rough set theory based systems, Opportunity/risks discovery, Data mining for Software Engineering and Knowledge Engineering. His most recent academic work has focused on Rough set theory based Inexact Field Learning, MML-based Causal Discovery, anomaly detection, data mining for Software Engineering and Knowledge Engineering, the development of advanced algorithms and optimization techniques for mining beyond data mining, and the enabling of Web technologies to facilitate E-systems. Dr. Dai has published more than 100 papers in refereed journals and conferences. Dr. Dai is currently the Program Committee Co-Chair of the 8th Pacific-Asia Conference on data mining and machine learning, Asia-Australia Contact Editor of the Informatics International Journal, Guest editor of the International Journal on Software Engineering and Knowledge Engineering, and the guest editor of the Informatica: An international journal of computing and informatics. Dr Dai completed his first degree in computational methods at Nanjing University in China, M.Sc. Degree in Software Engineering from Chinese Academy of Sciences, and he received his Ph.D in Computer Science from the RMIT University in 1995.

Invited Speaker: Jean-Luc Koning
Inpg-Esisar
50 rue La_emas - BP 54, 26902 Valence cedex 9, France
Email : Jean-Luc.Koning@esisar.inpg.fr

Title : Protocol Operational Semantics for Multiagent Systems

Abstract: In this invited talk, I will present a system for representing interaction protocols called POS which is both Turing complete and determine a complete semantics of protocols. This work is inspired by the Structured Operational Semantics in programming languages. I will precisely define POS and illustrate its power on extended examples. POS is a general agent conversation protocol engineering formalism that has proved efficient for the design of communities of software information agents. I will also show that POS is also valuable for robotic agents which have to operate in real time, like in the case of robot-soccer. It shows how an inherently symbolic abstract system like POS can be neatly integrated with agents whose internal architecture is reactive and relies on bottom-up behavior-based techniques.

Biography: Sep. 1987 _ Oct. 1990 Ph.D. in Computer Science, _Handling antagonistic decision rules for knowledge base systems_, University of Toulouse, France. Sep. 1985 _ June 1987 M.S. in Computer Science, _Use of Markov models for phonetic decoding_, University of Toulouse, France. Sep. 1982 _ June 1985 B.S. in Mathematics and Computer Science, University of Toulouse, France. Research and Teaching Experience Positions Vice-Director LCIS research laboratory, INPG, France. Dean of Education Computer and Network Engineering Department, Esisar, France.
Full Professor Technological University of Grenoble (INPG), Department of Computer Science, Research scientist Carnegie Mellon University, school of Computer Science, Pittsburgh, USA, (1990_1992).
Responsibilities
_ Leader of a sino-french advanced research project with the Chinese Academy of Sciences
_ Participant in the GEOMED research project sponsored by the European community.
_ Co-leader in a French national research project on Telecommunication.
_ Consultant for industrial projects in applied Computer Science.
_ Participant in the DARPA and AFOSR research project F49620-90-C-0003.

Invited Speaker: Markus Stumptner

Title: Model-Based Diagnosis and Debugging

Abstract: Model-based Reasoning was originally based on the realization that the description of physical devices and systems in declarative fashion can dramatically facilitate the flexibility of knowledge base construction when reasoning about the systems' behavior and function. Traditionally the main application for this has been in Model-Based Diagnosis where generic reasoning algorithms are applied to models (i.e., formal declarative descriptions) of basic components from a particular domain to identify and rank faults in complex systems composed from these components, in the presence of incomplete information and multiple simultaneous faults. Extensions of the paradigm have covered testing, repair and reconfiguration, and for several years also the application of model-based diagnosis to software artifacts. This area, model-based debugging, poses challenges both in the different kinds of models required and in the difficulties posed by finding diagnoses in a design environment. The talk will present the genesis of Model-Based Debugging from its diagnosis origins and the state of the art in MBD methods.

Biography: Markus Stumptner obtained his Ph.D. at the Databases and AI Group of Vienna University of Technology in 1990. He originally worked in Database Theory, Transaction Management, and Data Modeling and later led a series of projects in Model-Based Reasoning with industrial applications in intelligent product configuration, and model-based diagnosis of VLSI designs. His current main research areas are model-based debugging and the use of behavior descriptions for software and database integration.

MODEL ORGANIZATION CONSTRAINTS IN MULTI-AGENT SYSTEM

Xinjun Mao and Jiajia Chen
Department of Computer Science, National University of Defense Technology, China.
Email:xjmao21@21cn.com

Abstract: The organization concept is an important abstraction to analyze and design multi-agent system. In this paper, we argue, the organization constraints should be explicitly modeled and reasoned when developing multi-agent system. The characteristics of organization constraint are discussed, a systematic method to model and reason the organization constraints is put forward and a case is studied.

Key words: Multi-agent system, Organization Constraint, Maintenance Goal

1.   INTRODUCTION

Agent-oriented computing is rapidly emerging as a powerful paradigm for developing complex software system [1]. It provides us a number of high level abstract concepts to understand, model, analyze and design the entities and interactions in the complex system such as autonomous agent, social coordination, etc. Based on these concepts, there have been several attempts to develop the methodologies in support of analysis and design of multi-agent system such as Gaia[4], MaSE[5,6], AUML, etc. Recently, more and more agent-oriented methodologies borrow concepts and ideas from sociology and organization discipline to model and analyze multi-agent system such as role, responsibility, permission, organization, etc [1,2,3,4,6], based on which multi-agent system is modeled as an organization where there are a number of roles, each role has its tasks, responsibilities, and goals, different roles need to interact with each other to achieve their design objectives.

The organization abstraction and metaphor is important when developing multi-agent system. First, more and more multi-agent systems nowadays are intended to support real-world organizations, such as electric commerce, enterprise workflow management, etc. In such cases, an organization-based abstract and model can reduce the conceptual distance between real-word application and the software system. Therefore, it simplifies the development of the system and supports modeling the system in a natural fashion. Secondly, the organization abstract gives us a way to incorporate such high level concepts as role, responsibility, rule, etc to understand and model multi-agent system, which enables us to specify and analyze multi-agent system without considering the low-level and heterogeneous information. Such a way is natural and easy to understand not only for the software developer, but also for the stakeholders, users, etc.

In real-world, organization constraint is one of the organization elements and widely exists in applications in order to restrict the behaviors of autonomous agents in the organization. It defines the operation rules and guarantees the organization to behave in a consistent and coherent way. To model such organization constrain explicitly is of particular importance to understand, specify and analyze the system requirements, and further guide the design and implementation of multi-agent system.

Although organization metaphor and abstraction has gained many attentions, and organization rule concept has been integrated into some agent oriented methodologies like Gaia, MaSE, etc., there is little work to systematically analyze the characteristics of organization constraints. The organization constrains in multi-agent system are maybe complex, therefore it is necessary and helpful to provide a systematical method to model, analyze and reason them. The reminders of the paper are structured as follows. Section2 explains the characteristics of organization constrains. A systematical method to model and reason organization constraints is put forward by extending *i** framework in section3. Section4 introduces the related works. At last conclusions are made.

2.   CHARACTERISTICS OF ORGANIZATION CONSTRAINTS

In order to discuss the organization constraint and its characteristics, let us firstly consider a simple example from electric commerce application. Some company intends to develop a web system (called as InfoCenter system) based on Internet to publish the consuming and producing information about some kinds of products (e.g., computer sale, etc.) for its customers all around the world. The users that are the customers of the company and should have a valid account can post its consuming or producing information in the system. System can also automatically and actively send the posted information to any valid users who may concern about by semantics-based match analysis. Therefore, the consuming and producing information can be obtained and shared by the relevant customers in the system and they can further to conduct some business deals such as negotiations or bargains. In addition, the application has the following global constraints information: (1) All users who want to post information should have a unique and valid account; (2) The user should be truthful, he can not post the incorrect and unknown information; (3) system should guarantee that the valid user should log on the system before posting information. In general, organization constrain has such characteristics described as follows.

– Restricting system's elements

In most of cases, the organization constraint will restrict the elements in the system. Particularly, it will restrict the behaviors and plan choices of agents and the interactions among them in multi-agent system. For example, according to the third constrain in the sample, system can not permit the user to post information if he has not logged on.

– Global

In general, the organization constrain is global and will restrict all of the elements in the organization.

– Mutually Consistent

The multiple organization constrains in one organization should be consistent. It will be impossible that an application has organization constraints φ and $\neg\varphi$. If that so, the agents in the organization will be confused and don't know well which organization constraints should be obeyed and the system may disorder. For example, you should not require that the users be not only truthful but also untruthful. However, the organization constraints of multiple organizations may be inconsistent.

– Satisfiable

The organization constraints should be satisfiable, which means the agents in the organization should have some effective way to obey or respect them. The unsatisfiable organization constraints will be meaningless because they will never be obeyed.

– Consistent With Agent's Goal

The organization constraints should be consistent with the agent's goal. If the inconsistency between organization constraints and agent's goals takes place, agents will be confused and be unable to make decision about their behaviors. Therefore, there should have some ways to solve the inconsistency, which may be agent-dependent and application-dependent.

For example, if the organization constraints have high level priority, then agent should modify its goals to adapt the organization constraints in order to solve the inconsistency between them.

– Non-conflict With Agent's Goal

The organization constraints should be non-conflict with the agent's goal, which means that the abidance of organization constraints should not hinder the agent's goals from being achieved, and vice versa. If the conflict between organization constraints and agent's goal takes place, there should have some ways to resolve the conflict, which may also be application-dependent and agent-dependent.

– Mutually Non-Conflict

The multiple organization constraints should not be conflict. The conflict between multiple organization constraints means that the abidance of one organization constraint will definitely hinder the other from being obeyed. If that so, it signifies that there are some problems in the system requirements about organization constraints.

– Stable

The organization constraint embodies the organization setting and generally remains constant throughout the analysis and design process. This is in contrast to other elements such as system structure, agent's goals, plan choice, belief, etc., that may be dynamically changed from time to time.

– Persistent

Generally, the organization constraints will persist during the life cycle of system. This is in contrast with the other system elements such as goals, tasks, etc that will be changed during the life cycle of agent and system.

3.   MODELING ORGANIZATION CONSTRAINTS

In this section, we will introduce the method to model the organization constraints in a structural and systematic fashion by extending i* framework. The i* framework was once developed for modeling and analyzing organizations to help support business process reengineering and requirements engineering. The framework focuses on modeling intentional and strategic relationships among actors in the organizations. It consists of two types of models: the Strategic Dependency (SD) model and the Strategic Rationale (SR) model. The SD model is used to capture and specify the actors in the system and the network of relationships that hold among them. The SR model describes in more detail the alternative methods that the actors have for accomplishing their goals and tasks, etc [7,8].

A SD model is a graph consisting of nodes and links among the nodes. Each node in the model represents an *actor*, and each link between the actors represents the *dependency* among them, which specified how one actor depends on another for something in order to accomplish its goals and tasks. An actor in the model is an active entity that carries out actions to accomplish its goals and can be further differentiated into the concepts of *role, position,* and *agent.* A *role* is an abstract collection of coherent abilities and expectations. A *position* is a collection of roles that are typically occupied by one agent. An *agent* is an actor that has concrete manifestations such as human, hardware, or software, or combinations thereof. Four types of *dependencies* (i.e., *goal-, task-, resource- and softgoal-dependency*) are distinguished for indicating the nature of the freedom and control in the relationship among actors. A *softgoal* is similar to a *goal* except that the criteria of success are not sharply defined. The SD model provides one level of the abstraction for describing organizational environments and their embedded information system. It shows the macro or external (but nevertheless intentional) relationships among actors, while hiding the intentional constructs with each actor. It is useful in helping understand organizational and systems configurations as they exist, or as proposed new configuration.

The SR model provides a more detailed level of modeling by looking "inside" actors to model internal intentional relationships. It shows the micro or internal constructs and relationships in actor. The SR model is a graph consisting of four main types of nodes: *goal, resource, softgoal* and *task,* which appear in the SR model not only as external dependencies, but also as internal elements linked by some relationships. There are three main types of links in SR model: *means-ends, task decomposition* and *contribution* link. *Task decomposition* link describes how a task can be decomposed into s number of subtasks. *Means-ends* link specifies how a goal may be accomplished. *Contribution* link describes how one node contributes to another node. The SR model provides a way to model stakeholders' interests, and how they might be met, and the stakeholders evaluation of various alternatives with respect to their interests.

3.1   Modeling Organization Constraints in Strategic Dependency Model

The first question related with organization constraint when analyzing and specifying the multi-agent system may be that *what* the organization constraints are in the system. Such a question is important for the stakeholders and the requirement analyzers to understand the organization constraints clearly and can be served as the basic and precondition to elaborate on and refine the organization constraints. The question should be dealt with in the first step to model the organization constraints.

In the macro level, the organization constraints should be specified when constructing the strategic dependency models of applications. In this step, the requirement analyzers should consider not only what the actors (e.g., stakeholders and system itself) that the application has and the dependencies among them, but also whether there exist some organization constraints and what they are. The whole applications can be regarded as an organization, and the organization constraints of it should be specified explicitly and the relationship between the organization constraints and the dependencies of stakeholders should also be considered.

In order to support modeling the organization constraint in the macro level, the strategic dependency model in *i** framework is extended. A modeling element to denoting organization, which has explicit constraint specification and border to distinguish the actors in the organization that will be affected by the organization constrains from the actors outside that will not, is introduced (see *Figure1*).

In addition, the requirement analyzer should investigate whether the organization constraints specified are necessary and natural, and there are any inconsistencies and conflicts between them. There may need some tradeoffs about the degree of the organization constraints. Too strong constraints may lose the autonomy and proactive properties of agents in the organization and further lose the flexibility of the system. Too weak constrains, however, will impose little influences on the autonomous agent's behaviors. The macro modeling of the organization constraints are important, as well-defined specification and tradeoff of organization constraints will facilitate the micro-level reason and specification of organization constraints.

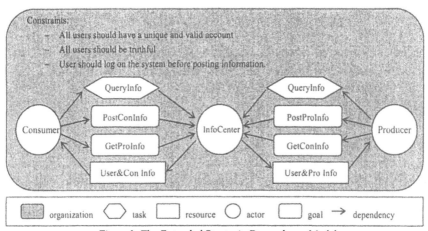

Figure1. The Extended Strategic Dependency Model

For the example described in section 2, we can identify the following three actors in the early requirement analysis phase: Consumer, Producer and

InfoSystem, where Consumer and Producer actors are actually the stakeholders of the system. They together constitute an organization and will be influenced by the organization constraints. The Consumer depends on InfoCenter to achieve goals of PostConInfo (denoting posting the consuming information) and GetProInfo (denoting getting the producing information), and to fulfill the task of QueryInfo (denoting querying the information). However, InfoCenter depends on Consumer to get the resource such as the Consumer user's information and the consuming information to be post. The organization constraints also are depicted in figure 1 as a part of organization specification.

3.2 Modeling Organization Constraints in Strategic Rationale Model

After specifying what the organization constraints are, the second question that should be dealt with may be that *how* the organization constraints influence the actors. Such a question is important to elaborate on and refine the organization constraints, helpful to investigate the actors' behaviors and valuable to guide the system design. Therefore the question should be dealt with as the second step to model the organization constraints based on the first step result

In the micro level, the organization constraints should be further refined, reasoned and specified when constructing the strategic rationale model of system, which provides detail information to model the inside intentional information about actors. In this step, the requirement analyzers should consider how the organization constraints will restrict the behaviors of the actors in the organization. Therefore, they should not only investigate the goal, resource, softgoal and task that each actors have, and the relationships among them such as *means-ends* and *task decomposition,* but also reason and consider how the organization will influence the intentional constructs and relationships of them in the actors.

In order to support modeling the organization constraint in the micro level, the strategic rationale model is extended. Two different types of goal will be differentiated: achievement goal and maintenance goal. The achievement goal means to achieve some state of affairs, and actually corresponds to the concept of goal in strategic rationale model. The maintenance goal means to maintain some state of affairs, and is a new modeling element to be introduced into the extended strategic rationale model. The maintenance goal is the abstract representation of organization constraints in the actor, therefore acts as one part of actor's internal intentional structures (see *Figure 2*).

The mapping from the macro level model of the organization constraints to the micro level model of the organization constraints is very simple. Each item of the constraint organization in the strategic dependency model will be mapped as the corresponding maintenance goal of the related actors. However, more work should be performed in this step to specify and reason the organization constraints. The relationship between the maintenance goal and the other elements of actor such as achievement goal, tasks, etc., should also be explored and specified. For example, some maintenance goal may influence and contribute positively to some achievement goal of actor. Moreover, the requirement analyzers should investigate whether there are inconsistency and conflict between the maintenance goal and the task, achievement goal, etc in the actor. If that so, the negotiation will be needed to resolve the inconsistent and conflict requirements.

Figure2 shows the strategic rationale model of the sample focusing on the InfoCenter actor. The organization constraints depicted in strategic dependency model will be mapped as the maintenance goal of the related actors. For example, the Consumer actor has the maintenance goals such as being truthful and logged before posting; the InfoCenter actor has such maintenance goals as logged before posting for users and having unique account for users. The maintenance goal of having unique account for users will contribute positively to the maintenance goal of logged before posting for users, which will further restrict the achievement goal of "post information".

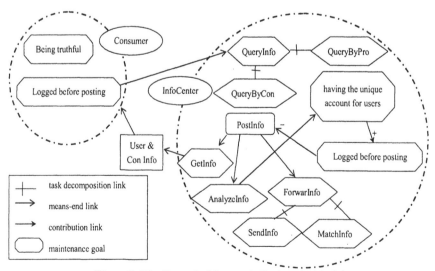

Figure2. The Extended Strategic Rationale Model

4.   RELATED WORKS

Shoham in [1] discussed the concept of social law for artificial agents in computational environment, which will guarantee the successful coexistence of multi-programs and programmers. He presented ways to the off-line design of social laws, and pointed out the social laws will on the one hand constraint the plan available to the programmer, but on the other hand will guarantee certain behaviors on the part of other agents. Zambonelli believed that the organization abstraction should play a central role in the analysis and design of multi-agent system, and introduced three additional organizational concepts: organizational rule, organization structure and organizational pattern that are necessary for the complete specification of computational organizations [2, 3]. He also discussed the importance and necessity of explicit identification of organization rules in the context of open agent system. In [4], Zambonelli further extended the Gaia methodology by introducing the modeling activity to identify, specify and analyze the organization rule in the requirement analysis phase. The organization rules, he pointed out, express the constraints on the execution activities of roles and protocols and are of primary importance in promoting efficiency in design and in identifying how the developing MAS can support openness and self-interested behavior. Another important work recently about the organization rule is [6]. DeLoach further extended the MaSE, an agent oriented methodology introduced in [5], by borrowing the concept of organization abstraction and integrating organizational rules into existing multi-agent methodology. Especially, he investigated how to integrate the existing abstractions of goals, roles, tasks, agents, and conversations with organizational rules and tasks. He used the approach similar to the notions used in the KAOS to represent the organization rules. It is not the first time for us to present the concept of maintenance goal. In [14], we had presented the concept of maintenance intention to investigate the agent's behaviors. The concept of maintenance goal can also be found in the formal Tropos [9] and KAOS.

5.   CONCLUSION

The organization concept is an important abstraction to analyze and design multi-agent system. Organization constraint is widespread in multi-agent system and will restrict the behaviors of agents in multi-agent system. The organization constraints have a number of important characteristics such as stable, consistent, non-conflict, persistent, etc. For complex multi-agent system, the specification and analysis of organization constraint may be difficult. In this paper, a structural and systematic way to model and analyze the organization constraints is presented by extending the *i** framework, an approach to model and reason the early requirement of system. In the macro level, the requirement analyzer should specify what the organization constraints in the system. Therefore, an organization modeling element, with explicit constraints specification and organization border is introduced into the strategic dependency model. In the micro level, the requirement analyzer should specify and reason how the organization constraint will restrict the behavior of agents in the multi-agent system. Therefore, an abstract cognitive concept of maintenance goal is introduced into the strategic rationale model. The steps are also described and a case is studied to show how to specify and analyze the organizational constraints from the macro level to the micro level.

6.   REFERENCES

1.   Y Shoham and M tennenholtz, On Social Laws for Artificial Agent Societies: Off-Line Design, Artificial Intelligence, Artificial Intelligence 73(1-2), 1995.
2.   F. Zambonelli, N. Jennings, M. Wooldridge, Organizational Rules as an Abstraction for the Analysis and Design of Multi-agent Systems , Journal of Knowledge and Software Engineering, 11(3), 2001.
3.   F Zambonelli, N R.Jennings, M Wooldridge, Organizational Abstractions for the Analysis and Design of Multi-agent System, AOSE'2001, LNCS2222, Springer, 2002.
4.   F. Zambonelli, N. R. Jennings, and M. Wooldridge, Developing Multiagent Systems: The Gaia Methodology, ACM Transactions on Software Engineering Methodology, 12(3), 2003.
5.   S A. Deloach, M F.Wood, and C H.Sparkman, Multiagents Systems Engineering, International Journal of Software Engineering and Knowledge Engineering, 11(3), 2001.
6.   S A. DeLoach, Modeling Organizational Rules in the Multiagent Systems Engineering Methodology, Proc. of the 15th Canadian Conference on Artificial Intelligence, Alberta, Canada. May 27-29, 2002.
7.   E. Yu, Agent-Oriented Modelling: Software Versus the World, Proc. Of Agent-Oriented Software Engineering, LNCS 2222, Springer-Verlag, 2001.
8.   E Yu, Towards Modeling and Reasoning Support for Early-Phase Requirements Engineering, Proceedings of the 3rd IEEE Int. Symp. on Requirements Engineering, 1997.
9.   A. Fuxman, et.al. Specifying and Analyzing Early Requirements: Some Experimental Results, Proceedings of the 11th IEEE International Requirements Engineering Conference, 2003.
10.   Wooldridge, N R.Jennings, and D.Kinny, The Gaia Methodology for Agent-Oriented Analysis and Design, International Journal of Autonomous Agents and Multi-agent System,3, 2000.

A MULTI-AGENT SYSTEM FOR MOBILE ENVIRONMENTS

Jianwen Chen[1,2] and Yan Zhang[2]
[1] *IBM Australia, 20 Berry Street, North Sydney, NSW 2060, Australia, jchen@au1.ibm.com*

[2] *School of Computing & IT, University of Western Sydney, Penrith South DC NSW 1797, Australia, yan@cit.uws.edu.au*

Abstract: In this paper, we present a framework/model for a logic programming multi-agent system in mobile environments. Such a system consists of a number of agents connected via wire or wireless communication channels, and we model the interactions between agents in our formalization. Our formalization is knowledge oriented with declarative semantics. Our model can be used to study the details of knowledge transaction in mobile environments.

Key words: multi-agent system, mobile environments, extended logic programming.

1.   INTRODUCTION

The advent of widespread portable computers has led to a wide variety of interesting hardware and software issues, and presented new challenges for researchers. Comparing to stationary environments, mobile environments have introduced a few specific features such as disconnection due to wireless network and mobility due to cell migration. In mobile environments, the communication channels can be wire or wireless. We believe that research on multi-agent system and knowledge transaction in mobile environments is important because this will significantly improve current development on both multi-agent systems and mobile systems. But so far no framework/model has been presented for multi-agent system in mobile environments and no study has been conducted for knowledge transaction in mobile multi-agent system. There seems to be a separation between multi-agent systems and the intelligent agents community on one side, and the mobile system community on the other side [13, 10, 17]. On mobile system community side, work in paper [4, 5, 12] has introduced calculus to describe the movement of processes and devices in mobile ambient, and the work in [3, 11, 6] has presented a Java based mobile agent to implement functionalities for mobile systems. The approaches above are not suitable for knowledge and have no declarative semantics. They are low level algorithms for "how to do" and have no high level "what to do" intelligent functionality. The details of transaction can't be specified in these approaches. On multi-agent and intelligent agent community side, a lot of frameworks/models have been developed for problem solving, knowledge representation and reasoning such as stable model/answer set, SMODEL, DLV and XSB model in paper [7, 15, 16]. But these models are only discussed and limited in classic non-mobile environments, and haven't be extended to mobile environments. In this paper we present a formalism and definition for a mobile logic programming multi-agent system (MLPMAS). With respect to previous work, our model has three advantages: 1) Our model is knowledge oriented and has declarative semantics inherited from logic programming; 2) It can specify details of knowledge transaction; 3) Our model can be used to study knowledge transaction in mobile environments.

The rest of this paper is organized as follows. In section 2, we give an overview of extended logic programming. In section 3, we introduce our knowledge study environmental model. In section 4, we formalize our mobile logic programming multi-agent system (MLPMAS). In section 5, we give an example to demonstrate how to specify a MLPMAS system in a particular problem domain. Finally, in section 6, we conclude our work.

2.   EXTENDED LOGIC PROGRAMS

Logic programming has been proved to be one of the most promising logic based formulations for problem solving, knowledge representation and reasoning. In non-mobile environments, traditional logic programming is used as a knowledge representation tool. An important limitation of this method is that logic programming does not allow us to deal directly with incomplete information, and therefore we only can get either *yes* or *no* answer from a query. When we study knowledge transaction in mobile environments, we should clearly understand that there is a major different between the scenario that the transaction fails and the transaction hangs on due to mobile user's sleep. The first scenario is transaction fails in the sense of its negation succeeds, it is a *no* answer for a query. The second scenario is transaction doesn't succeed because of incomplete information, the answer is *unknown* for a query transaction, but may become a definite answer *yes* or *no* after sometime. Therefore, in mobile environments, we need a method which can deal with incomplete information explicitly. The extended logic program [2, 8, 1] can overcome such a limitation, it contains classical negation $\neg$ in addition to negation-as-failure *not,* and includes explicit negative information. In the language of extended programs, we can distinguish between a query which fails in the sense that it does not succeed and a query which fails in the stronger sense that its negation succeeds.

Generally speaking, an extended logic program is a finite set of rules:

$L_0 \leftarrow L_1, ..., L_m, not\ L_{m+1}, ..., not\ L_n,$

where $n \geq m \geq 0$, and each L_i is a literal. A literal is a formula of the form A or $\neg A$, where A is an atom. We say logic program Π entails a literal L if L is always true in all answer sets of Π, this is denoted by $\Pi |= L$.

3.   ENVIRONMENTAL MODEL

When we study the transaction processing in mobile environments, we use the three level mobile environment model in the paper [9, 14] to represent the salient features of mobile environments. There is a Home Server (HS) acting as permanent storage of Mobile hosts' (MH) Files. There are Mobile Support Stations (MSS) providing services to a MH when it is within its cell. The MSS is connected to the HS via hardwires. The MH is continuously connected to a MSS via a wireless link while accessing data. It may become disconnected either voluntarily or involuntarily. In classical environments, an intelligent agent is an active object with the ability to perceive, reason and act. We assume that an agent has explicitly represented knowledge and a mechanism for operating on or drawing inferences from its knowledge. We also assume that an agent has the ability to communicate. In a distributed computing system, intelligent agent has been introduced to communicate with each other in order to achieve their goals.

Here we propose a new environment model to study knowledge base in mobile environments. This model integrates the features of both mobile environment [13, 10] and intelligent agents [17, 2] as shown in Figure 1.

In this environment model, we assume that every Mobile Host (MH) has its own knowledge base (KB) and intelligent agent (A11, A12, A21, A22), every MSS has knowledge base and agent residing on it as well, MSS1 and MSS2 represent different MSS in different geographic areas. Home Server (HS) level has a knowledge base and an agent that represents a set of rules of knowledge base. Every intelligent agent on MH will work on behalf of MH that resides on all the agents in the same geographic area will negotiate, communicate, and cooperate with each other to achieve the goal for themselves and their systems.

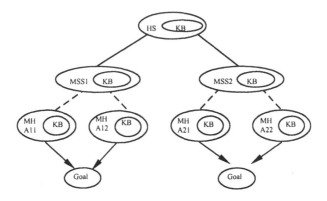

Figure 2. Knowledge Study Environment Model

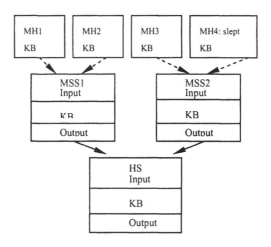

Figure 1. A MLPMAS

Mobile Logic Programming Multi-Agent System Formalization

In this section we formalize and define a Mobile Logic Programming Multi-Agent System (MLPMAS) in mobile environments, where each agent is represented by an extended logic program that contains its knowledge about itself and other agents. Agents communicate via communication channels.

We define and formalize the MLPMAS systems based on three layer environmental model. The model of A MLPMAS system is shown in Fig 2.

A mobile logic programming multi-agent system includes MH, MSS and HS three levels, the local knowledge base is located on each level. The system consists of a set of agents, the agent resides on MH, MSS and HS levels respectively, connected through communication channels. The agent on each level contains its own logic program representing its local information and reasoning method. Agents use information received from their incoming channels as input for their reasoning, where the received information may be overridden by other concerns represented in their programs. Agents produce output to their outgoing communication channels.

Definition 1: *A mobile logic programming multi-agent system,* or *MLPMAS*, is a pair $F = <A,C>$, where A is a set of agents: $A = A_{MH} \cup A_{MSS} \cup A_{HS}$, and $C \subseteq A \times A$ is a reflexive relation representing the communication channels between agents. For any $a_1, a_2 \in A$, if $<a_1, a_2> \in C$, then we say agents a_1 and $a2$ have a *communication channel*. Each agent $a \in A$, there is an associated extended logic programs *LocalKB(a)* which reprents agent a's *local knowledge base*.

Now we explain the definition of MLPMAS system above through the following Example 1. In our example, investor agent resides on MH, group agent resides on MSS, and fund manager agent resides on HS. Investor agent manages the local knowledge base and provides output to group agent on behalf of MH. Group agent collects information from investor agents, manages local knowledge base on MSS and sends output to fund manager agent. Fund manager agent collects information from group agents, does the investment decision and manages the local knowledge base on HS. Investor agent, group agent and fund manager agent are represented by a_{MH}, a_{MSS} and a_{HS} respectively.

Example 1: We have a mobile logic programming multi-agent system $F = <A,C>$, in this MLPMAS system, we have four mobile hosts MH1, MH2, MH3 and MH4, the investor agent resides on each MH:

$A_{MH} = \{a_{MH1}, a_{MH2}, a_{MH3}, a_{MH4}\}$

We have two mobile support station MSS1 and MSS2, group agent resides on each MSS:

$A_{MSS} = \{a_{MSS1}, a_{MSS2}\}$

We have one home server HS, fund manager agent resides on HS:

$A_{HS} = \{a_{HS}\}$

MH1 and MH2 are in geographic location of MSS1, MH3 and MH4 are in geographic location of MSS2. We have wireless communication channel between MH and MSS:

$<a_{MH1}, a_{MSS1}> \in C$, $<a_{MH2}, a_{MSS1}> \in C$,

$<a_{MH3}, a_{MSS2}> \in C$, $<a_{MH4}, a_{MSS2}> \in C$

We have wire communication channel between MSS and HS:

$< a_{MSS1}, a_{HS} > \in C, < a_{MSS2}, a_{HS} > \in C$

As we mentioned earlier, each agent is associated with an extended logic program of its local knowledge base.

We define input and output of agents in MLPMAS systems as follows.

Definition   2.   Let $F = < A, C >$ be   a   MLPMAS, where $A = A_{MH} \cup A_{MSS} \cup A_{HS}$. At MH, MSS or HS level, for $\forall a \in A$, we have two parts of inputs: *message input and knowledge input*, denoted by *MessageInput(a, X)* and *KnowledgeInput(a, Y)* respectively. That is,

Input(a) =< MessageInput(a, X), KnowledgeInput(a, Y) >

here $X \subseteq A, Y \subseteq A$, X, Y are subsets of A. Agent a collects message input from agents in X, and collects knowledge input from agents in Y, where

for $\forall b \in X$, we have $< a, b > \in C$, or $< b, a > \in C$ and

for $\forall b' \in Y$, we have $< a, b' > \in C$, or $< b', a > \in C$.

i.e. we know there is a communication channel between agent a and agent b, and agent a and agent b' respectively.

Message input is the information that an agent sends to another agent for the communication purpose. Such as one agents informs another agent that it will move into another MSS geographic area. This information will not cause any influence to the other agent's local knowledge base. While knowledge input is the information produced by the other agent's local knowledge base, and will be taken into the agent's local knowledge base, i.e. the answer set of a logic program.

For $\forall a \in A$, we have two parts of output, message output and knowledge output, denoted by *MessageOutput(a, X)* and *KnowledgeOutput(a, Y)* respectively. That is,

Output(a) =< MessageOutput(a, X), KnowledgeOutput(a, Y) >

here $X \subseteq A, Y \subseteq A$. Agent a sends message output to agents in X, and sends knowledge output to agents in Y.

Message output is information output for communication purpose, this information will not cause any influence to the other agent's local knowledge base, while knowledge output is the information that produced by the agent's local knowledge base and will have impact for the other agent's knowledge base.

Definition 3: We define *knowledge input and output* in MLPMAS systems on MH level as follows.

There is no input for MHs at MH level because this is the first level in MLPMAS systems, i.e.

KnowledgeInput(a_{MH}, Y) = ϕ (1)

The knowledge output can be derived from the equation:

KnowledgeOutput(a_{MH}, a_{MSS})

=an answer set of $[LocalKB(a_{MH}) \cup KnowledgeInput(a_{MH}, Y)]$ (2)

i.e. knowledge output is an answer set of the program formed by the local logic program of agent a_{MH} with extending of knowledge input from Y for agent a_{MH}. $LocalKB(a)$ is an extended logic program as we defined in Definition 1, $KnowledgeInput(a,Y)$ is a set of facts (beliefs). Note that $LocalKB(a_{MH}) \cup KnowledgeInput(a_{MH},Y)$ is viewed as a new logic program while fact $e \in KnowledgeInput(a,Y)$ is treated as a rule $e \leftarrow$.

Definition 4: We define *knowledge input and output* in MLPMAS systems on MSS level as follows.

The knowledge input can be derived from the equation:

$$KnowledgeInput(a_{MSS},Y)$$

$$= cons(\bigcup_{a_{MH} \in Y} KnowledgeOutput(a_{MH},a_{MSS}),S_F) \qquad (3)$$

where $cons(X)$ represents the maximal consistent subnet. The knowledge input of a_{MSS} is the maximal consistent subset of knowledge output from Y to agent a_{MSS} with respect to the select function S_F. S_F is the *selection function* of system F. For knowledge output, $\bigcup knowledgeOutput(b,a)$ may be inconsistent, S_F is introduced to solve such inconsistency by taking proper preference in the domain. Note that S_F is domain dependent, it can be a special logic programming rule for specific problem domain.

The knowledge output can be derived from the equation:

$$KnowledgeOutput(a_{MSS},a_{HS})$$

=an answer set of $[LocalKB(a_{MSS}) \cup KnowledgeInput(a_{MSS},Y)]$ (4)

i.e. knowledge output is an answer set of the program formed by the local logic program of agent a_{MSS} with extending of knowledge input of agent a_{MSS}.

Definition 5: *knowledge input and output* in MLPMAS systems on HS level as follows.

The knowledge input can be derived from the equation:

$$KnowledgeInput(a_{HS},Y)$$

$$= cons(\bigcup_{a_{MSS} \in Y} KnowledgeOutput(a_{MSS},a_{HS}),S_F) \qquad (5)$$

i.e. knowledge input of a_{HS} is the maximal consistent subset of knowledge output from Y to agent a_{HS} with respect to the select function S_F.

The knowledge output can be derived from the equation:

$$KnowledgeOutput(a_{HS})$$

=an answer set of $[LocalKB(a_{HS}) \cup KnowledgeInput(a_{HS},Y)]$ (6)

i.e. knowledge output is an answer set of the program formed by the local logic program of agent a_{HS} with extending of knowledge input of agent a_{HS}.

4.   AN EXAMPLE FOR MLPMAS SYSTEM

We will go through a completed example in this section to specify a MLPMAS system according to the formalization in section 4. We still use MLPMAS system Fig 2 in this example.

Example 2: In this example, we study a case in a specific investment problem domain. As showed in Figure 2, at MH level, we have MH1, MH2, MH3 and MH4. MH1 and MH2 are in the cell of MSS1, MH3 and MH4 are in the cell of MSS2. MSS1 and MSS2 are connected to the same HS. At MH level, each MH has a local knowledge base that includes a set of investment rules, investor agent resides on it. At MSS level, MSS has own knowledge base, MSS accepts the input from MHs and produces the output based on the input and own belief. The HS accepts the input from MSS level, it has own local knowledge base, investment decision will be made on HS level.

For the initial status, we assume MH1 and MH2 are all alive when transaction is processed in MSS1 cell. In MSS2 cell, the MH3 is alive, while MH4 is slept at the moment HS is requesting the transaction information from all related MH agents. The HS will need information from MH4 when the time it does the decision making.

MH Level:

On MH level, there is no input for the agent on MH. According to equation (2), we have

$KnowledgeOutput(a_{MH}, a_{MSS})$
=an answer set of $[LocalKB(a_{MH}) \cup KnowledgeInput(a_{MH}, Y)]$
= an answer set of $[LocalKB(a_{MH})]$

i.e. on MH level, the knowledge output is an answer set of local knowledge base. Based the local knowledge base on MHs, the knowledge outputs are derived as below on MH1, MH2, MH3 and MH4.

$KnowledgeOutput(a_{MH_1}, a_{MSS1}) = \{profit(share1), risk(share1), \neg cost(share1)\}$
i.e. it is high profit, high risk and low cost to invest share1 on MH1.

$KnowledgeOutput(a_{MH_2}, a_{MSS1}) =$
$\{profit(share1), \neg risk(share1), \neg cost(share1)\}$
i.e. it is high profit, low risk and low cost to invest share1 on MH2.

$KnowledgeOutput(a_{MH_3}, a_{MSS2}) =$
$\{profit(share1), \neg risk(share1), \neg cost(share1)\}$
i.e. it is high profit, low risk and low cost to invest share1 on MH3.

The MH4 is slept at the moment the information is retrieved from it.

MSS level:

On MSS level, according to equation (3), knowledge input on MSS1 is as below:

$$KnowledgeInput(a_{MSS_1}, Y)$$

$$= cons(\bigcup_{a_{MH} \in Y} KnowledgeOutput(a_{MH}, a_{MSS_1}), S_F)$$
$$= cons(KnowledgeOutput(a_{MH_1}, a_{MSS_1}) \cup$$
$$KnowledgeOutput(a_{MH_2}, a_{MSS_1}), S_F)$$

For agent a_{MSS1}, $risk(share1)$ is a belief in output of a_{MH1}, while $\neg risk(share1)$ is a belief in output of a_{MH2}, they are inconsistent. Here we assume selection function S_F takes positive atom as higher preference for investment risk, therefore $risk(share1)$ will become the input of a_{MSS1}.

We have knowledge input as below:

$$KnowledgeInput(a_{MSS1}, Y) = \{profit(share1), risk(share1), \neg cost(share1)\}$$

We can see that different knowledge input is derived with considering selection function in specific problem domain, therefore different answer set is derived for decision making due to selection function.

In the same way, we know the knowledge input of MSS2 agent equals:

$$KnowledgeInput(a_{MSS2}, Y)$$

$$= cons(\bigcup_{a_{MH} \in Y} KnowledgeOutput(a_{MH}, a_{MSS_2}), S_F)$$
$$= cons(KnowledgeOutput(a_{MH_3}, a_{MSS2}), S_F)$$

$$= \{profit(share1), \neg risk(share1), \neg cost(share1)\}$$

On MSS1, we have rule r1 related to this investment in its knowledge base

$$\{r1 : holds(inf\,o-requested(HS, MHi)) \leftarrow holds(slept(MHi))\}$$

On MSS2, we have rule r2 related to this investment in its knowledge base

$$\{r2: holds(\inf o - requested(HS, MHi)) \leftarrow holds(slept(MHi))\}$$

The r1 and r2 denote that if MHi is slept at the time the HS agent requests transaction information from MHs, HS will request information from MHi when HS does the decision making for the transaction.

According to the equation (4), the knowledge output can be derived:

$KnowledgeOutput(a_{MSS}, a_{HS})$

=an answer set of $[LocalKB(a_{MSS}) \cup KnowledgeInput(a_{MSS}, Y)]$

Thus, the knowledge output of MSS1 is derived as below:

$KnowledgeOutput(a_{MSS1}, a_{HS}) = \{profit(share1), risk(share1), \neg cost(share1)\}$

The knowledge output of MSS2 is derived as below:

$KnowledgeOutput(a_{MSS2}, a_{HS})$

$$= \left\{ \begin{array}{l} profit(share1), \neg risk(share1), \neg cost(share1), \\ \inf o - requested(HS, MH4) \end{array} \right\}$$

i.e. new belief *info-requested(HS, MH4)* is added to the answer set on MSS2 because of rule r2 in its local knowledge base.

HS level:

On HS level, based on the equation (5), knowledge input of HS agent equals:

$KnowledgeInput(a_{HS}, Y)$

$$= cons(\bigcup_{a_{MSS} \in Y} KnowledgeOutput(a_{MSS}, a_{HS}), S_F)$$

$$= cons(KnowledgeOutput(a_{MSS1}, a_{HS}) \cup KnowledgeOutput(a_{MSS2}, a_{HS}), S_F)$$

$$= \{profit(share1), risk(share1), \neg cost(share1), \inf o - requested(HS, MH4)\}$$

$risk(share1)$ is a belief of input on HS with considering the selection function.

We have rules r3-r9 in local knowledge base of HS.

$$
\begin{cases}
r3 : holds(invest(share1),s) \leftarrow holds(profit(share1),s), \neg holds(risk(share1),s), \\
\neg holds(cost(share1),s), holds(\inf o - get(MHi), res(request - \inf o(MHi),s)) \\
r4 : \neg holds(invest(share1),s) \leftarrow holds(risk(share1),s) \\
r5 : \neg holds(invest(share1),s) \leftarrow holds(cost(share1),s) \\
r6 : \neg holds(risk(share1),s) \leftarrow notholds(risk(share1),s) \\
r7 : \neg holds(cost(share1),s) \leftarrow notholds(cost(share1),s) \\
r8 : \neg holds(invest(share1),s) \leftarrow holds(\inf o - requested(HS, MHi),s), \\
\neg holds(\inf o - get(MHi), res(request - \inf o(MHi),s)) \\
r9 : \neg holds(\inf o - get(MHi),s) \leftarrow notholds(\inf o - get(MHi),s), \\
holds(\inf o - requested(MHi),s), holds(timeout(MHi),s)
\end{cases}
$$

The r3 denotes if it is high profit, low risk, low cost to invest share1 and HS gets requested information from ever slept MHi, HS will do the decision to invest share1. The r4, r5 and r8 denote if share1 is high risk or high cost on any MHi, or can't get information from ever slept MHi, HS will make the decision that share1 won't be invested. The r6 and r7 denote that if share1 hasn't be specified to be high risk or high cost for any MHi, then it is considered to be low risk or low cost. The r9 denotes that if HS hasn't got requested information from slept MHi until time is out, then HS will assume no information is available from MHi.

The knowledge output is derived as below according to the equation (6):

$KnowledgeOutput(a_{HS})$

=an answer set of $[LocalKB(a_{HS}) \cup KnowledgeInput(a_{HS},Y)]$

$risk(share1)$ is a belief of knowledge input of HS, according to the rule r4 of knowledge base, $\{\neg invest(share1)\}$ will be in every answer set of $[LocalKB(a_{HS}) \cup KnowledgeInput(a_{HS},Y)]$. Therefore we say $\{\neg invest(share1)\}$ is entailed, i.e. agent on HS makes the decision that share1 won't be invested. In this example, no matter what input from MH4, HS will do the decision that share1 can't be invested after considering the input from MH4. After HS has made decision that share1 will not be invested. The transaction decision will be sent to MSS, and all involved MHs will be noticed by broadcasting of MSS.

5.   SUMMARY

In this paper, we have presented and formalized a logic programming multi-agent system for mobile environments. Our formalization is knowledge based and has declarative semantics inherited from logic programming. Based on our formalized MLPMAS system, the details of knowledge transaction can be studied in mobile environments.

REFERENCES

1. Baral, C., Knowledge Representation, Reasoning and Declarative Problem Solving, Cambridge University Press, 2003.
2. Baral, C., and Gelfond, M., Logic Programming and Knowledge Representation, Logic Programming, 1994, pp. 73-148.
3. Bettini, L., et al, KLAVA: a Java package for distributed and mobile applications, Software Practice and Experience, 32 (2002) 1365-1394.
4. Cardelli, L., A. Gordon, D., Mobile Ambients, Theoretical Computer Science, 240 (2000), 177-213.
5. Cardelli, L., A. Gordon, D., Types for the Ambient Calculus, Information and Computation 177 (2002), 160-194.
6. Deugo D. Choosing a mobile agent messaging model, Proceedings of ISADS 2001. IEEE Press, 2001;278-286.
7. Eiter, T., and et al., A deductive system for nonmonotonic reasoning, in proceedings of the 4th International conference on Logic Programming and Nonmonotonic Reasoning (LPNMR97), pp 363-374. LNAI, Vol. 1265, 1997.
8. Gelfond, M., and Lifschitz, V., Classical Negation in Logic Programs and Disjunctive Databases, New Generation Computing, 1991, pp. 365-385.
9. Imielinski, T., and Korth, H.F., Mobile computing, Kluwer Academic Publishers, 1996.
10. Komiya, T., et al, Mobile Agent Model for Transaction Processing on Distributed Objects, Information Sciences, 2003, pp.1-16.
11. Lange D, Oshima M., Programming and Deploying Java Mobile Agents with Aglets, Addision-Wesley: Reading, MA, 1998.
12. Milner, R., et al,, A calculus of mobile processes, Parts 1-2, Information and Computation, 100 (1) (1992) 1-77.
13. Milojicic, D. Mobile Agent Applications, IEEE Concurrency, 1999, pp. 80-90.
14. Mirghafori, N., and Fontaine, A., A Design for File Access in a Mobile Environment, in proceedings of the IEEE - Conference on Mobile Computing, 1995, pp. 57-61.
15. Rao, P., et al, XSB: A system for efficiently computing well-founded semantics, in Proceedings of the 4th International Conference on Logic Programming and Nonmonotonic Reasoning, pp 2-17. LNAI, vol. 1265, 1997.
16. Vos, M. D., and Vermeir, D., Extending Answer Sets for Logic Programming Agents, in Proceedings of the Logic in Artificial Intelligence (Jelia2000) workshop, 2000.
17. Wooldridge , M., An Introduction to Multiagent Systems, John Wiley & Sons, LTD, 2002.

AGENT INTERACTION MANAGEMENT AND APPLICATION IN A VIRTUAL COLLABORATIVE ENVIRONMENT

Aizhong Lin, Igor T. Hawryszkiewycz, Brian Henderson-Sellers*
* Faculty of Information Technology, University of Technology, Sydney. POBox 123, Broadway, NSW 2007, AUSTRALIA. {alin, igorh, brian}@it.uts.edu.au.

Abstract: The intention of managing agent interactions between agents residing in a virtual collaborative environment is to obtain some useful beliefs that can be used in agent reasoning and decision making in order to optimize further agent interactions. Agent business relationships (such as trust, loyalty, understanding and friendship) are such beliefs. This research provides an approach to the management and application of agent interaction instances. The paper firstly introduces the multi-agent system architecture built in the virtual collaborative environment. Secondly, it presents the interaction protocols designed for the software agents. Then, it describes the design and implementation of the management of interactions. Finally, it depicts a specific belief revision function for personal agents to dynamically update agent business relationships in terms of the management of agent interaction instances.

Key words: Agent, Agent Interaction, Agent Interaction Protocol, Agent Interaction Management, Agent Business Relationship, Agent Belief Revision

1.   INTRODUCTION

A virtual collaborative environment called LiveNet [6] has been developed to support web-based group work. Software agents (or simply agents) built and run in the virtual collaborative environment are reusable components to manage workspace instances, goal instances, workflow instances, activity instances, groups, participants and resources. Some agents have capabilities of creating workspaces, goals, roles, participants and resources, while other agents have capabilities of gathering participants or resources from various places (e.g., Internet or Intranet) and, finally, other agents are able to create workflow instances for specific goal instances.

When undertaking group work, we may need an agent to create a workspace instance, a goal instance and activities for the achievement of goals. Meanwhile, we may need another agent to gather participants and resources for the work. In addition, we may also need another agent to create a workflow for the work to specify its resolution. These agents all have to cooperate with each other to achieve the common goal. Their cooperation is realized by their interactions. Therefore, an important property of agents is that of interaction, leading to the notion of societies of agents.

An interaction instance occurs for a specific goal, follows a specific interaction protocol, involves a set of agents and results in a number of messages being exchanged between the agents. In LiveNet, an agent can interact with other agents for *goal delegation*, *knowledge sharing* and *cooperative group formation*. There are many interaction instances occurring among agents when they achieve common goals. Those instances require management. The benefits of managing agent interactions are:

Classifying messages based on interaction instances increases the performance of interactions

Browsing interaction history is made easier

Obtaining new beliefs for agents from agent interactions performed earlier becomes possible

The first two benefits listed above are easily understood. The third benefit introduces an application of managing agent interaction instances. The application aims to obtain specific agent beliefs - agent business relationships - from the managed agent interaction instances. Agent business relationships reflect business relationships between human users represented by the agents. The beliefs can be revised from agent interaction instances performed earlier and play important roles on further action reasoning and decision-making of the agents.

The business relationships we identify in this research are *friendship* relationships, *trust* relationships, *loyalty* relationships and *understanding* relationships. In these relationships, friendship relationships are more in-depth than other business relationships. Human users in good friendship relationships are called friends who *trust* each other, *cooperate* with each other, are *loyal* to each other and *understand* each other [11]. Polson defines "*friendships* are in-depth relationship combining trust, support, communication, loyalty, and understanding" [13]. Consequently friendship relationships combine trust relationships, loyalty relationships and understanding relationships.

Our research provides an approach to the management and application of agent interaction instances. This paper describes the approach in four major sections. The first section introduces the multi-agent system architecture built in LiveNet; the second section describes the interaction protocols defined for software agents; the third section presents the design and implementation of the management of agent interaction instances; and the last section introduces the application of managing agent interaction instances.

2.   THE MULTI-AGENT ARCHITECTURE IN LIVENET

LiveNet is built on a collaborative semantic model as shown in Figure 1. The concept "activity" in this semantic model is the implementation of a workspace. It produces well-defined outputs using many workitems, actions and interactions. A role is a collection of a group of participants. A view is a folder containing a collection of artifacts that are electronic documents produced by participants. A workflow specifies the solution for a goal in an activity. A workitem is a set of actions and interactions needed to produce intermediate outcomes that eventually produce an activity output.

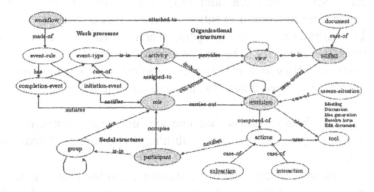

Figure 1: The collaborative semantic model of LiveNet [5]

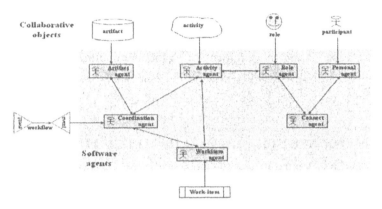

Figure 2: The multi-agent system architecture in LiveNet

The multi-agent system architecture is illustrated in Figure 2. The basic considerations for building agents in LiveNet are:

- Each participant has one and only one personal agent, which has capabilities to monitor the events related to the participants.
- Each role has one and only one role agent, which has capabilities to monitor the events related to all participants who take the role.
- Each activity has one and only one activity agent, which has capabilities to monitor events occurring in this activity.
- Each artifact may have an agent, which has capabilities to trigger a workflow instances to be started to process the artifact.
- Each workflow instance has a workflow instance monitor agent, which has capabilities to manage and monitor the workflow instance.
- Each workitem instance has one and only one workitem instance monitor agent, which has capabilities to manage and monitor the workitem instances.

The interactions between agents are classified into two dimensions. In the first dimension, considering a workspace, a personal agent could interact with a connect agent, which may interact with a role agent, to form a cooperative group for collaborative work. An artifact agent could ask a coordination agent to create or monitor a workflow instance that specifies the activities and workitem instances to produce the artifact. In the second dimension, considering different workspaces, any agent in one workspace may interact with the correspondent agent in another workspace in order to delegate a goal, share a piece of knowledge or form a cooperative group.

3.   AGENT INTERACTION PROTOCOLS

Three types of agent interactions - the "delegate" type, the "share" type and the "call for joining" type - are supported by agents in LiveNet. The "delegate" type interaction is used by two agents to delegate a goal from one to the other. The "share" type interaction is used by two agents to share a piece of knowledge such as a document or a graph. The "call for joining (cfj)" type interaction is used by agents to form a cooperative working group.

In an interaction, messages are exchanged between two or more agents. An interaction instance is normally realized by a series of messages exchanged between or among agents. In LiveNet agents, messages are represented using the Agent Communication Language (ACL) [4]. Table 1 lists the performatives that are used in the three interaction protocols ("x" means that the protocol uses the performative).

Table 1: Performatives used in interaction protocols

type	performative	delegate	share	Cfj
initial	delegate	x		
	share		x	
	cfj			x
middle	ask	x	x	x
	acknowledge	x	x	x
	answer	x	x	x
	request			x
	approve		x	x
	commit	x		
	accept		x	x
	decline	x	x	x
	inform			x
terminal	freeze	x	x	x

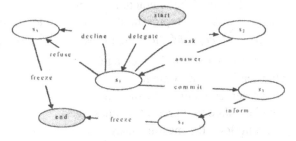

Figure 3: The "delegate" interaction protocol FSM

Interaction protocols are represented using Finite State Machines (FSMs). Figure 3 is the FSM of the delegate interaction protocol. An interaction FSM has two basic states - start and end - and one or more middle states. When an interaction message is sent to a receiver, the interaction instance reaches a specific state. Based on the interaction protocol, the receiver agent can decide on the next message. For example, suppose using a delegate protocol, agent ag_1 sends a "delegate" message to agent ag_2, consistent with the delegate FSM (Figure 3), the current state is s_1. Agent ag_2 can choose one from four different messages (decline, refuse, commit, or ask) to reply to the "delegate" message. If agent ag_2 chooses a "commit" message, the state of Figure 3 goes to s_3. Before the FSM reaches the "end" state, agents can exchange messages according to the protocol for an interaction instance.

4.   MANAGING AGENT INTERACTIONS

The management of agent interactions is modelled. as a pair of components *(R, F)*, in which *R* represents the interaction instances and *F* = *{f}* is a set of management functions.

An agent interaction instance is represented by a nine-tuple: $ii = (n, g, pr, pa, A, M, r, st, et) \in II$, in which, *II* is a set of interaction instances and:

- *n*:   the name of the interaction instance
- *g*:   the goal of the interaction instance
- *pr*:   the protocol of the interaction
- *pa*:   the patron of the interaction instance
- *A*:   the set of the names of the agents involved in this interaction instance
- *M*:   the set of messages exchanged in this interaction instance
- *R*:   the set of results of the interaction instances
- *st*:   the start time of the interaction instance
- *et*:   the end time of the interaction instance

An   message   is   represented   by   a   eight-tuple: $m = (p, ag_s, ag_t, l, o, c, st, rt) \in M$, in which *M* is a set of messages and:

- *p*:   the performative of the message
- ag_i: the sender agent of the message
- ag_j: the receiver agent of the message
- *l*:   the language to represent the message
- *o*:   the ontology the message uses
- *c*:   the content of the message
- *st*:   the send time of the message
- *rt*:   the receive time of the message

A   interaction   result   is   represented   by   a   four-tuple: $r = (gr, rl, rt, ru) \in R$, in which *R* is a set of results and:

- *gr*:   the general result that indicates if the interaction goal is achieved (true) or not (false)
- *rl*:   the result that indicates it is true or false that "if the patron agent ag_i of the interaction instance asks another agent ag_j to do something, the ag_j commits to do it"
- *rt*:   the result that indicates it is true or false that "if agent ag_j in the interaction instance will do what ag_j commits to do for the patron agent ag_i of the interaction instance"
- *ru*:   the result that indicates it is true or false that "if agent ag_j commits to do something and does it that what ag_j does is what the patron agent ag_i of the interaction instance wanted ag_j to do"

The major functions of interaction management are message generation, store, classification, retrieving and removing.

- *generate*: The "generate" function is provided in an agent to decide the next message or messages during an interaction instance. It is formalized as:

$$m_{i+1} = f_{gen}(pa, M_i)$$

where m_{i+1} is the message to be sent; pa is the name of the interaction protocol, its value belonging to the set *{delegate, share, cfj}*; and M_i is the set of messages that have been exchanged between agents before m_{i+1} is sent. The management function f_{gen} consists of two steps. The first step is to derive which messages it is possible to send using the finite state machine of pa. The second step is to decide which message from the message option to send.

- *store*:   The "store" function is provided in an agent to save a message in an interaction instance or save an interaction instance to the interaction instance repository, which resides in the agent.
- *classify*:   The "classify" function is provided in an agent to index interaction instances or messages in terms of given keywords. The keyword could be an interaction protocol (index interaction instances using the interaction protocol name), a patron (list the interaction instances that have this patron), an agent name (list the messages sent by this agent) and so on.
- *retrieve*:   The "retrieve" function is provided in an agent to retrieve specific interaction instances or messages from the interaction repository in terms of given keywords.
- *remove*:   The "remove" function is provided in an agent to delete specific interaction instances or messages from the interaction repository in terms of given keywords.

- *remove*:   The "remove" function is provided in an agent to delete specific interaction instances or messages from the interaction repository in terms of given keywords.

An interaction instance is managed in the agent whose user is the patron of the instance. The interaction instances of a personal agent are listed as shown in Figure 4. An interaction record can be created, opened, and removed. When opening an interaction, all ACL messages belong to this interaction are listed. An ACL message record has an attribute to save the interaction identifier so that an ACL message belongs to an interaction instance.

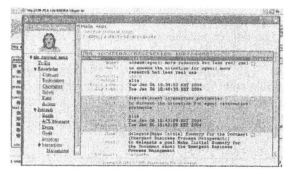

Figure 4: The list of agent interaction instances

5.   AN APPLICATION OF INTERACTION MANAGEMENT

The managed agent interaction instances have many uses. Here, we consider one of its applications - to obtain agent business relationships from agent-managed agent interaction instances and apply agent business relationships to the formation of cooperative agent work team.

A LiveNet personal agent works on behalf of one and only one human user. Similarly to its human user, an agent is normally self-interested [8]. To make a group of individually self-interested agents become a "cooperative" work team, we design three strategies:

- To give opportunities to the agents who are new to the team
- To advise the agents who are not cooperative
- To encourage the agents who are cooperative

To judge an agent that is cooperative or uncooperative in a work team, the agent business relationships that can be obtained from managed agent interaction instances are employed. For example, suppose an agent ag_i is going to delegate a subprocess to another agent, the agent ag_i classifies its

- the second group contains the uncooperative agents (the agents for which ag_i believes the friendship between ag_i and those agents is less than 0.5); and
- the third group contains the cooperative agents (the agents for which ag_i believes the friendship between ag_i and those agents equals or is larger than 0.5).

After the three groups are ready, the agent ag_i will choose one agent to be responsible for the sub process in terms of the three strategies:

- firstly chooses an agent ag_j from the new agent group and delegate the sub process to ag_j;
- send a message containing an advice such as "The friendship between us is low. I think we should improve it. May I do something for you?" to all agents in the uncooperative group; and
- send a message containing an encouragement such as "You are very friendly to me. I believe we should keep this forever. I will be there when you want." to all agents in the cooperative group.

5.1   The Model of Agent Business Relationships Revision

Figure 5 is a model to harvest business relationship between agents. It is illustrated in five steps (from the bottom up, based on Figure 5):

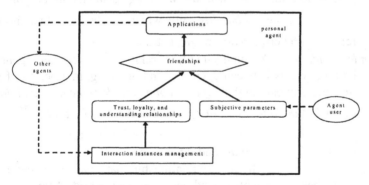

Figure 5: A model of agent business relationships revision

- During their activation, agents interact with each other by exchanging messages. An interaction message is contained in a message record and this record is contained in an interaction instance record that is saved in the knowledge base of the agent that initiates the interaction.
- After an interaction is completed, from the recorded interaction messages, the agent observes the interaction results.

- Using the interaction results, business relationships such as loyalty, trust and understanding are harvested.
- Using these business relationships and subject parameters that are set up by agent users, agent friendships are harvested.
- Finally, the business relationships are applied to assist the agent to reason and make decisions for further agent work, which returns the belief revision model back to its initial state.

5.2   The Definitions of Agent Business Relationships

As noted in Section 1, the business relationships between agents are friendship relationships, loyalty relationships, trust relationships and understanding relationships. They are defined as follows.

- *loyalty*   A loyalty relationship that an agent ag_i believes exists between agent ag_i and agent ag_j in a period of time pt is the proposition that "*if ag_i asks ag_j to do something, the ag_j will commit to do it*". $loy_{pt}^{ag_i,ag_j}$ is the *probability* with which ag_i believes that the loyalty relationship between ag_i and ag_j is true.

- *trust*   A trust relationship that an agent ag_i believes exists between agent ag_i and agent ag_j in a period of time pt is the proposition that "*ag_j will do what ag_j commits to do for ag_i*". $tru_{pt}^{ag_i,ag_j}$ is the *probability* with which ag_i believes that the trust relationship between ag_i and ag_j is true.

- *understanding*   An understanding relationship that an agent ag_i believes exists between agent ag_i and agent ag_j in a period of time pt is the proposition that "*if ag_j commits to do something and does it that what ag_j does is what ag_i wanted ag_j to do*". $und_{pt}^{ag_i,ag_j}$ is the *probability* with which ag_i believes that the understanding relationship between ag_i and ag_j is true.

- *friendship*   A friendship relationship that an agent ag_i believes it exists between agent ag_i and agent ag_j in a period of time pt is the proposition that "*ag_j is a friend of ag_i*". $fri_{pt}^{ag_i,ag_j}$ is the *probability* with which ag_i believes that the friendship relationship between ag_i and ag_j is true. A friendship relationship is the combination of the previous three business relationships.

5.3   The Method of Agent Business Relationships Revision

Typically, an agent uses the Prolog [9] logic programming language as the language of interaction message content (the Prolog language is also used to specify the beliefs of agents). Since an agent has an embedded Prolog engine for reasoning and decision-making, it can understand interaction message contents. After an interaction is completed, an assessment method, which belongs to the interact function, is activated to assess if the goal of the interaction is achieved and, meanwhile, to obtain a value for each element of R. A human process participant could also access her agent's interaction records to set or revise the value for each element of R.

The trust relationship between agents is expressed by using a real number in [0, 1]. The greater the number is, the stronger is the relationship between them. Similarly, the loyalty and understanding relationship between agents is also expressed by using a real number in the interval [0, 1]. They are calculated as:

- $tru_{pt}^{ag_i,ag_j}$ = (the total of the rt of the interactions between ag_i and ag_j in pt) / (the number of the interactions between ag_i and ag_j in pt)

- $loy_{pt}^{ag_i,ag_j}$ = (the total of the rl of the interactions between ag_i and ag_j in pt) / (the number of the interactions between ag_i and ag_j in pt)

- $und_{pt}^{ag_i,ag_j}$ = (the total of the ru of the interactions between ag_i and ag_j in pt) / (the number of the interactions between ag_i and ag_j in pt)

in which pt is a period of time, pt = (pst, pet), where pst and pet are respectively the start time and end time of this period. The greater the pt we use, the more accurate the business relationships between agents we get. To calculate the strength of the friendship relationship from these three business relationships, an agent user has to set the weights between the friendship relationship and these three business relationships as shown in Table 2 (set up by the agent user of agent ag_{alan}).

Table 2: Examples of weights between the friendship and other three relationships

Business relationships	Weight for friendships
Trust	0.98
Loyalty	0.90
Understanding	0.7

The weights of "trust", "loyalty", and "understanding" are denoted as w_{tru}, w_{loy}, and w_{und} respectively, and the formula to calculate the friendship relationship is:

$$fri_{pt}^{ag_p,ag_q} = \left(tru_{pt}^{ag_p,ag_q} * w_{tru} + loy_{pt}^{ag_p,ag_q} * w_{loy} + und_{pt}^{ag_p,ag_q} * w_{und}\right) \Big/ \left(w_{tru} + w_{loy} + w_{und}\right)$$

6.   RELATED WORK

Managing agent interaction instances can benefit group work and group members. Related work regarding agent interaction management includes that (1) the conversation layer is provided by FIPA-OS [14] to support various interaction protocols for agents; (2) the COOL language [2] was designed and implemented for agents to dynamically specify flexible interaction protocols; and (3) conversation managers [10] have been incorporated into multi-agent systems to enhance the high-level communication capability of multi-agent systems. In addition, a number of issues regarding conversation management (rather than agent conversation management) have been discussed [17] [1] [3]. However, these issues of conversation management focus on conversation analysis. The conversation layer of FIPA-OS, the COOL language and conversation managers concern more the interaction protocols than the interaction instance management.

Our examination of revising and applying agent business relationships extends previous work, particularly the following: (1) Panzarasa *et al.* [15] explore agent social relationships in an agent community by providing an agent social structure to represent the agent community and discuss the social relationships between agents in that community. (2) Hogg and Jennings [7] explore agent social attitudes (selfless, selfish, balance, social tendency and selfish tendency) that affect agent social decision-making strategies. Their social attitudes determine the agent social relationships. (3) Polson and the group in Global Friendship [13] surveyed the relationships between friendships and a set of attributes in a group of university teachers and students (200 persons) and found the most related attributes of friendship are trust (171 out of 200), honesty (113 out of 200), fun (69 out of 200), understanding (63 out of 200) and loyalty (59 out of 200). The survey tells us that friendships are closely related to trust, honesty, fun, understanding, and loyalty. (4) Marsh [12] explores the "trust" property of agents. He provides a formalization of trust, the tools necessary for trust revision and the basis for trusting artificial agents, which could form stable coalitions, take 'knowledgeable' risks, and make robust decisions in complex environments. Finally, (5) Simon [16] discussed relationships between friendliness and interaction using mathematical methods. He concluded that "friendliness increases interaction" and "interaction increases friendliness".

7.   CONCLUSION AND FUTURE WORK

Managing interaction instances benefits agents and their users in three aspects: (1) classifying messages based on interaction instances increases the performance of interactions; (2) browsing interaction history is made easier; (3) harvesting new agent beliefs from interactions performed becomes possible. This paper describes the management and application of agent interaction instances. In future, we will focus on more agent beliefs in terms of the managed interaction instances.

ACKNOWLEDGEMENTS

We wish to thank the Australian Research Council for providing funding for building reusable agents in collaborative environment. This is contribution number 04/02 of the Centre for Object Technology Applications and Research.

REFERENCES

1. Benford S., Bullock A., Cook, N., Harvey P., Ingram R. and Lee O. K., "A Model of Conversation Management in Virtual Rooms". *Proceedings of Applica '93*, Lille, France, March 1993.
2. Barbuceanu M. and Fox M. S., "COOL: A language for describing coordination in multiagent systems". *Proceedings of the First International Conference on Multi-Agent Systems* (V. Lesser, ed.), San Francisco, CA, pp. 17-24, MIT Press, 1995.
3. Finlay S. J. & Faulkner G., "Actually I Was the Star: Managing Attributions in Conversation". *Forum: Qualitative Social Research*, Volume 4, No. 1, Jan. 2003
4. FIPA, "Agent Communication Language". *http://www.fipa.org/specs/fipa00003/*
5. Hawryszkiewycz, I.T. (2002): "Designing Collaborative Business Systems". *Proceedings of IFIP 17th World Computer Congress, TC* Stream on Information Systems: The e-Business Challenge*, ed. Roland Traunmiller, Montreal, August 2002, Kluwer Academic Publishers, Boston, pp. 131-146.
6. Hawryszkiewycz, I.T., "Describing Work Processes in Collaborative Work". *Proceedings of The Fifth International Conference on Computer Supported Cooperative Work in Design*, IEEE Computer Society, Hong Kong, November, 2000, pp. 264-268.
7. Hogg L. M. and Jennings N. R., "Variable Sociability in Agent-Based Decision Making". *Proceedings of 6th Int. Workshop on Agent Theories Architectures and Languages (ATAL-99)*, Orlando, FL, 276-289.

8. Kraus S., "Contracting tasks in multi-agent environments". *Technical Report CS-TR 3254 UMIACS-TR-94-44*, U of Maryland, 1994.

9. Kim, S. H., "Knowledge Systems through Prolog". New York, New York: Oxford University Press, Inc.

10. Lin F., Norrie D. H., Flores, R.A., and Kremer R.C., "Incorporating Conversation Managers into Multi-agent Systems". *Proceedings of the Workshop on Agent Communication and Languages, Fourth International Conference on Autonomous Agents (Agents'2000)*. Barcelona, Spain, pp. 1-9.

11. Lewis M. and Rosenblum L.A. (eds.). Friendship and Peer Relations. N.Y. Wiley, 1975

12. Marsh P. S., Formalising Trust as a Computational Concept, *PhD Thesis*, University of Stirling, Scotland. Available http://www.iit.nrc.ca/~steve/Publications.html

13. Polson B., *http://www.cyberparent.com/friendship/what.htm*

14. Poslad S, Buckle, P and Hadingham R., "The FIPA-OS Agent Platform: Open Source for Open Standards". *Proceedings of the 5th International Conference and Exhibition on the Practical Application of Intelligent Agents and Multi-Agents*, UK, pages 355-368, 2000.

15. Panzarasa P., Norman T. J. and Jennings N. R. Modelling Sociality in a BDI framework, *Proceedings of 1st Asia-Pacific Conf. on Intelligent Agent Technology*, Hong Kong, 202-206.

16. Simon H. A.. Models of Man. *Social and Rational, Mathematical Essays on rational human behavior in a social setting*. New York: John Wiley, 1957

17. Whittaker S., Jones Q., Terveen L., "Managing long term communications: Conversation and Contact Management". *http://citeseer.nj.nec.com/472510.html*

AN INTEGRATED APPROACH TO BATTLEFIELD SITUATION ASSESSMENT

Yang Fan, Chang Guocen, Duan Tao and Hua Wenjian
The Telecommunication Engineering Institute, Air Force Engineering University, Xi'an, Shaanxi 710077, China

Abstract: Situation assessment (SA) is the basis for many of the planning activities performed by the battlefield commander and staff. And as a very complex military process, it requires the cooperation of lots of information processing technology. Multi-agents system (MAS) is a useful method to model the complex Command and Control (C2) system. In this paper, we present a multi-agents model for situation assessment. The three main components of this model, which are computation, reasoning and communication, were designed in detail by integrating series of new and useful technology. The computation component calculates the Battlefield Initiative; the reasoning component makes the situation prediction; and the communication component gives a help to interchange situation information among the Situation Assessment Agents (SA-Agents).This model can integrate qualitative reasoning, quantitative computing and multi-source communicating as a whole, and give the result of situation assessment and the risk value to take it, which is very useful in the C2 system simulation.

Key words: situation assessment; multi-agents system; command and control

1. INTRODUCTION

Situation assessment is the basis for many of the planning activities performed by the battlefield commander and staff. Improved SA may lead to faster, better planning. There is no general definition of situation assessment, but we can give a functional description, that SA is an explanation of battlefield view according to the force disposition, operation ability and efficiency of both sides in the battle, a procession of analysis to hostile attempts and operation plans[1].

As a very complex military information fusion process, SA has no fixed, mature theory. Because we cannot get a satisfied SA by using any single ready-made approach, it is necessary to integrate them to accomplish this task. And there are some methods based on the information fusion theory to get some degree of SA, such as Plate-based or AI-based technology. In our work, we concern that how to create a framework for integration of such methods.

More and more applications have shown the agent to be a valuable software concept with the potential to be more widely used in command and control system modeling[2]. The ability of agents to perform simple tasks autonomously has aroused much interest in the potential military applications. Key characteristics of agents which make them attractive are their:

- Autonomy;
- High-level representation of behavior;
- Flexible behavior;
- Real-time performance;
- Suitability for distributed applications; and
- Ability to work cooperatively in teams.

And the agent as described here is an autonomous piece of software, which has explicit goals or desires to achieve, and is pre-programmed with plans or behaviors to achieve these goals under varying circumstances. For example, when the BDI agent set to work, it pursues its given goals, adopting the appropriate plans, or intentions, according to its current beliefs of the state of the world, so as to perform the role it has been given. To use the MAS in modeling C2 System can integrate much useful technology.

In this paper, we present a multi-agents model for an important military application — situation assessment. And the paper is organized as follows: Section 2 is dedicated to the framework of the SA-Agents. In section 3 to 5 we discuss the three main components of SA-Agent in detail. Finally section 6 concludes.

2.   FRAMEWORK OF SA-AGENT

SA-Agent is an intelligent program that takes the task of SA. The main purpose of SA-Agents is to make sure that which side takes the advantage of the battlefield under the situation currently, and to foresee how this kind of advantage develops. And the challenge in the structure design of SA-Agent comes to combination of quality and quantity. So there should be three kinds of capabilities that SA-Agents must be equipped with, calculating, foreseeing and communicating. According to this, the framework consisted of three components: computation Reasoning and communication; while communication component consisted of advice encoder/decoder and system I/O. The structure of SA-Agent is shown in fig 1.

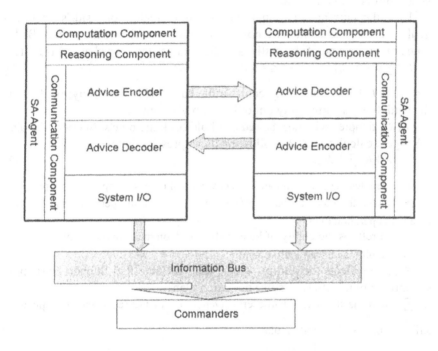

Figure 1. The Framework of SA-Agent

Though there are only two SA-Agents in the Fig.1 (limited by the paper), when more SA-Agents join this system, we can get their structures and relationships similarly according to fig 1.In an SA-Agent, Computation Component does the quantitative computing of Battlefield Initiative; Reasoning Component does the qualitative situation reasoning of the battlefield situation development; and Communication Component helps
. SA-Agents interchange situation information in the form of Advice. All the three components are discussed in detail in the next three sections.

3.   COMPUTATION COMPONENT

One of the most important tasks of SA-Agents is to determine which side takes the advantage of the current battlefield. And SA-Agent uses the BI (Battlefield Initiative) to make the judgment. BI denotes the degree how one side controls the battlefield[1].

How the current situation is propitious to realize one side's operation goals is the key to make sure how to calculate the BI. Set the current BI for blue army (one side of the battle, and the contrary side is red army) is I, then

$$I = \sum_i k_i \times F(R_i) \qquad (-1 \leq I \leq 1) \tag{1}$$

where, If $I=1$, the blue army controls the battlefield completely; or if $I= -1$, the battlefield is completely out of blue army' s control.

$F(R_i)$ denotes whether the red can hold back the blue's ith operation plan. SA-Agent calculates $F(R_i)$ following the expression below.

$$V = X_i Y_i R_i \Big/ \sum_j L_j M_j B_{ij} \tag{2}$$

where R_i denotes the potential battle effectiveness of blue' s ith operation plan;

B_{ij} denotes the potential battle effectiveness of red's jth operation plan to strike blue's ith operation plan;

X_i (L_j) reflects the ability of blue (red) 's C2(command and control) System to control the blue's ith (red's jth) operation plan;

Y_i (M_j) reflects the ability of blue (red)'s Battlefield Support System to support the blue's ith (red's jth) operation plan;

$\sum_j L_j M_j B_{ij}$ is the actual battle effectiveness of all the red's operation plans to strike the blue's ith operation plan.

$$F(R_i) = \begin{cases} 1, & V > U_{UP} \\ 0, & U_{DOWN} \leq V \leq U_{UP} \\ -1, & V < U_{DOWN} \end{cases} \tag{3}$$

where U_{DOWN}, U_{UP} are the upper limit and lower limit, which are created by the system and will be adjusted in the practice.

And in (1), k_i denotes the contribution of blue's ith operation plan to I, the Battlefield Initiative. k_i reflects the SA-Agent's value judgment to ith operation plan.

$$K_i = R_i \Big/ \sum_n R_n \tag{4}$$

All the parameters related would be obtained by the battlefield sensors system and inputted to the framework through the system I/O before situation assessment begins. The detailed computation methods of (1),(2) are not listed here, because that are beyond this paper's topic. Here, we just set up a kind (maybe not the perfect kind) of computation mechanism with which SA-Agent can get the quantificational Battlefield Initiative.

4.   REASONING COMPONENT

Inspired by the Stirling's multiple agent decision-making model[3], an epistemic system of SA- Agent was designed. Given a situation assessment system, Consider a finite number, N, of SA-Agents, denoted SA-Agent$_i$, ...SA-Agent$_N$; the epistemic system can be denoted by the triple (K_{xi}, G_{xi}, B_{xi}), consisting of the following:

K_{xi}, a situation knowledge corpus;

G_{xi}, a system of information valuation;

B_{xi}, a system of truth valuation.

A situation prediction is made by considering the informational value of the prediction versus its truth value.

Let U_i denote the set of possible situation prediction of SA-Agent$_i$, and assume that K_{xi} entails exactly one element of U_i, and that all elements of U_i are consistent with K_{xi}. U_i is said to be an ultimate patition for SA-Agent$_i$. A potential situation prediction for SA-Agent$_i$ occurs if SA-Agent$_i$ is able to reject all and only members of a subset of U_i(see more details in 3).

But in the SA-Agent reasoning model, unlike the other general agents, the knowledge corpus will keep unchanged until the new situation information is obtained. Because the main purpose of the reasoning component of SA-Agent is to make a prediction for the current situation, the SA-Agent needs not add the "right" prediction to the knowledge corpus. Even SA-Agent will not take any action but prediction, the tradeoff between the utility of avoiding error and the utility of getting more information still exists.

For any $g \subset U_i$, define the utility of SA-Agent$_i$ accepting g in the interest of avoiding error as $T_i(g,l)$, with $l \in \{t, f\}$ denoting whether g is true (t) or false (f), according to K_{xi} and B_{xi}, where

$$T_i(g,l) = \begin{cases} 1 & if \quad l = t \\ 0 & if \quad l = f \end{cases} \qquad (5)$$

Equation (5) defines the utility of avoiding error, and the utility of getting more information should be defined, too. To assess the utility of information that a situation prediction carries, SA-Agent$_i$ may assign an information value to each $g \subset U_i$. The potential predictions may be partially ordered with respect to information value. For example, let $g_1 \subset U_i$, g2 $\subset U_i$ be two potential predictions, if $\tilde{g}_1 \subset \tilde{g}_2$, but $\tilde{g}_1 \neq \tilde{g}_2$, then g_1 is less valuable informational than g_2, because accepting g_2 rejects more elements of U_i than does accepting g_1.

The informational value of a potential prediction is the sum of the values assigned each element of U_i that is rejected according to the potential prediction. Assume $U_i = \{h_{i1}, h_{i2}, ..., h_{in_i}\}$, and let $M_i(h_{ij}) \geq 0$ denotes the value

X_i assigns to h_{ij}, according to G_{xi}, then $\sum_{j=1}^{n_i} M(hi_j) = 1$. For any set $g \subset U_i$, define

$$M_i(g) = \sum_{h_{ij} \in g} M_i(h_{ij}) \tag{6}$$

as the SA-Agent$_i$'s informational value of rejecting g. And we can define

$$C_i(g) = 1 - M_i(g) \tag{7}$$

Then we get the utility function, $T_i(g,l)$, of avoiding error and the utility function, $C_i(g)$, of getting information. So the epistemic utility function for situation prediction can be defined as a convex combination:

$$u_i(g,l) = \alpha_i T_i(g,l) + (1 - \alpha_i)C_i(g) \tag{8}$$

where the quantity α_i represents the relative importance that SA-Agent$_i$ attaches to avoiding error versus getting more information. Equation (8) is the basis for SA-Agent to make tradeoff in the process of situation prediction. Similar to section 3, the detailed reasoning process will not be discussed here, but notice that, for the suitability for agent technology in military command and control, α_i usually be restrict in (0.5, 1).

5.   COMMUNICATION COMPONENT

In Section 3 and Section 4, we have discussed how a SA-Agent calculates the Battlefield Initiative and reasons out a situation prediction. But the two methods for situation assessment are both for single agent, and we must consider the communication, interaction and coordination among the SA-Agents to make better use of the virtues of MAS. And we do not concern the communication protocol here, instead our focus are the interchange of situation information and the cooperation on the situation prediction.

A SA-Agent must get some computation or reasoning parameters in order to make situation assessment. How to get and send those parameters correctly is the key problem in the Communication Component. As the framework we gave in section 2, SA-Agents send and receive these parameters in the form of Advice[4]. An Advice from SA-Agent$_i$ to SA-Agent$_j$ can be designed as follow:

Advice$_{ij}$ (ID_ parameter, Truth_ parameter, Trust_ Agent$_i$)   (9)

where ID_ parameter is the unique mark to identify the parameter; Truth_ parameter is the numerical value that SA-Agent$_i$ sends to SA-Agent$_j$; Trust_ parameter is the Trust of SA-Agent$_i$. And every SA-Agent has an encoder/decoder in its communication component to operate these Advices.

Trust is an important member of advice, and it is a very useful concept in the coordination in MAS, too[5]. Trust implies some form of risk, and that entering into a trusting relationship is choosing to take an uncertain path that can lead to either benefit or cost depending on the behavior of others.

The perceived risk of cooperating with a particular SA-Agent is determined by that SA-Agent's reliability, honesty, etc., embodied by the notion of trust. Thus a SA-Agent can use its trust in others as a means of assessing the risk involved in cooperating with them. An inverse relationship between trust, T, and risk, R, is as follows.

$$T = \frac{1}{R} \tag{10}$$

In assessing the reliability of a parameter sent by others, a SA-Agent must make a judgment about the risk attached to cooperation with the sender, by examining the trust value in the Advice sent.

Suppose that a SA-Agent knows of n others, SA-Agent$_1$, SA-Agent$_2$, ... SA-Agent$_n$, with the required parameter for performing a situation assessment, and ordered such that $T_{SA-Agent_{x-1}} \geq T_{SA-Agent_x}$, where $T_{SA-Agent_x}$ denotes the trust in SA-Agent$_x$. Then the risk R to take these advices (use the parameter) is:

$$R = \frac{1}{\sum_{1}^{n} \frac{T_{SA-Agent_i}}{i}} \tag{11}$$

For a Battlefield Initiative computation or a situation prediction making with m parameters, $a_1, a_2, \ldots, a_m$, the total risk C for this situation assessment is:

$$C = \sum_{i=1}^{m} R_{a_i} \tag{12}$$

Now a result of a situation assessment ω (which may be a Battlefield Initiative or a situation prediction) and the risk C related are gotten, so the Assessment Quality Q can be given as follow:

$$Q = \omega \times C \tag{13}$$

Finally, through the system I/O, all these results are sent to the information bus, which carries all these results and other C2 information to Battle Commander, and carries the environment information to SA-Agents or to other entities in distributed C2 system, as presented in Fig 1.

By now a process of battlefield situation assessment is accomplished. With the change of battlefield, the system I/O takes the task of interchange information between the situation assessment system and the environment again, and a new assessment process begins.

6.   CONCLUSION

To get a good assessment result needs integration of much technology. The agent-based approach in this paper gives us an intelligent environment to achieve this goal. SA-Agents can use the parameters in Advice, which gives not only the true number but also the Trust of these parameters. With these parameters, lots of technology whether is qualitative or quantitative can be integrated in this framework. And the more important is that with the help of SA-Agents, Commanders can get a clearer, more credible situation assessment for a better operation plan.

REFERENCES

1. Yang Fan, Study on Battlefield Situation Assessment in Command Automation of Air Unit, *master thesis*, (Air Force Engineering University, Xi'an, China, 2002).
2. Clinton Heinze, Simon Goss, and Adrian Pearce. Plan Recognition in Military Simulation: Incorporating Machine Learning with Intelligent Agents. In: *Proceedings of the Sixteenth International Joint Conference on Artificial Intelligence, Workshop on Team Behavior and Plan Recognition*, (Stockholm, Sweden, 1999), pp.53—63.
3. Wynn Stirling, A Model for Multiple Agent Decision Making, In: *Proceedings of the 1991 IEEE Conference on Systems, Man, and Cybernetics*. (New York, 1991), pp.2073--2078.
4. Mazda Ahmadi, Mehran Motamed and Jafar Habibi, Arian: A General Architecture for Advisable Agents, In: *International Conference of Machine Learning; Models, Technologies and Applications (MLMTA'03)*, (Las Vegas, Nevada, 2003), pp.17-23.
5. Nathan Griffiths and Michael Luck, Cooperative plan selection through trust. In: Multi-Agent System Engineering: Proceedings of the Ninth European Workshop on Modelling Autonomous Agents in a Multi-Agent World, edited by F. J. Garijo and M. Boman, (Springer, 1999), pp.162-174.

NEGOTIATION BASED ON PERSONALITY

Hong Zhang and Yuhui Qiu
Faculty of Computer and Information Science,Southwest China Normal University,Beibei, Chongqing, , P.R.China,zhangh, yuqiu@swnu.edu.cn

Abstract: Negotiation is the highlight of e-commerce and artificial intelligence. This paper applies the idea of personality to BDI models and therefore attempts to present new negotiation architecture and to illustrate the protocol and algorithm. Through the experiments this paper analyses and proves that the personality (temperament) exerts great influence on concession rates in negotiation, and therefore affects the choices of negotiation strategy.

Key words: personality negotiation e-commerce BDI mode

1.   INTRODUCTION

Software agent plays various roles in BtoB or BtoC commercial activity. Recently, people tend to use CBB model or BBT model to describe individual phases of e-commerce. In the two models mentioned, negotiation is an important link to which many researchers apply the advanced agent technology.

The negotiation in the e-commerce can be defined as the process of the transaction carried on by a group of agents to achieve a mutually acceptable agreement about the properties of some merchandizes. There also exists another definition in a stricter sense, that is, the process of deciding and reasoning supported by the artificial intelligence technology and mathematic technology (including logic, case based reasoning, belief correction optimization and game theory) and at the same time based on the agent's own inference of the belief, desire and intention. This demonstrates the importance of the psychological state to both sides of the negotiation during the process. Among the studies of the analysis and modeling of the agent's behavior, the BDI model (Belief, Desire and Intention) is one of the most representative ones. Belief and Desire represent the informational and evaluative state of the agent. While Intention represents the past decision of the agent, which is the key to the ideal performance under the limitation of given condition. A great deal of research work has been done on the form of the BDI model, focusing on describing its nature and behavior. The recognition of the agent's behavior is based on reasoning and goal driving (such as the intentional behavior). While the determining of the goal, the choosing and deciding of the parameter, the semantic and behavior are all based on his beliefs. Therefore the construction of the BDI model plays a very important role in the constructing negotiation models. However, it is regret that many models that had been recently constructed failed to relate the individual psychological factor to them. The present paper is attempting to explore the BDI model from this point.

2.   BDI MODEL BASED ON PERSONALITY

The psychological process during the negotiation between the purchaser and the bargainer is the amalgamation and consolidation of the three processes of cognition, emotion, and consciousness, which are derived from the transformation of the properties of the goods into the currency. The psychological phenomenon of the behaviors between the purchaser and the bargainer is the psychological manifestation of an individual in a group as a "person", which is inevitably controlled by the individual psychological characteristics. In commercial activities a person can have various psychological activities — such as perception, apperception, memory, association, attention, imagination, thinking, will and so on, which exhibit the common rules of human psychological activities. As an individual, the person in commercial activities always acts as both purchaser and bargainer, no matter what might be the content in every specific negotiation. And he will keep those steady and essential psychological qualities in a unique combination. This is called consumer individuality. In the negotiation process this personality displays the disparity in the aspects of ability, character, temperament, interest and so on. Thus the difference in the behaviors of the negotiation process comes into being.

In commercial activities, the basis of the psychological process between the purchaser and bargainer includes the common process of psychological activities, consumers' individual psychology, consumption needs, and purchasing motives and so on. In the commercial activities of BtoB which are carried on the basis of a fixed relationship and in an atmosphere of friendliness, the need, certainly, is the precondition for the negotiation between the purchaser and bargainer; and therefore, their motivation are naturally favorable. Therefore, we hold that under such circumstance, personalities play a crucial role in the negotiation process.

The following is an observation of the situations of the BDI Model after the personalities are added to it. In the process of negotiation, the belief, desire and intention in it are always influenced by cognition, emotion and consciousness. And if we add the common personalities to the BDI Model (BDI-P), we can get the following graph (figure 1).

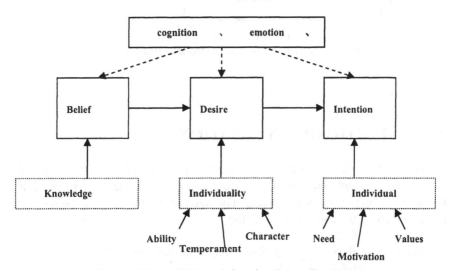

Figure 1. Figure 1 BDI mode based on Personality (BDI-P)

3.   CONCESSION RATE BASED ON TEMPERAMENT

In this paper, two individual mental (temperament and character) factor will be added in experiments. Temperament as defined here refers to individual in behavioral style. Carl Jung asserted that people are fundamentally different and can be classified into "psychological types" based on their particular preferences. The four pairs of opposite preferences are Extraverting (E) and Introverting (I), Sensing (S) and intuiting (N), Thinking (T) and Feeling (F), and Judging (J) and Perceiving (P). Within each pair of opposite preferences, a person leans toward one or the other in most cases

In various tactics (for seller agent), the predominant factor is personality of counter's agent, which decide which concession rate will be adopted.

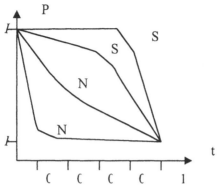
Figure 2. Various concession rate based on temperament

4.   TACTIC OF NEGOTIATION

This tactic determines the recommended price based on the amount of time remaining and concession rate related time for the agent. . Assume that the agent is biding at time $0 \leq t \leq t_{max}$. The agent bids from P_{max} as beginning price ,when t=0, and at t=t_{max}, the agent can't get reasonable price, negotiation is failed.

To calculate the bid value at time t, the following expressing is used:
$$p(t) = F_{cr}(t) \times p_{max}$$
When $F_{cr}(t)$ is a polynomial function of he form:
$$F_{cr}(t) = 1 - K_{cr}(t/t_{max})CR_i(t)$$
K_{cr} is a constant that determined the value of the end bid of the agent in negotiation. $CR_i(t)$ is function relation to temperament. $i \in \{SJ,SP,NT,NF\}$ By varying the value of $F_{cr}(t)$, a wide range of time dependant function can be defined from those that start biding near p_{max}, to those that only bid near $P_{max}(1-K_{cr})$, to all possibilities between. The only condition is that

$$0 \leq F_{cr}(t) \leq 1, F_{cr}(0) = 1, F_{cr}(t_{max}) = 1 - K_{rt}, and 0 \leq k_{rt} \leq 1$$

5.   CONCLUSION AND FUTURE WORK

Psychologists have identified human temperament as predominant factor in the patterns of human behavior. Neuroscience research indicates that temperament is an innate property of the brain. The potential for employing human temperament as an effective negotiation is strong. The mode based on personality proposed a solution to characterize concession rate in negotiation by taking human factor, particularly human temperament into considerations. Our main line of work is to further explore the development of strategies for our negotiation agent. Since the process in which the negotiation in e-commerce is running is highly dynamic, we intend to extend this work by using a revolution method to classify the users, and develop various strategies for different temperament people.

REFERENCES

1. Keirsey, David, and Marilyn Bates, "Please Understand Me,"Del Mar, Ca: Prometheus Nemesis Books, 1978.
2. P. Faratin, C. Sierra and N. R. Jennings (2000) "Using similarity criteria to make negotiation trade-offs" Proc. 4th Int. Conf on Multi-Agent Systems, Boston, 119-126.
3. P. Faratin, C. Sierra, and N. R. Jennings (1998) "Negotiation decision functions for autonomous agents" Int. J. of Robotics and Autonomous Systems 24 (3-4) 159-182.
4. N. R. Jennings, P. Faratin, A. R. Lomuscio, S. Parsons, C. Sierra and M. Wooldridge(2001) "Automated negotiation: prospects, methods and challenges" Int. J. of GroupDecision and Negotiation 10 (2) 195-215.

MIAM: A ROBOT ORIENTED MOBILE INTELLIGENT AGENT MODEL

Wu Shandong and Chen Yimin
School of Computer Engineering and Science, Shanghai University

Abstract: This paper proposes a robot oriented Mobile Intelligent Agent Model-MIAM, composed of core function, mobile ability, intelligent engine and communication interfaces, which provide flexible multi-mode robot control solutions for intelligent control and remote control.

Key words: robot, agent, MIAM, intelligent control, remote control

1. INTRODUCTION

Intelligent control and remote control are two important control modes for robot. The software agent technique provides an effective way for constructing multi-modes robot control system [1]. Focusing on providing high adaptability, this paper proposed a robot oriented Mobile intelligent Agent Model-MIAM and, the architecture and an applications example are introduced in detail.

2. MIAM-MOBILE INTELLIGENT AGENT MODEL

MIAM model is illustrated in Fig. 1. MIAM is a compound architecture, with no particular emphasis on intelligent agent or mobile agent. MIAM is designed for robot intelligent control and remote control and it is composed of four parts namely, core function, mobile ability, intelligent engine and communication interface. Below is a detailed introduction of the architecture of MIAM.

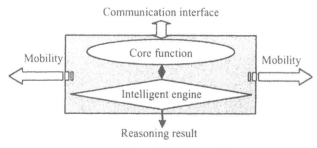

Figure 1. MIAM model

2.1   Core function

The core function is specified function of the agent itself, that is to say, what it could do naturally. In a robot control system there are several kinds of agent as follows with different core functions.

- Target agent. To perform target tasks directly such as conducting welding and conveying.
- Simulate agent. To trace and simulate the robot's motion process.
- Status agent. To monitor the motion and provide real time status message.
- Message agent. To send or receive none-real time messages.
- Collaboration agent. To manage working agents in a group as a chief.

2.2   Mobile ability

The free mobility of agent on network leads to more flexibility of the robot control system. For a remote robot object, mobile agent is able to move freely to the desired computer node to execute robot control task. User and robot are located on a fixed position. However, the mobile ability of agent provides a strong base for remote robot control mode.

The MIAM based remote robot control acts as following: the user sets up a task model, organizes various agents to form an appropriate agent team, and assigns subtasks to agents and configures the collaboration rules and relations, and then dispatches agent team to conduct robot control. Agents move automatically according to the itinerary initialized to the destination node. Agent could clone itself as need arises. During work time, the collaboration relations among agents may be changed or reorganized dynamically, usually under coordination of the collaboration agent. After finishing the task, agent may either return to the user, dispose of itself, or set stored in a new medium waiting to be re-actived. However, user could retract any dispatched agent home at any time.

2.3   Intelligent engine

The intelligent engine provides agent with intelligence. The advanced characteristics of agent depend on the intelligence in a higher degree. Our desire is that agent could as highly be intelligent as a person and be autonomous in solving the problems if faces, while asking little help from people. For MIMA model, we made agent possess both forward and backward directions intelligent reasoning abilities. The forward reasoning would make robot fully self-adaptability, that is to say, at any time and situation agent could reason out the next step's action. On the other hand, the backward reasoning is suitable for resolving questions inversely.

There exist multiple agents in the whole robot control system. Each single agent has its own local intelligent reasoning engine, which provides intelligence support for its own functions. For the agent collaboration, a global reasoning engine is required, which provides information sharing and fusing to support group intelligence. The global agent collaboration and reasoning engine is lightweight but with higher intelligence, which aims at resolving and processing the vital global questions, correspondingly, more partial and detailed questions are throw to agents for further processing.

2.4   Communication interface

In multi-agent system, communication between agents is a natural requirement and the basis of agent collaboration. MIAM agent is equipped with two kinds of communication interface. One is the Point to Point (P2P) interface, which enables agent to communicate directly and quickly with another desired agent. The other is a public interface for information sharing among multiple agents. Because each agent has its own knowledge, ability and apperception from environment, an ISC (Information Share Centre) is required in the system to make agents share or interchange information. Information sharing and fusing are the key basics for the agent collaboration, accordingly, besides providing and broadcasting static message, the ISC should be combined with agent collaboration rules.

Besides interface, another key issue remaining is agent communication language. A perfect protocol can provide standardized agent interface. Some famous protocols such as KQML, KIF and ACL are available.

3.   MIAM BASED APPLICATION EXAMPLE

According to the MIAM model introduced above, taking PT500 robot as the control objects, we built a multiple modes robot control system. A user can organize different kinds of agent dynamically and purposefully to form a work team to perform robot intelligent control or remote control. Below is a brief introduction of MIAM implementation in this system.

The kernel function of MIAM is aimed at controlling PT500 robot to motion and assemble. The control functions mainly include robot program interpreting, instruction library, control card driver, etc. The detailed robot functions are introduced in the related reference [2].

The MIAM communication language is KQML. The communication contents include control command and robot joints position data. The later is used to simulate robot motion, or may be transferred to the global reasoning engine to analyze and predict whether collision would happen between two robots. The former include the commands such as STOP, PAUSE robot, which come from the user or the reasoning engine.

The reasoning engine of MIAM is implemented by Jess [3]. Because the robot instructions of PT500i s obtained through teaching, the main intelligent engine in MIAM is forward reasoning. Two reasoning scripts are designed for single robot motion and the collaborative control of two robots.

The mobility of MIAM is implemented by Aglet [4]. Each aglet is equipped with a task interface which is used to assign robot program, viz. a set of robot instructions, in the remote robot control model. Aglet will move to desired remote robot nodes to interpret and execute the robot program to drive the robot.

4.   CONCLUSION

This paper proposes a Mobile Intelligent Agent Model and constructed a multi-mode robot control system for PT500 robot applying MIAM. MIAM is suitable for robot intelligent control and remote control, and the experience shows that the control system has a favorable control performance.

REFERENCES

1. P. Bellavista, A. Corradi, C. Stefanelli, Mobile Agent Middleware for Mobile Computing, IEEE Computer, Vol. 34, No. 3, pages 73-81, March 2001
2. WU Shan-dong, CHEN Yi-min, HE Yong-yi, Development Technique of High Level Software System for Industrial Robot Controller Base on WIN 9X/NT, Journal of Shanghai University, Dec. 2001, Vol.7, No.6, pp. 532-535
3. Ernest Friedman-Hill, Jess, http://herzberg.ca.sandia.gov/jess/main.html, Sandia National Laboratories, Livermore, CA, 1995
4. IBM Aglets, http://www.trl.ibm.co.jp/aglets/

INCORPORATING ELEMENTS FROM CAMLE IN THE OPEN REPOSITORY

C. Gonzalez-Perez, B. Henderson-Sellers, J. Debenham and G.C. Low, Q.-N.N. Tran
University of Technology, Sydney, Australia
University of New South Wales, Australia

Abstract: The CAMLE approach offers a methodological framework for the development of multi-agent systems. However, this approach does not provide full coverage of the needs often found in information systems development, lacking, for example, an appropriate capability for customization or links to infrastructural, non-engineering processes. By adopting a method engineering perspective, it is possible to integrate the best parts of CAMLE into the OPEN repository so organizations can create and own customized variants of CAMLE as necessary.

Key words: agent-oriented methodologies, CAMLE, OPEN, method engineering

1. INTRODUCTION

The CAMLE method [12] provides a fairly comprehensive language and environment for multi-agent software systems development. As with many other methods, it has been defined using natural language, which lacks the level of formalism needed to cater for extensions and customizations.

While individual methodologies may be useful for creating specific agent-oriented information systems, they have no flexibility as systems requirements change over time or as new concepts are understood and accepted. In contrast to these very rigid, single methodologies, the concept of situational method engineering (SME) provides a much more flexible environment in which to create a standard and useful methodological approach for systems design ([13], [10]). Here, we utilize one particular,

SME-focused methodological approach – that provided by the OPEN Process Framework [3], originally developed for creating object-oriented systems, but more recently expanded into "Agent OPEN" to include support for agent-oriented systems development [2, 6, 7]. As well as supporting SME, OPEN is formally defined using a metamodel. This means that individual method fragments are easily generated as instances of classes in the metamodel and, consequently, specific methods can be derived. In this paper, we show how the OPEN repository can be used to generate CAMLE. However, before this is possible, we need to evaluate the extent of existing support (in terms of repository-housed method fragments) in OPEN, particularly with respect to some of CAMLE's idiosyncratic features for multi-agent systems development.

In this paper, the major aspects of CAMLE are captured and integrated into OPEN. This is beneficial for both approaches, since CAMLE obtains a higher level of formalism (by being re-defined from a metamodel) and the OPEN repository is augmented with new contents. Section 2 briefly describes CAMLE and its main features, focussing on the major characteristics that differentiate it from other agent-oriented methods. Section 3 describes the OPEN Process Framework and its underpinning paradigm of method engineering. Section 4 provides a catalogue of new method fragments that are defined within the OPEN repository from CAMLE specifications. Finally, Section 5 presents our conclusions.

2.   BRIEF DESCRIPTION OF CAMLE

CAMLE, as defined by its authors, is a caste-centric agent-oriented modelling language and environment [12]. It is caste-centric because *castes*, analogous to classes in object-orientation, are argued to provide the major modelling artefact over the lifecycle by providing a type system for agents. A significant difference is claimed between castes and classes: while objects are commonly thought of as statically classified (i.e. an object is created as a member of a class and that is a property for its whole lifetime), agents in CAMLE can join and leave castes as desired thus allowing dynamic reclassification.

CAMLE provides a graphical notation for caste models (similar to class models in OO methodologies), collaboration models and behaviour models. Caste diagrams are similar to conventional class diagrams in that they depict the types involved in the system as surrogates for the actual instances that will comprise it at run-time In CAMLE, these instances are agents and types are castes. In addition to inheritance and UML-style composition and aggregation relationships (see [9], sec. 2.7.2.2), caste diagrams include notation for *congregation*, a kind of whole/part relationship in which the parts are detached from their type (i.e. caste) when the whole is destroyed; this is possible in CAMLE since dynamic classification of instances is fully supported. Similarly, notation for *migration* and *participation* relationships is available, representing cases of agents leaving their caste and joining a new one (migration) or agents that join a new caste without leaving their current ones (participation).

Collaboration diagrams depict the interactions between agents or castes. Unlike in UML collaboration diagrams ([9], sec. 3.65), interactions in CAMLE are produced by an agent observing the actions of other agents rather than by direct message sending or operation invocation. Therefore, arcs in CAMLE collaboration diagrams are labelled with an action name of the source agent rather than an operation name of the target. This suits well the autonomous and loose coupling nature of agents.

Behaviour models can be expressed in CAMLE using two kinds of diagrams. Scenario diagrams take the perspective of a given caste, describing a specific situation to which it must respond and what the response must be. A scenario diagram is necessary for each situation. Multiple scenario diagrams can be combined into a behaviour diagram, similar to a UML activity diagram ([9], sec. 3.84), which depicts the overall behaviour of a given caste.

From the process side, CAMLE defines three stages:

- the analysis and modelling of the existing information system
- the design of the new system as a modification of the existing one
- the implementation of the new system

CAMLE relies heavily on the fact that an information system already exists when a new project is started, so that the new system is designed as a modification to the current one. Although this situation is indeed common, the construction of systems from scratch also happens. CAMLE, however, seems to ignore this possibility.

At the same time, CAMLE defines a set of six activities that comprise the process of agent-oriented analysis and modelling, supposedly covering the two first stages in the list above. These activities produce caste models, collaboration models and behaviour models using an iterative and recursive approach. Agent castes that are too complex to be directly implemented are treated as complete systems and decomposed into component castes, applying the same activities to them recursively.

3.   BRIEF DESCRIPTION OF METHOD ENGINEERING AND OPEN

The method engineering paradigm, introduced by the works of, for example, Kumar and Welke [8], Brinkkemper [1], Rolland and Prakash [10], and Saeki [11], advocates the definition of a method (or methodology) as a collection of *method fragments*, i.e. self-contained chunks that define work products, tasks, techniques or processes[1] independently of their potential context. Once a repository of such components has been constructed, a method engineer can select a sub-set and connect them together into a *situated method*. It is called "situated" because it is constructed purposefully for a particular means, usually a specific project or organization.

The OPEN Process Framework (see, e.g., [3-5]) adopts a process engineering perspective and defines a *framework* composed of a metamodel plus a repository of method fragments. The metamodel establishes what concepts and relationships can be utilized to define these method fragments. For example, the OPEN metamodel defines the concepts of Activity ("a major Work Unit that models a cohesive yet heterogeneous collection of Tasks that achieves a related set of goals", [4], p. 98) and Work Product ("any significant thing of value that is developed during an Endeavour", [4], p. 65), and states that each activity produces zero or more work products ([4], fig. G.4). The OPEN repository is populated with method fragments that are instances of the concepts defined in the metamodel; following our example, the OPEN repository could contain an activity named "Requirements Engineering" (an instance of Activity) plus a work product named "System Requirements Specification" (an instance of WorkProduct), plus a link between them (an instance of the association between Activity and WorkProduct).

The OPEN metamodel is often seen as something fixed and given to method engineers "as is". Having an unchanging background on which everything else is based is useful for the common understanding and compatibility between methodologies. Each method engineer, however, is free to utilize the method fragments already pre-defined in the OPEN repository or create new ones if necessary. In fact, the addition of new method fragments to the repository comprises OPEN's major mechanism for extension and customization. This paper studies the CAMLE method and creates new OPEN repository method fragments based on CAMLE's specification, thus incorporating the process and work product definitions of the latter. Once this is done, CAMLE exists embedded in the OPEN

---

[1] We are using these terms here in their conventional sense. No technical meaning is attached.

repository as a collection of method fragments, and CAMLE itself or any variant of it, even those involving method fragments other than CAMLE's, can be generated.

4.   INTEGRATING CAMLE ELEMENTS INTO OPEN

This section explores different aspects of CAMLE from the perspective of the OPEN metamodel. For those CAMLE aspects that can be satisfactorily represented by an already-existing method fragment, this method fragment is identified. For those aspects of CAMLE that cannot be modelled by any method fragment in the OPEN repository, a new method fragment is introduced and fully defined.

4.1   Lifecycle

An OPEN lifecycle is the span of time associated with the development of a given software system. In this respect, CAMLE uses an iterative and recursive lifecycle that fits well into OPEN's *Iterative, Incremental, Parallel Lifecycle*. No new method fragments need to be introduced.

4.2   Phases and Activities

An OPEN phase is a large-grained span of time within a lifecycle that works at a given level of abstraction. An OPEN activity is a large-grained unit of work that specifies what to do in order to accomplish some results. Activities state *what* to do, while phases set the temporal frame stating *when* to do it.

CAMLE does not make a difference between what and when to do things. On the contrary, it defines three "stages" that involve work description and temporal issues altogether. First of all, the existing information system is analysed and modelled, which is likely to comprise an appropriate mix of requirements engineering and legacy mining. OPEN's activities *Requirements Engineering* plus probably *Component Selection* and *Environment Engineering*, assembled into an *Initiation* phase, are appropriate to model this.

Secondly, the new system is designed as a modification of the existing one. This is basically a design job that can be satisfactorily represented by OPEN's activity *Design*. Finally, the new system is implemented, which can be modelled by OPEN's activities *Implementation* and *Integration*. All these design and implementation activities can be packaged into a *Construction* phase.

CAMLE always assumes that an existing system is present and that the new system is constructed as a modification from it. OPEN does not impose this perspective on the phases of the lifecycle, or any other for that matter. In any case, the three "stages" defined by CAMLE can be easily mapped to already existing OPEN activities and phases, and therefore no new method fragments need to be introduced.

4.3   Tasks

An OPEN task is a small-grained, atomic unit of work that specifies what must be done in order to achieve some stated result. CAMLE defines six "activities", all within the second "stage", namely system design (see Section 4.2). No "activities" are described for the other two "stages". CAMLE "activities" semantically correspond to OPEN's tasks.

First, agents and their roles in the system are identified according to their functionality and responsibilities, and then grouped into castes. This produces a caste model. Agent OPEN's *Analyse use requirements*, *Identify CIRTs* and, most importantly, *Model agents' roles* and *Construct the agent model* are suitable tasks to model this. CIRT stands for "class, instance, role or type" and, in the context of CAMLE, the concept of CIRT can be extended to castes as well.

Then, inheritance and whole/part relationships between castes are modelled, augmenting the caste model with new information. Agent OPEN's *Construct the agent model*, again, can be used to model this.

The third "activity" involves identifying the communication links between castes in terms of how agents influence each other, producing a first version of the collaboration model. Agent OPEN's *Evaluate the design* (since the already existing caste model must be evaluated and possibly modified) and *Construct the agent model* can be used to model this.

Then, visible actions and state variables of each caste are identified and associated with communication links in the collaboration model. OPEN does not include any task appropriate to representing the identification of actions, so a new one must be introduced. Agent OPEN does, however, include the task *Construct the agent model*, which is appropriate to model the identification of state variables.

The newly proposed OPEN Task (to support CAMLE) is defined as follows:

OPEN Task

Task Name:	*Determine Caste Actions*
Relationships:	Semantically close to *Identify CIRTs* and *Construct the object model.*
Focus:	Dynamic modelling
Typical supportive	Techniques: *Responsibility identification, Responsibility-driven design, Delegation analysis, Event modelling, Interaction modelling*
Explanation:	This task defines the visible actions that a given agent caste is capable of performing.

Then, scenarios in the operation of the system as a whole are identified. OPEN's *Analyse user requirements* and *Design user interface* can be used to model this. Subtask Use case modelling deals predominantly with use cases using techniques such as *Hierarchical task analysis* and *Scenario development.*

Finally, each caste's response to each of the identified system scenarios is analysed and described, producing a behaviour model for each caste. Design-focussed tasks in OPEN, useful here, include *Capture the design, Document the design* and *Refactor*; with many techniques such as *Collaborations analysis, Relationship modelling* and *Robustness analysis.*

4.4　　Work Products

An OPEN work product is an artefact of interest for the performed work units. Work products usually comprise models and documents. CAMLE defines several kinds of diagrams, which can be modelled as OPEN work products.

A caste diagram in CAMLE is similar to a conventional class diagram, but it incorporates new constructs such as congregation, migration and participation relationships. In addition, the CAMLE literature does not mention the usage of UML-style associations ([9], sec. 3.41) in caste diagrams, which is probably an additional difference. Therefore, a new method fragment needs to be introduced.

OPEN Work Product

Name:	*Caste Diagram*
OPEN classification:	Static Architecture set of work products
Brief description:	A caste diagram depicts the castes in a system, together with the inheritance and whole/part relationships among them. Whole/part relationships include the conventional composition and aggregation relationships plus the newly proposed relationships of congregation, migration and participation [12].

A collaboration diagram in CAMLE is similar to a UML collaboration diagram, but incorporates the major difference of having the arcs labelled with a sender's action rather than a receiver's operation. This is a large enough distinction as to require the introduction of a new method fragment.

OPEN Work Product

Name: *Caste Collaboration Diagram*
OPEN classification: Dynamic Behaviour set of work products
Brief description: A caste collaboration diagram depicts the interactions between agent castes by showing what actions of what castes are observed (and reacted to) by other castes. Arcs in the diagram are labelled with the source caste's action name.

Behaviour models in CAMLE describe how a specific caste behaves from its own perspective. In particular, scenario diagrams show how agents of a given caste act when in a given scenario. Although scenario diagrams are similar to UML statechart diagrams ([9], sec. 3.74), they incorporate additional notation for predicates, state assertions and logic connectives. A new method fragment is necessary to reflect this.

OPEN Work Product

Name: *CAMLE Scenario Diagram*
OPEN classification: Dynamic Behaviour set of work products
Brief description: A CAMLE scenario diagram depicts the sequence of actions and state assertions that agents of a given caste go through when in a given scenario. Single and repetitive actions, as well as simple and continuous state assertions can be depicted, using logical connectives (and, or, not) if necessary.

Behaviour diagrams combine all the scenario diagrams of a given caste into a single diagram showing its overall behaviour and hiding the details of each single scenario. A new method fragment is introduced here.

OPEN Work Product

Name: *CAMLE Behaviour Diagram*
OPEN classification: Dynamic Behaviour set of work products
Brief description: A CAMLE-derived behaviour diagram depicts the interrelations between scenarios, preconditions and actions of a given agent caste. All the notation available for scenario diagrams is available, as well as a conflux notation that can be used to represent a logical conjunction of scenarios and/or preconditions.

4.5   Other Method fragments

CAMLE does not provide any information on appropriate techniques, necessary roles or other kinds of method fragments. Therefore we must assume that the repository of OPEN method fragments is already rich enough for the implementation of CAMLE.

5.   CONCLUSIONS

We have shown in this paper how the major elements of CAMLE can be re-defined formally in terms of the OPEN metamodel, and how the OPEN repository is augmented with method fragments made out of them. This results in an increased level of formality for CAMLE, which enables it to be extended, customized and integrated with other method fragments already present in the OPEN repository. It also results in a benefit for OPEN, since it gains additional content for its repository that enhances its capability to tackle agent-oriented systems development.

ACKNOWLEDGEMENTS

We wish to acknowledge financial support from the University of Technology, Sydney under their Research Excellence Grants Scheme and from the Australian Research Council. This is Contribution number 04/22 of the Centre for Object Technology Applications and Research.

REFERENCES

1. Brinkkemper, S., 1996. *Method Engineering: Engineering of Information Systems Development Methods and Tools.* Information and Software Technology. **38**(4): p. 275-280.
2. Debenham, J. and B. Henderson-Sellers, 2003. *Designing Agent-Based Process Systems - Extending the OPEN Process Framework, in Intelligent Agent Software Engineering*, V. Plekhanova (ed.). Idea Group. p. 160-190.
3. Firesmith, D.G., 2004. *Firesmith OPEN Process Framework (OPF) Website* (web site). Accessed on 27th April 2004. http://www.donald-firesmith.com/
4. Firesmith, D.G. and B. Henderson-Sellers, 2002. *The OPEN Process Framework.* The OPEN Series. London: Addison-Wesley.
5. Graham, I., B. Henderson-Sellers, and H. Younessi, 1997. *The OPEN Process Specification.* The OPEN Series. Harlow (Essex), UK: Addison-Wesley Longman.
6. Henderson-Sellers, B., J. Debenham, and Q.-N.N. Tran, 2004. *Adding Agent-Oriented Concepts derived from Gaia to Agent OPEN.* In *Procs. CAiSE 2004.* Springer-Verlag: Berlin, Germany.

7. Henderson-Sellers, B., J. Debenham, and Q.-N.N. Tran, 2004. *Incorporating the Elements of the MASE Methodology into Agent OPEN.* In *Procs. of the 6th International Conference on Enterprise Information Systems 2004.* 4.

8. Kumar, K. and R.J. Welke, 1992. *Methodology Engineering: a Proposal for Situation-Specific Methodology Construction*, in *Challenges and Strategies for Research in Systems Development*, W.W. Cotterman and J.A. Senn (eds.). John Wiley & Sons: Chichester, UK. p. 257-269.

9. OMG, 2001. *Unified Modelling Language Specification.* formal/01-09-68 through 80 (13 documents). Object Management Group.

10. Rolland, C. and N. Prakash, 1996. *A Proposal for Context-Specific Method Engineering.* In *Procs. IFIP WG8 International Conference on Method Engineering.* Atlanta, GA.

11. Saeki, M., 2003. *CAME: the First Step to Automated Software Engineering.* In *Procs. OOPSLA 2003 Workshop on Process Engineering for Object-Oriented and Component-Based Development.* Anaheim, CA, 26-30 October 2033. COTAR: Sydney.

12. Shan, L. and H. Zhu, 2004. *CAMLE: A Caste-Centric Agent-Oriented Modeling Language and Environment.* In *Third International Workshop on Software Engineering for Large-Scale Multi-Agent Systems.* Edinburgh, 24-25 May 2004. [in press]. Springer-Verlag.

13. ter Hofstede, A.H.M. and T.F. Verhoef, 1997. *On the Feasibility of Situational Method Engineering.* Information Systems. **22**(6/7): p. 401-422.

REPRESENTING HUMAN SPATIAL BEHAVIOR BY SELF-ORGANIZING NETWORKS

Takamitsu Mizutori and Kenji Kohiyama
Keio University Graduate School of Media and Governance, Design Studio B, 5322 Endoh Fujisawa, Kanagawa 252-8520 JAPAN, Tel:(+81)466-47-5000(ext.53665), e-mail: {mizutori, kohiyama}@sfc.keio.ac.jp

Abstract: In this paper, we propose a way for mobile applications to recognize the daily spatial behavior of a user in the duration of a day. A feature representation of the user's spatial behavior is created from the accumulation of GPS location data logged in the user's everyday lives. By referencing this representation - called "Behavior Map", mobile applications could infer a path the user will take, and behave proactively for locations where the user will be in.

Key words: Mobile agents; Distributed intelligence; Neural Computing.

1.   INTRODUCTION

In various pervasive computing scenarios, location information has been used to associate virtual objects with users' living environments (Harter et al., 1999; Jebara et al. 1999). Typical in these computing environments is that only the current position of a user is referred to invoke several computational events (e.g. retrieve reminders (Rodes, 1997)). In this paper, we propose a way for mobile applications to recognize not only the current location of the user, but her spatial behavior in the duration of a day.

2.   ORGANIZING A BEHAVIOR MAP

Our internal knowledge representations about familiar environments (Downs and Stea, 1973; Kuipers, 1982) are called "Cognitive Maps". Alternative knowledge representations for mobile applications to recognize our familiar paths are created in this paper. We call this representation as

"Behavior Maps". A Behavior Map is created by GPS location logs collected by the system shown in Figure 1. Using a GPS capable cellular phone, a user obtains her location information and attaches it to an e-mail and sends to a server where a map organizing agent organizes a Behavior Map.

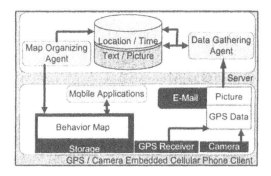

Figure1. System architecture

From a location log - (longitude, latitude, time of log), an input node of three -element vector (x, y, t) is created by normalizing the log by the Eq.(1). In Eq. (1), *m* is the number of the inputs, *minute$_i$* is the minute value of the time of log, and the constant number 1440 is the minute value of one day.

$$x_i = longitude_i / \left\{ \max_{j=1...m}(longitude_j) - \min_{j=1...m}(longitude_j) \right\}$$

$$y_i = latitude_i / \left\{ \max_{j=1...m}(latitude_j) - \min_{j=1...m}(latitude_j) \right\}$$

$$t_i = minute_i / 1440 \tag{1}$$

A learning network is constructed by a fixed number of output nodes in order to finally organize a Behavior Map. An output node is a three-element vector - (x, y, t), each element of which is initially given a pseudo random value ranging from 0 to 1. The output nodes are monotonically connected as a chain from node 0 to node N. The learning process is based on the self-organizing neural network (Kohonen, 1995). For each input node, every output node calculates the distance to that input node as,

$$DIST(I,O) = \sqrt{\alpha\left\{ (x_{out} - x_{in})^2 + (y_{out} - y_{in})^2 \right\} + \beta(t_{out} - t_{in})^2} \tag{2}$$

where α and β is the weight to define the relation between space and time (both α and β values are 1 in the experiment). The output node with the minimum DIST value, which is called "winner node", and its neighborhood output nodes update their vectors as,

$$O_i(t+1) = O_i(t) + \alpha(t)\beta_{ij}(t)\big(I(t) - O_i(t)\big)$$ (3)

where j is the id of the winner node, and $O_i(t)$ is the vector of the output node i at iteration t. $\alpha(t)$ is the learn rate at iteration t defined as, $\alpha(t) = \alpha(t_o)\big(\alpha(T)/\alpha(t_o)\big)^{t/T}$. $t_o = 0$, and T is the maximum iteration number given as, $T = num\_outputs \times 500 / num\_inputs$. $\beta_{ij}(t)$ is the neighborhood-learn rate defined as, $\beta_{ij}(t) = \exp(-|i-j|^2/\sigma(t)^2)$, where $\sigma(t)$ is the number of the neighborhood nodes to be updated. After iterating the process of Eqs.(2)-(3) to the all inputs by T times, the leaning network organizes a sequence of representative spatio-temporal points of the user's spatial behavior, which we call Behavior Map.

3.   EXPERIMENT

Behavior Maps of two users' week-day behaviors were created from their 75 and 88 location logs. The initial and final learn rate is 0.3 and 0.1 respectively in $\alpha(t)$ of Eq.(3). $\sigma(t)$ in $\beta_{ij}(t)$ starts from five, is decreased by one every time T/5 iterations passed, and ends to one (including only the winner node). The accuracy of the GPS receiver is 10 meters without any obstacles, 24-30 meters on arcaded streets, and more than 100 meters inside buildings (Sasaki, 2003). Behavior Maps were organized by different numbers of output nodes. Average distances between an input node and the nearest output node in the Behavior Maps are shown in Figre2. In the optimal Behavior Maps with 55 output nodes, shown in Figure3, the actual average distances in space and time are (689 meters, 32 minutes) for the user A, and (879 meters, 51 minutes) for the user B.

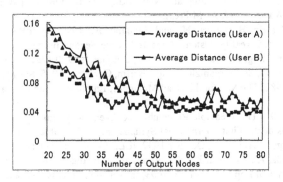

Figur2. Average distance between each input node and the nearest output node (User A)

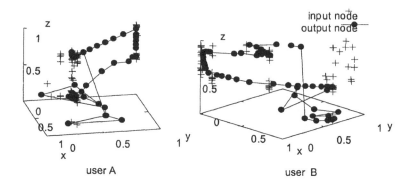

Figure 3. The Behavior Maps with 55 output nodes

4.   CONCLUSION

In this paper, we propose a computational model to create a representation of a user's daily spatial behavior from partial and distributed location logs. This representation is named "Behavior Map". Mobile systems could infer the user's spatial context by querying his/her current position to the Behavior Map. The experiment on two users' location logs showed that, even from discrete instances of the users' spatial behavior, effective representations could be created.

5.   REFERENCES

1. Downs, R. M., and Stea, D., 1973, Cognitive maps and spatial behavior. In Image and Environment, pages 8-26, Chicago, IL, U.S.A., 1973. Aldine Publishing Company.
2. Harter, A., Hopper, A., Steggles, P., Ward, A., and Webster, P., 1999, The anatomy of a context-aware application. In Proceedings of the Fifth Annual ACM/IEEE International Conference on Mobile Computing and Networking, MOBICOM'99, pages 59-68, Seattle, WA, U.S.A., August 1999. ACM Press.
3. Jebara, T., Schiele, B., Oliver, N., and Pentland, A., 1999, DyPERS: A Dynamic and Personal Enhanced Reality System. Appeared in the Second International Symposium on Wearable Computing, Pittsburgh, PA, U.S.A., October 1999. IEEE Computer Society.
4. Kohonen, T., 1995, Self-Organizing Maps, Berlin, Germany, 1995. Springer-Verlag.
5. Kuipers, B., 1982, The Map in the Head Metaphor, Environment and Behavior, 14(2):202-220, 1982.
6. Rhodes, B., 1997, The Wearable Remembrance Agent: a system for augmented memory. In Proceedings of the First International Symposium on Wearable Computing, pages 123-128, Cambridge, MA, U.S.A., October 1997. IEEE Computer Society.
7. Sasaki, I., Goda, K., Kogawa, K., H. Tarumi, 2003, Evaluation of the Space Tag System. IPSJ SIG Technical Reports, GN47-5, 2003, Information Processing Society of Japan.

MULTI-AGENT SYSTEM DEVELOPMENT KIT
MAS SOFTWARE TOOL IMPLEMENTING GAIA METHODOLOGY

Vladimir Gorodetski, Oleg Karsaev, Vladimir Samoilov, Victor Konushy, Evgeny Mankov and Alexey Malyshev
St. Petersburg Institute for Informatics and Automation, 14th line, 39,SPIIRAS, St. Petersburg, 199178, Russia
Phone: +7-812-2323570, fax: +7-812-3280685, E-mail:
{gor, ok, samovl, kvg, eman, A.Malyshev }@mail.iias.spb.su,
http://space.iias.spb.su/ai/gorodetski/gorodetski.jsp

Abstract: Recent research in area of multi-agent technology attracted a growing attention of both scientific community and industrial companies. This attention is stipulated by powerful capabilities of multi-agent technology allowing to create large scale distributed intelligent systems, and, on the other hand, by practical needs of industrial companies to possess an advanced and reliable technology for solving of practically important problems. Currently one of the topmost questions of the research is development of powerful methodologies for engineering of agent-based systems and development of more effective and efficient tools supporting implementation of applied systems. The paper presents one of such tools, Multi Agent System Development Kit, based on and implementing of Gaia methodology. It supports the whole life cycle of multi-agent system development and maintains integrity of solutions produced at different stages of the development process.

Key words: Software engineering, Multi agent systems, Methodology, Software tool

1. INTRODUCTION

Although agent-oriented software engineering is being a subject of active research for over a decade, it does not still come to the age of maturity required to be rated as an industrial technology. In spite of rich theoretical achievements in this area, there practically exist no powerful Multi-Agent System (MAS) software tools capable to support the whole life cycle of industrial MAS comprising analysis, design, implementation, deployment and maintenance, although to date a lot of MAS software tools are developed. Among them, the most mature and popular are AgentBuilder [18], Jack [16], JADE [3], ZEUS [7], FIPA-OS [11], agentTool [9], etc.

Analysis of the existing software tools allows understanding potential directions that can bring necessary results for considerable increasing powerfulness and maturity of MAS software tools. One of them is exploitation and adaptation of the experience accumulated within object-oriented approach and existing (at least, de-facto) "standards" of analysis, design and implementation commonly used in the information technologies [5]. In this respect, several initiatives are currently undertaken, and one of them is Agent UML project [1] that is being carried out by two leading international organizations, FIPA and OMG, focused on standardization within advanced information technology scope.

The other source of evolution and perfection of the MAS software tool is further development of the existing methodologies of agent–based system engineering that should potentially provide designers with new opportunities. Among the existing methodologies, Gaia [19], MESSAGE [6], MaSE [10], Prometheus [17], Adelfe [4], Tropos [12] and some others pretend to be very promising. Gaia methodology considers two stages of applied MAS development that are (1) analysis and (2) design. The objective of the analysis is to reach "*an understanding of the system and its structure (without reference to any implementation details)*" [19]. This stage assumes design of solutions of a high-level of abstraction concerning system organization, i.e. discovery MAS tasks, discovery roles and their responsibilities within particular MAS applications, description of roles' tasks and high-level scheme of roles' interactions during fulfillment of the MAS tasks, etc. The objective of the design stage is "*to transform the abstract models derived during the analysis stage into models at a sufficiently low level of abstraction that can be easily implemented*" [19]. This stage assumes formal specification of how the community of agents interacts in order to solve the MAS tasks and also formal specification of each particular agent of applied MAS under development.

Thus, the current trends in MAS technology prompt that sound methodology enriched by ideas and experience from object–oriented design scope can considerably improve MAS technology providing it with such properties as consistency and integrity of solutions being produced at the subsequent stages of MAS engineering life cycle.

The paper presents a recently developed software tool, Multi-agent System Development Kit 3.0 (MASDK) providing support for the whole life cycle of applied MAS development. This software tool is based on Gaia methodology integrated with ideas of object–oriented design of MAS resulted from the Agent UML project. This software tool was the subject of research during last years and the current version is the third one. Previous versions of MASDK [13] were used for rapid prototyping of different MAS applications [14, 15]. The experience accumulated so far allowed understanding of the drawbacks and limitations of the previous two versions of MASDK and developing adequate requirements to its current version, 3.0.

MASDK 3.0 software tool is now being evaluated based on design of applied MAS for detection of intrusions in computer network, situation assessment and design activity support. In the rest of the paper, section 2 outlines general ideas of MASDK supported technology. Sections 3, 4 and 5 describe the analysis, design, and implementation stages respectively of MAS technology. Conclusion outlines the paper results and future work.

2. OUTLINE OF MASDK 3.0 SOFTWARE TOOL AND TECHNOLOGY SUPPORTED

MASDK 3.0 software tool consists of the following components (Fig.1): (1) *system kernel* which is a data structure for XML–based representation of applied MAS formal specification; (2) *integrated* set of the user friendly *editors* supporting user's activity aiming at formal specification of an applied MAS under development at the analysis, design and implementation stages; (3) library of C++ classes of reusable agent components constituting what is usually called *Generic agent*; (4) communication platform to be installed in particular computers of a network; and (5) builder of software agent instances responsible for generation of C++ source code and executable code of software agents as well as deployment of software agents over already installed communication platform.

Specification of applied MAS in the system kernel is being carried out by use of editors structured in three levels. Editors of the *first one* provide support for meta–level specification of applied MAS corresponding to the

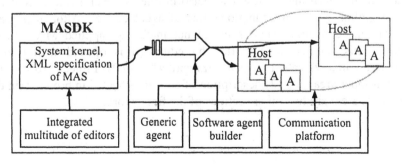

Figure 1. MASDK software tool components and their interaction

analysis stage in Gaia methodology. The set of the first level editors includes (1) *application ontology* editor, (2) editor for *description of roles, names of agent classes, and high-level schemes of roles' interactions,* (3) editor of *roles' interaction protocols.* Editors of the *second level* support the design activities and primarily aim at specification of agent classes. The following editors are used for this purpose: (1) editor specifying *meta-model of agent classes' behavior*; (2) editor specifying *particular agent functions and behavior scenarios* in terms of state machines; (3) editor specifying software *agent private ontology* inheriting the notions of shared domain ontology.

Editors of the *third level* support implementation stage of applied MAS and aim at (1) implementing (in C++ language) a *set of particular components and functions* specified in design stage; (2) specifying *sub-network* within which the designed MAS is to be deployed; (3) specifying *lists of agents instances of all classes* with the references to their locations (hosts names), and (4) initial states of *mental models* of each agent instance.

Applied MAS specification produced by designers exploiting the above editors is stored as XML file in the system kernel. This specification, including set of particular components and functions implemented in C++, and *Generic Agent* reusable component form the input of the software agent builder generating automatically software code based on *XSLT* technology.

3. ANALYSIS STAGE: APPLIED MAS META-MODEL

At the analysis stage conceptual description of applied MAS is produced. While having the MAS high–level tasks determined, the first step of problem domain analysis assumes (1) discovery and description of roles, (2) high–level mapping of role interactivities to protocol list, (3) determination of agent classes' names, and (4) designation of roles to them. At that, information about roles, interaction protocols, their mapping and textual description of the roles behavior according to respective protocols are used for defining the set of agent classes and assigning of roles to them. It is assumed that each agent class can perform one or several roles. Actually, this mapping determines functionalities of agent classes. Altogether these descriptions constitute what is called hereinafter an applied MAS meta–model. This activity is supported by editor (it is opened within main MASDK window) called "*Agent Framework*" (Fig.2). Project browser (in the left-upper area) and (2) description of element selected in browser (in the left-down area) are two other sections of the framework.

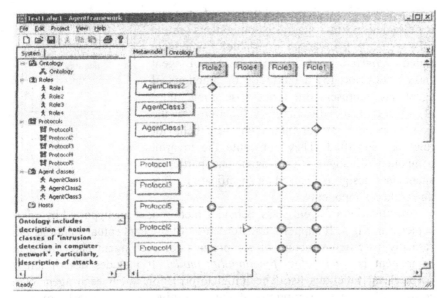

Figure 2. Meta-model editor

Detailed description of the roles interaction protocols is one of the key tasks of the analysis stage. Realizing the importance of this task was perhaps one of the reasons motivated the Agent UML project [1] initiated by both FIPA and OMG. Let us remind that the project objective is an extension of UML language to agent–based system specification language, and one of the focuses of this Project is development of a language directly destined for specification of agent interaction protocols [2].

MASDK 3.0 includes graphical editor of roles' interaction protocols that makes use of main principal solutions of Agent UML project. Not all the proposals of Agent UML project, pretending to develop future standards of MAS, are used in MASDK 3.0, because Agent UML is currently in progress and, thus, some of its proposals are tentative while others seem to be not well grounded or too overloaded with secondary notations, what makes it difficult both to understand and to implement such notations. For example, agent interaction protocol specification language used in MASDK 3.0 is a simplified version of the analogous language of Agent UML although the former preserves basically the expressive power of the latter.

4. DESIGN STAGE: AGENT CLASSES

Applied MAS meta-model developed at the analysis stage is further used as an input of the design stage. Specification of agent classes is a key point

of this stage. Generalized architecture of an agent
is presented in Fig.3. Its basic components are the
followings: (1) invariant (reusable) component
called *Generic Agent*, (2) meta-model of agent
class's behavior, (3) a multitude of functions of
agent class represented in terms of state machines;
(4) library of specific auxiliary functions. In the
first component, the common agent meta–behavior
rules are specified. They constitute the invarint
component of any software agent and particular
agent class design is focused on specification of its
three other components.

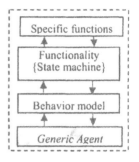

Figure 3. Agent structure

    Specification of agent class' behavior meta-model is supported by editor
depicted in Fig.4. It supports transformation of the conceptual solutions into
formally specified structure of components for each agent class. Its main
component is *Agent class functionality model.* It includes description of
agent class' functions list. The initial information about each agent class
consists of textual descriptions of the respective roles and tasks of roles
(defined at analysis stage of MAS development) allocated for execution to
agent class. Detailed specification of the above functions is the designer's
responsibility. An example of the set of such functions represented as state
machines is demonstrated graphically in Fig.4.
    The rest of the agent class components can be divided into two groups.
The first of them specifies event classes initiating execution of functions
specified within the following four components:
    Input messages. This component indicates relations between certain
protocols and functions. The sense of these relations is to point out the
protocols in which agent class in question takes part if the above protocols
are initiated by certain other agent classes. These protocols are determined
formally by use of meta-model of applied MAS developed at the analysis
stage. Let us note that the first messages of protocols play the roles of events
initiating execution of the respective functions.
    User commands. This component is present in agent class if it interacts
with user initiating certain agent class behavior in certain situations. In this
component, if any, the user commands mapped to respective functions are
specified.
    Pro-active model. If non-empty, it includes specification of rules in the
form *"When ... if ... then ...".* The precondition "*When*" indicates events
(e.g., time instants) when the second condition has to be the subject of
checking. The condition "*if*" specifies the agent class mental state when the
function indicated in the third part of the rule has to be executed.

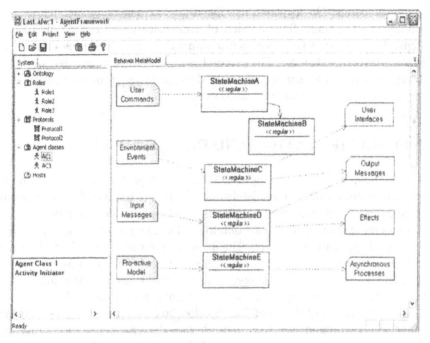

Figure 4. Meta-model of agent class behaviour

Environment events. Content of this component specifies classes of environmental events and respective behavior of agent class.

The second group of components describes actions that can be or has to be performed during execution of respective functions. They are 1) initiation of interaction protocols, 2) dialogs with user, 3) effects on environment and 4) execution of specific functions in asynchronous mode. In contrast to the components of the first group, which must be completely specified at this stage, specification of the components of second group is considered as specific application-dependent requirements to be taken into account in the subsequent steps of the design stage. The editor supports graphical mode of representation of the relationships between components and functions in form of explicit connections between them. Connections between functions represent the facts that certain functions are nested ones and their execution is invoked by other functions.

Each function is represented (specified formally) in terms of state machine composed of the following standard components: (1) state machine states; (2) transitions and conditions determining the transition selection depending on the agent current state; (3) state machine behavior corresponding to each particular state. Specification of the first and the second components is executed at the design stage and it is supported by graphical editor. On the contrary, the third component is specified at the implementation stage. Specification of state machines is carried out in two steps. The first step is carried out automatically based on meta-models of agent classes' behavior. The second step in carried out by designer developing the first step specification through insertion of new states with respective updating of the transitions structure.

5. IMPLEMENTATION AND DEPLOYMENT

The next stage of an applied MAS development corresponds to its implementation that is completely based on the results of two previous stages. Implementation technology consists of the following activities:

1) Implementation of the private ontology of each agent class, which inherits the shared application ontology. The inherited notions of shared ontology are used in specification of agent class messages content. The rest of notions specified in the private ontology of agent class (they can also inherit the notions of shared ontology) represent the agent class mental model.

2) Implementation of the library of specific auxiliary C++ classes of all the agent class components specified at the design stage. These classes correspond to scripts of agent classes behavior in particular states of state machines and functions (see Fig.3).

3) Specification of the applied MAS configuration, in particular, specification of instances of each agent class and indication of their locations in computer network where applied MAS under development is deployed.

4) Specification of initial mental model of each agent.

The next step of implementation stage is destined for generation of software agent instances and their placing in the respective hosts of computer network according to their addresses. While generating software code of an agent instance, three types of its components are combined. These components are (1) reusable component called *Generic agent*; (2) C++ library that is software implementation of particular functions; and (3) software components implementing meta-models of behavior and state machines of agent classes. It should be noted that software code of the last component and agents as a whole are generated automatically.

6. CONCLUSION

MASDK environment described in the paper possesses a number of practically important advantages allowing noticeably decrease the total amount of efforts and costs of multi–agent systems development. Among them, the most important ones are the followings:

1) Development process is carried out according to a well grounded methodology that is the Gaia methodology, whose abstract notion classes closely interrelate with the other ones used at the subsequent stages of applied MAS design and implementation.

2) User friendly multitude of graphical editors of MASDK provides clear presentation and simple understanding of all the stages of applied MAS development process. Together with the property mentioned in the item 1, graphical mode of the development process provides simple and clear cooperation between designers and programmers during the whole life cycle of applied MAS.

3) Due to well structured set of abstract notion classes, the MASDK environment provides development process with a capability of consistency maintenance and checking of integrity at all stages of process.

4) Representation of interaction protocols that is one of the key tasks of agent-based systems specification, based on solutions evolving experience of object-oriented approach makes the resulting applied MAS potentially compatible with the de-facto standards that are being developed within OMG and FIPA efforts within Agent UML project.

5) The developed technology is strongly based on reusability idea and *Generic agent* library, which includes necessary set of reusable solutions/software components, allows reducing the development process to specification of application-oriented knowledge.

Due to these advantages MASDK environment pretends to be a sufficiently effective and efficient tool with industry-oriented potential.

Currently the basis components of MASDK software tool are implemented and it is being validated via its use for development of applied MAS in such application domains as data fusion, computer network security, and design activity support and monitoring.

ACKNOWLEDGEMENT

This research is supported by grants of European Office of Aerospace R&D (Project #1993P) and Russian Academy of Sciences (Department of Information Technologies and Computer Systems), Project # 4.3.

REFERENCES

1. Agent UML: http://www.auml.org/

2. Bauer, B., Muller, J. P., Odell, J.: Agent UML: A Formalism for Specifying Multiagent Interaction. In: Ciancarini, P. and Wooldridge, M. (eds): Agent-Oriented Software Engineering, Springer-Verlag, Berlin, (2001) 91-103

3. Bellifemine, F., Caire, G., Trucco, T., Rimassa, G.: Jade Programmer's Guid. JADE 2.5 (2002) http://sharon.cselt.it/projects/jade/

4. Bernon, C., Gleizes, M.P., Peyruqueou, S., Picard, G.: Adelfe, a methodology for Adaptive Multi-Agent Systems Engineering. In: Third International Workshop "Engineering Societies in the Agents World" (ESAW-2002), Madrid, (2002)

5. Booch, G.: Object-Oriented Analysis and Design, 2nd ed., Addison-Wesley: Reading, MA, (1994)

6. Caire, G., Leal, F., Chainho, P., Evans, R., Garijo, F., Gomez, J., Pavon, J., Kearney, P., Stark, J., and Massonet, P.: Agent-oriented analysis using MESSAGE/UML. In: Wooldridge, M., Ciancarini, P., and Weiss, G., (editors): Second International Workshop on Agent-Oriented Software Engineering (AOSE-2001), (2001) 101-108

7. Collis, J. and Ndumu, D.: Zeus Technical Manual. Intelligent Systems Research Group, BT Labs. British Telecommunications. (1999)

8. Dam, K. H., and Winikoff, M.: Comparing Agent-Oriented Methodologies. http://grial.uc3m.es/~dcamacho/resources/papersAOSE/dam03comparing.pdf

9. DeLoach S. and Wood, M.: Developing Multiagent Systems with agentTool. In: Castelfranchi, C., Lesperance Y. (Eds.): Intelligent Agents VII. Agent Theories Architectures and Languages, 7th International Workshop, LNCS. Vol.1986, Springer Verlag, (2001)

10. DeLoach, S. A., Wood, M. F., and Sparkman, C. H.: Multiagent systems engineering. In: International Journal of Software Engineering and Knowledge Engineering, 11(3), (2001) 231-258

11. FIPA-OS: A component-based toolkit enabling rapid development of FIPA compliant agents. http://fipa-os.sourceforge.net/

12. Giunchiglia, F., Mylopoulos, J., and Perini, A.: The Tropos software development methodology: Processes, Models and Diagrams. In: Third International Workshop on Agent-Oriented Software Engineering, Jula (2002)

13. Gorodetski, V., Karsaev, O., Kotenko, I., Khabalov, A.: Software Development Kit for Multi-agent Systems Design and Implementation. In: Dunin-Keplicz, B., Navareski, E. (Eds.): From Theory to Practice in Multi-agent Systems. Lecture Notes in Artificial Intelligence, Vol. # 2296, (2002) 121-130

14. Gorodetski, V., Karsaev, O., Konushi, V.: Multi-Agent System for Resource Allocation and Schedulling. In: Lecture Notes in Artificial Intelligence, Vol. # 2691, (2003) 226-235

15. Gorodetsky, V., Karsaev, O., Samoilov, V.: Multi-agent Technology for Distributed Data Mining and Classification. In: Proceedings of the IEEE Conference Intelligent Agent Technology (IAT-03), Halifax, Canada, (2003) 438-441

16. Jack. Jack intelligent agents – version 3.1, agent oriented software pty. Ltd., Australia, http://www.agent-software.com.au .

17. Padgham, L. and Winikoff, M.: Prometheus: A pragmatic methodology for engineering intelligent agents. In: Proceedings of the OOPSLA 2002 Workshop on Agent-Oriented Methodologies, Seattle, (2002) 97-108

18. Reticular Systems Inc: AgentBuilder An Integrated Toolkit for Constructing Intelligent Software Agents. Revision 1.3. (1999) http://www.agentbuilder.com/.

19. Wooldridge, M., Jennings, N.R., Kinny, D.: The Gaia Methodology for Agent-Oriented Analysis and Design. In: Journal of Autonomous Agents and Multi-Agent Systems, Vol.3. No. 3 (2000) 285-312

LIMITATIONS IN AUML'S ROLES SPECIFICATION

Jean-Luc Koning & Ivan Romero Hernández
Institut National Polytechnique de Grenoble, LCIS Research Laboratory
50 rue Laffemas, BP 54, 26902 Valence cedex 9, France
{Jean-Luc.Koning,Ivan.Romero}@esisar.inpg.fr

Abstract   Roles have gained a fair amount of attention from researchers in the multiagent system domain, given its recurrent appearance on most application examples using an agent-oriented approach. This attention is understandable, because the role an agent takes within any given system defines every one of its actions, i.e., what it thinks and what it says.

The Agent-UML specification language presents a notion of Role that could be related to previous works such as actors and objects. However, AUML gives roles a totally different, more agent-oriented approach, by considering that roles are a *dynamic property* of the entities conforming the system (agents).

This paper focuses on the limitations of the current AUML specifications and its related implications on dynamic roles.

1.   A Pragmatic Definition of a Role

Roles have gained a fair amount of attention from researchers in the multiagent system (MAS) domain, given its recurrent appearance on most application examples using an agent-oriented approach. This attention is understandable, because the role an agent takes within any given system defines every one of its actions, i.e., what it thinks and what it says.

The notion of role affects many spheres of the agent activity, and not only one specific aspect. In the internal sphere it affects the agent's goals, desires and intentions —using a BDI terminology [5]. While it is evident that a complete notion of role needs to include those more abstract notions to be considered as such, it is impossible right now (given the state of the art), to give a thorough definition that encompasses all the possible dependency relations between roles and all the subtle aspects of agency. For this reason, we are going to choose a pragmatic approach: to give a definition of our own, that follows closely what it is interesting within our research work.

For our interests, **a role is a finite stereotypical behavior an agent takes through its existence within a MAS system.**

By *stereotypical* we mean a *repetitive, more or less predictable* sequence of messages and processing that happens when some condition is met, and by *finite* we mean it doesn't matter how complex the agent gets, there is always a condition known as *final state*. We do not focus on the actual mechanisms that specify how an agent reaches the beginning of any of these stereotypical behaviors, because these are directly linked to the cognitive sphere of the agent, which is well beyond a mere observationally descriptive approach as this one.

We are however, interested in (1) proving that once the system makes the decision of acquiring a stereotypical response, this chosen behavior eventually reaches its final state, and if not, (2) in detecting how this condition come to be in order to prevent it.

2.   Roles are Everywhere

As mentioned above, the notion of role has, indeed, gained a central *role* in some recent publications related to the agent oriented software engineering domain [4]. In the particular case of the AUML proposal, roles are everywhere [6].

AUML presents a notion of Role that could be related to previous works. It is already present on other domains of research, in particular that of *concurrent object actors* [1] [2] and within the more usual object oriented (OO) approach. In the actor approach, the system is defined by modular subdivision and detailed specification of any possible message sequence that any given entity could produce through time. This follows a revisited analogy to the real-world theater piece, where every possible dialog is perfectly specified to every possible actor. In the case of monolithic OO systems, a notion of role comes along with that of *class*, which allow a slightly role-like specification of the system in the form of public methods and encapsulation, but not necessarily enforcing a well defined sequence of message (method) exchange.

However, AUML gives roles a totally different, more agent-oriented approach, by considering that roles are a *dynamic property* of the entities conforming the system (agents).

By *dynamic property* we mean a transient, time dependent attribute related to an agent. In that view, an agent could decide to take or leave a role depending on its mental state, even allowing agents to take or leave a role in the middle of an ongoing interaction process.

3.   Limitations of the Current AUML Specification

As far as we are concerned, this possibility gives birth to some very particular problems unlike those already present on the distributed systems or concurrent objects domain, and likely unseen anywhere else. We have essentially identified four problems.

Role dynamics awareness.   If we have systems where an agent could choose to take another role, every other agent already involved inside an interaction process with the changing agent, should be aware of that change, before pursuing the normal flow of the interaction and any notation pretending to represent this should be explicit enough to represent it. There are some conceivable automatic delegation schemes applicable to particular application examples [3], that could eventually allow an agent to leave its role without affecting the overall function of the rest of the system, but in most cases we believe an explicit notification process will be indispensable.

Interaction integrity.   Once all the agents know a role change has happened, there must be a mechanism ensuring all the necessary roles are *properly* taken within the system, and if roles are or are not *vital* or *indispensable* it would be good to have a explicit way to know it. It is easy to see that any improperly made role-change could severely affect the overall functioning of the system. On the real world, people within an organization usually do not leave their assigned functions without delegating them first, if those functions are relevant enough to the overall functioning of the system. It is also important to note that not all roles are as important and others. For example, within an auction market scenario, it could happen that auctioneers and vendors could desist whenever they wish, even exchange places, but auction house managers can not do so.

Mental state consistency.   When roles are *relevant* to the system functioning, it could be necessary to ensure that the mental state of any possible delegate agent taking over this role is compatible and consistent with the original. This is a necessary condition if we want to assure that the delegate is able to take over the function left by one of their peers.

Location dependency.   In some cases agents are located within an environment, performing a very specific task related to its abstract or real location. These agents could take another role, but not leave a particular vital one which justifies their very existence.

4.   Implications of AUML Dynamic Roles

We believe that the dynamic nature of roles, as defined by the AUML proposal, has some interesting implications to the kind of multiagent systems AUML is capable of modeling. If we accept the fact that roles could change over time, according to the agent's mental state, we are also implying that there are mechanisms embedded within the final system to handle this role change.

Strangely enough there is very few, if any, publications on these issues. At this point, we essentially suggest two possible directions.

An explicit role-change notification mechanism made implicit.   There should be a way for the MAS as a whole to know when an agent has changed its role within the system, in order to assure a minimal functioning.

Usually in most MAS it is assumed that an agent knows which role it has and that it is able to detect which role their peers have too, either guessing by the sequence of messages they provide or through a explicit request. But most importantly, once an interaction process begins, it is executed until its end, without sudden roles changes. So we could insure that agent's mental state is consistent at the end of the interaction.

If we accept that an agent's role (or roles) could change over time according to the agent's mental state, even within an ongoing interaction process, we are implying that there is an implicit mechanism to notify the others that a change took place. It is either that or an advanced delegation mechanism.

An advanced delegation mechanism.   If agents could change role transparently without explicitly notifying to their peers every time they change their role, there must be a delegation mechanism taking the responsibility for them. This is in order to insure the continuity of the system function.

Those mechanisms *know* which roles belong to which agents and are capable of locating an agent capable of taking over the function given away by a third one. Such mechanisms *do exist* in some experimental multiagent systems [3], but are relatively far from the usual approach taken by most MAS platforms; where agents have well defined communication channels. They must find out by themselves if there is another agent capable of satisfying their needs; for example, through a ContractNet interaction protocol.

These advanced delegation systems have another severe limitation: mental state consistency is hard to satisfy. It restricts the kind of roles that could be delegated to a small subset of all the imaginable scenarios.

Besides, such delegation schema only works for a rather limited number of settings,i.e., in case there is no strong dependance between the internal variables (agent's mental state), like for instance in middle-ware agents or proxys.

5.   Mental State Consistency and Communication Integrity

Left apart the fact that AUML seems to already suggest some kind of infrastructure within the modeled system —which is against the intended purpose of platform independence behind such a notation—, there still is the problem of mental state consistency and communication integrity on dynamic role-change scenarios.

If we use a simplified internal versus external approach to the agent domain, it is not surprising to see in every MAS example available, that an agent's mental state is closely related to its history of interactions, and that this mental state is also decisive on the course those interactions will take from the present. The very notion of agent is based on this idea that the capacity of agents learning from past experiences (through interaction with the environment or with other agents) and the ability to choose what to do next according to this experience.

For specialists interested in multiagent system modeling, there are many methodological approaches that are more or less satisfying depending on their particular interests. For people interested in interaction, most agent oriented systems could be modeled in a manner analogous to most communicating systems, i.e., using a model checking approach (EFSM, Boochy automatas, Petri nets, CCS, Pi-calculus) and validated through model checkers, or a fully logics approach validated through theorem proving systems.

References

[1] G. Agha and P. V. Thati. Actors: A model for reasoning about open distributed systems. In *Formal methods for distributed processing: An object oriented approach*, chapter 8. Cambridge University Press, 1986.

[2] Jean-Pierre Briot. Actalk: A testbed for classifying and designing actor languages in the smalltalk-80 environment. In S. Cook, editor, *ECOOP-89*, pages 109–129, Nottingham, 1989. Cambridge University Press.

[3] Denis Jouvin and Salima Hassas. Dynamic multiagent architecture using conversational role delegation. In *International Workshop on Agent Oriented Software Engineering (AOSE-2003)*, LNCS, Melbourne, Australia, July 2003.

[4] Elizabeth A. Kendall. Agent roles and aspects. In *ECOOP Workshop*, page 440, 1998.

[5] D. Kinny, A. Rao, and M. Georgeff. A methodology and modeling technique for systems of bdi agents. In W. Van de Velde and J. Perram, editors, *Agents Breaking Away: 7th Workshop on Modeling Autonomous Agents in a Multi-Agent World (MAAMAW-96)*, volume LNAI 1038, pages 56–71, Eindhoven, The Netherlands, 1996. Springer-Verlag.

[6] James Odell, Harry Van Dyke Parunak, and Mitch Fleischer. The role of roles in designing effective agent organizations. In Alessandro Garcia, C. Lucena, F. Zambonelli, A. Omicini, and J. Castro, editors, *Software engineering for large-scale multiagent systems*, volume 2603 of *Lecture Notes on Computer Science*, pages 22–28. Springer, Berlin, 2003.

THE RESEARCH OF GEOMETRIC CONSTRAINT SOVING BASED ON THE PATH TRACKING HOMOTOPY ITERATION METHOD

Cao Chunhong, Lu Yinan and Li Wenhui
College of computer science and technology, Jilin University

Changchun 130012, P.R.China

Abstract: Geometric constraint problem is equivalent to the problem of solving a set of nonlinear equations substantially. Nonlinear equations can be solved by classical Newton-Raphson algorithm. Path tracking is the iterative application of Newton-Raphson algorithm. The Homotopy iteration method based on the path tracking is appropriate for solving all polynomial equations. Due to at every step of path tracking we get rid off the estimating tache, and the number of divisor part is less, so the calculation efficiency is higher than the common continuum method and the calculation complexity is also less than the common continuum method.

Key words: Geometric constraint solving, under-constraint, homotopy iteration method, path tracking

1.   INTRODUCTION

Geometric constraint solving approaches are made of three approaches: algebraic-based solving approach, rule-based solving approach and graph-based solving approach. One constraint describes a relation that should be satisfied. Once a user defines a series of relations, the system will satisfy the constraints by selecting proper states after the parameters are modified. The idea is named as model-based constraints. Constraint solver is a segment for the system to solve the constraints. In the practical project application, there are three basic needs for the geometric constraint problems: real-time quality (the speed must be fast), integrality (all the solutions must be gained) and stability (a small change from the solutions to the problems it cannot lead to a large change).

Geometric constraint problem is equivalent to the problem of solving a set of nonlinear equations substantially. In constraint set every constraint corresponds to one or more nonlinear equations, all the unattached geometric parameters in the geometric element set constitute the variable set of nonlinear equations. Nonlinear equations can be solved by Newton-Raphson algorithm. When the size of geometric constraint problem is large, the scale of the equation set is very large. Furthermore, the geometric information in the geometric system will not be treated properly and we cannot deal with under- and over-constrained design system well when all the equations must be solved. Accordingly, we can differentiate the geometry constraint method based on algebra method the method based on numerical value and based on symbol. Symbol solving can solve closed formal analytical solution of the problem, it is certainly the most perfect method, but sometimes, its difficulty is also very high. Along with the accretion of the problem's mathematical model, the process of eliminating variable is more and more complicate. [2]

The most universal method is Newton Iteration method, for example, the method proposed by Gossard[3], Assuming the constraint equations F_i $(x_i) = 0$, then the Newton-Raphson iteration formula is

$$X_i^{n+1} = X_i^n - \left[F_i'(X_i^n)\right]^{-1} F(X_i^n),$$

Here $\left[F_i'(X_i^n)\right]$ is a Jacobi matrix.

Given the initialized value X_i^0, we can calculate the new value X_i^1, X_i^2, ... , X_i^k according to iteration formula, until it satisfy (i) $\|F_i(X_i^k)\| < \delta$, or (ii) $k > N_{max}$. Condition (i): It can indicate that the iteration is convergent in a given time, and success in getting the solution; Condition (ii): indicate that the iteration isn't convergent in a given time, and fails in getting the solution. Generally, the method can get the solution quickly, but it needs a nice initialization value and it is quite sensitive to the initialized value. Using the method, when the initialization value changed a little, it may lead to emanative or converge to the solution that the user doesn't want. The analysis span method that [4] put forward is convergent in quite range, and we can judge if there is no solution in a given range, by the method we can also solve all the solutions in the range if there exist solutions, but there still exist problem choosing appropriate range of the initialization value. Homotopy can overcome this shortcoming[5, 6, 7] in a certain degree. Homotopy is an effective numerical iterative method, it has a strong whole convergence, and it can solve all the solution or a set of the isolated solution of the equations reliably. But the equations from the geometry constraint problem is sometimes under-constraint, so when using the homotopy method to get the solution, we should adopt the homogeneous homotopy method or the coefficient homotopy method, it need to predispose the problem, it not only makes the solving process more complicated, but also needs specific disposal for specific problem, then it decreases the universality of the solving process. For the big scale and under-constraint problem, the calculating efficiency of solving also restricts the practical appliance of the method. [8-13]

Based on the spirit the Homotopy continuum, we put forward a new numerical iterative method that integrates the Homotopy function with the traditional iteration method; we define it as Homotopy iteration method. Similarly with the usual Homotopy method, Homotopy iteration method can effectively solve all numerical solution of the non-linear equations without choosing appropriate initialization value. For the under-degree equation, it not only needn't to predispose such as homogeneous Homotopy or coefficient Homotopy, but also has a higher calculation efficiency and reliability of getting all the solutions.

2.   HOMOTOPY ITERATION METHOD

2.1   The Summarization of the Homotopy Method

Homotopy itself is the conception in the Analisissitus. Homotopy algorithm is a whole algorithm that can solve non-linear equations. In 1976, Kellogg and Yorke.Li, solved the global astringency problem of the Homotopy algorithm by differential coefficient topology tools, and proved the theorem's constructive character of Brouwer fixed point, from then on scientists began to restudy the Homotopy method. In several decades, this algorithm became a successfully algorithm and is applied to the Economics, the design of the electronic circuitry, auto control, computer aided design, computer aided manufacture and many other areas and so on.

The main spirit of the Homotopy is that: firstly, choose a simple equation $f(x)=0$, which solution is known, then construct the Homotopy mapping $H(x,t)$ which contains parameter, such that $H(x,0) = f(x)$, $H(x,1) = g(x)$. In a given condition, the solution of the H(x,t) = 0 can define the curve x(t) which starts from the solution of f(x) = 0, x(0) = x^0, when t approximates to 1, the curve achieve to the solution x*=x(1) of the g(x) = 0, this is just Homotopy method.

Therefore, Homotopy method can be disparted into two steps: *Step1*. Insert the equations P(x) into a cluster of the equations H(x,t), this is just the reason why we call it as Homotopy. *Step2*. Carry numerical track to the solution curve by the Homotopy-Continuation Method.

Definition1: Homotopy H(x,t) = 0 is defined as a set of equations as follows:

$$H(x,t) = c (1-t)^k f (x) + t^k g (x) = 0, \quad k \in N, \quad c \in C \backslash \{0\}, \quad t \in [0, 1],$$

here t is a homotopy parameter.

When K=1, we usually call it as Protruding Linear Homotopy; When K>1, when the every solution path just starts or almost ends, the lengths of step are both quite short. But the Homotopy mapping H(x,t): $R^n \times [0, 1] \rightarrow R^n$ has original equation f(x) = 0, its solution is called as original solution, then g(x) = 0 is called as target equation, and for any $t \in R$, every H (x, t) is a polynomial equation set about x .

Homotopy method may also constringe to an unexpected solution. But because of its property of explaining itself, the terminate state can be found in the process of the solving, the user can easily find out where is wrong at his initial hypothesize, in this way, they then can backtrack to former state and correct the mistake.

2.2   Homotopy iteration method

Common continuum method's calculation efficiency is quite low when it is applied in solving big under-constraint equations. Although efficient method can preclude many emanative paths, it leaves large numbers of emanative paths at most conditions; furthermore, its preprocessing course needs to specific proposal for specific problem and sometimes some skills are needed. Coefficient Homotopy method is a quite high effective method when solving the polynomial equations which has the same structure and different coefficients, but when it is applied to solving common initial equations, it still needs to adopt the common continuum method or efficient method, thus it come back to the problem of getting solutions using this two methods.

Based on calculation practice, [14],[15] brought forward a new method solving under-constraint polynomial equations, the main spirit is: (1) to construct Homotopy function H(t, x)= (1-t) F (x) +tγG (x) for the equations F(x)=0 which is to be solved, here G (x) is an initial function whose solutions are known. It isn't required that G (x) and F (x) are of the same efficient characters, commonly G_i (x) $= x_i^{d_i}$-1, in which d_i is the degree of F_i (x) , t is a Homotopy parameter, γ is a random constant plural number whose imaginary part is not zero. (2) For every solution to the G (x) =0, by the Newton iteration(or any traditional iteration) , calculate directly the solution of the H (t, x) =0 when t=0.5; (3) Adopt the solution as an initial value which is solved at the former step, using Newton iteration, calculate directly the solution to the H (t, x) =0 when t=0 . If the iteration emanative, then preprocess the above course from another solution to the G (x) =0 again; if the iteration is convergent, then we can get the solution to the F (x) =0. Repeat the process described above until getting all the solutions of the G (x) =0 . The common Homotopy method is 10-20 times slower than the Newton-Raphson method when it comes to non-linear equations, but in practice, the essence of following tracking precept is the application of Newton method (or other traditional iterations) many times. Traditional iteration mostly requires choosing an appropriate initial value to ensure its local convergence, however, choosing an initial value is usually of blindfold character which blocks the efficiency of the method. Now by the Homotopy function, we can resolve the problem well. The Homotopy iteration method based on the following tracking precept is appropriate for solving all polynomial equations. Due to at every step of path tracking we get rid off the estimating tache, and the number of divisor part is less, therefore the calculation efficiency is higher than the common continuum method, and the calculation complexity is also less than the common continuum method.

2.3   The Solving of Geometrical Constraint Based on Path Tracking Homotopy Iteration method

The steps of the algorithm based on the Path Tracking Homotopy Iteration method are as follow:

Step1.   Assuming the constraint equations are F(x)=0, for polynomial equations F(x)=0, we can construct aided equations G (x) =0 whose full solutions are known or can be got easily, generally adopting G_i (x) =x_i^{di}-1, in which d_i is the degree of F_i (x) ;

Step2.   Construct Homotopy function H(t,x)= $(1-t)$ $\bar{t}$ +tγG (x) , in which t$\in$ [0,1], γ=$e^{i\theta i}$ is a random constant plural number whose imaginary part is not zero;

Step3.   Choose and input the iteration controlling parameter, which includes the iteration degree k, for a given precision d and emanative condition number, select the increment $\sqcup$ t of Homotopy parameter t or the interval number n (=1/$\sqcup$ t), and $\bar{t}$ =1-$\sqcup$ t;

Step4.   Select a solution $X^{(0)}$ as an initial value to the G (x) =0;

Step5. Adopting Newton method (or another traditional numerical iteration method), to get a solution $X^{(1)}$ of the $H(\bar{t}, x)=0$;

Step6. If $\sum \|H(\bar{t}, X^{(1)})\| < d$, then convert to the step9;

Step7. If $\sum \|H(\bar{t}, X^{(1)})\| > f$, then turn to the step10;

Step8. If the times of the iteration is less than k, then let $X^{(0)} = X^{(1)}$, turn to the step5;

Step9. Set $\bar{t} = \bar{t} - \sqcup t$, If $\bar{t} \geq 0$, then adopt $X^{(0)} = X^{(1)}$, convert to the step5; if $\bar{t} < 0$, we can get the solution $X^* = X^{(1)}$ of F(x)=0, convert to the step11:

Step10. The process of the iteration is emanative。

Step11. If there is any solution to the G (x) =0, then convert to the step4; Else the calculation is end.

To make the above algorithm can be processed quickly and efficiently, we should select appropriate Homotopy parameter increment $\sqcup$ t (or the interval division number n), the control parameter k, and the parameters d and f. Especially, the size of the interval division number n can affect directly the speed and precision of the calculation, so the choosing principle is given as follows: If the DOD of the polynomial equations is larger, then the n become larger too, in which DOD is under-degree of equations; DOD=(TD−the number of the equations) × 100%/TD。

3.   RESULT

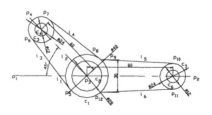

Figure 1. An example of devising

In the figure 1, there are 6 line segments and 6 circles. And 6 line segments can be decomposed 6 lines and 12 line segment nodes, so there are 24 geometric elements, the freedom degree is 54 and the constraint degree is 49. Here we change DIST_PP (p_{c1}, p_{c3}, 80) to DIST_PP (p_{c1}, p_{c3}, 60), VDIST_PP (p_9, p_{12}, 32) to VDIST_PP (p_9, p_{12}, 30), ANGLE_LL (l_1, l_2, $\pi/6$) to ANGLE_LL (l_1, l_2, $\pi/4$). If we use 49 nonlinear equations to superpose in order to solve 54 position variables corresponding to 24 geometric elements, the solving will be very inconvenient. Here we use the solving of geometrical constraint based on path tracking Homotopy iteration method, the result is as follows.

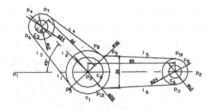

Figure 2. The solving result

We can see that when DOD=0(all the solutions of the equation needing to solve are 0), if n is larger, the area is set off more detailed, the time spent on tracking every route is more, the precision of tracking is higher, so the probability of getting all of the solutions is higher. For the under-system of DOD>0, if we set a smaller n value, the are of division is larger, we can judge many emanative routes, decrease the calculating time. For the hyper-under system (DOD $\geq$ 90%), n can be the minimum $n_{min}=2$, corresponding⊔ $t_{max}=1/ n_{min}=0.5$. This is the homotopy iteration method of two-step tracking mentioned in[18],[19] . The number of emanative condition f will have an effect on the calculating efficiency and the probability of getting all the solutions will increase. The experiment indicates in most conditions the homotopy iteration method will get the same solution many times, though it can improve the reliability of getting all of the solutions, In order to decrease unnecessary iteration computation the appropriate scope of value of f is 10^3-10^{10},which should make about half of the routes converge. When there is short of experiment, we can select f =10^7, 10^8 firstly, then adjust by computing some routes. The select of d and k will affect computation efficiency, precision and the probability of getting all of the solutions, but they are less important than the parameters n and f.

Usually the value of d is about 10^{-6}-10^{-4}, and the value of k is small about 10-20 in the beginning of tracking(for example two-step tracking t=0.5), and the value of k is large about 200-500 before the tracking ceases(for example two-step tracking t=0).

We can see that when DOD=0(all the solutions of the equation needing to solve are 0), if n is larger, the area is set off more detailed, the time spent on tracking every route is more, the precision of tracking is higher, so the probability of getting all of the solutions is higher. For the under-system of DOD>0, if we set a smaller n value, the are of division is larger, we can judge many emanative routes, decrease the calculating time. For the hyper-under system(DOD ≥ 90%), n can be the minimum n_{min}=2, corresponding⊔ t_{max}=1/ n_{min}=0.5. This is the homotopy iteration method of two-step tracking mentioned in[18],[19] . The number of emanative condition f will have an effect on the calculating efficiency and the probability of getting all the solutions will increase. The experiment indicates in most conditions the homotopy iteration method will get the same solution many times, though it can improve the reliability of getting all of the solutions, In order to decrease unnecessary iteration computation the appropriate scope of value of f is 10^{3}-10^{10},which should make about half of the routes converge. When there is short of experiment, we can select f =10^{7}, 10^{8} firstly, then adjust by computing some routes. The select of d and k will affect computation efficiency, precision and the probability of getting all of the solutions, but they are less important than the parameters n and f. Usually the value of d is about 10^{-6}-10^{-4}, and the value of k is small about 10-20 in the beginning of tracking(for example two-step tracking t=0.5), and the value of k is large about 200-500 before the tracking ceases(for example two-step tracking t=0).

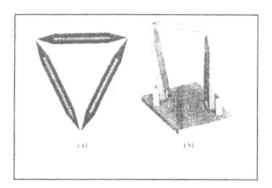

Figure 3. The example of Tracking Homotopy Iteration method

For the two examples in the figure 3, the results by different methods are indicated in table 1. The comparison of the result indicated that the solving efficiency can be improved greatly by our method.

We can see the advantages of Homotopy Iteration method are: (1) has a good universality. We can adopt a uniform solving method to the nonlinear equations; (2) can deal with the complex constraint solving; (3) when the figure has a great change, it can also achieve to convergence. (4) can have a not high demand for the iteration initialized value. The shortages are: (1) because of iteration solving, the speed is still slow. If the number of equations is large, it is not convenient to realize. (2) can't choose a solution using geometric information when there are many solutions.

Table 1. The comparison of result by different methods

	Newton Method	ordinary homotopy method	Path Tracking Homotopy Iteration method
Fig.3 (a) convergence	not convergent	convergent	convergent
time of solving(s)	-----	<100	<5
Fig.3 (b) convergence	not convergent in most conditions	convergent	convergent
time of solving(s)	<1 (if convergent)	<60	<3

ACKNOWLEDGEMENTS

This research has been supported by National Nature Science Foundation of China. (No. 69883004)

REFERENCES

1. Yuan Bo, Research and Implementation of Geometric Constraint Solving Technology, Doctor dissertation, Tsinghua University, 1999
2. Chen Yong, Li Yong, Zhang Jian, Yan Jing, an iteration method based on the homotopy function—homotopy iteration method, *the numerical calculation and computer appliance.* 2: 6 (2001), 149-155

3. Light R, Gossard D, Modification of geometric models through variational geometry[J], *Computer Aided Design*, 1982, 14(4): 209-214

4. Zhang Jiyuan, Shen Shoufan, Span analysis method determined framework kinematics solutions, *Mechanism Engineering Journal*, 27: 2（1991）,75-79

5. E.L.Allgower & K.Georg，Numerical Continuation Methods, An Introduction. *Springer-Verlag*, 1990

6. E.L.Allgower & K.Georg，Continuation and Path Following，*Acta Numerical*, 1993, p.1-84

7. T.Y.LI，Numerical Solutions of Multivariate Polynomial Systems by Homotopy Continuation Methods，*Acta Numerical*, 1997, Vol.6，p.399-436

8. Wang Ketang, GaoTangan, the introduction of homotopy method，Chongqing Press, 1990

9. Tsai，L.W.，Morgan，A.，Solving the Kinematics of the Most General Six-and-Five-Degree of Freedom Manipulators by Continuation Methods，*ASME Journal of Mechanisms，Transmissions and Automation in Desig*, 107（1985），189-200

10. Morgan，A.P.，Solving Polynomial Systems Using Continuation for Engineering and Scientific Problems, *Prentice-Hall*,1987.

11. Li，T.Y.，Yorke，J.A.，The Random Product Homotopy and deficient Polynomial Systems, *Numerische Mathemetik*, 51(1987), 481-500

12. Li，T.Y.，Yorke，J.A.，The Cheater's Homotopy: An efficient Procedure for Solving System of Polynomial Equations, *SIAM, Journal of Numerical Analysis*, 18:2(1988), 173-177.

13. Morgan，A.P.，Sommese, A.J., Coefficient Parameters Polynomial Continuation, *Appl. Math. Comput.*29(1989),123-160.oyouniurougan

14. Chen Y.，Yan，J., An iteration Method Based on Homotopy Function For Solving Polynomial Systems and Application to Machanisms Problems, *Journal of Southwest Jiaotong University*, 5: 1（1997），36-41

15. Chen .Y.,Yan J.,The Homotopy Iteration and its application in the a general 6-SPS Parallel Robert Position Problem, *Mechanism Science and Technology* ,16: 2（1997），189-194

FAST STEREO MATCHING METHOD USING EDGE TRACTION

Zheng-dong Liu, Ying-nan Zhao and Jing-yu Yang
Department of Computer Science,Nanjing University of Science and Technology, Nanjing 210094, P.R. China

Abstract: Combining the reliable edge feature points and area similarity, the fast stereo matching algorithm using edge traction was presented. First, find valid disparity set of feature points and traverse combinations of adjacent points' disparities, obtain the valid disparity set of featureless points using dynamic program, then, generate the initial sparse disparity space using area similarity. The algorithm reduces the computation complexity of disparity space and decreases the possibility of mismatching illusion. Under the uniqueness constraint, integral dense disparity map and occlusion area can be obtained by collision detection. Experiment on real visual images is performed to verify the feasibility and effectiveness of this algorithm.

Key words: Stereo Matching, Edge Feature, Disparity, Occlusion Detection

1. INTRODUCTION

The stereo matching is used for obtaining reliable, dense and smooth disparity maps. The area-based methods can produce dense disparity map [1][2], but the match is very sensitive to noise and light reflection. The feature-based methods can obtain highly reliable match of the feature points [3][4], but dense disparity map is available only by interpolation.

For the research of moveable machine with visual system, real-time is more required then high precision. In this paper, we present a fast stereo algorithm using edge traction. Combining area-based and feature-based methods can produce more precise disparity map. Relatively reliable edge is used to restrict the calculation of disparity scope of featureless points, which also helps to decreases the possibility of mismatch illusion when detect occlusion area. To demonstrate the effectiveness of the algorithm, we provide experimental data from a real image pair. Conclusion is drawn at last.

2.   FAST STEREO MATCHING USING EDGE TRACTION

Edge feature points are relatively less sensitive to noise. We use the LoG method to get the feature image $F'(x, y)$. Construct a feature point label set:

$$J = \{j_1, j_2, ..., j_n\} \tag{1}$$

The n is the number of feature points, j_i is the valid disparity set of feature point i. Disparities outside the label set are considered as forbidden area. The valid disparity set of featureless point can be obtained by the assortment of disparities of the adjacent feature points using dynamic program. Assume $(x_a, y) \in F'$ and $(x_b, y) \in F'$ are adjacent feature points. Define left compatible sequence L and right compatible sequence R.:

$$L = \{l_i \mid x_a < l_i < x_b, 0 < i \le M\}$$
$$R = \{r_j \mid x_a + d_a < r_j < x_b + d_b, d_a \in j_a, d_b \in j_b, 0 < j \le N\} \tag{2}$$

We use dynamic compatibility to match two sequences. Let $H(L, R)$ represents the total minimal accumulated distortion distances. For $l_i \in L$, $r_j \in R$, their distortion distance $h(l_i, r_j)$ is absolute value of difference. According to the continuity constraint, the result of compatibility matching is monotonic increasing. If $H(l_i, r_j)$ is the minimal accumulated distortion distance at (l_i, r_j), the new distance value can be defined as:

$$H(l', r') = \min \{H(l_i, r_j) + h(l_{i+1}, r_j), H(l_i, r_j) + 2h(l_{i+1}, r_{j+1}),$$
$$H(l_i, r_j) + h(l_i, r_{j+1})\} \tag{3}$$

The final minimal accumulated distortion distance is:

$$H(L, R) = \frac{1}{M + N} H(l', r') \tag{4}$$

Traveling through all the assortments of j_a and j_b, we can find out the valid disparity set of each featureless point. Area outside the valid disparity set is also defined as forbidden area. Based on the valid disparity set of each point, the disparity space with sparse match values can be constructed. Most methods traverse all disparities and pixels to construct the disparity space [2][5]. For $M \times N$ gray image, $W \times W$ correlative window and D maximal disparity, their computation complexity is $O(M \times N \times W^2 \times D)$, a computation complexity of this algorithm was reduced to $O(M \times N \times D^2)$.

Define the left line of sight LS and corresponding right line of sight RS at pixel (x_i, y_i) as a point set in the disparity space:

$$LS = \{(x, y, d) \mid x = x_i, y = y_i, 0 < d < d_{max}\}$$
$$RS = \{(x, y, d) \mid x = x_i + (d - d_i), y = y_i, 0 < d < d_{max}\} \qquad (5)$$

In General, points in occlusion area have smaller match values along their line of sight. The point with the highest match value, if had conflict on its left line of sight, is marked as unmatchable point. When all the points which have a larger match values than threshold are marked as unmatchable points, they can be determined as occlusion area. Otherwise, disparity with the highest match value could be the final matching disparity. In many instances, there are some feature points between occluded areas, it restricts valid disparity scope of featureless points and avoid mismatching illusion when search incorrect area with high match values.

3.   EXPERIMENTAL RESULTS

We have applied the algorithm to the corridor images from Carnegie Mellon University. Figure 1(a), (b), and (e) show the image pair and its ground-truth disparity map. Figure 1(c) shows the image of feature image by LoG Filter with $\sigma = 0.5$. Disparity map of edge feature points was shown in 1(d). Figure 1(f) shows the disparity map as a result. Black areas in the disparity map are detected occlusions. Running time was only 3.2s for decreasing valid disparity scope and processing without iteration. Table 1 shows the statistics data of the experiment.

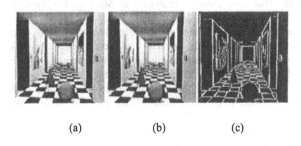

(a)   (b)   (c)

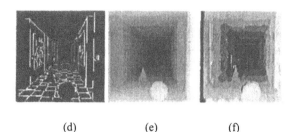

(d)   (e)   (f)

Figure 1. Experimental Results. (a) Left image, (b) right image, (c) left edge features image, (d) feature disparity map, (e) ground true disparity map, (f) disparity map as a result.

Table 1. Statistics data of the experimental result

	Pixel Found	Correct Match	%Correct Rate
Available Feature	7817	7766	99.35
Featureless	54558	47329	86.75
Occluded Points	3161	1020	32.27
Total	65536	56115	85.62

4.   CONCLUSION

In the algorithm, the edge feature point restricted valid disparity set of the featureless points under the uniqueness and continuity constraint. There are the following advantages. First, Computational complexity and searching area was reduced. Efficiency of matching was improved for request of real-time processing. At last, searching along the lines of sight and threshold of match value can determine occlusion and avoid illusion in a certain extent.

REFERENCES

1. T. Kanade, M. Okutomi. A stereo matching algorithm with an adaptive window: Theory and experiment. IEEE Trans. on Pattern Analysis and Machine Intelligence, 1994, 16(9): 920~932.
2. C. L. Zitnick, T. Kanade. A Cooperative Algorithm for Stereo Matching and occlusion Detection. IEEE Trans. on Pattern Analysis and Machine Intelligence, 2000, 22(7): 675~684.
3. H. Baker, T. Binford. Depth from Edge and Intensity Based Stereo. In: Proceedings of the 7th International Joint Conference on Artificial Intelligence, Vancouver, 1981. 631~636.
4. W. Grimson. Computational experiments with a feature based stereo algorithm. IEEE Trans. on Pattern Analysis and Machine Intelligence, 1985, 7(1): 17~34.
5. Qiuming Luo, Jingli Zhou. Stereo matching and occlusion detection with integrity and illusion sensitivity. Pattern Recognition Letters, 2003, 24(9-10): 1143~1149.

HYBRID COLOR IMAGE SEGMENTATION BASED FULLY AUTOMATIC CHROMA-KEYING SYSTEM WITH CLUTTERED BACKGROUND

Li Shijin, Zhu Yuelong, Yang Qian and Liu Zhe
School of Computers and Information Engineering, HOHAI University, Nanjing, P. R. China, 210098

Abstract: In this paper, we present a fully automatic digital chroma-keying system, which is based on the integration of color image segmentation algorithm and improved alpha estimation technique. Chroma-keying is a critical technology in virtual studio system. When used with cluttered background, it calls for much intelligence. According to the characteristics of frame images in the target application, a hybrid color image segmentation algorithm is put forward, which makes good use of both chromatic and luminance information. Then, refinement measures are further taken to deal with the color distribution in the neighborhood of the boundary through modified Ruzon-Tomasi alpha estimation algorithm. In contrast to the previously reported methods, our system needs no human interaction in the whole procedure. Experimental results on China sports lottery TV programs show that the proposed fully automatic keying system is viable and can be applied to the real program post production process of TV stations.

Key words: Virtual studio, color image segmentation, chroma-keying, alpha estimation.

1.   INTRODUCTION

Chroma-keying is a critical technology in virtual studio system [1]. By using this technology, actors in the studio, who have performed in front of a blue screen, are shown on the TV with new background, which is composed by a computer using graphics or animations. Because of the composition of the computer, the background can be rapidly changed, which not only improves the efficiency of the program production and the availability of the studio, but also makes the background much more splendid and attractive than the usual physical one.

Traditional chroma-keying adopts blue-screen technology [2], which means that the actor is recorded in front of a solid color background (blue, green etc). In recent years, chroma-keying in a hybrid color or a cluttered background becomes a hotspot in the research community [3-6](in some technical papers, it is also called matting [2,3]). When used with cluttered background, it calls for much intelligence. All these methods are based on the following basic composition equation:

$$C = \alpha F + (1-\alpha) B$$

Where C represents the output signal of the composition of foreground and background signals, F is the foreground signal, B denotes the background signal, and α is the key signal, which is also known as alpha. So in some papers, it is also called alpha estimation technique [4].

For the unlimited color distribution of the background, alpha estimation algorithm loosens the strict requirement (the solid color background) in the blue-screen scenario, and the only thing needed is the boundary. The common features of all the current algorithms based on this idea are that first manually segment the image into three parts –the foreground, the background and the unknown region (i.e. the contour of the foreground), and then estimate values of foreground colors, background colors and the alpha respectively.

With this kind of algorithms, it will cost a lot of money and human resources to manually deal with every frame in the video, furthermore, too many human interactions may lead to the poor quality of the final result. So more effective methods are needed to improve this situation. If the actor keeps staying in the same place when broadcasting in the air, we can use image segmentation to pick up the rough contour of the anchor person automatically, which can reduce or even eliminate the human interactions.

The basic idea of the new algorithm proposed in this paper is to firstly exert color image segmentation to outline the rough contour of the foreground object, and then carefully refine the boundary using modified Ruzon-Tomasi alpha estimation algorithm [4]. Experimental results on China sports lottery TV programs show that the proposed fully automatic keying system integrates the advantages of the image segmentation and alpha estimation algorithms and greatly extend the application scenario of virtual studio keying system.

2.   COLOR IMAGE SEGMENTATION

Along with the development of color imaging and its relevant techniques in recent years, color image segmentation techniques become a hot research topic in the image processing domain. Since the color image has more useful information (hue, saturation etc) than grayscale (only has brightness information), we can use statistical features of such information to segment it. Because the conclusions drawn from different color spaces are so much different that sometimes they are even contradictory, the selection of color spaces is not important, considering their unsuitability to all types of image. In this paper we choose the HSI color space for its similarity to the characteristics of human vision [7].

2.1   Multi-channel information fusion based hybrid color image segmentation

For the application in this paper, firstly, we have to refine the contour of the hostess in China sports lottery TV programs with a cluttered background, and then insert the virtual background to produce the virtual synthesis video shown on different TV stations. For the usually adopted H information can't separate the foreground object from the background effectively, the segmentation in this paper is mainly based on the S and I information in HSI color space. Figure.1 shows an original frame image in our application.

Figure1. One frame color image from the video and its corresponding HSI components

In figure 1, both the original color image of the hostess and the corresponding HSI component pictures illustrate that S and I information are useful in our image segmentation task.

At present, color image segmentation algorithms can be classified into three sorts of methods [8]: fusion of chromatic based on gray image segmentation; multidimensional gradient thresholding and color vector analysis. Having adopted the first segmentation methodology in this paper, we employ the optimal edge detection operator, which has been put forward by Shen in [9], to binarize the triple channel images in HSI space before the integration of the result of each part. Before giving the specific realization of our segmentation strategy, a brief introduction will be made about the optimal edge detection operator theory and its recursive implementation.

Based on Gaussian function, D. Marr [10] proposed the LOG operator whose precision of edge detection is varied following the change of the variance of Gaussian function. After carefully analyzing the previous boundary detection filters, upon the symmetric exponential filter, Shen [9] worked out an optimal edge detection operator which can not only effectively reduce the noise by an infinitely large size window, but also makes the central part of the filtering function sharp enough to enhance the boundary location precision.

The symmetric exponential filter has the following form:

$$F(x, y) = C_1^2 \times C_2^{|x|+|y|} \tag{1}$$

where $C_1 = a_0 \big/ (2 - a_0)$; $C_2 = 1 - a_0$, $a_0 \in (0, 1)$. When a_0 is near 1, F(x,y) becomes narrower, and the anti-noise capability is lower, while the precision of edge localization is higher; when a_0 becomes smaller, the anti-noise capability is higher, but more detailed edges will be lost. Assuming f(i,j) denotes the original image, and it is filtered by the above filters, Shen [9] has proved that the filtering process can be decomposed into the cascading of two-pass filtering in row and column directions respectively and can be implemented by two recursive filters in two passes. Firstly, the filtering is done in row direction:

$$f_1(i, j) = f_1(i, j-1) + a_0 \times [f(i, j) - f_1(i, j-1)] \quad j = 1, 2, \cdots, n$$
$$f_2(i, j) = f_2(i, j+1) + a_0 \times [f_1(i, j) - f_2(i, j+1)] \quad j = n, n\text{-}1, \cdots, 1 \tag{2}$$

Where $f_2(i, j)$ is the output of the filtering in row direction. Then, the filtering in column direction is conducted based on the previous results.

$$f_3(i, j) = f_3(i-1, j) + a_0 \times [f_2(i, j) - f_3(i-1, j)] \quad i = 1, 2, \cdots, n$$
$$f_4(i, j) = f_4(i+1, j) + a_0 \times [f_3(i, j) - f_4(i+1, j)] \quad i = n, n\text{-}1, \cdots, 1 \tag{3}$$

Hence,

$$f_4(i, j) = f(i, j) \times C_1^2 \times C_2^{|i|+|j|} \tag{4}$$

$$f_4(i, j) - f(i, j) \approx \frac{1}{2C_1 \ln C_2} \times \nabla^2 F(x, y) \times f(i, j) \tag{5}$$

And the last output results are the Laplacian image of the original one [9].

In our application scenario, we separate the two-pass filtering and conduct it using different parameters, i.e., the 'a0' in Equation 2) and 3) can take different values, and we use the parameter pair (a0, b0) to characterize the procedure. So we can configure different parameters to detect different oriental edges in images.

We divide the image into three sections (the section above the head, the section with head and the section with body) according to the image characteristics in this specific application, and choose diverse segmentation strategies in different channels of each section. By the way, through the vertical projection, we can get the positions of the two dividing lines (the up line and the down line), which separate the image into three parts.

Because the brightness in the section above the head is high and the color information is reduced by the glaring for the highlighting in the studio, we segment it in the brightness channel. The edge of head is mostly in vertical direction, so we mainly consider the vertical orientation filtering in Shen optimal edge detector, and in operation we only filter in vertical direction. The parameters take the value of $(a0, b0) = (0.0625, 1)$.

In the section with the head, since the color similarity of hair and the background Chinese characters leads to the unapparent distinction of hue, we segment the image in S channel, which is very high in the hostess for their densely make-up. The edge of this part is in mostly horizontal direction, so we mainly consider the horizontal orientation filter in Shen optimal edge detection, and in practice we only filter in horizontal direction. The parameters take the value of $(a0, b0) = (0.5, 0.125)$.

As the body section is concerned, for the distinction of colors in hostess and background is apparent and the background is nearly the solid yellow, we adopt the classical Otsu histogram thresholding [11] in H channel to accomplish the segmentation.

After the segmentation of these three parts individually, we compose them into a whole image. The results are given in Fig.2 (a) ~ (d), and the 2(d) image is the result of initial integration.

2.2   Post-processing

Getting the binary image after segmentation, we go on with the post processing, which includes the removal of the small noise region, the combination of the segmented regions belonging to the hostess and the brim fairing using the mathematical morphology operations.

Firstly, we take the edge tracing in the binary image after the segmentation. Among the connected regions in the image, the area containing the body of hostess is the largest one, so we set the lower limit area of the bound rectangles, which surround the connect region, 100 to eliminate the small connect regions. After computing the area of the largest bordering rectangle, in order to remove the noise interference, we eliminate the connected regions far from the center of the rectangle, and incorporate the connected region near the contour. Then trace this largest region and go on with mathematical morphology processing to smooth the edge and filling the holes. Fig. 3 illustrates the aforementioned procedure.

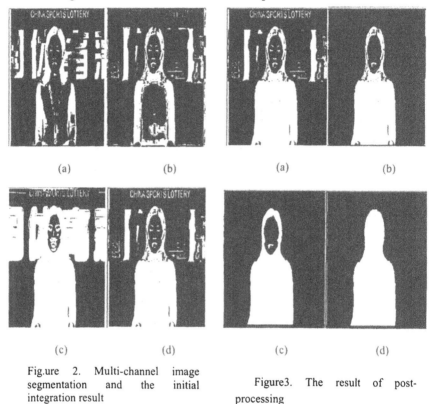

Fig.ure 2. Multi-channel image segmentation and the initial integration result

Figure3. The result of post-processing

Compared with the original image, result of single frame image segmentation is relatively satisfying. Although the foreground object is almost completely extracted, the zigzag and unsmooth hair brim is unable to show the nicety of the hair, and some ends of the hair around the shoulder still can not be refined. If the segmented frames are composed into one AVI file, the resulting video makes the audiences visually uncomfortable. To improve this situation, we employ the alpha estimation technique after the traditional image segmentation process is conducted.

3.   ALPHA ESTIMATION

Alpha channel or α channel in short, determines the transparency of each pixel besides tricolor channels in digital image. α channel is also called opacity or coverage percentage. Put forward by Porter and Duff in 1984[12], the conception of α channel is that one pixel can be described in four channels (r, g, b, α) and the distributions of colors (red, green and blue) in each pixel can be measured by the product of α and the value of each color.

In the real world, the boundary between objects area is not very sharp, but a gradual transition. Since each boundary pixel receives the light from many objects and the color penetration, the exact segmentation could not be achieved just depending on the use of image segmentation or boundary extraction. To solve the problem alpha estimation technique emerges.

Ruzon-Tomasi alpha estimation algorithm [4] is employed in this paper. Firstly, we automatically segment the boundary region into many sub-regions, then build a box to surround each sub-region containing those pixels already known in the foreground object and background. The surrounding pixels in the foreground are from the sampling function of P(F), while the pixels in the background are with the sampling function of P(B). All these pixels are divided into different color clusters – each has a Gaussian distribution in the color space, so we can regard the foreground color distribution as a mixture of Gaussian distributions. Like the foreground, all the background pixels can also be divided into different clusters according to their colors, and each cluster in the background is related to one foreground color cluster.

After building the color cluster distribution network, which map the foreground cluster to the background one, we treat the observed color C coming from an intermediate distribution P(C), which is located between foreground and background. The intermediate distribution is also defined as a mixture of Gaussian distributions, each of which has a new expectation located at a certain position in the diagonal, connecting a pair of foreground and background color clusters. An optimum alpha is claimed with the intermediate distribution, which makes the observed color have the maximum probability. The foreground and background colors are estimated as a post-process using a weighted sum of the foreground and background cluster means. These values are then perturbed, so that a line segment with endpoints at F and B, goes through C and also satisfies the basic composition equation. The detailed algorithms can be found in [4].

In this paper, we make some modifications to the color quantization in the algorithm in [4]. Because the foreground and the background are manually picked out in [4], the color quantization is global, i.e. the colors of all the pixels in the image are quantized. That may lead to some disadvantages. Since there may be millions of colors in an image, the to-be-segmented region in the image may only have very few color samples and they may be ignored by the global quantization algorithm, which will lead to the mismatch of the color codebook and the actual color in the boundary region. In this paper, because the preceding image segmentation can tell the sub-region of the boundary, only the pixels nearby the boundary are quantized and the precision and color fidelity are further guaranteed. In the implementation, after the four times dilatations and erosions of the segmentation outcome, we "XOR" the two resulting images to get the boundary region needed in alpha estimation algorithm. Also because the color quantification only deals with the original image in the boundary region above, the precision of alpha estimation algorithm has been further improved.

4.   EXPERIMENTAL RESULTS AND DISCUSSIONS

Proven by a great deal of experiments on many samples, the automatic chroma-keying method which integrates color image segmentation and alpha-estimation is able to pick-up the fine and translucent complex region in the foreground from the background without the limitation that the background must be in purely colors. The system proposed in this paper can achieve the high quality of refined image and greatly extend the application scenarios of virtual studio. The procedures of the algorithm, and the corresponding results are presented in Fig.4.

The experiments demonstrate the feasibility of using automatic chroma-keying method which is based upon the color segmentation and alpha-estimation in the field of video keying technology, and they also demonstrate that the apparent improvement of the object refinement upon the simply image segmentation algorithm is meaningful to extend the application scenario of virtual studio. Furthermore, the proposed technology can be applied in other similar situations, such as the weather forecast program production. However, there are still some limitations in the system proposed in this paper. In various foregrounds and backgrounds, we have to adopt different segmentation algorithms without a uniform solution. Snake or active contour models [13] are currently being considered as an alternative. How to apply the technique proposed in this paper to more complex situations and how to further improve the capability of the algorithm are the main research directions in the future.

ACKNOWLEDGEMENTS

We are grateful to Mr. Wang Hui for the experimental videos he provided and the inspiring discussions with him are also appreciated.

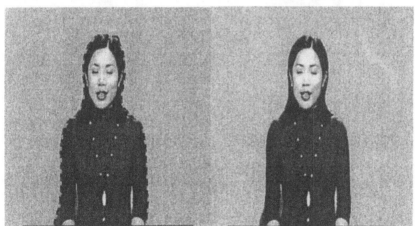

Figure 4. Alpha estimation procedure illustration and the last result

REFERENCES

1. Luo Yuhua, Virtual studio system: an overview, China Journal of Image and Graphics, 1996, Vol. 1, No.3, pp220-224.
2. Smith A. and Blinn J. Blue screen matting. In Proc. SIGGRAPH'96, pp.259–268, 1996.

3. Chuang Y., Curless B., and Salesin D., et al, A bayesian approach to digital matting, in Proceedings of IEEE Conference on CVPR 2001, Vol.2, pp.264-271.

4. Ruzon M. and Tomasi C., Alpha estimation in natural images, in Proceedings of IEEE Conference on CVPR 2000, Vol.1, pp. 18-25.

5. Mitsunaga T., Yokoyama T. and Totsuka T., AutoKey: Human assisted key extraction, in Proceedings of SIGGRAPH'95, pp. 265–272, 1995.

6. Qian R. J. and Sezan M. I. Video background replacement without a blue screen. in Proceedings of ICIP 1999, pp. 143–146, October, 1999.

7. Wei Baogang, Li Xiangyang, Lu Dongming, Survey of the segmentation of color images, China Journal of Computer Scien-ces, 26(4): 59-62.

8. Ruzon M., Early vision using distributions, Ph.D thesis, Computer Science Dept., Stanford Univ., Stanford, Calif., Apr. 2000.

9. Shen J., The optimal linear edge detection operator, China Journal of Pattern recognition and Artificial intelligence, 1987, Vol. (1): 86-103.

10. Marr D. and Hildreth E., Theory of Edge detection, Proc. Royal Soc. London, Vol. B207, pp.187-217, 1980.

11. Otsu N., A threshold selection method from gray-level histograms, IEEE Trans. Systems Man Cybernetics, SMC-9, 62-66, 1979.

12. Porter T. and Duff T. Compositing digital images. In *SIGGRAPH 1984*, pages 253–259, July 1984.

13. Kass, M., Witkin, A., and Terzopoulos, D., "Snakes: active contour models," International Journal of Computer Vision, Vol.1, No. 4, pp. 321-331, 1987.

RESEARCH ON TECHNIQUES OF APPROXIMATE RECOGNITION OF CONTINUOUS DEFORMATION OF IMAGES WITH MULTI-GREY-LEVELS*

Feng Zhi-quan, Li Yi and Qu Shou-ning
School of Information and Science Engineering, Jinan University,Jiwei Road 106, Jinan, Shandong, P R China, 250022, fzqwww@263.net

Abstract: A new algorithm of recognition of continuous deformation of the images with multi-gray-levels is put forward in this paper, which the following steps are made: the fist is the adoption of griddings procedures, the other is the classification of continuous deformation into continuous deformation with preserving topological structure and continuous deformation with non-preserving topological structure , and introduction of a new method approximate identifying continuous deformation. The main characteristics of this algorithm are the flexible modulations between accuracy to calculate and time to process, and so the needs from different applications be satisfied easily. Finally, a few examples are given to test the versatility of the techniques, from which it is verified that the algorithm developed here exhibits good performance.

Key words: Continuous deformation, gridding, Recognition techniques

1.   INTRODUCTION

The recognition to continuous deformation images is not only one of the most important issues in the field of pattern recognition in computer science, but also has significant theoretically value and wide applications in the field of robot vision systems.

Colonna de et. al [1] present a method named phase-shifting techniques, and discuss its application in the field of metrology. Colonna et. al[2]

improve its some demerits which desires to keep the stability of phase in deformation, by means of comprehensive consideration continuous five frames for phase of some point. However, computing point by point limits its speed and therefore affecting time gap between continuous frames. Zhu Zhongtao et.al [3,4] propose put forward a new method by means of studying image arithmetic operators, obtaining differential invariance of image under boundary, but getting transform clots is not a easy job there being some theoretical issues to be solved. As a whole, the mainstream is adoption of various invariance[5-16],but it is difficult to harmonize the conflict between sufficient conditions and necessary conditions.

As a tool, gridding has been introduced into research on continuous deformations in [18], but ignore the relationship between gridding and continuous deformations.

Hopfield network can realize association recognition of network model by means of constructing energy function and finding the network status minimizing energy, which is suitable for limited noise and deformation. However, its storage capacity is limited and must be told models to be recognize, which makes it difficult to recognize objects with arbitrary and random deformations. Therefore, we propose a new similar invariance in [19], upon which discusses the recognition issue on the continuous deformation objects. But it limits the meaning of objects.

2.   BASIC DEFINITIONS

2.1   Edge-gridding

If a gridding covers at least two different greys on its four edges, this gridding is called as a edge-gridding. Especially, when the height and width of a edge-gridding are 1 pixel, this edge-gridding is called a edge point of the image.

2.2   Topological relationship

Topological relationship, means adjacent relationships among areas of the given objects.

2.3   Continuous deformation

Let the edge images of i-th and i+1 th frames are I_i and I_{i+1} respectively, and the time gap between continuous frames is Δt, if

$$\lim_{\Delta t \to 0} I_{i+1} = I_i \tag{1}$$

and I_i and I_{i+1} is homoeomorphism, we call the deformation from frame i to frame i+1 is a continuous deformation with precision Δt.

2.4   Gridding features

The features, such as grey sequence, grey number, dimension of the gridding, gridding coordinate and so on, are calledthe gridding features of the gridding. The coordinate of upper-left point of the gridding is referenced as gridding coordinate of the gridding.

2.5   The condition NS

For an arbitrary edge-gridding, （i, s, a）, among which s is the coordinate of the edge-gridding and a is the feature of the gridding of frame i, U(i, s) notes the eight neighbors gridding of the gridding, if U(i+1,s) $\supset$ (I,s,a),we call the gridding (i,s) satisfies the condition NS

2.6   The condition NC

For an arbitrary edge-gridding, （i, s, a）, among which s is the coordinate of the edge-gridding and a is the feature of the gridding of frame i, U(i, s) notes the eight neighbors gridding of the gridding, if
$$U(I,s) \supset (i+1,s,a)$$
We call the gridding (i,s) satisfies the condition NC

2.7   Escapable gridding

Under allowed precision, a gridding is called escapable gridding, if it need not be further refined into sub-gridding.

2.8   The continuous deformation with topological structure holding

If the relationship keeps unchangeable during deformation of the images, this deformation is referenced as the continuous deformation with topological structure holding.

2.9   Topology break

This is the case when adjacency relationship among areas of the deformed images changes. For example, if some two areas is separated ,or one area is divided into two or more different areas after deformation, a topology break takes place. The another example is the case that two or more different areas are conglutinated into one area.

2.10   The continuous deformation with topological structure non-holding

The continuous deformation with topological structure non-holding is a deformation in which topological breaks are allowed to appear in limited scope and limited time.

3.   RECOGNITION ALGORITHM

First of all, we give our overall algorithm flow chart as follows(Figure 1).

3.1   Basic theorem

Theorem 1   the sufficient and necessary condition of being a continuous deformation with topological structure holding between two adjacent frames is that the condition NS and condition NC are be satisfied at the same time.
Proof:
Firstly, proof sufficient condition is true. If the condition NS is satisfied, no split occurs after deformation, meaning that two areas are still connected after deformation if they are connected before deformation. Otherwise, if one area is divided into two or more different areas, there are no griddings with the same feature girddings in the neighbor of breaking point in frame i+1, compared with the image before deformation, which is a conflict with the definition of the condition NS. Similarly, if the condition NC is satisfied, no conglutination occurs after deformation, meaning no new connection among areas is produced. Otherwise, if produces new connection among areas, exists a neighbor areas round the new connection in the frame i and doesn't include any griddings with the same feature at the same position as frame i in frame i+1, which is a conflict with the definition of condition NC.
Necessary condition is clear and need not further proof.

```
┌─────────────────────────┐
│      Initalization       │
└─────────────────────────┘
```

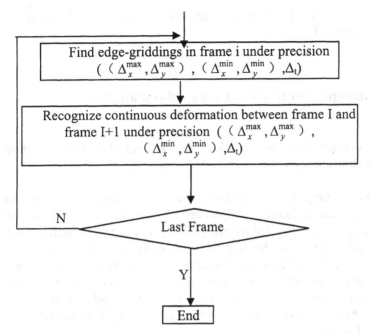

Figure 1. The Overall Diagram of our algorithm

3.2   An algorithm to find edge-griddings

The main purpose of an algorithm to find edge-griddings is to identify all edge-griddings under desired precision, essentially, obtaining the edges with some difference and rudeness. The algorithm is given as follows.

Step1: Set edge-gridding collection with null;

Step2: $\Delta_x = \Delta_x /2$, $\Delta_y = \Delta_y /2$, and if the condition $(\Delta_x, \Delta_y) > (\Delta_x^{min}, \Delta_y^{min})$ is satisfied, turn Step3 else turn Step9;

Step3: divide each griddings into four griddings, with sub-griddings with width and height Δ_x and Δ_y;

Step4: Find gridding features of each sub-griddings;

Step5: For a gridding, s, if its grey number is more than two, turn Step7 else turn next step;

Step6: Is the condition $(\Delta_x, \Delta_y) > (\Delta_x^{max}, \Delta_y^{max})$ satisfied? If yes, turn Step8 else turn Step2;

Step7: Add this gridding into new edge-gridding collection, turn Step2;

Step8: Return.

In initalization, Δ_x is the width of the image, and Δ_y is the height of the image, Counter=0.

3.3   Recognition to continuous deformation

3.3.1   The continuous deformation with topological structure holding with precision (($\Delta_x^{max}, \Delta_y^{max}$) , ($\Delta_x^{min}, \Delta_y^{min}$) , Δ_t)

Generally speaking, it is impossible to recognize accurately a continuous deformation by the definition on account of time gap Δ_t between two adjacent frames. So, we consider recognizing to continuous deformation with topological structure holding with precision ((Δ_x^{max} , Δ_y^{max}) , ($\Delta_x^{min}, \Delta_y^{min}$) Δ_t). The continuous deformation with topological structure holding demand objectively no separation or conglutination in the procedure of deformation, meaning that the condition NS and the condition NC should be checked between two frames with time gap Δ_t We describe our algorithm as follows:

Step1: Initalization the current griddings;
Step2: Is the condition NS satisfied? if yes turn Step3 else turn Step6;
Step3: Is the condition NC satisfied? if yes turn Step4 else turn Step6;
Step4: s=next gridding;
Step5: Are all griddings finished? if yes turn Step7 else Step2;
Step6: failure, return.
Step7: successful, return.

The continuous deformation with topological structure non-holding with precision (($\Delta_x^{max}, \Delta_y^{max}$) , ($\Delta_x^{min}, \Delta_y^{min}$) , Δ_t , Σ)

The continuous deformation with topological structure non-holding allows of topology break of local topological structure after deformation. Based upon the algorithm with topological structure holding, it is easy to obtain the following algorithm to recognize the continuous deformation with topological structure non-holding with precision ((Δ_x^{max} , Δ_y^{max}) , ($\Delta_x^{min}, \Delta_y^{min}$) , Δ_t, Σ).

Step1: Initalization the current griddings;
Step2: Is the condition NS satisfied? if yes turn Step3 else turn Step6;
Step3: Is the condition NC satisfied? if yes turn Step4 else turn Step6;
Step4: s=next gridding;
Step5: Are all griddings finished? if yes turn Step7 else Step2;
Step6: T=T+1;
Step7: If $\dfrac{T}{TOTAL} < \Sigma$, be successful and return else failure and return.

Once a topology break occurs, the algorithm counts the number of griddings related to topology break,. When all griddings are dealt with, if the ratio of T to total number of griddings,TOTAL, is in limited scope, we believe occurs a continuous deformation with topological structure non-holding with precision (($\Delta_x^{max}, \Delta_y^{max}$) , ($\Delta_x^{min}, \Delta_y^{min}$) , Δ_t , $\sum$).

3.4   Match with database

Some typical static images are stored in a database in advance. After recognizing to each image, compare it with every image in the database, checking the condition NS and the condition NC. In a continuous image sequence, as long as exists a image matches with a image in the database, continue to identify whether or not the last image matches with the first frame.

4.   PERFORMANCE ANALYSIS OF THE ALGORITHM

We compare this algorithm with that put forward in [19]. In paper[19], the time complexity is $O(s*n)$, among which s is the number of circle in object and n is the number of vertex in each circle. So $s*n$ stands for the total number of vertex in original image, showing that our time complexity is improved, to some extent.. Furthermore, the time complexity is not related to the complexity of topological structure of image, which is another important feature of our algorithm .

5.   EXPERIMENTAL RESULTS

Example 1   Take continuous deformation of face as a example, getting satisfactory result. We obtain a video with number camera and divide it into a image sequence with time gap 1ms. Figure 2 is a snippet we arbitrarily cut. Our programming results show that this is a The continuous deformation with topological structure holding with precision with precision (($\Delta_x^{max}, \Delta_y^{max}$) , ($\Delta_x^{min}, \Delta_y^{min}$) , Δ_t)= ((10, 10), (3, 3), 1) . By further experiment, if let Δ_t =1 and ($\Delta_x^{min}, \Delta_y^{min}$) = (2, 2) , the recognition fails.

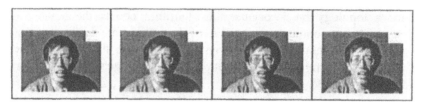

Figure 2. a continuous deformation sequence of a real example

So, $(\Delta_x^{min}, \Delta_y^{min})$ affects the recognition precision.

Example 2 Word Recognition

Figure 3 shows a 3DSMAX move, which is by our programming, a continuous deformation with topological structure non-holding with precision ($(\Delta_x^{max}, \Delta_y^{max})$, $(\Delta_x^{min}, \Delta_y^{min})$ Δ_t)= ((12, 12), (2, 2), 1) , occurring a topology break.

Figure 3. a continuous deformation with topological structure

Example 3 a example of non-continuous deformation

Figure 4 shows a example of non-continuous deformation , in which occurs a break in background and the scope of changes exceeds our limitation $\sum$ (here $\sum$=30%) .

Figure 4. a non-continuous deformation

6.   CONCLUSIONS

On one hand, our world is complex and is of diversity; on the other hand, error occurs everywhere when we collect data from objects, and the process speed is limited by hardware conditions. Taking all above factors into consideration, to find a algorithm suitable for all situation to recognize continuous deformation is not a easy job. In this paper, we just put forward an approximate and rude method in attempt to deal with this issue.

ACKNOWLEDGEMENTS

This work is supported by Ji Nan University Fund (Y0203).

REFERENCE

1. Colonna de Lega X, Jacquot P, "Deformation measurement using object induced dynamic phase-shifting", Applied Optics, received 21 December 1995, revised manuscript received 15 March 1996
2. Colonna de Lega, "Continuous deformation measurement using dynamic phase-shifting and wavelet reansforms", IOP Publishing Ltd, sep. 1996:261-267
3. Zhu ZhongTao, Zhang Bo, Zhang ZaiXing. The Differential Invariance of Image Under Boundary Extracting Operator. Chinese J.Computers, 1999, 22(9): 903–910.
4. Zhu ZhongTao, Zhang Bo, Zhang ZaiXing.The quasi-invariants of curves under the topological deformation. Chinese J.computers, 1999, 22(9): 897–902
5. J Perantonis, P J G Lisboa. Translation, rotation, and scale invariant pattern recognition by high order neural networks and moment classifiers. IEEE Trans Neural Networks, 1992, 3(2): 241-251.
6. E Rivlin, I Weiss. Local invariance for recognition. IEEE Trans Pattern Anal. Mach. Intell., 1995, 17(3): 226-238.
7. J Wood. Invariant pattern recognition: a review. Pattern Recognition, 1996, 29(1):1-17.
8. J Wood, J Shawe-Taylor. Representation theory and invariant neural networks. Discrete Applied Mathematics, 1996, 69(1-2):33-60.
9. Weiss I. Projective invariants of shapes. Proceedings of DARPA Image Understanding Workshop, Cambridge, 1998: 1125-1134.
10. Zhao Lei, Fengzhiquan, LiJingping. Research Advances on the Theory of Visual Invariants in Computer Vision. The theories and applications of Modern Information Technology:CIE-YC'2002.HeFei,China,2002,589-593.
11. Zhang Ling, Zhang Ba, Wu Chaofu.Multilayer Neural Networks for Motion Invariant Pattern Recognition.Chinese J.Computers, 1998, 21(2): 127–136.
12. Yan Sunzhen, Sun Jixiang.The Research and Application of Moment Invariants in Object Shape Recognition.Journal of National University of Defense Technology, 1998, 20 (5): 75~80.
13. Liao yuan, Yuan jie.Recognition of Occluded Target with Fused Data of Several Invariances.Journal of Wuhan University),1998, 44 (1): 81~84.
14. Zhao Nanyuan.The Topology Properties Algorithm of Image.Journal of Tsinghua University, 1989, 29 (4): 74-79.
15. Guo Lianqi, Li Qingfen.A study of the Graphic Recognition Method by Using the Topological Relation.Journal of Harbin Engineering University, 1998, 9(4):38~43.
16. Feng ZhiqQuan. A New Kind of Similar Invariant and Its Apply to Object Recognition Algorithm. Computer Science,2002,29(9):360-361

17. Musse, O.; Heitz, F. Topology preserving deformable image matching using constrained hierarchical parametric models. Image Processing, 2000. Proceedings. 2000 International Conference on Computer Vision and Pattern. 2000 vol.1:505-508

18. Zhu; M. Gotoh . "Automatic remeshing of 2D quadrilateral elements and its application to continuous deformation simulation: part I. remeshing algorithm" , Journal of Materials Processing Technology. 1999, vol.87, no.1-3 .165:178

19. Feng Zhiquan, Lijingping, Dong et al..Computer Recognition of 2-D Objects with Continuous Deformation. Chinese Journal of Computers.2003. Vol.26(12):1637-1644.

RECOGNITION OF IMAGE WITH NATURAL TEXTURES BASED ON LEARNING OF INFORMATION AUGMENTATION

Cheng Xian-Yi[1,2],Yuan Xiao-Hua[1],Li Shu- Qin[1] and Xian De-Shen[1]
[1]*Department of Computer Science , NanJing University of Science&Technology,Nianjing 219004, P.R.china*
[2]*State Key Laboratory for Novel Software Technology at Nanjing University, Nianjing, 210093,P.R.China*
[3]*Computer Science & Communication Engineering Institute of Jiangsu University. Zhenjiang,212013,P.R. China*

Abstract: The efficiency of pattern recognition depends heavily on that if feature extraction and selecting are effective. Complicated image such as medical image and remote sensing image, belong to image with natural textures, this kind of image is always of high resolution, with many layers of gray degree, and a very intricate shape structure. Because there are no obvious shapes, but only distributions of some gray degrees and colors in these images, so for them, there are no good methods yet for feature extraction and region recognition. In this paper, based on information augmentation and kinetics, we present a learning algorithm, which can be used to do region classification of the above-mentioned images with natural textures. We applied our algorithm to recognition of image with natural textures and obtained a good result.

Key words: pattern recognition; information entropy augmentation; machine learning; NN

1. INTRODUCTION

In many medical images, such as cardia and cerebrum, they are neither any obvious edge nor clear boundary between different tissues; we call these images natural textures. For this kind of medical images, it is very difficult to do region recognition. For example, when classifying   human cerebrum tissues in clinical application by computer, features used mostly are ectocinerea, alba, cerebrorachidian liquid, pallium and background etc. In image of Magnetic resonance imaging(MRI), although different tissues and background may have different gray degrees, each tissue doesn't belong to a single gray degree but belong to a gray degree scope, and the gray degree distributions of cerebrum tissues can be nearly taken as gaussian distribution, and further more, the distributive functions of the gray degree of these tissues overlay each other, we can see this from Fig. 1.(data come from document[1], p93).

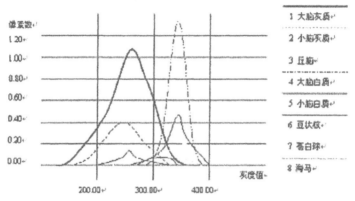

Fig. 1 Gray degree distribution of human cerebrum tissues in MRI

All that mentioned above, we classify these tissues neither by gray degree thresholds nor by lower feature, which based statistics, such as color, texture, shape, etc, because these features are not competent for describing image with natural textures. So in this paper, to aim at the difficulty of region recognition of image with natural textures, based on the information augmentation and kinetics, we put forward a learning algorithm, which transform a minimizing problem of information entropy augmentation into a learning process of dynamic system. Applied our learning algorithm in interesting regions recognition of human cerebrum, we got a satisfied result.

2.   INFORMATION AND INFORMATION AUGMENTATION

Information theory, also called statistical communication theory, firstly set up by Shannon to solve problems from information transfer (communication) process, it is a theory to study the generation, obtaining, measuring, transformation, transfer, processing, recognizing and application of information. Information entropy is a measure of the uncertain degree in information[2,3]. The related concept, we summarize as follow:

(1)Self information of event. If S represent a group of event marked as E_1 , E_2 , $\cdots$, E_n , their corresponding probabilities are $P(E_j) = p_j$, $0 \le p_j \le 1$, and the regularization constraints on p_j is

$$p_1 + p_2 + \ldots + p_n = 1 \qquad (1)$$

Then the self information of event E_j is defined as $I(E_j) = -K \ln p_j$ $i = 1,2,\ldots n$, where $K = \log_2 e$.

(2)Entropy of S. Entropy of S is the statistical mean of S's Self information, we note it as $H(s)$

$$H(s) = E(I) = -K \sum_j p_j \ln p_j \qquad (2)$$

some remarks related to (2) are:
· if $H(s) = 0$, then there exists only one possibility and no uncertainty.
· if the occurring possibility of n events are the same, namely, to event E_j, $P(E_j) = 1/n$,
then $H(s)$ achieve it's maximum $-K \ln n$, and
the corresponding system is with the largest uncertainty.
· If $P(E_j)$ closing to each other, then $H(s)$ is large, and vice versa.

(3)Information augment. Rewriting formula (2) as formula (3)

$$H(s) = \sum_j p_j (-K \ln p_j) = \sum_j p_j I(E_j) \qquad (3)$$

Then we have

$$I(E_j) - I(E_j') = -K \ln p_i + K \ln p_j' = K \ln\left(\frac{p_j}{p_i'}\right) \qquad (4)$$

Averaging formula (4), and take the result formula (5) as the measure of mean changes of information (we call it information augmentation)

$$VI(S,S') = K \sum_j p_j \left(\frac{p_j}{p_i'}\right) \qquad (5)$$

Assume that p_j, p_j' meet(1), then it can be proved that $VI(s) \ge 0$, and that only when S is of an uniform distribution, equation (5) come into exist.

3.   LEARNING BASED INFORMATION AUGMENTS

Let $f(q)$ be an actual pattern distributive function, and $\tilde{f}(q)$ be the guessed distributive function generated by the system, if we take information augmentation as the measure of the similarity degree between the two distributive function above, then we can denote information augmentation as below (might as well let $K=1$):

$$VI(S,\widetilde{S}) = \int f(q)\ln\left(\frac{f(q)}{\widetilde{f}(q)}\right)d^nq \geq 0 \qquad (6)$$

Where $f(q)$ and $\widetilde{f}(q)$ satisfy two regularization constraints in (7)

$$\int f(q)d^nq = 1 \quad \text{and} \quad \int \widetilde{f}(q)d^nq = 1 \qquad (7).$$

We can rewrite (6) as (8)

$$VI(S,\widetilde{S}) = \int f(q)\ln f(q)d^nq - \int f(q)\ln \widetilde{f}(q)d^nq \qquad (8)$$

Because $f(q)$ having an invariant value, so we can get the minimum of $VI(S,\widetilde{S})$ as long as maximizing (9)

$$\int f(q)\ln \widetilde{f}(q)d^nq = \max \qquad (9).$$

Let $q = (q_1, q_2, \ldots, q_n)$, then the problem left is how to estimate $\widetilde{f}(q)$ by measuring all the moments in (10)

$$< q_i >, < q_i, q_j >, < q_i, q_j, q_k >, < q_i, q_j, q_k, q_l > \qquad (10),$$

In accordance with maximum information(entropy) theory, the estimating formula of $\widetilde{f}(q)$ is of form as

$$\widetilde{f}(q) = N\exp(\sum_j \lambda_j q_j - \sum_{ij}\lambda_{ij}q_i q_j + \sum_{ijk}\lambda_{ijk}q_i q_j q_k - \sum_{ijkl}\lambda_{ijkl}q_i q_j q_k q_l)$$

and because $\widetilde{f}(q)$ is regularization constrained under space of q, the odd moments need to be assumed to be zero, such we have

$$\widetilde{f}(q) = N\exp(-\sum_{ij}\lambda_{ij}q_i q_j - \sum_{ijkl}\lambda_{ijkl}q_i q_j q_k q_l) \qquad (11).$$

formula（11）can be realized by using a NN with 4 layer, then λ_{ij} and λ_{ijkl} are the corresponsive

connective weights, and then solving (9) is transformed to solving for λ_{ij} and λ_{ijkl}. Below we will

deduce the learning process in which λ_{ij} and λ_{ijkl} are solved:let

$$N = \exp(-\lambda), V_{j'} = \left\{\begin{array}{ll} q_i q_j & \text{if } j' = ij \\ q_i q_j q_k q_l & \text{if } j' = ijkl \end{array}\right\}, \text{ and}$$

$$\lambda_{j'} = \left\{\begin{array}{ll} \lambda_{ij} & \text{if } j' = ij \\ \lambda_{ijkl} & \text{if } j' = ijkl \end{array}\right\}$$

then (11) changes to （12）

$$\widetilde{f}(q) = \exp(-\lambda - \sum_j \lambda_j V_j) \qquad (12)$$

multiply the left side of (9) by -1, and according to (11), there is

$$W = -\int f(q)\ln \tilde{f}(q)d"q = \lambda \int f(q)d"q + \int f(q)\sum_j \lambda_j V_j d"q,$$

and because of (7), there is

$$W = \lambda + \int f(q)\sum_j \lambda_j V_j d"q \qquad (13)$$

where λ_j was controlled by the strategy of gradient evolvement, namely λ_j subjects to (14)

$$\dot{\lambda}_j = -\gamma \frac{\partial W}{\partial \lambda_j} \qquad (14).$$

From (7) and (12), we get

$$e^{-\lambda}\sum_j \exp(-\sum_k \lambda_k V_k) = 1,$$

and consequently there is

$$\lambda = \ln \sum_j \exp(-\sum_k \lambda_k V_k) \qquad \text{or}$$

$$\lambda = \ln \int \exp[-\sum_j \lambda_j V_j]d"q \qquad (15)$$

put (15) into (13) and take the derivation of (13) in direction of λj, we can get PDEs as (16)

$$\frac{\partial W}{\partial \lambda_j} = -\left\{(\int \exp[-\sum_j \lambda_j V_j]d"q)^{-1}\int V_j \exp[-\sum_j \lambda_j V_j]d" \right\} + \int f V_j d"q \qquad (16).$$

It is apparently that the expression in the big bracket in (16) can be interpreted as the mean value of V_j on the distributive function of $\tilde{f}(q)$, namely $\{......\} = <V_j(q)>_{\tilde{f}}$, and the second term of the right side is the same mean value namely $<V_j(q)>_f$ of the distributive function prescribed by outside, then (14) can be rewritten with a more simply form as (17)

$$\dot{\lambda}_j = \gamma(<V_j(q)>_{\tilde{f}} - V_j(q)>_f) \qquad (17),$$

Because each mean value is just its corresponding measure moment, so as concerned to the distributive function given by experiment, to decide the mean value of V_j is very simply. In practice, we can do that in this way: assuming that $f(q)$ is an uniformly distributive function of an incoming signal, and that these signal arrive at discrete time τ, then each incoming signal can be described as a corresponding q_τ. When there have been L surveyed results, we will have:

$$<V_j(q)>_f = \frac{1}{L}\sum_{\tau=1}^{L} V_j(q_\tau) \to \frac{1}{T}\int_0^T V_j[q(\tau)]d\tau.$$

Because time consumed to compute $<V_j(q)>_{\tilde{j}}$ is too more if using the above formula, so alternately, we make use of the properties of a steady stochastic process, and we can do so just because there is

$$V_j(q) = <V_j(q)>_{\tilde{j}} + p_j(t)$$

Where $p_j(t)$ is a fluctuate variant that satisfy $<p_j(t)>= 0$. From all above, (17) become

$$\dot{\lambda}_j = \gamma(V_j(q) - \frac{1}{T}\int_0^T V_j[q(\tau)]d\tau \tag{18}$$

The formula (18) Shows that to solving for $\lambda_j(t)$, we must use $\lambda_j(t-1)$ decided in the before step, so the process solving for $\lambda_j(t)$ become a learning process.

4.   LEARNING ALGORITHM

We summarize our learning algorithm as follow:

step 1. Initial feature space $q = (q_1, q_2, \ldots, q_n)$, learning time T, learning step length Δt, learning parameter γ, $t = 0$, $\lambda_i(t) = 0$, $i = 1, \ldots, n$, actual pattern distributive function $f(q)$, error threshold ε, the largest learning step length T', and let the initial learning step length $\Delta t = 0.005$.

step 2. Compute $V_j(q)$, $\frac{1}{T}\int_0^T V_j[q(\tau)]d\tau$, $j=1,\ldots,n$.

step 3. Update λ:

$$\lambda_j(t+1) = \lambda_j(t) + \gamma\{V_j(q) - \frac{1}{T}\int_0^T V_j[q(\tau)]d\tau\}, \; j=1,\ldots,n.$$

step 4. Compute $\tilde{f}(q)$ according to (11).

step 5. If $|f(q) - \tilde{f}(q)|< \varepsilon$, then Learning succeeds and go to step 9.

step 6. If $t \leq T$, then set $t = t+1$, and go to step 2.

step 7. If $t > T$ and $\Delta t \leq T'$, then let $\Delta t = \Delta t + 0.005$, $t = 0$, and go to step 2.

step 8. If $t > T$, $\Delta t > T'$ and $\gamma \leq 1$, then let $\Delta t = 0.005, t = 0$, and go to step 2, else learning process fail.

step 9. end.

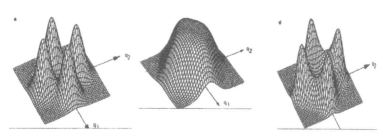

Fig. 2 running samples of learning algorithm

5.   CONCLUSIONS

In this paper, by utilizing the information entropy augmentation and dynamic process, we transformed a complicate recognition process into a learning process of the NN connecting weight, so solved the recognition problem of image with natural textures.

ACKNOWLEDGEMENTS

This work was supported by Education Office of Jiangsu province,China under Grant 02KJD520004.

REFERENCES

1   Luo shu-qian and Zhou guo-hong, Medical image processing and analysis. Science press,Beijing, China, 2003 .
2   Chang Jiong. Information theoretical foundation[J].Tsinghua University Press, Beijing,China, 2001.
3   Haken. Harmonizing. Computer and cognizing - the from above to below method of NN [J]. Tsinghua University Press, Beijing, China, 1994:78-79.

IMPROVEMENTS ON CCA MODEL WITH APPLICATION TO FACE RECOGNITION

Quan-Sen Sun[a, b], Mao-Long Yang[a], Pheng-Ann Heng[c] and De-Sen Xia[a]
[a]Department of Computer Science, Nanjing University of Science &Technology, Nanjing 210094,People' Republic of China. [b]Department of Mathematics, Jinan University, Jinan 250022, People' Republic of China. [c]Department of Computer Science and Engineering, The Chinese University of Hong Kong, Hong Kong

Abstract: Two new methods for combination feature extraction are proposed in this paper. The methods are based on the framework of CCA in image recognition by improving the correlation criterion functions. Comparing with CCA methods, which can solve the classification of high-dimensional small size samples directly, being independent of the total scatter matrix singularity of the training simples, and the algorithms' complexity can be lowered. We prove that the essence of two improved criterion functions is partial least squares analysis (PLS) and multivariate linear regression (MLR). Experimental results based on ORL standard face database show that the algorithms are efficient and robust.

Key words: canonical correlation analysis(CCA); feature extraction; feature fusion; partial least squares (PLS); multivariate linear regression(MLR); face recognition

1. INTRODUCTION

In recent years, feature level fusion plays an important role in the process data fusion, which has achieved delightful development [1]. The advantage of feature level fusion is obvious, different feature vectors extracted from the same pattern always reflects different features of patterns. By optimizing and combining these different features, it not only keeps the effective discriminant information of multi-feature, but also eliminates redundant information to certain degree. This is especially important to the problem of classification and recognition.

There exist two feature fusion methods. One is to group two sets of feature vectors into one union-vector [2], and then to extract features in a higher-dimension real vector space. Another one is to combine two sets of feature vectors by a complex vector[1], and then to extract features in the complex vector space. Both feature fusion methods aim at increasing the recognition rate.

In paper [3], we have proposed a new feature fusion strategy based on the idea of CCA, by creating a framework of CCA in image recognition. We have obtained good results in the application of the framework in the fields of face recognition and handwritten character recognition.

The work in detail is presented in this paper. The relation between the CCA, PLS and MLR was built by improving the correlation criterion function. PLS and MLR have been applied in the field of feature fusion. Comparing with CCA methods, the advantage of PLS and MLR is that they can solve classification problem of high-dimensional space and small sample size, be independent of the total scatter matrix singularity of the training simples, and the algorithms' complexity is lowered greatly. Experimental results based on ORL standard face database show that the algorithms are efficient and robust, which are superior to experimental results of classical Eigenfaces and Fisherfaces.

2.   A FRAMEWORK OF CCA IN IMAGE RECOGNITION

2.1   The basic idea of CCA

In Multivariate Statistical Analysis, the correlation problem of two random vectors are often studied, that is to convert the correlation research of two random vectors into that of a few pairs of variables, which are uncorrelated. H. Hotelling developed this idea in 1936 [4].

Considering two zero-mean random vectors X and Y, CCA finds a pair of directions α and β that maximize the correlation between the projections $x^{*} = \alpha^{'}x$ and $y^{*} = \beta^{'}y$. This correlation is called the canonical correlation.

In general, the projective directions α and β are obtained by maximizing the correlation criterion function as follows:

$$\rho = \frac{E[\alpha^T xy^T \beta]}{\sqrt{E[\alpha^T xx^T \alpha] \cdot E[\beta^T xy^T \beta]}} = \frac{\alpha^T S_{xy} \beta}{\sqrt{\alpha^T S_{xx} \alpha \cdot \beta^T S_{yy} \beta}}.$$

Where S_{xx} and S_{yy} denote the covariance matrixes of x and y respectively, while S_{xx} is their between-set covariance matrix.

2.2   The theory of combine feature extraction

Suppose $\omega_1, \omega_2, \cdots, \omega_c$ are c known pattern classes. Let $\Omega = \{ \xi \,|\, \xi \in R^n \}$ be a training sample space. Given $A = \{ x \,|\, x \in R^p \}$, $B = \{ y \,|\, y \in R^q \}$, where x and y are two feature vectors of the same sample ξ extracted by different means. We will discuss the feature fusion in the transformed training sample feature space A and B.

Our idea is to extract the canonical correlation features between x and y based on the idea of CCA proposed in Section 2.1, we denote them as $\alpha_1^T x$ and $\beta_1^T y$ (the first pair), $\alpha_2^T x$ and $\beta_2^T y$ (the second pair), $\cdots$, $\alpha_d^T x$ and $\beta_d^T y$ (the d th pair). Given the following:

$$X^* = (\alpha_1^T x, \alpha_2^T x, \cdots, \alpha_d^T x)^T = (\alpha_1, \alpha_2, \cdots, \alpha_d)^T x = W_x^T x;$$
$$Y^* = (\beta_1^T y, \beta_2^T y, \cdots, \beta_d^T y)^T = (\beta_1, \beta_2, \cdots, \beta_d)^T y = W_y^T y.$$

In paper [3], we had already given two feature fusion strategies:

$$\text{FFS I} : Z_1 = \begin{pmatrix} X^* \\ Y^* \end{pmatrix} = \begin{pmatrix} W_x^T x \\ W_y^T y \end{pmatrix} = \begin{pmatrix} W_x & 0 \\ 0 & W_y \end{pmatrix}^T \begin{pmatrix} x \\ y \end{pmatrix} \tag{1}$$

$$\text{FFS II} : Z_2 = X^* + Y^* = W_x^T x + W_y^T y = \begin{pmatrix} W_x \\ W_y \end{pmatrix}^T \begin{pmatrix} x \\ y \end{pmatrix} \tag{2}$$

Two linear transformations (1) and (2) are used for classification by the projected feature vectors correspondingly, while the transformation matrix is:

$$W_1 = \begin{pmatrix} W_x & 0 \\ 0 & W_y \end{pmatrix} \text{ and } W_2 = \begin{pmatrix} W_x \\ W_y \end{pmatrix}, \text{where } W_x = (\alpha_1, \alpha_2, \cdots \alpha_d), W_y = (\beta_1, \beta_2, \cdots \beta_d).$$

Define. We call α_i and β_i as the ith pair of canonical projective vectors (CPV) of x and y, and $\alpha_i^T x$ and $\beta_i^T y$ as the ith canonical features of x and y. We also call Z_1 and Z_2 as the canonical discriminant features.

Next, we will discuss how to obtain the value and quality of CPV as follows:

Supposed S_{xx} and S_{yy} are positive definite, and $S_{xy}^T = S_{yx}$, $r = rank(S_{xy})$.

We can give the criterion function as follows:

$$J(\alpha, \beta) = \frac{\alpha^T S_{xy} \beta}{(\alpha^T S_{xx} \alpha \cdot \beta^T S_{yy} \beta)^{1/2}} \tag{3}$$

Let $\alpha^T S_{xx} \alpha = \beta^T S_{yy} \beta = 1$ \hfill (4)

Then the problem is equivalent to finding the CPV α and β with constraint (4) which maximizes the criterion function (3).

Supposing the first pair of CPV (α_1, β_1) has been computed, after the first $(k\text{-}1)$ CPV $(\alpha_1, \beta_1), (\alpha_2, \beta_2), \cdots (\alpha_{k-1}, \beta_{k-1})$ have been chosen, the kth one can be computed by solving the following optimization problem:

$$\text{Model 1} \begin{cases} \max J(\alpha, \beta) \\ \alpha^T S_{xx} \alpha = \beta^T S_{yy} \beta = 1 \\ \alpha_i^T S_{xx} \alpha = \beta_i^T S_{yy} \beta = 0 \ (i = 1, 2, \cdots, k-1) \end{cases} \tag{5}$$

According to the method of Lagrange multipliers, the question can be transformed to the solving of two generalized eigenproblem:

$$\begin{cases} S_{xy} S_{yy}^{-1} S_{yx} \alpha = \lambda^2 S_{xx} \alpha & (6) \\ S_{yx} S_{xx}^{-1} S_{xy} \beta = \lambda^2 S_{yy} \beta & (7) \end{cases}$$

In order to obtain the solution under the restricted condition (5), supposing that $H = S_{xx}^{-1/2} S_{xy} S_{yy}^{-1/2}$. Applying Singular Value Decompose (SVD) theorem on matrix H, we obtain $H = \sum_{i=1}^{r} \lambda_i u_i v_i^T$, where $\lambda_1^2 \geq \lambda_2^2 \geq \cdots \geq \lambda_r^2$ are entire nonzero eigenvalues of $G_1 = H^T H$ and $G_2 = HH^T$, u_i and v_i are the orthogonal eigenvectors of G_1 and G_2 corresponding to the nonzero eigenvalue λ_i^2, where $i = 1, 2, \cdots, r$.

From above, we can refer to the important theorem [3]:

Theorem 1. Given $\beta_i = S_{yy}^{-1/2} v_i$, $\alpha_i = \lambda_i^{-1} S_{xx}^{-1} S_{xy} \beta_i$, $i = 1, \cdots, r$. Then

(1) α_i and β_i are the eigenvectors of generalized eigenequation (6) and (7) corresponded to λ_i^2;

(2) $\begin{cases} \alpha_i^T S_{xx} \alpha_j = \beta_i^T S_{yy} \beta_j = \delta_{ij} \\ \alpha_i^T S_{xy} \beta_j = \lambda_i \delta_{ij} \end{cases}$ $(i, j = 1, 2, \cdots, r)$. where $\delta_{ij} = \begin{cases} 1 & i = j \\ 0 & i \neq j \end{cases}$ \hfill (8)

From the above discussion, we can draw the following conclusion:

Theorem 2. Under criterion (3), the number of the efficient CPV satisfying the restricted condition(4) and (5), is r pair(s) at most($r = rank(S_{xy})$) , and getting $d(\leq r)$ pair CPV are compose of the eigenvectors corresponding to first d maximum eigenvalues of two generalized eigenequation (6) and (7) that satisfy Eq.(8).

3.   THE IMPROVEMENTS OF THE MODEL

From the above we can find that the matrices S_{xx} and S_{yy} must be positive definite when solving the projections and the discriminant features based on the criterion function (3). In the field of pattern recognition, especially in face recognition, cases of high-dimensional space and small sample size are common, where the total scatter matrix of the training simples is singular. A solution, where S_{xx} and S_{yy} are singular, was proposed in paper [3], which can obtain the projective vectors in low–dimensional feature space. Two ways are proposed as follow by improving the criterion function (3).

3.1   Improvement 1: PLS

In the denominator of the criterion function (3), replacing both S_{xx} and S_{yy} by the unit matrices, the criterion function can be written as:

$$J_P(\alpha,\beta) = \frac{\alpha^T S_{xy}\beta}{(\alpha^T\alpha \cdot \beta^T\beta)^{1/2}} \tag{9}$$

Then the problem is equivalent to finding the projections α and β with constraint (10) which maximizes the criterion function (9).

$$\alpha^T\alpha = \beta^T\beta = 1 \tag{10}$$

Based on the criterion function (9), the process of obtaining projection and correlation feature with the constraint (10) shares exactly the same idea with partial least squares analysis, namely PLS [5].

The step of feature fusion and image recognition, which employ PLS, is similar to what we have discussed in section 2: to solve the projection; then to extract combination features by FFS I and FFS II. So we can write model 1 as:

$$\text{Model 2} \begin{cases} \max J_p(\alpha, \beta) \\ \alpha^{\mathrm{T}}\alpha = \beta^{\mathrm{T}}\beta = 1 \\ \alpha_i^{\mathrm{T}}\alpha = \beta_i^{\mathrm{T}}\beta = 0 \ (i = 1, 2, \cdots, k-1) \end{cases} \tag{11}$$

Then the generalized eigenequations (6) and (7) can be written as:

$$\begin{cases} S_{xy}S_{yx}\alpha = \lambda^2\alpha \tag{12} \\ S_{yx}S_{xy}\beta = \lambda^2\beta \tag{13} \end{cases}$$

We can obtain the optimal solutions satisfying model 2 from eigen-equations (12) and (13) as follows:

Theorem 3. Under the criterion (9), the number of effective projective vectors, which satisfy restricted constraints (10) and (11), is r ($r = rank(S_{xy})$) pairs at most. $d(\leq r)$ pairs of projective vectors are composed of vectors which are selected from the eigenvectors corresponding to the first d maximum eigenvalues of eigenequations (14) and (15) and satisfying:
(a) all the eigenvectors should satisfy: $\alpha_i = \lambda_i^{-1}S_{xy}\beta_i, \beta_i = \lambda_i^{-1}S_{yx}\alpha_i, i = 1, \cdots, r$;

(b) $\begin{cases} \alpha_i^{\mathrm{T}}\alpha_j = \beta_i^{\mathrm{T}}\beta_j = \delta_{ij} \\ \alpha_i^{\mathrm{T}}S_{xy}\beta_j = \lambda_i\delta_{ij} \end{cases}$ $(i, j = 1, 2, \cdots, r)$.

where λ_i^2 is the non-zero eigenvalue of the two eigenequations, where eigenvectors are α_i and β_i ($i = 1, 2, \cdots, r$), respectively.

Proof. By the method of Lagrange multipliers, function $L(\alpha, \beta)$ is defined

as $L(\alpha, \beta) = \alpha^{\mathrm{T}}S_{xy}\beta - \dfrac{\lambda_1}{2}(\alpha^{\mathrm{T}}\alpha - 1) - \dfrac{\lambda_2}{2}(\beta^{\mathrm{T}}\beta - 1)$. Let $\dfrac{\partial L}{\partial \alpha} = \dfrac{\partial L}{\partial \beta} = 0$, then the

following can be derived:

$$\begin{cases} S_{xy}\beta - \lambda\alpha = 0 \\ S_{yx}\alpha - \lambda\beta = 0 \end{cases} \Rightarrow \begin{cases} \alpha = \lambda^{-1}S_{xy}\beta \\ \beta = \lambda^{-1}S_{yx}\alpha \end{cases} \tag{14}$$

Then eigenequations (12) and (13) can be derived from Eq.(14). Both $S_{xy}S_{yx}$ and $S_{yx}S_{xy}$ are symmetric matrices, $rank(S_{xy}S_{yx}) = rank(S_{xy}) = r$, so that the two eigenequations have the same non-zero eigenvalue $\lambda_1^2 \geq \lambda_2^2 \geq \cdots \geq \lambda_r^2 > 0$, and the r pairs of eigenvectors corresponding to them are orthonormal, namely $\alpha_i^{\mathrm{T}}\alpha_i = \beta_i^{\mathrm{T}}\beta_i = \delta_{ij}$. Conclusion (a) is true because Eq.(16), and conclusion (b) is true as $\alpha_i^{\mathrm{T}}S_{xy}\beta_j = \alpha_i^{\mathrm{T}}S_{xy}(\lambda_j^{-1}S_{yx}\alpha_j) = \lambda_j^{-1}\alpha_i^{\mathrm{T}}(\lambda_j^2\alpha_j) = \lambda_j\delta_{ij}$, too.   □

3.2   Improvement by MLR:

In the denominator of the criterion function (3), replacing S_{yy} by the unit matrices, the criterion function can be written as

$$J_M(\alpha, \beta) = \frac{\alpha^T S_{xy} \beta}{(\alpha^T S_{xx} \alpha \cdot \beta^T \beta)^{1/2}} \tag{15}$$

In this sense, the problem is equivalent to the finding of projections α and β with the constraint (16) which maximizes the criterion function (15):

$$\alpha^T S_{xx} \alpha = \beta^T \beta = 1 \tag{16}$$

Based on the criterion function (15), the process of obtaining the projection and correlation feature with the constraint (16) implies the idea of multivariate linear regression, namely MLR.

In fact, under the condition of Section 2.1, the goal of MLR is to minimize following the square error[6]:

$$\varepsilon^2 = E[y^T y] - 2\theta \alpha^T S_{xy} \beta + \theta^2 \alpha^T S_{xx} \beta \tag{17}$$

where θ is a regression coefficient. Let

$$\frac{\partial \varepsilon^2}{\partial \theta} = 2(\theta \alpha^T S_{xx} \alpha - \alpha^T S_{xy} \beta) = 0 \Rightarrow \theta = \frac{\alpha^T S_{xy} \beta}{\alpha^T S_{xx} \alpha} .$$

By inserting this expression into Eq. (17), we get

$$\varepsilon^2 = E[y^T y] - \frac{(\alpha^T S_{xy} \beta)^2}{\alpha^T S_{xx} \alpha} .$$

In order to minimize ε^2, what should be done is just to maximize the following quotient function:

$$\rho = \frac{\alpha^T S_{xy} \beta}{(\alpha^T S_{xx} \alpha)^{1/2}} = \frac{\alpha^T S_{xy} \beta}{(\alpha^T S_{xx} \alpha \cdot \beta^T \beta)^{1/2}} \tag{18}$$

where $\beta^T \beta = 1$.

Comparing function (15) with function (18), one will find that they go all the way if constraint (16) is satisfied.

The discussion on the application of feature fusion and image recognition by MLR is similar to that in section 3.1, which is omitted.

3.3   Comparison of the three methods

In order to depict clearly, we call the three methods as CCA, PLS, MLR respectively for short, and call the projection and the discriminant feature by criterion functions (3), (9), and (14) as correlation projective vector (CPV) and correlation discriminant feature vector (CDV), respectively.

All three methods can solve the problem of compressing the pattern feature dimensions effectively. They all make the two sets of feature having maximal correlation based on maximizing their covariance in order to identify the projection. But their restrictions to projection are different: the projection should be conjugate orthogonal for S_{xx} and S_{yy} in CCA, and should be orthonormal in PLS, while one set projection should be orthonormal, the other should be conjugate orthogonal for S_{xx} or S_{yy} in MLS.

The two methods of PLS and MLR can be seen as the special instances of the first method (CCA) in some sense, so the process in solving the CPV and the CDV is coincident. On the other hand, PLS is superior to CCA in arithmetic complexity, while MLR's is between that of PLS and CCA.

PLS has a better generalization capability than the other two methods because it is independent of the total scatter matrix singularity of the training simples. Moreover, PLS is effective on the classification of both large size simples and small ones. MLR can make up the influence caused by the total scatter matrix when it is singular. We only need to make sure that the total scatter matrix is composed of one of the two set features of the same pattern is nonsingular.

4.   EXPERIMENT AND ANALYSIS

Experiment is performed on the ORL face image database. There are 10 different images for 40 individuals. For some people, images were taken at different times. And the facial expression (open/closed eyes, smiling/ nonsmiling) and facial details (glasses/no glasses) are variables. The images were taken against a dark homogeneous background and the people are in upright, frontal position with tolerance for some tilting and rotation of up to $20°$. Moreover, there is some variation in scale of up to about 10%. All images are grayscale and normalized with a resolution of 92×112. Some images in ORL are shown in Fig.1.

Fig.1. Ten images of one person in ORL face database

In this experiment, we use the first five images of each person for training and the remaining five for testing. Thus, the total amount of training samples and testing samples are both 200.

In the experiment, the rank of the total covariance matrix S_t is computed first, and it is equal to 199. Then, we translate the original image vectors into 199 dimensional feature space $\Omega = \{\xi \mid \xi \in R^{199}\}$ by K-L transform, and then decompose it into 2 parts: 59D and 140D, namely $\xi = \begin{bmatrix} x \\ y \end{bmatrix}$, which composes the feature sub-space $A = \{x \mid x \in R^{59}\}$ and $B = \{y \mid y \in R^{140}\}$, respectively.

Then the CPV and the correlation discriminant feature vector are solved by the above three methods, respectively, and the combination features are extracted by the two feature fusion strategies FFSI and FFSII, which are classified finally by the minimum distance classifier and the nearest-neighbor classifier, respectively. The corresponding recognition rates are shown in table 1.

Furthermore, we present the recognition results on ORL face image database of classical Eigenfaces method[7] and Fisherface method[8] in table 1.

Table 1 Recognition rates of different classifier

Classifier	FFS1			FFS2		Eigenface	Fesherface
	CCA	PLS	MLR	PLS	MLR		
M-distance	0.915	0.920	0.940	0.925	0.935	0.895	0.885
N-neighbor	0.905	0.950	0.910	0.945	0.905	0.930	0.885

Table 1 shows that the recognition rates of the three methods by FFSI and FFSII with the minimum distance classifier are higher than those of the Eigenfaces method and the Fisherfaces method, which can be up to 91%. MLR, moreover, is better than CCA and PLS by FFSI and FFSII, of which the optimal recognition correct rates can be up to 94%.

Recognition rates of the PLS by FFSI and FFSII with the nearest-neighbor classifier are higher than that of the other methods which can be up to 95%, while the rates of CCA and MLR are less than the Eigenfaces method, but higher than that of the Fisherfaces method.

Experimental results have shown that the two improved models (PLS and MLR) are superior to previous methods (CCA) in arithmetic complexity and classification capability.

5.   CONCLUSION

We have presented two new feature fusion methods — PLS and MLR by improving the combination feature extraction methods — CCA, which broaden the field of combination feature extraction. Experimental results show that the improved methods are superior to the original methods, which arithmetic complexities are reduced significantly.

ACKNOWLEDGEMENTS

We wish to thank the CUHK fund from HKSAR Government under Grant No. 4185 / 00E for supporting.

REFERENCES

1. Yang Jian, Yang Jing-yu, Zhang David, Lu Jian-feng, Feature fusion: parallel strategy vs. serial strategy, Pattern Recognition, 36 (2003) 1961-1971.
2. Liu C J, Wechsler H, A shape-and texture-based enhanced Fisher classifier for face recognition, IEEE Transactions on Image Processing, 10 (4) (2001)598-608.
3. Quan-Sen Sun, Sheng-Gen Zeng, Yan Liu, Pheng-Ann Heng, De-Shen Xia. A new method of feature fusion and its application in image recognition. Pattern Recognition(USA), in review.
5. A. Höskuldsson, PLS regression methods, Journal of Chemometrics, 2(1988)211-228.
6. M. Borga, Learning Multidimensional Signal Processing, Linköping Studies in Science and Technology, issertations, No.531, Department of Electrical Engineering, Linköping University, Linköping , Sweden, 1998.
7. Turk M and Pentland A. Eigenfaces for recognition. J. Cognitive Neuroscience, 1991, 3(1):71-86.
8. Peter N. Belhumeur, et al. Eigenfaces vs. Fisherfaces: Recognition using class specific linear projection. IEEE Trans. Pattern Anal. Machine Intell. 19(7) (1997) 711-720.

PERFORMANCE OF SEVERAL TYPES OF MEDIAN FILTERS IN SPECTRAL DOMAIN

O. Uma Maheshwari, G.B. Vanisree, Dr. D. Ebenezer
Uma_o@annauniv.edu, gbvanisree@yahoo.com, Ebenez26@mailcity.com

Abstract: Median filter is well known for removing impulsive noise and preserving edges. Repeatedly filtering of any one-dimensional signal with a median filter will produce a root signal. Any impulses in the input signal will be removed by sufficient number of passes of median filter, where any root like features in the input signal will be preserved. A signal of finite length will be filtered to a root signal after a finite number of passes of a median filter of a fixed window, results in the convergence of the signal. In this paper, root signal and its properties are analyzed for One-dimensional signal. Adaptive length median filter, weighted median filter, FIR hybrid median filter and Linear combination of weighted median filter have been taken and their root signals are obtained. Their performances are analyzed by determining Power spectrum density, Mean square error and Signal to noise ratio.

Key words: Median filtering, Root signal, Power spectrum density, Mean square error, Signal to noise ratio

1.   INTRODUCTION

Impulse noise occurs frequently in image processing [11]. It may be caused by transmission channel error (e.g., binary symmetric channel noise), sensor faults, edge sharpening procedures, engine sparks, ac power interference and atmospheric electrical emissions. Due to the strong amplitude of impulse noise, human visual perception is very sensitive to it and the removal of such noise is a important issue in image processing.

Linear filters have poor performance in the presence of noise that is not Additive. If a signal with sharp edges is corrupted by high frequency noise, however, as in some noisy image data, then linear filters designed to remove the noise also smooth out signal edges. In addition, impulse noise cannot be reduced sufficiently by linear filters.

A nonlinear scheme called 'median filtering' has been used with success in these situations. Some interesting results and analyses for median filters have been obtained recently [11].

The success of median filters is based on two intrinsic properties:

1. Edge preservation.
2. Efficient noise attenuation with robustness against impulsive noise.

A median filter maps a class of input signal into an associated set of root sequences.

2. ROOT SIGNAL AND ITS PROPERTIES

Repeated application of the median filter on a defined signal of finite length ultimately results in a sequence, termed a root signal, which is invariant to additional passes of the median filter [12].

The characteristics of root signals are based on the local signal structures, summarized for a median filter with window size W=2N+1, as follows:

➢ A *Constant neighborhood* is a region of at least N+ 1 consecutive identically valued sample.

➢ A *Edge* is a monotonically rising or falling set of samples surround on both sides by constant neighborhood of different values.

➢ An *Impulse* is a set of at most N samples whose values are different from the surrounding regions and whose surrounding are identically valued constant neighborhoods.

➢ An *Oscillation* is any signal structure which is not a part of constant neighborhood, an edge or an impulse

➢ A *root* is an appended signal which is invariant under filtering by particular median filter.

A filter is said to be idem potent if its output signal converge to a root in only one pass of the filtering process for any input signal. The root signal retains the spatial characteristics of the input signal, such as edges, while at the same time; it deletes redundant impulses and oscillations (which are defined above).

Since the output of the median filter is always one of its input samples, it is conceivable that certain signal could pass through the median filter unaltered. A filter is said to be 'idem potent' if its output signal converge to a root in only one pass of the filtering process for any input signal. The root signal retains the spatial characteristics of the input signal, such as edges, while at the same time; it deletes redundant impulses and oscillations (which are defined above).

The analysis of the root signal can be explained by taking binary signals and the theory can be extended to multilevel signals and two-dimensional image. For a window of width 2N+1, any signal of length L will converge to a root $i_3 \left\lceil \dfrac{L-2}{2(K+2)} \right\rceil$

It is obtained by considering binary signals first, then extending it to multi-level signals via the threshold decomposition (Peter 1986). For N>1, this bound is much lower than the

$$\left| \frac{L-1}{2} \right|$$

The inverse dependence on the window width that appears in this convergence bound allows limiting operations to be performed. Slow convergence of binary signal into a root signal.

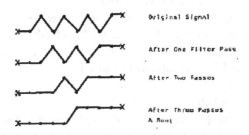

Figure 1. Slow convergence of a binary signal

3.   PRINCIPLES OF SEVERAL TYPES OF MEDIAN FILTERS

In this section the principles of several types of median filters are discussed. The root signal for the filters discussed is analyzed in the next section. Their performances are analyzed by determining Power spectrum density, Mean square error and Signal to noise ratio.

Weighted median filter

The weighted median filter is a extension of median filter which gives more weights to some values within the window. For a discrete time continuous valued input vector $X = [X_1, X_2, X_3... X_N]$, the output Y of the WM filter of span X associated with the integer weights $W = [W_1, W_2, W_3... W_N]$ is given by,

$Y = MED[W_1 \lozenge X_1, W_2 \lozenge X_2, ..., W_N \lozenge X_N]$

Where MED {.} denotes the median operation and $\lozenge$ denotes duplication, i.e.,

$$K \; times$$
$$K \lozenge X = (X, ... , X.)$$

FIR Hybrid median filter

A new class of generalized median filters, which contain linear substructures. The root signals types as well as the noise attenuation properties of these FIR median hybrids (FMH) filters are similar to those of the standard median filters. The FMH filters require, however less computations than the standard median filters [10].

The simplest FMH filter is the averaging FMH filter consisting of two identical averaging filters.

$$k \qquad k$$
$$Y(n) = MED [(1/k) \Sigma x(n-1), s(n) ,(1/k)\Sigma x(n+1)]$$

$$i = 1 \qquad i = 1$$

Linear combination of weighted medians

A class of linear combination of weighted median (LCWM) filters that can offer various frequency characteristics including LP, BP and HP responses. The scheme is modeled on the structure and design procedure of the linear-phase FIR HP filter.

Design procedure for the LCWM filter:

Design an N-tap prototype FIR filter h using frequency specifications.

Choose a weight vector w of the M-tap SM sub filter (smoother)(M<N).

Using the row-searching algorithm, find $B_{N,M}$ and convert it into B_p.

Using SSP's and 1/Ms, transform B_p into B.

Using alpha = $h*B^{-1}$

Adaptive median filter

Median filters employing adaptive length algorithms, based on noise detection, exhibit improved performance for impulse noise removal. The detection algorithm is fundamentally different from other commonly used adaptive or threshold algorithms, which are based on statistical parameters and /or edge detection, and which seen les suitable for impulse noise smoothing. Impulse noise generally has a lower probability of occurrence and a considerably higher probability for large amplitude. A smooth region with impulse noise, and an edge with smaller amplitude, is difficult to recognize from some simple statistical parameters. To detect impulse noise deterministically thus seems a more proper procedure. The algorithm is insensitive to specific threshold values, and its realization is feasible and efficient. One dimensional median filters can be used to remove either positive or negative impulse noise of low density. Such filters can achieve quite good performance with very efficient realizations [1].

4.   ALGORITHM FOR THE PERFORMANCE ANALYSIS OF THE FILTERS

1. A signal is generated which contains proper edges, constant regions and randomly variably noise. Such a signal is termed as '**test signal**'.
2. The generated test signal is allowed to pass through the designed filters like Adaptive median filter, Weighted median filter, FIR hybrid median filter and Linear combination of weighted medians .
3. The time domain and frequency domain model of the signal is plotted.
4. The output signal of the respective filters are repeatedly passed through the same filter. Root signal is determined for each type of filter.
5. Frequency domain model of the root signal is plotted for each output.
6. Next, the mean square error, power spectrum and signal to noise ratio are calculated, by varying the intensity of the noise.
7. The performance is analyzed from the values obtained above.

5. ROOT ANALYSIS OF SEVERAL TYPES OF FILTERS

The signal that is invariant to subsequent passes is said to be root signal. The performance analysis is done by determining the root signal for each type of filter. A common test signal is generated and the signal is allowed to pass through several types of filters repeatedly to get the root signal. The root properties for Adaptive median length, Weighted median filter, FIR Hybrid median filter and Linear Combination of weighted median are analyzed below.

From the spectrum of the outputs of the test signal, the shape of the root signal is same, It is seen from the results in table 1, table 2 the information carried by the original Signal retained Adaptive length median compared to the weighted medians.

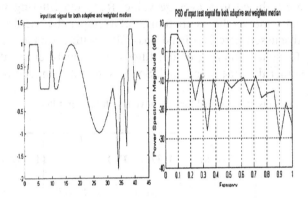

Figure 2. Figure(a),Figure(b)

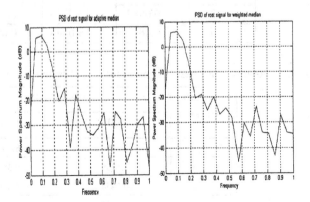

Figure 3. Figure(c),Figure(d)

Results of the test signal: (a) Model test signal. (b) Spectrum of original signal. (C). Spectrum for root of Adaptive median. (d) Spectrum for root of Weighted median

Results of the Sinusoidal signal: (a) Spectrum of original signal . (b) Spectrum of corrupted signal. (C). Specturm for root of Adaptive median. (d) Spectrum for root of Weighted median Similarly the analysis is carried for a test signal. The root signal is determined for the test signal. The analysis is extended to two dimensional image. The root signal is determined for Adaptive median filter. The results are not satisfactory, blurring of the image is seen. This can be improved by new class or some recent modification in the Adaptive median filter.

The signal is not converged to a root for the case of a LCWM and FMH filter. The reasons are discussed below. The FMH filter discussed here is a averaging type filter. Hence the impulses are not completely removed but they are reduced to a average value. Repeated filtering with a FMH filter does not removes the oscillations, but averages the oscillations. The LCWM filter discussed here is a band pass filter with a frequency range of 0.32 to 0.7. Repeated filtering of the filter continuously eliminates the frequency range other than the prescribed. So the signal does not converge to a root.

Table 1. Results of test signal for Adaptive length Median filter.

NOISE POWER	ITERATION I		ITERATION II	
	MSE	PSNR	MSE	PSNR
0	0.28330	8.4932	0.2981	8.2719
1	0.1774	9.2981	0.1776	9.2932
2	0.1158	9.3622	0.1529	8.1526
3	0.0983	10.0755	0.1017	9.99255
4	0.0612	15.0448	0.0804	13.8580

Table 2. Results of test signal for Adaptive length Median filter

NOISE POWER	ITERATION I	
	MSE	PSNR
0	0.2850	8.4680
1	0.1738	9.3876
2	0.1454	8.3745
3	0.1131	9.4636
4	0.0808	13.8770

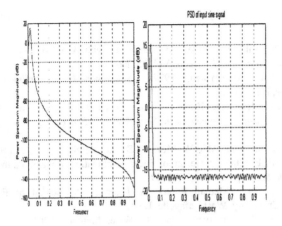

Figure 4. Figure(a),Figure(b)

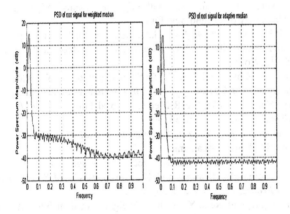

Figure 5. Figure(c),Figure(d)

6.   CONCLUSION

In this project the root analysis for several types of filters like adaptive length median filter, fir hybrid median filter, weighted median filter and linear combination of weighted medians is performed. The root signals are obtained for one-dimensional signal of adaptive median filter and weighted median filter. For the case of FIR Hybrid median and Linear combination of weighted median, the input signal is not converged to root signal, the reasons were discussed. The root performance are compared from the results of mean square error, signal to noise ratio and power spectrum density.

REFERENCES

1. Ho-Ming Lin, Alan N. Willson, (1988), "Median Filter with Adaptive Length", *IEEE Transaction action on Circuits and systems*, Vol. 35, No. 6.
2. Jaakko Astola and Pauli Kuosmanen, (1977), *"Fundamentals of nonlinear digital Filtering"*, CRC Press, New York.
3. Jaakko Astola and Pekka Heinonen, (1987), "On Root Structures of Median and Median – Type Filters", *IEEE Transaction on Acoustic Speech Signal Processing*, vol. ASSP 35, No. 8.
4. Kang-Sun Choi, Student Member, Aldo W. Morales, Senior Member, IEEE, and Sung-Jea Ko, Senior Member, IEEE, (2001), " Design of linear combination of weighted medians", *IEEE Transaction on Signal processing*, Vol. 49.
5. Neal G. Gallagher, (1988), "Median Filters: A Tutorial", Jr. School of Electrical Engineering, Purdue University, West Lafayette, USA.
6. Neal G. Gallagher, Jr. Member, IEEE, Gary L. Wise, Member, IEEE (1981), "A Theoretical Analysis of Properties of Median filters", *IEEE Transaction on Acoustic Speech Signal Processing*, Vol. ASSP 29, No. 6.
7. Olli yli- Harja, Heikki Huttunen, Antti Niemisto & karan Egiazarian, "Design of Recursive weighted median filters with negative weights", Signal processing laboratory, Tampere University of Technology, Finland.
8. Patrick fitch, Edward J. Coyle and Neal C. Gallegher, (1985), "Root Properties and Convergence Rates of Median Filters", *IEEE Transaction on Acoustic Speech Signal Processing*, vol. ASSP 33, No. 1.
9. Peter D. Wendt, Edward J. Coyle and Neal C. Gallagher, (1986) " Some Convergence Properties of Median filters", *IEEE Transaction on Circuits and systems*, Vol. 33, No. 3.
10. Pekka Heinonen, Yrjo Neuvo, (1987), " FIR-Median Hybrid Filters", *IEEE Transaction on Acoustic Speech Signal Processing*, Vol. 35, No. 6.
11. Pitas. I and Venetsanopoulos. A.N. (1990), " *Nonlinear Digital Filters: Principles and Applications"*. Boston, MA. Kluwer Academic.
12. Thomas A. Nodes, Student Member, IEEE and Neal. C. Gallagher, Jr, Member IEEE (1982), "Median filters: Some Modifications and Their Properties", *IEEE Transaction on Acoustic Speech Signal Processing*, vol. ASSP 30, No.5.
13. Yin. L, Yang.R, Gabbouj.M, and Neuo.Y, (1996), "Weighted median filter: A tutorial," *IEEE Transaction on Circuits Syst*. Vol.4.

FUZZY AND ROUGH SET
Combining Fuzzy Set and Rough Set for Inductive Learning

Hong Jing[1], Lu Jingui[1], Shi Feng[2]
[1]*Department of Computer Science and Engineering, Nanjing University of Technology, Nanjing,210009;* [2]*National Die & Mold CAD Engineering Research Center, Shanghai Jiaotong University,Shanghai,200030*

Abstract: A fuzzy-rough set model is presented based on the extension of the classical rough set theory. The continuous attributes are fuzzified. The indiscernibility relation in classical rough set is extended to the fuzzy similarity relation. Then an inductive learning algorithm based on fuzzy-rough set model (FRILA) is proposed. Finally, with comparison to the decision tree algorithms, the effectiveness of the proposed method is verified by an example.

Key words: Fuzzy set, Rough set, Fuzzy similarity relation, Inductive learning

1. INTRODUCTION

In the early 1980s, Pawlak Z proposed rough set theory, which combines knowledge with classification and provides a new approach to vague and uncertain data analysis [1]. However, there are some limitations with the classical rough set. The original rough set cannot deal with the continuous attributes well. And it is based on the indiscernibility relation. Pawlak proposed that both fuzzy set and rough set were not competitive but complementary [2]. Dubois and Prade also proposed that they were related but distinct and complementary theories [3]. Hence, it is possible to combine the two theories.

2.   FUZZY-ROUGH SET MODEL

2.1   Fuzzifying the continuous attributes

Practically, there are many continuous or numerical attributes in the decision table. Each attribute a is fuzzified into k linguistic values T_i, $\forall i=1,\ldots,k$. The slop of triangular membership functions are selected in the way that adjacent functions cross at the membership value 0.5, so the only parameters to be determined are the set of k centers $M=\{m_i, i=1,2,\ldots,k\}$. The center m_i can be calculated through Kohonen's feature-map algorithm.

2.2   New definitions based on fuzzy similarity relation

The classical lower and upper approximations are originally introduced with reference to an indiscernibility relation (reflexive, symmetric, and transitive). Practically, it can be extended to fuzzy similarity relation.

In order to obtain the partition of U given the fuzzy similarity relation $\widetilde{R}$, an algorithm is designed as follows: *Algorithm 1*:

Input: fuzzy similarity matrix $\widetilde{R}$ and level value λ

Output: U/IND($\widetilde{R}_\lambda$)

1) Calculate normal similarity relation matrix $\widetilde{R}_\lambda$; 2) $x_i \in U$, $X \Leftarrow \phi$, $Y \Leftarrow \phi$; 3) $j \Leftarrow 0$; 4) If $r_{ij}=1$ and $x_j \notin X$, then $X \Leftarrow X \cup \{x_j\}$, $Y \Leftarrow Y \cup \{x_j\}$; 5) $j \Leftarrow j+1$; 6) If $j<n$, then GOTO 4; otherwise, GOTO next step; 7) If $card(Y)>1$, then select $x_i \in Y$ and $Y \Leftarrow Y-\{x_i\}$, GOTO 3; otherwise, GOTO next step; 8) Output the set X and let $U \Leftarrow U-X$; 9) If $U=\phi$, then end; otherwise, GOTO 2. Where $card$ (Y) denotes the cardinality of set Y.

Considering a subset $X \subseteq U$ and a fuzzy similarity relation $\widetilde{R}_\lambda^A$ defined on U, the lower approximation of X, $\widetilde{R}_{\lambda-}^A$ (X) , and upper approximation of X, $\widetilde{R}_\lambda^{A-}$ (X) , are respectively defined as follows: $\widetilde{R}_{\lambda-}^A$ (X) = $\cup\{Y:Y \in$ U/IND($\widetilde{R}_\lambda^A$) ,$Y \subseteq X$); $\widetilde{R}_\lambda^{A-}$ (X) = $\cup\{Y:Y \in$ U/IND($\widetilde{R}_\lambda^A$),$Y \cap X \neq \varnothing$). Assuming U/IND($\widetilde{R}_\lambda^C$) and Y are two partitions on U, where U/IND($\widetilde{R}_\lambda^C$) = $\{X_1, X_2,\ldots,X_k\}$ and Y=$\{Y_1,Y_2,\ldots,Y_r\}$, the positive region $POS_C^\lambda(Y)$ is defined as follows: $POS_C^\lambda(Y) = \cup\{\widetilde{R}_{\lambda-}^C(Y_i) : Y_i \in Y\}$.

2.3   Fuzzy similarity relation based attribute reduction

Assuming a condition attribute set C and a decision attribute set D, the degree of dependency of C on D, denoted by γ(C, D), is defined as:γ(C,D)=$card(POS_C$ (D))/$card$(U), where $card$(X) denotes the cardinality of set X and $0 \leq \gamma$ (C,D) ≤ 1. According to the definition of the degree of dependency, the attribute significance for every attribute $a \in C$-R can be defined as follows: SIG $(a, R, D) = \gamma(R \cup \{a\}, D) - \gamma(R, D)$.

In order to obtain the minimal reduction, a hierarchy attribute reduction algorithm is constructed as follows: *Algorithm 2:*

Input: decision table T=<U, C∪D, V, f>

Output: the minimal attribute reduction set R.

1) Let $R \Leftarrow \phi$; 2) Compute SIG (x, R, D) for every attribute $x \in C$-R; 3) Select attribute x with maximum SIG (x, R, D) and let $R \Leftarrow R \cup \{x\}$; 4) If $\gamma(R,D) = \gamma(C,D)$, then GOTO 5; otherwise, GOTO 2; 5) Return R.

3.   DESCRIPTION OF FRILA

Based on the fuzzy-rough set model, FRILA can be described as follows.
1) Calculate the center m_i and fuzzify the continuous attributes. 2) Calculate the fuzzy similarity matrix for every attribute; 3)Calculate fuzzy partition U/IND($\tilde{R}_\lambda^{\{a\}}$) given the fuzzy similarity relation $\tilde{R}_\lambda^{\{a\}}$ with the value set λ ;
4) Calculate the minimal attribute reduction; 5) Calculate the attribute core of the condition attribute with respect to the decision attribute and obtain the minimal reduction of the condition attribute, then delete the redundant objects; 6) For every object, calculate the value core of the condition attribute, and then delete the redundant attribute values and objects;7) Delete the same objects in decision table and translate the decision rules.

4.   A CASE STUDY

In Reference [4], there is a simple relational database system shown as Table 1.

Tab. 1 A relational database

ID	Degree	Experience	Salary	ID	Degree	Experience	Salary
1	Ph. D.	7.2	63,000	12	Master	3.6	41,000
2	Master	2.0	37,000	13	Master	10	68,000
3	Bachelor	7.0	40,000	14	Ph. D.	5.0	57,000
4	Ph. D.	1.2	47,000	15	Bachelor	5.0	36,000
5	Master	7.5	53,000	16	Master	6.2	50,000
6	Bachelor	1.5	26,000	17	Bachelor	0.5	23,000
7	Bachelor	2.3	29,000	18	Master	7.2	55,000
8	Ph. D.	2.0	50,000	19	Master	6.5	51,000
9	Ph. D.	3.8	54,000	20	Ph. D.	7.8	65,000
10	Bachelor	3.5	35,000	21	Master	8.1	64,000
11	Master	3.5	40,000	22	Ph. D.	8.5	70,000

Firstly, two continuous attributes, denoted by E and S respectively, are fuzzified. The Kohonen's feature-map algorithm is used to determine the center m_i and. Secondly, The fuzzy similarity relations of three attributes are constructed. Then given the level values, the fuzzy similarity matrix is transformed to the normal similarity matrix. Thirdly, the fuzzy partition U/IND($\tilde{R}_\lambda^{\{a\}}$) given the fuzzy similarity relation $\tilde{R}_\lambda^{\{a\}}$ is calculated, where the level values are as follows: λ_D=1.0, λ_E=0.7 and λ_S=0.7. Finally, calculate the attribute reduction and there is no redundant attribute in this case. Then we use FRILA to generate 6 fuzzy rules.

In Reference [4], the ID3-like algorithms, named by FCLS, tend to involve more attributes than FRILA. In other words, the rules induced by FCLS algorithms have redundant attributes and are not more concise than FRILA. The more concise rules and fewer rules lead to a more efficient classification; on the other hand, more rules lead to a higher classification accuracy. These two factors have to be traded off to satisfy application-dependent specifications. The comparison of FCLS and FRILA is shown as Table 2, where the level values λ_D=1.0 and λ_S=0.7.

*Table 2.*Comparison of FRIFA and FCLS

Algorithms	FCLS	FRILA			
		λE=0.6	λE=0.7	λE=0.9	λE=0.95
Number of rules (num)	17	4	6	7	12
Coverage rate (%)	100	84	100	100	100
Accuracy rate (%)	100	64	77	91	100

Compared to the decision tree algorithms, the proposed algorithm has the following advantages:

1) The method can deal with both discrete and continuous attributes.

2) The induced rules are more concise. Due to the root node attribute exists all the rules, the rules induced by decision tree have redundant attributes.

3) The method generates fewer fuzzy rules. It is shown that when both accuracy rate and coverage rate are 100%, FRILA generates 12 rules, whereas FCLS generates 17 rules.

REFERENCES

1. Z. Pawlak, AI and intelligent industrial applications: the rough set perspective. Cybernetics and Systems: An International Journal, 31(4), pp. 227-252, 2000
2. Z. Pawlak, Rough sets and fuzzy sets. Fuzzy Sets and Systems, 17(1), pp.88-102, 1985
3. D. Dubois and H. Prade, Rough fuzzy sets and fuzzy rough sets[J]. Int. J. General Systems, 17, pp.191-208,1990
4. S. M. Chen and M. S. Yeh, Generating fuzzy rules from relational database systems for estimating null values. Cybernetics and Systems: An International Journal, 28(8), pp. 695-723, 1997

ALGEBRAIC PROPERTY OF ROUGH IMPLICATION BASED ON INTERVAL STRUCTURE

Xue Zhan-ao, He Hua-can and Ma Ying-cang
School of Computer Science, Northwestern Polytechnical University, Xi'an 710072, China

Abstract: Due to the shortage of rough implication in [4] ~ [6], rough set and rough implication operators are redefined by using interval structure in [7], the shortages have been e improved. We have investigated the characteristics of the rough implication, and also point out that the good logic property of the rough implication in [7]. In this paper, we will study the algebraic properties of the rough implication in depth.

Key words: Rough Logic, Algebraic Property, Rough Implication, Approximation Spaces

1.   INTRODUCTION

Rough set theory, introduced by Zdzislaw Pawlak in the early 1980s [1-3], is a new mathematical tool to deal with many problems such as vagueness, uncertainty, incomplete data and reasoning. Now there are lots of papers about rough logic idea and its abroad application [1~9], but some rough implication operators exist defects, for instance, $B^c \to A^c = A \to B$ doesn't hold in [4], $A \to A$ is not Theorem in [5,6], etc.. In order to eliminate those defects we redefine rough set system, and new rough operators such as intersection, union, complement and implication are expressed by using interval structure in [7]. The characteristics of this implication were investigated, and logic properties of rough implication were pointed out in [7]. Further, we will study the algebraic properties of the rough implication in this paper.

2.   ROUGH SET THEORY

Definition2.1 Let U be the universe set and R be an equivalent relation on U. A pair

(U, R) is called an approximate space. If $X \subseteq U$ is an arbitrary set, then two approximations are formally defined as follows:

$$\underline{X} = \{x \mid x \in U, [x]_R \subseteq X\}, \qquad \overline{X} = \{x \mid x \in U, [x]_R \cap X \neq \phi\}.$$

Where $[x]_R$ is an equivalent class containing x. $\underline{X}$ is called lower approximation of X, $\overline{X}$ is called upper approximation of X. The approximate set X lies between its lower and upper approximations: $\underline{X} \subseteq X \subseteq \overline{X}$.

We get $-\overline{X} \subseteq -X \subseteq -\underline{X}$, where, $Z \subseteq U$ and $-Z$ is the complement of Z in U.

For each $X \subseteq U$, a rough set is a pair $\langle \underline{X}, \overline{X} \rangle$. We denote the empty set ϕ by $\langle \underline{\phi}, \overline{\phi} \rangle = \langle \phi, \phi \rangle$, the universe set U by $\langle \underline{U}, \overline{U} \rangle = \langle U, U \rangle$ and the power set of U by $\Re(U)$.

Definition 2.2 Let $A, B \in \Re(U)$, the inclusion relation of two rough sets is defined by $A \widetilde{\subseteq} B$ if and only if $\overline{A} \subseteq \overline{B}$ and $\underline{A} \subseteq \underline{B}$;

The equivalent relation of two rough sets is defined by

$A = B$ if and only if $\overline{A} = \overline{B}$ and $\underline{A} = \underline{B}$.

Definition 2.3 The intersection of two rough sets A and B is a rough set in approximate space, and is defined by $A \cap B = \langle \underline{A} \cap \underline{B}, \overline{A} \cap \overline{B} \rangle$,

The union of two rough sets is a rough set in approximate space, and is defined by $A \cup B = \langle \underline{A} \cup \underline{B}, \overline{A} \cup \overline{B} \rangle$,

The complement of A is a rough set in approximate space, and is defined by $A^c = \langle -\overline{A}, -\underline{A} \rangle$,

The pseudo complement of A is a rough set in approximate space, and is defined by $A^* = \langle -\underline{A}, -\underline{A} \rangle$,

Where $X \subseteq U$, $-X$ is the complement of X in U.

Theorem 2.4 Suppose $A, B \in \Re(U)$, then

$$\underline{A \cap B} = \underline{A} \cap \underline{B}, \quad \overline{A \cap B} \subseteq \overline{A} \cap \overline{B};$$
$$\underline{A \cup B} \supseteq \underline{A} \cup \underline{B}, \quad \overline{A \cup B} = \overline{A} \cup \overline{B}.$$

Proof. Theorem 2.4 follows from [1] ~ [3] and [8] ~ [9].

Theorem 2.5 If A^c is the complement of A in U, A^* is the pseudo complement of A in U, then

(1) $A^c \subseteq A^*$;   (2) $A^{**} \subseteq A^{c*}$;   (3) $A^c \cup A^* = A^*$, $A^c \cap A^* = A^c$;

(4) $A^{c*c} = A^{c**} = \langle -\overline{A}, -\overline{A} \rangle$;   (5) $A^{cc*} = A^{*c*} = A^{***} = A^{**c} = A^{*cc} = A^*$;

(6) $A^{ccc} = A^c$;   (7) $A^{c*c*} = A^{c*}$.

Proof. Theorem 2.5 can be proved easily from Definition 2.3.

Theorem 2.6 Let $A, B \in \Re(U)$, then,

$(A \cap B)^c = A^c \cup B^c$; $(A \cup B)^c = A^c \cap B^c$;

$(A \cap B)^* = A^* \cup B^*$; $(A \cup B)^* = A^* \cap B^*$.

Proof. Theorem 2.6 is easy to be proved by Definition 2.3.

3. ALGEBRAIC PROPERTIES OF ROUGH IMPLICATION

We redefine the implication operator in [7], which to improve the shortage of

rough implication in [4]~[6]. In this section, we will directly cite the definition implication operator $\rightarrow$, and will investigate its algebraic properties.

Definition 3.1 Let $mng\,(\varphi) = \langle \underline{A}, \overline{A} \rangle$, $mng\,(\psi) = \langle \underline{B}, \overline{B} \rangle$, $mng\,(\beta) = \langle \underline{C}, \overline{C} \rangle$, and mng is a bijection, for any $\varphi, \psi, \beta, 0, 1 \in P$, we have

$$mng(\varphi \wedge \psi) = \langle \underline{A} \cap \underline{B}, \overline{A} \cap \overline{B} \rangle ; \qquad mng(\varphi \vee \psi) = \langle \underline{A} \cup \underline{B}, \overline{A} \cup \overline{B} \rangle ;$$

$$mng(\varphi^c) = \langle -\overline{A}, -\underline{A} \rangle ; \qquad mng(\varphi^*) = \langle -\underline{A}, -\underline{A} \rangle ; \qquad mng(0) = \langle \phi, \phi \rangle ;$$

$$mng(\varphi^{c*}) = \langle \overline{A}, \overline{A} \rangle ; \qquad mng(\varphi^{c*c}) = \langle -\overline{A}, -\overline{A} \rangle ; \qquad mng(1) = \langle U, U \rangle .$$

$$(\varphi \vee \psi)^c = \varphi^c \wedge \psi^c ; \qquad (\varphi \wedge \psi)^c = \varphi^c \vee \psi^c ; \qquad (\varphi \vee \psi)^* = \varphi^* \wedge \psi^* ;$$

$$(\varphi \wedge \psi)^* = \varphi^* \vee \psi^* ; \qquad \varphi^{c*c} = \varphi^{c**} ; \qquad \varphi^{ccc} = \varphi^c ;$$

$$\varphi^{c*c*} = \varphi^{c*} ; \qquad \varphi^{cc} = \varphi^{*c*} = \varphi^{***} = \underline{\varphi}^{**c} = \varphi^{*cc} = \varphi^* .$$

$$mng(\varphi \rightarrow \psi) = mng(\varphi^c \vee \psi \vee (\varphi^* \wedge \psi^{c*})) = \langle -\overline{A} \cup \underline{B} \cup (\overline{B} \cap -\underline{A}), -\underline{A} \cup \overline{B} \rangle$$

(I)

Theorem 3.2 $(P, \vee, \wedge, ^c, 0, 1)$ is a boundary lattice.

Proof. Theorem3.2 is easy to prove from definition 3.1 and [7].

Theorem 3.3 Let $A, B \in \Re(U)$, the following are equivalent:

(1) $A \rightarrow B = \langle -\overline{A} \cup \underline{B} \cup (\overline{B} \cap -\underline{A}), -\underline{A} \cup \overline{B} \rangle$;

(2) $A \rightarrow B = \langle ((-\underline{A} \cup \underline{B}) \cap (-\overline{A} \cup \overline{B}), -\underline{A} \cup \overline{B} \rangle$.

Proof. Theorem 3.3 is easy to be proved from (I).

Proposition 3.4 Suppose $(P, \vee, \wedge, ^c, 0, 1)$ is called a boundary lattice which is inverse ordered involution, and $\rightarrow$ is rough implication operator, the following are satisfied:

(IA.1) $\varphi \rightarrow (\psi \rightarrow \beta) = \psi \rightarrow (\varphi \rightarrow \beta)$ (IA.2) $\varphi \rightarrow \varphi = 1$

(IA.3) $\varphi \rightarrow \psi = \psi^c \rightarrow \varphi^c$ (IA.4) if $\varphi \rightarrow \psi = \psi \rightarrow \varphi = 1$, then

$\varphi = \psi$

(IA.5)

$\varphi \vee \psi \rightarrow \beta = (\varphi \rightarrow \beta) \wedge (\psi \rightarrow \beta)$ (IA.6) $\varphi \wedge \psi \rightarrow \beta = (\varphi \rightarrow \beta) \vee (\psi \rightarrow \beta)$

Proof. The formulas can be proved by Theorem 3.3 and (I).

Proof of (IA.1)

$$\varphi \rightarrow (\psi \rightarrow \beta) = \varphi^c \vee (\psi \rightarrow \beta) \vee (\varphi^* \wedge (\psi \rightarrow \beta)^{c*})$$

$$= \varphi^c \vee (\psi^c \vee \beta \vee (\psi^* \wedge \beta^{c*})) \vee (\varphi^* \wedge (\psi^c \vee \beta \vee (\psi^* \wedge \beta^{c*}))^{c*})$$

$$= \varphi^c \vee \psi^c \vee \beta \vee (\psi^* \wedge \beta^{c*}) \vee (\varphi^* \wedge (\psi^* \vee \beta^{c*} \vee (\psi^* \wedge \beta^{c*})))$$

$$= \varphi^c \vee \psi^c \vee \beta \vee (\psi^* \wedge \beta^{c*}) \vee (\varphi^* \wedge \psi^*) \vee (\varphi^* \wedge \beta^{c*}) \vee (\varphi^* \wedge \psi^* \wedge \beta^{c*})$$

$$\psi \rightarrow (\varphi \rightarrow \beta) = \psi^c \vee (\varphi \rightarrow \beta) \vee (\psi^* \wedge (\varphi \rightarrow \beta)^{c*})$$

$$= \psi^c \vee (\varphi^c \vee \beta \vee (\varphi^* \wedge \beta^{c*})) \vee (\psi^* \wedge (\varphi^c \vee \beta \vee (\varphi^* \wedge \beta^{c*}))^{c*})$$

$$= \psi^c \vee \varphi^c \vee \beta \vee (\varphi^* \wedge \beta^{c*}) \vee (\psi^* \wedge (\varphi^* \vee \beta^{c*} \vee (\varphi^* \wedge \beta^{c*})))$$

$$= \psi^c \vee \varphi^c \vee \beta \vee (\varphi^* \wedge \beta^{c*}) \vee (\psi^* \wedge \varphi^*) \vee (\psi^* \wedge \beta^{c*}) \vee (\psi^* \wedge \varphi^* \wedge \beta^{c*})$$
$$= \varphi^c \vee \psi^c \vee \beta \vee (\psi^* \wedge \beta^{c*}) \vee (\varphi^* \wedge \psi^*) \vee (\varphi^* \wedge \beta^{c*}) \vee (\varphi^* \wedge \psi^* \wedge \beta^{c*})$$

Hence, $\varphi \rightarrow (\psi \rightarrow \beta) = \psi \rightarrow (\varphi \rightarrow \beta)$

Proof of (IA.2)   Obviously, $\varphi \rightarrow \varphi = 1$

Proof of (IA.3)

$$\varphi^c \rightarrow \psi^c = \varphi^{cc} \vee \psi^c \vee (\varphi^{c*} \wedge \psi^{cc*}) = \psi^c \vee \varphi \vee (\psi^* \wedge \varphi^{c*})$$
$$\psi \rightarrow \varphi = \psi^c \vee \varphi \vee (\psi^* \wedge \varphi^{c*})$$

Hence, $\varphi \rightarrow \psi = \psi^c \rightarrow \varphi^c$.

Proof of (IA.4)

Because of $A \rightarrow B = \langle (-\underline{A} \cup \underline{B}) \cap (-\overline{A} \cup \overline{B}), -\underline{A} \cup \overline{B} \rangle$ $A \rightarrow B = U$ iff
$A \rightarrow B = \langle (-\underline{A} \cup \underline{B}) \cap (-\overline{A} \cup \overline{B}), -\underline{A} \cup \overline{B} \rangle = \langle U, U \rangle$ iff $-\underline{A} \cup \underline{B} = U, -\overline{A} \cup \overline{B} = U, -\underline{A} \cup \overline{B} = U$
iff $\underline{A} \subseteq \underline{B}$ and $\overline{A} \subseteq \overline{B}$ iff $A \widetilde{\subseteq} B$.

Analogously we have $B \rightarrow A = U$ iff $B \widetilde{\subseteq} A$.

Hence, (IA.4) is proved.

Proof of (IA.5)

$$(\varphi \rightarrow \beta) \wedge (\psi \rightarrow \beta) = (\varphi^c \vee \beta \vee (\varphi^* \wedge \beta^{c*})) \wedge (\psi^c \vee \beta \vee (\psi^* \wedge \beta^{c*}))$$
$$= (\varphi^c \wedge \psi^c) \vee (\varphi^c \wedge \beta) \vee (\varphi^c \wedge \psi^* \wedge \beta^{c*}) \vee (\beta \wedge \psi^c) \vee \beta \vee (\beta \wedge \psi^* \wedge \beta^{c*})$$
$$\vee (\varphi^* \wedge \psi^c \wedge \beta^{c*}) \vee (\beta \wedge \varphi^* \wedge \beta^{c*}) \vee (\varphi^* \wedge \psi^* \wedge \beta^{c*})$$
$$= (\varphi^c \wedge \psi^c) \vee \beta \vee (\varphi^* \wedge \psi^* \wedge \beta^{c*})$$
$$(\varphi \vee \psi) \rightarrow \beta = (\varphi \vee \psi)^c \vee \beta \vee ((\varphi \vee \psi)^* \wedge \beta^{c*}) = (\varphi^c \wedge \psi^c) \vee \beta \vee (\varphi^* \wedge \psi^* \wedge \beta^{c*})$$

Hence, $\varphi \vee \psi \rightarrow \beta = (\varphi \rightarrow \beta) \wedge (\psi \rightarrow \beta)$.

Proof of (IA.6)

$$(\varphi \wedge \psi) \rightarrow \beta = (\varphi \wedge \psi)^c \vee \beta \vee ((\varphi \wedge \psi)^* \wedge \beta^{c*}) = (\varphi^c \vee \psi^c) \vee \beta \vee ((\varphi^* \vee \psi^*) \wedge \beta^{c*})$$
$$= (\varphi^c \vee \psi^c) \vee \beta \vee (\varphi^* \wedge \beta^{c*}) \vee (\psi^* \wedge \beta^{c*})$$
$$(\varphi \rightarrow \beta) \vee (\psi \rightarrow \beta) = (\varphi^c \vee \beta \vee (\varphi^* \wedge \beta^{c*})) \vee (\psi^c \vee \beta \vee (\psi^* \wedge \beta^{c*}))$$
$$= (\varphi^c \vee \psi^c) \vee \beta \vee (\varphi^* \wedge \beta^{c*}) \vee (\psi^* \wedge \beta^{c*})$$

Hence, $\varphi \wedge \psi \rightarrow \beta = (\varphi \rightarrow \beta) \vee (\psi \rightarrow \beta)$.

The poor is complete.

Proposition 3.5 Suppose $(P, \vee, \wedge, ^c, 0, 1)$ is called a boundary lattice which is inverse ordered involution, and $\rightarrow$ is rough implication operator which is expressed by interval structure, then $(\varphi \rightarrow \psi) \rightarrow \psi \neq (\psi \rightarrow \varphi) \rightarrow \varphi$

Proof.

$$(\varphi \rightarrow \psi) \rightarrow \psi = (\varphi^c \vee \psi \vee (\varphi^* \wedge \psi^{c*}))^c \vee \psi \vee ((\varphi^c \vee \psi \vee (\varphi^* \wedge \psi^{c*}))^* \wedge \psi^{c*})$$
$$= (\varphi \wedge \psi^c \wedge (\varphi^{*c} \vee \psi^{c*c})) \vee \psi \vee ((\varphi^{c*} \vee \psi^* \wedge (\varphi^{**} \vee \psi^{c**})) \wedge \psi^{c*})$$
$$= (\varphi \wedge \psi^c \wedge \varphi^{*c}) \vee (\varphi \wedge \psi^c \wedge \psi^{c*c}) \vee \psi \vee (\varphi^{c*} \wedge \psi^* \wedge \varphi^{**} \wedge \psi^{c*}) \vee (\varphi^{c*} \wedge \psi^* \wedge \psi^{c**} \wedge \psi^{c*})$$
$$= (\psi^c \wedge \varphi^{*c}) \vee (\varphi \wedge \psi^{c*c}) \vee \psi \vee (\psi^* \wedge \varphi^{**} \wedge \psi^{c*})$$

Analogously, $(\psi \rightarrow \varphi) \rightarrow \varphi = (\varphi^c \wedge \psi^{*c}) \vee (\psi \wedge \varphi^{c*c}) \vee \varphi \vee (\varphi^* \wedge \psi^{**} \wedge \varphi^{c*})$

Hence, $(\varphi \rightarrow \psi) \rightarrow \psi \neq (\psi \rightarrow \varphi) \rightarrow \varphi$ (except for $\varphi = \psi$).

Remark If $(P, \vee, \wedge, ^c, 0, 1)$ is lattice implicative algebra [11~13], then it is satisfied Proposition 3.4 (IA.1) ~ (IA.6) and $(x \rightarrow y) \rightarrow y = (y \rightarrow x) \rightarrow x$. Since the equivalence of lattice implicative algebra is normal *FI*-algebra [11,

[14], the operator $\rightarrow$ is not satisfied $(x \rightarrow y) \rightarrow y = (y \rightarrow x) \rightarrow x$. Hence, $(P,\vee,\wedge,^c,0,1)$ is not lattice implicative algebra, but it is FI-algebra [11, 14].

4.   CONCLUSION

The study of rough implication operators is the emphasis and difficulty in the field of rough logic. Due to definition the shortages of the rough implication operator in [4] ~ [6], we can not imply $B^c \rightarrow A^c = A \rightarrow B$ in [4], i.e. the inversely negative proposition and original proposition are not equivalent, and A→A isn't Theorem in [5, 6], etc... We redefine the rough intersection, rough union, rough complement and rough implication operator from the view of interval structure, which their relations and properties have been investigated in [7]. In this paper, we_study the algebraic properties of the rough implication in a deep way, and also point out that $(P,\vee,\wedge,^c,0,1)$ is not lattice implicative algebra, but it is FI-algebra, because the formula $(x \rightarrow y) \rightarrow y = (y \rightarrow x) \rightarrow x$ doesn't hold.

ACKNOWLEDGEMENTS

This paper is supported by the National Natural Science Foundation (No.60273087) and Beijing Nature Science Foundation of China (No.4032009).

REFERENCES

1. Pawlak Z. Rough Sets. International Journal of Computer and Information Sciences, 1982, 11: 341~356.
2. Pawlak Z. Rough Sets-Theoretical Aspects of Reasoning about Data. Kluwer Academic Publishers. Dordrecht, 1991.
3. Pawlak Z. Vagueness and Uncertainty: A Rough Set Perspective, Computational Intelligence. 1995, 11:227~232.
4. Duntsch 1. Logic for Rough Sets. Theoretical Computer Sciences, 1997, 179:427~436.
5. E.Orlowska Reasoning about Vague Concepts. Bull. Pol. Ac: Mathematics, 1987, 35:643~652.
6. Ceng H L. Rough set theory and Application. Chongqing University Press, Chongqing, 1998(in Chinese).
7. Xue Z A. and He H C. Rough Implication. Journal of Computer and Sciences (in Chinese). 2003, 30(11):18~20.
8. Zhang Wenxiu etc... Rough set theory & method. Science Press, Beijing, 2001.7 (in Chinese).
9. Zhu F. He H C. The Axiomatization of the Rough Set. Journal of Computer (in Chinese). 2000, 23(3):330~333.

10. Wong S.K.M. Wang L.S. Yao Y.Y. On Modeling Uncertainty with Interval Structures. International Journal of Computational Intelligence. 1995, 11(2):406~426.

11. Wang G J. MV-Algebras, BL-Algebras, R_0-Algebras, and Multiple-Valued Logic. Fuzzy Systems and Mathematics (in Chinese).2002, 16(2):1~15.

12. Chang C C. Algebraic analysis of many-valued [J]. Trans.Amer.Math.Soc.1958, 88:467~ 490.

13. Xu Y. Lattice implicative algebra. Journal of Southwest Jiao tong University, 1993, 28(1): 20~26.

14. Jakubi'k J. Direct product decomposition of MV-algebras. Czechoslovak Mathematical Joural, 1994, 44:725~793.

RESEARCH ON INFORMATION REQUIREMENT OF FIRST-ORDER UNIVERSAL IMPLICATION OPERATORS IN FUZZY REASONING

Fu Lihua and He Huacan
Department of Computer Science & Engineering, Northwestern Polytechnical University, Xi'an 710072, P.R. China

Abstract: Based on the definition of *linear specificity measure*, this paper discusses detailedly the conditions on which the *first-order universal implication operators* satisfy the information boundedness principle in fuzzy reasoning, and gets the corresponding conclusion: when fuzzy propositions have positive measuring errors for their membership grades, *first-order universal implication operators* satisfy the information boundedness principle only if they are rejecting or restraining correlative; when they have negative ones, the operators satisfy the principle only if they are restraining correlative. This conclusion has important directive meaning for how to give the value of the *general correlative coefficient h* in practical control application.

Key words: Universal logic, First-order universal implication, General correlation, General self-correlation, Measure of specificity, Information boundedness principle

1.   INTRODUCTION

As is well known, fuzzy reasoning now has become a theoretical basis and an important method for the design and analysis of fuzzy controller. However, an important problem involved in fuzzy reasoning is how to define the implication operator. People have presented many different definitions[1-5], but the majority usually relies on the subjective experience without theoretical guide and analyses of their effectiveness, which are often given at will and blindly. In 1996, *Universal Logic* proposed by *Prof. He* provided a valid path to resolve this problem[10-12]. *Universal implication* is the implication connective of *Universal Logic*, which is a cluster of *R*-implications determined by the *general correlation coefficient h* between propositions. In practical application, according to the inherent correlation between propositions, we can take a corresponding implication operator from the cluster, so that overcome effectively the blindness.

In fuzzy reasoning, the *starting objects* and the *resulting object* are all fuzzy sets, and the semantic interpretation associated with the output of the *FMP* process depends on the value of the resulting fuzzy subset at all points in its domain. Thus, in considering the appropriateness of the implication operator used in *FMP*, account must be taken of the whole resulting fuzzy subset, not only some points in its domain[7-9]. So, *Yager* proposed the global requirements for implication operators in fuzzy reasoning, called as information boundedness principle[8].

In practical control application, how to determine the value of *h* between propositions has been a problem for further studies. When taking no account of the measuring errors for the membership grades of propositions, we have proceeded the detailed research on information requirement of *zero-order universal implication operators*, and get an important conclusion[17]. However, in practical application, the measuring errors are ineluctable. Therefore, based on the information boundedness principle, this paper discusses further the information requirement of *first-order universal implication operators* in a specific way, and draws the general conclusion, which has important directive meaning for how to give the value of *h*.

2.   FUNDAMENTAL CONCEPTS

2.1   Basic model of fuzzy reasoning

In fuzzy reasoning, the basic model of *FMP* can be represented as follows:

$$\begin{array}{ll} \text{rule} & A \rightarrow B \\ \text{for given} & A* \\ \hline \text{to determine} & B* \end{array} \tag{1}$$

where A and $A*$ are the fuzzy sets in X, and B and $B*$ are the fuzzy sets in Y.

2.2   Basic idea of *Universal Logic*[10-12]

1. Basic idea of *Universal Logic*

Based on the investigation on the general regulation of the logics having existed, in 1996, *Prof. He* proposed firstly a kind of totally new theoretical frame of mathematical logic, called as *Universal Logic*. It is a continuous and parameterized logic system and describes the logic regulation of the flexible world. And it contains every kind of logics and reasoning forms. Its basic idea can be summarized as follows: it is the general correlation between propositions that makes logic operators are uncertain.

He leads the Chinese classical philosophic thought into the theory of flexible logics, which is all things in the world are correlative, namely either mutual promoting or restraining. So he uses the general correlation to explain why the logic operators of proposition connectives are not unique. The general correlation is the inherent character of things and contains *general correlation* and *general self-correlation*, which represent the correlation between fuzzy propositions and the measuring errors of the membership grades of fuzzy proposition, respectively.

And he uses *general correlation coefficient h* to describe *general correlation*, changing continuously from 1 to 0. *General correlation* changes continuously from the max-attracting state to the max-restraining state. As the tolerance decreasing from its maximum, *general correlation* decreases continuously from its max-attracting state($h=1$) to the independent correlation state($h=0.75$), and then to the max-rejecting state(namely the min-restraining state, $h=0.5$). After that, with the restraint increasing, it continues decreasing from its min-restraining state($h=0.5$) to the max-restraining state($h=0$) through its deadlock one($h=0.25$). Similarly, *general self-correlation coefficient k* is used to describe *general self-correlation*, changing continuously from 0 to 1, too. For example, if measuring errors are the positive maximums, then $k=1$, if they are the negative ones, then $k=0$, and if there are no measuring errors, then $k=0.5$. Thus, based on the theory of norms and the *correlation coefficients*, we can get the corresponding clusters of operators for different connectives. The operators can change continuously, and the ones gotten with the same *correlation coefficient* are corresponding with one another.

As long as the values of h and k are given, the corresponding operators of connectives can be gotten. So, in practical application, we can get the appropriate operators of connectives by the inherent correlation between propositions, this avoiding effectively giving them at will and blindly.

2. *First-order universal implication*

In *Universal Logic, first-order universal implication* is defined as:

Definition 1[12] *First-order universal implication* is the cluster

$$I(x, y, h, k)=ite\{1|x\leq y;0|m\leq 0,y=0,x\neq 0;\Gamma^{1}[(1-x^{mn}+y^{mn})^{1/(mn)}]\}. \tag{2}$$

where $m = (3 - 4h) / (4h(1 - h))$, $h \in [0, 1]$, $m \in R$, $n=-1/log_2k$, $k \in [0, 1]$, $n \in R^+$.

Remark: the conditional expression $ite\{\beta | \alpha; \gamma\}$ represents that if α is true, then the result is β, otherwise γ. Similarly, $ite\{\beta 1 | \alpha 1; \beta 2 | \alpha 2; \gamma\}=ite\{\beta 1 | \alpha 1; ite\{\beta 2 | \alpha 2; \gamma\}\}$. And $\Gamma'[x]=ite\{1 | x>1; 0 | x<0$ or x is an imaginary number; $x\}$.

For the sake of convenience, the following piecewise form is given[16]:

$$I(x,y,h,k) = \begin{cases} ite\{y \mid x = 1;1\} & \{0\} \times (0,1] \cup (0,0.75) \times \{1\} \\ min(1, y/x) & [0,1] \times \{0\} \cup \{0.75\} \times (0,1] \\ ite\{1 \mid x \le y; y\} & (0.75,1] \times \{1\} \cup \{1\} \times (0,1) \\ 1 & x \le y, (0,0.75) \times (0,1) \cup (0.75,1) \times (0,1) \\ 0 & x > y, y = 0, (0.75,1) \times (0,1) \\ (1 - x^{mn} + y^{mn})^{1/(mn)} & else \end{cases} \quad (3)$$

where suppose that $\lim_{h \to 0.75}(\frac{3 - 4h}{4h(1 - h)}) \times \lim_{k \to 1}(-\frac{1}{log_2 k}) = 0$, $\lim_{h \to 1}(\frac{3 - 4h}{4h(1 - h)}) \times \lim_{k \to 1}(-\frac{1}{log_2 k}) = 0$, $\lim_{h \to 0}(\frac{3 - 4h}{4h(1 - h)}) \times \lim_{k \to 0}(-\frac{1}{log_2 k}) = 0$, $m=(3-4h)/(4h(1-h))$, $h \in [0, 1]$, $m \in R$, $n=-1/log_2k$, $k \in [0, 1]$, $n \in R^+$, $\{0\} \times [0, 1]$ represents $h=0$ and $k \in [0,1]$, and the others are similar.

The *first-order universal implication* is a continuous super-cluster of implication operators determined by h and k. In practical application, according to the *general correlation* between propositions and the *general self-correlation*, we can take the corresponding one from the cluster.

3. Some common properties of *first-order universal implication*

For the sake of convenience, some common properties of *first-order universal implication* are given [12, 16]:

I1 If $x_1 \le x_2$, then $I(x_1, y, h, k) \ge I(x_2, y, h, k)$, where $h \in [0,1]$, $k \in [0,1]$.

I2 If $y_1 \le y_2$, then $I(x, y_1, h, k) \le I(x, y_2, h, k)$, where $h \in [0,1]$, $k \in [0,1]$.

I3 $I(0, y, h, k) = 1$, where $h \in [0,1]$, $k \in [0,1]$.

I4 $I(1, y, h, k) = y$, where $h \in [0,1]$, $k \in [0,1]$.

2.3   Information boundedness principle

Most of the discussions about the selection of the implication operator have been based on satisfaction to a number of properties associated with the classical binary implication operator[5, 8], such as the famous D-P conditions[6]. However, these properties except continuity are all local or pointwise requirements. As said above, in considering the appropriateness of the implication operator used in *FMP*, account must be taken of the whole resulting fuzzy subset, not only some points in its domain[7-9]. Therefore, *Yager* proposed the information boundedness principle, which requires that the information contained in a fuzzy granule resulting from an inference must be no greater than the information contained in the consequent of the *if-then* proposition and that the information contained in inferences under two different inputs should be ordered by the matching degree between the input and the antecedent of the *if-then* proposition[8]. In fact, if the implication operator satisfies the property I4, the latter contains the former. So, in the following sections, we will emphasize to discuss the latter.

In [13], *Yager* proposed a characterization of *measure of specificity*, which provides an appropriate measure of the information contained in a proposition.

Definition 2[13] Suppose that X is a finite set of cardinality n and A is a fuzzy subset in X. A measure $Sp: F(X) \to [0, 1]$ is called a *measure of specificity* if it satisfies the following properties:

1) $Sp(A)=1$ if and only if A is a singleton set, $A=\{x\}$.

2) $Sp(\emptyset) = 0$.

3) If B and C are normal fuzzy sets in X and $B \subset C$, then $Sp(B) \geq Sp(C)$.

Of course, in practical application, we can define many different concrete models of *measure of specificity*. In this paper, we will use a class of specificity measures, called as *linear specificity measure*[15]:

Definition 3 [15] Suppose that X is a finite set of cardinality n, A is a fuzzy subset in X and a_j is the jth largest membership grade in A. A *linear specificity measure* is defined as

$$Sp(A)=a_1- \sum_{j=2}^{n} w_j a_j \qquad (4)$$

where and the w_j's are a set of weights satisfying: 1) $w_j \in [0, 1]$; 2) $\sum_{j=2}^{n} w_j =1$; 3) $w_i \geq w_j$ for $i < j$.

3. INFORMATION REQUIREMENT OF *FIRST-ORDER UNIVERSAL IMPLICATION* IN FUZZY REASONING

3.1 Information requirement of implication operators

Without loss of generality, we assume that Y is a finite set of cardinality n: $\{y_1, y_2, \ldots, y_n\}$ and its elements have been indexed such that $\mu_B(y_i) \geq \mu_B(y_j)$ for $i < j$ in $Eq.(1)$. And suppose that all propositions have the same level of measuring errors, namely the equal values for k in an application. In fuzzy control, the input x corresponding to the state variable is crisp, $x = x^*$, then A' is a singleton, that is, $\mu_{A'}(x) = 1$ if $x = x^*$, and $\mu_{A'}(x) = 0$ if $x \neq x^*$. Thus, we will get the following expression using the CRI method:

$$\mu_{B^*}(y) = \sup T_{h_1,k}(\mu_{A^*}(x), I_{h_2,k}(\mu_A(x), \mu_B(y)))$$
$$= I_{h_2,k}(\mu_A(x^*), \mu_B(y)) \qquad (5)$$

where $T_{h_1,k}$ and $I_{h_2,k}$ are the *first-order universal conjunction operator* and the *first-order universal implication operator* determined by the h_1, h_2 and k between propositions, respectively.

According to the reasoning process in [17], we can similarly get the following conclusions:

Proposition 1 In fuzzy reasoning, the implication operators satisfying the information boundedness principle should satisfy the requirement, that is, the truer the consequent of the *if-then* proposition is, the more insensitive $I_{h,k}(x, y)$ is to the change of x.

Proposition 2 In fuzzy reasoning, the implication operators satisfying the information boundedness principle should satisfy the requirement, that is, $D(v)=I_{h,k}(v, a)-I_{h,k}(v, b)$ is a non-decreasing function of v for all $a>b$.

Obviously, *Prop.*1 and *Prop.*2 are equal, which describe the different aspects of one thing.

3.2 Information requirement of first-order universal implication

In this section, we will analyze the information requirement of the *first-order universal implication* in detail, and give the general conclusion. According to its piecewise definition, we have:

1. Suppose that $m \to -\infty$, $n \in (0, +\infty)$, that is, $h=1$, $k \in (0, 1)$. So $I_{h,k}(x, y)$ is *Gödel* implication operator $R_G(x, y) = ite\{1| x \le y; y\}$.

$D(v) = I_{h,k}(v, a) - I_{h,k}(v, b) = ite\{1|v \le a; a\} - ite\{1| v \le b; b\}$.

1) If $v \le b < a$, then $D(v) = I_{h,k}(v, a) - I_{h,k}(v, b) = 1 - 1 = 0$.

2) If $b < v \le a$, then $D(v) = I_{h,k}(v, a) - I_{h,k}(v, b) = 1 - b \ge 0$.

3) If $b < a < v$, then $D(v) = I_{h,k}(v, a) - I_{h,k}(v, b) = a - b \le 1 - b$.

According to the above analyses, $I_{h,k}(x, y)$ do not satisfy the principle.

2. Suppose that $m \in (-\infty, 0)$, $n \to +\infty$, that is $h \in (0.75, 1]$, $k=1$. So $I_{h,k}(x, y)$ is *Gödel* implication operator R_G. According to the above analyses, $I_{h,k}(x, y)$ do not satisfy the principle.

3. Suppose that $m=0$, $n \in (0, +\infty)$, namely, $h=0.75$, $k \in (0, 1]$. So $I_{h,k}(x, y)$ is *Goguen* implication operator $R_{Go}(x, y) = ite\{1| x=0; min(1, y/x)\}$.

$D(v) = I_{h,k}(v, a) - I_{h,k}(v, b) = ite\{1|v=0; min(1, a/v)\} - ite\{1|v=0; min(1, b/v)\}$

If $v=0$, then $D(v) = I_{h,k}(v, a) - I_{h,k}(v, b) = 1 - 1 = 0$.

2) If $0 < v \le b < a$, then $D(v) = I_{h,k}(v, a) - I_{h,k}(v, b) = 1 - 1 = 0$.

3) If $b < v \le a$, that is, $a/v \ge 1 > b/v$, then $D(v) = 1 - b/v > 0$, and $1 - b/v$ is a non-decreasing function of v.

4) If $b < a < v$, that is, $1 > a/v > b/v$, then $D(v) = a/v - b/v = (a-b)/v$, and $(a-b)/v$ is a non-increasing function of v.

Due to the above analyses, $I_{h,k}(x, y)$ do not satisfy the principle.

4. Suppose that $m \in (-\infty, +\infty)$, $n \to 0$, namely, $h \in [0, 1]$, $k=0$. So $I_{h,k}(x, y)$ is *Goguen* implication operator R_{Go}. Due to the above analyses, $I_{h,k}(x, y)$ do not satisfy the principle.

5. Suppose that $m \in (0, +\infty)$, $n \to +\infty$, that is, $h \in (0, 0.75)$, $k=1$. So $I_{h,k}(x, y)$ is a variant of the *Standard Sharp* implication $R(x, y)=ite\{y \mid x=1; 1\}$.

$D(v) = I_{h,k}(v, a) - I_{h,k}(v, b) = ite\{a \mid v=1; 1\} - ite\{b \mid v=1; 1\}$.

1) If $v \neq 1$, then $D(v)=I_{h,k}(v,a) - I_{h,k}(v,b)=1-1= 0$.

2) If $v=1$, then $D(v)= I_{h,k}(v, a) - I_{h,k}(v, b)= a-b>0$.

Based on the above analyses, $I_{h,k}(x, y)$ satisfy the principle.

6. Suppose that $m \to +\infty$, $n \in (0, +\infty)$, that is, $h=0$, $k \in (0, 1]$. So $I_{h,k}(x, y)$ is a variant of the *Standard Sharp* implication. Based on the above analyses, $I_{h,k}(x, y)$ satisfy the principle.

7. Suppose that $m \in (-\infty, 0)$, $n \in (0, +\infty)$, namely, $h \in (0.75, 1)$, $k \in (0, 1)$. According to *Def.* 1, we have

1) If $v \leq b < a$, then $D(v)=I_{h,k}(v, a)-I_{h, k}(v, b)= 1-1=0$.

2) If $b = 0$, then $v>0$ and $a>0$.

i) If $v \leq a$, then $D(v)=I_{h,k}(v, a) - I_{h,k}(v, b)=1-0= 1$.

ii) If $v>a$, then $D(v)=\Gamma^{1}[(1-v^{mn}+a^{mn})^{1/(mn)}] - 0= \Gamma^{1}[(1-v^{mn}+a^{mn})^{1/(mn)}]$. Due to the property I1, $D(v)$ is non-increasing.

So, if $h \in (0.75, 1)$ and $k \in (0, 1)$, then the *first-order universal implication operators* do not satisfy the principle.

8. Suppose that $m \in (0, +\infty)$, $n \in (0, +\infty)$, that is, $h \in (0, 0.75)$, $k \in (0, 1)$. According to *Def.* 1, we have

1) If $v \leq b < a$, then $D(v) = I_{h,k}(v, a)-I_{h, k}(v, b) = 1-1=0$.

2) If $b<v \leq a$, then $D(v)=1-\Gamma^{1}[(1-v^{mn}+b^{mn})^{1/(mn)}] \geq 0$. Due to the property I1, $D(v)$ is a non-decreasing function of v, which take its maximum at $v=a$:

$$D_1(v) = 1- (1-a^{mn}+b^{mn})^{1/(mn)} \tag{6}$$

3) If $b<a<v$, then $b^{mn}<a^{mn}<v^{mn}$ and $b^{mn}, a^{mn}, v^{mn} \in [0, 1]$. So we have

$$I_{h, k}(v, a) = \Gamma^{1}[(1-v^{mn}+a^{mn})^{1/(mn)}]= (1-v^{mn}+a^{mn})^{1/(mn)} \tag{7}$$

$$I_{h, k}(v, b) = \Gamma^{1}[(1-v^{mn}+b^{mn})^{1/(mn)}]= (1-v^{mn}+b^{mn})^{1/(mn)} \tag{8}$$

According to *Eq.*(7) and *Eq.*(8), we have:

$$D(v) =I_{h, k}(v, a)-I_{h, k}(v, b)=(1-v^{mn}+a^{mn})^{1/(mn)}-(1-v^{mn}+b^{mn})^{1/(mn)} \tag{9}$$

that is,

$$\partial D(v)/\partial v=v^{mn-1}[(1-v^{mn}+b^{mn})^{1/(mn)-1}-(1-v^{mn}+a^{mn})^{1/(mn)-1}] \tag{10}$$

) Suppose that $n \in (1, +\infty)$, that is, $1/n \in (0, 1)$, $k \in (0.5, 1)$, fuzzy propositions have positive measuring errors for their membership grades, and we have

) $m \in [1,+\infty)$, that is, $h \in (0, 0.5]$, propositions are restraining correlative.

So, $mn>1$, that is, $1/(mn)-1<0$, and we have $(1-v^{mn}+b^{mn})^{1/(mn)-1}>(1-v^{mn}+a^{mn})^{1/(mn)-1}$, namely, $\partial D(v)/\partial v >0$. Thus, $D(v)$ is a non-decreasing function of v, which take its minimum at $v=a$:

$$D_2(v)=(1-a^{mn}+a^{mn})^{1/(mn)} - (1-a^{mn}+b^{mn})^{1/(mn)}=1- (1-a^{mn}+b^{mn})^{1/(mn)} \tag{11}$$

According to *Eq.*(6) and *Eq.*(11), we have $D_1(v)=D_2(v)$.

Thus, if $k \in (0.5, 1)$, $h \in (0, 0.5]$, that is, propositions have positive measuring errors for their membership grades and are restraining correlative, then the *first-order universal implication operators* satisfy the principle.

) $m \in (1/n, 1)$, namely, propositions are rejecting correlative with $h \in (0.5, ((n+1)-(n^2-n+1)^{1/2})/2)$.

So, $mn > 1$, that is, $1/(mn)-1 < 0$. Similarly, $D(v)$ is a non-decreasing function of v, which take its minimum at $v=a$, and $D_1(v)=D_2(v)$.

Thus, if propositions have positive measuring errors and are rejecting correlative with $h \in (0.5, ((n+1)-(n^2-n+1)^{1/2})/2)$, then the *first-order universal implication operators* satisfy the principle.

) $m = 1/n$, that is, $mn = 1$, and propositions are rejecting correlative with $h = ((n+1)-(n^2-n+1)^{1/2})/2$.

So, we have
$$D(v) = I_{h,k}(v,a) - I_{h,k}(v,b) = \Gamma^1[(1-v^{mn}+a^{mn})^{1/(mn)}] - \Gamma^1[(1-v^{mn}+b^{mn})^{1/(mn)}]$$
$$= (1-v+a) - (1-v+b) = a-b$$
and $D_1(v) = 1-(1-a^{mn}+b^{mn})^{1/(mn)} = 1-(1-a+b) = a-b$.

Thus, if propositions have positive measuring errors and are rejecting correlative with $h = ((n+1)-(n^2-n+1)^{1/2})/2$ then the *first-order universal implication operators* satisfy the principle.

) $m \in (0, 1/n)$, that is, propositions are rejecting correlative with $h \in (((n+1)-(n^2-n+1)^{1/2})/2, 0.75)$.

So, $mn > 1$, that is, $1/(mn)-1 > 0$ and we have $(1-v^{mn}+b^{mn})^{1/(mn)-1} < (1-v^{mn}+a^{mn})^{1/(mn)-1}$, namely, $\partial D(v)/\partial v < 0$. Thus, $D(v)$ is a decreasing function of v.

Thus, if propositions have positive measuring errors and are rejecting correlative with $h \in (((n+1)-(n^2-n+1)^{1/2})/2, 0.75)$, then the *first-order universal implication operators* do not satisfy the principle.

) Suppose that $n \in (0, 1)$, that is, $1/n \in (1, +\infty)$, $k \in (0, 0.5)$, fuzzy propositions have negative measuring errors for their membership grades, and we have

) $m \in (1/n, +\infty)$, that is, propositions are restraining correlative with $h \in (0, ((n+1)-(n^2-n+1)^{1/2})/2)$.

So, $mn > 1$, that is, $1/(mn)-1 < 0$. Similarly, $D(v)$ is a non-decreasing function of v, which take its minimum at $v=a$, and $D_1(v)=D_2(v)$.

Thus, if propositions have negative measuring errors and are restraining correlative with $h \in (0, ((n+1)-(n^2-n+1)^{1/2})/2)$, then the *first-order universal implication operators* satisfy the principle.

) $m = 1/n$, that is, $mn = 1$, and propositions are restraining correlative with $h = ((n+1)-(n^2-n+1)1/2)/2$.

Similarly, we have $D(v) = a-b = D_1(v)$.

) $m=1/n$, that is, $mn=1$, and propositions are restraining correlative with $h=((n+1)-(n^2-n+1)1/2)/2)/2$.

Similarly, we have $D(v)=a-b=D_1(v)$.

Thus, if propositions have negative measuring errors and are restraining correlative with $h=((n+1)-(n^2-n+1)^{1/2})/2$, then the *first-order universal implication operators* satisfy the principle.

) $m\in[1, 1/n)$, that is, that is, propositions are restraining correlative with $h\in(((n+1)-(n^2-n+1)^{1/2})/2, 0.5]$.

So, $mn<1$, that is, $1/(mn)-1>0$. Similarly, $D(v)$ is a decreasing function of v.

Thus, if propositions have negative measuring errors and are restraining correlative with $h\in(((n+1)-(n^2-n+1)^{1/2})/2, 0.5]$, then the *first-order universal implication operators* do not satisfy the principle.

) $m\in(0,1)$, that is, $h\in(0.5,0.75)$, and propositions are rejecting correlative.

So, $mn<1$, that is, $1/(mn)-1>0$. Similarly, $D(v)$ is a decreasing function of v.

Thus, propositions have negative measuring errors and are rejecting correlative, then the operators do not satisfy the principle.

) Suppose that $n=1$, that is, $k=0.5$, fuzzy propositions have no measuring errors for their membership grades. Then *first-order universal implication* changes into *zero-order universal implication*.

So, we have the conclusion that when propositions are restraining correlative, that is, $h\in[0, 0.5]$, the *universal implication operators* satisfy the information boundedness principle[17].

Fig.1-2 shows $I_{h,k}(v, a)$, $I_{h,k}(v, b)$ and $D(v)$ for several representative values of h, where $a=0.6$, $b=0.1$, with $k=0.7$ or 0.125, respectively.

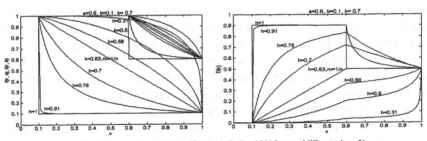

Fig.1 When measuring errors are positive, $I(v, a)$, $I(v, b)$ and $D(v)$ for several different values of h

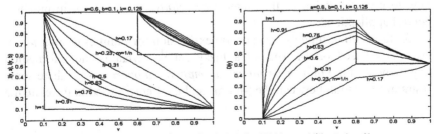

Fig.2 When measuring errors are negative, $I(v, a)$, $I(v, b)$ and $D(v)$ for several different values of h

Based on the above analyses about information requirement of the *first-order universal implication operators*, we can draw the conclusion as follows:

When propositions are attracting correlative, namely, $h \in [0.75, 1]$, the *first-order universal implication operators* do not satisfy the information boundedness principle with propositions having positive or negative measuring errors;

When propositions have positive measuring errors, if they are rejecting correlative with $h \in (((n+1)-(n^2-n+1)^{1/2})/2, 0.75)$, then the *first-order universal implication operators* do not satisfy the principle; and if they are rejecting correlative with $h \in [0.5, ((n+1)-(n^2-n+1)^{1/2})/2]$ and restraining correlative with $h \in [0, 0.5]$, then the operators satisfy the principle;

When propositions have negative ones, if they are rejecting correlative with $h \in (0.5, 0.75]$ and restraining correlative with $h \in (((n+1)-(n^2-n+1)^{1/2})/2, 0.5]$, then the *first-order universal implication operators* do not satisfy the principle; and if they are restraining correlative with $h \in [0, ((n+1)-(n^2-n+1)^{1/2})/2]$, then the operators satisfy the principle;

When propositions have positive maximal measuring error, namely $k=1$, if they are rejecting or restraining correlative, then the *first-order universal implication operators* satisfy the principle; and when they have negative maximal one, namely $k=0$, all operators do not satisfy the principle.

4.   CONCLUSIONS

Based on the definition of *linear specificity measure*, this paper has discussed detailedly the conditions on which the *first-order universal implication operators* satisfy the information boundedness principle in fuzzy reasoning, and get the conclusion: When propositions have positive measuring errors, if they are rejecting correlative with $h \in [0.5, ((n+1)-(n^2-n+1)^{1/2})/2]$ or restraining correlative with $h \in [0, 0.5]$, then the *first-order universal implication operators* satisfy the principle; and when propositions have negative ones, if they are restraining correlative with $h \in [0, ((n+1)-(n^2-n+1)^{1/2})/2]$, then the *first-order universal implication operators* satisfy the principle. This conclusion has important directive meaning for how to give the value of the *general correlative coefficient h* in practical control application.

As far as other models or a general expression for families of *measure of specificity* based on t-norms of a fuzzy set [14], what is the information requirement of the *first-order universal implication operators*? Is there some restraining relation between the t-norms and the t-norms used to generate the corresponding *first-order universal implication operators*? These problems will be further studied elsewhere.

ACKNOWLEDGEMENTS

This work was supported by the Foundation of Natural Sciences under Grant 60273087, the National Plan of 863 under Grant 2002AA412020 and the Foundation of Natural Sciences of Beijing under Grant 4032009.

REFERENCES

1. Mizumoto M, Zimmermann H. Comparison of Fuzzy Reasoning Method. Fuzzy Sets and Systems, 1982, 8:253-283
2. Fernandez F. G., Kreinovich V. Fuzzy Implication Can be Arbitrarily Complicated: A Theorem. Int. J. Intelligent Systems, 1998, 13:445-451
3. Turksen I. B., Kreinovich V., Yager R. R., A new class of fuzzy implications. Axioms of fuzzy implication revisited. Fuzzy Sets and Systems, 1998, 100:262-272
4. Dujet C., Vincent N. Force implication:A new approach to human reasoning. Fuzzy Sets and Systems,1995, 69:53-63
5. Klir G. J., Bo Y. Fuzzy Sets and Fuzzy Logic: Theory and Application, Prentice-Hall, NJ, 1995
6. D. Dubois, H. Parde. Fuzzy sets in approximate reasoning part I: inference with possibility distributions, Fuzzy Sets and Systems, 1991, 40:143-202
7. Yager R. R. Measures of information in generalized constraints. Int. J. uncertainty, fuzziness and knowledge-based systems, 1998, 6:519-532
8. Yager R. R. On global requirements for implication operators in fuzzy modus ponens. Fuzzy S. and S.,1999,106:3-10
9. D.Chen, Information measure requirement of implication operator in fuzzy reasoning,Comp. Sci.,2001,28(8):124-126.
10. H.C. He, Generalized logic in experience thinking, Science in China(Series E), 1996, 39(3):225-234.
11. H.C. He, Studies on generalized implication operation and generalized series reasoning operation, Journal of Software, 1998, 9(6):469-473(in Chinese).
12. H.C. He, Universal logics principle. Science Press, Beijing, 2001 (in Chinese).
13. R. R. Yager, On the specificity of a possibility distribution, Fuzzy Sets and Systems, 1992, 50:279-292.
14. L. Garmeridia, On t-norms based measures of specificity, Fuzzy Sets and Systems, 2003, 133:237-248.
15. R. R. Yager, Default knowledge and measures of specificity, Inform. Sci. 1992, 61:1-44.
16. Y.C. Ma, The properties of universal implication, to appear(in Chinese).
17. L.H. Fu, Research on information requirement of zero-order universal implication operators in fuzzy reasoning, The 5th WCICA, (accepted)

AN EXTENDED ROUGH SETS APPROACH TO ANALYSIS OF CUDT

Hua Wenjian and Liu Zuoliang
The Telecommunication Engineering Institute, Air Force Engineering University, Xi'an Shaanxi 710077,China

Abstract: Classical Rough Sets Theory (CRST) is thought to be an effective mathematical approach to discovering rules from Decision Table (DT). Every entry in DT must be unique and certain qualitative value of attribute. However, there are always heterogeneous entries in DT from complex decision problem, that is, entries with a continuous quantitative attribute, unknown entries or multi-valued entries, and these types of entries often occur in same DT. The DT with these entries named Continuous Uncertain Decision Table (CUDT) cannot be analyzed directly by CRST. Fortunately, by modeling those three types of entries in CUDT with Fuzzy Sets theory (FST), we found that CUDT can be transformed into a special DT called Extended Decision Table (EDT) in which each entry is associated with a membership degree. An extended CRST is proposed to transform the CUDT into EDT and to calculate the lower approximations and the boundaries of decision concepts in EDT.

Key words: continuous uncertain decision system; extended Rough Sets Approach; Approximation of concepts

1. INTRODUCTION

In CRST, Decision system (DS) is a 4-tuple $\langle U, A \cup D, V_{A \cup D}, g \rangle$, where U is a finite set of objects; A and D are called as condition attributes and decision attributes respectively, such that $A \cap D = \varnothing$; $V_{A \cup D} = \bigcup v_{r_i}$, $r_i \in A \cup D$, $i = 1, \cdots$, $|A| + |D|$; $g : U \rightarrow V_{A \cup D}$. DS can be represented as a table of two dimensions called Decision Table (DT) with unique entries and certain qualitative value of attribute. However, we are always faced with a continuous uncertain decision table (CUDT) characterized by the heterogeneous entries: entries with multiple possible values, entries of continuous quantitative attributes and unknown entries[1]. The latter two types of heterogeneous entries can be analyzed by many methods but not based on FST[5-8]. In this paper, by fuzzy modeling of these heterogeneous entries, we proposed an approach to transforming the CUDT into EDT in which every entry is associated with a degree of possibility, and extending CRST to operate approximation of the decision concepts in EDT. Next section, modeling of heterogeneous entries is discussed. Section 3 contains the method of approximating concepts in EDT. Section 4 gives a summary and prospect of this method.

2.   MODELING OF HETEROGENEOUS ENTRIES

Discretization of continuous qualitative attributes by FST actually is the procedure that the appropriate fuzzy subsets labeled by the qualitative linguistic terms on the domain V_{a_i} of a continuous attribute are defined and map a value of attribute to a linguistic term. Assume that a set of discrete linguistic terms, denoted by $LS^i = (ls_1^i, ls_2^i, \cdots, ls_m^i)$, corresponding to a continuous quantitative attribute $a_i \in A$ given by the experts. Then for $\forall ls_k^i \in LS^i$ ($1 \leq k \leq m$), there is a fuzzy subset $\mu_k^i : V_{a_i} \to (0,1]$ on V_{a_i}, where membership degree $\mu_k^i(a_i(u_j))$ means the degree of possibility that entry $[u_j, a_i]$ is discretized to ls_k^i. But we find that the supports of the fuzzy subsets often overlap, which results in a value of attribute in the overlapped part corresponding to at least two linguistic terms. We can describe discrete result of any entry $[u_j, a_i]$ in this situation as follows:

$$\{ (ls_1^i, \mu_1^i(a_i(u_j))), (ls_2^i, \mu_2^i(a_i(u_j))), \cdots, (ls_m^i, \mu_m^i(a_i(u_j))) \}, \tag{1}$$

where $\mu_k^i > 0$, if the supports of fuzzy subsets of linguistic terms overlap; otherwise, not all μ_k^i more than 0. There is another situation we have to consider that entry may be a fuzzy number $\tilde{a}_i(u_j)$. We can describe this entry by analogy with the above formula (1) as formula (1'):

$$\{ (ls_1^i, \mu_1^i(\tilde{a}_i(u_j))), (ls_2^i, \mu_2^i(\tilde{a}_i(u_j))), \cdots, (ls_m^i, \mu_m^i(\tilde{a}_i(u_j))) \}. \tag{1'}$$

Calculating the membership degree in (1) and (1') is as follows.

Let $x \in U$; A, a attribute set, $a_i \in A$, $1 \leq i \leq |A| = n$; V_i is value domain of a_i, $V_i \subset R$, and R is real number set; $\tilde{v}_{ih}$ is the h th fuzzy subset on V_i, and its membership degree is $\mu_{\tilde{v}_{ih}}(a_i(x))$, $h = 1, \cdots, m_i$, where m_i is the number of fuzzy subsets on V_i, a linguistic term of $\tilde{v}_{ih}$ labeled accordingly by v_{ih}. Let $\pi(\bullet, \tilde{v}_{ih})$ denote the membership degree that $\bullet$ is discretely described as v_{ih}. We can get that if $a_i(x)$ is crisp, then

$$\pi(a_i(x), \tilde{v}_{ih}) = \sup_{a_i(x) \in V_i} \{\min[1, \mu_{\tilde{v}_{ih}}(a_i(x))]\} = \mu_{\tilde{v}_{ih}}(a_i(x)) ; \tag{2}$$

and if $\tilde{a}_i(x)$ is a fuzzy number on V_i, then

$$\pi(\tilde{a}_i(x), \tilde{v}_{ih}) = \sup_{a_i(x) \in V_i} \{\min[\mu_{\tilde{a}_i(x)}(a_i(x)), \mu_{\tilde{v}_{ih}}(a_i(x))]\} = \mu_{\tilde{v}_{ih}}(\tilde{a}_i(x)). \quad (3)$$

Complementarity for unknown entries is actually a procedure of obtaining the most possible entries according to other known entries under the same attribute. We are sure that the unknown entry must be the element of the set of linguistic terms given by the analysts. The set of linguistic terms is equal either to the set or to the subset of discrete linguistic terms of the attribute of the unknown entry. We assume that entry $[u_j, a_i]$ is unknown. The idea of complementarity for unknown entry is formally declared by FST as below. There is a fuzzy set $\mu_i : LS^i \to (0,1]$ meaning that for every ls_k^i, membership degree $\mu_i(ls_k^i)$ indicates the possible degree of complementarity for $[u_j, a_i]$ with ls_k^i. The entry $[u_j, a_i]$ after complementarity can be:

$$\{(ls_1^i, \mu_1^i(ls_1^i)), (ls_2^i, \mu_2^i(ls_2^i)), \cdots, (ls_m^i, \mu_m^i(ls_m^i))\}. \quad (4)$$

The multi-valued entries generally occur in decision entries of some military command decision problems we are faced with[1]. Transforming the multi-valued entries into single-valued entries is such a process that the most possible decision value can be selected from the alternative decision values. Let d_i denote the ith decision attribute, and $S^i = \{s_1^i, s_2^i, \cdots, s_m^i\}$ denote discrete linguistic terms of d_i; Assume that $[u_j, d_i]$ is a multi-valued entry, and $[u_j, d_i]$ is represented as $s_1^i, s_2^i, \cdots, s_m^i$. The idea of a multi-valued entry description similar with the above complementarity is formally described as follows.

There is a fuzzy set on S^i, $\mu_i : S^i \to (0,1]$, for every $s_k^i \in S^i$ ($1 \le k \le m$), $\mu_i(s_k^i)$ meaning the possible degree that $[u_j, d_i]$ takes s_k^i. Accordingly, $[u_j, d_i]$ could be represented as :

$$\{(s_1^i, \mu_i(s_1^i)), (s_2^i, \mu_i(s_2^i)), \cdots, (s_m^i, \mu_i(s_m^i))\} \quad (5)$$

For DT of CRST, there is only one membership degree equal to 1 in formula (5), and the other all are 0. But for CUDT, there are at least two membership degrees more than 0 in formula (5).

Definition 1. Unified description of Heterogeneous Entry (HE). Let W_i be a set of linguistic terms of attribute $a_i \in A$, where $W_i = \{w_{ih}\}$, $h = 1, \cdots, m_i$, $m_i = |W_i|$; If the value domain of a_i is continuous quantitative, fuzzy discretization of a_i make the $w_{ih} \in W_i$ the label of fuzzy subset $\tilde{w}_{ih}$ on the value domain of a_i ; if the value domain of a_i is discrete, any entry of a_i can take the element of W_i directly. So the unified description of heterogeneous entry in CUDT is

$$[x, a_i] = \{(w_{ih}, \pi_{ih}(x)) \mid w_{ih} \in W_i \, and \, \pi_{ih}(x) > 0\}, \quad (6)$$

denoted by $HE(x, a_i)$, where $\pi_{ih}(x)$ means degree of possibility that $x \in U$ is described by the h th linguistic term of the i th attribute,

$$\pi_{ih}(x) = \begin{cases} \pi(\tilde{a}_i(x), \tilde{w}_{ih}) & a_i \text{ is continuous quantitative}, \tilde{a}_i(x) \text{ is fuzzy} \\ \pi(a_i(x), \tilde{w}_{ih}) & a_i \text{ is continuous quantitative}, a_i(x) \text{ is crisp} \\ \pi(a_i(x), w_{ih}) & a_i \text{ is discrete} \end{cases} \quad (7)$$

3.   EXTENED ROUGH SET APPROACH

A HE information system $\tilde{I}_{HE} = \langle U, A, W, \tilde{\varsigma}_{HE} \rangle$ means that every entry can be regarded as the complex of the pairs of linguistic terms and possibility degrees on a_i, denoted by

$$[x, a_i] = \{(w_{ih}, \pi_{ih}(x))\}, \ \pi_{ih}(x) > 0, \ 1 \le h \le m_i, m_i = |W_i|. \tag{8}$$

There is a suggestion of subdivision of uncertain dataset proposed by Salido, Murakami and Bodjanova respectively[2,3]. Their method substitutes the complex (a_i, w_{ih}) for a_i, where $1 \le h \le m_i$, $m_i = |W_i|$ is the number of linguistic terms. Their approach causing the larger number of attributes may be too computational complexity during the operation of reduction and rule induction[4]. However, our approach declared below could avoid this despite of demanding much computational space.

Definition 2. Let $P \subseteq A$ be the attribute set describing $x \in U$. W_i is the linguistic term set of the ith attribute $q_i \in P$, and $m_i > 1$ means the number of element of W_i more than 1. $[x, q_i] = \{(w_{ih}, \pi_{ih}(x))\}$, $\pi_{ih}(x) > 0$, let $\Pi_i(x)$ denote the set consisting of all degrees of possibility $\pi_{ih}(x)$ in pair $(w_{ih}, \pi_{ih}(x))$ of $[x, q_i]$. If x^j is a subobject of x, then $[x^j, q_i] = (w_{ih}, \pi_{ih}(x^j))$, $\pi_{ih}(x^j) \in \Pi_i(x)$. If only one attribute in P has multi-valued entries, then $j = 1, \cdots, p_i$, $p_i = |\{h \mid \pi_{ih}(x) > 0\}| \le m_i$; if more than one attribute in P have multi-valued entries, then $j = 1, \cdots, \Pi_{i:p_i > 0} p_i$, $p_i = |\{h \mid \pi_{ih}(x) > 0\}| \le m_i$. So, there must be a vector of x^j related to P:

$$((w_{1h}, \pi_{1h}(x^j)), \cdots (w_{ih}, \pi_{ih}(x^j)) \cdots, (w_{nh}, \pi_{nh}(x^j))). \tag{9}$$

And P possible degree $\pi_P(x^j)$ that P describe x^j is modeled by fuzzy T-norm operator as:

$$\pi_P(x^j) = \min\{\pi_{1h}(x^j), \pi_{2h}(x^j), \cdots, \pi_{nh}(x^j)\}, n = |P|. \tag{10}$$

Definition 3. Let p be the number of x^j, and P possible degree that P describe x^j is $\pi_P(x^j)$, then the relative coefficient is

$$\eta_p(x^j) = \frac{\pi_p(x^j)}{\sum_{i=1}^{p} \pi_p(x')}, \tag{11}$$

which means the scale of the part of x occupied by x^j related to P.

Definition 4. Extended Information Table is a 5-tuple $\tilde{I} = \langle U', \eta, A, W, \tilde{\varsigma} \rangle$, where U' is the finite set of all subobjeccts; η is the set of relative coefficients, i.e. $\eta = \{\eta_A(x')\}$, $x' \in U'$; A is the finite set of condition attributes; $W = \bigcup_{i:a_i \in A} W_i$, W_i is set of qualitative value domain of $a_i \in A$, or called as the set of qualitative linguistic terms of a_i; $\tilde{\varsigma}$ is called as the extended information function, such that $x' \in U', a_i \in A$, $\tilde{\varsigma}(x', a_i) = (w_{ih}, \pi_{ih}(x'))$.

Definition 5. $\tilde{I} = \langle U', \eta, A, W, \tilde{\varsigma} \rangle$ is an extended information system. For $P \subseteq A$, $\forall q_i \in P$, $x' \in U'$, $y' \in U'$, $\tilde{R}_P = \{(x', y') : q_i(x') = q_i(y') = w_{ih}\}$ is the P-indiscernibility relation on U', where $q_i(x') = w_{ih}$, $w_{ih} \in W_i$.

There must exist a partition of U' : $A = U'/\widetilde{R}_P = \{[x']_P : x' \in U'\}$, where $[x']_P = \{y' : (x', y') \in \widetilde{R}_P\} = \{y' : q_l(y') = q_l(x')(\forall q_l \in P)\}$. $(U', \widetilde{R}_P)$ is a Pawlak approximation space. We call $[x']_P$ in A as a P-equivalence class. But how do we measure degree of possibility of using w_{lh} to describe $[x']_P$.

Let $\pi_{ih}(x'_i)$ be the degree of possibility that $x'_i \in [x']_P$ is described by w_{ih}. Then degree of possibility of using w_{lh} to describe $[x']_P$ is $\pi_{ih}([x']_P) = \min_{x'_i \in [x']_P} \{\pi_{ih}(x'_i)\}$.

Definition 6. The relative coefficient of subobject $y' \in U'$ is $\eta_P(y')$, and then the cardinality of $[x']_P$ is $Card([x']_P) = \sum_{y' \in [x']_P} \eta_P(y')$.

Definition 7. $(U', \widetilde{R}_P)$ is a Pawlak approximation space, $[x']_P \in A$. For any $Y \subseteq U'$, P-lower and P-upper approximation of Y related to $(U', \widetilde{R}_P)$ are as follows respectively:

$$\underline{\widetilde{R}}_P(Y) = \{x' \in U' : [x']_P \subseteq Y\} = \bigcup \{ [x']_P : [x']_P \subseteq Y\}, \tag{12}$$

$$\overline{\widetilde{R}}_P(Y) = \{x' \in U' : [x']_P \cap Y \neq \varnothing\} = \bigcup \{[x']_P : [x']_P \cap Y \neq \varnothing\}; \tag{13}$$

P-boundary of Y related to $(U', \widetilde{R}_P)$ is:

$$\widetilde{Bn}_P(Y) = \overline{\widetilde{R}}_P(Y) - \underline{\widetilde{R}}_P(Y) \tag{14}$$

Definition 8. Accuracy of Y related to approximation space $(U', \widetilde{R}_P)$ is

$$\alpha_{\widetilde{R}_P}(Y) = \frac{Card(\underline{\widetilde{R}}_P(Y))}{Card(\overline{\widetilde{R}}_P(Y))} \text{, where} \tag{15}$$

$$Card(\underline{\widetilde{R}}_P(Y)) = \sum_{[x']_P \subseteq \underline{\widetilde{R}}_P} Card([x']_P) = \sum_{x' \in \underline{\widetilde{R}}_P} \eta_P(x') \text{, } Card(\overline{\widetilde{R}}_P(Y)) = \sum_{[x']_P \subseteq \overline{\widetilde{R}}_P} Card([x']_P) = \sum_{x' \in \overline{\widetilde{R}}_P} \eta_P(x').$$

Definition 9. Let Ω be the classification on U', $\Omega = \{\omega_i\}$, $\omega_i \subseteq U'$, such that $\omega_i \cap \omega_j = \varnothing$, $1 \leq i \neq j \leq n$, the lower approximation and the upper approximation of Ω are respectively:

$$\underline{\widetilde{R}}_P(\Omega) = \{\underline{\widetilde{R}}_P(\omega_1), \underline{\widetilde{R}}_P(\omega_2), \cdots, \underline{\widetilde{R}}_P(\omega_n)\} \text{, } \overline{\widetilde{R}}_P(\Omega) = \{\overline{\widetilde{R}}_P(\omega_1), \overline{\widetilde{R}}_P(\omega_2), \cdots, \overline{\widetilde{R}}_P(\omega_n)\};$$

And P- approximation quality of Ω is:

$$\gamma_{\widetilde{R}_P}(\Omega) = \frac{\sum_{l=1}^{n}(Card(\underline{\widetilde{R}}_P(\omega_l)))}{Card(U')} \tag{16}$$

Assuming that the original decision table has been subdivided to be $\widetilde{I}$ but still with multi-valued decision entries, we can subdivide x^j into x^{jk}, called as secondary subobject. So a x^{jk} is a secondary subobject that can be actually described as a vector with both condition single-valued entry and decision single-valued entry.

Relative coefficient of x^{jk} which means the scale of the part of x^j occupied by x^{jk} related to D is:

$$\eta_D(x^{jk}) = \frac{\pi_D(x^{jk})}{\sum_{g=1}^{l} \pi_D(x^{jg})}, \tag{17}$$

where $\pi_D(x^{jk}) = \min\{\pi_{1h}(x^{jk}), \pi_{2h}(x^{jk}), \cdots, \pi_{|D|h}(x^{jk})\}$.

The relative coefficient of x^j, denoted by $\eta_A(x^j)$, the relative coefficient of x^{jk}, denoted by $\eta_D(x^{jk})$, $\eta_{A,D}(x^{jk}) = \eta_A(x^j) \bullet \eta_D(x^{jk})$ is interpreted as comprehensive relative coefficient of x^{jk} which means the scale of the part of x occupied by x^{jk} related to A and D.

Definition 10. Extended Decision System is a 5-tuple $\tilde{D}T = \langle U'', \eta, Q, W, \tilde{\varsigma} \rangle$, where U'' is the set of secondary subobjects; η is the set of comprehensive relative coefficients, i.e. $\eta = \{\eta_{A,D}(x'')\}$, $x'' \in U''$; $Q = A \cup D$, and $A \cap D = \varnothing$, A and D are condition attribute set and decision attribute set respectively; $W = \bigcup_{i \wedge q_i \in Q} W_i$, W_i is the set of linguistic terms on attribute q_i; $\tilde{\varsigma}$ is satisfied with $\tilde{\varsigma}(x'', q_i) = (w_{ih}, \pi_{ih}(x''))$, where $\pi_{ih}(x'')$ means the degree of possibility that x'' is described by the h th linguistic term of the i th q_i.

4.   CONCLUSION

This paper proposed an approach based on extended Rough Sets Theory to computing the lower and upper approximation of the concepts in EDT, which can be as input to the rule induction algorithm, i.e. LEM2[4]. Some concepts, however, such as reduction before LEM2, cover and minimal rule set in LEM2, must be extended according to extended Rough Sets Theory above discussed. This is just the problem we are focusing on.

REFERENCES

1. Hua Wenjian, Liu zuoliang and Yang fan, A novel knowledge representation and induction of decision rules. *Journal of Air Force Engineering University (Natural Science Edition)* 4(6), 44-48(2003).
2. J.M Fernandez Salido, S. Murakami., Rough set analysis of a general type of fuzzy data using transitive aggregation of fuzzy similarity relations. *Fuzzy Sets and Systems* 139(3), 635-660(2003).
3. Slavka Bodjanova., Approximation of fuzzy concepts in decision making. *Fuzzy Sets and Systems* 85(1), 23-29(1997).
4. Jerzy Stefanowski, On Rough set based approaches to induction of decision rules, in: *Rough sets in knowledge discovery 1*, edited by Lech Polkowski and Andrzej Skowron. (Physica-Verlag, Heidelberg, 1998), pp.500-529.
5. Wang Guoyin, *Rough Sets Theory and Knowledge Acquisition* (Xian Jiao Tong University Publisher Press, Xian, 2001).
6. Nguyen S.H. ,Skowron A, Quantization of real value attributes: rough set and Boolean reasoning approach, in: *Second Annual Joint Conference on Information Sciences (JCIS'95)*, edited by P.P. Wang (Wrightsville Beach, North Carolina, 1995), pp.34-37.
7. Ellis J. Clarke, Bruce A. Barton., Entroy and MDL discretization of continuous variable for Bayesian belief network. *International Journal of Intelligent Systems* 15(1), 61-92(2000).
8. Zhao Weidong, Dai Weihui and Cai Bin, The discretization of continuous attributes using genetic algorithms. *Systems Engineering Theory & Practice* 23(1),62-67(2003).

INTRUSION DETECTION BASED ON ORGANIZATIONAL COEVOLUTIONARY FUZZY CLASSIFIERS

Liu Fang and Chen Zhen-guo
School of Computer Science and Technology, Xidian University, Xi'an, 710071, China

Abstract:　　To solve the intrusion detection question, we introduce the fuzzy logic into Organization CoEvolutionary algorithm[1] and present the algorithm of Organization CoEvolutionary Fuzzy Classification (OCEFC). In this paper, we give an intrusion detection models based on OCEFC. After illustrating our model and applying it to the real-world network datasets KDD Cup 1999, we obtain the better performance than other traditional methods.

Key words:　　Intrusion detection; Organization CoEvolutionary; Anomaly detection; Fuzzy Logic

1. INTRODUCTION

An intrusion detection system (IDS) is a component of the computer and information security framework. Many intrusion detection techniques have been used to IDS. Using data mining techniques over system audit data[2]. Using short sequences of system calls performed by running programs as discriminators between normal and abnormal [3]. In this paper, we present a new approach, based on OCEFC, to anomaly detection over network.

2. ORGANIZATIONAL COEVOLUTIONARY (OCE)

In OCE [1], the objects having some similarities in the value of attributes are gathered firstly. Then, the significance of attributes is used to guide the evolutionary process. The set of objects whose decision attribute have the same values form a target class: $DC_a = \{O \mid O \in U \wedge a \in V_D \wedge O_D = a\}$. A parameter called attribute significance CI_c is introduced to weigh the influence of each attribute.

Details about the OCE can be seen in [1].

3. AN INTRUSION DETECTION BASED ON OCEFC

In 1965 Lotfi Zadeh[4] first published a description and analysis of Fuzzy Logic. This is a true superset of Boolean Logic and permits the description of functions and processes with a degree of vagueness or uncertainty.

3.1. Organizational CoEvolutionary Fuzzy Classification

We redefine the $SAME_{ORG}$ viewing from the fuzzy logic.

Definition 1: Same Attribute is a condition attribute whose value of all objects in organization ORG has the same logic value.

The algorithm of the evolution of attribute significance can be seen in [1].

Algorithm 1 Organizational CoEvolutionary Fuzzy Classification

Step1: Each object in every target class is added to the corresponding population $P_i(0)$ as a free organization. $i = 1, 2, \cdots, |V_D|$; $t = 0, i = 1$

Step2: If $i > |V_D|$, go to Step8; else go to Step3;

Step3: If the number of organizations in $P_i(t)$ is larger than 1, go to Step4, otherwise go to Step7;

Step4: Two parent organizations ORG_{p1}, ORG_{p2} are randomly selected from $P_i(t)$; The **evolutionary operator**[1] will act on ORG_{p1}, ORG_{p2}, and we can get child organizations ORG_{c1}, ORG_{c2};

Step5: Compute the continuous attributes fuzzy logic value and Compute the fitness of child organizations ORG_{c1}, ORG_{c2};

Step6: Perform **selection mechanism**[1] on ORG_{p1}, ORG_{p2} and ORG_{c1}, ORG_{c2}, move the rest organization in $P_i(t)$ to $P_i(t+1)$, go to Step3;

Step7: $i = i+1$, go to Step2;

Step8: If meet the stopping criteria, go to Step9, otherwise, $t = t+1$, $i = 1$, go to Step2;

Step9: After the evolutionary process ends, we can extract the rules.

Definition 2: *weight* : the confidence of knowledge; CON : the condition set. M_O is the number of object when $x = a$, $a \in \{VeryLow, Low, Medium, High, VeryHigh\}$ and $class = c$, N_O is the number of object where $class = c$, SV_a^c is a statistic value and can be get by M_O / N_O. So we can get the confidence of knowledge by following equation: $weight = MIN\{SV_a^c(x)\}$, where x belongs to CON. $SV_a^c(x)$ is corresponding x.

Definition 3: Two organizations ORG_{p1}, ORG_{p2} are randomly selected from a population firstly, IF $USE_{ORG_1} \subseteq USE_{ORG_2}$ OR $USE_{ORG_2} \subseteq USE_{ORG_1}$, $THEN$ $ORG = ORG_1 \cup ORG_2$, $USE_{ORG} = USE_{ORG_1} \cap USE_{ORG_2}$.

Definition 4: The $SCALE_{ORG}$ is the scale of organization. The *weight* can determine the class that an object belongs to. If $weight_{object} > \lambda$, class=c, we can get $object_{decision} = c$ ($\lambda > 0.6$). It can get by following equation: $SCALE_{ORG} = |ORG|/|DC_a|$, where a is the value of decision attribute in ORG.

Algorithm 2 Rules extract

Step1: $i \leftarrow 1$, $RULES \leftarrow \varnothing$;

Step2: If $i > |V_D|$, go to Step4; Otherwise, Two organizations ORG_{p1}, ORG_{p2} are randomly selected from P_i, according to Definition 3: $P_i \leftarrow (P_i / \{ORG_1, ORG_2\}) \cup ORG$, until $\forall ORG_1, ORG_2 \in P_i$ not satisfy the Definition 3, go to Step3.

Step3: Extract rule from the same Attribute set of each ORG in P_i. Compute $SCALE_{ORG}$, then $RULES \leftarrow RULES \cup rule$; $i \leftarrow i+1$, go to Step2;

Step4: Sort by the $SCALE_{ORG}$ and get $RULES$.

Where P_i, $i=1,2,\cdots$, $|V_D|$ is the evolutionary result; $RULES$ is the rules set; In this section, we provide a definition of the intrusion detection model.

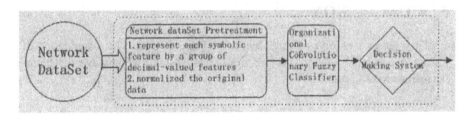

Figure 1: The IDS based on Organizational CoEvolutionary Fuzzy Classification

4. SIMULATION

In this paper, we use the dataset from original 10% KDD Cup 1999. To get a fuzzy dataset, where each numerical value in the dataset we normalized between 0.0 and 1.0 according to the equation: $x' = \ln(rx)/\ln(r\beta)$ $\alpha r \geq 1$, where x is the value of numerical attribute, β and α are separately the maximum and minimum value as the same attribute with x, r is a constant.

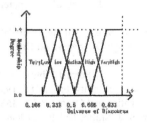

Figure 2: Fuzzy space for KDD-CUP99 dataset

For each continuous attribute we assign the fuzzy space shown in figure 2.

4.1. The Results of Simulation

We compared performance of OCEFC with the other methods. We use 20% randomly sampled as training data to evaluate the performance of a model. Another 40% randomly form the threshold determination set, which has no overlap with the training set. We use two performance measures in our simulation: FAR (false alarm rate) and TDR (true detection rate).

After running 100 times, we compare the average result based on OCEFC with other methods in *Table 1*. Ours method has better performance.

Table 1: Comparison of IDS performance based on OCEFC with others method

Method	OCEFC	GA	RIPPER-Artificial Anomalies [5]
FAR (%)	2.75	7.0	2.02
TDR (%)	99.23	93.14	94.26

5. CONCLUSION

This paper has investigated the use of OCEFC as one component of intrusion detection system. As the simulation shown, we achieve the better performance than others.

ACKNOWLEDGEMENTS

This work was Supported by the National Natural Science Foundation of China under Grant Nos. 60372045, 60133010; National High Technology Development 863 Program of China under Grant No. 2002AA135080.

REFERENCES

1. Liu Jing, Zhong Wei-Cai, Liu Fang, Jiao Li-Cheng. Classification based on organization coevolutionary algorithm. Chiense Journal of Computers, 2003, 26(4): 446-453 (in Chinese).
2. W. Lee, S. J. Stolfo, and K. W. Mok, "Mining audit data to build intrusion detection models", Proc. Int. Conf.Knowledge Discovery and Data Mining (KDD'98), pages 66-72, 1998.
3. S. A. Hofmeyr, A. Somayaji, and S. Forrest, "Intrusion detection using sequences of systems call", Journal of Computer Security, 6:151-180, 1998.
4. Zadeh, L..A.. Fuzzy Sets. Information and Control 8:338:353 1965
5. W. Fan, W. Lee, M. Miller, S. J. Stolfo, and P. K.Chan, "Using artificial anomalies to detect unknown and know network intrusions", Proceedings of the First IEEE International Conference on Data Mining, 2001.

SIMPLE FUZZY LOGIC RULES BASED ON FUZZY DECISION TREE FOR CLASSIFICATION AND PREDICTION PROBLEM

J. F. Baldwin and Dong (Walter) Xie

Department of Engineering Mathematics, Faculty of Engineering, University of Bristol
Bristol, BS8 1TR, United Kingdom
Jim.Baldwin@bristol.ac.uk   D.Xie@bristol.ac.uk

Abstract: In data mining for knowledge explanation purposes, we would like to build simple transparent fuzzy models. Compared to other fuzzy models, simple fuzzy logic rules (IF … THEN… rules) based on triangular or trapezoidal shape fuzzy sets are much simpler and easier to understand. For fuzzy rule based learning algorithms, choosing the right combination of attributes and fuzzy sets which have the most information is the key point to obtain good accuracy. On the other hand, the fuzzy ID3 algorithm gives an efficient model to select the right combinations. We therefore discover the set of simple fuzzy logic rules from a fuzzy decision tree based on the same simple shaped fuzzy partition, after dropping those rules whose credibility is less than a reasonable threshold, only if the accuracy of the training set using these rules is reasonably close to the accuracy using fuzzy decision tree. The set of simple fuzzy logic rules satisfied with this condition is also able to be used to interpret the information of the tree. Furthermore, we use the fuzzy set operator "OR" to merge simple fuzzy logic rules to reduce the number of rules.

Key words: Simple shaped fuzzy partition, fuzzy ID3 decision tree, simple fuzzy logic rules (SFLRs), classification problem, prediction problem.

1.   INRODUCTION

The classification and prediction problems, where the target attribute is respectively discrete (nominal) or continuous (numerical), are two main issues in data mining and machine learning fields. General methods for these two problems discover rules and models from a database of examples. IF ... THEN ... rules, neural nets, Bayesian nets, and decision trees are examples of such models.

To be able to handle imprecision and uncertainty of the representation of concepts and words in the real world, these models have been used with fuzzy logic [3] introduced by Zadeh in 1965. These fuzzy models overcome the sharp boundary problems [5], providing a soft controller surface and good accuracy in dealing with continuous attributes and prediction problem.

In classification and prediction problems, we would like the fuzzy model to be as simple as possible and provide an easy means of providing an explanation for the result. The fuzzy logic rules (IF ... THEN... rules) are good choice, because they are not only much simpler than the other models but also formulate human reasoning and decision-making into a set of easily understandable linguistic clauses. For explanation purpose, we have to use the simple triangular or trapezoidal shape fuzzy sets, so that simple fuzzy logic rule model based on these fuzzy sets are produced.

In order to use less number of simple fuzzy logic rules to provide reasonable accuracy, we firstly discover a fuzzy ID3 decision tree with post-pruning [2][4] based on the simple triangular fuzzy sets, and transfer the tree into a set of simple fuzzy logic rules after dropping those rules whose credibility is less than a reasonable threshold, only if the accuracy of the training set using simple fuzzy logic rules is reasonably close to the accuracy using fuzzy decision tree.

In Fril [1], a symbolic AI uncertainty logic programming system combining fuzzy reasoning, possibility and probability reasoning, we interpret the simple fuzzy logic rules as conditionalisations rather than as implications. Defuzzification in Fril takes a very simple form.

To reduce the complexity of our model, we merge simple fuzzy logic rules with neighbouring fuzzy sets to give trapezoidal fuzzy sets.

2. SIMPLY SHAPED FUZZY PARTITION AND FUZZY ID3 DECISION TREE

2.1 Simply triangular or trapezoidal shape fuzzy sets

When Zadeh proposed fuzzy set theory [3] in 1965, the use of simple linguistic words in place of numbers for computing and reasoning was one of the key ideas. This provides fuzzy logic with a simplified explanation power of being a suitable interface between human users and computing systems. This power does, though, depend on the form of fuzzy sets. If the fuzzy sets are simple triangular or trapezoidal in shape, then they can be given an easy interpretation. If they have a complicated shape, such as Figure 1, they do not provide a useful linguistic description.

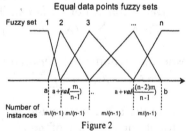

Figure 1

Optimised fuzzy sets, such as neuro-fuzzy sets [1], are used to obtain good accuracy but they have no explanation power because of their complicated shape. We investigate methods of deriving rules and models using a simple shaped fuzzy partition for each attribute, which is defined as a family of triangular or trapezoidal fuzzy sets in Definition 1 such that for any argument value the memberships add to 1. [1][2]

Definition 1: A *simply shaped fuzzy partition* $\{f_i\}$ is a set of triangular or trapezoidal fuzzy sets such that

$$\sum_i \chi_{f_i}(x) = 1 \quad \text{for any data point } x \in X \text{ where } X \text{ is the universal set.}$$

2.2   Fuzzy partition model and membership function

In this paper, we use equal data points fuzzy sets (EDP-FS) model in Definition 2 for continuous (numerical) attributes, which are normally asymmetric, and still use crisp sets as a special case of fuzzy sets for discrete (nominal) attributes.

Definition 2: Equal data points fuzzy sets (EDP-FS)

In this model, the number of data examples in each interval covered by a triangular fuzzy set in the universal set [a, b] is equal. For n fuzzy sets and m examples in database sorted in ascending order, if the value of example x is $val(x)$ where $x \in [1, m]$, then the fuzzy partition is illustrated in Figure 2.

Equal data points fuzzy sets

Figure 2

Mass Assignment Theory [1][2] proposed by Baldwin in 1991 integrated fuzzy logic and probability theory, points out that for simple shaped fuzzy partition $\{f_i\}$ of *kth* attribute, input such as $x = g$, where g can be point value, fuzzy set or probability distribution, is translated into distribution over fuzzy sets of words using membership function $\chi_f : X \rightarrow [0, 1]$ [3]. The membership values $\chi_f(x)$ where $x \in X$ is the conditional probability of each fuzzy set given input $Pr(f_i \mid g)$. [1][2]

Definition 3: *Membership value* $\chi_{f_i}(x) = Pr(f_i \mid g)$, where if g is the point value, then $Pr(f_i \mid g)$ $\chi_{f_i}(g) = $, otherwise we will use point value semantic unification [1][2] to calculate it.

2.3   Fuzzy ID3 decision tree

Fuzzy ID3 algorithm [2][4] developed by Baldwin and co-workers and described below is an efficient algorithm to generate fuzzy decision tree.

Input 3 parameters of model: training set S, the number of fuzzy sets f and the depth of decision tree l,
Start to form fuzzy decision tree from the top level,
Do loop until [1] the depth of the tree gets to l or [2] there is no node to expand
   a) Determine expected entropy $EE(A_k)$ for each attribute of S not already expanded in this branch,
   b) Expand the attribute x with the minimum expected entropy $EE(A_x)$,
   c) Stop expansion of the leaf node A_{kf} of attribute k if entropy $E(A_{kf}) = 0$ or nearly 0,
   d) Use post pruning to prune the tree and stop.
End do loop

During the process of learning fuzzy decision tree, the leaf nodes A_{kf} in each stage have the entropy

$$E(A_{kf}) = \sum_i Pr(t_i \mid A_{kf}) \times Ln(Pr(t_i \mid A_{kf}))$$

where the node belongs to the *kth* attribute and *fth* fuzzy set, and t_i is *ith* class or fuzzy set of the target attribute. $Pr(t_i \mid A_{kf})$ is the conditional probabilities associated with each class in the target attribute.

Definition 4: For the *kth* attribute, the *expected entropy* is

$$EE(A_k) = \sum_f Pr(A_{kf}) \times E(A_{kf})$$

where the renormalized **branch probability** passed in each branch is

$$Pr(A_{kf}) = ReNorm(\sum_T \sum_{A_{1f}} \cdots \sum_{A_{(k-1)f}} \sum_{A_{(k+1)f}} \cdots \sum_{A_{nf}} Pr(A_{1f\ldots}A_{nf}, T))$$

where the subscript f could be the different number of fuzzy sets in each attribute and the set of nodes $\{A_{1f}, \ldots, A_{kf}, \ldots, A_{nf}, T\}$ comprises the branch which is the path of the target T.

We modify Laplace's formula to prune the fuzzy decision tree. The error of the *fth* children node S_f of any node S in fuzzy decision tree is

$$Error(S_f) = \frac{N \times Pr'(S_f) - N \times Pr'(S_f) \times Pr(t_i \mid S_f) + k - 1}{N \times Pr'(S_f) + k}$$

where N is the number of examples in the training set, and $Pr'(S_f)$ is the probability passed in the branch before renormalization in Definition 4. Then, we calculate backup error of node S. If BackUpError(S) $\geq$ Error(S), the tree is pruned by halting at S and cutting all its children nodes. [2]

3.   SIMPLE FUZZY LOGIC RULES BASED ON FUZZY DECISION TREE

For machine learning and data mining purpose, various types of fuzzy rules and models can be used, such as general Fril rules [1], fuzzy decision trees, fuzzy Bayesian nets and IF…THEN…fuzzy logic rules. Depending on the simply shaped fuzzy sets, fuzzy logic rules provide a simple transparent formulation of human reasoning and hence can be explained easily. Though those rules over optimised fuzzy sets would provide good accuracy, they lose their main advantage of fuzzy logic rules in original. We therefore only use those over simply triangular or trapezoidal shape fuzzy sets that are called as simple fuzzy logic rules in this paper.

3.1   Simple fuzzy logic rules (SFLRs)

Suppose there are k attributes and the jth attribute is the target attribute, the simple fuzzy logic rule (SFLR) based on the simple shaped fuzzy sets is of the form shown in (1):

$$(A_j \text{ is large}) \text{ IF} \hspace{4cm} (1)$$
$$(A_1 \text{ is small}) \text{ AND} \ldots \text{AND} (A_{j-1} \text{ is small}) \text{ AND} (A_{j+1} \text{ is medium}) \text{ AND} \ldots \text{AND} (A_k \text{ is large})$$

where the term on the left side of IF is the head of this rule and the set of terms on the right is the body, and the clauses of the terms are words of attributes defined by fuzzy sets. Every SFLR has support and credibility defined as below.

Definition 5: The joint probability p_r = Pr(A_1 is small $\wedge \ldots \wedge A_{j-1}$ is small $\wedge A_j$ is large $\wedge A_{j+1}$ is medium $\wedge \ldots \wedge A_k$ is large) is the *support* of the simple fuzzy logic rule in (1). [2]

The support of a SFLR represents the frequency of occurrence of the particular combination of attribute values in the SFLR in the training set.

Let p = Pr(A_1 is small $\wedge \ldots \wedge A_{j-1}$ is small $\wedge A_{j+1}$ is medium $\wedge \ldots \wedge A_k$ is large)

$= \sum_{A_j \text{ is large}} \text{Pr}(A_1 \text{ is small} \wedge \ldots \wedge A_k \text{ is large})$, then

Definition 6: the value of $\frac{p_r}{p}$ is the *credibility* (confidence) of the simple fuzzy logic rule in (1). [2]

The credibility of a SFLR represents how often it is likely to be true.

Only the SFLRs whose credibility is greater than or equal to the credibility threshold ε are chosen. Those SFLRs are likely to be true, if ε is reasonably high.

3.2   Simple fuzzy logic rules from fuzzy ID3 decision tree

All kinds of decision trees can be changed into IF...THEN...rules. In our model, fuzzy ID3 decision tree is transferred into a set of SFLRs with one of the model parameters --- a credibility threshold ε. The head of a SFLR is the class or fuzzy set of a leaf node with maximum conditional probability, and this conditional probability is equivalent to the credibility of the SFLR transferred. The body is the path of this target in the tree. Any SFLR whose credibility is less than ε is dropped.

For example, in the Pima Indian Diabetes classification problem, we discovered a fuzzy decision tree [2][4] shown in Figure 3 using 3 fuzzy sets defined in Definition 2 in each attribute and assigning the depth of tree as 3, where each pair of integer numbers in a bracket on the left side represents a node in the tree, and the first number represents an attribute number and the second represents a selected fuzzy set of this attribute. Those float numbers on the right side are the conditional probabilities associated with each class in the target attribute. For instance, the first path of the tree shows the node with 2nd attribute 1st fuzzy set leads to the target node with probability equal to 0.862725 for the 1st class and 0.137275 for the 2nd class.

	1.	(2 1)	(0.862725 0.137275)
	2.	(2 2)	(0.668541 0.331459)
Fuzzy decision	3.	(2 3)(8 2)	(0.308811 0.691189)
tree:	4.	(2 3)(8 3)	(0.275786 0.724214)
	5.	(2 3)(8 1)(7 1)	(0.814304 0.185696)
	6.	(2 3)(8 1)(7 2)	(0.525588 0.474412)
	7.	(2 3)(8 1)(7 3)	(0.236044 0.763956)

Credibility >= 0.6

	1.	(attribute_9 is class_1) IF (attribute_2 is fuzzy_set_1)
	2.	(attribute_9 is class_1) IF (attribute_2 is fuzzy_set_2)
	3.	(attribute_9 is class_2) IF
		(attribute_2 is fuzzy_set_3) AND (attribute_8 is fuzzy_set_2)
Simple fuzzy	4.	(attribute_9 is class_2) IF
logic rules		(attribute_2 is fuzzy_set_3) AND (attribute_8 is fuzzy_set_3)
(SFLRs):	5.	(attribute_9 is class_1) IF
		(attribute_2 is fuzzy_set_3) AND (attribute_8 is fuzzy_set_1)
		AND (attribute_7 is fuzzy_set_1)
	7.	(attribute_9 is class_2) IF
		(attribute_2 is fuzzy_set_3) AND (attribute_8 is fuzzy_set_1)
		AND (attribute_7 is fuzzy_set_3)

Figure 3

As we can see in Figure 3, these SFLRs with information of fuzzy ID3 decision tree have the simpler form and are easier to understand than the decision tree.

Our model has two uses: one is to efficiently discover a set of SFLRs with good accuracy, when their training set accuracy is reasonably close to the fuzzy decision tree; the other is to use the set of SFLRs transferred from

·fuzzy decision tree to interpret the information of the tree, if the training set accuracy of SFLRs is reasonably close to the accuracy of fuzzy decision tree.

3.3 Using simple fuzzy logic rules (SFLRs) to evaluate new case for classification or prediction problem

In Fril we interpret the IF...THEN... simple fuzzy logic rules as conditionalisations rather than as implications [1]. This makes more sense when uncertainties are involved since it is the conditional probabilities that are naturally apparent in data.

To evaluate a new example $\{x_1,...,x_k\}$ over k attributes using the SFLR in (1), we calculate Pr (body) = Pr (small | x_1) × ... × Pr (small | x_{j-1}) × Pr (medium | x_{j+1}) × ... × Pr (large | x_k) over k-1 attributes in the body. Let Pr (body) = ϕ, Fril inference of the SFLR is formulated as Pr (head) = Pr (head | body) × Pr (body) + Pr (head | ¬ body) × Pr (¬ body) = 1 × ϕ + [0, 1] × (1 - ϕ) = [ϕ, 1] [1][2]

Definition 7: For $\{t_i\}$ classes in the target attribute, the Fril inference of SFLRs will give $\{t_i : [\phi_i, 1]\}$ for each class. We therefore choose the class t_i of the target attribute as the predicted class that has maximum inference $\underset{t_i}{MAX} (\phi_i)$.

Definition 8: For $\{f_i\}$ fuzzy sets in the target attribute, the Fril inference of SFLRs will give $\{f_i : [\phi_i, 1]\}$ for each fuzzy set, where there is $\sum_i \phi_i \leq 1$. Let $\chi_{f_i}(m_i) = 1$, the predicted value is:

$$x = (x_u + x_l)/2, \text{ where}$$
$$x_u = \underset{\{\theta_i\}}{MAX} \sum_i m_i\theta_i \ s.t \ \phi_i \leq \theta_i \leq 1 \ (all \ i), \sum_i \theta_i = 1$$
$$x_l = \underset{\{\theta_i\}}{MIN} \sum_i m_i\theta_i \ s.t \ \phi_i \leq \theta_i \leq 1 \ (all \ i), \sum_i \theta_i = 1$$

The predicted value x equals to the average of possible maximum value x_u of x and possible minimum value x_l. In the formula, we take the maximum value m_i of each fuzzy set i ($\chi_{f_i}(m_i) = 1$) that is multiplied by the probability distribution θ_i associated with ith fuzzy set. To make x_u maximal, we keep probability distribution θ as much as possible in the fuzzy set whose maximum value m is maximal among all fuzzy sets, and then the rest of θ_i is assigned to the associated Fril inference ϕ_i. Vice versa for x_l.

For example, suppose we have Firl inferences $\{f_{small} : [0.2, 1], f_{medium} : [0.5, 1], f_{large} : [0.1, 1]\}$, where $\chi_{small}(1) = 1$, $\chi_{medium}(5) = 1$, and $\chi_{large}(9) = 1$.

Then $x_u = 1 \times 0.2 + 5 \times 0.5 + 9 \times (1 - 0.2 - 0.5) = 5.4$ and $x_l = 1 \times (1 - 0.5 - 0.1) + 5 \times 0.5 + 9 \times 0.1 = 3.8$. The predicted value $x = (5.4 + 3.8) / 2 = 4.6$. This provides the defuzzification.

3.4   Merging simple fuzzy logic rules (SFLRs)

The number of rules is the main measurement of the complexity of rule-based model. To reduce the number of SFLRs, we merge those rules where their heads are the same, and fuzzy sets separately in one term of their bodies are neighbouring but the other terms are same, by using fuzzy set operator "OR". The Fril inference of one merged rule equals the sum of inferences of those rules before mergence shown in Figure 4, because of Definition 1. The mergence therefore would not affect the accuracy of classification or prediction at all.

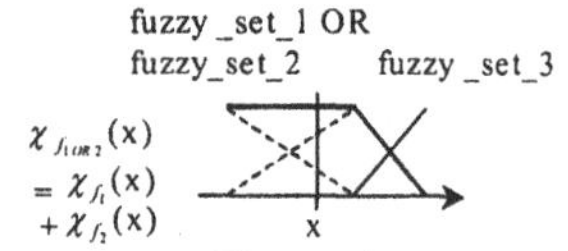

Figure 4

For example, the first 4 SFLRs in Figure 3 can be merged into two rules: (attribute_9 is class_1) IF (attribute_2 is [fuzzy_set_1 OR fuzzy_set_2]) and (attribute_9 is class_2) IF (attribute_2 is fuzzy_set_3) AND (attribute_8 is [fuzzy_set_2 OR fuzzy_set_3]). In result, the number of SFLRs in Figure 4 is reduced from 6 into 4.

4.   EXPERIMENTS

To evaluate our models, we choose some typical databases in UCI Machine Learning Repository [6] to separate each of them into training set and test set by selecting database examples randomly, and then use the same training set and test set to get the accuracy each time.

In the following tables, "Number of Fuzzy Sets" represents the number of fuzzy sets we used for each attribute of database. "Depth of Tree" and "Credibility Threshold" are also model parameters mentioned in section 2.3 and 3.2. "Number of Leaf Nodes" and "Number of Rules" respectively show the complexity of fuzzy decision tree and SFLRs, where the number on the left of "→" is the number of SFLRs before merging and one on the right is after merging. The accuracy for "Training set" and "Test set" using fuzzy ID3 decision tree and SFLRs are in the percentage format and respectively calculated in (2) or (3) for classification or prediction problems:

$$\text{Accuracy} = \frac{\text{the number of successfully classified instances}}{\text{the number of instances in total in the dataset}} \qquad (2)$$

$$\text{Accuracy} = 1 - \frac{|\, T_{predicted} - T_{original}\,|}{range\,(T)} \qquad (3)$$

where $T_{predicted}$ is the predicted target value, $T_{original}$ is the original target value in the dataset, and $range(T)$ is the range of the target attribute T.

In the bottom of tables, we use models of Weka [7] to compare our model in classification problem using the same training set and test set.

Tree examples in classification are shown in Table 1, 2, 3 below.

Table 1. Pima Indians Diabetes Database

Number of Fuzzy Sets	Depth of Tree	Leaf Nodes	Training Set (ID3)	Test Set (ID3)	Credibility Threshold	Number of Rules	Training Set (SFLRs)	Test Set (SFLRs)
3	1	3	71.09 %	76.82 %	0.6	3 → 3	71.09 %	76.82 %
3	5	9	72.13 %	75.52 %	0.6	9 → 6	71.35 %	75.78 %
4	5	19	75.26 %	78.64 %	0.6	18 → 11	75.26 %	78.64 %
5	5	69	80.21 %	79.17 %	0.6	64 → 41	78.38 %	79.43 %
Weka J48 (C4.5 decision tree)					7 leaf nodes*		76.30 %	78.12 %
Weka Naïve Bayes							74.22 %	77.60 %
Weka Neural Network					7 nodes**		80.47 %	77.60 %

Table 2. Sonar Data

Number of Fuzzy Sets	Depth of Tree	Leaf Nodes	Training Set (ID3)	Test Set (ID3)	Credibility Threshold	Number of Rules	Training Set (SFLRs)	Test Set (SFLRs)
3	5	37	90.38 %	87.50 %	0.6	37 → 29	89.42 %	84.61 %
5	5	65	93.27 %	71.15 %	0.6	62 → 33	92.31 %	71.15 %
Weka J48 (C4.5 decision tree)					8 leaf nodes*		97.11 %	74.03 %
Weka Naïve Bayes							75.96 %	73.08 %
Weka Neural Network					33 nodes**		100 %	84.61 %

Table 3. Vision Data

Number of Fuzzy Sets	Depth of Tree	Leaf Nodes	Training Set (ID3)	Test Set (ID3)	Credibility Threshold	Number of Rules	Training Set (SFLRs)	Test Set (SFLRs)
4	5	28	65.75 %	65.78 %	0.4	27 → 15	67.18 %	68.25 %
5	5	37	66.98 %	67.15 %	0.4	33 → 14	65.42 %	65.97 %
6	5	71	68.41 %	69.07 %	0.4	56 → 23	68.04 %	68.86 %
Weka J48 (C4.5 decision tree)					625 leaf nodes*		91.45 %	73.18 %
Weka Naïve Bayes							49.36 %	50.47 %
Weka Neural Network					20 nodes**		76.47 %	75.69 %

* The tree is pruned by using Weka's default pruning. [7]

** Those nodes include all of nodes (internal and external nodes) in the neural network.

Table 4 is a example in prediction, where the 3-attribute and 529-data-point training set is created by function Z = Sin(X*Y) plotted in Figure 6, but the test set has 2209 data points. "5-6-6" in Table 4 represents using 5 fuzzy sets in the target attribute and 6 fuzzy sets in the other attributes.

Table 4. Function SinXY

Number of Fuzzy Sets	Depth of Tree	Leaf Nodes	Training Set (ID3)	Test Set (ID3)	Credibility Threshold	Number of Rules	Training Set (SFLRs)	Test Set (SFLRs)
5-6-6	2	31	90.66 %	90.68 %	0.3	29 → 17	92.35 %	92.40 %
5-8-8	2	57	94.54 %	94.46 %	0.3	57 → 34	96.25 %	96.42 %
5-10-10	2	82	95.36 %	95.33 %	0.3	82 → 44	95.69 %	95.90 %
5-12-12	2	122	97.16 %	97.03 %	0.3	122 → 55	96.02 %	96.44 %
13-13-13	2	145	97.89 %	97.66 %	0.2	145 → 107	98.02 %	98.04 %

Figure 6: Original Function   Figure 7: Test Set (SFLRs) 5-10-10 Figure 8: Test Set (SFLRs) 13-13-13

As we can see, if the training set accuracy using the set of SFLRs transferred from fuzzy decision tree is reasonably close to the training set accuracy using decision tree, the test set accuracy using SFLRs is reasonably close to the other or even better than it.

Furthermore, comparing other models, the SFLRs based on decision tree have a reasonable accuracy with less complexity (the number of rules). Considering their advantages of simplicity, transparency, and linguistic explanation power ability, it is one of most useful models in data mining and machine learning.

REFERENCES

1. J. F. Baldwin, T. P. Martin and B. W. Pilsworth, "Fril – Fuzzy and Evidential Reasoning in Artificial Intelligence", Research Studies Press Ltd. (John Wiley), 1995.
2. Jim Baldwin, http://www.enm.bris.ac.uk/teaching/enjfb/emat31600/
3. Lotfi A. Zadeh, George J. Klir, "Fuzzy Sets, Fuzzy Logic, and Fuzzy Systems: Selected Papers by Lotfi A. Zadeh", World Scientific Publishing Company, May 1996.
4. Jim Baldwin, Sachin Karale, "New Concept of Fuzzy Partition, Defuzzification and Derivation of Probabilistic Fuzzy Decision Trees", Proceedings of the 2003 UK Workshop on Computational Intelligence.
5. Susan M. Bridges, Rayford B. Vaughn, "Fuzzy Data Mining and Genetic Algorithms Applied to Intrusion Detection", 23rd National Information Systems Security Conference, 2000.
6. UCI Machine Learning Repository, http://www1.ics.uci.edu/~mlearn/MLSummary.html
7. University of Waikato, Weka 3.4, http://www.cs.waikato.ac.nz/ml/weka/

A RESEARCH ON KNOWLEDGE REDUCTION OF INFORMATION SYSTEMS BASED ON SUB-CONSCIOUSNESS

Wei Huang, Cong Liu, Xiao-ping Ye
School of Information Science and Technology, Sun Yat-sen University

Abstract: The *information system based on sub-consciousness* is a new type of information system developed from the incomplete information system by introducing the new concept of *sub-consciousness* based on the possible relations among the domains of the attributes in the information system. In this paper, we will discuss the knowledge reduction in the information system based on sub-consciousness, we also propose the concept of rationally guided emotional reduction in the information system based on sub-consciousness which is then compared with the rational reduction and the emotional reduction in the information system based on sub-consciousness.

Key words: Information system, Sub-consciousness, Knowledge reduction, Reduction of sub-consciousness

1 INTRODUCTION

The classical *Rough Set Theory* has been very successful in knowledge acquisition in the complete information system [1]. In consideration of that some of the attributes in the information system might have absent value, the complete information system was developed into the incomplete information system. [2]-[5] are several extensions to the classical rough set theory considering some different connotations of the absent value respectively. In the theoretical framework of the information system based on sub-consciousness proposed in [6], the complete information system with the classical rough set method and those with extended rough set method can be regarded as some special cases. The knowledge reduction is more complicated in the information system based on sub-consciousness than those of the complete and incomplete information systems with the introduction of the mechanism of sub-consciousness, so in this paper, we will propose the concept of rationally guided emotional reduction in the information system based on sub-consciousness.

2   A NEW KIND OF EMOTIONAL REDUCTION

In this section, the definition of a new kind of emotional reduction in the information system based on sub-consciousness is given that is different from that defined in reference [6]. All the symbolic and denotational convention in this paper is conform to that in reference [6]. Because of space limitation, readers are recommended to reference [6] for related concepts and denotations.

Definition 2.1 Let $c(c1,c2,...,cn)$ and $d(d1,...,dm)$ to be vectors, A and B are sets of attributes (where $|A|=n$, $|B|=m$). We define a function Replace(c, d, A, B)=e=($e1,...,en$), where $ei=dj$, if $ai \in A$, $bj \in B$ and $ai=bj$; $ei=ci$ otherwise.

Definition 2.2 Let $B \subseteq AT(B=\{b1,b2,...,bm\})$, then for any $x,y \in U$, we have $B(x)=(b1(x),...,bm(x))$. For any attribute $ai \in AT$, if there is an attribute $bj \in B$ such that $ai=bj$, we mark the arbitration function h_i on ai as h_{bj}, and use $h(B,x,y)$ to represent the vector $(h_{b1}(x,y),...,h_{bm}(x,y))$.

Definition 2.3 An attribute set B is called *emotionally reducible* if and only if $(\forall x,y \in U)(\exists d \in \prod_{0<i<n+1}$ and $_{ai \in B}D_i)$ $((F(x,y)=H(c)) \to (H(c)=H(Replace(c,d,AT,B))))$ holds. If there is no another attribute set $C(B \subset C \subseteq AT)$ that is emotionally reducible, the $A=AT-B$ is called the *knowledge reduction for the experiential data* S or *emotional reduction* and d is called the *origin*.

From definition 2.3, we know that the knowledge reduction in the traditional complete and incomplete information system is the emotional reduction, where origin d takes the form (true,..., true) (the number of true is $|AT-A|$ totally). If we replace part <1> of the configuration of sub-consciousness Ψ with $D_i=Bool$, part <3> with $H(c1,c2,...,cn)=c1 \lor c2 \lor ... \lor cn$, then for the information system S with sub-consciousness Ψ, the origin takes the form (false,..., false) (the number of false is $|AT-A|$).

3   THE RATIONALLY GUIDED EMOTIONAL REDUCTION IN THE INFORMATION SYSTEM BASED ON SUB-CONSCIOUSNESS

For we have introduced the sub-consciousness Ψ and its attribute correlation function H into the information system based on sub-consciousness, we could use their definition to guide the knowledge reduction. The attribute correlation function could be defined as a conjunction form (or a disjunction form), that is the definition of H could appear as H(c1,c2,...,cn)=f1(C1)$\wedge$......$\wedge$fs(Cs) (or f1(C1)$\vee$......$\vee$fs(Cs)), where Ck(0<k<s+1) are subsets of {c1,c2,...,cn}, fk(0<k<s+1) are some middle functions whose range is Bool. If we regard the definition of H as a predicate form, each fs(Cs) could be regarded as its sub conjunction form (or sub disjunction form). In fact, each Ck corresponds to one of the subsets Ak of the attribute set AT, and all Ck make up an coverage of the attribute set AT. If we restrict the reduction to the subset of {A1,...,As}, when s<<n, the complexity of the reduction will be reduced largely.

Definition 3.1 Let AT (AT={a1,a2,...,an}) be the rational reduction of information system S, and sub-consciousness Ψ to be the reduced sub-consciousness of the information system S, and its attribute correlation function could be written as H(c1,c2,...,cn)=f1(C1)$\wedge$......$\wedge$fs(Cs) (or f1(C1)$\vee$......$\vee$fs(Cs)). We construct a new information system S''(U'',BT) based on S, where BT(BT={b1,b2,...,bs}) is the attribute set of S''. For each object x in S, there is a object x'' in S'' which corresponds to x, where bi(x'')=Ai(x)(0<i<s+1). We establish a sub-consciousness Ψ'' in the information system S'' as follows:

<1>D''$_i$=Bool, where 0<i<s+1.

<2>h''$_i$(bi(x''),bi(y''))=fi(h(Ai,x,y)), where 0<i<s+1.

<3>H''(c1,c2,...,cs)=c1$\wedge$c2$\wedge$...$\wedge$cs   (or   c1$\vee$c2$\vee$...$\vee$cs),   where c1,c2,...,cs$\in$Bool.

Let it is the emotional reduction D={d1,d2,...,dr}={b$_{d1}$,b$_{d2}$,...,b$_{dr}$} of the information syste S'' (its origin takes the form (true,...,true) or (false,...,false)), then we call the attribute set A the *rationally guided emotional reduction* (or the *emotional reduction guided by sub-consciousness Ψ*) if and only if ($\forall$a$\in$A)($\exists$i)((0<i<r+1)$\wedge$(a$\in$A$_{di}$)). Similar to the definition of the rationally (or emotionally) reduced sub-consciousness, the rationally guided emotional reduced sub-consciousness Ψ' is created by removing the range D$_i$ and the arbitration function h$_i$ that correspond to the attribute that is in AT-A, and by removing from the definition of the attribute correlation function H the sub conjunction forms or the sub disjunction

forms (i.e. fi(Ci)) that correspond to the emotionally reduced attributes in the information system S''.

From definition 3.1 we know that for any $x,y \in U$ there are corresponding $x'',y'' \in U''$ such that $F(x,y)=F''(x'',y'')$. So, we could get the following theorem directly.

Theorem 3.1 Let A be the rationally guided emotional reduction of the information system S(U, AT) with sub-consciousness Ψ, and the sub-consciousness Ψ' to be corresponding reduced sub-consciousness, then any $x \in U$: $SIM_\Psi(x)=SIM_{\Psi'}(x)$ and $SIM_\Psi^{-1}(x)=SIM_{\Psi'}^{-1}(x)$.

Whether the definition of H is $H(c1,c2,...,cn)=f1(C1) \wedge ...... \wedge fs(Cs)$ or $f1(C1) \vee ...... \vee fs(Cs)$, each $fi(Ci)(0<i<s+1)$ could be regarded as a predicate form. We can regard (U, Ai) as a new information system Si, and that part <1> and part <2> of the sub-consciousness configuration are the corresponding domain of the attribute set Ai and the arbitration function in the original information system, the <3> part, i.e. the definition of the attribute correlation function H, is fi(Ci). Since all fi(Ci) $(0<i<s+1)$are predicate forms, they could also be conjunction form or disjunction form, and the rationally emotional reduction could also be performed on them. Therefore, the process to perform rationally guided emotional reduction in the whole information system is a hierarchical process, which could be top-down or bottom-up. Comparing definition 3.1 and definition 2.3, we could get the following theorem.

Theorem 3.2 If the attribute set B is emotionally reducible in the information system S with sub-consciousness Ψ, it is not certain whether it is rationally guided emotionally reducible, vice versa.

Practically, when performing reduction on an information system, the rational reduction should be performed first, and then the rationally guided emotional reduction to reduce the attribute set, and finally performing the emotional reduction on the attribute set with the newly reduced sub-consciousness.

Our next research is to find some efficient algorithms for the rational reduction, emotional reduction, the rationally guided emotional reduction and especially the hierarchical rationally guided emotional reduction.

REFERENCES

1. Z.Pawlak, J.GBusse, R.Slowinski *et al.* Rough sets. Communications of the ACM, 1995, 38 (11) : 89～95.
2. Kryszkiewicz M. Properties of incomplete information systems in the framework of rough sets. In Pollkowski L.,Skowron A.(eds.) Rough Sets in Data Mining and Knowledge Discovery,Physics-Verlag,1998,422-450.
3. Kryszkiewicz M. Rough set approach to incomplete information systems, Information Sciences 112(1998), 39-49.

4. Stefanowski J, Tsoukias A. On the extension of rough sets under incomplete information, On 7th international workshop, RSFDGrC'99 Yamaguchi, Japan, November 9-11, 1999 Proceedings. 73-81.
5. Wang Guoyin, Extension of rough set under incomplete information systems. journal of computer research and development, 39(10)2002, 1238-1243.
6. Wei Huang, Cong Liu, Gang Zhang. Information system based on sub-consciousness and its rough set method. Proceedings of ICMLC2004, Shanghai, China, August 26-29, 2004. To be published by IEEE.

OPTIMAL DESIGN OF CONIC-CYLINDRICAL GEAR REDUCTION UNIT USING FUZZY PHYSICAL PROGRAMMING

Hong-Zhong Huang[1,2], Xu Zhang[1], Zhi-Gang Tian[1] Chun-Sheng Liu[2] and Ying-Kui Gu[1]

[1]*School of Mechanical Engineering, Dalian University of Technology, Dalian, 116023, China*

[2]*Department of Mechanical Engineering, Heilongjiang Institute of Science and Technology, Harbin, 150027, China*

Abstract: Conic-cylindrical gear reduction unit as a high-performance power transmission device is widely used to build various machineries. There are lots of fuzzy factors in its manufacturing process and operation environment, which should be taken into consideration in the design process. Fuzzy physical programming is an effective multiobjective optimization method which incorporates fuzziness in its problem formulation. The fuzzy physical programming model for the optimal design of two-stage conic-cylindrical gear reduction unit is developed in this paper, and genetic algorithm is used to solve the model. An example is given to illustrate that fuzzy physical programming can consider the fuzziness of conic-cylindrical gear reduction unit substantially, and conforms more perfectly to the engineering realities.

Key words: conic-cylindrical gear reduction unit, multiobjective optimization, physical programming, fuzzy physical programming

1. INTRODUCTION

Generally, mechanical design has been taken as the multiobjective problem and the design process is actually an optimizing process, considering multi-restricted conditions. Multiobjective optimization has been applied widely in the field of mechanical design. In recent years, some new algorithms for the multiobjective optimization appear, such as collaborative optimization[1], interactive multi-objective optimization[2], physical programming[3] and VEGA (Vector Evaluated Genetic Algorithm)[4]. These algorithms have characteristics of their own, and have found applications in various engineering practical problems.

There are lots of fuzzy factors in manufacture process and operation environment[5]. The key sources of fuzziness are as follows: the complexity of system's structure and mechanism; the limitation of test conditions; the limitation and subjectivity of human being. Because of the existence of fuzziness, the product performances (weight, price, volume, etc.) are thus fuzzy sets.

Fuzzy physical programming is a new efficient multiobjective optimization method[6], which inherits the advantages of physical programming and considers the fuzziness of multiobjective systems. Fuzzy physical programming can solve fuzzy multiobjective design problems and get the design results considering fuzzy factors by incorporating fuzziness in design variables, objective functions and constraints.

Conic-cylindrical gear reduction unit as a high-performance power transmission system is widely used to make various machineries, and its structure and performance has distinct influence on robust, noise level, bearing capacity and service life of the whole machinery. Currently, there are rare researches in this area. Regarding geometry structure and bearing capacity are as main optimization objectives, and considering the fuzziness of the design variables and objectives substantially, this paper develops the fuzzy physical programming model for optimal design of conic-cylindrical gear reduction unit. Genetic Algorithms is applied to solve the formulated fuzzy physical programming model.

2.   FUZZY PHSICAL PROGRAMMING

2.1   PHSICAL PROGRAMMING

Physical programming is a new effective multicriteria optimization method first brought forward by Achille Messac in 1995[7], which reduces the computational intensity of large problems and places the design process into a more flexible and natural framework. It can capture the designer's physical understanding of the desired design outcomes by forming the aggregate objective function. Designers specify ranges of different degrees of desirability (desirable, tolerance, undesirable, etc.) for each design metric.

Once the designers' preferences are articulated, obtaining the corresponding optimal design is a non-iterative process.

Design objectives are classified into four different categories. Each class comprises two cases, hard and soft, subject to the sharpness of preference. The qualitative meaning of soft preference function is depicted in Figure 1[8]. The value of the objective function, g_i, is on the horizontal axis, and the corresponding preference function, $\bar{g}_i$, is on the vertical axis. No matter which category, the smaller the value of preference functions is, the better it is.

2.2   Mathematical model of fuzzy physical programming[6]

With fuzzy parameters X, the design objective value of fuzzy system, $\tilde{g}_i(X)$, is a fuzzy set. Supposing that $\tilde{g}_i(X)$ is represented using normal membership function, and takes the form

$$\mu_{\tilde{g}_i(x)}(g_i) = e^{-\left[\frac{g_i - g_i(x)}{\delta_i}\right]^2}, \delta_i > 0 \qquad (1)$$

$fp_i(\tilde{g}_i(X))$ is used to represent the preference function with respect to fuzzy set $\tilde{g}_i(X)$. Referring to the definition of satisfying degree function for generalized fuzzy constraint[5], $fp_i(\tilde{g}_i(X))$ takes the form

$$fp_i(\tilde{g}_i(X)) = \frac{\int_{g_i(X)-3\delta_i}^{g_i(X)+3\delta_i} \bar{g}_i(g_i) \cdot \mu_{\tilde{g}_i(X)}(g_i) dg_i}{\int_{g_i(X)-3\delta_i}^{g_i(X)+3\delta_i} \mu_{\tilde{g}_i(X)}(g_i) dg_i} \qquad (2)$$

The fuzzy aggregate objective function, $fp_i(\tilde{g}_i(X))$, is formulated by synthesizing the fuzzy preference functions for all the design metrics

$$fp(X) = \log_{10}\left\{\frac{1}{n_{sc}}\sum_{i=1}^{n_{sc}} fp_i(\tilde{g}_i(X))\right\} \qquad (3)$$

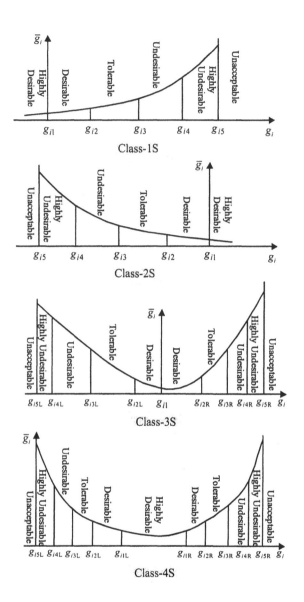

Figure 1. Preference function ranges for *i*th generic metric

With the fuzzy aggregate objective function described above, the fuzzy physical programming problem model takes the following form[6]

$$\min_{X} fp(X) = \log_{10}\left\{\frac{1}{n_{sc}}\sum_{i=1}^{n_{sc}} fp_i(\tilde{g}_i(X))\right\} \qquad \text{(for soft classes)}$$

st. $g_i(X) \le g_{i5}$ (for class 1 - S)

        $g_i(X) \ge g_{i5}$ (for class 2 - S)

        $g_{i5L} \le g_i(X) \le g_{i5R}$ (for class 3 - S and 4 - S)   (4)

        $g_i(X) \le g_{iM}$ (for class 1 - H)

        $g_i(X) \ge g_{im}$ (for class 2 - H)

        $g_{im} \le g_i(X) \le g_{iM}$ (for class 3 - H and 4 - H)

        $x_{jm} \le x_j \le x_{jM}$

where g_{im}, g_{iM}, x_{jm} and x_{jM} represent minimum and maximum values, and n_{sc} is the number of soft design metrics that the problem comprises. The process of formula transforming is similar to that in physical programming problem model[8,9].

2.3   Computational procedure of fuzzy physical programming

The solution to the multiobjective optimization problem using the proposed fuzzy physical programming approach can be determined using the following step-by step procedure.

a) Determine design objectives and design variables.

b) Specify the membership function for each design metric.

c) Specify the class type for each design metric (class 1S-4H).

d) Provide the range limits for each design metric.

e) Form the fuzzy physical programming problem model.

f) Solve the problem model, and obtain the optimal design.

In conventional optimization methods, multiobjective is converted into single objective, which only can obtain local optimum. In this paper, Genetic Algorithms is used in solving the formulated fuzzy physical programming model, and has demonstrated its ability to obtain the global optimum even if there exists local optimums.

3.   EXAMPLE

In the section, the case of two-stage conic-cylindrical gear reduction unit, which is used in chain moving machinery, is studied using fuzzy physical programming approach. A pair of conic gears is used as high-speed gears, while a pair of cylindrical gears is used as the low-speed gears. The performance of fuzzy physical programming is compared with that of physical programming. The objective is to minimize volume and minimize difference of power delivered between high-speed gear and low-speed gear [10, 11].

3.1 Problem formulation

The design vector x is
$$x = [m_1, \psi_R, Z_1, m_2, \psi_a, Z_3, i_1, \beta]$$
where m_i is the module value of the ith gear set, Z_i represents the tooth numbers of the ith pinion, ψ_R is the face width of the conic gear set, ψ_a is the face width of the cylindrical gear set, i_1 represents the gear ratio of the high-speed gear, β is the helix angle. The values of the primary design parameters refer to reference 10.

The objective of the minimum volume of the gear reduction unit takes

$$V = 0.392669 \left[m_1^3 \psi_R Z_1^2 \left(1 - \psi_R + \frac{\psi_R^2}{3} \right)(i + i_1^2) + m_2^3 \psi_a Z_3^3 \left(1 + \frac{i}{i_1} \right)\left(1 + \frac{i^2}{i_1^2} \right)\frac{1}{\cos^3 \beta} \right] \quad (5)$$

where i is the general gear ratio.

The objective of minimum difference of power delivered between high-speed gear and low-speed gear is represented by

$$\Delta P = |P_h - P_l| \quad\quad\quad\quad (6)$$

where

$$P_h = \frac{\psi_R(1 + 0.5\psi_R)^2 i_1 m_1^3 Z_1^3}{Z_E^2 Z_H^2 k} \cdot \frac{n_1 [\sigma]_{HL}^2}{4 \times 9.55 \times 10^6}$$

$$P_l = \frac{\psi_a m_2^3 Z_3^3 i}{k Z_E^2 Z_H^2 Z_\varepsilon^2 i_1^2 \cos^3 \beta} \cdot \frac{n_1 [\sigma]_{HL}^2}{4 \times 9.55 \times 10^6}$$

The mathematical model of the multi-stage gear reduction unit optimization problem is formulated as follows:
minimize V, minimize ΔP

s.t.

$$0 \le i_1 \le 5 \tag{7}$$

$$8\pi/180 \le \beta \le 25\pi/180 \tag{8}$$

$$0.2 \le \psi_R \le 0.33 \tag{9}$$

$$0.4 \le \psi_a \le 0.6 \tag{10}$$

$$Z_1 - 17m_1/\sqrt{1+i_1^2} \ge 0 \tag{11}$$

$$Z_2 - 17\cos^3 \beta \ge 0 \tag{12}$$

$$\frac{1}{2\pi}\left\{\frac{Z_1}{\cos(\tan^{-1}(1/i_1))}\left[\tan\left(\cos^{-1}\frac{Z_1\cos(\pi/9)}{Z_1+2\cos(\tan^{-1}(1/i_1))}\right)\right]+ \right.$$
$$\left.\frac{Z_1 i_1}{\sin(\tan^{-1}(1/i_1))}\left[\tan\left(\cos^{-1}\frac{Z_1 i_1 \cos(\pi/9)}{Z_1 i_1 + 2\sin(\tan^{-1}(1/i_1))}\right)-\tan(\pi/9)\right]\right\}-1.6 \ge 0 \tag{13}$$

$$\left[1.88 - 3.2\left(\frac{1}{Z_3}+\frac{i_1}{iZ_3}\right)\right]\cos^3\beta - 1.3 \ge 0 \tag{14}$$

$$\frac{\psi_a Z_3(1+i/i_1)\sin\beta}{2\pi m_2}-1 \ge 0 \tag{15}$$

$$[\sigma]_{HL}^2 - \frac{4kT_1 Z_E^2 Z_H^2}{\psi_R(1-0.5\psi_R)^2 m_1^3 Z_1^3 i_1} \geq 0 \tag{16}$$

$$1 - \frac{4kT_1 Y_{F_1} Y_{S_1}}{\psi_R(1-0.5\psi_R)^2 m_1^3 Z_1^2 \sqrt{1+i_1^2} [\sigma]_{F_1}} \geq 0 \tag{17}$$

$$1 - \frac{4kT_1 Y_{2_1} Y_{S_2}}{\psi_R(1-0.5\psi_R)^2 m_1^3 Z_1^2 \sqrt{1+i_1^2} [\sigma]_{F_2}} \geq 0 \tag{18}$$

$$1 - \frac{Z_E Z_H Z_\varepsilon}{[\sigma]_{HL}} \sqrt{\frac{2kT_2(2+\psi_R)\cos^3 i_1}{m_2^3 Z_2^3 \psi_R \sqrt{1+i_1^2}} \left(1+\frac{i_1}{i}\right)} \geq 0 \tag{19}$$

$$1 - \frac{2kT_2(2-\psi_R)\cos^3 \beta}{m_2^3 Z_2^3 \psi_R \sqrt{1+i_1^2} [\sigma]_{F_3}} Y_{F_3} Y_{S_3} Y_{\beta_3} Y_{t_3} \geq 0 \tag{20}$$

$$1 - \frac{2kT_2(2-\psi_R)\cos^3 \beta}{m_2^3 Z_2^3 \psi_R \sqrt{1+i_1^2} [\sigma]_{F_4}} Y_{F_4} Y_{S_4} Y_{\beta_4} Y_{t_4} \geq 0 \tag{21}$$

Eq. (7) is the range of the gear ratio, Eq. (8) is the range of the helix angle, Eqs (9)-(10) reflect the face width constraints, Eqs (11)-(12) represent the interference constraints, Eqs (13)-(15) represent the limit of overlap ratio, and Eqs (16)-(21) represent the strength constraints.

3.2   Results and discussions

Subject to the foregone conditions, we can establish the fuzzy physical programming problem model as Eq. (4). Region limits and the parameter δ_i of the design objections are show in Table 1. Genetic algorithms is used to solve the formulated model, and the optimal results are obtained and depicted in Table 2 and 3. The deviation between the result of fuzzy physical

·programming and physical programming is shown in Table 4. Considering the fuzzy factors of the system, the largest deviations of design objective and design variable are 5.9% and 13.2%, respectively. It is obvious that neglecting the fuzzy factors in the system will not lead to true optimal solution.

Table 1 Region limits and the parameter δ_i of the design objections

Design objective	Type of preference function	g_{i5}	g_{i4}	g_{i3}	g_{i2}	g_{i1}		δ_i
$V(m^3)$	1-S	0.020	0.018	0.016	0.014	0.010	-∞	0.0000280
$\Delta P(kW)$	1-S	0.025	0.024	0.022	0.019	0.015	-∞	0.0000420

Table 2 The design variables' value

Design variable	m_1	ψ_R	Z_1	m_2	ψ_a	Z_2	i_1	β
FPP	3.849	0.203	19.817	3.675	0.400	21.379	4.76	0.140602
PP	3.856	0.208	19.923	3.774	0.425	21.220	4.72	0.140855

Table 3. The design objective functions' value

Design objective	$V(m^3)$	$\Delta P(kW)$
FPP	0.0125	0.0175
PP	0.0144	0.0182

Table 4. The deviation between the result of fuzzy physical programming and physical programming (%)

Design variable and Design objective	m_1	ψ_R	Z_1	m_2	ψ_a	Z_2	i_1	β	V	ΔP
Deviation	1.2	2.4	0.5.	2.6	5.9	0.7	5.7	0.2	13.2	3.8

4.   CONCLUSIONS

The fuzzy physical programming model for the optimal design of two-stage conic-cylindrical gear reduction unit is developed in this paper, and genetic algorithm is used to solve the model. Compared with the physical programming approach, fuzzy physical programming is a more reasonable method for complex engineering systems. Combining with genetic algorithms, fuzzy physical programming approach can obtain the global optimum. The example illustrates that fuzzy physical programming can consider the fuzziness of conic-cylindrical gear reduction unit substantially, and conforms more perfectly to the engineering realities.

REFERENCES

1. Tappeta R V, Renaud J E. Multiobjective collaborative optimization. ASME, Journal of Mechanical Design, 1997, 119(9): 403~411
2. Tappeta R V, Renaud J E. Interactive multi-objective optimization design strategy for decision based design. ASME, Journal of Mechanical Design, 2001, 123(6): 205~215
3. Messac A, Gupta S, Akbulut B. Linear physical programming: A new approach to multiple objective optimization. Transactions on Operational Research, 1996, 8: 39~59
4. Tapabrata R, Kang T, Kian C S. Multiobjective design optimization by an evolutionary algorithm. Engineering Optimization, 2001, 33(4): 399~424
5. Huang H-Z. Fuzzy design. Beijing: China Machine Press, 1999
6. Tian Z-G, Huang H-Z, Guan L-W. Fuzzy physical programming and its application in optimization of through passenger train plan. Proceedings of the Conference on Traffic and Transportation Studies, ICTTS, 2002, 1: 498~503
7. Messac A, Hattis P D. High speed civil transport (HSCT) plane design using physical programming. AIAA/ASME/ASCE/AHS Structures, Structural Dynamics & Material Conference – Collection of Technical Papers. 1995, 3: 10~13
8. Messac A. Physical programming: Effective optimization for computational design. AIAA Journal, 1996, 34(1): 149~158
9. Huang H-Z, Tian Z-G, Guan L W. Neural networks based interactive physical programming and its applications in mechanical design. Chinese Journal of Mechanical Engineering, 2002, 38(4): 51~57
10. Wei H, Zhang J-S. The multi-aim optimization design for conic-cylindrical reducer. Journal of Lianyungang College of Chemical Technology, 1999, 12(1): 11~14
11. Huang H-Z. Mechanical fuzzy optimization: Principle and application. Beijing: Science Press, 1997

NLOMJ--NATURAL LANGUAGE OBJECT MODEL IN JAVA

Jiyou Jia(1), Youfu Ye(2), Klaus Mainzer(3)
(1)(3) Institute for Interdisciplinary Informatics, University of Augsburg, Germany
(2) Information Technology Designing & Consulting Institute, China

Abstract: In this paper we present NLOMJ—a natural language object model in Java with English as the experiment language. It describes the grammar elements of any permissible expression in a natural language and their complicated relations with each other with the concept "Object" in OOP. Directly mapped to the syntax and semantics of the natural language, it can be used in information retrieval as a linguistic method. Around the UML diagram of the NLOMJ the important classes (Sentence, Clause and Phrase) and their sub classes are introduced and their syntactic and semantic meanings are explained.

Key words: natural language processing (NLP), object oriented programming (OOP), natural language object model in Java (NLOMJ)

1. BACKGROUND

We have developed an innovative web-based human-computer-interaction system with natural language for foreign language learning: CSIEC (Computer Simulator in Educational Communication) [1]. The kernel of this system is the natural language understanding mechanism (NLML, NLOMJ and NLDB) and the communicational response (CR). NLML (Natural Language Markup Language) is a markup language to describe the grammar of an expression in a natural language. It is produced to an expression of this natural language by a parser written according to the grammar rules and lexicon of this language [2]. We use English as the experiment language in our system.

With the simple structure of the markup language the NLML can be easily parsed by an OOP language to construct the object model of the nodes in the markup language. As for the NLML the nodes are just the grammar elements of the natural language. So we have selected Java, the typical OOP language, to parse the NLML and to represent the grammar elements and their relations with the concept of Object. We call this technique NLOMJ. It enables us to extract the information we need from any permissible expression of a natural language, hence can be used as a linguistic method in intelligent information processing.

The UML diagram for the whole NLOMJ is shown in figure 1. In the following paragraphs we introduce the content of NLOMJ around this diagram in the order of sentence, clause and phrase very structurally.

2.   SENTENCES

2.1   Super class "Sentence" and Interface "Sentence_operation"

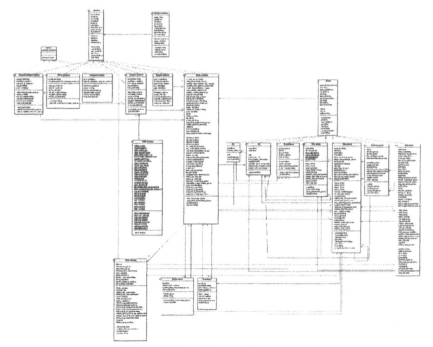

Figure 1. UML diagram for NLOMJ

All sentences with diverse complexity, tense, mood and voice must have at least one subject and one verb phrase. So we use the class "Sentence" to generalize the common features of the sentences. Because there are great structure differences for the sentences with different complexity, the compound complex sentence, compound sentence, complex sentence and simple sentence are all treated as the subclass of the class "Sentence".

The attributes in the super class "Sentence" include "mood", "input", etc, which are all with the type "String". The "mood" represents the mood of the sentence therefore may have one of the values--"statement", "question", "order", etc. The attribute "input" is the input from the user, whereas the "text" is inferred by the parser from the "input" and other attributes. So the "input" does not always equal the "text". The "nlml" is the parsing result in NLML format. The "description" is the syntactic and semantic description of the "text".

In order to get the object model from the NLMLs a method for the parsing of the NLML should be implemented in every subclass of the "sentence". So an Interface "Sentence_operation" is written with only this method "parse_nlml".

2.2   Sentences with different complexity

The "Compound_complex_sentence" consists of a subordinate "Simple_ sentence" and an "And_or_sentence". The attribute "subordinator" with the type "String", the "sub" with the type "Simple_sentence", and the "main" with the type "And_or_sentence" represent the subordinator, the subordinate sentence, and the main sentence, respectively. The key is the semantic decomposition of the compound complex sentence into simple sentences, e.g. the compound complex sentence with the conjunction "and" connecting N main clauses can be decomposed into N complex sentences, each of which has the same subordinate clause.

The "And_or_sentence" consists of a coordinator ("and", or "or") represented by the attribute "coordinator" and several instances of the class "Complete_sentence" represented by the array "complete_sentences".

The "Complete_sentence" consists of a subordinator, a subordinate clause and a main sentence represented by the attribute "subordinator", by the sub" with the type "Simple_sentence", and by the "main" with the type "Simple_sentence", respectively. If the subordinator of an instance is null, the "sub" is meaningless, and this instance is essentially the same as an instance of "Simple_sentence". The array "complete_sentences" in the class "Complex_compound_sentence" and the "Compound_sentence" uses this special case. But if either the "subordinator" or the "sub" is null, this instance is the same as an instance of the class "Complex_sentence". In other words the "Complete_sentence" is either a "Complex_sentence" or a "Simple_sentence". It does not exist in the real language, however is useful to describe the personality of the "chatting robot" in the "CSIEC" project, as some personalities can be stated by simple statement sentences as the facts, whereas others are states or behaviors happening only with some conditions, which should be represented by the "Complex_sentence".

The "Compound_sentence" consists of the conjunctions represented by the attribute "coordinator" and several complete sentences represented by the array "complete_sentences".

The "Complex_sentence" consists of a subordinator, a subordinate clause and a main sentence. Here the subordinator can not be null.

Summarily the simple sentence is the most elementary sentence and the end point of the parsing of all sentences with different complexities.

2.3   Simple sentence

This kind of sentence has at least one verb phrase. It may contain relative clause and noun clause which contain also verb phrases. So we deal with them at first, i.e., search the tag "noun_clause" and "relative_clause" and replace their contents with a noun phrase and a preposition phrase, respectively, then parse every noun clause and relative clause, and save them in the arrays. In the UML diagram the blue arrow with the number "0...." from the class "Simple_sentence" to the "Noun_clause" and to the "Relative_clause" indicates this relation.

We should think over the parsing with different moods. For example, if the mood is "np", "what terse exclamation", or "about", the sentence treats essentially one noun phrase, therefore can be parsed as a noun phrase. The attribute "np" in the class "Simple_sentence" stands for it.

The sentence may have several subjects. They are all represented by instances of the class "Noun_phrase" and saved in the array "subjects". In order sentences and some clauses like infinitive, gerund, etc, there may be a negative phrase like "don't", "not". So it should be parsed firstly via the tag "neg". Finally we get the verb phrase via the tag "verb_phrase". If the content of the tag "verb_phrase_connector" is null, there is only one verb phrase; otherwise there are several which can be sequentially got via the tags "verb_phrase_part". They are put into the array "verb_phrases".

The key point is how to combine these subjects, verb phrases and circumstances. The conjunction connecting the noun parts and the conjunction connecting the verb phrases are: "and", "or", "neither...nor". It is common that either the subject or the verb phrase is made up of several parts, e.g., N parts. In this case this simple sentence can be decomposed into N basic sentences. If the conjunction is "and", these N basic sentences are independent; if it is "or", the relation among these basic sentences is single choice; if it is "neither_nor", we can form N independent basic sentences through negative operation. The circumstances are suitable for every basic sentence.

The method in the "Simple_sentence", "contruct_basic_sentences()", implements this operation of combination. Then the basic sentences are stored into the two dimensional array "basic_sentences". The values of the attribute "text" and "description" are also calculated according to the "mood" and the element values of "basic_sentences". The concept "basic sentence" used here represents the sentence with no more than one subject phrase and one verb phrase. It is represented by the class "Basic_sentence", which is just a subclass of the class "Sentence", as its instance is not formed by parsing the NLML, but constructed by the given subject phrase, verb phrase, and other parameters.

3.   CLAUSES

In NLOMJ the relative clause and noun clause are defined as subclass of the "Simple_sentence", for they either are full simple sentences or can be extended to semantically equal simple sentences. The attributes and operations in the "Simple_sentence", such as "text", "subjects", "verb_phrases", "construct_basic_sentences", etc, can be still applied in the two subclasses. Additionally some special attributes and operations are needed.

3.1   Noun clause

There are several types of noun clauses:

"that", "whether", "whether or not": the noun clause consists of a preceding word and then a simple statement sentence without noun clause. The "implied_text" equals the "text".

"query clause": the implied text is a question and can be obtained with the same method as that used in obtaining the "text" in the Basic_sentence with the mood "question". The key is how to get the auxiliary verb and the other parts in the verb phrase, which is realized in the class "Verb_phrase".

"query_to": in this type there is no subject, so it is more difficult to infer the implied question. If the noun clause is the subject of the main sentence, this question may be suitable to all people. In this situation we assign "*a person*" as the subject of the question. If the noun clause is the object in the main sentence or the object in a prepositional phrase, we can assign the subject in the main sentence as the subject of the noun clause.

"normal_to": there is also no subject in the noun clause. If this type of infinitive appears as the object of some special verbs, which are shown in the various construction forms of the verb phrase, we don't have to obtain the implied statement with great efforts, because the subject of the infinitive clause is the same as the subject in the main sentence and the whole verb phrase including both the main verb word and the infinitive clause expresses a mental state of the subject and the semantics can not be expressed by the main verb word or the infinitive clause alone.

3.2   Relative clause

The relative clause is a full relative clause if it has a subject; otherwise it is a terse relative clause, whose actual subject is evidently the noun phrase it modifies. The full relative clause starts with a query word (if there is none it is "which") which points to the modified noun phrase in front of it. So we can infer the implied statement sentence by two steps: firstly get the statement sentence with the query noun phrase in the way we use in the noun clause, secondly replace the query word with the modified noun phrase.

For the terse sentence it is difficult to set the tense of the implied statement sentence. If it is the present participle, the implied statement sentence may have the tense "progressive". If it is the past participle, the implied statement sentence may have the tense perfect or past. This character is labeled by the tag "voice" with the value "passive". If it is passive infinitive clause, we can set the tense with the value "future" or use the model verb "should".

4.   PHRASES

4.1   Super class "Phrase"

The sentence consists of various phrases, so at the end of the parsing of the sentences comes the parsing of the phrases. On other side the phrase exists in the sentence and has its syntax und semantic function in the context of its existing sentence. The super class "Phrase" in NLOMJ represents its common feathers. Its attributes include the "nlml", "text", and "description" which are similar with those in the class "Sentence". Besides it has also the following ones: the "parent" with the type "Simple_sentence" representing the simple sentence where this phrase exists; the "part_connector" with the type "String" representing the conjunction word if this phrase consists of several parts; the "kernel" with the type "String" representing the kernel word in the phrase; etc.

Every subclass of the "Phrase" has some special attributes and its own method "parse_nlml()" to parse the "nlml" in order to form an instance of this subclass. Now we introduce the subclasses of the "Phrase".

4.2   Adverb

The class "Adv" represents the adverb and has two attributes: "grad" and "np". The string "grad" represents the grad of the adverb and is obtained via the tag "grad", i.e. "abso" (absolute), "comp" (comparative), or "supl" (superlative). The "np" with the type "Noun_phrase" is obtained through the parsing of the other parts in the NLML, if the type of this adverb is "so_that", "so_as", "enough_to", "too_to", or "adv_than", because these types of sentences express the result or the extent of the adverb with a compared noun phrase, a statement sentence or a noun clause (infinitive clause), all of which can be parsed with the class "Noun_phrase".

4.3   Adjective

The class "Adj" represents the adjective. It has two attributes: "grad" and "advs". The "grad" is similar with that in "Adv". The array "advs", whose elements are instances of the class "Adv", represents the adverbs modifying it.

4.4   Circumstance

The class "Circumstance" represents the circumstance. It can be adverb, prepositional phrase or noun clause (infinitive clause or participle clause), what is decided by the attribute "type". Its attribute "position" represents the position of the circumstance in the sentence: pre, mid or post, and the "attribute" represents its semantic function in the whole sentence: place, time, way, and others.

4.5   Prepositional phrase

The class "Prep_phrase" represents the prepositional phrase. It has the attribute "prep" with the type "String" representing the preposition word and the attribute "np" with the type "Noun_phrase" representing its object.

4.6   Noun phrase

The "Noun_phrase" represents the noun phrase and has many special attributes such as "personality", "number", "case", etc. It may have several parts connected by conjunction and every part can be in the normal form: pre modifiers + kernel + post modifiers. The kernel can have different types, like "countable noun", "number", etc, what is decided by the attribute "type". The pre modifiers can be adjective, article, determiner, quantifier, etc. The post modifier can be prepositional phrase or relative clause. The noun clause as a noun phrase is specially considered.

4.7   Predicate phrase

The "Predicate_phrase" represents the predicate which may be adjective, noun phrase or prepositional phrase, what is encoded in the attribute "type". For the adjective a noun phrase or noun clause can be attached by "as...as", "than", "too...to", "enough...to", or "so...that" to express the compared object, the extent or the result of the adjective.

4.8   Verb phrase

The class "Verb_phrase" represents the verb phrase and is the most important and complicated phrase in constructing a sentence and may consist of all other types of phrases. It describes the actions or the states of the subject, or the subject's relation with other things or persons which can be described by direct and (or) indirect objects represented by the two instances of "Noun_phrase" ("direct_object" and "indirect_object"), or predicates represented by the instances of "Predicate_phrase" ("predicate"). The concrete pattern of the verb phrase is decided by the attribute "verb_type". In the parsing firstly the verbal attributes are obtained, such as "personality", "number", "voice", "tense", "kernel_tense", "verb_type", etc. Then the other parts in the verb phrase are obtained corresponding to the "verb_type". At last the verb words are obtained successively.

REFERENCES

1.   Jia, J. CSIEC (Computer Simulator in Educational Communication): An Intelligent Web-Based Teaching System for Foreign Language Learning. In Proceedings of ED-MEDIA04 (17th World Conference on Educational Multimedia, Hypermedia and Telecommunications), P. 4147-4154.

2. Jia, J. NLML--a Markup Language to Describe the Unlimited English Grammar. Submitted to German conference for artificial intelligence 2004. Also available at http://arxiv.org/abs/cs.CL/0404018.

FINGERPRINT RIDGE LINE RECONSTRUCTION
Using Sampling-based Tracing Method

Yaxuan Qi

Department of Automation , Singh University , Beijing China, 100084 , qiyx98@mails.tsinghua.edu.cn

Abstract: Reconstruction of fingerprint ridge lines is a critical pre-processing step in the identification of poor quality fingerprint images. This paper presents a new fingerprint ridge line reconstruction approach by way of ridge line tracing. In our research, the fingerprint ridge line in a gray scale image is viewed as a track of a ridge segment moving along the ridge. The curve tracing problem is solved by the target tracking technique in computer vision. We first formulate the model of fingerprint ridge line segments and then apply a target tracking method to trace each of the ridge lines. In addition, a feedback technique is adopted to correct the fingerprint directional image in each tracing step in order to improve tracing accuracy. By connecting all the traced ridge line segments, a polyline reconstruction of the ridge line can be obtained. We objectively assess the performance of this approach by using NIST fingerprint images.

Key words: sampling, fingerprint, reconstruction.

1. INTODUCTION

Because of the uniqueness and immutability, fingerprint identification is adopted in many highly reliable automatic authentication systems. Fingerprints in a gray scale image appear to be ridges and ravines. The uniqueness of fingerprint identification is mainly determined by the ridge structure characteristics and their correlation [3]. The most prominent ridge characteristics, called minutiae, are ridge bifurcations and ridge endings.

In fingerprint identification, minutiae are taken as discriminating and reliable fingerprint features. Most fingerprint identification or verification systems are so far based on fingerprint minutiae matching. Various approaches to automatic minutiae detection have been proposed. Most of these approaches consist of a series of processing steps:
- Getting ridge line structure;
- Binarization and thinning;
- Minutiae extraction.

Since the last two steps may produce false minutiae without clear ridge line structure, the first step becomes much more important. Our research focuses on the problem of how to obtain clear and reliable ridge line structures. In this paper we present a new approach to reconstruct fingerprint ridges through ridge line tracing.

The difficulty of ridge line structure reconstruction lies in the fact that the quality of the input fingerprint image is usually poor. Noise, deformation and contrast deficiency may produce false ridge line structures. Therefore, it is considerably difficult to achieve reliable fingerprint ridge line structures from poor quality images. This problem has been thoroughly studied but not yet completely solved.

In the published literatures, most approaches to obtain ridge line structures are based on two different techniques: One technique first enhances the ridge line structure by applying filtering approach to the original images and then obtain ridge lines through binarization and thinning process. The other technique extracts ridge lines directly from gray scale images. O'Gorman and Nickerson proposed an enhancement technique based on the convolution of the image with a filter oriented according to the directional image [2]. Hong Lin and A.K. Jain presented a formula that Gabor function is used in fingerprint enhancement, taking fingerprint ridge orientation and ridge frequency as filtering parameters [3]. In addition, M. T. Leung introduced a neural network based approach to minutiae detection by employing a multilayer perception in analyzing the output of a rank of Gabor's filters applied to the gray scale image [5]. To binarize the fingerprint image, several thresholding methods, local thresholding for instance, have been proposed. Moayer and Fu presented a binarization technique based on the iterative application of a Laplacian operator and a dynamic threshold [6]. Some thinning algorithms have been studied in order to obtain a skeleton of the fingerprint ridge lines. These methods are listed in the Reference section of this paper [7] [8]. Instead of using a conventional thinning method Weber proposed an algorithm which detects the minutiae starting from the thick-ridges in the binary image [9].

Though some of the techniques presented so far provide good results by producing high-quality fingerprint images, they are sometimes either inaccurate or not robust enough for poor quality images. The poor performance of these methods when inputting low quality fingerprint images is due to the following reasons. Firstly, filtering techniques rely on global data such as ridge line direction and ridge line frequency. These data are obtained area by area in fingerprint images and fail to provide enough local information of fingerprint ridge line structures. Secondly, a lot of data are lost during binarization processes, especially when applied to poor quality images.

Maio and Maltoni proposed a new approach in their resent work to detect minutiae directly from the gray scale fingerprint images [4]. The method does not follow the binarization and thinning steps. The principle of their method is to trace the ridge lines on the gray scale image by "sailing" in accordance with the fingerprint directional image. Their results are far superior in terms of efficiency and robustness to the conventional thresholding and thinning approaches. However, the method is still limited in the following two aspects. On one hand, it still depends on the accuracy of the directional image. In practice, it is difficult to obtain precise ridge direction from low quality images. On the other hand, the approach adopts a symmetric gauss silhouetted mask to do convolution with lines of pixels on the ridge and orthogonal to the ridge line direction. Because convolution can change the local gray scale distribution, the ridge line structures may thus be deformed in some area of fingerprint images.

This paper presents a new ridge line reconstruction approach through ridge line tracing. In our study, each ridge line in the input fingerprint image is treated as a track of a ridge segment moving along the ridge line. Within the framework of tracking technique in computer vision, a sampling-based tracing method is applied to the fingerprint ridge line reconstruction. We first formulate a ridge line model and then use a sampling method to trace each ridge line piecewise. The approach does not change any of the original fingerprint gray scale images so as to exploit more useful information directly from the original image. In addition, a feedback technique for directional image is employed in this study. To obtain more accurate ridge line structure information, the directional image after each tracing step is adjusted in accordance with the ridge line has been traced.

The rest of the paper is organized as follows: In Section 2, we built the ridge line model for sampling-based ridge line tracing. Section 3 is devoted to the feedback technique applied to the directional image. Experimental results are reported in Section 4 and conclusions are outlined in Section 5 of the paper.

2.   RIDGE LINE MODELLING

Let I be an $a*b$ gray scale image with 0 to $g-1$ gray levels, and $G(i,j)$ be the gray level of pixel (i,j) of I, $i=1,...,a, j=1,...,b$. Let $z=G(i,j)$ be the discrete surface corresponding to the image I. By associating the dark pixels with the gray levels near $g-1$ and the bright pixels with the gray levels near zero, the fingerprint ridge lines correspond to the surface ridges and the spaces between the ridge lines correspond to the surface ravines (Fig. 1).

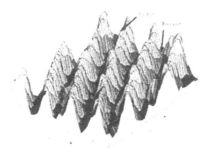

Figure 1. A surfaces corresponding to a small area of a fingerprint gray scale image. Fingerprint ridges and ravines are shown.

At each ridge line tracing step, our algorithm attempts to locate a point representing the local ridge line segment in a section along the ridge line direction. By connecting all the traced points, a polyline approximation of the ridge line can be obtained.

Both the structure and the distribution of ridge lines in fingerprint images have some specific characteristics. Out of these characteristics, there are two main aspects:

-   *Continuity.* Each of the fingerprint ridge lines distributes continuously, i.e., the directions of a series of ridge line segments do not change abruptly;
-   *Correlation.* The neighboring fingerprint ridge lines have some strong correlation. For example, if a ridge line has an up-left direction in a certain area; its neighboring ridge lines in a near area follow the same direction.

Starting from these two characteristics, we take the ridge line as a track of a ridge segment moving from one end of the ridge line to the other. Based on such a tracking technique in computer vision, we adopt sampling-based tracking technique to trace the fingerprint ridge line. In order to apply the tracking technique to static fingerprint images, a dynamic model is built for the ridge line tracing problem. The following part of this section illustrates the proposed ridge line tracing model as compared with the general dynamic model for target tracking.

2.1   Formulation of Ridge Line Tracing Problem

In the framework target tracking (see [10]), the target state at time t is denoted by X_t. The task of tracking is to infer X_{t+1} based on both the last state X_t and the observed image evidence Y_{t+1}, where Y_t is the image measurement at time t, i.e., to estimate $p(X_{t+1} | Y_{t+1}, X_t)$. Such a probabilistic dynamic system can be depicted graphically by Fig. 2.

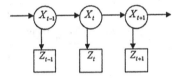

Figure 2. Relationship between target state X_t and image observation Y_t

In the fingerprint ridge line tracing problem, the moving target in visual tracking is taken as a segment on the ridge line. The segment is represented by its center point at $P_t = (i_t, j_t)$ which is the coordinates of the center point in the fingerprint image. Target state X_t is defined as the ridge line direction D_t at point P_t and the observation Y_t is defined as the gray level distribution Z_t in a certain area centered at point P_t. Their relations are shown in Fig. 3.

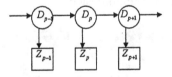

Figure 3. Relationship between ridge line direction D_t and fingerprint image observation Z_t

The key problem is the estimation of D_{t+1} given Z_{t+1} and D_t. The expectation of D_{t+1} over $p(D_{t+1} | Z_{t+1}, D_t)$ is:

$$E(D_{t+1} \mid Z_{t+1}, D_t)$$

$$= \int D_{t+1} p(D_{t+1} \mid Z_{t+1}, D_t)$$

$$= \int D_{t+1} p(D_{t+1}, D_t \mid Z_{t+1}) p(D_{t+1} \mid D_t) \qquad (1)$$

$$= \int D_{t+1} p(D_{t+1} \mid Z_{t+1}) p(D_{t+1} \mid D_t)$$

2.2   Sampling

If we have N i.i.d samples $D_{t+1}^{(i)}$ ($i = 1, ..., N$) and associate each sample with a weight $w(D_{t+1}^{(i)}) \propto p(D_{t+1} \mid Z_{t+1}) p(D_{t+1} \mid D_t)$ then, by Monte Carlo simulation,

$$E(D_{t+1} \mid Z_{t+1}, D_t) = \sum_{i=1}^{N} \tilde{w}^{(i)} D_{t+1}^{(i)} \qquad (2)$$

Where

$$\tilde{w}^{(i)} = \frac{w(D_{t+1}^{(i)})}{\sum_{j=1}^{N} w(D_{t+1}^{(j)})} \qquad (3)$$

Direction samples $D_{t+1}^{(i)}$ ($i = 1, ..., N$) are formed by point samples $P_{t+1}^{(i)}$ ($i = 1, ..., N$) and the starting point P_t. Since ridge line points can be defined as a sequence of maximum and saddle points in fingerprint gray scale image $imgD$ [11], samples of $P_{t+1}^{(i)}$ are all local maximum and saddle points in area A_t. Here A_t is a searching area defined as a circular sector with radius r and is oriented to the direction of D_t. The central angle of A_t is $\pi/2$. Fig. 4 is an illustration of the sampling step.

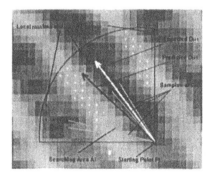

Figure 4. Search for the samples of $P_{t+1}^{(i)}$ in area A_t.

For computation convenience, $p(D_{t+1} | D_t)$ is set to be a uniform distribution. Thus the weight for each sample point is in direct proportion to $p(D_{t+1} | Z_{t+1})$. The weight $w(D_{t+1}^{(i)})$ is then obtained from the following three aspects:

- Let $D_{t+1}^{(i)}$ be the direction defined by the starting point P_t and sample point $P_{t+1}^{(i)}$. Then from P_t to $P_{t+1}^{(i)}$, a rectangle is established. The average gray level within this rectangle is recorded by $G^{(i)}$;
- The variance of the gray level within this rectangle is recorded by $V^{(i)}$;
- The variance of the gray level within this rectangle is recorded by $V^{(i)}$. There is an included angle between $D_{t+1}^{(i)}$ and D_t for each sample point. This angle is recorded by.

Thus the weight is computed by

$$w(D_{t+1}^{(i)}) = w(P_{t+1}^{(i)}) = \exp(-K(g - G^{(i)})V^{(i)}I^{(i)}) \quad (4)$$

Where K is a constant through 10 to 100. By applying Equ.2 and 3, we obtain the expected tracing direction D_{t+1} along which the starting point D_t is to be moved to the next point P_{t+1} with μ pixels (in the proposed algorithm, μ is set to be 5 to 8 pixels).

3. DIRECTION FEEDBACK AND STOP CRITERIA

3.1 Direction Feedback

Once the ridge line tracing direction is obtained, the directional image can be corrected in accordance with it. Because of the continuity and correlation of fingerprint ridge lines, the directions in area A_t around point P_t are similar to a certain extent. Therefore, the feedback of the included angle convoluted with a 2D gauss mask can be used to correct the directions in area A_t. Precision of the directional image is thus increased with the feedback of the local ridge line information.

3.2 Stop criteria

The stop criteria are some events which stop the ridge line tracing, including:
- Exit from the interested area. The new point P_{t+1} is external to a rectangular window representing the sub-image whose ridge lines are to be traced;
- Termination. The searching area A_t is lack of local maxima as compared with the number of local minima. According to this criterion the ridge line tracing stops independently on the gray level of the current region,

and the algorithm can work on both saturated regions and contrast-deficient regions without particular enhancement;
-   Intersection. The next starting point P_{l+1} has been previously labeled as a point belonging to another ridge line.

As an overview of the approach, Figure 5 is a flowchart of the fingerprint ridge line tracing algorithm.

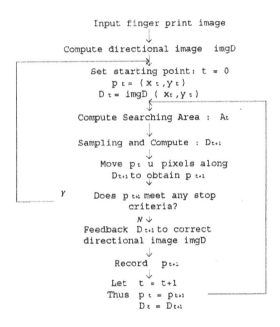

Figure 5. The flowchart of the ridge line tracing algorithm.

4.   RESULTS AND PERFORMANCE ANALYSIS

The aim of this section is to demonstrate the experimental results of the proposed ridge line tracing approach. We objectively assess the performance of this approach by using NIST fingerprint images. Figure 6(a) is a high quality fingerprint image, and the result of ridge line reconstruction is shown in Figure 6(b). For poor quality image, such as the one shown in Figure 7(a), the proposed ridge line reconstruction algorithm can also provide clear and accurate ridge line structures (see Figure 7(b)).

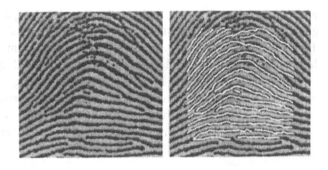

(a)   (b)

Figure 6. (a)A NIST fingerprint image of high quality. (b) The ridge line reconstruction result.
The ridge structures are shown in (b) by bright polylines.

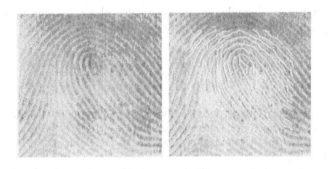

(a)   (b)

Figure 7. (a) A NIST fingerprint image of poor quality. (b) The ridge line reconstruction
result. The ridge structures are shown in (b) by bright polylines.

5.   CONCLUSION AND FUTURE WORK

We have described a sampling-based method to reconstruct the
fingerprint ridge lines regardless of fingerprint image noise, contrast
deficiency and effects of lighting conditions. Our approach fits the target
tracking techniques widely used in computer vision in estimating the tracing
direction of fingerprint ridge lines. A prominent advantage of the proposed
approach is that, in order to obtain more accurate result, we just focus on
how to give a more precise ridge line model without changing the
framework of the approach.

The contribution of this study can be summarized as follows. Firstly, we
introduce a sampling approach for tracing lines directly in a gray scale image,
depending on the continuity and correlation of the lines. This is considerably
different from the tracing method in computer vision where series of images
are required. Secondly, we use a feedback technique to make the directional

image more accurate in local areas. Both of these two techniques can be adopted to general continuous curve tracing problems in static images.

One of the goals in our future study is to solve the print-to-print matching problem. The resulting ridge line structures can be directly used to address the minutiae detection problem for fingerprint matching. Another consideration in our future work is to generate fingerprint representations normalized with respect to scale and rotation. Such representations are to be worked out to avoid rotating fingerprint images and to match fingerprints among all possible orientations in print-to-print matching.

ACKNOWLEDGEMENTS

We gratefully acknowledge our many useful discussions with Prof. Qi from Hainan M.C. and Dr. Ma from National AI Laboratory.

REFERENCES

1. Xudong Jiang, Wei-Yun Yau, Wee Ser: Detecting the Fingerprint Minutiae by Adaptive Tracing the Gray-level Ridge, Pattern Recognition 34 (2001) 999-1013
2. L. O'Gorman, J.V. Nickerson: An Approach to Fingerprint Filter Design, Pattern Recognition 22 (1989) 29
3. L. Hong, Y. Wan, A.K. Jain: Fingerprint Image Enhancement: Algorithm and Performance Evaluation, IEEE Trans. Pattern Anal. Mach. Intell. 20 (1998) 777
4. D. Maio, D. Maltoni: Direct Gray-scale Minutiae Detection in Fingerprints, IEEE Trans. Pattern Anal. Mach. Intell. 19
5. M. T. Leung, W. E. Engeler, and P. Frank: Fingerprint Image Processing Using Neural Networks, Proc. Tenth Conf. Computer and Communication System, pp. 582-586, Hong Kong, 1990
6. B. Moayer, K. Fu: A Tree System Approach for Fingerprint Pattern Recognition, IEEE Trans. Pattern Anal. Mach. Intell. 8 (1986) 376
7. R. Stefanelli, A. Rosenfeld: Some Parallel Thinning Algorithms for Digital Pictures, J. ACM 18 (1971) 255
8. C. Arcelli, G.S.D. Baja: A Width Independent Fast Thinning Algorithm, IEEE Trans. Pattern Anal. Mach. Intell. 7 (1984) 463
10. Michael Isard and Andrew Blake: Contour Tracking by Stochastic Propagation of Conditional Density. In Proc. of European Conf. on Computer Vision, Cambridge, UK, 1996
11. Carlotta Domeniconi, Sibel Tari, Ping Liang:Direct Gray Scale Ridge Reconstruction in Fingerprint Images. 1997

DESIGN AND IMPLEMENTATION OF AUTOMATED DATA MINING USING INTELLIGENT AGENTS IN OBJECT ORIENTED DATABASES

V. Saravanan [1] and Dr. K. Vivekanandan [2]

1.Dept of Computer Science & Engineering, Bharathiar University, Coimbatore – 641 046, INDIA, tvsaran@hotmail.com

2.School of Management, Bharathiar University, Coimbatore – 641 046, INDIA,

vivek1958@hotmail.com

Abstract: Data Mining is the process of posing queries and extracting useful information, patterns and trends previously unknown from large quantities of data. Agents are defined as software entities that perform some set of tasks on behalf of users with some degree of autonomy. This research work deals about developing a automated data mining system which encompasses the familiar data mining algorithms using intelligent agents in object oriented databases and proposing a framework. Because the data mining system uses the intelligent agents, a new user will be able to interact with the data mining system without much data mining technical knowledge. This system will automatically select the appropriate data mining technique and select the necessary fields needed from the database in a right time without expecting the users to specify the specific technique and the parameters. Also a new framework is proposed for incorporating intelligent agents with automated data mining. One of the major goals in developing this system is to give the control to the computer for learning automatically by using intelligent agents for the exploratory data mining.

Key words: Data Mining, Cluster analysis, Intelligent agents

1.   1. INTRODUCTION

Data Mining is the process of posing queries and extracting useful information, patterns and trends previously unknown from large quantities of data [Thu, 00]. It is the process where intelligent tools are applied in order to extract data patterns   [JM, 01]. This encompasses a number of different technical approaches, such as cluster analysis, learning classification and association rules, and finding dependencies. Agents are defined as software entities that perform some set of tasks on behalf of users with some degree of autonomy. This research work deals about developing a automated data mining system which encompasses the familiar data mining algorithms using intelligent agents in object oriented databases and proposing a framework. Because the data mining system uses the intelligent agents, a new user will be able to interact with the data mining system without much data mining technical knowledge. This system will automatically select the appropriate data mining technique and select the necessary field needed from the database at the appropriate time without expecting the users to specify the specific technique and the parameters. Also a new framework is proposed for incorporating intelligent agents with automated data mining. One of the major goals in developing this system is to give the control to the computer for learning automatically by using *intelligent agents.*

2.   REVIEW OF LITERATURE

How the data mining systems uses right algorithms and correct data types for the data anlaysis is the big issues in the data mining [Thu, 00]. Many familiar data mining systems are also analysed in this research project. This includes DBMINER 2.0, Polyanalyst, Miner3D, Knowledge Miner etc.,. Even though all these systems supports for the data mining techniques like Finding dependencies, Cluster analysis and Classification analysis, it is the user who has to select the appropriate parameters for performing data analysis. As given in [LJLL, 01], an intelligent data mining system was developed in the Hong Knog Polytechnic University for a dispersed manufactured network. It works like other data mining systems for performing data analysis. It also doesn't have an integrated and automated approach with it.

Also most of the data mining systems are application dependent, no data mining system has the facility of selecting the parameters automatically from the given database for the given problem domain. By taken these points in view the new system has been proposed.

3.   NEED OF THE PROPOSED SYSTEM

The concept of domain knowledge is very important in data mining. In order to get the correct knowledge from the data mining system, the user must define the objective and specify the algorithms and its parameters exactly. If the data mining system produces large number of meaningful information by using a specialized data mining algorithm, it will take more time for the end-users to choose the appropriate knowledge. In some cases, even choosing the correct data mining algorithm involves more time and the domain knowledge. This proposed system deals about using intelligent agent based approach in solving data mining problems. If the user is using the system frequently the previous results also will be prompted when he enters in the system next time. Since the new system selects the algorithm and the parameter automatically, the user can perform different types of data analysis without wasting much time. Also the new system uses Intelligent agents, selecting the appropriate parameter for the given problem domain will be done by the system itself.

4.   USING INTELLIGENT AGENTS

Agents, special types of software applications, have become a very popular paradigm in computing in recent years. Some of the reasons for this popularity are their flexibility, modularity and general applicability to a wide range of problems. With the explosive growth of information source available on the Internet, and on the business, government, and scientific databases, it has become increasingly necessary for the users to utilize automated and intelligent tools to extract knowledge from them [Ays, 99]. Intelligent agents are an emerging technology that is making computer systems easier to use by allowing people to delegate work back to the computer. They help do things like find and filter information, customize views of information, and automate work. An Intelligent agent is software that assists people and acts on their behalf. Intelligent agents work by allowing people to delegate work that they could have done, to the agent software. [Gil, 97]

Using Intelligent Agents in data mining is quite interesting and also it will automate the process. Also automating the entire process may not be viable solution [AST, 00]. Because of the incorporation of multiple technologies to discover the knowledge, the new users will be able to interact with the system more efficiently. In this research work the following points are incorporated. Certain parameters like, user name, the database name, field name, type of algorithm used are also stored in data base with the knowledge component. If the user is using the system many times for data analysis, the intelligent agent will choose the resultant database for giving the knowledge back to the users without mining one more time. Also, the featured system will prompt the results given to the user during the previous time. Whenever an update occurs, the intelligent agent program will caution the user and if the need arises, it will analyze only the updated part.

5.   ALGORITHMS USED

The following recent data mining algorithms were used in this research work to design and implement the automated data mining using intelligent agents in object oriented databases
   a)   Association Algorithms (APriori Algorithm, FP-Tree Growth Algorithm, Border Algorithm)
   b)   Clustering Algorithms (BIRCH Algorithm, CURE Algorithm, CACTUS Algorithm)
   c)   Classification Algorithms (K-Means / K-Medoid Algorithm, C4.5 Algorithm, CHAID Algorithm)
The new system uses any one of the above techniques to perform data analysis. If the user is using an algorithm initially, he/she may go for choosing another algorithm with different paameters also in the next time to get better / accurate results. As the preliminary step in the research, only few algorithms are considered for the development and implementation of the system. Many algorithms will be added in the future.

6.   DATABASE USED

For implementing the above system a object data warehouse has been taken which has 1,50,000 records. The structure of the database is as follows
   "Age,   Work-class,   education,   education-number,   marital-status, occupation, relationship, race, sex, hours-per-week, native country, Income"
The above object database is used to input to any one of the algorithms specified in the section vi. If the need arises the same database can be used with the different algorithm and parameters for performing sophisticated data analysis. From the above defined database, the associations between age and workclass, age and education, marital status and occupation, marital status and hours per week and many more can be analysed by using the

different techniques available. The other data mining techniques can also be used to perform the same with different parameters.

Object that share a common set of properties can be grouped into an object class. Each object is an instance of its class. Object classes can be organized into class / subclass hierarchies so that each class represents properties that are common to objects in that class. Object oriented databases are becoming increasingly popular in industry and applications. [JM, 01]. Because of this features the new system uses the object oriented concept.

7.   FRAMEWORK OF THE NEW SYSTEM

The framework of the newly developed system is represented diagrammatically as follows. The automated data mining system gets the input from the given database (after the cleaning). Apart from getting the data alone, it gets the other information like, user information, and metadata. If the user is repeating the task, the new system will get the input from the storage also. Intelligent agent is used in the system to select the data mining technique and to get back the results from the storage. If the need arises, visualization tools may also be applied with the resultant database for pattern analysis.

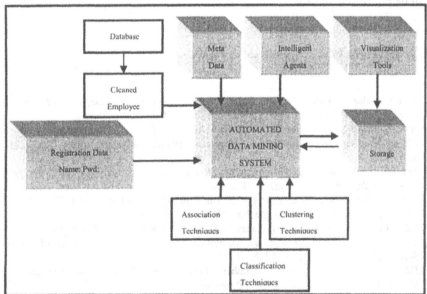

Figure 1: Framework of the newly developed automated data mining system

8.   PERFORMANCE EVALUATION

The user needs only minimum time to perform the analysis in the newly developed system because of the using automated approach and intelligent agents. This in turn improves the overall efficiency of the system. Also the results produced by the new system will be better than the results produced by the existing system. The Prototype development of the proposed system is on the way using Visual Basic. The database is available in Oracle.

9.   CONCLUSIONS

Data Mining is not the answer to all problems and sometimes it has been over emphasized [Thu, 00]. It is expensive to carry out the entire process and therefore has to be thought out clearly. Since the proposed system uses multiple technologies such as learning agents, data mining to discover the knowledge, the results produced by this system shall be more relevant and interesting than the results produced by any data mining system. Also the new users / end users will get better results quickly while operating this data mining system because of the easiness and user friendliness. Also, this research project is in the finishing level, the results and the future directions will be published shortly.

REFERENCES

1. [AST, 00] Alex Berson, Stephen Smith, Kurt Thearling, *"Building   Data Mining Applications for CRM"*, Tata McGrawhill Publishers, 2000.
2. [Ays, 99] Ayse Yasemin Seydim, *"Intelligent Agents: A Data Mining Perspective"*, Dept of Computer Science and Engineering, Southern Methodist University, Dallas, TX 75275, May 1999.
3. [Thu, 00]   Bhavani Thuraisingam, *"Data Mining: Technologies, Techniques, Tools, and Trends"*, CRC Press, 2000. Pages: 1, 4, 6, 93.
4. [Gil, 97]   Don Gilbert, *"Intelligent Agents: The Right Information at the Right Time"* IBM Corporation, Research Triangle Park, NC USA, May, 1997
5. [LJLL, 01]   H.C.W. Lau, Bing Jiang, W.B. Lee and K.H. Lau, *"Development of an intelligent data mining system for a dispersed manufacturing network"*, Journal of Expert Systems, September 2001, Vol 18, No 4.
6. [JM, 01] Jaiwei Han & Miceline Kamber, *"Data Mining: Concepts and   techniques"*, Morgan Kaufmann   Publishers, 2001, Pages 5-7.
7. [Puj, 01] Arun K Pujari (2001), *"Data Mining Techniques"*, University Press, First Edition, Pages 79-173.

A BAYESIAN OPTIMIZATION ALGORITHM FOR UAV PATH PLANNING

X. Fu , X. Gao and D. Chen
Northwestern Polytechnical University, Xi'an 710072, China

London South Bank University, London SE1 0AA, UK

Abstract: A Bayesian optimization algorithm (BOA) for unmanned aerial vehicle (UAV) path planning is presented, which involves choosing path representation and designing appropriate metric to measure the quality of the constructed network. Unlike our previous work in which genetic algorithm (GA) was used to implement implicit learning, the learning in the proposed algorithm is explicit, and the BOA is applied to implement such explicit learning by building a Bayesian network of the joint distribution of solutions. Experimental results demonstrate that this approach can overcome some drawbacks of other path planning algorithms. It is also suggested that the learning mechanism in the proposed approach might be suitable for other multivariate encoding problems.

Key words: UAV, path planning, Bayesian network, genetic algorithm, Bayesian optimization algorithm

1.   INTRODUCTION

Flight path planning is a part of unmanned aerial vehicle (UAV) mission planning, and has received a lot of research attention [1] [2]. In essence, flight path planning is ultimately responsible for the generation of a trajectory in space which, when followed, maximizes the likelihood of the UAV completing its assigned tasks. However, most previous approaches have their drawback. For example, the planning result needs to be optimized further to make it flyable to UAV [2], or the algorithm might get stuck in local minima [1]. In this paper, we propose an algorithm that can overcome these drawbacks.

In the presented algorithm, an initial set of path genotype strings will be generated randomly. From the current population, the better promising set of strings will be used for building a Bayesian network of the joint distribution of solutions. Subsequently, another set of path genotype strings will be generated in terms of the joint distribution, some of which will replace previous strings based on fitness selection. If stopping conditions are not satisfied, the constructed Bayesian network will be updated again using the current set of promising path genotype strings.

2.   BOA FOR PATH PLANNING

This section discusses the proposed Bayesian optimization algorithm for path planning, including genetic representation, chromosome decoding, and multivariate *K2* metric for measuring the quality of the constructed Bayesian network. For a detailed description of the UAV path planning problem and the BOA see, for example, [1] [3] [4] [5].

2.1   Genetic Representation

In the presented algorithm, a chromosome consists of different sequences of positive integers that represent a sequence of speed and heading transitions at discrete times $\{t_k, k= 0, 1... n\}$, respectively. The possible transitions, assumed to be triggered at the start of each t_k interval, are listed in Table 1, where Δu and $\Delta \varphi$ denote increment in velocity and heading of the UAV, respectively. Note that the ordering of the transitions in Table 1 is arbitrary and the transitions mean that all turns are made at the maximum possible turn rate $\dot{\varphi}_{max}$ and all accelerations/decelerations are made at the maximum value a_{max}. This corresponds to aggressive maneuvering of the UAV.

Table 1. Genetic representation

Parameter	Genetic representation								
	1	2	3	4	5	6	7	8	9
Δu	+	-	0	-	0	+	0	+	-
$\Delta \varphi$	-	-	-	0	0	0	+	+	+

Thus, the jth individual of a population can be expressed as a sequence of transitions that reflect the nature of changes in the motion state to be initiated at time instant k^{th} :

$$\vec{P}^j = [I_1 \quad I_2 \quad ... \quad I_\ell]$$

(1)

where I_k indicates the type of change to be initiated at sampling interval k^{th}, and ranges from 1 to 9 in our case.

2.2   Chromosome Decoding

Given a sequence of transitions in speed and heading as discussed above, it is then necessary to generate a corresponding expected trajectory for the flight. This trajectory is typically required for evaluating the performance of a trial solution. In a 2-dimensional case, given a constant acceleration and turn rate as defined by the transition rules in Table 1, the motion of the UAV over an interval is described by the equations:

$$u[k+1] = u[k] + \Delta u$$
$$\varphi[k+1] = \varphi[k] + \Delta \varphi$$
$$x[k+1] = x[k] + u[k+1]\cos(\varphi[k+1]) \qquad (2)$$
$$y[k+1] = y[k] + u[k+1]\sin(\varphi[k+1])$$

where u is the UAV velocity with $u_{min} \le u \le u_{max}$, φ is the UAV heading with $|\varphi| \le \varphi_{max}$, Δu and $\Delta \varphi$ are the inputs, and (x, y) are inertial UAV position coordinates.

The rationale for using the kinematics model is based on the assumption that there exist inner and outer loop navigation control laws, which enable the UAV to track a trajectory as long as changes in speed and heading are within the UAV's motion limits.

2.3   Multivariate *K2* Metric

The traditional BOA uses bivariate chromosome to construct Bayesian network. In our algorithm multivariate chromosome is employed, and therefore the metric used is different to that in the traditional BOA. For each pair of positions i and j, the count of each combination of values can be summarized as the following contingency table:

Table 2. Count of each combination

$I_i \backslash I_j$	1	2	...	r_j	Σ
1	$n_{i,j}(1,1)$	$n_{i,j}(1,2)$	...	$n_{i,j}(1,r_j)$	$n_i(1)$
2	$n_{i,j}(2,1)$	$n_{i,j}(2,2)$	...	$n_{i,j}(2,r_j)$	$n_i(2)$
...	...	...	...	...	...
r_i	$n_{i,j}(r_i,1)$	$n_{i,j}(r_i,2)$	...	$n_{i,j}(r_i,r_j)$	$n_i(r_i)$
Σ	$n_j(1)$	$n_j(2)$	...	$n_j(r_j)$	N

where $n_{i,j}(r_i, r_j)$ denotes the count of each combination of values I_i and I_j in positions i and j at the same time, N denotes the size of a population, and $r_j = r_i = 9$.

The multivariate marginal frequency $p_{i,j}(I_i, I_j)$ is defined as the frequency of individuals in parent population, which has I_i and I_j in positions i and j at the same time:

$$p_{i,j}(I_i, I_j) = n_{i,j}(I_i, I_j)/N \tag{3}$$

Conditional probability of occurrence of the value I_i in the ith position in the case of occurrence of I_j in the jth position is determined by

$$p_{i,j}(I_i | I_j) = p_{i,j}(I_i, I_j)/p_j(I_j) \tag{4}$$

The dependency information is used to build up a Bayesian network and the following metric is used to measure the quality of the constructed network [7]:

$$(5) \quad K2_{i,j} = \left(\prod_{l=1}^{r_i} \frac{(r_j)!}{(r_j + n_i(l))!} \prod_{s=1}^{r_j} (1 + n_{i,j}(l,s))! \right) \Big/ \left(\frac{(r_j)!}{(r_j + N)!} \prod_{z=1}^{r_j} (1 + n_j(z))! \right)$$

This equation is derived from $K2$ metric used in BOA algorithm [4] [5], which is a special case of Bayesian Dirichlet (BD) metric for measuring the quality of the network. The $K2$ metric is used when no prior information available about the problem under consideration. This is the case for path planning as usually there is no any prior information about the distribution of the population. Therefore, $K2$ metric is employed in our algorithm.

3.   EXPERIMENTAL RESULTS

In this section, some results of path planning experiments using the proposed BOA are presented, which are further compared to the results given by the standard genetic algorithm based on the same dataset.

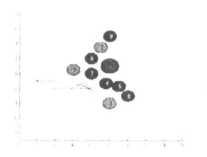
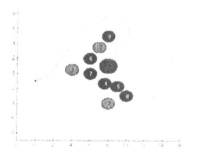

Figure 1. Planning result by GA   Figure 2. Planning result by BOA

The UAV is assumed to be initially at $(x_0, y_0) = (0, -1)$ with speed $u[0] = 2$ and heading $\varphi[0] = 0$. Speed changes are limited to 1 with the UAV speed constrained to be an integer in the range [1, 3]. Changes in heading are limited to $\pm 30^0$. The environment through which the UAV must navigate consists of three threats and six obstacles located at the positions as indicated in Figure 1. A target is located at $(x_T, y_T) = (8, 1)$.

Figure 1 shows the planning result by genetic algorithm, which traps in a local minimum. We can use fitness sharing to counteract the attraction towards the local minimum. Figure 2 shows the result of path planning generated by the presented BOA, which overcomes the drawback of the standard genetic algorithm.

4.   CONCLUSIONS

In this paper a new path planning algorithm is presented based on Bayesian networks. The approach is novel because it is the first time that a Bayesian network model has been applied to the field of UAV path planning. Experimental results have demonstrated the strength of the proposed Bayesian optimization algorithm. The standard GA uses problem-independent recombination operators that may break good building blocks in order to converge to a local optimum. The proposed approach takes advantage of global information about the set of promising solutions to estimate their distribution and this estimate can be used to generate new candidate solutions. Although we have presented this work in terms of path planning problem, it is suggested that the main idea of the approach could be applied to many other multivariate encoding problems. In the future, we will attempt to use the BOA to resolve path planning for multiple UAVs.

ACKNOWLEDGEMENTS

This research work was supported by the National Nature Science Foundation of China (grant No.90205019) and the Research Fund for the Doctoral Program of Higher Education (grant No.20020699001).

REFERENCES

1. Brain J. Capozzi. Evolution-based Path Planning and Management for Autonomous Vehicles. PhD thesis, University of Washington, 2001.
2. Bortoff S. Path planning for UAVs. Proceeding of American Control Conference., Chicago, USA, 2000, pp.364-368.
3. Martin Pelikan, Kumara Sastry, David E. Goldberg. Evolutionary Algorithm+Graphical Models=Scalable Black-Box Optimization. IlliGAL Report No.2001029.
4. Martin Pelikan, David E. Goldberg. BOA: Bayesian Optimization Algorithm. IlliGAL Report No.99003, 1999.

5. Josef Schwarz, Jiøí Oèenášek. Experimental Study: Hyper Graph Partitioning Based on the Simple and Advanced Genetic Algorithm BMDA and BOA. Proceedings of the Mendel '99 conference, BRNO, CZ, FSI VUT, 1999, pp. 124-130.

DILATED CHI-SQUARE: A NOVEL INTERESTINGNESS MEASURE TO BUILD ACCURATE AND COMPACT DECISION LIST

Yu Lan*, Guoqing Chen*, Davy Janssens** and Geert Wets**

* *School of Economics and Management, Tsinghua University, Beijing 100084, China*

  Email: {yul1; chengq} @em.tsinghua.edu.cn

***Limburg University Centre, Universitaire Campus, gebouw D,B-3590 Diepenbeek, Beigium*

  Email: {davy.janssens; geert.wets} @luc.ac.be

Abstract: Associative classification has aroused significant attention in recent years. This paper proposed a novel interestingness measure, named dilated chi-square, to statistically reveal the interdependence between the antecedents and the consequent of classification rules. Using dilated chi-square, instead of confidence, as the primary ranking criterion for rules under the framework of popular CBA algorithm, the adapted algorithm presented in this paper can empirically generate more accurate and much more compact decision lists.

Key words: dilated chi-square, associative classification, CBA

1.   INTRODUCTION

In recent years, extensive research has been carried out to integrate classification and association rules [1-5]. By focusing on a limited subset of association rules, i.e. those rules where the consequent of the rule is restricted to the class attribute, it is possible to build more accurate classifiers.

Associative classification is first proposed in CBA system [1], which uses a slightly adapted version of the well known Apriori algorithm [6] in order to extract meaningful association rules with their consequents limited to class labels. These rules are then primarily sorted by descending confidence and pruned in a way to get a minimal number of rules that are necessary to cover the training data and to achieve satisfactory accuracy. The aim of this paper is to improve CBA algorithm and generate a more accurate and compact decision list. Instead of confidence, a novel interestingness measure called dilated chi-square is applied as the primary sorting criterion.

The remaining of the paper is arranged as follows. Section 2 elaborates on the weakness of confidence. Section 3 describes in detail the design of dilated chi-square to overcome it. The empirical research is presented in section 4. Section 5 gives our concluding remarks.

2.   LIMITS OF CONFIDENCE

The rules in CBA are sorted primarily by descending confidence, which will determine to a large extent the accuracy of the final classifier. Confidence is a good measure for the quality of (class) association rules but it also suffers from certain weaknesses [7].

First, the confidence of a rule $X => Y$ is invariable when the size of $s(Y)$ or D varies. $s(Y)$ is the subset of the samples which are covered by the consequent of the rule, while D is the total samples in the dataset. The confidence of rule $X=>Y$ is $Supp(X \cup Y)/Supp(X)$. Keeping the numerator and denominator fixed, the confidence is stable when the size of $s(Y)$ or D changes. Nevertheless, the rule $X =>Y$ is more likely to happen when the size of $s(Y)$ increases or when the size of D decreases.

Second, the minimal support is always set to 1% or even lower in practice. It might very well happen that some rules have a high confidence but on the other hand they might be confirmed by a very limited number of instances, and that those rules stem from noise only.

Therefore, a novel interestingness, i.e. dilated chi-square was designed to overcome these two drawbacks. The next section elaborates on this.

3.   DILATED CHI-SQUARE

Traditional Chi-square test statistics (χ^2) is a widely used method for testing independence or correlation. This statistic is based on the comparison between the observed and the corresponding expected frequencies.

For each rule $X=>Y$ generated from a training dataset D, a 2*2 contingency table can be derived as Figure 1:

	Y	¬Y	Row Total
Satisfy X	m_{11}	m_{12}	Support count of X
Not Satisfy X	m_{21}	m_{22}	$|D|$-Support count of X
Column Total:	Support count of Y	$|D|$-Support count of Y	$|D|$

Figure 1. A 2*2 contingency table for rule $X=>Y$ and dataset D

The chi-square value for rule X=>Y can be calculated as

$$\chi^2 = \frac{(m_{11}m_{22} - m_{12}m_{21})^2 |D|}{(m_{11} + m_{12})(m_{21} + m_{22})(m_{11} + m_{21})(m_{12} + m_{22})} \tag{1}$$

However, simply using the traditional chi-square value will be favorable in a situation where the distribution of the row total is close to that of the column total distribution. We then adjust it according to local and global maximum chi-square that we define.

*Definition 1:*Given a dataset D, the local maximum chi-square, denoted as $lmax(\chi^2)$, is the maximum chi-square value for a fixed support count of X.

*Definition 2:*Given a dataset D, the global maximum chi-square, denoted as $gmax(\chi^2)$, is the maximum chi-square value for any possible support count of X.

Property 1: $lmax(\chi^2) = (n_1 n_2)^2 |D| / [(m_{11}+m_{12})(m_{21}+m_{22})(m_{11}+m_{21})(m_{12}+m_{22})]$, where $n_1 = \min(\min(m_{11}+m_{12}, m_{21}+m_{22}), \min(m_{11}+m_{21}, m_{12}+m_{22}))$ and $n_2 = \min(\max(m_{11}+m_{12}, m_{21}+m_{22}), \max(m_{11}+m_{21}, m_{12}+m_{22}))$. The local maximum chi-square value is arrived at the largest deviation from the expected frequency, assumed that the support count of X is given.

Property 2: $gmax(\chi^2) = |D|$. The equation is arrived when $m_{21}+m_{22} = m_{12}+m_{22}$ and $m_{11}+m_{12} = m_{11}+m_{22}$, i.e. the distribution of row total equals that of column total.

Chi-square value has a bias to different row total distributions. We adjust it to a more uniform and fare situation and get a novel interestingness measure called dilated chi-square value, denoted as $dia(\chi^2)$. More concretely, we heuristically use formula 3 to dilate the chi-square value according to the relationship between the local and global maximum chi-square values for current rule and database. The dilation procedure is nonlinear and empirically achieved excellent results, as shown in the next section.

$$\frac{dia(\chi^2)}{\chi^2} = \left(\frac{gmax(\chi^2)}{lmax(\chi^2)}\right)^\alpha = \left(\frac{|D|}{lmax(\chi^2)}\right)^\alpha, where \quad 0 \le \alpha \le 1 \tag{2}$$

Therefore

$$dia(\chi^2) = \left(\frac{|D|}{lmax(\chi^2)}\right)^\alpha \chi^2 \tag{3}$$

The parameter α is used to control the impact of global and local maximum chi-square values and can be tuned for different classification problems. It is visible that the dilated chi-square value is sensitive when the size of s(Y) or D varies. Furthermore, for these rules with high confidence and very low support, dilate chi-square values estimate their interestingness in a more cautious way.

We now adapted CBA by taking dilated chi-square as the primary criteria to sort the class association rules. Rule r_i has a higher rank than *rule* r_j if it has a larger value of dilated chi-square. When two rules have the same values of dilated chi-square, they are ranked according to the ranking mechanism of the original CBA.

4.   EMPIRICAL SECTION

This part is to validate our adapted CBA algorithm on 16 binary classification datasets from UCI [8]. The average results of 10-fold cross validation are described in table 1:

Table 1. Results on UCI datasets

Datasets	Adapted CBA(α=best)		Original CBA		C4.5 [9]	NB
	error rate	no. of rules	error rate	no. of rules	error rate	error rate
austra	13.04%	12.4	14.35%	130.5	13.48%	18.70%
breast	3.58%	28.3	3.86%	42.2	4.43%	2.58%
cleve	16.13%	9.6	17.16%	63.8	20.79%	16.17%
crx	13.04%	12.4	14.93%	138.2	12.75%	18.99%
diabetes	21.74%	10.7	22.26%	38.5	22.92%	24.22%
german	26.80%	19.7	26.70%	134	27.60%	25.30%
heart	16.67%	7.4	17.78%	37.6	18.89%	14.81%
hepati	16.83%	11.3	16.21%	25.2	16.77%	15.48%
horse	14.12%	1	19.03%	87.9	15.22%	20.92%
hypo	0.85%	10.9	1.64%	30	0.85%	1.90%
iono	6.55%	18.5	8.25%	44.8	9.69%	8.26%
labor	8.33%	4.4	10.00%	12.5	15.79%	8.77%
pima	22.00%	10.7	23.43%	38.3	22.66%	25%
sick	3.25%	1	2.64%	47.4	2.07%	4.32%
sonar	18.74%	21.8	22.60%	41	18.75%	25.48%
ti-tac	3.34%	9	0.00%	8	14.20%	29.65%
average	12.81%	11.82	13.80%	49.34	14.80%	16.28%

As shown in Table 1, adapted CBA has a lowest average error rate on these benchmarking datasets if the best parameter α is selected. The average number of rules that adapted CBA generated on these datasets is nearly one fourth of the original CBA! We also run the adapted CBA with α set at 0.8 for all datasets. The average error rate and number of rules are respectively 14.02% and 12.7.

Wilcoxon signed-rank test was used to give statistical comparisons between adapted CBA (for best α) and each of other classifiers considered in this paper. The results are depicted in Table 2.

Table 2. P-values of the Adapted CBA algorithm versus other classifiers

p-values for one tail test	Original CBA	C4.5	Naïve Bayes
Adapted CBA (α =best)	0.0107	0.0035	0.0125

5.   CONCLUSION

A novel interestingness measure name dilated chi-square is proposed in this paper. We adapt CBA algorithm, which can be used to build classifiers based on class association rules, by coupling it with dilated chi-square. More concretely, dilated chi-square is adopted as the primary criteria to rank the class association rules at the first step of the database coverage pruning procedure in the CBA algorithm. Experiments on wide-range datasets proved that this adapted CBA, compared with original CBA, C4.5 decision tree and Naive Bayes, achieves significantly better performance and generates classifiers much more compact than CBA.

ACKNOWLEDGEMENT

The work was partly supported by the National Natural Science Foundation of China (79925001/70231010), the MOE Funds for Doctoral Programs (20020003095), and the Bilateral Scientific and Technological Cooperation Between China and Flanders/Czech.

REFERENCES

1.   B.Liu, W.Hsu, and Y.Ma. Integrating Classification and Association Rule Mining. in the 4th International Conference on Discovery and Data Mining. 1998. New York,U.S.: pp. 80-86.
2.   G.Dong, et al. CAEP:Classification by aggregating emerging patterns. in 2nd International Conference on Discovery Science,(DS'99),volume 1721 of Lecture Notes in Artificial Intelligence. 1999. Tokyo,Japan: Springer-Verlag: pp. 30-42.
3.   W.Liu, J.Han, and J.Pei. CMAR: Accurate and efficient classification based on multiple class-association rules. in ICDM'01. 2001. San Jose, CA: pp. 369-376.
4.   X.Yin and J.Han. CPAR:Classification based on predictive association rules. in 2003 SIAM International Conference on Data Mining (SDM'03). 2003. San Fransisco,CA: pp. 331-335.
5.   K.Wang and S.Zhou. Growing decision trees on support-less association rules. in KDD'00. 2000. Boston,MA: pp. 265-269.
6.   R.Agrawal and R.Srikant. Fast algorithm for mining association rules. in the 20th International Conference on Very Large Data Bases. 1994. Santiago,Chile: pp. 487-499.
7.   Janssens, D., et al. Adapting the CBA-algorithm by means of intensity of implication. in the First International Conference on Fuzzy Information Processing Theories and Applications. 2003. Beijing, China: pp. 397-403.
8.   C.L.Blake and C.J.Merz, UCI repository of machine learning databases.1998, Irvine,CA:University of California, Dept. of Information and Computer Science. http://www.ics.uci.edu/~mlearn/mlrepository.htm.
9.   J.R.Quinlan, C4.5 programs for machine learning. 1993: Morgan Kaufmann.

POST SEQUENTIAL PATTERNS MINING
A New Method for Discovering Structural Patterns

Jing Lu[1], Osei Adjei[2], Weiru Chen[1] and Jun Liu[1]

[1] *School of Computer Science and Technology, Shenyang Institute of Chemical Technology, Shenyang 110142, China. Email: Jing.Lu@luton.ac.uk, Tel:44-1582-743716*
[2] *Department of Computing and Information Systems, University of Luton, Park Sq. Luton, LU1 3JU,UK*

Abstract:
In this paper we present a novel data mining technique, known as Post Sequential Patterns Mining, which can be used to discover Structural Patterns. A Structural Pattern is a new pattern, which is composed of sequential patterns, branch patterns or iterative patterns. Sequential patterns mining plays an essential role in many areas and substantial research has been conducted on their analysis and applications. In our previous work [12], we used a simple but efficient Sequential Patterns Graph (SPG) to model the sequential patterns. The task to discover hidden Structural Pattern is based on our previous work and sequential patterns mining, conveniently named Post Sequential Patterns Mining. In this paper, in addition to stating this new mining problem, we define patterns such as branch pattern, iterative pattern, structural pattern, and concentrate on finding concurrent branch pattern. Concurrent branch pattern is thus one of the main forms of structural pattern and will play an important role in event-based data modelling.

Key words:
Post Sequential Patterns Mining, Sequential Patterns Graph, Structural Pattern, Concurrent Branch Patterns

1. INTRODUCTION

Sequential pattern mining proposed by Agrawal and Srikant [1] is an important data mining task and with broad applications that include the analysis of customer behaviors, web access patterns, process analysis of scientific experiments, prediction of natural disasters, treatments, drug testing and DNA analysis etc. Over the last few years considerable attention has been focused on the achievement of better performance in sequential pattern mining[1,5,10,14,15,16], but there is still the need to do further work in order to improve on results achieved so far. Questions that are usually asked with respect to sequential pattern mining are: What is the inherent relation among sequential patterns? Is there a general representation of sequential patterns? Based on these questions, we proposed a novel framework for sequential patterns called Sequential Pattern Graph (SPG) as a model to represent relations among sequential patterns [12].

From our previous work on SPG and sequential patterns mining, other new patterns such as branch pattern, iterative pattern or structural pattern could be discovered. These patterns were first proposed in [11]. In order to find such patterns, we present a new mining technique known as Post Sequential Patterns Mining. Structural Pattern is the combination of sequential pattern, branch pattern and iterative pattern. Discovering Structural Pattern is the ultimate goal of the Post Sequential Patterns mining task. In this paper, we focus on concurrent branch pattern and its mining algorithms.

The organization of this paper is as follows: We introduce the concept of branch pattern, iterative pattern, and structural pattern and Post Sequential Pattern Mining problem in section 2. In section 3, we present concurrent branch pattern mining. The algorithms used in this approach are also outlined in this section. Section 4 reviews some related work whilst section 5 concludes the study and identifies further work.

1.1 Structural patterns and Post Sequential Patterns Mining Problem Statement

Before introducing the Post Sequential Patterns Mining problem, we formally define some new patterns.

1.2   Structural pattern

All the definitions of terminologies in relation to sequential patterns mining presented in [1] are followed in this paper. Recall that the **support** of sequence s, denoted by $s.sup$, is the number of data sequences containing s divided by the total number of data sequences in DB. The minsup is the user specified minimum support threshold. A sequence s is a **frequent sequence**, or called **sequential pattern**, if $s.sup \geq minsup$. The aim of sequential pattern mining is to discover all the sequential patterns or maximal sequence.

Based on these definitions, some new concepts are introduced first. This introduction is necessary for the understanding of Post Sequential Patterns Mining, which will be proposed in the next subsection.

Definition 1 (Mono-pattern) A sequential pattern that contains only one element is called a **mono-pattern** and it is denoted by <*(itemset)*> or <*item*>.

A mono-pattern is a frequent itemset of the result of association rule mining. Patterns <a>,<(a, b)> and <(b, c)> are all examples of mono-patterns.

Definition 2 (Sub-pattern) A sub-pattern is part of a pattern that includes some elements and their sequence order relations.

The pattern <cd> is an example of a *sub-pattern* of the patterns <abcd>, <acbd>, <cabd>, and <acbde>.

Definition 3 (Branch Pattern) A **branch pattern** is a combination of some sequential patterns if and only if those patterns have the same prefix and/or postfix, and the *support* of the combination is greater than or equal to *minsup*. Notation $[s_i,s_j]$ denotes that two *sub-patterns* s_i and s_j appear in different branches pattern. Sub-patterns s_i,s_j are called the *branches* of a branch pattern.

For example, sequential patterns <eacb> and <efcb> have the same prefix <e> and the same postfix <cd>. If the support of those two patterns occur in the same customer sequence is above the *minsup*, then they can constitute a new branch pattern and denoted by < e[a,f]cd >.

Note that in branch pattern such as <a[b,c]d >, *b* and *c* are the *branches*. The order of those two branches is indefinite, therefore <a[b,c]d > occurs as *abcd* or *acbd* in a database.

Branch pattern can be divided into three categories: concurrent, exclusive and trivial.

In the following description, notation **sup(a∧b)** is used to denote the support for two sub-pattern *a* and *b* which appear in the same customer sequence at the same time.

- **Concurrent Branch Pattern.** For any two given sub-patterns s_i and s_j, if $sup(s_i \wedge s_j) \geq minsup$, then they constitute a concurrent branch pattern and denoted by $[s_i \ominus s_j]$. Concurrent branch pattern mining is discussed in detail in section 3.

- **Exclusive Branch Pattern.** For any two given sub-patterns s_i and s_j, if $sup(s_i) \geq minsup$, $sup(s_j) \geq minsup$ and $sup(s_i \wedge s_j) \leq maxsup$, then they constitute an exclusive branch pattern and denoted by $[s_i \ominus s_j]$. The maximum support *maxsup* is defined as an acceptable maximum probability for some event to occur.

- **Trivial Branch Pattern.** A branch pattern which is neither an exclusive branch pattern nor a concurrent branch pattern is called **trivial branch pattern.**

Definition 4 (Iterative Pattern) A sequential pattern is called an **iterative pattern** if it is made up of only one sub sequential pattern S, which appears at least *n* times ($n \geq 2$), and at most *m* times ($m \geq n$). The expression $<\{S\}_n^m>$ denotes the iterative pattern. If a sub-pattern S can be repeated **at most** m times, the iterative pattern will be denoted by $<\{S\}^m>$, and if a sub-pattern S can be repeated **at least** n times, the iterative pattern will be denoted by $<\{S\}_n>$. Hence the expression $<\{S\}_2>$ means S occurs **at least** twice (i.e. n=2).

As an example, a sequential pattern $<a\ a>$ is an iterative pattern since it is made up of two *a*s and denoted by $<\{a\}^2>$. A sequential pattern $<(a,b)\ (a,b)$ $(a,b)>$ is also an iterative pattern made up of 3 *(a,b)*s and denoted by $<\{(a,b)\}^3>$.

Definition 5 (Structural Pattern) A **structural pattern** is a general designation of mono-pattern, sequential pattern, branch pattern, iterative pattern, and their composition, it is made up of some elements and their sequence order relations.

For example, $<a\ \{(b,\ c)\}\ [\{d\}^5_3,\ \{e\ (f,\ g)\}^4,\ a\ h]\ i>$ is a structural pattern.

Definition 6 (Pattern Size) The maximal length of all sub sequential pattern of a structural pattern p is called **Pattern Size,** and denoted by**PSize(p).**

For example, patterns $<acd>,<a[a,b]c>$and $<[a,b,c,d,e]f[a,j]>$ are all have the same size of 3.

1.3   Post Sequential Pattern Mining Problem Statement

The mining task based on the sequential patterns mining is Post Sequential Patterns Mining. The ultimate goal of this new mining task is to discover the hidden branch pattern, iteration pattern and structural pattern. This new mining task is complex and there are many questions to be asked. For example: (i) How does one find each part of structural patterns? (ii) What is a better way to find them? (iii) What are the actual meanings of these patterns? (iv) Where and how can these patterns be applied? This paper only focuses on tasks with respect to concurrent branch pattern mining.

2.   CONCURRENT BRANCH PATTERN MINING

One of our contributions is the definition of branch pattern, iterative pattern and structural pattern. The main form of branch pattern is concurrent branch pattern, which indicates that the sequences in different branches may appear in the same customer sequence within a believable probability. In this section, the concurrent branch pattern mining problem is tackled.

2.1   Concurrent Group and Maximal Concurrent Group Set

Before we present a mining algorithm to discover all concurrent branch patterns, we propose another new concept called concurrent group.

Definition 7 (Concurrent Group, *CG*) Given customer sequences, set of items (or itemset) that have transaction support above *minsup* makes up a **concurrent group** and it is denoted by *CG* for brief.

Example 1 Consider the following customer sequences and let *minsup* be 50%:<a (a,b,c)(a,c)d(c,f)>,<(a,d) c (b,c) (a,c)>,<(e,f) (a,b) (d,f) c b>,<e g (a,f) c b c>.

Items (or itemset) sets {a,b,c,d}, {(a,b),c,d,f} and {(a,c),b,d} are all examples of *concurrent group* since the condition in the definition is satisfied. From definition 7 we know that concurrent group is a set and the elements in this set can be an item or an itemset. Consider {(a,b),c,d,f} for example, four elements are contained in this concurrent group, one is an itemset *(a,b)* and the other three are items *c,d,* and *f.*

Further explanation concerning the Concurrent Group is as follows:

- For any itemset element of a concurrent group *CG*, items in the itemset can also be considered as an item element of *CG* when this *CG* is compared with another set. For example {(a,b),c,d,f} can also be considered as {a,b,c,d,f}. This is useful in understanding the rough concurrent branch pattern which will be introduced in section 3.2.
- Any two elements of a *CG* should not include each other. For example, {(a,c),a,c,b,d} is not a concurrent group , for its elements *a* and *c* are included by another element *(a,c)*.

Definition 8 (Maximal Concurrent Group, *MCG*) A concurrent group is called a **maximal concurrent group** if any of its superset is not a concurrent group. The set of Maximal Concurrent Group Set is denoted by *MCGS* for abbreviation.

Example 2 Consider the previous example, among these following three concurrent groups{a,b,c,d}, {(a,b),c,d,f} and {(a,c),b,d}. The group {(a,b),c,d,f} is a maximal concurrent group but {a,b,c,d} is not, since its superset {(a,b),c,d,f} is a concurrent group.

The set of Maximal Concurrent Group of example 1 is MCGS={{(a,b),c,d,f}, {(a,c),(b,c),d}, {a,b,c,e,f}}.

If each customer sequence is considered as a transaction, then discovering concurrent group from customer sequence is identical to the association rules mining from the transaction.

2.2   Rough Concurrent Branch Pattern

Following the definition of the maximal concurrent group in the previous section, we investigate the relation between the Maximal Sequence Set (*MSS*) discovered in sequential patterns mining and the maximal concurrent group proposed.

Definition 9 (Rough Concurrent Branch Pattern, *RCBP*) Let *C* be a maximal concurrent group in MCGS. *Concurrent sequences* can be obtained by the *sequential intersection operation* of *C* and each element in *MSS* respectively. These concurrent sequences constitute a **rough concurrent branch pattern (RCBP)**.

Sequential intersection operation can be treated as a normal intersection, and the sequence relations among elements after this operation will be consistent with that in the original sequence pattern. The notation of sequential intersection is

Sequential pattern or Sequential pattern set ∩ Concurrent Group

The main goal of our work is to discover concurrent branch pattern. We start by finding the rough concurrent branch pattern and then refine it as presented in section 3.3.

Algorithm 1 (Getting a RCBP)

Input: Maximal Concurrent Group *C* and Maximal Sequence Set *MSS*.

Output: Rough Concurrent Branch Patterns *RCBP(C)*.

Method: Finding rough concurrent branch patterns in the following steps.

1   Let rough concurrent branch pattern for *C, RCBP(C)*, be empty.

2   For each element *ms* in *MSS*
     Add *ms* to *RCBP(C)*;
     For each element (item or itemset) *i* in *ms*, test if *i* is an element of *C* or *i* is included in one element of *C*;
     If neither condition is satisfied, then delete *i* from *ms*.

3   Delete the element in *RCBP(C)* which contained by another pattern in the *RCBP(C)*.

4   The result is *RCBP(C)*.

Example 3 Given *MSS*={<eacb>, <efcb>, <a(b,c)a>, <(a,b)dc>, <fbc>, <(a,b)f>, <ebc>, <dcb>, <abc>, <acc>,<(a,c)>}. Let us find the rough concurrent branch pattern for the maximal concurrent group in example 2.

The *sequential intersection* of maximal concurrent group {(a,b),c,d,f} and each element in *MSS* is MSS∩{(a,b),c,d,f}={<acb>, <fcb>, <aa>,<(a,b)dc>, <fbc>,<(a,b)f>, <dcb>,<abc>, <acc>}. This is the rough concurrent branch pattern RCBP(1). Similarly, MSS∩ {(a,c),(b,c),d}={<acb>, <a(b,c)a>, <dcb>, <abc>, <acc>, <(a,c)>}=RCBP(2); MSS∩ {a,b,c,e,f}={<eacb>, <efcb>, <aa>, <fbc>, <ebc>, <abc>, <acc>}=RCBP(3).There are three rough concurrent branch patterns in this example.

The following theorem can ensure the correctness of algorithm 1.

Theorem 1 *All concurrent sequences obtained by sequential intersection operation in a RCBP constitute a concurrent branch pattern.*

Proof. Concurrent sequences in a *RCBP* are the sequential intersection of a maximal concurrent group C and each element in *MSS* respectively. Since we know that:

- All concurrent sequences are sequence patterns, for they are all from *MSS*;
- All elements in any one sequence of *RCBP* are concurrent, for they are all from C, a maximal concurrent group in *MCGS*.

Therefore theorem 1 is true.

2.3 Refining of Rough Concurrent Branch Pattern

RCBPs are only rough concurrent branch patterns, which should be refined for getting the most accurate concurrent branch patterns. What does an accurate concurrent branch pattern mean? Consider [<abc>⊖ <afg>] and <a[<bc>⊖ <fg>]> for example. <a[<bc>⊖ <fg>]> is obtained by combining the common prefix a in [<abc>⊖ <afg>]. The latter is considered more accurate than the former.

Definition 10 (Common Item/Itemset Set, *CIS*) Given any two patterns s_i and s_j, item/itemset i is called a common item/itemset of s_i and s_j if i is contained in both patterns. All *common item/itemset* for a group of patterns constitute a **common item/itemset set (*CIS*)**.

For example, for patterns <acc> and <(a, c)>, their Common Item/Itemset Set is *CIS* = {a, c}. For <eacb> and <efcb>, *CIS*={*e, c, b*}.

Definition 11 (Common Pattern Pair, *CPP*) A pair of patterns a and b are called **common pattern pair** if they share a common item (or itemset).

There maybe several *common pattern pairs* for each $ci \in$ CIS. The notation **CPP(ci)** is used to denote the set of *common pattern pairs* of ci.

Example 4 Consider <eacb> and <efcb>, CIS={e, c, b}, if pattern size is set to 2, i.e. PSize(CPP)=2, we have CPP(e)={<e[a,f]>,e[a,c]>,<e[a,b]>,<e[f,c]>,<e[f, b]>,<e[b,c]>}.

Definition 12 (Accurate Concurrent Branch Pattern, *ACBP*) Concurrent sequences in RCBP are accurate if there are no common pattern to be taken out to reconstruct a new concurrent branch pattern. Accurate concurrent branch pattern is the refined result of rough concurrent branch pattern.

Example 5 Consider concurrent sequences [<abc>⊖ <cdf>⊖ <xy>] for example, no common pattern can be founded. Therefore, it is an accurate concurrent branch pattern.

Definition 13 (Concurrent Structural Pattern, *CStruP*) A pattern which is made up of sequential patterns and concurrent branch patterns is called **concurrent structural pattern (*CStruP* for brief)**. RCBP is a special form of concurrent structural pattern. From definition 12, we can define that a concurrent structural pattern is accurate if all the concurrent branch patterns are accurate. *ACStruP* is used to denote an accurate concurrent structural pattern. An accurate concurrent branch pattern defined in definition 12 is a special form of *ACStruP*.

Example 6 [<[a⊖ b]c>⊖ <xy> ⊖ <c [d⊖ b]>] is a concurrent structural pattern since it is composed of sequential patterns <xy> and two concurrent branch patterns <[a⊖ b]c> and <c [d⊖ b]>. This concurrent structural pattern is accurate since these two concurrent branch patterns are accurate.

Next, the notation MSS(*CStruP*) is used to represent the Maximal Sequential Set for concurrent structural pattern. The MSS(*CStruP*) can be considered as one operation. All sequential patterns of *CStruP* and *branches* in branch patterns of *CStruP* are included in MSS(*CStruP*).

Theorem 2 *For a given pattern set* $P=\{p_1,p_2,...,p_n\}$, *MSS(P)* = $MSS(MSS(\{p_1\}) \cup MSS(\{p_2\}) \cup... \cup MSS(\{p_n\}))$.

Theorem 3 *For three given patterns set P, P1 and P2 where* $P1=\{p_{11},p_{12},...,p_{1m}\}$, $P2=\{p_{21},p_{22},...,p_{2n}\}$, *and if the condition* $P= P1 \cup P2$ *holds, then it is concluded that* $MSS(P) = MSS(MSS(P1) \cup MSS(P2))$.

The above two theorems form the theoretical foundations for concurrent patterns refining. The definition of concurrent patterns refining is given as follows:

Definition 14 (Concurrent Patterns Refining, *CPR*) The process that refines Concurrent Structural Pattern *CStruPs* is called **concurrent patterns refining**. This process can be denoted by CPR(*CStruP*). The refined result is that MSS(ACStruP) is equal to MSS(∪ CStruPs).

Theorem 4 *For a given RCBP, suppose* $RCBP=\{P\} \cup RCBP'$, *where P is an element of RCBP, RCBP' is a sub set of RCBP when P is deleted from RCBP, then* $CPR(RCBP)=CPR(\{P\} \cup CPR(RCBP'))$.

Theorem 4 is the foundation of the CPR algorithm to be discussed in the next section. Proofs of theorem 2,3and 4 are omitted due to the restriction on the paper length.

2.4   Concurrent Branch Patterns Mining Algorithm

The following algorithm is used to find the concurrent branch patterns.
Algorithm 2 (Finding Concurrent Branch Pattern)
Input: A transaction database *DB* and a minimum support *minsup*.
Output: Concurrent branch patterns *CBP*.
Method: Finding concurrent branch patterns in the following steps.
1   Find Maximal Concurrent Group Set (*MCGS*) from customer sequences in DB using traditional algorithm such as association rules mining.

2 Find *MSS* from customer sequences using traditional sequential patterns mining algorithm.

3 Calculate Rough Concurrent Branch Patterns *RCBPs* using Algorithm 1 based on the *MCGS* and *MSS*.

4 Find the Accurate Concurrent Structural Pattern *ACStruP* for each *RCBP* by calling Algorithm 3.

5 The Union of all the *ACStruPs* is the concurrent branch patterns set *CBP*.

Algorithm 3 (Finding the ACStruP for a RCBP)

Input: Rough Concurrent Branch Pattern *r*.

Output: Accurate Current Structural Pattern *ACStruP*

Method: Call CPR(*r*)

Procedure CPR(*r*)

{

if *r* contains only one sequential pattern, then return r. /*r is the result*/

Decompose *r* into two parts such that $r = \{p\} \cup r1$, where *p* is the first element of *r* (also a sequential pattern), and *r1* is the set of the left patterns by removing *p* from *r*.

return the result by calling CPR_2P(*p*, CPR(*r1*)) /* CPR_2P is shown in algorithm 4*/

}

The definition of *Common Item/Itemset Set* and *Pattern Size* introduced previously will be useful in the understanding of the following algorithm.

Algorithm 4 (Finding accurate concurrent structural pattern for two patterns)

Input: Patterns *p1* and *p2*, where *p1* must be a sequential pattern, *p2* may be an *ACStruP*.

Output: Accurate Current Structural Pattern *P*

Method: Call CPR_2P(*p1,p2*)

Procedure CPR_2P(*p1,p2*)

{

Let $P=\{p1\} \cup \{p2\}$. /* P will be used as the result of CPR_2P */

Calculate the common item/itemset set *CIS* for *p1* and *p2*.

Let pattern size variable *PSize*=2.

Do while *CIS* is not empty {

For each element $ci \in CIS$, find *CPP(ci)*. *CPP(ci)* must satisfy the conditions: *CPP(ci)* should not be sub-patterns of any pattern in *P*, and PSize(*CPP(ci)*) is *PSize*.

For each possible pattern in *CPP(ci)*, test if its support is above *minsup*. If it satisfies the condition then let it be included into *P*.

For any element *ci* in CIS, if the *support* of every element in CPP(*ci*) is all below *minsup*, then delete *ci* from *CIS*.

Clear up *P* by deleting patterns, which have any super pattern in *P*.
Let *PSize=PSize+1.*}
return P.
}

A concrete example of the algorithm 4 for readers' understanding is given follows:

Example 7   Consider the customer sequences in example 1 and suppose *minsup*=50%: <a (a,b,c) (a,c) d (c,f)>, <(a,d) c (b,c) (a,c)>, <(e,f) (a,b) (d,f) c b>, <e g (a,f) c b c>. Let patterns <eacb> and <efcb> be the input patterns of CPR_2P. While calling CPR_2P:

1   P={<eacb>, <efcb>},CIS={e, c, b}, PSize=2.
2   For the first element of CIS e, CPP={< e[a,f]> }.
3   Since the support of < e[a,f]> is above minsup, add it into P. Thus, P={<eacb>,<efcb>,<e[a⊖ f]>}. Note that <e[a,c]>,<e[a,b]>,<e[f,c]> and <e[f, b]> are not in CPP, for they are sub patterns of some elements of P.
4   Similarly, for element of CIS, c and b, the result is P={<eacb>, <efcb>, < e[a⊖ f]>, <[a⊖ f]c>,<[a⊖ f]b>}.
5   When Psize is 4, P={<eacb>, <efcb>, <e[a⊖ f]cb>}.
6   Delete <eacb> and <efcb> from P for they are sub-patterns of <e[a ⊖ f]cb>.
7   The final result is P={<e[a⊖ f]cb>}.

3.   RELATED WORK

Discovering Structural Patterns seems to be new to data mining. There are, of course, several topics in which related issues have been considered. A theoretical framework and practical methods are described in [13] for finding event sequence decompositions. These methods used the probabilistic modelling of the event generating process. Recently, a simple and efficient data mining algorithm presented in [6] to discover all fragments that satisfy certain conditions. A fragment is an ordering of a subset of variables in a 0-1 dataset. They describe the criteria, frequency and violation fraction, to be used for finding potentially interesting fragments of order. However, the emphasis of our work is on finding structural patterns (including sequential pattern, branch pattern or iterative pattern) based on the result of sequential patterns mining.

We mentioned that we can apply the post sequential pattern mining into event-based modelling. In traditional workflow modelling process, a designer has to construct a detailed workflow model accurately describing the routing of the work. It is time consuming and the initial design is often incomplete and subjective. Since WfMSs (Workflow Management Systems) log many events that occur during process executions, so a technique called workflow mining (also referred to as process mining) was proposed to solve the problem in workflow model design. Workflow mining is an approach to reverse the process and the information collected at run-time can be used to derive a model. The process mining is not new [2,3,4,7,8,9], however most process mining results are limited to sequential behavior. Not much work has been done to find concurrent or iterative behavior. Our approach in workflow modelling is one of the key directions for further research.

4.   CONCLUSIONS AND FUTURE WORK

One of the future research directions of data mining is to propose new mining task or discover various patterns. Post sequential patterns mining is just for this purpose. This novel mining task is based on sequential patterns mining. In this paper we first reviewed the Sequential Patterns Graph (SPG) as proposed in [12]. It is clear from the previous work that SPG is a bridge from discrete sequences set to structural knowledge and it is also the foundation of post sequential patterns mining.

The main purpose of post sequential patterns mining is to discover the hidden structural patterns in event-based data. Before addressing the problem of post sequential patterns mining, we defined formally some new patterns including branch pattern, iterative branch and structural pattern. Concurrent branch pattern is an important pattern, which occurs in many event-based data. Thus, we concentrated on concurrent branch pattern mining in this paper.

An important phase for our work is to perform more experiments to support our theories. In our previous work, we implemented the algorithm for constructing SPG and analyzed the efficiency of that approach. In our existing research work, we anticipate that more experiments are needed to demonstrate the affective nature and efficiency of concurrent branch patterns mining algorithms. This paper has been theoretical, experimentation is on going to establish the validity of our algorithms. In addition to the above, we intend to extend the method to cover concurrent branch patterns to exclusive branch patterns mining or iterative patterns mining. This, we envisage will be our ultimate goal.

REFERENCES

1. R. Agrawal and R. Srikant. *Mining Sequential Patterns*. Eleventh Int'l Conference on Data Engineering, Taipei, Taiwan. IEEE Computer Society Press, pages 3-14, March 1995.
2. R. Agrawal, D. Gunopulos and F. Leymann.*Mining Process Models from Workflow Logs*. Proceedings of the Sixth International Conference on Extending Database Technology (EDBT), 1998.
3. J.E. Cook and A.L Wolf. *Discovering Models of Software Processes from Event-Based Data*. ACM Transactions on Software Engineering and Methodology, 7(3), pages 215-249, 1998.
4. J.E. Cook and A.L Wolf. *Software Process Validation: Quantitatively Measuring the correspondence of a Process to a Model*. ACM Transactions on Software Engineering and Methodology, 8(2), pages 147-176, 1999.
5. M. Garofalakis, R. Rastogi, and K.Shim . *SPRIT: Sequential Pattern Mining with Regular Expression Constraints*. Twenty-fifth International Conference on Very Large Data Bases, Edinburgh, Scotland, UK, Morgan Kaufmann, pages 223-234, September 1999.
6. A. Gionis, T. Kujala and H. Mannila. *Fragments of Order*, *SIGKDD'*03, pages129-136, Washington, DC,USA, August 2003.
7. J. Herbst. *A Machine Learning Approach to Workflow Management*. Proceedings of European Conference on Machine Learning (ECML-2000), Lecture Notes in Artificial Intelligence No. 1810, pages 183-194, 2000.
8. J. Herbst. *Dealing with Concurrency in Workflow Induction*. In Proceedings of the 7th European Concurrent Engineering Conference, Society for Computer Simulation (SCS), pages 169- 174, 2000.
9. J. Herbst and D. Karagiannis. *Integrating Machine Learning and Workflow Management to Support Acquisition and Adaptation of Workflow Models*. International Journal of Intelligent Systems in Accounting, Finance and Management, 9: pages 67-92, 2000.
10. M.Y.Lin and S.Y. Lee. *Fast discovery of sequential patterns by memory indexing*. DaWaK, pages. 150-160, 2002.
11. J.Lu, O.Adjei, X.F.Wang and F.Hussain. *Sequential Patterns Modeling and Graph Pattern Mining*. the forthcoming IPMU Conference ,Perugia, July, 4-9,2004.
12. J. Lu, X.F.Wang, O.Adjei and F.Hussain. *Sequential Patterns Graph and its Construction Algorithm*. Chinese Journal of Computers, 2004 Vol. 6.
13. H.Mannila and D. Rusakov. *Decomposing Event Sequences into Independent Components*, In V. Kumar and R. Grossman, editors, the First SIAM Conference on Data Mining,*Proc.*, pages 1-17, *SIAM*,2001.
14. J. Pei, J.W. Han, B. Mortazavi-Asl,.and H. Pinto. *PrefixSpan: Mining Sequential Patterns Efficiently by Prefix-Projected Pattern Growth*. Seventh Int'l Conference on Data Engineering, Heidelberg, Germany, 2001.
15. R. Srikant, R. Agrawal. *Mining Sequential Patterns: Generalizations and Performance Improvements* .Fifth Int'l on Extending Database Technology,EDBT, vol. 1057, Avigon, France, pages 3-17, March 1996.
16. M.J. Zaki. *SPADE: An efficient algorithm for mining frequent sequences*. Machine Learning, 42(1/2), pages 31-60, 2001.

EXTENDED CONSTRAINT HANDLING FOR CP-NETWORKS

Yonggang Zhang and Jigui Sun
College of Computer Science and Technology, Jilin University, Changchun, 130012, China

Abstract: CP-networks are an elegant and compact qualitative framework for express preference, in which we can represent and reason about preference rankings given conditional preference statements. However, represent constraints in such framework is one difficult problem. We therefore propose a new approach, i.e. mapping CP-networks to constraint hierarchy, thus we can reason preferences with constraint solving algorithms. We compare it with related work finally.

Key words: CP-networks, constraint hierarchy, preference, reasoning

1. INTRODUCTION

Representing and reasoning about preference is an area of increasing interest in theoretical and applied AI[1]. In many real life problems, we have both hard and soft constraints and qualitative conditional preferences. Now, there are few work on reasoning with these information. For example, constraint hierarchy (CH) solvers [2] are good at hard and soft constraint solving, while CP-networks[3]are most suited for representing qualitative conditional preference statements. In this paper, we combine two approaches, so that we can handle both constraints and preference efficiently.

2. CONSTRAINT HIERARCHY

A constraint hierarchy is a finite set of labeled constraints defined over some set of values D called domain, e.g. real numbers. Given a constraint hierarchy H, H_0 is a vector of required constraints in H in some arbitrary order with their labels removed. Similarly, H_1 is a vector of the strongest non-required constraints in H etc. up to the weakest level H_n, where n is the number of non-required levels in the hierarchy H. We set $H_k =\varnothing$ for k>n. Recall, that if i<j then the constraints in H_i are stronger (more preferred) than the constraints in H_j. We call the sets H_j hierarchy levels.

A assignment for the set of constraints is a function that maps variables in the constraints to elements in the domain D over which the constraints are defined. A solution to the constraint hierarchy is a set of assignments for the variables in the hierarchy such that any assignment in the solution set satisfies at least the required constraints, i.e., the constraints in H_0, and, in addition, it satisfies the non-required constraints, i.e., the constraints in H_i for i>0, at least as well as any other assignment that also satisfies the required constraints.

3.   CP-NETWORKS

CP-networks were introduced as a tool for compactly representing qualitative preference relations[3]. First it consist of a set of features, {A,B,C,···}.Each feature can have a finite domain of values. Without loss of generality, we assume features have just two possible values (true or false), written a or a'. The user has a preference ranking, a total preorder>on assignments of values to features.

Example 3.1 Consider the CP-network N with the CPT: a>a' , b>b', (a ∧ b') ∨ (a' ∧ b):c>c', c: d>d'.

a>a' is n unconditional preference statement, it has the semantics that whatever values are taken by the other features, we will prefer an assignment to A of a over a'. c:d>d' is a conditional preference statement, it has the semantics that having assigned a to A, we will prefer an assignment of b to B over b'.

One important question is whether one assignment is better than another, i.e. a dominance query[3], we employ another semantics[5].A refined notation of dominance would consider all the features that are at the same level w.r.t the hierarchy included by the preference statements.

Definition 3.1 Assume the CP-networks N is acyclic, the corresponding hierarchy N_H consists of n levels: level 1 is the node (feature) with an indegree of zero, and level 2 is the node whose father nodes are in level, until level n, there no other nodes remained.

Definition 3.2 Consider one acyclic CP-network N and it's hierarchy N_H, s_1 and s_2 are two assignment, we say s_1 dominates s_2, written as $s_1 \triangleright s_2$, iff started at the highest level, its assignments win on the majority at the same level, we call this the majority lexicographic order.

Example 3.2 See the CP-network in example 3.1, the corresponding hierarchy is $N_H=\{l_1:<A,B>,\ l_2:<C>,l_3:<D>\}$, consider two assignment $s_1=ab'cd$ and $s_2=a'bc'd'$, and $s_1 \rhd s_2$.

4. MAPPING CP-NETWORKS TO CONSTRAINT HIERARCHIES

Thanks to Rossi[4], whose study enlightens us on the connection with constraint hierarchy, we can transform a cyclic CP-networks N to the constraint hierarchy CH_N, following show the procedure with pseudocode.

Trans(N_H, CH_H)
for i=1 to k do
  $H_i= \emptyset$;
  for every feature in l_i do
    consider the preference statement about feature A_i ;
    if its form is $a_i>a_i'$ then $H_i=H_i \cup \{X_{ai}=a_i\}$
    else if its form is $b_i \wedge \cdots : a_i>a_i'$ then $H_i=H_i \cup \{X_{bi}=b_i \wedge \cdots \wedge X_{ai}=a_i\}$
    else if its form is $(b_i \wedge b_j \cdots) \vee \cdots : a_i>a_i'$
            then $H_i=H_i \cup \{(X_{bi}=b_i \wedge X_{bj}=b_j \cdots \wedge X_{ai}=a_i) \vee \cdots\}$
  enddo
  i=i+1;
enddo

Given a cyclic CP-networks N and its hierarchy N_H, after running the procedure, we get the constraint hierarchy, thus reasoning about CP-networks i.e. solving of the constraint hierarchy.

Example 4.1 The constraint hierarchy of the CP-networks in example 3.1 is: $H_1=\{X_A=a,\ X_B=b\};H_2=\{(X_A=a \wedge X_B=b' \wedge X_C=c') \vee (X_A=a' \wedge X_B=b \wedge X_C=c')\}$; $H_3=\{X_C=c \wedge X_d=d\ \}$

We can use the comparator to compare two assignments. for the sake of keep identical semantics of CP-network, we define a global comparator.

Definition 4.1 Let c be a constraint and θ is a assignment, the expression $c\theta$ is the boolean result of applying θ to c, the trivial error function $e(c\theta)$ is defined: $e(c\theta)=0$, if $c\theta$ holds, otherwise $e(c\theta)=1$.

Definition 4.2 If a assignment θ is better than σ, written as $\theta \succ \sigma$, there is level k in the constraint hierarchy such that for i<k, $g(E(H_i\theta))=g(E(H_i\sigma))$,and at level k, $g(E(H_i\theta)) < g(E(H_i\sigma))$, where < is a lexicographic ordering, E is the form of e operate on the constraints set, and g is sum-better combining function, $g(v)= \Sigma\ v_i$, $i=1,\cdots,|v|$, v is a vector.

Example 4.2 See the hierarchy in example3, given two assignment, $\theta_1=\{X_A=a,\ X_B=b',\ X_C=c,\ X_D=d\}$ and $\theta_2=\{\ X_A=a',\ X_B=b,\ X_C=c',\ X_D=d'\ \}$, using the trivial error function, we get two vectors $<<0,1>,<1>,<0>>$ and $<<1.0>,<0>,<1>>$, then using the sum-better global comparator we get $<1,1,0>$ and $<1,0,1>$, show that $\theta_1 \succ \theta_2$.

Theorem 4.1 The constraint hierarchy CH_H generated from an acyclic CP-networks N, is an information preserving of it, i.e. for each pair of assignments s_1 and s_2, we have $s_1 \triangleright s_2 \Rightarrow s_1 \succ s_2$.

5. CONCLUSION

There are another approaches, e.g. combining the CP-networks with semiring-based CSPs[5,6] and logic programming framework[7], and etc. [5]provides the connection between the CP-nets and soft constraints machinery. But as far as the semiring-based CSPs itself is concerned, efficient algorithms are still under development. The work presented in [7] based on a reduction to the problem of computing stable models for nonmonotonic logic programs, thus provide a new techniques for computing optimal outcomes. Furthermore, we will combine our approaches with HCLP, which would be comparable with the work in [7].

ACKNOWLEDGEMENTS

The work described in this paper was supported by China Natural Science Foundation under grant No.60073039.

REFERENCES

1. Hansson, S.O. Preference Logic. In Gabbay, D.M. and Guenthner, F., editors, Handbook of Philosophical Logic, volume 4, pages 319-394, Kluwer, 2001.
2. Borning, A., Freeman-Benson, Wilson, M. Constraint hierarchies. Lisp and Symbolic Computing, volume5, pages 223-270, 1992.
3. Boutilier,C., Brafman, R., Hoos, H., Poole, D. Reasoning with Conditional Ceteris Paribus Preference Statements. In Proc. of UAI-99, 1999.
4. Rossi, F., Venable, K.B. CP-networks: semantics, complexity, approximations and extensions, In Proc. IJCAI, 2003.
5. Domshlak, C., Rossi, F., Venable, K.B., Walsh, T. Reasoning about soft constraints and conditional preferences: complexity results and approximation techniques. In Proc. Of IJCAI, 2003.
6. Meseguer, P., Bouhmala, N., Bouzoubaa, T., Irgens, M., Sanchez, M. Current Approaches for Solving Over-Constrained Problems. Journal of Constraints, volume8, pages 9-39, 2003.
7. Brafman, R., Dimopoulos, Y. Extended Semantics and Optimization Algorithms for CP-Networks. 2003.

SOLVING CSP BY LAGRANGIAN METHOD WITH IMPORTANCE OF CONSTRAINTS

Takahiro Nakano and Masahiro Nagamatu
Graduate School of Life Science and Systems Engineering, Kyushu Institute of Technology

Abstract: We proposed a neural network called LPPH-CSP for solving constraint satisfaction problem (CSP). The LPPH-CSP is not trapped by any point which is not a solution of the CSP, and it can update all neurons simultaneously. In this paper, we propose two methods to improve the efficiency of the LPPH-CSP. Though the LPPH-CSP can deal with several types of constraints of the CSP, it treats all constraints evenly. One of the proposed methods distinguishes the types of constraints for solving the CSP more efficiently. Another one of the proposed methods applies fast local search (FLS) to the LPPH-CSP. Experimental results show the effectiveness of our proposals.

Key words: CSP; constraint satisfaction problem; neural network; Lagrangian method.

1.   INTRODUCTION

Many AI problems can be represented by the CSP (Constraint Satisfaction Problem). The CSP is a problem to find a variable assignment which satisfies all given constraints. We proposed a neural network called LPPH-CSP[1] for solving the CSP by extending a neural network called LPPH[2] which is proposed for solving the SAT which is a problem to find an assignment of truth values to the variables which satisfies the given CNF (Conjunctive Normal Form).

In this paper, we propose two methods to improve the LPPH-CSP. First we apply the FLS (Fast Local Search)[3] which is useful for the speedup of the neighborhood search process. Next, we extend the LPPH-CSP by introducing importance of the types of the constraints. The LPPH-CSP can deal with several types of constraints of the CSP, however, it treats all constraints evenly. Our extended LPPH-CSP distinguishes the importance of the types of constraints. It can solve the CSP more efficiently.

2.   CSP

The CSP is a combinatorial problem to find a solution which satisfies all given constraints. The CSP is defined by a triple (X, D, C). $X=\{X_1,X_2,\dots,X_n\}$ is a finite set of variables. $D=\{D_1,D_2,\dots,D_n\}$ is a finite set of domains. Each domain D_i is a finite set of values and each variable X_i is assigned a value in D_i. $C=\{C_1,C_2,\dots,C_m\}$ is a finite set of constraints. A solution of the CSP is a variable assignment to X which satisfies C. Let x_{ij} be a Boolean variable which represents "variable X_i is assigned the jth value of D_i". x_{ij} is called a VVP (Variable-Value Pair). Constraint C_r consists of a set of VVPs. In this paper we consider ALT(n,S) [at-least-n-true constraint][1] which requires that at least n of VVPs in S must be true where S is a finite set of VVPs. We also consider ALF(n, S) [at-least-n-false constraint], AMT(n, S) [at-most-n-true constraint], and AMF(n, S) [at-most-n-false constraint].

3.   LPPH-CSP

From now on, each VVP x_{ij} is not a Boolean variable, but a variable which has a continuous value between 0 and 1. The dynamics of the LPPH-CSP is defined as follows[1]:

$$\frac{dx_{ij}}{dt} = x_{ij}\left(1-x_{ij}\right)\sum_{r=1}^{m} w_r s_{rij}\left(x\right),$$

$$\frac{dw_r}{dt} = -\alpha w_r + h_r\left(x\right),$$

(1)

where $s_{rij}(x)$ represents a force put on x_{ij} for satisfying constraint C_r, w_r is the weight of constraint C_r, $h_r(x)$ represents the degree of unsatisfaction of constraint C_r, α is a constant called attenuation coefficient. The LPPH-CSP searches a solution of the CSP by numerically solving the above dynamics.

3.1   Applying the fast local search to LPPH-CSP

Bently[4] proposed the approximate 2-opt method for the TSP (traveling salesman problem). The FLS (Fast Local Search)[3] is a generalization of the approximate 2-opt method. In the FLS algorithm, the neighborhood of the problem is broken down to a small number of sub-neighborhoods and an activation bit is attached to each of them. Only the sub-neighborhoods with the activation bit set to 1 are searched. These sub-neighborhoods are called active sub-neighborhood, and the other are called inactive sub-neighborhood, and they are not searched. We applied the FSL to the LPPH-CSP by the following algorithm:

1. Initially, assign activation bit to all neuron (initial value of activation bit is 1).
2. According to (1) update x_{ij}'s of neurons for which the activation bit is 1. Inactivate a neuron x_{ij}, if x_{ij} does not change its value and all constraints which contain x_{ij} are satisfied. Otherwise activate a neuron x_{ij}.
3. Update weights by (1).
4. Repeat 2 and 3 until the LPPH-CSP find a solution.

3.2   Considering importance of constraints

We consider four types of constrains which are ALT, ALF, AMT and ALF. The LPPH-CSP treats these constraints equally. We extended the LPPH-CSP so as to deal with the importance of the types of constraints. This is called LPPH-CSP with IC (Importance of Constraints). For the dynamics of LPPH-CSP with IC, we replace $w_r s_{rij}(x)$ with $\rho_r w_r s_{rij}(x)$ in (1). ρ_r indicates the importance of constraint C_r. The value of ρ_r depends on the types of constraint C_r.

4.   EXPERIMENTAL RESULTS

We examined the efficiency of proposed methods by experiments. Fig.1 shows the average CPU time for solving Car Sequencing Problems and N-Queen Problems. The average of each problem is calculated by changing initial points 30 times. Furthermore the average of these average CPU time is calculated for the problems in each problem class. The constraints in Car Sequencing Problems and N-Queen Problems are represented by ALT and AMT. We tried various values of ρ_r for CSPs. As the result, we obtained that the best values of ρ_r for solving Car Sequencing Problems and N-Queen problems is around $\rho_r = 1$ for ALT and around $\rho_r = 2$ for AMT.

From experimental results, we can see that the LPPH-CSP with FLS &IC is most effective within the four methods.

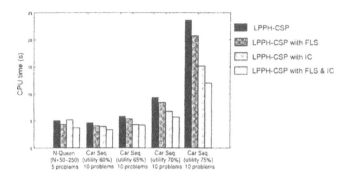

Figure 1. CPU time of proposed methods for N-Queen Problems and Car Seaquencing Problems

5.   CONCLUSION

We proposed two acceleration methods for the LPPH-CSP. First, we applied the FLS which can speed up the neighborhood search process of the LPPH-CSP. Next, we extended the LPPH-CSP so as to deal with the importance of constraints.

Experimental results show that these methods are effective especially for hard problems. For future works we are going to study theoretical analysis of experimental results obtained in this paper, and we plan to determine more effective values of ρ_r's of the LPPH-CSP with IC.

REFERENCES

1.   T. Nakano and M. Nagamatu, "Solving CSP via Neural Network Which Can Update All Neurons Simultaneously", *In Proceedings of the SCIS & ISIS 2004*, (to appear).
2.   M. Nagamatu and T. Yanaru, "On the Stability of Lagrange Programming Neural Networks for Satisfiability Problems of Propositional Calculus", *Neurocomputing*, 13, 119-133, 1995.
3.   C. Voudouris, and E. Tsang, "Partial Constraint Satisfaction Problems and Guided Local Search", *In Proceedings of the PACT-96*, 337-356, 1996.
4.   J.L.Bently, "Fast Algorithms for Geometric Traveling Salesman Problems", *ORSA Journal on Computing* , 4, 387-441, 1992.

COMPONENT RETRIEVAL USING CONVERSATIONAL CASE-BASED REASONING

Mingyang Gu1, Agnar Aamodt2 and Xin Tong3
1,2,3Department of Computer and Information Science, Norwegian University of Science and Technology, Sem Sælands vei 7-9, N-7491, Trondheim, Norway +47 7359 7410 {1Mingyang, 2Agnar, 3Tongxin}@idi.ntnu.no

Abstract: Component retrieval, about how to locate and identify appropriate components, is one of the major problems in component reuse. It becomes more critical as more reusable components come from component markets instead of from an in-house component library, and the number of available components is dramatically increasing. In this paper, we review the current component retrieval methods and propose our conversational component retrieval model (CCRM). In CCRM, components are represented as cases, a knowledge-intensive case-based reasoning (CBR) method is adopted to explore context-based semantic similarities between users' query and stored components, and a conversational case-based reasoning (CCBR) technology is selected to acquire users' requirements interactively and incrementally.

Key words: Software Component Retrieval, Conversational Case-Based Reasoning, Knowledge-Intensive Case-Based Reasoning, Semantic Similarity Calculation, Incrementally Query Acquisition

1.   INTRODUCTION

One of the major problems associated with component reuse is component retrieval[1, 2, 3], which is concerned with how to locate and identify appropriate components to satisfy users' requirements. This problem becomes more critical as the emergence of several component architecture standards, such as, CORBA, COM, and EJB. These standards make software components interoperate more easily. Therefore component reuse surpasses the limitation of a single software company, that is, instead of getting components from an in-house component library, users search for desired components from component markets[4] (web-based software component collections provided by vendors or third parties), which separate component users and component vendors from each other.

A large and rapidly increasing number of reusable components put more strict demands on the retrieval efficiency[5]. If it is acceptable for users to look through tens of available components to identify the most appropriate ones, it is intolerable for them to look through hundreds, or thousands of candidate components, to select what they really need.

Several methods have been put forward to address the component retrieval problem. Most of them assume users can define their component query clearly and accurately, which puts too much impractical burden on component users. Based on the analysis of current retrieval methods, we propose a component retrieval model combining knowledge-intensive case-based reasoning technologies and conversational case-based reasoning methods.

Case-Based Reasoning (CBR) is a problem solving method[6]. The main idea underlying CBR is that when facing a new problem, we will search in our memory to find the most similar previous problem, and reuse the old solution to help solve the new problem.

A CBR process can be divided into four phases: retrieve, reuse, revise and retain, as described in[6]. Our research, as reported in this paper, focuses on the retrieve phase.

In the retrieve phase, a new case (new problem description) is compared to the stored cases, and the most similar one (ones) will be retrieved. Partial matching is adopted in the retrieve phase. Note that the CBR notion of partial matching, i.e. the matching of a group of features in order to return a best match, and where each feature typically has its own weight, distinguishes this technology from information retrieval and database access methods in general. Some CBR methods are 'knowledge-poor', which only consider superficial or syntactical similarities between a new case and stored cases, while other systems take both the syntactical similarity and the semantic similarity into account by combining case-specific knowledge and general domain knowledge. The latter approach is referred to as knowledge-intensive CBR[7].

Conversational case-based reasoning (CCBR) is an interactive form of case-based reasoning. It uses a mixed-initiative dialog to guide users to facilitate the case retrieval process through a question-answer sequence[8]. In the traditional CBR process, users are expected to provide a well-defined problem description (a new case), and based on such a description, the CBR system can find the most appropriate case. But usually users can not define their problem clearly and accurately. So instead of letting users guess how to describe their problem, CCBR calculates the most discriminative questions automatically and incrementally, and displays them to users to extract information to facilitate the retrieval process.

CCBR has been probed in several application domains, for instance, the customer support domain[9], and products or services selection in E-Commerce[10]. To our knowledge, current CCBR methods are to a large extent based on superficial feature properties, and there are so far no published results on CCBR applied to software component retrieval. In our research, we combine knowledge-intensive CBR and conversational CBR in an attempt to resolve the component retrieval problem.

The rest of this paper is organized as follows. In section 2, we review current existing retrieval methods, briefly discuss their advantages and disadvantages; in section 3, our conversational component retrieval model (CCRM) is proposed and some examples are illustrated; in section 4, we discuss the current status of using CBR technologies in the component retrieval field, and identify the advantages and limitations of our component retrieval model. In the end, we discuss our results so far, and point to future work (section 5).

2.   CURRENT COMPONENT RETRIEVAL METHODS

A component retrieval method can be described from three aspects: component representation, component query (users' requirements) specification, and component retrieval process. A popular component retrieval method, named free-text-based retrieval method[11, 12], comes from the information retrieval community. In this method, components are represented as free-text-based documents, while a component query is described using keywords. The retrieval process is to look up the keywords in all component description documents. The components with most matched keywords will be selected. Vector space and indexing technology are used to facilitate documents organizing and matching. This method has low scores on both recall and precision[5]. Researchers and practitioners have proposed to use general thesaurus to extend keywords, by including their synonyms and antonyms, to get more relevant components[13]. In addition, general domain knowledge is also used to extend initial keywords to get more semantically relevant components[5]. However, both of these two improvements increase retrieval recall at the cost of retrieval precision.

Instead of free-text-based component and query descriptions, the following four types of retrieval methods represent components and specify queries using structural information from different perspectives. The pre-enumerated vocabulary method uses a set of pre-defined vocabularies to express both components and queries[14]. In this way, both recall and precision are increased at the cost of the flexibility to describe components and specify component queries. The signature matching method[15] describes both components and queries using signatures which specify the interfaces of components, for instance, the number and the type of input, and output variables. This approach is suitable for components implemented using strongly-typed programming languages. Its weakness is its lack of domain and searching context information. The behavior-based retrieval method[16] is based on the special characteristic of software components being executable. Components take the form of executable codes, and queries are represented by a set of input samples and their desired outputs. The retrieval proceeds by selecting samples, and executing components using the selected samples. The components that satisfy the desired output are retrieved. This method is designed for executable software components and has low efficiency because of long execution time.

The final method we want to mention in this category is faceted selection. This approach predefines a set of dimensions, called facets, which are used to classify components from different perspectives[14]. Users can find their desired components by searching down the stratified categories. This method is getting increasing attention because it takes domain knowledge into account when designing facets. But there exists a design embarrassment: If facets are designed too simple or few, there will be too many components in final categories, which will ask users to select further manually. On the other hand, if facets are designed too complex, it is hard for users to understand them and hard for designers to classify all components into different categories[17, 18]. In addition, the faceted selection method essentially uses the exact matching process. However, it is very hard to get the appropriate components through exact matching because of the universal differences between component requirements and components descriptions[19].

All the retrieval methods mentioned above have one common assumption, that is, users can well define their component queries, and the retrieval system can find one or a few appropriate components according to users' queries. However, this assumption is not always realistic. People often lack clear ideas about what they need while they begin searching for components and usually can not define their queries accurately. They need retrieval system to guide them refining their queries incrementally. Hence, an efficient component retrieval system should be able to support partial matching, select components based on both the syntactical similarity and the semantic similarity, and guide searchers to refine their component query incrementally. Conversational case-based reasoning, extended with knowledge-intensive CBR methods, provides a possibility for satisfying these requirements.

3. THE CONVERSATIONAL COMPONENT RETRIEVAL MODEL (CCRM)

3.1 CCRM Overview

As illustrated in Fig. 1, our conversational component retrieval model (CCRM) includes six parts: a knowledge base, a new case generating module, a knowledge-intensive CBR module, a component displaying module, a question generating and ranking module, and a question displaying module.

The knowledge base stores both component-specific knowledge (cases) and general domain knowledge (including a domain ontology). The new case generating module can set up a new case based on users' initial query and their later answers to discriminative questions. Given a new case, the knowledge-intensive CBR module calculates the similarities between the new case and stored component cases, and returns the components whose similarities surpass a threshold (the threshold is specified initially and can be adjusted following the execution of the system). The component displaying module displays the candidate components to users, ordered by their similarities. In the question generating and ranking module, possible unknown questions are identified, and an information gain algorithm[20] is used to rank the possible questions according to how much information it can provide if it has been answered. Then general knowledge is used to filter out those questions whose answers can be inferred from the initial query or previously answered questions. These ordered questions are further reordered according to some constraints inferred from general knowledge, for example, people normally prefer to answer the high level questions before answering low level ones. The question displaying module selects the most discriminative question, in order to optimize search towards a meaningful answer.

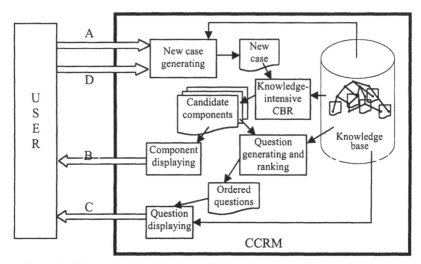

Figure 1. The architecture of conversational component retrieval model (CCRM).

Arrows: A, B, C and D, are interactive processes between users and CCRM. A: users input their initial query; B: the system provides users with top matched components; C: the system displays the most discriminative question to users; D: users select a displayed question and provide their answer to the system. Other processes are completed in the system automatically.

The retrieval process in the CCRM model can be described as the following steps:

1. Users provide their initial query, which takes the form of free-text-based terms.
2. The new case generating module transforms the initial query into a new case. In this step, a general thesaurus and a domain ontology are used to transform the free-text-based initial query into standard terms used in the internal system, and formalize them into a new case.
3. The knowledge-intensive CBR module calculates the similarities between the new case and stored cases through combining both component specific knowledge and general domain knowledge, and the components whose similarities surpass a threshold are returned.
4. If users find their desired component from the displayed candidate components, they can terminate the retrieval process. Otherwise, the conversational process is activated.
5. The question generating and ranking module identifies the unknown questions from the candidate components, and ranks them according to their information gains. Further, the ordered questions are filtered and reordered using general domain knowledge.

6. The question displaying module selects the most discriminative question, and displays it and its meaningful answers to users in a readable format.
7. Users provide the system with their answer to the displayed question. Otherwise, if users can not answer a displayed question, the question displaying module will display the next most discriminative question.
8. The new case generating module combines the previous new case and the newly gained answer to set up a new case.
9. The iterations from 3 to 8 continue until users find their desired component or there are no other discriminative questions left.

3.2   Component Representation in CREEK

In CCRM, we adopt a frame-based knowledge representation and reasoning system, CREEK[21], which can unify component-specific cases and general domain knowledge within a single representation system. In CREEK, all knowledge is represented as concepts, and a concept takes the form of a frame-based structure, which consists of a list of slots. A slot acts as a relation from the concept to a value related with another concept. Viewed as a semantic network, a concept (frame) corresponds to a node, and a relation (slot) corresponds to a link between nodes. Slot values have types or roles, referred to as facet. Typical facets include current value, default value, value class, and value constraint. So the knowledge in CREEK is represented in a 4-level structure, frame, slot, facet and value.

```
OutputComponent (partial)
    subclass-of                value            Component
    has-instance               value            Write BMP
    has-instance               value            Write TIFF
    has-instance               value            Write JPEG
    has-error                  value            file-open-error
    has-number-of-parameter    default          1
    has-image-color-space      value-class      Color-space
    has-image-dimension        value-class      Image-Dimension
    has-image-file-type        value-class      Image-file-type
    has-size-constraints       value-constraint (and (> 0 Bytes) (< 100 MB))
    ...
```

Fig. 2 gives, in a frame view, an example to illustrate how a part of an image OutputComponent class is represented in CREEK. Fig. 3 shows, in a network view, a part of the knowledge base for components used in the image processing field. General domain knowledge can be represented as relations between different values. For example, the "extract to" relation from "3D" to "2D" means that 3 dimension images can be extracted to 2 dimension images. Similarly, the two relations "convert to" between "XYZ" and "RGB" mean that images described using "XYZ" color space and

images described using "RGB" color space can be converted to each other
without losing any information.

Figure 3. A part of the knowledge base (implemented in the CREEK system) for
components in the image processing field.

Component query (partial)	
has-number-of-parameter	1
has-image-color-apace	RGB
has-image-dimension	3D
has-image-file-type	BMP file
has-error	file-open-error
has-file-size-constraints	5 megabyte
...	

Write BMP component (partial)	
has-number-of-parameter	1
has-image-color-apace	XYZ
has-image-dimension	2D
has-image-file-type	BMP file
has-error	file-open-error
has-file-size-constraints	(and (> 0 Bytes) (< 100 Megabyte))
...	

Figure 4. The partial frame contents of the component query and the stored component
'Write BMP'.

3.3   Knowledge-Intensive Similarity Calculation

In CCRM, we use an explanation-driven similarity calculating method[7],
which can be divided into three steps, ACTIVATE, EXPLAIN and FOCUS.
ACTIVATE determines what knowledge in the knowledge base is involved
in the retrieval process, and calculates the similarities between the new case
and activated stored cases based on a rather syntactical or superficial
similarity measuring. The output of the ACTIVATE step is a set of
components whose similarity values surpass a certain threshold. EXPLAIN
is used to evaluate the similarities between the new case and stored cases,
selected in the ACTIVATE step, based on general domain knowledge. The
evaluation task concerns justifying that the well-matched slots are relevant to

the problem goal, and "explaining away" the mismatched slots that are unimportant. According to evaluation results, similarity values are adjusted. For instance, if one mismatched slot is evaluated as important for the problem goal, the total similarity value of the involved component is reduced. Otherwise, the similarity value is increased or keeps unchanged.

In the example shown in Fig. 4, there are two mismatched slots, "has-image-color-space" and "has-image-dimension", between the component query and the stored component. With the domain knowledge that "RGB convert to XYZ" and "XYZ convert to RGB", we can explain that "since the source image using RGB color space can be converted to an image using XYZ color space and vice versa, it is possible to use this stored component to realize the required task", and the similarity value generated in the ACTIVATE step can be kept unchanged or increased. On the contrary, there is not any explanation path from 2D to 3D, which means it is impossible for images with 2 dimensions to be converted to images with 3 dimensions, so the mismatch on the "has-image-dimension" slot can not be explain as unimportant and the similarity value of this stored component is reduced.

3.4   Question Selecting and Ranking

There are at least two requirements on the mixed-initiative question-answer interaction in conversational CBR. First, displayed questions should be easy to understand. Second, the selected question should be the most informative or discriminative one.

As to the first requirement, we predefine a question and its possible answers to each slot. For example, on the slot "has-image-file-type", we predefine a question that "what type of images do you want to deal with in this component?" and the possible answers, "BMP", "TIFF", "JPEG", or "Text". All the slots that appear in the candidate components, returned by the knowledge-intensive CBR module, but not in the new case are identified and transformed into unknown questions. Whether or not a possible answer is displayed to users in the conversational process depends on whether this answer appears in the candidate components.

As to the second requirement, "selecting the most informative question", we adopt the information gain metric[20] to quantitatively measure the information one slot (question) can provide (if we know the value of this slot).

The core concept in information gain is entropy. Given a collection S, its entropy value in state m can be calculated using the following formula:

$$Entropy(S_m) = \sum_{i}^{c} - p_i \log_2 p_i$$

The number c means how many sub-groups the collection can be divided into, and p_i means the proportion of the ith sub-group. If we can not classify a collection of components into sub-groups, its entropy is 0 (c=1, p_i=1). After we acquire information on slot n, the collection can be classified into different sub-groups according to their various values on slot n, and the collection's entropy is increased. Information gain of slot n is defined as:

$$InformationGain(slot\_n) = Entropy(S_{have-information-about-slot\_n}) - Entropy(S_{have-no-information-about-slot\_n})$$

Different slots have different information gain. The larger the information gain one slot has, the more information it can provide if we know the value for this slot. That is, to find the most informative question is to find the slot with the largest information gain.

For instance, there is a candidate component collection with the number of 100, and there are two unknown slots in the new case, "has-image-file-type" and "has-image-color-space". According to the different values of the slot "has-image-file-type", appearing in the candidate components, "BMP", "TIFF" and "JPEG", the collection can be divided into three sub-groups with the numbers, 30, 30 and 40 respectively. According to the different values on "has-image-color-space", "RGB" and "XYZ", the collection can be divided into two sub-groups with the numbers, 30 and 70 respectively. In this case, the information gains of these two slots are calculated using the above formulae:

$$InformationGain(S_{has-image-file-type}) = 1.5711 \quad InformationGain(S_{has-image-color-space}) = 0.8814$$

So the question based on the slot "has-image-file-type" is more informative than that of "has-image-color-space". The question, "what type of images do you want to deal with in this component?" is displayed to users with three possible answers, "BMP", "TIFF", or "JPEG".

4.   RELATED RESEARCH AND DISCUSSION

Software is used to resolve practical problems, and software components are existing solutions to previous problems, so component reuse can be described as "trying to use the solutions to previous similar problems to help solve the current problem". Therefore, it is very natural to use CBR methods to support component reuse. In fact, various types of CBR methods have been explored and found useful for component reuse.

Object Reuse Assistant (ORA)[2] is a hybrid framework to use CBR to locate appropriate components in an object-oriented software library (small-talk component library). In this framework, both small-talk classes and small-talk methods take the form of stored cases. The concepts in small-talk, for instance, c-class, c-method and c-data-spec, and their instantiated objects are connected together as a conceptual hierarchy. Though the conceptual hierarchy can be seen as a representation method combining case-specific knowledge and general knowledge, the retrieval process is knowledge-poor (a new case is compared with stored cases based on how many attributes two cases have in common).

IBROW[22] is an automated software application configuration project. Users' tasks (queries) can be decomposed into sub-tasks by matched task decomposers, and sub-tasks can be decomposed further. Tasks or subtasks can finally be solved by matched stored components. Both task decomposers and components are referred to as PSMs (problem solving methods). The output is an application configuration composed of stored components, which satisfies users' query. CBR is used at two levels in IBROW. The high level is called constructive adaptation. In this level, PSMs take the form of cases, which are represented using feature terms, and a knowledge-poor matching method (term subsumption) is adopted when searching the possibly applied PSMs. At the low level, CBR is used as a heuristic algorithm to realize the best-first searching strategy. Previously solved configurations are stored as cases, and represented as feature terms. For each intermediate state, the newly added PSM is considered. The stored configurations in which the same PSM appears as a part are identified, and the similarities between each of these configurations and the new problem are calculated. The most similar configuration is selected, and its similarity value is taken as the heuristic value to the involved intermediate state. As the ORA system, IBROW uses a knowledge-poor retrieval process and only supports tentative and manual interactions between users and the system.

Compared with these two CBR-based component retrieval systems, our proposed conversational component retrieval model (CCRM) has two advantages:

The first is that components are selected based on both their syntactical similarities and semantic similarities. Selecting components based on their semantic similarities with users' query rather than only on syntactical similarities is a promising research topic. However, the existing research concerned with this topic mainly use domain knowledge to refine users' queries before the searching process[5, 17, 23]. In CCRM, besides the query refinement using general thesaurus and domain-ontology, a special type of knowledge-intensive CBR method, explanation-driven CBR, is adopted to explore components' context-based semantic similarities with a query during the retrieval process.

The second is that users' requirements are acquired interactively and incrementally. Normally, component users prefer to provide their initial query only based on their necessary requirements in order to avoid excluding possibly appropriate components. Because of the looseness of the initial query and the large number of available components, users usually still get numerous candidate components. In CCRM, instead of letting users guess and try what requirements they should specify further, an information gain algorithm is used to provide users with the most discriminative questions to refine their query interactively and incrementally.

A limitation of our method is its dependence on knowledge engineering. The knowledge base combining both component specific cases and general domain knowledge is assumed to exist initially. The construction of this initial knowledge base puts a significant workload on the knowledge engineering process.

5.   FUTURE WORK

The evaluation of CCRM is in process. The knowledge-intensive similarity measuring process has been realized in the CREEK system, and the conversational process is being added. We are building a knowledge base for the components existing in the DynamicImager system, a visual and dynamic image processing experimentation environment, in which there are about 200 different image operating components.

Our current research focus is to use the knowledge-intensive method to facilitate the discriminative question selection. Though the information gain algorithm can select the most discriminative question automatically and incrementally, it is knowledge-poor essentially. We plan to use knowledge-intensive methods, especially the explanation-driven method, to remove the candidate slots (questions) whose values can be inferred from users' initial query or previously answered questions, and to adjust the priorities between slots which represent semantic relations, such as, abstraction, causality, dependency and part-of relations. The hypothesis is that this will help to identify the most informative question, shorten dialog length, and reduce users' cognitive workload.

REFERENCES

1. Mili, A., R. Mili, and R.T. Mittermeir, (1998), A survey of software reuse libraries. Annals of Software Engineering, 5(0): p. 349 - 414.
2. Fernández-Chamizo, C., et al. (1996), Supporting Object Reuse through Case-Based Reasoning. European Workshop on Case-Based Reasoning. Lausanne, Switzerland.
3. Iribarne, L., J.M. Troya, and A. Vallecillo. (2002), Selecting software components with multiple interfaces. 28th Euromicro Conference.
4. Ravichandran, T. and M.A. Rothenberger, (2003), Software reuse strategies and component markets. Communications of the ACM, 46(8): p. 109 - 114.
5. Klein, M. and A. Bernstein. (2001), Searching for Services on the Semantic Web Using Process Ontologies. The First Semantic Web Working Symposium. Stanford, CA, USA.
6. Aamodt, A. and E. Plaza, (1994), Case-Based Reasoning: Foundational Issue, Methodological Variations, and System Approaches. AI Communications, 7(1): p. 39-59.
7. Aamodt, A. (1994), Explanation-driven case-based reasoning. Topics in Case-based reasoning: Springer Verlag.
8. Aha, D.W. and L.A. Breslow, (2001), Conversational Case-Based Reasoning. Applied Intelligence, 14(1): p. 9-32.
9. Muñoz-Avila, H., et al., (1999), HICAP: An Interactive Case-Based Planning Architecture and its Application to Noncombatant Evacuation Operations.
10. Shimazu, H., (2002), ExpertClerk: A Conversational Case-Based Reasoning Tool for Developing Salesclerk Agents in E-Commerce Webshops. Artificial Intelligence Review, 18(3-4): p. 223 - 244.
11. Frakes, W.B. and B.A. Nejmeh, (1987), Software reuse through information retrieval. ACM SIGIR Forum, 21(1-2): p. 30-36.
12. Helm, R. and Y.S. Maarek. (1991), Integrating information retrieval and domain specific approaches for browsing and retrieval in object-oriented class libraries. Conference on

Object Oriented Programming Systems Languages and Applications. Phoenix, Arizona, United States.

13. Magnini, B., (1999), Use of a lexical knowledge base for information access systems. Journal of Theoretical & Applied Issues in Specialized Communication, 5(2): p. 203 - 228.

14. Prieto-Daz, R., (1991), Implementing faceted classification for software reuse. Communications of the ACM, 34(5): p. 89 - 97.

15. Zaremski, A.M. and J.M. Wing, (1995), Signature matching: a tool for using software libraries. ACM Transactions on Software Engineering Methodology, 4(2): p. 146 -170.

16. Park, Y., (2000), Software retrieval by samples using concept analysis. Systems & Software, 54(3): p. 179-183.

17. Sugumaran, V. and V.C. Storey, (2003), A Semantic-Based Approach to Component Retrieval. The DATA BASE for Advances in Information Systems, 34(3): p. 8-24.

18. Vitharana, P., F.M. Zahedi, and H. Jain, (2003), Design, retrieval, and assembly in component-based software development. Communications of the ACM, 46(11): p. 97-102.

19. Redondo, R.P.D., et al. (2002), Approximate Retrieval of Incomplete and Formal Specifications Applied to Vertical Reuse. International Conference on Software Maintenance. Montreal, Quebec, Canada.

20. Quanlan, J.R., (1986), Induction of decision trees. Machine Learning, 1(1): p. 81-106.

21. Aamodt, A. (1994), A Knowledge Representation System for Integration of General and Case-Specific Knowledge. International Conference on Tools with Artificial Intelligence. New Orleans.

22. IBROW, (2004), Website. http://www.swi.psy.uva.nl/projects/ibrow/home.html.

23. Bernstein, A. and M. Klein. (2002), Towards High-Precision Service Retrieval. International Semantic Web Conference. Sardinia Italy.

MIXED PARALLEL EXECUTION OF ALGORITHMS FOR SATISFIABILITY PROBLEM

Kairong Zhang   and   Masahiro Nagamatu
Graduate School of Life Science and Systems Engineering, Kyushu Institute of Technology, Kitakyushu, Japan

Abstract: LPPH has been proposed to solve the satisfiability problem (SAT). In order to solve the SAT more efficiently, a parallel execution has been proposed. Experimental results show that higher speedup ratio is obtained by using this parallel execution of the LPPH. In this paper, we propose a method of mixed parallel execution of several algorithms for the SAT. "Mixed" means the parallel execution of the LPPH and local search algorithms. In the experiments, we used the LPPH with attenuation coefficient generating function and the GSAT. Results of experiments show mixing these two algorithms yield excellent performance.

Key words: Satisfiability problem; parallel execution; neural network; Lagrangian method

1.   INTRODUCTION

We have proposed a parallel execution of the LPPH[1,2,3], and experimental results show that higher speedup ratio is obtained by using this parallel execution of the LPPH. In this paper, we propose a mixed parallel execution of the LPPH and local search algorithms. We did experiments in which the LPPH with attenuation coefficient generating function[4] and the GSAT[5] are used. Results of the experiments show the mixed parallel execution can be more efficient than the parallel execution of the LPPH only or the parallel execution of the GSAT only for many problems.

2. PARALLEL EXECUTION OF LPPH

We have proposed a parallel execution of the LPPH: (1) Prepare plural neural networks of the LPPH. (2) Start the LPPHs simultaneously from different initial points from each other. (3) When any of the LPPHs finds a solution, halt all LPPHs and return the solution. It is very easy to realize this parallel execution of the LPPH by hardware. Only we have to do is preparing plural neural networks. The total system is very simple and executable at high-speed.

Suppose that a parallel execution of p LPPHs is done. Let t_j be the execution time of jth LPPH for finding a solution. Then, $T_p = \min\{t_j \mid 1 \le j \le p\}$ is the execution time of the parallel execution. We will call T_p and pT_p, "execution time" and "total execution time", respectively. Sometimes we will use "number of updates" instead of "execution time", because these are proportional when the problem is fixed. The result of experiment is shown in Fig.1. The horizontal axis indicates the number of LPPHs, and the vertical axis indicates the speedup ratio, namely $E(T_p)/E(T_1)$, where E means the average. In this experiment, parallel execution of p (p=1, 2, ... , 50) neural networks of LPPH is used. Randomly generated 3-SAT problems are used in this experiments. They are exp-r300 (300 variables and 1275 clauses), exp-r200 (200 variables and 860 clauses), exp-r100 (100 variables and 430 clauses), and exp-r50 (50 variables and 215 clauses). From Fig.1, it is shown that higher speedup ratio is obtained. This is remarkable for large and difficult problems, e.g. exp-r300.

3. MIXED PARALLEL EXECUTION OF LPPH AND GSAT

The local search algorithms find solutions from randomly selected initial points. Therefore they can be used in our parallel execution. In this paper, we propose a mixed parallel execution of local search algorithms and the LPPH as follows:
(1) Prepare plural solvers of the SAT, such as the LPPH and local search algorithms. These solvers may be neural networks, electronic circuits or software processes executed on computers.
(2) Start the solvers simultaneously from different initial points.
(3) When any of the solvers finds a solution, halt all solvers and return the solution.

The mixed parallel execution also has the same advantage with the parallel execution of the LPPH, and also do not need any communication overhead.

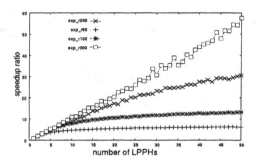

Figure1. The speedup ratio for random 3-SAT

4. EXPERIMENT

We did experiments which use the LPPH with attenuation coefficient generating function and the GSAT for the mixed parallel execution. Results of experiments are shown in Figure 2 and Figure 3. Figure 2 and Figure 3 are the results of a random 3-SAT of 200 variables and 860 clauses, and a 20-Queen problem, respectively. In these graphs, horizontal axes indicate the number of solvers and vertical axes indicate the average of the total CPU times of 200 trials. In these graphs, 3 types of parallel execution are compared. In the first type, all solvers are the LPPH with attenuation coefficient generating function. We call this type PA_{LPPH}. In the second type, all solvers are GSAT (PA_{GSAT}). In the third type, they are mixed into halves (PA_{mixed}). For many problems we have results similar to Figure2 and Figure 3. From these results, we can say PA_{LPPH} is more efficient than PA_{GSAT}, if p is small, and PA_{mixed} is at least as efficient as the better one of PA_{GSAT} and PA_{LPPH}. Furthermore, it is not so rare, to our surprise, that PA_{mixed} becomes more efficient than PA_{GSAT} and PA_{LPPH} as shown in Figure 3.

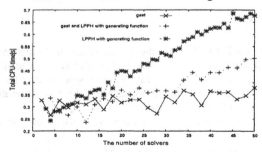

Figure 2. Comparison of several parallel execution methods
for random 3-SAT of 200 variables and 860 clauses

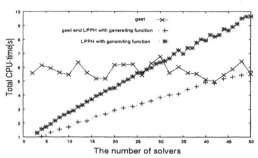

*Figure3.   Comparison of several parallel execution
methods for 20 —queen*

5.   CONCLUSION

It is easy for the LPPH to achieve a parallel processing when neurons are implemented individually by electronic circuits or on different computers (neuron-level parallel processing). Many researches of neuron-level parallel processing had been done. In this case several kinds of communication overheads are needed, such as space overhead or time overhead.

We have proposed a parallel execution of the LPPH (we call this a network-level parallel processing). This method achieves the high speedup ratio and low communication overhead. In this paper, we extend this to the mixed parallel execution of the LPPH and the GSAT. The experimental results show that for many problems the mixed parallel execution is at least as efficient as the better one of the two non-mixed parallel executions. Furthermore, for some problems, the mixed parallel execution becomes more efficient than non-mixed parallel executions. The future work for us, is to study about the reason of the efficiency of mixed parallel execution.

REFERENCE

1. M. Nagamatu and T. Yannaru, "On the stability of Lagrange programming neural networks of satisfiability problems of propositional calculus", Neurocomputing, 13, 119-133, 1995.
2. M. Nagamatu and T. Yannaru, "Parallel state space search for SAT with Lagrange Programming Neural Network", proceedings of the fifth International Conference on Neural Information Processing. October, 1998
3. K. Zhang and M. Nagamatu, "Parallel execution of neural networks for solving SAT" (to appear).
4. K. Zhang and M. Nagamatu, "Solving SAT by execution of neural network with probabilistic attenuation coefficient generator" (to appear)

5. B.Selman, H. Levesque and D.Mitchell, "A new method for solving hard satisfiability problem," AAA-92, Proceedings Tenth National Conference on Artifical Intelligence, pp.440-6,1992

CLUSTERING BINARY CODES TO EXPRESS THE BIOCHEMICAL PROPERTIES OF AMINO ACIDS

Huaiguo Fu, Engelbert Mephu Nguifo
CRIL-CNRS FRE2499, Université d'Artois, Rue de l'université SP 16, 62307 Lens cedex. France
{fu,mephu}@cril.univ-artois.fr

Abstract   We study four kinds of binary codes of amino acids (AA). Two codes of them are based respectively on biochemical properties, and the two others are generated with artificial intelligence (AI) methods, and are based on protein structures and alignment, and on Dayhoff matrix. In order to give a global significance of each binary code, we use a hierarchical clustering method to generate different clusters of each binary codes of amino acids. Each cluster is examined with biochemical properties to give an explanation on the similarity between amino acids that it contains. To validate our examination, a decision tree based machine learning system is used to characterize the AA clusters obtained with each binary codes. From this experimentation, it comes out that one of the AI based codes allows to obtain clusters that have significant biochemical properties. As a consequence, it appears that even if attributes of binary codes generated with AI methods, do not separately correspond to a biochemical property, they can be significant in the whole. Conversely binary codes based on biochemical properties can be insignificant when forming a whole.

Keywords: Bioinformatics and AI, Amino acids, Classification, Clustering

1.   Introduction

More and more methods and techniques of Artificial Intelligence (AI) are applied to solve problems of molecular biology such as protein secondary or tertiary structures prediction. Such techniques are generally based on AA mutation matrices. However there are a lot of symbolic AI techniques based on binary representations that could be applied in this domain. These works used single representation which does not catch many biochemical properties of AA. If the biochemical properties of AA can be perfectly described with certain binary codes, it will improve performance accuracy on the prediction of protein structure and function from its AA sequences [1]. Hence in this paper we will focus on binary representation for AA.

Expressing binary rules is more understandable for human-expert and could be helpful for providing efficient results explanation to the expert. Many symbolic AI systems deal with binary representations. They are unable to treat numerical values as that encodes in AA mutation matrices. If several research works are being devoted to AA indices or mutation matrices, our investigation of the literature gives rise only to four works on binary representation of AA:

Dickerson & Geis (DG) [2], Marlière & Saurin (MS) [3], De la Maza (DM) [1], and finally
Gracy & Mephu (GM) [4].

In this study, we compare and analyse these 4 methods of AA binary representation. In order
to search for a global significance of each binary code, firstly, we use a clustering algorithm to
group AA. Then a machine learning system is used to explain the significances of the clusters
using biochemical data. If the clusters perfectly correspond to certain biochemical properties of
Amino acids, we consider this binary code as a good binary representation. In order to validate
and explain the clusters of AA, the decision tree C4.5 is used to characterize the AA clusters.

The paper is organized as follows. The four AA binary representations are presented in next
section. In the third section, we present hierarchical clustering to generate clusters of binary
representations, and discuss the results obtained. And then a decision tree system C4.5 is used
to validate the clusters of representations of AA in the fourth section.

2.   Binary representations of amino acids

Binary representation of AA is a table of twenty rows and different columns. Each column
is a property which can correspond to a biochemical property. Each row corresponds to an AA.

2.1   Binary Codes based on biochemical properties

Two representations based on biochemical properties of AA are described by: DG and MS.

DG's binary representation considers following properties of AA: aliphatic, aromatic, charged,
polar, size of AA and hydrophobic. The table of the properties of AA could be easily transform
to a binary representation.

DG make an analysis of some protein sequences of the heavy and light chains of immunoglob-
ulines to create this representation. A problem with this representation is that some AA have
exactly the same physical and chemical properties in their classification, so the binary representations can't be distinguished. A way to solve this problem could be to add additional properties
that allows to distinguish them.

MS propose to represent AA with 8 biochemical properties [3]. On the basis of these 8
biochemical properties, each AA can be represented by a bit string like with the DG's code. For
example, we use 00010100 to represent the amino acid I (Isoleucine).

This coding is a topologic description of AA.The coding appears sharply particular choices
to certain types of studies, because certain criteria such as hydrophobicity in particular are debatable. This coding can be spread with the addition of other properties such as hydrophobicity,
hydrophilic, etc. With such coding, it is also necessary to explicitly or implicitly add negation
of properties in order to avoid inclusion between two AA codes.

2.2   Binary codes based on AI methods

DM's [1] and GM's [4] codes apply AI algorithms to generate binary representations. They
propose a complete system to generate and test the binary representations of AA.

They use different techniques, but the whole structure is the same. In order to generate best
binary representations, they use searching algorithms to find the best solution for representation
of AA, from some data of AA or protein.

DM used the primary and secondary structure of proteins to create AA representations that
facilitate secondary structure prediction. A genetic algorithm searches the space of AA representations. The quality of each representation is quantified by training a neural network to
predict secondary structure using that representation. The genetic algorithm then uses the per-

formance accuracy of the representation to guide its search and to create AA representations (see an example in [1]) that improve the performance accuracy.

DM [1] describes a system that synthesizes regularity exposing attributes from large protein databases. After processing primary and secondary structure data, this system discovers an AA representation that captures what are thought to be the three most important AA characteristics (size, charge, and hydrophobicity) for tertiary structure prediction.

GM's method uses the Dayhoff matrix and simulated annealing algorithms to generate the binary code of representation of 20 AA. Using this method, we can get different representations of AA by changing its parameters.

3.   Clustering analysis of binary representations of AA

In the previous section, four methods to represent AA with binary codes are briefly presented. However, we face some questions: What's the significance of each binary representation? Which is a good AA representation? To answer these questions, we use a clustering algorithm and decision tree system to validate the AA binary representations.

3.1   Hierarchical Clustering

We use different hierarchical clustering methods available inside the SAS datamining package: Ward's method, Average Linkage method, and Centroid method. For example,using Ward's method with the 24 bits representation of GM's method, when the number of clusters is 5, the result obtained is: Cluster 1: Asp, Glu, His, Lys, Asn, Pro, Gln, Arg. Cluster 2: Gly, Met, Val. Cluster 3: Cys, Ser, Thr. Cluster 4: Ala, Ile, Leu. Cluster 5: Phe, Trp, Tyr.

3.2   Examination of clusters

The AA biochemical properties are at the basis of the interpretation of clusters of binary representations. We modify and extend the representation of chemical properties of AA proposed by DM. Modifications and extensions come from discussion reported in recent publications on biochemistry. We add some properties such as the mass, the number of atoms, and the hydrophobicity scale.

As an example, the result of 5 clusters with the 24 bits representation of GM, is well-adapted to biochemical conditions and these clusters of AA have a certain logic of biochemical affinity:

Phenylalanine, Tryptophane and Tyrosine : aromatic AA with cyclic side chain and no charged. Alanine, Isoleucine and Leucine : AA with side chains aliphatic. Cysteine, Serine and Threonine : the Threonine differs of Serine by a grouping methyl and the Cysteine differs of serine by the presence of one atom of sulfur in the place of the atom of oxygen. Asp, Glu, His, Lys, Asn, Pro, Gln, Arg: are more hydrophilic. Gly, Met, Val are hydrophobic.

From the examination of all the sets of clusters obtained, it appears very often that there were always two or three clusters with debatable similarity, except for the previous one: the set of 5 clusters of 24-bits representation of GM. With the coding of DM, we didn't obtain the same clusters as that reported in [1]. This may be due to the fact that DM uses the Cobweb clustering algorithm which is different from the Ward's method. With the coding based on biochemical properties, we were unable to find a set with good clusters.

From this first observation, it appears that coding based on AI method can have a good global significance, whenever coding based on biochemical properties could not be significant in a whole. This global significance arises from the fact that similarity between AA is expressed inside the Dayhoff matrix in the case of GM, or inside protein sequence alignment and protein structure in the case of DM.

A second observation is made on properties of AI based coding. For the binary representation based on biochemical properties, each column corresponds to one biochemical property. For representations based on AI methods, we find that properties of binary codes do not separately correspond to biochemical properties.

4.   Interpretation of clusters

In order to verify the clusters of binary representations of AA using biochemical data, we use a public domain of decision tree system C4.5 to predict the cluster of an AA.

From the results of decision tree, the representation based on AI methods can be shown that it corresponds to some biochemical properties of AA in varying degrees. It validates the accuracy of the clusters of AA representations.

However, even with the clusters and biochemical properties reported in [1], we were unable to find the explanation tree obtained with the decision tree system as mentioned in the paper.

The results show that the clustering results of the 24-bits representation produced by GM's method are correct and can be characterize with biochemical properties. This is in concordance with the results of our examinations by hand. This shows that the 24-bits representation produced by GM's method is one of the best binary representations of AA. This corroborates previous results reported in [4], where this representation allows to find good alignment when dealing with weakly homologous protein sequences.

For biochemical based representations, the decision tree can't give an understandable explanation of the clusters. This is in concordance with our analysis by hand. Thus biochemical properties based representations need to be preprocessed before being used, in order to express a whole significance.

From the results of clustering and decision tree process, we know that the methods of DM, and of GM based on AI methods can generate good binary representations of AA. These representations are significant in a whole, and allow to take into account biochemical properties when dealing with protein primary structure.

5.   Conclusion

This paper reviews two kinds of AA binary representations respectively based on biochemical properties, and on searching methods. A comparative study of these codes is described, and provides some significant results.

Good AA representations can facilitate the prediction of proteins secondary or tertiary structure, can allow to find good alignment of proteins primary sequences. This work could allow to improve results of AI methods when dealing with protein folding problem as it is well-established that data representation is one of the keys of success of AI methods.

References

[1] De la Maza M. Generate, Test and Explain: Synthesizing Regularity Exposing Attributes in Large Protein DataBases. In *Proc. of (HICSS)*, pages 123–129, Hawaï, USA, 1994.

[2] Dickerson R.E. and Geis I. The structure and actions of proteins. *Harper & Row Publishers,New York, NY*, pages 16 – 17, 1969.

[3] Sallantin J., Marlière P., and Saurin W. Description logique des contextes spatiaux dans les protéines: application à la conception de polypeptides artificiels. In *Actes des journées Point Curie*, pages 141–153, Paris, France, 1984. Institut Curie.

[4] E. Mephu Nguifo. *Concevoir une abstraction à partir de ressemblances.* Thèse de doctorat d'université, Université de Montpellier II, Mai 1993. 276 pages.

NATURAL LANGUAGE INTERFACE TO MOBILE DEVICES

Lina Zhou, Mohammedammar Shaikh and Dongsong Zhang
University of Maryland, Baltimore County, Baltimore, MD 21250, U.S.A.

Abstract: Natural language interface (NLI) facilitates the human use of computers. In this paper, we review the state-of-the-art NLI application. Based on the extant literature, we design process flow of an NLI system enabling easy information access via mobile devices.

Key words: natural language interface, natural language processing, mobile device

1. INTRODUCTION

Natural Language Interface (NLI) is an interface that allows users to interact with the computer using a human language, such as English or Chinese, as opposed to using a computer language, command line interface, or a graphical user interface [1]. NLI essentially provides an abstract layer between users and computers by enabling computers to understand human language instead of the other way around. It allows the user to enter natural language search queries in written or spoken text.

Mobile devices (e.g., PDAs, cell phones) present usability challenges to users and system designers due to small screens and limited input methods, unreliable network connectivity, customer apathy, and other factors [2]. NLI has been used for a variety of applications including database query, question-answering, personalization and so on [3-5]. Despite the potential of NLI in improving the usability of mobile devices, the extant work on NLI has primarily focused on desktop computer systems. Thus, investigating NLI to mobile devices can extend our knowledge on NLI from both theoretical and practical perspectives.

In this paper, we focus on NLI that enables easy access to information repositories via mobile devices.

2.   NATURAL LANGUAGE INTERFACE TO MOBILE DEVICES

Natural language processing is the core technology in support NLI systems. A natural language system [6] should not only have an understanding of what a word means and how to combine words into phrases and sentences, but also know what a sentence means in various contexts. The potential of NLI was first demonstrated with LUNAR [7] - a natural language dialogue system. It led to a stream of research on natural language query interfaces to database (e.g., [5]). NLI has been extended to help users navigate the site by accepting and processing questions such as search queries in natural language and responding in natural language [4]. This is particularly useful for transforming customer service capabilities. For example, consumers can issue intuitive and natural commands or queries rather than being asked to follow complex menus and adjust to difficult interfaces. NLI also allows users to control systems by carrying out directions and executing business transactions. The natural language is also viewed as a compelling enabling technology for information personalization [8]. In sum, NLI demonstrates advantages such as efficiency, flexibility, economy, and expressiveness. Speech-based interface can further increase the speed of accessing a computer system by allowing hand-free human computer interaction, which is not possible when using the standard keyboard and mouse.

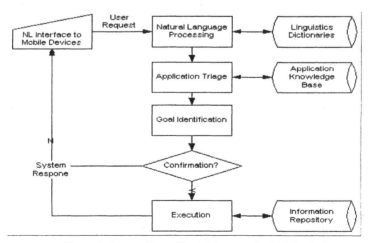

Figure 1. Process Flow of an NLI system for Mobile Devices

Mobile devices users can benefit from NLI by increasing the efficiency and effectiveness of information management. Mobile devices are identified as the best alternative to paper-based tools in managing information [9]. The physical limitations of mobile devices can be mitigated with the help of natural language. For example, finding an appropriate application and inserting the information into the right place in an application consumes a large amount of users' time. An NLI to applications may help user locate the right application and update information in the corresponding database or information repository.

Drawing from the literature on NLI (e.g., [10, 11]), we design process flow of an NLI system for mobile devices, as shown in Figure 1. Brief descriptions of each component are provided as follows:

NL Interface: The NL interface provides an easy-to-use and unified interface to mobile applications. It accepts text or speech input in natural language.

Natural Language Processing: The user request is processed with natural language techniques.

Application Triage: Based on the understanding result, the user request is triaged to an appropriate application on mobile devices.

Goal Identification and Confirmation: Once the application is identified, a course of action will be initiated by updating information in the application. In addition, confirmation gives users an opportunity to either proceed with the action or return to the NL interface.

Execution: Action is taken in response to user request.

The above processes and related knowledge source and information repository will be updated periodically based on users' interaction history. It is suggested that the challenges of developing satisfactory NLI should never be underestimated [1] and both competence and performance errors should be expected. The effectiveness of the proposed process flow will be evaluated by studying usability of prototype systems in future.

3.   CONCLUSION

The pragmatic goal of natural language and multimodal interfaces [8] (including speech recognition, keyboard entry, and pointing, among others) is to enable ease-of-use for users/customers in performing more sophisticated human-computer interactions. Information management on mobile devices is an emerging and challenging issue. The NLI presented in this paper suggested potential solutions to addressing the above challenges. We hope that this study will motivate more research and applications of NLI to mobile devices.

ACKNOWLEDGEMENTS

This work is partially supported by the National Science Foundation of USA under Grant# IIS-0328391. Any opinions, findings and conclusions or recommendations expressed in this material are those of the authors and do not necessarily reflect the views of the National Science Foundation (NSF).

REFERENCES

1. C. W. Thompson and K. M. Ross, Natural-language interface generating system, in *U. S. Patent.* U.S., 1987.
2. S. Sarker and J.D.W., Understanding Mobile Handheld Device Use and Adoption, *Communications of the ACM*, vol. 46, pp. 35-40, 2003.
3. J. F. Kelley, An Iterative Design Methodology for User-Friendly Natural Language Information Applications, *ACM Transactions on Information Systems*, vol. 2, pp. 26 - 41, 1984.
4. E. Paek and H.-j. Jeon, A Natural Language Interface for Simple Classification Tasks, presented at Flairs-97 Preliminary Conference, Gainesville, FL, 1997.
5. A. Yates, O. Etzioni, and D. Weld, A Reliable Natural Language Interface to Household Appliances - EXACT, presented at IUI'03, Miami, FL, 2003.
6. J. Allen, *Natural Language Understanding*: The Benjamin/Cummings Publishing Company, Inc., 1995.
7. W. Woods, R. Kaplan, and B. Nash-Weber, The Lunar Sciences Natural Language Information System, Bolt Beranek and Newman 2378, June 1972.
8. W. Zadrozny, M. Budzikowska, J. Chai, N. Kambhatla, S. Levesque, and N. Nicolov, Natural language dialogue for personalized interaction, *Communications of the ACM*, vol. 43, pp. 116 -120, 2000.
9. C. Campbell and P. Maglio, Supporting Notable Information in Office Work, presented at Conference on Human Factors in Computing Systems, Ft. Lauderdale, FL, 2003.
10. E. Zoltan-Ford, How to Get People to Say and Type What Computers Can Understand, *International Journal of Man-Machine Studies*, vol. 34, pp. 527-547, 1991.
11. A. Dix, J. Finlay, G. Abowd, and R. Beale, *Human-Computer Interaction*: Prentice Hall, 1998.

RESEARCH AND APPLICATION IN WEB USAGE MINING OF THE INCREMENTAL MINING TECHNIQUE FOR ASSOCIATION RULE

Sulan Zhang and Zhongzhi Shi
Key Lab of Intelligent Information Processing, Institute of Computing Technology
Chinese Academy of Sciences, Beijing, 100080, China
Email: zhangsl@ics.ict.ac.cn

Abstract: The paper analyzes some existing incremental mining algorithms for association rule and presents an incremental mining algorithm for association rule fit for Web Usage Mining. Because there are some characteristics of web logs which are dynamic, attributed, smaller and updated frequently, the algorithm uses BORDERS algorithm when mining single log file, and takes advantage of partition algorithm when mining many log files simultaneously.

Key words: Web Usage Mining, association rule, access patterns, incremental mining

1.   INTRODUCTION

Web Usage Mining is to mine the user access patterns on user's access records reserved on server. Main techniques include the path analysis technique peculiar to web mining and some traditional techniques in data mining such as association rule mining, Sequential patterns mining, Clustering, Classification and etc.

The rules mined out can only reflect the current status of the database. The alteration of data source can probably cause new rules and make some old rules invalid. To improve the rules' stability and reliability, the rules maintaining defined as incremental mining is necessary. A direct and simple solution is to run mining algorithm on the whole database after being altered, but it has obvious defectiveness which can't take advantage of the anterior results and the efficiency is very low when data source is very big or the mining results are very dense. The research of incremental mining technique for association rule in web usage mining is very important. For one thing, association rule can be the reference for bettering web site, the evidence for market development on web and heuristic rule for prefetching the web page for remote customers. For another, server access logs, the object of data mining in web usage mining, are updating perpetually and the size of the union of several logs in some days on an usual web site is very big, so it is inefficient to mine on those logs all over again. In the paper, we will discuss and analyze the incremental mining technique for association rule, then present an incremental algorithm fit for Web Usage Ming according to the characteristics of web logs.

2.   RESEARCH AND ANALYSIS OF RELATED THEORIES AND METHODS

The process of association rule mining can be divided into two sub-processes: finding frequent itemsets and producing association rule. Association rule Mining can be simplified as frequent itemsets mining because the second sub-process can be finished directly. Similarly, the essence of association rule incremental mining is to find new frequent itemsets of database after being altered. Cheung believes that maintain of frequent itemsets includes looking for the following two kinds of itemsets:

The defeater: the itemsets that are frequent before data source being altered but infrequent after data source being altered.

The winner: the itemsets that are infrequent before data source being altered but frequent after data source being altered.

The association rule maintaining was introduced in the reference [1] at first. The paper presented FUP algorithm that updates association rule when new transactions are added into database. A more general algorithm FUP2 was presented [2], the algorithm updates association rule when insertion, deletion or modification is applied on data source. The two algorithms are based on the principle of Apriori algorithm and need to scan database $O(n)$ times (n is the number of items in the biggest frequent itemset). They take advantage of anterior mining results to decrease works and improve the efficiency of incremental mining when mining new rules, but the general and long-term price of them is not small. The DELI algorithm [3] uses sampling and statistics technique to estimate the distinction of association rule sets between before alteration and after alteration. The necessity of updating is judged from the distinction, then too frequent updating can be avoided and a large amount of resource and long-term price can be saved. Thomas and Feldman presented the BORDERS algorithm at the same time [4,5]. The algorithm uses the negative border notion presented by Toivonen [6] to judge the necessity of checking every candidate itemset on database. The biggest contribution of the algorithm is that it needs only a time at most to scan database for updating frequent itemsets when the alteration of database gives rise to expansion of the negative border of frequent itemsets. The algorithm is fit for frequently-updated database, but it is not fit for very large database because the negative border reserved during computing process will occupy a large memory. It can be processed collaterally.

3.   UPDATE_BP ALGORITHM PRESENTED

When a manager of web site wants to analyze the user access patterns in some days, the log files in these days should be mined. It is a most usual means to union all log file in these days and mine them simultaneously, but its efficiency is not high because data is too much and those results mined separately from these logs are not used. Now an incremental mining algorithm on web logs Update_BP is presented to solve the problem.

Because there are some characteristics of web log which are dynamic, attributed, smaller and updated frequently, the algorithm Update_BP uses BORDERS algorithm which has been introduced above when mining a single log file, and fulfill in virtue of partition algorithm[7] when mining many log files.

The data in web server access logs is different with market basket. It is changed into appropriate data format fit for association rule mining before mining. The following is the description of algorithm Update_BP:

The algorithm has the same description of terminology (p_i, C_k^P, L_k^P, L^P, C_k^G, C^G, L_k^G, L^G) as the reference [7] does.

(1) n= Number of Log files
(2) For i=1 to n begin
(3) L^i=gen_large_itemsets(p_i)
(4) End
(5) For(j=2; $L_1^j \neq \Phi$, j=1,2,...,n; i++) do
(6) $C_1^G = \cup_{j=1,2,...,n} L_1^j$ // union
(7) For i=1 to n begin
(8) For all candidates $c \in C^G$ gen_count(c,p_i)
(9) End
(10) $L^G = \{c \in C^G | c.count \geq minsup\}$

Figure 1 Update_BP

The function gen_large_itemsets is achieved with the BORDERS algorithm whose input is single log file and output is local frequent itemsets with a variety of length of the log file. All local frequent itemsets with same length of every log file are merged into the whole candidate itemset with the same length in the step (6). In the step (7) to step (9), the whole support of every candidate is computed on all log files. The whole frequent itemset is built in step (10). The function gen_count was in the reference [7]. If some log files have already been mined separately, the step (3) that builds local frequent itemsets can be omitted and the time for mining can be reduced.

All-round analysis of the performance of BORDERS algorithm and Partition algorithm has been made in the original papers and will not be iterated in this paper. The simulation of the algorithms in lab verified that the two algorithms can be used in web usage mining and can improve largely the efficiency of log incremental mining.

4.   CONCLUSIONS

The paper actualizes the incremental mining of web log in the light of BORDERS algorithm and Partition algorithm. The experiment has proved that the algorithm can improve largely the efficiency of log mining. In the following research, more incremental mining algorithms for other patterns such as Sequential patterns, Clustering, Classification and etc. in web mining should be developed.

REFERENCES

1. D.Cheung, J.Han, V.Ng and C.Y.Wong. Maintenance of discovered association rules in large databases: An incremental updating technique. In ICDE'96, New Orleans, Louisiana, USA, Feb.1996
2. D.Cheung, S.Lee and B.Kao. A general incremental technique for maintaining discovered association rules. In Proc. Of the 5th International Conference on Database Systems for Advanced Applications, Melbourne, Australia, April 1-4,1997
3. S.Lee and D.Cheung. maintenance of discovered association rules: When to update? In DMKD'97, Tucson, Arizona, May.1997
4. S.Thomas, S.Bodagala, K.Alsabti and S.Ranka. An Efficient Algorithm for the Incremental Updation of Association Rules in Large Databases. In KDD'97, New Port Beach, California, Aug.1997
5. R.Feldman, Y.Aumann, A.Amir and H.Mannila. Efficient Algorithms for Discovering Frequent Sets in Incremental Databases. In DMKD'97, Tucson, Arizona, May.1997
6. H.Toivonen. Sampling Large Databases for Association Rules. In VLDB'96, pp.134-145
7. A.Savasere, E.Omiecinski, and S.Navathe. An efficient algorithm for mining association rules in large databases. Proceedings of the 21st International Conference on Very large Database,1995, pp.432-444

FACE RECOGNITION TECHNIQUE BASED ON MODULAR ICA APPROACH

CAO Wen-ming[1] LU Fei[1] YUAN Yuan[1] WANG shuojue[2]

[1]*Institute of Intelligent College of Information Engineering , Zhejiang University of Technology , Hangzhou 310014 , China,.*[2]*Institute of Semiconductors, Chinese Academy of Science, Beijing, 100083,China*

Abstract: In this paper, a face recognition algorithm based on modular ICA approach is presented. Compared whit conventional ICA algorithm, the proposed algorithm has an improved recognition rate for face images with large variations in lighting direction and facial expression. In the proposed technique, the face images are divided into smaller sub-images and the ICA approach is applied to each of these sub-images. Since some of the local facial features of an individual do not vary even when the pose, lighting direction and facial expression vary, we expect the proposed method to be able to cope with these variations. The accuracy of the conventional ICA method and modular ICA method are evaluated under the conditions of varying expression, illumination and pose using Yale face database[1].

Keywords: ICA; Face recognition: Modular ICA

1. INTRODUCTION

Face recognition is a difficult problem because of the generally similar shape of faces combined with the numerous variations between images of the same face. The image of a face changes with facial expression, age, viewpoint, illumination conditions, noise etc. The task of a face recognition system is to recognize a face in a manner that is as independent as possible of these image variations.

In this paper, a face recognition algorithm based on modular ICA approach is presented. Compared whit conventional ICA algorithm, the proposed algorithm has an improved recognition rate for face images with large variations in lighting direction and facial expression.

2.   REVIEW OF THE ICA METHOD

2.1   The principle of ICA

The ICA is usually used to process statistic signal. The principle of this algorithm is to denote a set of stochastic variables by a set of basis functions which are independent of each other. Let the observation signals from M channels are $x_i (i = 1,2, \cdots, M)$, and each signal is composed of N independent signal $s_j (j = 1,2, \cdots, N)$,namely:
$x_i = a_{i1}s_1 + a_{i2}s_2 + \cdots + a_{iN}s_N$ $(i = 1,2, \cdots, M)$. Which can be represented as follow formula:

$$X = A \bullet S, X = (x_1, x_2, \cdots, x_M), S = (s_1, s_2, \cdots, s_N), \qquad (1)$$

A is an unknown mixed matrix, S is an independent signal. After we figure out the mixed A, we can get $S = A^{-1} \bullet X = W \bullet X$. $W=A^{-1}$ was defined as separate matrix. There are two methods to realize the ICA algorithm: 1) Minimize or maximize assessment function, which need complex vector computation;2) Self-adaptive algorithm based on random grads lowering, which converges very slowly. Hyvärinen et al [2][3][4][5] putted forward a" Fast and Robust Fixed-Point Algorithms for Independent Component Analysis", which are very efficient.

According to [2], every independent heft can be recognized as an extremum of a peak. The peak of the projection of the stochastic variables X on a vector can be represented as follow:

$$Kurt(w^T X) = E\{w^T X\}^4 - 3(E\{w^T X\}^2)^2 \qquad (2)$$

The mean of X is zero, and $E\{(w^T X)^2\} = 1$. We can get iteration formula:

$$w^*(k) = C^{-1} E\{X[w(k-1)^T X]^3\} - 3w(k-1) \qquad (3)$$

$$w(k) = w^*(k)/[w^*(k)^T Cw^*(k)]^{1/2} \qquad (4)$$

$C = E\{XX^T\}$ is a covariance matrix; k is the number of iterations. If there is a stable extremum at peak $Kurt(w^T X)$, then the independent heft of stochastic variables X is:

$$s_i = \pm w_i^T X \quad (i = 1,2,\cdots,N) \tag{5}$$

2.2 Face recognition based on ICA

Let x_i represents the i-th image of a face. There are n stochastic variable in training set, namely $x_i (i = 1,2,\cdots,n)$. Each x_i is composed of m unknown independent heft. Then we can get $X = A \bullet S$, $x_i = [a_{i1}, a_{i2}, \cdots, a_{im}] \bullet [s_1, s_2, \cdots, s_m]'$ .The independent heft $s_j (j = 1,2,\cdots,m)$ describes the feature of a face.

When we test the face vector $test$, at first, we get the weight vector by projection of $test$ on S:

$$V = S \bullet test \tag{6}$$

Then we compute Euclid norm:

$$d_i = \|V - W_i\|, i = 1,2,\ldots N \tag{7}$$

$$W_i = S \bullet x_i \quad S = [s_1, s_2, \cdots s_m]^T, \quad i = 1,2,\ldots N \tag{8}$$

The i-th class corresponding to the least d_i is the same class with face $test$.

3. FACE RECOGNITION BASED ON MODULAR ICA

3.1 Modular ICA

The ICA based face recognition method is not very effective under the conditions of varying pose and illumination, since it considers the global information of each face image and represents them with a set of weights. Under these conditions the weight vectors will vary considerably from the weight vectors of the images with normal pose and illumination, hence it is difficult to identify them correctly. On the other hand if the face images were divided into smaller regions and the weight vectors are computed for each of these regions, then the weights will be more representative of the local information of the face. When there is a variation in the pose or illumination, only some of the face regions will vary and the rest of the regions will remain the same as the face regions of a normal image. Hence weights of the face regions not affected by varying pose and illumination will closely match with the weights of the same individual's face regions under normal conditions. Therefore it is expected that improved recognition rates can be obtained by following the modular ICA approach. We expect that if the face images are divided into very small region the global information of the face may be lost and the accuracy of this method may deteriorate.

There are N face images in our face database. Let vector $x_i (i = 1,2,\cdots N)$ represent the face images in our face database. In this method, each image in the training set is divided into H smaller images (as figure 1). Hence it can be represented as the follow formula:

Figure 1. Separate an image into four sub-images.

$$x_{ij}(m,n) = x_i (\frac{W}{\sqrt{H}}(j-1)+m, \frac{W}{\sqrt{H}}(j-1)+n)$$

$$i = 1,2,\cdots N \quad j = 1,2,\cdots H \quad m = 1,2,\cdots L/\sqrt{N} \quad n = 1,2\cdots L/\sqrt{N} \qquad (9)$$

Then, we can get independent hefts by the ICA method.

3.2   Classification

Let the independent heftses derived from sub-images are $S_j (j = 1,2,\cdots H)$. When we test the face vector *test*, at first, we separate it into H sub-images. Then, we compute the projection weight vectors of *test* on $S_j (j = 1,2,\cdots H)$:

$$V_j = S_j \bullet test_j \quad j = 1,2,\cdots,H \qquad (10)$$

And then, compute the mean Euclid norm:

$$d_i = \frac{1}{H}\sum_{j=1}^{H} d_{ij}$$

$$d_{ij} = \|V_j - W_{ij}\| \quad i = 1,2,\ldots N, \quad j = 1,2,\cdots,H \qquad (11)$$

$$W_{ij} = S_j \bullet x_{ij} \quad i = 1,2,\ldots N, \quad j = 1,2,\cdots,H \qquad (12)$$

The i-th class corresponding to the least d_i is the same class with face *test*.

4.   YALE FACE DATABASE [1]

The Yale database has 165 images of 15 adults, 11 images per person. The face images vary with respect to facial expression and illumination. The images have normal, sad, happy, sleepy, surprised, and winking expressions. There are also images where the position of the light source is at the center, left and right. In addition to these, there are images with and without glasses. Out of the 11images of a person, only eight were used for training and the remaining three were used to test the recognition rates.Fi g.2 and 3 show the set of images of a person used for training and testing respectively. The choice of the training and test images was made to facilitate comparison of performance of both the methods for test images with uneven illumination and partial occlusion.

subject01.centerl...   subject01.happy   subject01.noglasses   subject01.normal   subject01.sad

Figure 2. Images for training

subject01.glasses   subject01.rightlight   subject01.leftlight

subject01.sleepy   subject01.surprised   subject01.wink

Figure 3. Images for testing

In our experiment, each image is stretched to 64×64 pixels, and then normalized as follow:

$$x_i' = \frac{s\,\mathrm{var}}{\mathrm{var}}(x_i - mean) + smean$$

(13)

svar is the expecting mean square error, var is the square error of this image, smean is the expecting mean, and mean is the mean of this image.

5.   EXPERIMENT RESULT

Recognition method	Face recognition based on ICA	Face recognition based on modular ICA	
Recognition Rate	81.11%	Separate an image into 2 sub-images(separate by up and down)	80.00%.
		Separate an image into 2 sub-images(separate by left and right)	95.56%
		Separate an image into 4 sub-images	94.44%
		Separate an image into 16 sub-images	93.33%

A typical example:

With the ICA method, fig 4 (a) was classified to 4 (b). But with the modular ICA, fig 4 (a) was classified to 4 (c).

Figure 4. （a） subject01.rightlight   （b） subject08.centerlight   （c） subject01.happy

6.   CONCLUSION

We can conclude from the data that:

(1) . Because the position of the light source vary horizontally not vertically, the recognition rate of modular ICA is less than ICA when images are separated by up and down; the recognition rate of modular ICA is highest when images are separated by up and down. This phenomenon denotes that modular ICA keeps a high recognition rate when the face images vary with respect to illumination.

(2). When the images are separated into 16 sub-images, the recognition rate is lower than when the images are separated into 4 sub-images. That is because there is little global information when a image is separated into 16 sub-images.

To sum up, face recognition based on modular ICA is much better than based on ICA, especially for face images with large variations in lighting direction and facial expression.

REFERENCE

1. Yale face database,<http://cvc.yale.edu/projects/yalefaces/yalefaces.html>
2. A. Hyvärinen. Fast and Robust Fixed-Point Algorithms for Independent Component Analysis. IEEE Transactions on Neural Networks 10(3):626-634, 1999.
3. A. Hyvärinen and E. Oja. A Fast Fixed-Point Algorithm for Independent Component Analysis. Neural Computation, 9(7):1483-1492, 1997.
4. A. Hyvärinen and E. Oja. Independent Component Analysis: Algorithms and Applications. Neural Networks, 13(4-5):411-430, 2000.
5. A. Hyvarinen . Independent component analysis : A tutorial [OL]. http :/ / www. cis. hut . fi/ projects/ ica/ , IJCNN99-tutori-al2.html, 2002.

MODEL-BASED DEBUGGING
WITH HIGH-LEVEL OBSERVATIONS

Wolfgang Mayer and Markus Stumptner
University of South Australia
Advanced Computing Research Centre
Mawson Lakes, SA 5095, Adelaide, Australia.

{ mayer,mst }@cs.unisa.edu.au

Abstract   Recent years have seen considerable developments in modeling techniques for automatic fault location in programs. However, much of this research considered the models from a standalone perspective. Instead, this paper focuses on the highly unusual properties of the testing and measurement process, where capabilities differ strongly from the classical hardware diagnosis paradigm. In particular, in an interactive debugging process user interaction may result in highly complex input to improve the process. This work extends the standard entropy-based measurement selection algorithm proposed in (de Kleer and Williams, 1987) to deal with high-level observations about the intended behavior of Java programs, specific to a set of test cases. We show how to incorporate the approach into previously developed model-based debugging frameworks and to how reasoning about high-level properties of programs can improve diagnostic results.

Keywords: Model-based reasoning, Software engineering and AI, Diagnosis, Debugging

1.   INTRODUCTION

Debugging, i.e., detecting a faulty behavior within a program, locating the cause of the fault, and fixing the fault by means of changing the program, continues to be a crucial and challenging task in software development. Many papers have been published so far in the domain of finding faults in software, e.g., testing or formal verification (Clarke et al., 1994), and locating them, e.g., program slicing (Weiser, 1984) and automatic program debugging (Lloyd, 1987) work that is being continued in a series of workshops on debugging (Ducassé, 2000). In the 1990s model-based diagnosis techniques (Reiter, 1987) started to be examined for locating faults in software, originally for logic programs (Console et al., 1993), later for the debugging of large-scale concurrent hardware designs written in VHDL (Friedrich et al., 1999), and more recently imperative programs (Mayer et al., 2002a).

This paper extends prior research on model-based diagnosis for locating bugs in programs written in mainstream programming languages (e.g. Java). The idea behind the model-based debugging approach is (1) to automatically compile a program to its logical model or to a constraint satisfaction problem, (2) to use the model together with test cases and a model-based diagnostic engine for computing the diagnosis candidates, and (3) to map the candidates back to their corresponding locations within the original program. Formally, given a set of test cases on which the program is run, a (minimal) diagnosis is defined as a (minimal) set of incorrectness assumptions $AB(C)$ on a subset $C \in \Delta$ of components $COMP$ in the program (usually statements) such that $\{AB(C)|C \in \Delta\} \cup \{\neg AB(C)|C \in COMP \setminus \Delta\} \cup SD$ is consistent (Reiter, 1987). Here, SD is a logical theory describing the program's behavior under the assumption that components work correctly, and $AB(C)$ expresses that the program part modeled by C is possibly faulty (*ABnormal*) and can show arbitrary effects. Since the computation depends on observations in terms of test case output, unlike formal verification approaches, no separate formal specification is necessary – everything but the test cases is computed automatically from the source code. Conversely, where verification model checkers produce counterexamples, the outcome of the diagnosis process are code locations. Model-based debugging thus complements, rather than replaces verification techniques.

The models presented in (Mateis et al., 2000; Mayer et al., 2002c) have successfully been applied in the Jade project to debug Java programs, with tests performed on small to medium sized Java programs together with their faulty variants and given test cases. A comparison of the models and their effectiveness relative to each other as well as compared to a normal interactive debugger was given in (Mayer et al., 2002a). More recent work (e.g., (Mayer and Stumptner, 2003)) has added models based on the Abstract Interpretation Framework (Cousot and Cousot, 1977; Cousot and Cousot, 2000) and also moved to more efficient models that are based on test case specific representation of individual traces.

While considerable improvements in the modeling and diagnostic algorithms have been achieved, the interactive aspect of (semi-) automatic debugging has so far taken second seat behind the computational aspects. In particular, previous research prototypes combined a standard debugger-like interface with a variant of the standard entropy-based selection of measurements to identify points during program execution where the debugger user would be queried about the correctness of (parts of) the program status at that point in execution (the user serving as "oracle"). The experience was that answering these oracle queries posed by the system could be difficult in many cases. In particular, if the model of the program closely reflects the program's semantics, most queries can only be answered if the program behavior is hand-simulated up to that point. Therefore, to be useful for interactive debugging, an approach to queries is needed that is both more powerful and simple for the developer (debugger user) to apply. This work takes a step in this direction in that the measurement selection algorithm proposed in (de Kleer and Williams, 1987) is extended to deal with certain issues specific to the software domain. Furthermore, we introduce the notion of what we call *high-level observations* (HLO's) about the expected behavior of the program. Dedicated HLO predicates provide high level descriptions of program execution beyond the classical diagnosis test of whether a given part of the program state is correct or incorrect. We refer to an observation as high-level if it constrains multiple program states and/or locations. HLO's thus allow for debugging capabilities beyond current modeling approaches while keeping the information that has to be provided by the user at a minimum.

In addition to missing observations needed to refute unwanted diagnoses (we assume that there is a threshold on the maximal cardinality of fault candidates. Therefore, additional conflicts remove diagnosis candidates once the threshold is exceeded) an additional source of spurious fault candidates is approximate modeling. In contrast to many diagnostic models, where the behavioral description of each component is known in full, for programs approximations need to be made to avoid undecidability issues related to loops, recursive method calls, and dynamic data structures. The high-level observation approach also helps in this case, as refined modeling may diminish negative effects cause by coarse approximations.

Lastly, more effective control over the queries asked of the user is important. The application of the standard measurement selection proposed in (de Kleer and Williams, 1987) to the software domain is problematic. In particular, changing control- and data flow for multiple test cases and fault candidates results in non-comparable sets of variables and possible values, which renders the standard algorithm unsuitable. Furthermore, multiple test cases with widely varying value ranges need to be integrated.

Under these conditions entropy alone is not sufficient to effectively pinpoint measurements that discriminate between fault candidates. To make queries easily answerable, query complexity and reasoning over all test cases needs to be incorporated.

The rest of the paper is organized as follows. Section 2 investigates the sources of query complexity in model-based debugging and describes the concept of high-level observations. Section 3 provides an algorithm to select the "best" measurement and describes how to incorporate our measurements in the approach of (de Kleer and Williams, 1987). Finally, we discuss future extensions before we conclude the paper.

2.   DEBUGGING WITH HIGH LEVEL OBSERVATIONS

In our current scheme, HLO's are produced by presenting queries to the user that have been ranked high as measurements to be selected (see Section 3); the query specifies a high level condition and the user provides a HLO, or measurement outcome, by answering it. A query is a condition on the program state or actual execution. A query schema describes the possible HLO's the debugging system can deal with.

DEFINITION 1 *A query schema* $S = \langle P, C, Q \rangle$ *is a 3-tuple, where* P *denotes a first order formula representing the scope of* Q, C *is the complexity of the query, and* Q *represents a logical schema describing the actual condition (or "query") to be tested.*

For all components L in a model run (or program execution) R where $P(L)$ is true, $Q(L)$ is applicable. C is a positive number, predefined or assigned by the system, that estimates the complexity of the query as it will be experienced by the user. This is later used to rank easier queries first. We make the simplifying assumption that all query instances of the same query schema have equal complexity. Q (also denoted by $Q(S)$) denotes the condition that is to be confirmed or refuted by the user. We will see later that these conditions often coincide with the traditional notion of an invariant.

EXAMPLE 2 $\langle \_loop(L), 5, \text{allUpdated}(L) \rangle$ *denotes a query schema that tracks the property* allUpdated(L) *for all loops (all parts of the program code for which* $\_loop(L)$ *is true). The complexity associated with the query is 5.*

DEFINITION 3 *A query* $q = \langle T, L, C, Q, R_T, R_F, R_U \rangle$ *is an instance of a query schema* S, *where* T *is the test case that* q *is valid for,* L *denotes the location where the query takes place in the model describing* T, C *is the complexity (taken from the query schema), and* Q *is the query expression (invariant) specified by the query schema* $Q = Q(S)$ *with all free variables instantiated with information describing the context of the query (test case, location, context, complexity, question).* R_T *and* R_F *are the sets of fault candidates that predict* Q *to be true and false, respectively. Candidates in* R_U *are those that do not predict a value for* Q.

When debugging using a model that follows the program semantics closely, three main causes of complex queries can be identified. First, unless the observed variable is at a point close to the start or the end of the program execution, the user needs to simulate much of the programs behavior to compute the desired value. Second, frequent switching between different execution states makes it much harder for the user to build a model of the correct execution of a program. This is especially true if the execution states are deep in the middle of some complex computation. Finally, the user cannot rely on values of variables provided by the debugger, as these may have been influenced by the true program fault or the diagnostic assumptions.

Our current approach to tackling above problems is to abstract from concrete values of variables as much as possible and present simple high-level queries to the user, i.e., individual predicates but chosen for their suitability to

T_f : list.price $= [2, 10, 4, 8, 100, 40]$. T_c : list.price $= [0, 1, 7, 5]$

```
1    class PriceList {
2        float price;
3        PriceList next;
4    }
5    class Test {
6        static void increase(PriceList list) {
7            while (list != null) {
8                if (list.price < 10.0f)
9                    list.price += 1.0f;
10               else
11                   list.price *= 0.05f; // 1.05f
12               list = list.next;
13           }
14       }
15   }
```

T_f : list.price $= [3, 10.5, 5, 9, 105, 42]$. T_c : list.price $= [1, 2, 8, 6]$

Figure 1. Example program and test case.

extract parts of the design information from the user's mental model and use it for diagnostic purposes. Concrete values (heretofore our standard type of observations) are mainly used to define input values and to check the result of a program run. The HLO's provide the necessary information to prune conflicts and build refined models that help avoiding some approximations. Thus, while in general software diagnosis is more difficult than hardware diagnosis due to the absence of a correct model, in this case the ability to obtain a description of *intent* from the user (developer) makes observations potentially more powerful than with hardware. Generation and selection of suitable high level queries are described in sections 2 and 3, respectively.

EXAMPLE 4 *For illustration, consider the program in figure 1. Using a value-based model (Mateis et al., 2000) and the input and expected output values depicted in the figure for test case T_f, statements* list!=null$_7$, list.price*=0.05f$_{11}$, *and* list=list.next $_{12}$ *are identified as possible faults. In addition to the true fault in line 11, two spurious diagnoses are reported. By adding the observation that each member of the list must be assigned exactly once, it is derived that the loop must be bounded (because the data structure that is traversed is acyclic). (We assume that every program eventually terminates.) This information allows to build a refined model (Mayer and Stumptner, 2004), where* list!=null$_7$ *and* list=list.next $_{12}$ *are no longer considered as explanations.*

2.1   The HLO Catalogue

While there are no intrinsic requirements on the structure and subexpressions used in HLO's, in our current implementation each type of observation is separately implemented, in keeping with the assumption that it is advantageous to let the users deal with individual, dedicated predicates rather than asking them to form complex expressions interactively. Currently, our models can deal with the following different types of HLO predicates. (We omit the formal definition for space reasons. "A" refers to the attributes used by the predicate. Optional attributes are in brackets.)

Traversal properties: Elements of arrays and dynamic data structures are often processed such that either all of them are read or updated. If the underlying data structure is monotonic, this allows to bound the number of times the iterating loop or recursive function is executed, which in many cases allows to refine the model to avoid imprecision due to approximation and to exclude unwanted fault candidates. A: data structure (variable), type of access, [order of traversal].

Acyclicity: Knowledge that a data structure should be acyclic can be exploited to bound the number of loop iterations and method calls. Code that builds such data structures is also constrained in that any diagnosis candidate that implies a cycle is refuted. A: data structure (variable), path.

Read- and write-only: Observations that all elements of a data structure used as input to a loop or a method call are either only read or updated only. A: data structure, [type or path constraints]. The latter limit the effect of the assertion to a subset of all reachable elements.

Read-only assertions allow to ignore any attempted update to data structures passed to a loop or method call, and exclude diagnostic candidates implying such updates. This is most useful to bypass model limitations due to aliasing between references to dynamic data structures.

Write-only access is used to decouple the previous values of the data structure from the updated values, leading to smaller conflicts in case the update operation is abnormal.

Subproblem (in)dependence: Loops and recursive method invocations can be modeled differently if it is known that computations in different loop iterations and disjunct sub-structures of dynamic data structures are independent (Mayer and Stumptner, 2004) (modulo the loop variable, which is of course updated based on the previous value). This allows to construct behavioral descriptions with fewer approximation operators and fewer data dependencies between components, resulting in more precise values and smaller conflicts. A: loop statement.

Variable (in)dependence: Information about possible dependencies between variables can be utilized to infer missing statements or uses and updates of wrong variables (Jackson, 1995). In our approach, this is also used to shortcut conflict computation, especially if the dependencies relate method parameters and side-effects at the method exit. A: variable set. Dependency information could also be used to chose a suitable abstraction for dependent variables. For example using a relational model for local dependent variables may reduce spurious values (and fault candidates) compared to a purely non-relational approach.

Loop specific invariants: Loops based on counters or other induction variables (Gerlek et al., 1995) can often be bounded if monotonicity of the induction variable is assumed. Although it is possible to infer that property for large classes of loops using syntactic pattern-based and Abstract Interpretation (Cousot and Cousot, 1977) approaches, manual specification also eliminates the fault candidate where the update expression of the induction variable is assumed abnormal.

UML invariants: Invariants taken from UML class diagrams, such as type constraints and cardinality constraints for relations, are useful to detect conflicts as soon as the invariant is violated. Consequently, the number of components in a conflict is reduced. A further benefit of type invariants is that dynamic types can often be derived even if the concrete object is unknown.

Region reachability: Here, statements that should be executed always (or never, or at least once) are marked to remove paths that would otherwise contribute to spurious fault candidates. This is often used to indicate that a particular method invocation should not raise an exception. **A**: Statement set, frequency specification.

2.2   Generating High Level Queries

Queries about high-level properties are generated using an approach borrowed from the Daikon (Ernst et al., 2000) invariant detection tool. The idea is to track a set of properties while test cases are executing, and to eliminate all invariants that do not imply all properties. Statistical measures are used to discard invariants without sufficient support. Tracked properties consist of built-in predicates, such as $\geq$ and $=$null, and can be extended with user-specified predicates. For this work, we also add properties necessary to infer high-level observations. During model simulation, auxiliary variables are created to track the valid predicates. One important aspect is that tools like Daikon do not generate *real* invariants, but merely guesses based on a set of test cases. In our case that is not a problem as the purpose of queries is not to serve as explanations to the user, but as tests to obtain his agreement or disagreement.

While Daikon only supports forward execution where all values of a program state are known, our approach also allows backward reasoning and variables with unknown values. This is necessary to support invariant detection even if fault assumptions are present. Consequently, the predicates may not evaluate uniquely and are ignored in that case.

EXAMPLE 5 *Reconsidering the program in figure 1. Assume a HLO predicate allUpdated(L) is tracked to find loops L where all elements of the data structure references by L are traversed and updates. This can easily be checked by examining the assignments and the loop update expression in each iteration. Note that it is not necessary that the loop always traverses all values. It is sufficient that it does given the values predicted by the current test case and fault candidate.*

For each fault candidate, the model is simulated and the predicate is tracked:

Fault candidate	allUpdated($\boxed{while}_7$)
$\emptyset$	true
$\{ab(\boxed{list!=null}_7)\}$	?
$\{ab(\boxed{list.price*=0.05f}_{11})\}$	true
$\{ab(\boxed{list=list.next}_{12})\}$	?

For the second and the last candidate, the predicate cannot be evaluated uniquely, as the number of loop iterations is not known. The loop is modeled as an approximation only, where targets of assignments in different iterations cannot be determined reliably.

HLO's are instantiated into queries if the tracked property is not strongly refuted and the assumption of the HLO allows to eliminate some fault candidates. A property P is *strongly refuted* if there exist a test case T and a fault candidate that predicts false for P given T. The sets R_T is determined by assuming that the HLO predicate holds, to obtain a refined model P' which is subsequently used to analyze each candidate where the predicate may not hold. All candidates that imply contradictions in the new model are eliminated from R_T. R_F and R_U are empty, as there must not exist any candidates that predict false for P'. While simulation and candidate elimination is an expensive operation, this is alleviated to a certain extent by the measurement selection, which can rule out many potential queries based on the queries' locations alone.

EXAMPLE 6 (CONT. FROM EX. 5) *When checking either of the two candidates from example 5 for consistency, it is discovered that the invariant is never strongly refuted. Consequently, a refined model for the loop is built assuming* allUpdated($\boxed{\text{while}}_7$) *holds. As a consequence, the statements in lines 7 and 12 are no longer valid single faults, as the incorrect values are still derived (independent of the effects of* $\boxed{\text{list!=null}}_7$ *and* $\boxed{\text{list=list.next}}_{12}$).

Consequently, the query
$\langle T_f, \boxed{\text{while}}_7, 5, \text{allUpdated}(\boxed{\text{while}}_7), R_T, \emptyset, \emptyset \rangle$, *with* $R_T = \{\boxed{\text{list.price*=0.05f}}_{11}\}$
is instantiated.

3.   SELECTING MEASUREMENTS

A solution for selecting good measurements given a test case and a set of fault candidates was presented in (de Kleer and Williams, 1987). The algorithm utilizes entropy to find the variable that, when observed, on average eliminates the most candidates. Only fault probabilities for components and the values predicted by the fault candidates are required.

For the software domain, we obtain fault probabilities from the execution paths of correct and faulty test cases (Mayer et al., 2002b). Components that are executed for few correct test cases and many failing test runs are assigned a higher fault probability.

To integrate the HLO's and the IIO's into the measurement selection, we define auxiliary variables o_i for each query Q_i, with $\text{dom}(o_i) = \{true, false\}$. The sets R_T, R_F, and R_U are used to compute the entropy for o_i: $H(o_i) = p(o_i = true) \log p(o_i = true) + p(o_i = false) \log p(o_i = false) + p(R_U) \log 2$ (H denotes the entropy, $p(o_i = v) = p(S_v) + \frac{p(R_U)}{2}$, where S_v is the set of selected candidates where $o_i = v$, and $p(X)$ denotes the summed probability of all fault candidates in X). Finally, the measurement with maximal entropy is selected.

While this approach selects the variable that (on average) optimally discriminates fault candidates, it proved insufficient for interactive debugging, mainly due to the queries being too complex to answer with reasonable effort. For interactive debugging, selected queries must also conform to the following properties:

1 Queries that are deep in the execution trace of a program are difficult to answer, as the values predicted by fault candidates cannot be relied upon to judge correctness of invariants.

2 The selected queries should be focused (from a user's point of view). In particular, queries should not "jump around" in the execution trace, as

this prohibits the user from building a model of the correct execution of the program.

3 Subsequent queries should use the same test case, if possible.

To elude these problems, we propose to extend the entropy-based measurement selection with a heuristic approach, that sacrifices optimality in favor of low query complexity.

To minimize query complexity, for each query we compute a "distance" d_i between the location $l_i = L(Q_i)$ and the location of the closest answered query (or the program start or end point) for the same test case. d_i is derived from the execution profile of the test cases and all the fault candidates: Each statement that is executed for at least one fault candidate is marked. Also, the union of all the call graphs for each fault candidate is computed.

Starting at l_i, transitions between statements are explored to find the path to an answered query Q_j where the difference between the minimal nesting depth and the maximal nesting depth is minimal. To find the closest query, we apply a simple best-first search algorithm, following only transitions between marked statements. The nesting depth of a statement in a method is computed from the source code. For called methods, all possible call and return transitions are followed, according to the call graph generated earlier. The nesting depths for each method are summed.

EXAMPLE 7 *Reconsider the query from example 6 (for test case T_f). Assume further that no other queries have been answered. The nesting depth of line 7 is 0, as there is no enclosing scope other than the method. Lines 8 and 12 and lines 9 and 11 are at nesting depth 1 and 2, respectively. The call graph is empty, as there are no method calls. All statements are executed for at least fault candidate.*

The query is located at line 7 and has thus distance 0 to the start of the program.

Using the entropy, the query complexity, and d_i, the best possible measurement that is easy to answer and not too far from the a previously observed position is selected. The algorithm proceeds as follows:

1 **Compute entropy.** For each query Q_i, compute the entropy e_i using $R_T(Q_i)$, $R_F(Q_i)$, and $R_U(Q_i)$. For variables that are not associated with HLO's and IIO's use the standard algorithm from (de Kleer and Williams, 1987).

2 **Mark executed statements.** For each test case and each fault candidate, mark the statements that are executed.

3 **Compute call graph.** Build the graph containing all possible call sequences between methods and statements marked in the previous step.

4 **Compute distances.** For each Q_i, compute $d_i = \forall_{Q_j} \min \text{distance}(L(Q_i), L(Q_j))$. Start at $L(Q_i)$ and perform a best-first search, traversing only statements that are marked. Move between method according to the graph computed in the previous step.

5 **Find a good, close query.** Find the k queries where $e_i \cdot r + d_i \cdot (1 - r)$ is smallest. Discard all other queries.

6 **Pick the simplest.** From the remaining queries, return the one with minimal $C(Q_i)$. If there is more than one candidate, select the one with larger entropy (or lower complexity if entropy does not discriminate).

The parameters r and k are currently pre-specified, but could also be adapted according to the history of (un)answered queries.

EXAMPLE 8 *In our example, the fault probabilities for all statements are 0.5, with the exception of line 9, where the probability is 0.0. Given the sets R_T, R_F, and R_U from example 6, the entropy of the allUpdated($\boxed{\text{while}}_7$) observation is greater or equal than for any other observation.*

The predicate allUpdated($\boxed{\text{while}}_7$) is (by definition of our HLO library) simpler than queries of type 'Subproblem Independence'. Other HLO queries are not considered as either they are refuted by a test case, or they are always strongly derived. It is also simpler than the IIO queries for the same reason.

The HLO query is also the closest to the program start, as all other statements are embedded into the loop. It is therefore selected in step 6 of the above algorithm.

4.   FURTHER WORK & CONCLUSION

While the approach described in this paper has provided promising results on a set of small benchmark programs, there are open issues requiring further work. Currently, the measurement selection is not fully integrated in our debugging prototype, which makes further evaluation difficult. Further, it is not clear whether the parameters k and r must be preset or if there exist good heuristics to choose and update those values. The user interaction aspect of interactive debugging also requires more investigation, in particular, the question on what and how much context needs to be provided to the user to allow efficient query answering.

In contrast to other debugging and verification approaches (for example (Groce and Visser, 2003)), our method has the advantage that it does not require to specify the behavior of the program in a formal language. Rather, it is sufficient to provide properties and invariants that are *specific to a set of test cases*, which is usually much easier, especially as the behavioral description need not be complete. Also, complexity is lower than for verification, as we do not follow *all* possible executions of a program. Instead we focus on the program behavior specific to a set of test cases, which is usually good enough if the test set is large.

In summary, we have presented an approach to semi-automatic debugging that builds on a fixed library of predicates which can be used to analyze high-level properties of the program. Combined with the inference of test-case specific invariants, this allows for more expressive user interaction, leading to a more powerful oracle describing the expected behavior of the program. Interaction between specific types of HLO's and specific types of program constructs enables effective heuristics and provides a gateway for the choice of a correct model in a specific situations (a long-term goal of our research (Mayer et al., 2002b)).

References

Clarke, Edmund M., Grumberg, Orna, and Long, David E. (1994). Model Checking and Abstraction. *ACM Transactions on Programming Languages and Systems*, 16(5):1512–1542.

Console, Luca, Friedrich, Gerhard, and Dupré, Daniele Theseider (1993). Model-based diagnosis meets error diagnosis in logic programs. In *Proc. 13th IJCAI*, pages 1494–1499, Chambery.

Cousot, Patrick and Cousot, Radhia (1977). Abstract interpretation: A unified lattice model for static analysis of programs by construction of approximation of fixpoints. In *POPL'77*, pages 238–252, Los Angeles.

Cousot, Patrick and Cousot, Radhia (2000). Abstract interpretation based program testing. In *Proceedings of the SSGRR 2000 Computer & eBusiness International Conference*.

de Kleer, Johan and Williams, Brian C. (1987). Diagnosing multiple faults. *Artificial Intelligence*, 32(1):97–130.

Ducassé, Mireille, editor (2000). *Proceedings of the 4th International Workshop on Automated and Algorithmic Debugging, AADEBUG '00*. Munich.

Ernst, Michael D., Czeisler, Adam, Griswold, William G., and Notkin, David (2000). Quickly detecting relevant program invariants. In *Proceedings of the 22nd International Conference on Software Engineering*, pages 449–458, Limerick, Ireland.

Friedrich, Gerhard, Stumptner, Markus, and Wotawa, Franz (1999). Model-based diagnosis of hardware designs. *Artificial Intelligence*, 111(2):3–39.

Gerlek, Michael P., Stoltz, Eric, and Wolfe, Michael (1995). Beyond induction variables: Detecting and classifying sequences using a demand-driven SSA. *ACM Transactions on Programming Languages and Systems*, 1(17):85–122.

Groce, Alex and Visser, Willem (2003). What went wrong: Explaining counterexamples. In *SPIN Workshop on Model Checking of Software*.

Jackson, Daniel (1995). Aspect: Detecting Bugs with Abstract Dependences. *ACM Transactions on Software Engineering and Methodology*, 4(2):109–145.

Lloyd, J. W. (1987). Declarative Error Diagnosis. *New Generation Computing*, 5:133–154.

Mateis, Cristinel, Stumptner, Markus, and Wotawa, Franz (2000). A Value-Based Diagnosis Model for Java Programs. In *Proc. 11th Int'l Workshop on Principles of Diagnosis*, Morelia, Mexico.

Mayer, Wolfgang and Stumptner, Markus (2003). Model-based debugging using multiple abstract models. In *Proceedings of the 5th International Workshop on Automated and Algorithmic Debugging, AADEBUG '03*, pages 55–70, Ghent.

Mayer, Wolfgang and Stumptner, Markus (2004). Approximate modeling for debugging program loops. In *Proceedings of the Fifteenth International Workshop on Principles of Diagnosis*, Carcassonne.

Mayer, Wolfgang, Stumptner, Markus, Wieland, Dominik, and Wotawa, Franz (2002a). Can AI help to improve debugging substantially? Debugging Experiences with Value-Based Models. In *Proc. ECAI*, pages 417–421, Lyon.

Mayer, Wolfgang, Stumptner, Markus, Wieland, Dominik, and Wotawa, Franz (2002b). Towards an Integrated Debugging Environment. In *Proceedings of the European Conference on Artificial Intelligence (ECAI)*, pages 422–426, Lyon.

Mayer, Wolfgang, Stumptner, Markus, and Wotawa, Franz (2002c). Model-based Debugging or How to Diagnose Programs Automatically. In *Proc. IEA/AIE*, Springer LNAI, pages 746–757, Cairns, Australia.

Reiter, Raymond (1987). A theory of diagnosis from first principles. *Artificial Intelligence*, 32(1):57–95.

Weiser, Mark (1984). Program slicing. *IEEE Transactions on Software Engineering*, 10(4):352–357.

MAPPING SEARCH RESULTS INTO SELF-CUSTOMIZED CATEGORY HIERARCHY

Saravadee Sae Tan[1], Gan Keng Hoon[1], Chan Huah Yong[2], Tang Enya Kong[1] and Cheong Sook Lin[1]

[1]*Computer Aided Translation Unit (UTMK)*
School of Computer Sciences, Universiti Sains Malaysia, 11800 Penang, Malaysia

[2]*Grid Computing Lab*
School of Computer Sciences, Universiti Sains Malaysia, 11800 Penang, Malaysia
{saratan | khgan | hychan | enyakong | slcheong}@cs.usm.my

Abstract: With the rapid growth of online information, a simple search query may return thousands or even millions of results. There is a need to help user to access and identify relevant information in a flexible way. This paper describes a methodology that automatically map web search results into user defined categories. This allows the user to focus on categories of their interest, thus helping them to find for relevant information in less time. Text classification algorithm is used to map search results into categories. This paper focuses on feature selection method and term weighting measure in order to train an optimum and simple category model from a relatively small number of training texts. Experimental evaluations on real world data collected from the web shows that our classification algorithm gives promising results and can potentially be used to classify search results returned by search engines.

Key words: information retrieval, results classification, feature selection, self-customized categories

1.   INTRODUCTION

As the number of online information is growing rapidly, it becomes more and more difficult in finding relevant information. Two common tools that assist user in retrieving information from the web are *web search engines* and *web directories*. Search engines return a ranked list of results in response to a user search query. Nowadays, a simple query may return thousands (or even millions) of results. Results of different topics are mix together and the user has to browse through the long ranked list to find for relevant information. On the other hand, web directories such as Yahoo! and LookSmart classify web pages into hierarchical structured categories. However, the manual classification of web pages into directory makes web directories impossible to keep up with the rapid growth of the web.

Chen and Dumais [3] present a user interface that organizes web pages returned by a search engine into hierarchical structured categories. This approach combines the advantage of broad coverage in search engines and structured categories in web directories. Their study [4] shows that the category interface increase the speed in finding information compared to a long ranked list. Paper [3] more focuses on the category interface instead of the classification algorithm. In this paper, we present a classification algorithm that automatically classifies search results into user defined category hierarchy.

In our methodology, a user is allowed to define a set of categories of his interest by providing a set of training text for each category. Our classification algorithm automatically learns the characteristics of the categories from the training texts. Later, it would be able to map the results returned by a search engine into categories based on the knowledge learned. Intuitively speaking, the user has the flexibility to define the categories as well as the concepts in which each category represent. For this reason, he may foresee the information or content being classified in each category thus can directly focus on relevant topics. This gives more flexibility to the user compare to web directories, in which he is only allowed to browse the topic hierarchy defined by editors.

In our classification algorithm, characteristic of the categories are represented using a Category Model (CM). The CM consists of the categories along with a set of keywords for each category. The keywords are automatically generated from the training texts. The quality of CM will strongly affect the performance of the classification algorithm. Therefore, in this paper, we pay more attention on the feature selection method as well as the term weighting measure in order to increase the ability of our classification algorithm in selecting a set of optimum keywords from a relatively small number of training texts.

We have previously proposed a feature selection method in annotating a topic hierarchy [9]. In this paper, we show that the idea from our previous work is also applicable to text classification task.

2.   CLASSIFICATION ALGORITHM

The main aim of the classification task is to map search results into user defined categories. In order to apply real time classification, a classification algorithm with high accuracy and reasonable processing time is required. Figure 1 shows the processing flow of our results classification algorithm. It consists of two phase: category model generation phase and results classification phase.

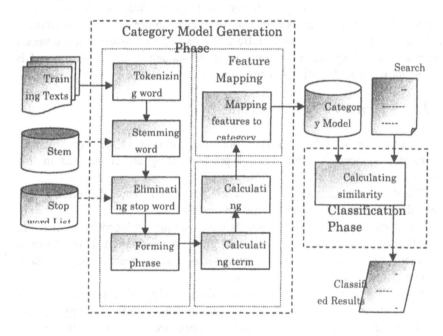

Figure 1. Processing flow of the classification algorithm

3.   CATEGORY MODEL (CM) GENERATION

Size and quality of a category model are major concerns in the performance of our classification algorithm. Since the CM is prepared beforehand, processing time is not a major issue and it will not affect the real time classification. Thus, we propose methods on feature generating and selecting in order to compose an optimum CM for higher accuracy and faster processing.

3.1   Document Representation

A simple and frequently used document representation is the feature vector representation. It is a 'bag-of-words' representation, in which each document is represented as a vector of features. Mladenic and Globelnik [6] extend the 'bag-of-words' representation to 'bag-of-phrases' representation by adding new features generated from word sequences, also know as N-grams.

In this paper, we define each distinct *term* or *phrase* corresponds to a feature. By using phrases as features, we attempt to preserve the information left out by single word representation. We use up to 3-grams feature vector representation. Experiments show that word sequences of length up to 3 is sufficient in most classification systems [6].

3.2   Feature Pre-Processing

In order to transform a text document into a feature vector, pre-processing is needed. Four type of pre-processing are considered in this paper.

Word tokenizing: Single words are extracted from documents. All capitalized letters are converted into lower case.

Word stemming: All single words extracted are replaced by their stem. Words variants usually only convey one piece of information. Thus, it would be more reasonable to reduce them into one representative for both efficiency and effectiveness concerns.

Stop word eliminating: The high dimensionality of a feature space is initially reduced by eliminating all stop words. Stop words are words that do not take semantic meaning themselves. They are not helpful to capture documents' semantic, hence they are irrelevant to classification. Two type of stop word are considered in this paper, 'general stop words' (e.g. *a, the, of...*) and 'web page stop words' (e.g. *html, home...*).

Phrase forming: Phrasal feature consist of up to 3 stemmed token occurring as a sequence in a document are formed.

3.3   Feature Selection

Feature selection is used as a basic step in the process of building a classifier. It is a process that chooses a subset of features from the original set of features so that the feature space is optimally reduced according to a certain criterion. This tends to produce classification models that are simpler, clearer, and computationally less expensive [7]. In our methodology, feature selection method is used to select the set of feature that compose the Category Model.

Various approaches of feature selection have been developed for dimensionality reduction in a classification task. Basically, these methods can be broadly divided into 2 main approaches, (i) Feature Selection in Machine Learning, and (ii) Feature Selection in Text Learning. Feature Selection in Machine Learning traverse a search space and evaluate every candidate subset in order to find the best subset. These methods are less practical when the number of features is large. On the other hand, Feature Selection in Text Learning evaluates every feature independently, in which a scoring criterion is used to measure the goodness of a feature. All features are sorted in a list and a predefined number of best features are selected. However, the number of features to be selected is a main experimental issue in these methods.

Feature selection method adopted in this paper is from the author's previous work. It combines the idea from both methods of feature selection in machine learning and text learning [9]. All features are sorted in a list according to their significance in term of discriminating power between categories. An optimum set of features is selected by finding a cut-off point in the list using consistency measure.

3.3.1   Term Weighting

Intuitively, frequency may be a main indicator of the importance of a term. This comes from two major concerns. A term is considered as representative if it appears many times *within* a document. On the other hand, a term is regarded as not informative if it appears too many times *among* documents [1]. These two aspects are commonly used in term weighting functions.

TFIDF is a commonly used term weighting function in a classification task [2][8]. TFIDF measures the importance of a feature in term of discriminating power between documents using the two aspects mentioned previously. The former addresses how frequent a term appears *within* a document, which is known as term frequency (TF). The latter measures how many documents that the term appears among all documents, which is known as inverse document frequency (IDF).

Term weighting function presented in this paper, named TFDF is an extension of TFIDF. TFDF measures the importance of a feature in term of discriminating power among categories. Frequency distribution of a feature across categories is taken as a basis in weighting a term. Two main aspects considered are:

Term Frequency (**TF**): TF of a feature f_i denotes the frequency occurrence of the term in a category C_k. An additional factor, total frequency of f_i in all other categories, is added in order to boost terms that occur more frequent in category C_k compare to other categories.

Although raw TF does emphasize those features with high frequency, normalization is needed because training texts are not of uniform length. Therefore, relative frequency is preferred. *Maximum frequency normalization* is used in this paper, in which the term frequency of a feature is divided by the highest frequency over all the features in category C_k.

$$W_{TF}(f_i, C_k) = \frac{TF(f_i, C_k)}{TF_{max}(C_k) \times \left(1 + \sum_{l \neq k} TF(f_i, C_l)\right)}$$

The rational behind term frequency is that the ability of a feature in discriminating categories depends on how frequently it occurs in a category as against the other categories.

Document Frequency (**DF**): DF of a feature f_i denotes the number of documents in category C_k in which the term occurs at least once. Again, we boost terms that occur in more documents in category C_k against the rest of categories. This is done by dividing DF with the total number of documents that contain f_i in other categories.

Since the number of training text in each category is different, we consider the relative frequency by normalizing DF with total number of documents in the category.

$$W_{DF}(f_i, C_k) = \frac{DF(f_i, C_k)}{DF_{total}(C_k) \times \left(1 + \sum_{l \neq k} DF(f_i, C_l)\right)}$$

The main idea of document frequency is that features that occur in more documents in a category against other categories are more discriminative than features that occur in many documents in many categories.

By combining both TF and DF weights together, we can obtain a final TFDF weight of a feature f_i in a particular category C_k, as follow.

$$TFDF(f_i, C_k) = W_{TF}(f_i, C_k) + W_{DF}(f_i, C_k)$$

3.3.2   Consistency Measure

The size of Category Model is a main concern in the processing speed of our classification algorithm. Thus, it is important to concern the set of features selected in order to compose an optimum CM. We expect that the selected features are informative enough to represent the concepts of the categories, neither too few to miss semantics or too many to burden the processing speed.

In this paper, a set of selected feature is evaluated by *class separability* measure. A feature subset is considered 'optimal' when it maximizes the class separability within a domain. Consistency measure is a conservative way of achieving class separability. It does not attempt to maximize the class separability but tries to retain the power of class separability defined by the original set of features. The idea is to find a smallest set of features that can distinguish classes as well as the full set of features. [5].

In our feature selection method, consistency measure is applied in the task of finding cut-off point in the list of features sorted by their weight. The measure is an inconsistency rate over the training text for a given feature set. This criterion heavily relies on the set of training text and it uses Min-Features bias in selecting a feature subset.

3.4 Mapping Feature to Category

From the definition of term weighting function in Section 3.3.1, the weight indicates the importance of a feature in discriminating a particular category from the rest of the categories. Thus, a feature is mapped to the category that has the highest weight. Intuitively speaking, a feature is treated as a descriptive keyword for the category, which can express the concept of the category more clearly.

4. RESULTS CLASSIFICATION

Every result is represented by a Boolean vector in our Category Model vector space in which the Boolean value denotes the occurrence of a particular feature in the result.

4.1 Similarity Calculating

Result classification is typically performed by comparing representation of the result with representation of categories and computing a measure of their similarity. The measure is a *cosine* value between two vectors. The smaller angle the two vectors has, the more similar the results and the contents of the category. The cosine value of a result r with every category C_k is calculated and the result is assigned to the most similar category.

$$\cos ine\,\theta(r, C_k) = \frac{r \cdot C_k}{|r||C_k|}$$

5.   EXPERIMENTS

5.1   Data Collection

In our experiments, we used a human edited directory of the web, Open Directory Project (ODP) as reference in defining our own categories. We selected a total of 9 categories as our category hierarchy. For each category, we collect a set of web pages as training text. These web pages are selected manually in which they can comprise the concepts represented by each category.

As testing text, we collect 892 distinct site listing from the ODP sub-categories pages. For every site listing, we generate two testing texts, the first testing text only contain a title and a short description provided by the editor in ODP. The second testing text is the full text of the web site.

The first set of testing text contains less content. However, the content is more 'clean' and 'informative'. This is because the title and description are provided by human editor and may fully describe a particular site. We include this set of testing text in order to provide an overview on how our classification algorithm can be applied on text data with limited content. This is because search result returned by search engines usually only contains a title and a short description about the site.

The full text of a web site may contain more 'noise' due to the heterogeneous of web pages. The contents vary from page to page, where some pages may contain useful textual information while others may contain only graphics, animation, multimedia and etc. Our classification algorithm considers only textual information in the classification task. In this paper, we use the text contain in the first page of the web site as our testing text.

Table 1 shows the number of training and testing text collected for every category.

Table 1: The data set used in the evaluation of our classification algorithm

Categories	Sub-Categories	No of Training Text	No of Testing Text	
			Title & Desc	Full Text
Artificial Intelligence	Artificial Life	43	100	100

	Fuzzy Logic	31	29	29
	Genetic Programming	33	48	48
	Neural Networks	39	87	87
Natural Language Processing	Information Management	60	135	135
	Language Analysis	41	92	92
	Machine Translation	34	69	69
	Speech Processing	38	184	184
High Performance Computing	-	59	148	148
Total		378	1784	

5.2   Performance Measure

Every testing text has one correct category (its ODP category). The performance is measured by calculating the accuracy of our classification algorithm.

$$\text{Accurac} \quad \frac{\text{Number of testing text that are assigned to the correct category}}{\text{Total number of testing text}}$$

5.3   Experimental Results and Discussion

We carried out experiments to test on the performance of our classification algorithm. The set of training text is used to train our Category Model (CM). Later, the CM is used to classify the testing text. Two type of testing text are prepared, (i) title and description of web sites and (ii) full text of the web sites.

We first compare the impact of different feature types ('single terms' and 'phrases') using the TFDF term weighting function presented in Section 3.3.1. 'Single term' means only individual word component are considered as features, whereas 'phrases' means phrases of length up to 3 are generated as features. Figure 1 and Figure 2 show the results of our classification algorithm using different top n% of features from the feature list to generate the category model.

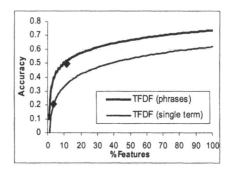

Figure 2. Accuracy of classification for 'Title & Desc' testing texts

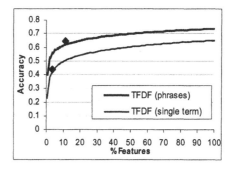

Figure 3. Accuracy of classification for 'Full Text' testing texts.

Figure 2 and Figure 3 show that the overall performance for 'phrases' feature type is better than 'single term'. The results prove that considering phrases as features can preserve the information left out by single words and thus increase the accuracy of our classification algorithm.

Figure 2 and Figure 3 also show a trend for the performance of our classification algorithm. The classification accuracy increases with the number of features that contain in our CM and become more stable after a certain point. More features may give us a better performance; however, the high dimensionality of feature space in CM may create a more complex classifier and increase the processing time. In order to find a compromise point between the accuracy and the size of CM, we apply the consistency measure to determine the size of our CM. We also show the cut-off point in our feature list using consistency measure discussed in Section 3.3.2.in the figures above. The consistency measure applied in our feature selection method can be useful in helping us to predict a compromise point between the accuracy and the size of our CM.

It is interesting to see how the performance of our classification algorithm can be improved by considering additional aspects in term weighting function as presented in Section 3.3.1. We test the performance of our classification algorithm using *raw term frequency* as term weighting function. The results comparison between raw TF and TFDF are shown in Figure 4 and Figure 5.

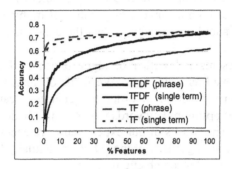

Figure 4. Results comparison of TF and TFDF for 'Title & Desc'

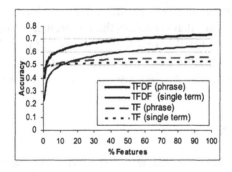

Figure 5. Results comparison of TF and TFDF for 'Full Text' testing texts.

For 'clean' and 'informative' testing texts, TF alone can give us encouraging results. However, in the situation where the testing texts contain a lot of 'noise' ('full text' testing texts), TFDF outperform TF. In this case, considering the distribution of a feature in documents among categories is useful in helping us to identify discriminative keywords.

6.   CONCLUSION AND FUTURE WORK

The quality of the classification task is mainly depends on two factors:

The inherent separation between categories selected. Clearly, even the best training and classification algorithm cannot achieve high accuracy if the categories are fuzzy and ambiguous. The categories selected should be mutually exclusive and 'well-separated' so that their intersection and overlapping is minimized.

The ability of the training process to capture the difference between categories from the training data. In order to generate a category model with reasonable size and high accuracy, the quality of training data is important. The training data should reasonably reflect the concepts of the category they belong.

This paper presents a classification algorithm that can be used to classify search results as well as web pages. We focus on feature selection method and term weighting function in order to generate a category model that consists of a set of optimum keywords which can fully describe the concepts of the categories. The results of our experiments are encouraging and shows that the classification algorithm proposed can potentially be used to classify search results returned by search engines.

In this paper, we only focus on linear classification. In linear classification, all categories are considered at the same level and the hierarchical structure of category hierarchy is not taken into account. As future research directions, we are interesting in developing a hierarchical classification algorithm that considers the hierarchical structure of categories. Intuitively, many potentially good keywords are not useful discriminators in non-hierarchical representation. We believe that considering the hierarchical structure of the categories can increase the accuracy of a classification task.

REFERENCES

1. C, Liu. (2004). A Survey: Automatic Text Categorization. *CS412 Report*, University of Illinois at Urbana-Champaign.
2. T, Joachims. (1997). A Probabilistic Analysis of the Rocchio Algorithm with TFIDF for Text Categorization. *In Proceedings of the 14th International Conference on Machine Learning (ICML97)*, pp143-151.
3. H, Chen. and S.T. Dumais. (2000). Bringing Order to the Web: Automatically Categorizing Search Results. *In Proceedings of the ACM SIGCHI Conference on Human Factors in Computing Systems (CHI 2000)*, pp145-152.
4. H, Chen., S.T. Dumais and E, Cytrell. (2001). Optimizing Search by Showing Results in Context, *In Proceedings of the ACM SIGCHI Conference on Human Factors in Computing Systems (CHI 2001)*. pp277-284.
5. H, Liu., H, Dash., and H, Motoda. (2000). Consistency Based Feature Selection, *In Proceedings of the Pacific-Asia Conference on Knowledge Discovery and Data Mining (PAKDD-2000)*

6. D, Mladenic. and M, Grobelnik. (1998). Word sequences as features in text-learning. *In Proceedings of ERK-98, the seventh Electro-technical and Computer Science Conference*, pp145-148.

7. M, Sahami. and D, Koller. (1996). Toward Optimal Feature Selection. In *Proceedings of the 13th International Conference on Machine Learning (ICML96)*, San Franscisco CA, Morgan Kaufmann, pp 284-292.

8. G, Salton. and C, Buckley. (1988). *Term Weighting Approaches in Automatic Text Retrieval*. In Technical Report, COR-87-881, Department of Computer Science, Cornell University.

9. S, S, Tan. (2002). *Topic Hierarchy Annotation using Feature Selection Technique*. MSc Thesis, School of Computer Science, Universiti Sains Malaysia.

RANK AGGREGATION MODEL FOR META SEARCH

An Approach using Text and Rank Analysis Measures

Gan Keng Hoon[1], Saravadee Sae Tan[1], Chan Huah Yong[2] and Tang Enya Kong[1]

[1]*Computer Aided Translation Unit (UTMK)*
School of Computer Sciences, Universiti Sains Malaysia, 11800 Penang, Malaysia

[2]*Grid Computing Lab*
School of Computer Sciences, Universiti Sains Malaysia, 11800 Penang, Malaysia
{khgan | saratan | hychan | enyakong}@cs.usm.my

Abstract: One problem domain of meta search is to combine and improve the precision of ranking results from various search systems. This paper describes a rank aggregation model that incorporates text analysis measure with existing rank-based method, e.g. Best Rank and Borda Rank, to aggregate search results from various search systems. This approach provides means to normalize the differences of rank methodology used by different search systems, justifying the potential of using contents analysis to improve the results relevancy in meta search. In this paper, we fully describe our approach on text normalization for meta search and present our rationality of using two rank-based methods in our model. We then evaluate and benchmark the performance of our model based on user judgment on results relevancy. Our experiment results show that when text analysis factor is taken into account, the results outperform the rank-based methods alone. This shows the potential of our model to complement current rank aggregation methods used in meta search.

Key words: Information retrieval, ranking, search results aggregation, meta search, normalization

1.   INTRODUCTION

Looking at the speed of information growth on the web, practically, it is not likely for a single search system to have coverage for the entire web. Meta search allows combination of the best search results from various search systems, at the same time utilizing all the underlying ranking methodologies deployed by these systems. One way to organize search results from various search systems is to combine them into a unified result list. The task of combining results involves re-ordering them into a list where the most relevant result is displayed on top of the result list. However, since each search system has its own rules and policies in listing its search results, combining ranks from multiple systems has become a research issue in the field of information retrieval.

Based on the simplicity or depth of methodology used in solving the issue, different rank combination methods and their variations are obtained, e.g. best rank, Borda's positional, scaled footrule, Markov chain methods etc ([8], [4], [10]). Major distinctions among these methods are that they can be classified based on the type of information utilized, whether: i) they rely on the rank, ii) they rely on the relevance score, and iii) they require training data or not [8], [9].

As an alternative to the existing methods, this paper proposes a rank aggregation model which includes text analysis in addition to the information stated above. The idea is to utilize text-based information such as title and description obtained from a search result to improve the quality of the combined results list. This paper makes the following contributions: i) we present method of normalization for text-based information across different query types and search systems. ii) while result's rank or position is simple and practically, yet widely used in most rank aggregation methods, we utilize and analyze both rank and text information in our rank aggregation model. We evaluate our model by using user judgment on the results relevancy, where positive results are achieved. iii) with minimal training, we get an optimized rank aggregation model, where the best combination of weights allocated for both rank and text analysis factors are obtained. iv) we benchmark our rank aggregation model against common rank-based methods.

Our experiments show initial evidence of success for the proposed model. The usage of text information provides a certain standard of normalization when outputs of different search systems need to be combined. This approach could be easily used to minimize the problem of not comparable search systems.

2.   RANK AGGREGATION MODEL

2.1   Preliminaries

We first present some definitions that will be used in this paper.

Query – A *query* consists one or more search terms, and will be used interchangeably with *topic* in our paper later. We denote n_{query} as the number of term(s) in a search query.

Term – A term is a series of characters without space in between any of the characters (including letters, numbers and symbols).

Let U denote the set of all web pages in the universe. In real situation, it is not possible or convenient for a search system to index the entire set of web pages. This situation is stated as partial rank list (detail references in [9], [4]) where it only rank some of the elements of U. Here, I denote the set of web pages indexed by a particular search system, where $I \subset U$.

Let τ denote the results list of a search system in response to a search query. τ consists set of results $x_1, x_2, ... x_{|\tau|}$ with each $x_i \in I$, in which lower numbered of i represents higher rank or preferred result. The position or rank of a result in τ is given by $\tau(i)$. $|\tau|$ is the size of the results list, where $|\tau| \leq |I|$.

Considering τ from different search systems, in rank aggregation model, we manipulate a set of results lists, R from k search systems, $R = \{\tau_1, \tau_2, ... \tau_k\}$. The union of unique results (e.g. elimination of results overlapping) in R is given as U_R. For our work, a unique result is referred by its URL.

Let X denote a result of our rank aggregated model. We obtain a scored results list, $U_R = \{X_1, X_2, ..., X_{|U_R|}\}$, and $X(i)$ = score for result i. Adhering to the generality rule, we assume that a higher score represents a better rank.

2.2   Rank Aggregation

In the problem domain of aggregating results from different search systems, a common issue arises is that the rank-based or score-based information obtained could not be compared. The results lists produced by different search systems are generated based on individual methodology, which is not comparable. Underlying each methodology, different research and method are carried out to increase the quality of the ranking algorithms. Thus, we see the situation of inequality of the performance of these search systems, as some are superior to others.

In the case where there are huge differences between the performances of search systems used, we are more likely to get an aggregated list which offers quantity rather than quality. This situation often causes the precision of the aggregated list to be less than the precision of the best search system. An alternative for this situation is to allocate different priorities to the search systems, where training data are required to get the list of ranked or weighted search systems. Moreover, the weight has to be dynamic following the increment or decrement of the search system's popularity against time. A search system comparison method is suggested in [4].

In our rank aggregation model, we attempt to leverage the differences of search systems by incorporating text analysis of contents (title text and description text of a result) together with ranks (or score) given by the search systems. Our justification is that rank (or score) generated by search system is undeniable important regardless the popularity level of the system. However, we observe that the contents i.e. title and description given by a search system is in fact a good resource that could help us to normalize the disparate search systems.

2.2.1   Text Analysis

First, we have identified some issues of text analysis that need to be considered in our rank aggregation model.

Types of text – In results aggregation, texts that can be used for analysis include title, description, URL, and full text (text from the web site). In our justification, title and description are both derived from the result's site, either extracted from full text or edited by human based on the contents of the web site. We could directly utilize these texts as they have been filtered by search systems (less noise compared to full text), and can be obtained in timely manner (does not need to retrieve full text). We did not consider URL text as it is more suitable for context-based analysis.

Location of terms – The location of terms, either in title text or description text indicates different level of importance. For most search systems, the title text is treated with a higher priority compared to description text.

Frequency of terms – For terms frequency, we consider factors as follows:

length of text and display format which vary for different search systems. This is particular noticeably in description text, where different display format can be seen.

spamming possibility where same term is repeated many times.

query length, e.g. query with many terms indirectly induce higher terms occurrences.

Second, we proceed with title and description analysis, together with score normalization for these two factors.

Title Normalization

In general, the text of title is short and is a direct extraction from the title tag of a result's site or document title of result's link. Therefore, we only take into account the density of unique terms occurrences in relative to the size of query. The nature of title text, where the multiple occurrences of the same term is uncommon, allows us to ignore consideration for repetitive term.

Density

n_{td} = the number of term(s) that occur at least once in title text.

$\tau(i)_{title}$ = the score of title analysis for result at position i in τ.

For a result $i \in \tau$,

$\tau(i)_{title} = \log_{n_{query} + 1}(n_{td} + 1)$, where $0 \leq n_{td} \leq n_{query}$

Description Normalization

For text analysis in description, we consider two cases, the total occurrences of any term in a query, and the density of occurrences for unique term in a query. This is due to high occurrences of terms for a query might not reflect that all terms in the query are represented. Thus we take the product of both cases for better measurement of description text.

Density

n_{dd} = the number of term(s) that occur at least once in description text.

$\tau(i)_{desc;\, d}$ = the score of description density analysis for result at position i in τ.

For a result $i \in \tau$,

$\tau(i)_{desc;\, d} = \dfrac{n_{dd}}{n_{query}}$, where $0 \leq n_{dd} \leq n_{query}$

Frequency

n_{df} = the total occurrences of term(s) in description text.

$\tau(i)_{desc;\, f}$ = the score of description frequency analysis for result at position i in τ.

In order to leverage the frequency of terms in description text, issues like display length, display format, spamming, are taken into accounts. Notice that the number of terms in a query also affects the total terms occurrences, therefore, we will also normalize total occurrences in relative to this variable.

We observe the distribution of total terms occurrences in description text using a terms occurrences scale. The scale is divided into two phases:

Phase I. $n_{df} \leq n_{query}$: If the number of total terms occurrences is less or equal to the number of terms in a query, we take the linear proportion of the total occurrences against the number of terms in the query. In this phase, our intention is to normalize the distribution of total terms occurrences against different query size.

Phase II. $n_{df} > n_{query}$: If the number of total terms occurrences is more than the number of terms in a query, we measure how many times of the occurrences against the query size. In this phase, we intend to control the size of total terms occurrences across various display format.

This scale is then normalized using logarithm function to uniform its score distribution.

For a result $i \in \tau$,
$$\tau(i)_{desc}; \left\{ = \begin{array}{l} \log_3 \left\lfloor \left(\dfrac{n_{df}}{n_{query}} \right) + 1 \right\rfloor, \text{where } 0 \leq n_{df} \leq n_{query} \\[3ex] \log_3 \left\lfloor \left(1 + \left(1 - \dfrac{n_{query}}{n_{df}} \right) \right) + 1 \right\rfloor, \text{where } n_{df} > n_{query} \end{array} \right.$$

2.2.2   Rank Analysis

For rank aggregation approach that only utilizes rank or position information, we differentiate the normalization method to two types, either depend or not depend on R [9]. Here, we consider rank analysis for both types, i.e. Borda Rank normalization which depends on R, and Simple Rank normalization which does not depend on R.

For both normalization methods, the top ranked result is given normalized score 1, and the bottom ranked result is given normalized score 0. However, there is a difference in score allocation. For rank normalization method, the score decreases with a factor of $1/|\tau|$ between two subsequent ranked results, while for Borda rank normalization, the score decreases with a factor of $1/|U_R|$. In the former, unranked results within a result list does not occur as each result, $i \in \tau$ is compared against its own list. Whereas the latter normalizes each result, $i \in \tau$ against the merged results list, U_R, where unranked results will be given an equal distribution of the left over scores. An exceptional case occurs when $|\tau| \in R$ equals $|U_R|$ (each results list is a full list with respect to the merged list), where we obtain same score allocation for both methods.

$\tau(i)$ = the position or rank of result at position i in τ.

$\tau(i)_{pos}$ = the score of rank normalization for result at position i in τ.

Simple Rank Normalization

For a result $i \in \tau$,

$$\tau(i)_{pos} = 1 - \frac{\tau(i) - 1}{|\tau|}$$

Borda Rank Normalization
For a result $i \in U_R$,

$$\tau(i)_{pos} \begin{cases} 1 - \frac{\tau(i) - 1}{|U_R|}, & \text{if } i \in \tau \\ \\ \frac{1}{2} + \frac{1 - |\tau|}{2 \cdot |U_R|} & \text{otherwise} \end{cases}$$

Few issues that we consider in rank analysis include:

1. Computational efficiency: For Simple Rank normalization, the score can be calculated whenever any list, τ is retrieved as it does not depend on the entire set of R to be available to begin processing the score. This method is more computational efficient, especially when k and $|\tau|$ are large.

2. Handling uneven lists: For Simple Rank normalization, the issue of uneven lists is solved by adapting different score factor, $1/|\tau|$ based on the size of individual list. For Borda Rank normalization, the score factor, $1/|U_R|$ is fixed, allow standardized score across the uneven lists as each result $i \in \tau$ is compared against U_R.

3. Single voter vs. multiple voters: Originally a voting model, where a winning candidate highly based on the number of voters, Borda Rank normalization adapts similar concepts for meta search by emphasizing on the preference of a result by multiple search systems rather than single system. In Borda Rank normalization, the score for a result very much rely on the number of voters (search systems) in addition to the position of the result. In contrast, Simple Rank normalization gives the authority to a single search system to decide the position of a result. When the positions collide between different systems, the authority will be given to a more preferred search system and so forth. This can also be applied for Borda Rank normalization when the voting results from multiple search systems collide.

3.   EVALUATION MEASURES

3.1   Data Sets

In order to evaluate our rank aggregation model, we use the search results obtained from three actual search systems, i.e. AllTheWeb, Alta Vista and Yahoo. These systems have been classified by Search Engine Watch [6] as major search engines on the web because of their well-known or well-used.

In selecting search queries, we have chosen a subset of topics (search queries) from TREC (Text Retrieval Conference) Web Topics, track on web searching [5]. The main reason we use topics from TREC test collections is because of the, i) fairness of selection of topics by a group of NIST assessors [7], ii) realistic web queries, e.g. TREC-9 topics where specifically generated from real web logs, containing the actual web log terms [5].

16 topics are selected from four TREC conferences (Table 1). This subset was chosen with awareness in topics diversity, e.g. length of query (number of keywords in a query) and type of query (statement or question). We anticipate that this subset is able to closely represent real search queries submitted to search systems.

Table 1. The search query data sets used in the evaluation of our rank aggregation model.

TREC Web Track	No.	Topic
TREC 2002 Topic Distillation (551-600)	585	Tornado basics
	566	Television violence
	560	Symptoms of diabetes
	552	Foods for cancer patients
TREC 2001 Web Topics (501-550)	543	radiography what are the risks
	529	history on cambodia?
	515	what about alexander graham bell
	513	earthquakes?
	511	diseases caused by smoking?

	05	5	edmund hillary; sir?
	02	5	prime factor?
TREC-9 Web Topics (451-500)	53	4	hunger
	51	4	What is a Bengals cat?
TREC-8 Ad-hoc and Small Web Topics (401-450)	23	4	Milosevic, Mirjana Markovic
	06	4	Parkinson's disease
	03	4	osteoporosis

3.2 Relevance Judgment

One way to assess the performance of our rank aggregation model is to see whether the model is able provides a higher quality results list as required by user compared to individual output by each search system. A quality results list ensures that the most relevant result required by user is placed at the upper most of the results list and so forth. Therefore, we will evaluate the performance of our model based on relevance judgment made by user.

In the relevance judging experiment, we collected the top 20 results from each search system. Our justification is that in results viewing, the mean of pages examined by user is 2.35, and more than three quarters of users did not go beyond first two pages [1]. A total of 30 user judges (as in Table 2) were recruited for the relevance judgment evaluation process. From our judges selection criteria, we believe that each judge has proper general knowledge to handle the topics assigned to them. All of them have web search experiences throughout the years mentioned.

Table 2. Selection of user judges for relevance judgment.

Qualifications*	Master Candidate	PhD. Candidate	Research Analyst	Junior Developer	Senior Developer
Percentage	25%	3%	6%	44%	22%

* Minimal requirements of first degree (3 years) with 1 year research or development experiences in the field of Computer Science/Information Technology.

All judges were required to work on a common topic, *529*, and additional topics that were assigned in random order. Each judgment made is independent, where a judge does not know the decision made by others. Given a results list, a user evaluates whether a search result is relevant according to the topic. A relevant result is able to give a comprehensive overview for someone wanting to learn about the topic based on the description and narrative provided by NIST. Referral to description and narrative allow our user judges to have the same understanding about what is needed for each topic (as in Figure 1). To prevent bias of search systems preferences, search results were reformatted and standardized.

```
<top>
<num> Number: 529
<title> history on cambodia?
<desc> Description:
Find accounts of the history of Cambodia.
<narr> Narrative:
A  relevant  document  will  provide  historical  information  on
Cambodia.
Current events in Cambodia are not relevant.
</top>
```

Figure 1. Topic 529 from TREC 2001 conference, web topics track

3.3   Performance Evaluation

Given the results ranked by our rank aggregation model, and the set of relevant results provided by user judges, we could estimate the strength of our model by using common retrieval measures like precision and recall, and the harmonic mean [3], as well as benchmarking with other methods.

3.3.1   Precision and Recall

We examine the quality (precision) and coverage (recall) of top 20 results ranked by our rank aggregation model, allowing us to measure whether top 20 results ranked by our model offers a better quality or coverage compared to the individual top 20 results retrieved by search systems.

Precision at Top 20

$$= \frac{\text{Relevant results ranked by rank aggregation model at Top 20}}{\text{Total results at Top 20}}$$

Recall at Top 20

$$= \frac{\text{Relevant results ranked by rank aggregation model at Top 20}}{\text{Total relevant results}}$$

3.3.2   The Harmonic Mean

In addition to precision and recall, we use the Harmonic Mean, F, to obtain a single effectiveness measure, allowing us to take into accounts both precision and recall value equally for evaluating our model.

$$F = \frac{2}{\dfrac{1}{\text{Recall at Top 20}} + \dfrac{1}{\text{Precision at Top 20}}}$$

4.   EXPERIMENTS AND RESULTS

4.1   Trade-off Between Text and Rank Analysis

We first carry out experiments to look at how text and rank analysis factors trade off against one another in our rank aggregation model. We obtain the average value of precision and recall of all topics using different variation of weight allocation, $[\alpha_{text}, \alpha_{rank}]$. Since our model is implemented under a meta search system, IDS (Internet Data Syndicator), we shall refer our model variations as IDS(a) for Text and Simple Rank Model, and IDS(b) for Text and Borda Rank Model.

Table 3. Precision, Recall and the Harmonic Mean for IDS(a) and IDS(b).

Sys. ID	Weight $[\alpha_{text}, \alpha_{rank}]$	IDS(a)			IDS(b)		
		Average Precision	Average Recall	F	Average Precision	Average Recall	F
I	[1.0,0 .0]	0.41 39	0.55 01	0.47 24	0.41 39	0.55 01	0.47 24
I I	[0.9,0 .1]	0.41 91	0.55 84	0.47 88	0.41 78	0.55 27	0.47 59
I	[0.8,0	0.42	0.57	0.48	0.42	0.57	0.48

II	.2]	29	07	58	64	37	92
I	[0.7,0	0.41	0.59	0.48	0.41	0.59	0.48
V	.3]	54	06	78	73	00	88
V	[0.6,0	0.42	0.58	0.49	0.44	0.60	0.51
	.4]	52	10	11	78	79	57
V	[0.5,0	0.43	0.59	0.50	0.45	0.61	0.52
I	.5]	18	50	05	48	81	40
V	[0.4,0	0.43	0.59	0.50	0.45	0.62	0.52
II	.6]	11	75	09	72	31	74
V	[0.3,0	0.42	0.58	0.48	0.46	0.63	0.53
III	.7]	18	36	97	74	81	96
I	[0.2,0	0.41	0.57	0.48	0.46	0.64	0.53
X	.8]	44	35	12	69	00	99
X	[0.1,0	0.40	0.56	0.47	0.45	0.63	0.52
	.9]	80	01	21	12	62	80
X	[0.0,1	0.39	0.55	0.46	0.42	0.58	0.49
I	.0]	87	67	46	28	60	12

In this experiment, we are interested to find out whether text analysis factor gives satisfy results when combined with common rank normalization method. Considering both factors have equal weight, we achieve positive results, where IDS(a)-VI shows precision of 0.4318 and recall of 0.5950, IDS(b)-VI shows precision of 0.4548 and recall of 0.6181. Our preliminary success shows the potential of incorporating text analysis factor with other rank-based or score-based methods.

We notice that when combined with rank-based method, text analysis factor causes increment or decrement in precision and recall depending on the weight allocated to that factor. By examine the performance distribution pattern under different weight allocation (Figure 2), we can predict proper weights, $[\alpha_{text}, \alpha_{rank}]$ for both factors, that further optimize the performance of our rank aggregation model. From the graph, we loosely predict the optimal F value and obtain IDS(a)-V, IDS(a)-VI, IDS(b)-VII and IDS(b)-VIII as the well performed systems.

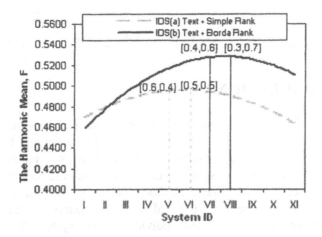

Figure 2. The Harmonic Mean, F across weight allocation [αtext, αrank] of IDS(a) and IDS(b).

4.2   Benchmarking

We benchmark our model against i) rank-based methods, i.e. Best Rank[10] and Borda Rank, and ii) three search systems used. From Table 4, we see that our model, IDS(a) and IDS(b) outperform the two rank-based methods. Although the results of Borda Rank is somehow similar to IDS(a), we have expected this due to the already noted performance of Borda Rank[8]. For evaluation fairness, we compare the result of Borda Rank with IDS(b), and see the performance of our model exceeds the performance of Borda Rank method. Similar achievement is gained when comparing IDS(a) and Best Rank method. The results of both IDS(a) and IDS(b) indicate room of improvement for rank aggregation in meta search whereby text analysis of search results can be adapted to yield a better quality of aggregated results.

In order to meaningful assess our model in meta search context, we examine the performance against the three search systems used as the input for our rank aggregation model. Assume that performance usually increases when more search systems are used [1], we expect our model to perform better than individual search system in overall, as displayed in Table 4.

Table 4. Benchmarking of IDS(a) and IDS(b) against rank-based methods and individual search systems.

	IDS(a)-V	IDS(a)-VI	IDS(b)-VII	IDS(b)-VIII	Best Rank	Borda Rank	SearchSys. I	SearchSys. II	SearchSys.III
Avg. Precision	0.4252	0.4318	0.4572	0.4674	0.3987	0.4228	0.2724	0.3151	0.3448

Avg. Recall	0. 5810	0. 5950	0. 6231	0. 6381	0. 5567	0. 5860	0. 3661	0. 4021	0. 4542

5.   CONCLUSIONS

We have described a rank aggregation model for meta search which incorporates text analysis of contents (title and description) from search results, with existing rank normalization method. We have tested the performance of our model and our findings show initial success as follows: i) when combined with rank-based method, analysis on text information help to increase the average precision and recall on results relevancy. ii) the performance of our model exceeds individual search system, thus satisfying the basic criterion as meta search ranking model. iii) with the usage of optimized weights, α_{text} and α_{rank}, the performance of our model increases, reflecting the importance of text analysis aspect in our model.

Our model offers advantages and prospective in rank aggregation, i) consideration of text information reduces the distance of the inequality of search systems, ii) with the assumption that text information obtained can well represent the context of its source, i.e. web site, web document etc., simple text analysis helps enhancing the quality of relevant results with respect to the search query submitted, iii) in addition to the rank given by search systems, we foresee the room of improvement for meta search to adapt suitable contents analysis in its rank aggregation model to achieve higher quality results.

REFERENCES

1. B.J. Jansen, "The effect of query complexity on Web searching results", *Information Research 6(1)*, 2000.
2. B.J. Jansen, A. Spink and T. Saracevic, "Real life, real users, and real needs: a study and analysis of user queries on the web", *Information Processing and Management 36(2) 207-227*, Elsevier, 2000.
3. B.Y. Ricardo and R. N. Berthier, *Modern Information Retrieval*, ACM Press Series/Addison-Wesley, New York, 1999.
4. C. Dwork, R. Kumar, M. Naor and D. Sivakumar, "Rank Aggregation Methods for the Web", *WWW10*, ACM, Hong Kong, 2001.
5. D. Harman, "The Development and Evolution of TREC and DUC", *NTCIR Workshop*, 2003.

6. D. Sullivan, "Search Engine Watch: Major Search Engines and Directories", http://searchenginewatch.com/links/article.php/2156221/, 2003.

7. E.M. Voorhess, "The Philosophy of Information Retrieval Evaluation", *2nd Workshop of the Cross-Language Evaluation Forum, CLEF 2001*, Darmstadt, Germany, 2001, pp. 355-370.

8. J.A. Aslam and M. Montague, "Model for Metasearch", *SIGIR'01*, ACM, New Orleans, Louisiana, USA, 2001, pp. 276-284.

9. M.E. Renda and U. Straccia, "Web Metasearch: Rank vs. Score Based Rank Aggregation Methods", *SAC2003*, ACM, Melbourne, Florida, USA, 2003.

10. M.S. Mahabhashyam and P. Singitham, "Tadpole: A Meta search engine", *CS276A Report*, Standford, 2002.

ON THE IMPORTANCE OF BEING DIVERSE:

ANALYSING SIMILARITY AND DIVERSITY IN WEB SEARCH

Maurice Coyle and Barry Smyth*
Smart Media Institute
University College Dublin, Dublin, Ireland
firstname.lastname@ucd.ie

Abstract   We argue that the emphasis normally placed on query-similarity in Web search limits search precision. We draw on related work in case-based reasoning (CBR) and recommender systems research, which shows how enhancing diversity can improve the quality of retrieved cases and recommendations. We investigate the use of related diversity-enhancing retrieval techniques in Web search, showing that similar benefits are available, i.e. that result diversity can be significantly enhanced without compromising query similarity or result precision and recall.

Keywords: Web search, diversity, relevance, topic coverage

Introduction

Web search engines are the primary tool for online information discovery and significant strides have been made to build upon their information retrieval (IR) origins in order to address the specific needs of Web users. Nevertheless, search engines frequently fail to deliver the right results at the right time.

It has been shown that users have a tendency to formulate under-specified queries consisting of between 2 and 3 search terms [15]. This coupled with the fact that most commercial search engines index over 1 billion documents leads to large result-lists with poor precision characteristics. Most search engines rank search results according to their similarity to the query terms and this can lead to result-lists with low diversity and poor topic coverage.

As an example, the first 200 Google results for the intentionally vague query 'lisp' all refer to the Lisp programming language with only a few references to other meanings, none of which refer to speech impediments. With a predominance of computer-related information on the Web, it's not hard to see why this

*The support of the Informatics Research Initiative of Enterprise Ireland is gratefully acknowledged

is the case, but with an increasing number of online users from non-computing backgrounds, there is no longer a corresponding bias among Web searchers.

The point is that given vague queries, result diversity in modern search engines is poor which will inevitably lead to search failures – a speech therapist will not be served well by a typical search engine for the term 'lisp' and will be left with no choice but to refine their query. Thus, researchers have focused their efforts on a number of different possible approaches. Recently, ranking metrics have been developed using factors other than query-page similarity [3].

In this paper we focus on diversity among search engine results for vague queries. Research in the areas of CBR and recommender systems has begun to question the similarity assumption, arguing that in many scenarios query-similarity can be sacrificed in favour of improved result diversity in order to maximise the coverage of the retrieved cases. A successful solution has involved a ranking metric incorporating diversity as well as similarity, rather than attempting to elaborate the queries or change the result presentation paradigm.

We adapt this diversity-enhanced approach for use in Web search and evaluate its performance on a range of test data (Sections 3 and 4). We show that the technique introduces result diversity without compromising overall query-page similarity or precision and recall characteristics of the result-lists (see Section 4). First, we will review a range of related research, covering context-sensitive search methods, result-clustering, and diversity-enhancing techniques.

1.   Background

1.1   Related Work

In related work, *search context* was introduced to elaborate vague queries and focus search [10] - this encompasses *explicit context manipulation* ([6, 11]) and *implicit context inference* ([4, 7]). The context-sensitive technique yielded promising results indicating that Web search can benefit from its use ([16, 17]).

1.2   Results Clustering

The IR community uses clustering both as a pre-retrieval process to speed up search performance [19] and as a post-retrieval document browsing technique for handling vague queries [5, 12]; it is the second paradigm that concerns us.

[21] and [22] are examples of early work on result clustering. A technique called *suffix tree clustering* (STC) is introduced which shows potential as a means of generating meaningful clusters. A fuzzy similarity metric is proposed in [8] as part of a relational fuzzy clustering algorithm that is $O(n^2)$ (STC is $O(n)$), apparently capable of producing more focused clusters than STC.

It is also worth mentioning [20] for their approach to clustering using connectivity information rather than textual content.

1.3   Towards Diversity-Enhanced Retrieval

The above strategies help users to find information following a vague query. However, they place different obligations on both search engine and searcher and move away from the accepted *ranked list presentation paradigm.*

A number of case retrieval systems have concentrated on improving the diversity of a single set of recommendations while preserving the query-similarity of these recommendations to a lesser or greater extent. [14] introduces a system focused on diversity, however although recommendations are maximally diverse from each other, query-similarity is compromised. Thus, the candidate cases must be sufficiently similar to the query to begin with.

[13] introduces *similarity layers* and *similarity intervals.* The former preserve case-query similarity while enhancing diversity and the latter achieve greater diversity by relaxing the constraint that query similarity must be preserved. It is worth noting that a retrieval technique may enhance diversity as a side-effect. *Order-based retrieval* is an example of such a technique [2], exhibiting an inherent ability to enhance the diversity of a set of retrieval results.

The above techniques are designed for use in case retrieval scenarios and as such it is not clear how they may be adapted for Web search. However, one of the earliest proposals for diversity-enhanced retrieval ([1],[18]) is sufficiently general for it to be directly applied to Web search. This technique is described in detail below and serves as the focus for the remainder of this paper.

2.   The Case for Diversity in Web Search

The average Web search is unlikely to result in a focused list of relevant results [9] and Web users are unlikely to venture beyond the first results page [15]. Thus, search engines must maximise the probability that a relevant result will be presented within the first page. Furthermore without any assessment of user preferences or search context, it is valuable to ensure that the first k search results reflect a representative sample of as many relevant results as possible.

In the next section we describe the Bounded Greedy Selection technique first introduced by [18]. We will argue that it provides a reasonable balance between similarity and diversity with only a small extra computational cost.

3.   Similarity vs. Diversity

We assume a standard similarity function for computing the similarity between a search query, q, and a page p_i, $Sim(q, p_i)$. Further, we assume that this function can also measure the similarity between two pages, $Sim(p_i, p_j)$.

$$Div(p_1, ..., p_n) = \frac{\sum_{i=1..n} \sum_{j=i..n} (1 - Sim(p_i, p_j))}{\frac{n}{2} * (n-1)} \tag{1}$$

We define the diversity of a set of pages, $p_1, ..., p_n$ to be the average dissimilarity between all pairs of pages in this set (see Equation 1). Standard search engines will tend to display a diversity profile which increases and a similarity profile which decreases, as result-list size increases (see Section 4.2). Thus the trade-off between query-similarity and result-diversity is a simple one: for small result-lists, high query-similarity means low diversity. We aim to optimise this trade-off, delivering result-lists that are diverse and that thus offer greater coverage of the result-space, without compromising their similarity to the query or their relevance to the end-user.

Table 1a. Greedy Algorithm.

q: target query, P: set of pages matching q, k: # results
1. `define GreedySelection(q,P,k)`
2. `begin`
3. `R:={}`
4. `For i := 1 to k`
5. `Sort P by Qual(q, p, R) ∀ p in P`
6. `R := R + First(P)`
7. `P := P - First(P)`
8. `EndFor`
9. `return R`
10. `end`

Table 1b. Bounded Greedy Algorithm.

q, P, k: as in Table 1a, b: bound
1. `define BoundedGreedySelection(q,P,k,b)`
2. `begin`
3. `P':=bk pages in P most similar to q`
4. `R:={}`
5. `For i := 1 to k`
6. `Sort P' by Qual(q, p, R) ∀ p in P'`
7. `R := R + First(P')`
8. `P' := P' - First(P')`
9. `EndFor`
10. `return R`
11. `end`

3.1   Greedy Selection

A novel approach to improving diversity, while at the same time maintaining similarity, is to explicitly consider both diversity and similarity during retrieval [18]. The *greedy selection* algorithm (Table 1a) achieves this by incrementally building a final result-list, R. During each step the remaining pages are ordered according to their *quality* with the highest quality page added to R.

The quality (see Equation 2) of a page p is proportional to the similarity between p and the current query q, and to the diversity of p *relative* to those pages so far selected, $R = \{r_1, ..., r_m\}$ (see Equation 3). The first page to be selected is always the one with the highest similarity to the query. During each iteration, the page with the highest quality value is selected.

$$Qual(q, p, R) = Sim(q, p) * RelDiv(p, R) \qquad (2)$$

$$
\begin{aligned}
RelDiv(p, R) &= 1 \quad if\ R = \{\}; \\
&= \frac{\sum_{i=1..m}(1 - Sim(p, r_i))}{m} \quad ,otherwise
\end{aligned}
\qquad (3)
$$

However, this algorithm is expensive. For an initial result-list of n pages, during each of the k iterations we must calculate the diversity of each remaining page relative to those so far selected. This means an average of $\frac{n-k}{2}$ relative diversity calculations, each one consisting of an average of $\frac{k}{2}$ similarity calculations. This gives an average total cost of $k * \frac{n-k}{2} * \frac{k}{2}$ similarity computations per retrieval. For example, for an initial result-list of 1000 pages, retrieving the top 3 pages can mean approximately 2250 similarity computations.

3.2   Bounded Greedy Selection

To reduce the complexity of the greedy selection algorithm we implement a bounded version adapted from that found in [18]. The *bounded greedy selection* algorithm (Table 1b) selects the best bk pages using their query-similarity (line 3) and then applies the greedy selection method to these (lines 4 - 9).

This algorithm has a greatly reduced cost since k pages are selected from bk pages instead of from n pages and $bk \ll n$ for typical low values of b and k. This only means a total of $k * \frac{k(b-1)}{2} * \frac{k}{2}$ extra similarity computations on top of the normal retrieval cost. For example, for a 1000 page initial result-list, retrieving the 3 best pages with $b = 2$ will now require about 7 extra similarity computations on top of the standard similarity-based retrieval cost.

We may miss a page with a marginally lower similarity value than the best bk pages but a significantly better diversity value. However, the likelihood of this decreases with page similarity so for suitable values of b it is unlikely.

[18] shows that the bounded greedy algorithm offers the best combination of diversity and efficiency, at least in CBR systems. Here we are interested in Web search and in our evaluation we investigate whether the advantages of this diversity preserving technique transfer into the Web search context.

4.   Evaluation

In this section we describe a recent evaluation to investigate this diversity-conscious ranking strategy. We compare the similarity-based and diversity-based methods and focus on their diversity and similarity characteristics, the degree of re-ordering that takes place as a result of introducing diversity and the effects of this on precision and recall characteristics.

4.1   Set-up

We produced 760 separate queries taken from 5 distinct topical domains (mammals, programming languages, researchers, computer science and travel). We also produced two search engines based on the Jakarta Lucene search engine. The *SIM* version of Lucene used standard similarity-based retrieval with TF*IDF term weighting, and corresponds to a standard Web search engine.

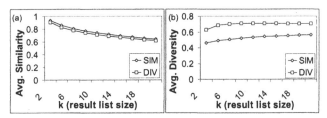

Figure 1. (a) Query-similarity profile, (b) Avg. diversity profile for SIM and DIV at various result list sizes

The *DIV* version was set up to incorporate the diversity-enhancing retrieval technique on top of the TF*IDF functions. Thus, for each query we were able to generate and compare result-lists of varying sizes for SIM and DIV.

Next we needed to populate our test search engines with a collection of Web pages and we also needed to establish a set of relevant pages for each query. To do this we adopted a similar approach to that reported by [16, 17]. Specifically, a basic or *non-contextualised* (e.g. 'java') and a *contextualised* (e.g. 'programming language java') version of each query was submitted to the HotBot search engine and the top 1000 results retrieved. To determine which results for the basic query were relevant, the intersection between the 2 lists for each query was taken. Thus, we had a list of relevant results for each query which was used to assess the precision and recall of the result-lists produced for the basic queries by the SIM and DIV search engines.

Finally, an index was created from the candidate result-lists produced for each of the queries, producing an index of approximately 250,000 pages.

4.2   The Similarity-Diversity Tradeoff

In this first experiment we evaluate the similarity-diversity trade-off – the degree to which query-similarity is compromised as we introduce diversity. We do this by submitting each query to the SIM and DIV (with $b = 4$) search engines to produce results-lists of various sizes, for $k = 2...20$. For each result-list produced by each search engine, we compute its average similarity (i.e., the average similarity between its results and the current query) and its average diversity (i.e., the average pairwise dissimilarity between its results).

The results are shown in Figure 1(a&b) as graphs of average similarity and diversity vs. result-list size. As expected, the diversity-enhanced technique used by DIV leads to a drop in query-similarity when compared to SIM. For example, the average similarity for DIV drops from 0.905 at $k = 2$ to 0.617 at $k = 20$ whereas for SIM it starts at 0.93 at $k = 2$ and falls to 0.639 at $k = 20$. So for different values of k there is only around a 3% drop in average query-similarity for the result-lists produced by DIV compared to those of SIM.

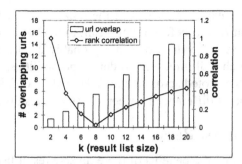

Figure 2.   Rank correlation and result overlap characteristics

Also as expected, in Figure 1(b) the advantage goes to DIV, which offers result-lists with significant diversity increases compared to those offered by SIM. For instance, the average diversity for DIV remains stable at approximately 0.7 for k>=4. This is in contrast with the average diversity of the SIM result-lists, which starts at 0.46 at $k = 2$ and grows to only 0.56 at $k = 20$.

The thing to note here is the difference between the scale of the drop in similarity versus the increase in diversity. A minor drop in query-similarity experienced by DIV is accompanied by a significant increase in result diversity.

4.3   A Comparison Of Rankings

Comparing the result-list produced by SIM, for a given k, to that produced by DIV for the same k should illustrate two things. First, DIV will have dropped some of SIM's results in favour of new, more diverse results from outside of SIM's top k results. Second, the results they have in common should be ordered differently to reflect their different quality contributions. Here we evaluate the extent to which this is happening by comparing result-lists from SIM and DIV and measuring the number of results that they have in common and their rank correlation (Spearman's rank correlation is used).

The results are shown in Figure 2 as graphs of overlap and rank correlation against result-list size. As expected, the number of shared results between SIM and DIV increases with k. To begin with, at $k = 4$ SIM and DIV share, on average, about 2.7 results and this increases to nearly 16 results at $k = 20$. Interestingly, this indicates that the percentage overlap grows slowly across the values of k, from an percentage overlap of about 66% at $k = 4$ to 79% at $k = 20$. Thus, on average the diversity-enhancing technique (at $b = 4$) tends to drop approximately 20% to 35% of SIM's top k results in producing its own top k diverse results. This percentage is at a suitably low level that we are not relying too heavily on diversity and not enough on query-page similarity.

The rank correlation results are also interesting. The rank correlation is seen to drop rapidly as k increases initially but then begins to increase slowly again beyond $k = 8$. For example, at $k = 4$ the rank correlation is 0.37 and this falls to near-zero at $k = 8$ before rising again to 0.43 at $k = 20$. The higher correlation values at low values of k are probably a reflection of the small result-set sizes which will limit the reordering possibilities. Nevertheless, the low correlation values noted across the different values of k indicate that there is a considerable order difference between the shared results in SIM and DIV.

4.4   Precision vs. Recall

We have shown that the benefits of more diverse result lists can be enjoyed without overly compromising the query-similarity of the selected results. However, if increasing diversity in the hope of improving result coverage reduces the precision and recall characteristics of the result-lists (where precision is the proportion of retrieved results that are relevant and recall is the proportion of relevant results that have been retrieved) then our approach is unlikely to bear fruit in practice. Here we consider this issue directly by estimating the accuracy of the SIM and DIV result-lists, in terms of precision and recall estimates on the generated result lists, using the relevant results identified earlier.

The precision and recall results, graphed against k (result-list size), are presented in Figure 3 for the mammals and travel domains. Each data-point represents the mean precision or recall results for either SIM or DIV ($b = 4$) calculated across all queries for the specific domain. The obvious point about these results is that they indicate an improvement in both precision and recall for DIV when compared to SIM. For example, in Figure 3(c) we see that SIM achieves an average precision score of 0.25 at $k = 2$ and that this grows to 0.31 at $k = 20$. In contrast, the same graph indicates that the DIV method achieves an average precision of just under 0.28 at $k = 2$, growing to around 0.35 at $k = 20$. For all result-list sizes we find that the precision characteristics of DIV represent improvements of between 12% and 23% over SIM.

In Figure 3(d) we find that DIV enjoys a similar benefit when it comes to recall. At $k = 2$ both SIM and DIV offer recall of just over 0.01 (actually 0.13 for SIM and 0.16 for DIV) but by $k = 20$ DIV's recall has grown to just under 0.20 whilst SIM has achieved only 0.17. For all values of k this means that DIV benefits from an improvement in recall over SIM by between 12% and 24%. Similar results can be seen for the mammals domain in Figure 3(a&b).

The significance of these results is based on the fact that DIV does not result in a drop in precision and recall – this was always a danger given that there is a reduction in query-similarity.

5.   Conclusions

Most search engines rely mainly on query-similarity when it comes to selecting and ordering search results. This often leads to a lack of diversity within

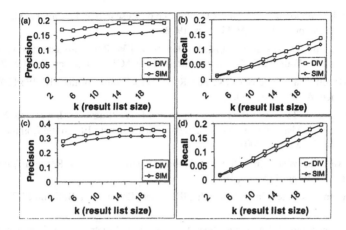

Figure 3. (a) Precision results for the mammals domain, (b) Recall results for the mammals domain, (c) Precision results for the travel domain, (d) Recall results for the travel domain

result-lists where the top-scoring documents may be very similar to the query but very similar to each other as well. A user looking for information on a different topic may need to sift through many similar but irrelevant results.

We have proposed a solution to this problem that employs the standard ranked-list presentation paradigm of today's search engines and that is general enough to work with all search engines that rank results according to a well-defined similarity metric. It calls for the introduction of diversity when it comes to selecting and ranking search results. This diversity-enhancing algorithm is efficient and effective, leading to significant increases in diversity and relatively minor compromises in query similarity. It reorders search results to maximise result diversity as well as query similarity and initial experiments indicate that it does not compromise precision and recall characteristics.

References

[1] K. Bradley and B. Smyth "Improving Recommendation Diversity", Proceedings of the 12th National Conference in Artificial Intelligence and Cognitive Science (AICS-01), pp. 75-84, Maynooth, Ireland, 2001.

[2] D. Bridge and A. Ferguson "Diverse Product Recommendations using an Expressive Language for Case Retrieval", Proceedings of the 16th European Conference on Case-Based Reasoning, pp. 43-57, 2002.

[3] S. Brin and L. Page "The Anatomy of A Large-Scale Hypertextual Web Search Engine", Proceedings of the 7th International World-Wide Web Conference, 2001.

[4] J. Budzik and K. Hammond "User Interactions with Everyday Applications as Context for Just-in-time Information Access", Proceedings of the International Conference on Intelligent User Interfaces, pp. 44-51, ACM Press, 2000.

[5] D. R. Cutting and D. R. Karger and J. O. Pedersen and J. W. Tukey "Scatter Gather: a cluster-based approach to browsing large document collections", Proceedings of

the 15h International ACM SIGIR Conference on Research and Development in Information Retrieval, pp. 318-29, ACM Press, 1992.

[6] E. Glover and S. Lawrence and M. D. Gordon and W. P. Birmingham and C. Lee Giles "Web Search - Your Way", Communications of the ACM, 44(12), pp. 97-102, 2000.

[7] T. H. Haveliwala "Topic-Sensitive PageRank", Proceedings of the 11th World-Wide Web Conference, ACM Press, 2002.

[8] Z. Jiang and A. Joshi and R. Krishnapuram and L. Yi "Retriever: Improving Web Search Engine Results Using Clustering", Managing Business with Electronic Commerce: Issues and Trends, Idea Press, 2001.

[9] R. Krovetz and W. B. Croft "Lexical Ambiguity and Information Retrieval", Information Systems, 10(2), pp. 115-141, 1992.

[10] S. Lawrence "Context in Web Search", IEEE Data Engineering Bulletin, 23(3), pp. 25-32, 2000.

[11] S. Lawrence and C. Lee Giles "Searching the Web: General and Scientific Information Access", IEEE Communications 37(1), pp. 116-122, 1999.

[12] A. Leouski and W. Croft "An Evaluation of Techniques for Clustering Search Results", Technical Report IR-76, Department of Computer Science, University of Massachusetts, Amherst, 1996.

[13] D. McSherry "Diversity-Conscious Retrieval", Proceedings of the 6th European Conference on Case-Based Reasoning, pp. 219-233, Aberdeen, Scotland, 2002.

[14] H. Shimazu "ExpertClerk: Navigating Shoppers' Buying Process with the Combination of Asking and Proposing", Proceedings of the 17th International Joint Conference on Artificial Intelligence, pp. 1443-1448, Seattle, Washington, USA, 2001.

[15] C. Silverstein and M. Henzinger and H. Marais and M. Moricz "Analysis of a Very Large AltaVista Query Log", Technical Report 1998-014, Digital SRC Technical Notes http://gatekeeper.dec.com/pub/DEC/SRC/technical-notes/abstracts/src-tn-1998-014.html, 1998.

[16] B. Smyth and E. Balfe and P. Briggs and M. Coyle and J. Freyne "Collaborative Web Search", Proceedings of the 18th International Joint Conference on Artificial Intelligence, pp. 1417-1419, Acapulco, Mexico, 2003.

[17] B. Smyth and E. Balfe and P. Briggs and M. Coyle and J. Freyne "I-SPY - Anonymous, Community-based Personalization by Collaborative Meta-search", Proceedings of the 23rd SGAI International Conference on Innovative Techniques and Applications of Artificial Intelligence, Cambridge, UK, 2003.

[18] B. Smyth and P. McClave "Similarity vs. Diversity", Proceedings of the 4th International Conference on Case-Based Reasoning, Vancouver, Canada, 2001.

[19] C. J. van Rijsbergen "Information Retrieval, 2nd Edition", Department of Computer Science, University of Glasgow, 1979.

[20] Y. Wang and M. Kitsuregawa "Link-based Clustering of Web Search Results", Lecture Notes in Computer Science, Advances in Web-Age Information Management, Second International Conference, 2118, pp. 225-237, WAIM 2001.

[21] O. Zamir and O. Etzioni "Web Document Clustering: A Feasibility Demonstration", Research and Development in Information Retrieval, pp. 46-54, 1998.

[22] O. Zamir and O. Etzioni "Grouper: A Dynamic Clustering Interface to Web Search Results", Computer Networks, 31(11-16), pp. 1361-1374, Amsterdam, Netherlands, 1999.

USING FINITE DOMAINS IN CONSTRAINT SATISFACTION PROBLEM

Ilie Popescu
Computer Science Department , University of Quebec in Outaouais , Gatineau, QuébecCanada, J8X 3X7

Abstract: Constraint satisfaction problem (CSP) methodologies are intended to solve (mostly combinatorial) problems especially in areas of planning and scheduling. Our paper focuses on a model enforcing arc consistency without changing the structure of the constraint network (CN), i.e., only by efficiently removing values from variable domains. The propagation of a variable domain to the constraints related to this variable allows the model to keep under control the size of the search space, by enumerating only the variable values which are part of a solution.

Key words: Constraint satisfaction problem, consistency, search space

1.   INTRODUCTION

Constraint satisfaction problems (CSPs) are very convenient formalisms for many real-life problems, like resource allocation, scheduling and planning problems, database systems, natural language processing, electrical circuit design, and many others [4,5,7]. Many combinatorial problems can be naturally expressed in the frame of CSP.

Finding a solution in a constraint network involves looking for value assignments for a set of variables so that all the constraints are simultaneously satisfied [3,6,8]. The proposed algorithms to solve these kind of problems make a systematic exploration of the search space, changing the original CSP into a new one removing values from domain variables which cannot belong to any solution of the CSP [2]. As long as the unassigned variables have values consistent with the current state of the CSP, they extend it by assigning values to these variables and change the current state to a new one. This process is called consistency technique and it is the core of most constraint satisfaction methodologies.

In this paper, we present a model based on constraint propagation. The motivation behind this is the desire to reduce the vast amount of deductions required by an expert system when executed on a logic program system. A key idea is to represent the relations among the rules as constraints and to integrate the rule chaining with constraint solving.

In order to reduce the size of the search space, we use the filtering techniques to enforce arc consistency by removing all local inconsistencies that otherwise would have been repeatedly found during search.

2.   PRELIMINARIES

A CSP is defined as a set of n variables $X = (X_1, \ldots, X_n)$, a set of n domains $D = \{D_1, \ldots D_n\}$ and a set of binary constraints between pairs of variables X_i and X_j, $C = \{C_{ij}(X_i, X_j)\}$ $i = 1..n$, $j = 1..n$, $i \neq j$.

$C_{ij}(v_i, v_j)$ is the Boolean value obtained when variables X_i and X_j are replaced by the values v_i and v_j respectively.

A solution to a constraint satisfaction problem is a function $f : X \to D^n$ such that all the sets of values $\{v_1, \ldots, v_n\} \in D^n = D_1 \times \ldots \times D_n$ for the variables $X_1, \ldots, X_n$ satisfy all the constraints belonging to R.

An arc (X_i, X_j) is arc consistent with respect to Cartesian product $D_i \times D_j$ iff $\forall\ v_i \in D_i$, $\exists v_j \in D_j$ such that $(v_i, v_j) \in C_{ij}$. Arc consistency is widely used in solving CSPs because it only changes the domains of variables.

3.   CONSISTENCIES ENFORCEMENT

Consistency is a process of removing values from domains which cannot be part of any solution of a CSP. The basic idea of consistency techniques is that if we can find an inconsistency in the CSP formulation, then tuples of values from the domains of variables implied in a constraint can be removed. By removing inconsistencies, we reduce a CSP to an equivalent but tighter problem. The arc consistency (AC) is the most widely used consistency technique [1]. There exits several arc consistency algorithms starting from AC-1 and concluding at AC-8. These algorithms are based on repeated revisions of variable domains by removing values which violate some constraints, until a consistent graph is reached.

In order to make an arc (X_i, X_j) consistent, the values VX_i of the variable X_i without support in the domain of X_j are deleted from the domain of X_i. If a value is not supported, it is removed from its domain. The main drawbacks of these algorithms are those many pairs of values are tested for consistency in every arc revision. These tests are repeated every time an arc is revised.

4.   CONSTRAINT OPTIMISATION

In many real-life problems, we do not want any solution but a good solution. Based on the above observation instead of handling a queue of arcs to be propagated, we can use a list of variables that have seen their domain modified. To implement this idea you can carry out a top-down procedure in the following four steps:

I.   Select and represent the variable domains as lists of values
II. For each variable X_i and each arc $C_{ij}(X_i, X_j)$ reduce the domain of X_i, propagate the new domain of X_i to all constraints $C_{ki}(X_k, X_i)$ and delete all the values of X_k which are not viable.
III. Add/delete new constraints on the existing variables.
IV. Stop the propagation when there are not changes in any variable domain or a variable domain is empty.

This model handles constrained problem arising in both static and dynamic environments and provides a general schema for implementing arc consistency techniques. The efficiency of this methodology resides mainly in the fact that the reduced domain of a variable X_i is propagated to all constraints $C_{ij}(X_k, X_i)$, $k \neq i$, implying the variable X_i: the domains of X_k, $k = 1,2,\ldots$ are reduced by eliminating values which lost their support in the new domain of X_i. On the other hand, the users of these systems often need to extend the constraints system with some constraints that are specific to the application at hand. This "glass-box" approach extends the well known constraints programming paradigm as a black-box. Applying traditional methods often suffice for developing industrial applications, but understanding their performances requires tools able to reinforce/modify the search strategy by adding/deleting constraints during the search progress.

5.   CONCLUSIONS

In this paper we have proposed a new model for solving CSPs that cope with the complexity NP-complete problems. The arc consistency techniques approach is essential to reduce the size of the search space and so to improve the efficiency of search algorithms. They can be used during a preprocessing filtering step to remove the local inconsistencies that otherwise are repeatedly found during the search.

The solution computation may still be too expensive time wise when the CSP is very large. One of the lessons learned so far from the application of constraint programming tools in practice is that domain specific information is needed. In such cases the model allows the addition/deletion of new domain-specific and problem-specific knowledge. Judging the importance of consistency techniques, integrating new constraints enhance the efficiency of the CSP solver.

REFERENCES

1. R. Bartak. On-line guide to Constraint Programming, Prague, 1998, http://kti.mff.cusni.ez/~ bartak/constraints/.
2. R. Debruyne, C. Bessière. Domains Filtering Consistencies. Journal of Artificial Intelligence Research 14, pages 205-230, 2001.
3. R. Dechter. Constraint networks. In Stuart C. Shapiro, editor, Encyclopedia of AI (second edition), volume 1, pages 276-284. John Wiley & Sons, 1992.
4. A.K. Mackworth. Constraint satisfaction. In Stuart C. Shapiro, editor, Encyclopedia of AI (second edition), volume 1, pages 285-293. John Wiley & Sons, 1992.
5. J.J. McGregor. Relational consistency algorithms and their applications in finding sub graph and graph isomorphism, Information Science 19, pages 229-250, 1979.
6. P. Meseguer. Constraint satisfaction problems: An overview. AICOM, 2, pages 3-17, 1989.
7. U. Montanari. Networks of constraints: Fundamental properties and applications to picture processing, Information Science (7) (2), pages 95-132, 1974.
8. E. Tsang. Foundations of Constraint Satisfaction. London, Academic Press, 1993.

RESEARCH ON RADAR TARGETS RECOGNITION BY EXTRACTING 3-D CHARACTERISTIC FROM ISAR IMAGES

Liu, Feng and Xu, Jiadong

Electronic Engineering Department, Northwestern Polytechnical University, Xi'an 710072
E-mail: Beaconliu@263.net, Tel: (86) 029-88491414

Abstract: Based on ISAR imaging technology and Computer Vision theory, a novel target recognition method extracting the 3-Dimensional characteristic of targets from ISAR images sequence is presented in this paper, which can get higher recognition rate with fewer samples.

Key words: ISAR, Scattering Centers, 3-Dimensional Characteristic, Target Identification

1. INTRODUCTION

With the developing of modern radar, a considerable amount of effort has been devoted to radar target identification [1]. Currently, most past work mainly focus on identifying targets with the one-dimensional feature of radar echo [2-3], which need a large numbers of training samples [2-3]. However, just as the 3-dimesional structure of a object could be estimated by its images shooting at different angles [4], similarly, the 3-D structure characteristic of the scattering centers of motion target can be determined through their ISAR (Inverse Synthetic Aperture Radar) image sequence. Furthermore, the target's 3-D structure characteristic is possible to be used to identify different targets. In this paper, we present the method to extract the radar target's 3-D structure parameters from the target's ISAR image sequence, and the experimental identification results for simulated targets.

2.   ABOUT ISAR IMAGE SEQUENCE

The theory and approach of the ISAR imaging are depicted in [5-6].

If the processing of ISAR imaging is constantly done several times for a dynamic target, the target's ISAR image sequence could be gained. An actual target's ISAR image sequence given in [6] is shown here in Figure1.

Figure 1. Actual target's ISAR image sequence

3.   THE METHOD OF EXTRACTING 3-D CHARACTERISTIC FROM ISAR SEQUENCE

The geometrical structure of the main scattering centers that distinctly illuminates the characteristic of a target. It is shown in Fig.1, that the information of the target's scattering centers included in the target's ISAR images is displayed as discrete spot cells distributing in different grayscale and area on the images. Conveniently, in this paper, the spot cell is defined as "Imaged Cell of Scattering Center (ICSC). In order to extract the 3-D structure of the target's scattering centers, the method of Optical Flow Estimation in Computer Vision field [7] is applied in the paper.

3.1   Determining and tracking CICSC

As to compute the ICSC's optical flow, firstly, the Centroid of Imaged Cell of Scattering Center (CICSC) should be determined and tracked to match the ICSCs between the frames. CICSC defined as the average point in an ICSC according to the grayscale (intensity of echo). In order to predict and track the moving trace of the ICSC between frames, the filtering model is applied as follows:

$$X(k+1) = \begin{bmatrix} 1 & T & 0 & 0 \\ 0 & 1 & 0 & 0 \\ 1 & 0 & 0 & 0 \\ 0 & 0 & 0 & 0 \end{bmatrix} X(k+1) + \begin{bmatrix} T^2/2 & 0 \\ T & 0 \\ 0 & 0 \\ 0 & 0 \end{bmatrix} \begin{bmatrix} W_1(k) \\ W_2(k) \end{bmatrix}$$

$$Z(k) = \begin{bmatrix} 1 & 0 & 0 & 0 \\ 1 & 0 & -1 & 0 \end{bmatrix} X(k) + \begin{bmatrix} V_1(k) \\ V_2(k) \end{bmatrix} \tag{1}$$

where $X(k)$ is the position state composed of the centroid position, the centroid offset, and the ecntroid position of last frame; $Z(k)$ is composed of the measured values of the centroid position and offset; W and V is the noise; T is the interval between frames. From (1), the motion and position parameters of CCICS in the frames can be estimated by applying Kalman filtering method.

3.2   3-D reconstruction of scattering centers based on optical flow

In case of ground based radar, the motion of a scattering center of the target in the virtual projection space [8] is equivalent to a rotation followed by a translation [4]

$$\begin{bmatrix} X' \\ Y' \\ Z' \end{bmatrix} = \begin{bmatrix} t_1 \\ t_2 \\ t_3 \end{bmatrix} + \begin{bmatrix} \omega_1 \\ \omega_2 \\ \omega_3 \end{bmatrix} \times \begin{bmatrix} X \\ Y \\ Z \end{bmatrix} \tag{2}$$

In the virtual projection space, the image-space coordinates of a CICSC are related with the corresponding scattering center coordinates by the following equation:

$$\begin{cases} x = f_x \cdot \dfrac{X}{Z} \\ y = f_y \cdot \dfrac{Y}{Z} \end{cases} \tag{3}$$

where $(x, y)^T$ are the image-space coordinates of the CICSC; f_x and f_y are the Virtual Focal Length (VFL) [8] in abscissa and ordinate. For the ISAR image sequence, the optical flow of CICSC $(u, v)^T$ can be completely described by its displacement between the frames [9]

$$\begin{cases} u = dx / dt \\ v = dy / dt \end{cases} \tag{4}$$

Substituting (3) and (4) into (2) gives

$$Z = \frac{t_1 f_x - x t_3}{u + [xy\omega_1 / f_y - (f_x + x^2 / f_y)\omega_2 + y\omega_3 f_x / f_y]} \tag{5}$$

$$= \frac{t_2 f_y - y t_3}{v + [(f_y + y^2 / f_y)\omega_1 - xy\omega_2; / f_x - x\omega_3 f_y / f_x]}$$

Generally, we call Z as the depth of the scattering center in the virtual projection space. From (5), associating with X and Y, the 3-D parameters of

4.   EXPERIMENTAL IDENTIFICATION RESULTS

The experimental identification results for 5 types of simulated targets are shown in Table 1. The 5 targets are clearly identified just with 9 group samples for each target in the aspect angle range of ±30°, while more than 60 samples must be obtained by the method of using range profiles [2-4]. The average recognition rate is also measured to 89.5%.

Table 1. Experimental identification results for 5 types of simulated targets

Targets	A	B	C	D	E
Recognition rate(%)	87.5	92.5	90	87.5	90

5.   CONCLUSION

A method of extracting the 3-D characteristic of targets from ISAR images sequence of the targets is presented in the paper. And, the target's 3-D structure characteristic is possible to be used to identify different radar targets.

REFERENCES

1. Smith C. R., Goggans P. M.. Radar target identification. IEEE. Antenna and Propagation Magazine, 1993,35(2):23-33
2. Li H. J., Yang S. H.. Using range profiles as feature vectors to identify aerospace objects. IEEE Trans. on Aerospace and Electronics System, 1993, 29(3):741-748
3. Hudson S., Psaltis D.. Correlation filters for Aircraft identification from radar range profiles. IEEE Trans. AES, 1993 29(3):741-748
4. David V. . Machine vision. Prentice Hall, 1991
5. Haiqing Wu, Gilles Y. Delisle. Precision tracking algorithms for ISAR imaging. IEEE Trans. Aerospace and Electronic System, 1996, 32(1):243-254
6. Toshiharu Itoh, Hachiro Sueda. Motion compensation for ISAR via centroid tracking. IEEE Trans. Aerospace and Electronic System, 1996, 32(3):1191-1197
7. B. Horn, B. Schunck. Determining optical flow. Artificial Intelligence, 1981, 17: 185-203
8. Feng Liu. Target 3-dimensional Feature Extraction Based on Radar Image Sequence Analyzing. Northwestern Polytechnical University Ph.d dissertation, 2004.
9. K. Kanatani. Geometric computation for machine vision. Oxford: Oxford Science Publications, 1993

UNCERTAIN REASONING AND DECISION MAKING

Qing Zhou
The Software Institute of Zhongshan University, Guangzhou, Guangdong, P.R.China, 510275
lnszq@zsulink.zsu.edu.cn

Wei Peng
Science and Technology Institute of GRC, Guangzhou, Guangdong, P.R.China, 510060
pengwei99@tom.com

Abstract   In this paper we discuss uncertain reasoning and decision making. Our proposal is based on the knowledge we have and entirely formalized within the so called classical two valued logic, so it has a solid foundation. Basic notions of various items are defined formally; formulas of supporting degree for uncertain reasoning and supporting degree with safety for decision making are introduced. Evaluation of "weighted facts", which represents the different importance of facts, is clearly presented within our proposal without anything else. The relation between uncertain reasoning and decision making is discussed in detail. Examples in the paper are comprehensively exhibited, which shows that our proposal is reasonable and computer-operative.

Keywords: uncertainty, decision making, knowledge-based systems

1.   Introduction

In this paper we discuss the uncertain reasoning and decision making on the base of knowledge. As our discussion is entirely built on the base of the so called classical two valued logic, it has a strong foundation.

Our purpose is to find a method similar to the way we often use when we deal with uncertain problems. So first let us take a look at what we usually do in such situations:

Suppose P is a problem, $h_1, ..., h_k$ are propositions about the solution of P, called the hypothesis. Our problem is to decide which of $h_i, 1 \leq i \leq k$, is true. If such a h_i can be deduced from a set K (corpus of knowledge) of propositions, which has been accepted as true, the question is solved definitely and hence P is certain; otherwise, P is uncertain. Then our problem turns to whether there is a further way to solve the question when P is uncertain.

A common way used by experts can be described as follows: 1. Gather an evidence set E as completely as possible. 2. Try to infer h_i form $K \cup E$. If (2) successes, the question is solved, and the uncertainty of h_i is removed absolutely. Otherwise, 3. try to estimate the degree of the possibility for h_i to be true under $K \cup E$.

From the above discussion, we can see that several concepts are basic. To determine the truth value of a proposition called a hypothesis, we need some knowledge, which is a set of formulas syntactically. The set is called a corpus of knowledge, which are regarded as true such as logical axioms, basic laws in a field, etc. When the hypothesis is uncertain, we employ some evidences, which are usually some facts (closed formulas, syntactically) on the specific problem P, to help us determine the truth value of the hypothesis. It is only required that all of the evidences are closed formulas, although they are supposed to be true for our purpose.

From the view point of uncertain reasoning, the most important part is, of course, to find a method to estimate the degree of the possibility for h_i to be true. Here we bring in an easy fact from classical logic: As indicated above, due to the limitation of our knowledge, an uncertain problem is an undecidable formula in the logical system which contains our knowledge. This means that our knowledge on the problem is incomplete, hence it has many models by the Completeness Theorem; In some of them h_i is true, while in others h_i is false, so our purpose is to determine which model is the one we want. Now since all the evidences are true in the model we want, h_i should have some common consequences with evidences if h_i is also in the model since all the consequences of evidences and h_i have to be true in the model from the definition of models. Then it is logical to believe that if h_i has more common consequences with evidences than h_j, it is more possible to be true than h_j. The following example illustrates the point:

EXAMPLE 1 *Suppose we are in a murder case and we have a corpus of knowledge: If x is the murder, 1. x was in scene of the crime during certain time period; 2. x has a reason of murdering; 3. x has the weapon in the crime. Now after investigation, we found the evidences: Michael was in the scene of the crime during the time period and has a reason of murdering, John has a weapon like the one in crime. Then we have reasons to believe that Michael did the crime more likely than John as he has more suspicions than John.*

The above example shows that the more same consequences of $K \cup \{h_i\}$ and $K \cup E$ we have, the more likely we believe h_i to be true. So it makes sense to consider these common consequences as important facts which support the solution h_i. Then number of common consequences of each possible solution h_i represents the strength of the supports of it from the evidences we have. This is the idea of this paper.

We will describe this process formally and on the base of the two-valued classical logic we will develop a computer-operative method of finding out the strength of believing h_i when h_i is uncertain.

An important area of applications of uncertain reasoning is decision making. Actually, all decision making problems are uncertain since all the knowledge we have now is about the past and the results of our decisions will happen in the future. This makes decision problems difficult. With the help of uncertain reasoning in this paper, we will propose a knowledge based method of decision making. The method is an analogue of "what...if..." analysis method, which is often used by experts. The following example is a simple decision making problem:

EXAMPLE 2 *John wants to make an investment and he has 3 choices: in a bar, a restaurant or a super market. Investing in a bar needs small investment and most of the investment is in the dinner equipments but produces small profits. Investing in a restaurant needs large investment and most of the investment is in the dinner equipments and produces large profits. Investing in a super market needs large investment and most of the investment is in the merchandiser and produces large profits. John thinks that large profits is very important for his investment and he has to consider the possibility of changing his mind when he has to. Now if he choose to invest in a restaurant, he can have large profits and he can easily shift to a bar when he wants. So John gains more advantages from investing in restaurant than the other choice, and hence he has reasons to choose investing in a restaurant.*

So in a decision making problem, we always analyze the result under the assumption that we take a specific choice (what ... if ... analysis) to try to have the most advantages and consider the easiness of changing our mind to reduce risks. This consideration will be embodied into the formalizations in the paper, too.

The rest of this paper breaks into three sections. The basic notions about uncertain reasoning are given in the first section. The supporting degree of uncertain reasoning is also introduced here. All of these are completely done within the classical two valued logic. In the second section we deal with "weighted facts". This is important since it often happens that some facts are believed more important than others during the uncertain reasoning or decision making in our real life. We show in this section that one needs nothing else to deal with weighted facts with our method, weighted facts can be represented in our method without any extra efforts. The last section takes care of the decision making problem. As indicated above, our decision making method is built on the method of uncertain reasoning discussed in the first section. A method of evaluation of "overlapped" facts is also discussed in the section, which help us to make smart decision with less risks.

2.   Uncertain Reasoning and Its Supporting Degree

Now we formalize our propose within the classical logic. Let T be a fixed first order reasoning system, and L its language. In the following discussion, we will use K to be the corpus of knowledge, which is a finite set of formulas of L. Further it is assumed that K is consistent; E to be the evidence set, which is a finite set of closed formulas of L. It is also assumed that $K \cup E$ is consistent; P to be a formula of L, which is called problem. Semantically P is the problem we want to solve and K consists of those basic rules on P and E consists of some facts related to P.

Let X be a set of formulas of L. If a formula A of L can be derived from X, we use $X \vdash A$ to denote it.

Now we define that a closed formula s is uncertain if K can not deduce both s and $\neg s$. Then let $H = \{h_1, ..., h_n\}$ be the set of hypotheses for the problem P. From the discussion in the Introduction, for all $h_i \in H$, h_i is undecidable in K, i.e. we have no way to determine whether a proposition is certainly true or false from the knowledge and the facts we have got. So we define:

DEFINITION 3 *We call a set of closed formulas H a hypotheses set and for $h_i \in H$, we call h_i a hypothesis, if every sentence in H is undecidable in K.*

As indicated in the Introduction, common consequences of both the hypothesis h_i and the evidence set E play important roles in the uncertain reasoning. So we define the common consequence set D_{h_i} as:

DEFINITION 4 *Let h_i be a hypothesis. Then*
$$D_{h_i} = \{A : A \text{ is a closed formula of } L \text{ and } K \cup E \vdash A \text{ and } K \cup \{h_i\} \vdash A\}$$

Then we say that $A, B \in D_{h_i}$ are equivalent in D_{h_i}, denoted as $A \sim B$, if $K \cup E' \vdash A$ if and only if $K \cup E' \vdash B$ for all $E' \subseteq E$. It is trivial to show that $\sim$ is an equivalent relation defined on D_{h_i}. Now we define

DEFINITION 5 *B_{h_i} be the equivalent class on D_{h_i}, i.e. $B_{h_i} = \{U : U \subseteq D_{h_i}$ and for any $A, B \in U, A \sim B\}$.*

Then it is easy to see that B_{h_i} is finite.

From above definitions, it is obvious that for any $A \in D_{h_i}$, A is a common consequence derived by both E and h_i, so it supports h_i. Then it is logical to believe that the more elements B_{h_i} has, the more facts support h_i. From this observation, we use the word "the supporting degree " to formalize it which are given in the following definition:

DEFINITION 6 *The supporting degree of a hypotheses h_i in H, $s(h_i, H)$, is a real number:*
$$s(h_i, H) = \frac{|B_{h_i}|}{|\bigcup\limits_{h_k \in H} B_{h_k}|}$$

EXAMPLE 7 *Let us take a look on how to use the above system to solve the Example 1. in the Introduction.*

The reasoning system we construct is:

Our language L has the following formulas::

1. $murderer(x)$, which indicates that x was the murderer semantically;

2. $inscene(x)$, which indicates that x was in scene of the crime during certain time period semantically;

3. $reason(x)$, which indicates that x had a reason of murdering;

4. $weapon(x)$, which indicates that x had the weapon in the crime;

Here x can be assigned a constant in $\{Michael, John\}$. which indicates the man with such a name, semantically.

The corpus of knowledge K consists of the following axioms:

1. $murder(x) \rightarrow inscene(x)$, which semantically indicates that if x was the murder, x was in scene of the crime during certain time period;

2. $murder(x) \rightarrow reason(x)$, which semantically indicates that if x was the murder, x had a reason of murdering;

3. $murder(x) \rightarrow weapon(x)$, which semantically indicates that if x was the murder, x had the weapon in the crime;

4. $murder(x) \rightarrow \neg murderer(x_1)$, which semantically indicates that if x was the murder, x_1 was not;

5. $murder(x) \vee murder(x_1)$, which semantically indicates that x or x_1 was the murder.

Here $x, x_1 \in \{Michael, John\}$ and $x \neq x_1$. Formula 4 and 5 show that only one was the murder among $John$ and $Michael$.

We also assume that the system has two deduction rules: 1. if $A \rightarrow B$ and A, then B; 2. if $A \vee B$ and $\neg A$, then B.

The evidence set E consists of:

$inscene(Michael), reason(Michael), weapon(John)$

The hypotheses set:

$H = \{murder(Michael), murder(John)\}$

Now we have done our construction of the reasoning system. Let us look at what we can have with the system.

Obviously, from $K \cup \{murder(Michael)\}$ we can have from the rules and the corpus of knowledge that: $inscene(Michael), reason(Michael)$ and $weapon(Michael)$.

And from $K \cup E$ we can have: $inscene(Michael), reason(Michael)$

So $|B_{murder(Michael)}| = |\{inscene(Michael), reason(Michale)\}| = 2$

From $K \cup \{murderer(John)\}$ we can deduce the following,

$inscene(John), reason(John)$ and $weapon(John)$.

And from $K \cup E$ we can have: $weapon(John)$

So $|B_{murder(Jhon)}| = |\{weapon(John)\}| = 1$

Then we can get $s(murder(Michael), H) = 2/3 > s(murder(John), H) = 1/3$.

Therefore from our system we have that Michael did the murder more likely than John did. This is exact what we should believe from the evidences we have, since Michael has more suspicions than John has.

3.   Evaluations for "Weighted Facts"

It seems that we can get the best solution by comparing $|B_{h_i}|$ for all $h_i \in H$. But in reality it is not so simple. It often happens that some facts are supposed to be more important than others. For example, when John wants to invest in a project he thinks that the profit is more important than other factors. So, our uncertain reasoning system should reflect the difference in numbers. But in the supporting degree introduced in the last section every common consequence of E and the hypothesis is used only once and hence every common consequence plays the same role as others. So the importance of some evidences seem to be ignored.

Now we show that "weighted facts" can be easily represented in our system without any extra efforts.

Let S be a first order reasoning system. Suppose F is a fact which is assumed to be more important than others. We do not know whether F can be derived from our system or not. But what we want is as soon as F is derived we count it twice. Can this be represented in our system? The answer is Yes.

To this end, we add two new predicates, $dummy$ and $dummy1$, to the system S. Then we add rules $F \wedge dummy \rightarrow dummy1$ and $h_i \rightarrow dummy1$ for all $h_i \in H$ to the corpus of knowledge K, and add $dummy$ to the evidence set E. We use S_1 to denote the resulting system. Then the following results show that with the supporting degree introduced in the last section, B_{h_i} will be the same in both S and S_1 if F is not in D_{h_i} and B_{h_i} in S_1 will be 1 more than in S if F is in D_{h_i}.

THEOREM 8   *In S_1, $F \in D_{h_i}$ if and only if $dummy1 \in D_{h_i}$.*

Now we use $B_{h_i}^S$ and $B_{h_i}^{S_1}$ to B_{h_i} in S and S_1, respectively. Then from the theorem we immediately get:

COROLLARY 9   *If $F \in D_{h_i}$ then $|B_{h_i}^{S_1}| = |B_{h_i}^S| + 1$.*

This theorem shows that "weighted facts", i.e. the importance of facts, can be reflected by the increments in number.

4.   Uncertain Reasoning in Decision Making

As well known, decision making is an important application area of uncertain reasoning. In our life, we always face decision problems which can be described as follows: We have a problem P, which could be our goal, or a difficulty in our life. To reach our goal or overcome the difficulty we have a few choices $c_1, ..., c_n$ which are supposed to be the possible solutions. The decision problem is to find out the best solution from the choice set $\{c_1, ..., c_n\}$.

As indicated in the Introduction, the main difficulty of making a choice is that there always is uncertainty on what will exactly happen since we can only have knowledge on the past and the result of our decision is about future.

Now suppose we have a choices set $\{c_1, ..., c_n\}$ and we have to make a decision. As there are always some uncertainties on what will exactly happen, decision making problems are uncertain and we can use uncertain reasoning for such problems. So for the discussion of decision making we should first define the notion "choice" formally.

In the real life, before we choose one from the choice set we always consider what results it will bring to us, i.e. what...if... analysis. Different choices will make different resulting sets. Among these different resulting sets, if one contains more advantages than others, we have reasons to take the one which produces this set. These results are usually able to be derived from the knowledge we have when a choice c_i is assumed and they can be supported by evidences we gathered, that is, they can be deducted from both $K \cup E$ and $K \cup \{c_i\}$.

In terms of Model Theory the decision making problem is to choose the best model, then if some evidences are in the same model as c_i they should have something in common with c_i, i.e. they and c_i should have common consequences. From this observation, we say that a subset of E favorites c_i if it has a common consequence with c_i. (Due to the length limitation, we only consider those evidences which give advantages in this paper, for the case of disadvantages, one can easily have the formulation from the idea of this paper.)

Now let $C = \{c_1, ..., c_n\}$ be the set of choices for the problem P. From the discussion above, for all $c_i \in C$, c_i is undecidable in K, i.e. we have no way to determine whether a choice is certainly true or false from the knowledge and the facts we have got. So we define:

DEFINITION 10 *We call a set of closed formulas C a choices set and for $c_i \in C$, we call c_i a choice, if every sentence in C is uncertain.*

Comparing this definition with the one for hypothesis in the first section, we can easily see similarity of them. So it is reasonable to use the formulas in the first section and choose the choice from the choice set which has the largest supporting degree. Actually, from the discussions above, this is what we always do when we are in the cases that we have to make decisions in some simple situations, but in many cases, we will miss some important factors if we only use that supporting degree.

In the real world, some common results might be derived by more than one choices. In the example in the Introduction, the dinner equipments are needed for both bars and restaurants, so it will be easier for John to change investment in a restaurant to a bar when he has to. This is certainly an important factor he has to consider when he is making decision on his investment. Of course, this is also an important factor we have to take account of when we consider decision making problems. We call such a fact the "overlapped problem" in the field of decision making. Described formally, for two choice $c_i, c_j \in C$, we say that they are overlapped if they have same consequences, i.e. $B_{c_i} \cap B_{c_j} \neq \varnothing$.

Obviously different decisions between two overlapped choices c_i and c_j will make different results. Our problem is how to evaluate the common results $B_{c_i} \cap B_{c_j}$ derived by both of them and use it to help us make decision. We think that such results play different roles for c_i and c_j. Suppose our choice is c_i. Then we will have all the advantages in B_{c_i}, but also have partial advantages in B_{c_j}, i.e. the $B_{c_i} \cap B_{c_j}$ part in B_{c_j}. Therefore, to give a measurement to this partial advantage for c_j when c_i is chosen it is logical to consider the number $\frac{|B_{c_i} \cap B_{c_j}|}{|B_{c_j}|}$; which we call "*the relevancy coefficient* ":

DEFINITION 11 *For two choices c_i and c_j, the relevancy coefficient of c_i to c_j in C, $rc(c_i, c_j, C)$, is a real number:*

$$rc(c_i, c_j, C) = \frac{|B_{c_i} \cap B_{c_j}|}{|B_{c_j}|}$$

It is also obvious that not only the supporting degree of a choice but also the common effects of all choices in the choices set should be taken account when we want to make a smart decision and consider the situations that we may have to change our mind later. The number rc could measure the effects of such common consequences in each of the choices in our decision making procedure. We will use it in the following discussion.

Because $B_{c_i} \cap B_{c_j}$ contains those common consequences which support both c_i and c_j and they can still work for c_j even when c_i is chosen and c_j is not, $rc(c_i, c_j, C)$ measures the advantages for c_j, so it represents the possibility of changing c_i to c_j. The relevancy coefficient represents the degree of the easiness of changing from one choice to another. The larger $rc(c_i, c_j, C)$ is, the easier we change c_i to c_j. It is very important and necessary when we are in the decision-making cases in which we have often to change our mind due to situations. We define $rc(c_i, c_j, C) = 0$ if $|B_{c_j}| = 0$. Then it is easy to have the formula for taking care of such consideration, which we call "*the supporting degree with safety*":

DEFINITION 12 *For any choice $c_i \in C$, the supporting degree with safety $ssd(c_i, C)$ of c_i is defined to be:*

$$ssd(c_i, C) = s(c_i, C) + \sum_{c_j \in C, c_j \neq c_i} rc(c_i, c_j, C) \times s(c_j, C)$$

LEMMA 13 $ssd(c_i, C) \leq |C|$

This definition gives a balanced consideration which is often needed in reality while making decisions. Once we have the safe supporting degree of c_i for every c_i in the choice set C, we can easily make our decision: It is the one which has the largest safe supporting degree as it is the most possible solution for the problem and has the least risk from the knowledge we have now. Of course in many cases we do not have chances to change our plan then we can omit the safe degrees and take one with the highest supporting degree instead.

With our purpose, some emotional factors, such as one's interests or hobbies, are not taken in our proposal because they are very hard to be represented completely within the classical logic.

EXAMPLE 14 *Now we consider the Example 2. in the Introduction.*

To solve the problem we have to build up a reasoning system for it first.
We define a first order language L as follows:
We will use the symbols BAR, RST and SM to denote a bar, a restaurant or a super market respectively and the letter x to denote the variables representing a project which John will invest to. Obviously $x \in \{BAR, RST, SM\}$.
Also L contains the following predicate:
$Invest(x)$: a predicate which represents that John invests to the project x ;
$SI(x)$: a predicate which represents that the project x needs small investment;
$LP(x)$: a predicate which represents that the project x produces large profits;
FA: a predicate which represents most of the investment is in the fixed assets(dinner equipments);
$dummy$, $dummy1$: two predicate symbols without any sense.
Then our problem turns out to determine which can satisfy John's needs more in the choice set $C = \{c_1 = Invest(BAR), c_2 = Invest(RST), c_3 = Invest(SM)\}$.
Now we can construct our corpus of knowledge K as following:
$Invest(BAR) \rightarrow SI(BAR)$: which means that the investment in a bar needs small investment;
$Invest(BAR) \rightarrow FA$: which means that most of the investments in a bar is for fixed assets(dinner equipment);
$Invest(RST) \rightarrow FA$: which means that most of the investments in a restaurant is for fixed assets(dinner equipment);
$Invest(RST) \rightarrow LP(RST)$: which means that the investment in a restaurant produces large profits;

$Invest(SM) \rightarrow LP(SM)$: which means that of the investment in a restaurant produces large profits ;

$LP(x) \wedge dummy \rightarrow dummy1$: which mean that large profits of an investment is important;

$Invest(Bar) \rightarrow dummy1$, $Invest(Bar) \rightarrow dummy1$, $Invest(SM) \rightarrow dummy1$: meaningless, only for the completeness as in the Section 2.

Then our evidence set E consists of the facts: $SI(BAR)$, $LP(RST)$, $LP(SM)$, FA, $dummy$.

So from $K \cup \{c_1\}$ and $K \cup E$ we can get $B_{c_1} = \{[SI(BAR)], [FA]\}$; From $K \cup \{c_2\}$ and $K \cup E$ we can get $B_{c_2} = \{[LP(RST)], [FA], [dummy1]\}$; From $K \cup \{c_3\}$ and $K \cup E$ we can get $B_{c_3} = \{[LP(SM)], [dummy1]\}$. So

$$\left| \bigcup_{c_k \in C} B_{c_k} \right| = |\{[SI(BAR)], [FA], [LP(RST)], [LP(SM)], [dummy1]\}| =$$

5. Then we can get the supporting degrees as:

$s(B_{c_1}, C) = \frac{2}{5}, s(B_{c_2}, C) = \frac{3}{5}, s(B_{c_3}, C) = \frac{2}{5}$

The relevancy coefficients are: $rc(B_{c_1}, B_{c_2}, C) = \frac{1}{3}, rc(B_{c_2}, B_{c_1}, C) = \frac{1}{2}$ and $rc(B_{c_3}, B_{c_1}, C) = rc(B_{c_1}, B_{c_3}, C) = rc(B_{c_2}, B_{c_3}, C) = rc(B_{c_3}, B_{c_2}, C) = 0$

So we can get the supporting degrees with safety for such choices: $ssd(B_{c_1}, C) = \frac{2}{5} + \frac{2}{5} \times \frac{1}{2} = \frac{3}{5}$,, $ssd(B_{c_2}, C) = \frac{3}{5} + \frac{3}{5} \times \frac{1}{3} = \frac{4}{5}$, and $ssd(B_{c_3}, C) = \frac{2}{5}$

Thus John has more reasons to invest in a restaurant. If we do not consider the importance of large profits of investment, investing in a restaurant gains the same advantages as that in a bar. But when the importance is considered, we get different results. It shows that our purpose can work for such problems.

References

Doyle, J., Maintenance and Belief Revision, in Belief Revision, Ed. by P. Gardenfors, Cambridge University Press, 1992.

Kanal, L., Lemmer, J.F., Uncertainty in Artificial Intelligence, North-Holland, Amsterdam, New York, Oxford, Tokyo, 1986.

Russell, S., Norvig, P. Artificial Intelligence - A Modern Approach, Chapter 16 "Making Simple Decisions", Prentice Hall, 1995.

George J. Klir, Richard M. Smith, On Measuring Uncertainty and Uncertainty-Based Information: Recent Developments, Annals of Mathematics and Artificial Intelligence, Volume 32, Issue 1-4, 2001

Guerlain, S., Brown, D. and Mastrangelo, C. (2000). Intelligent decision support systems. Proceedings of the IEEE Conference on Systems, Man, and Cybernetics, Nashville, TN, pp. 1934-1938.

Zhou, Q., Peng, W., KURS: a Knowledge-based Uncertain Reasoning System, Artificial Intelligence & Its Applications, Proceedings of the ICAAI'03, 2003

Chansarkar, S.R., Expert System Shell: A Case Study, Artificial Intelligence & Its Applications, Proceedings of the ICAAI'03, 2003

DIAGNOSING JAVA PROGRAMS WITH STATIC ABSTRACTIONS OF DATA STRUCTURES

Rong Chen [1, 2], Daniel Koeb [1] and Franz Wotawa [1] *

[1] *Technische Universitaet Graz, Institute for Software Technology, 8010 Graz, Inffeldgasse 16b/2, Austria;* [2] *Institute of Software Research, Zhongshan University, Xingangxilu 135, 570215 Guangzhou, China*

Abstract: Model-based software debugging helps users to find program errors and thus to reduce the overall costs for software development. In this paper, we extend our previous work to diagnose common data structure errors. The proposed logical program model derives from a collection of indexed object relations, which capture the underlying data structures at the abstraction level of objects. A case study suggests that the counterexample with the diagnoses can help the user to understand the nature of program errors and thus speed up error correction.

Key words: Automatic reasoning, model-based diagnosis, fault localization

1.   INTRODUCTION

Model-based software debugging (MBSD) helps users to find program errors and thus to reduce the overall costs for software development [1]. MBSD starts from a description of a working piece of software. This description can be automatically extracted from the software and captures its structure and behavior. Using this model, one can make predictions in terms of values of variables under certain circumstances. If any of these values contradict the test case (i.e., the software does not behave as expected), the diagnostic system will isolate which statement or expression accounts for this contradiction.

* Authors are listed in alphabetical order. The work presented in this paper was funded by the Austrian Science Fund (FWF) P15265-N04, and partially supported by the National Natural Science Foundation of China (NSFC) Project 60203015 and the Guangdong Natural Science Foundation Project 011162.}

To diagnose common data structure errors, we, in this paper, propose a logical program model, derived from a collection of indexed object relations, which capture the underlying data structures at the abstraction level of objects. A case study suggests that the counterexample with the diagnoses can help the user to understand the nature of program errors and thus speed up error correction.

2.   ABOUT OBJECT STORE

The Object Store is defined by locations (to represent run-time objects), indexed location relations (defined over locations) and variable assignments (associated with indexed location relations). We briefly introduce the Object Store by using the *List* program shown in the leftmost column of Table 1, where L is abbreviated for *List*.

Table 1. The Object Store of the *remove* method in Fig. 1

Program/statements	Object Store	
class List {	Points-to	Indexed location relations
List next;		
int value;		
. remove(int v) {		
1. List c = this;	$(c_1, 0)$	
2. List p = this;	$(p_1, 0)$	$L.next_1 = \{\ \}_{\{c/0,\ p/0\}}$
3. **while** ((c.next != null)&&(v > c.value)){ 3.1 p = c; 3.2 c = c.next; } /* case (a): loop body not executed */		
		$L.next_1 = \{\ \}_{\{c/0,\ p/0\}}$
/* case (b): unfold loop once */		
3.1 p = c;	$(p_2, 0)$	
3.2 c = c.next;	$(c_2, 1)$	$L.next_2 = \{(0, 1)\}_{\{c/1,\ p/0*\}}$ (from $L.next_1$)
/* case (c): unfold loop two times */		
3.1 p = c;	$(p_3, 1)$	
3.2 c = c.next;	$(c_3, 2)$	$L.next_3 = \{(0, 1), (1, 2)\}_{\{c/2,\ p/1*\}}$ (from $L.next_2$)
/* merge location relations for various cases*/		
		$L.next_4 = \phi(L.next_1, L.next_2)$
		$L.next_5 = \phi(L.next_2, L.next_3)$
4. **if** (v = p.value) { 4.1 p.next = c; } 4.1 p.next = c;		$L.next_6 = \{(0, 0)\}_{\{c/0,\ p/0*\}}$ (from $L.next_1$)
		$L.next_7 = \{(0, 1)\}_{\{c/1,\ p/0\}}$ (from $L.next_2$)
		$L.next_8 = \{(0, 1), (1, 2)\}_{\{c/2,\ p/1\}}$ (from $L.next_3$)
/* merge location relations of the if-statement */		
		$L.next_9 = \phi(L.next_1, L.next_6)$
		$L.next_{10} = \phi(L.next_2, L.next_7)$
		$L.next_{11} = \phi(L.next_3, L.next_8)$
} }		

L -- List

Locations, denoted by positive integers, are abstract representations of run-time objects. A **points-to relation** is a binary relation that relates an object variable and its locations. Since variables/relations might be defined/updated at different program points, we distinguish them by assigning a unique index. In our example, statement *List c = this* is converted into a pair $(c_1, 0)$ in a points-to relation in Table 1, which means variable c points to the object at location 0 (i.e. *this*).

A **location relation** is used to relate multiple locations.

Definition 1 A location relation, denoted by $T.f$, is a set of n-tuples in the form $(i_1,...,i_n)$ where $i_k(1 \leq k \leq n)$ are integers (not *nil*) representing locations, T is a class name, and f, of reference type, is a field of class T.

Furthermore, let an n-tuple $(i_1,...,i_n) \in T.f$, we say location i_j can **reach** i_k (or i_k is **reachable**) when $1 \leq j < k \leq n$.

We distinguish location relations by assigning a unique index (thus called **indexed location relations**) and a **variable assignment,** which is a set of variable-location associations that describe the points-to pairs at a certain program point. In table 1, $L.next_2 = \{(0, 1)\}_{\{p/0,c/1\}}$ is an indexed location relation, where a location pair $(0, 1)$ is placed because locations 0 and 1 are of type *List*, and the object at location 1 is reachable from the object at location 0. Moreover, the variable assignment $\{p/0, c/1\}$ means variables p and c point to locations 0 and 1 respectively.

Note that locations are introduced for modeling a reference variable, a field access and a parameter of method call. A **used location** is a location which is explicitly used in class creation statements, or when its content is explicitly used. In our example, location 0 becomes a used location because its content *next* is explicitly used when modeling the field access expression *c.next* on statement 3.2 (In Table 1 a star is used for marking used locations).

With the notations that we have already introduced, we can formally define the Object Store as follows:

Definition 2 Object Store is a collection of points-to relations and indexed location relations.

The Object Store in Table 1 is extracted from the input program *List* automatically by accessing the structure of the data and converting the statements into points-to relation and indexed location relations. Since there are various control flows that may update location relations, we adopt the static single assignment form (SSA, see [2]); that is, we insert extra pseudo-assignments (known as ϕ-functions) at control flow merge points. In our example, $L.next_1$ arises from the then-branch of if-statement 4, and $L.next_6$ from the else-branch. Then we insert a pseudo-assignment $L.next_9 = \phi(L.next_1, L.next_6)$ right after the if-statement 4. If the path of execution comes from the then-branch, the ϕ-function takes the value of $L.next_1$; otherwise, it takes the value of $L.next_6$.

3.   DIAGNOSING WITH LOGICAL RULES FROM THE OBJECT STORE

Since our diagnostic system uses a theorem prover to find conflict sets and thus to compute diagnoses [1,3], we map each certain indexed location relation into a logical rule. In our example, the Object Store is mapped into the following logical rules:

$$\neg AB(1) \wedge \neg AB(2) \to ok(L.next_1) \tag{1}$$
$$\neg AB(3) \wedge ok(L.next_1) \to ok(L.next_2) \tag{2}$$
$$\neg AB(3) \wedge ok(L.next_1) \wedge ok(L.next_2) \wedge \neg ok(L.next_4) \to \perp \tag{3}$$
$$\neg AB(3) \wedge ok(L.next_2) \to ok(L.next_3) \tag{4}$$
$$\neg AB(3) \wedge ok(L.next_2) \wedge ok(L.next_3) \wedge \neg ok(L.next_5) \to \perp \tag{5}$$
$$\neg AB(4) \wedge ok(L.next_1) \to ok(L.next_6) \tag{6}$$
$$\neg AB(4) \wedge ok(L.next_1) \wedge ok(L.next_6) \wedge \neg ok(L.next_9) \to \perp \tag{7}$$
$$\neg AB(4) \wedge ok(L.next_2) \to ok(L.next_7) \tag{8}$$
$$\neg AB(4) \wedge ok(L.next_2) \wedge ok(L.next_7) \wedge \neg ok(L.next_{10}) \to \perp \tag{9}$$
$$\neg AB(4) \wedge ok(L.next_3) \to ok(L.next_8) \tag{10}$$
$$\neg AB(4) \wedge ok(L.next_3) \wedge ok(L.next_8) \wedge \neg ok(L.next_{11}) \to \perp \tag{11}$$

Where predicate $AB(i)$ means statement i is abnormal. Moreover, we expect the following properties:

Property 1 *If the list is not empty before, then one cell with the target value is   removed afterward.*

Property 2 *If the list is acyclic before, then it is acyclic afterwards.*

The Object Store provides an appropriate computing environment for checking user-expected properties. In our example, $L.next_6$ violates Property 2 because location 0 can reach itself. Since $L.next_9 = \phi(L.next_1, L.next_6)$, one observation is $\neg ok(L.next_9)$. By calling the diagnosis engine with rules (1)~(11), we get one conflict set $\{\neg AB(1), \neg AB(2), \neg AB(4)\}$, which tells us that one of statements 1, 2 and 4 is faulty (i.e., diagnoses, see [3]).

Furthermore, $L.next_7$ and $L.next_8$ are counterexamples of Property 1 because they are the same as their parent locations $L.next_2$ and $L.next_3$. Therefore, the diagnoses and the counterexamples $L.next_6$, $L.next_7$ and $L.next_8$ give the user some hints, help him to understand the nature of program misbehavior, and then correct the program error quickly.

REFERENCES

1. C. Mateis, M. Stumptner, and F. Wotawa. Modeling Java Programs for Diagnosis, ECAI 2001, Berlin Germany.
2. R. Cytron, J. Ferrante, B. K. Rosen, M. N. Wegman and F. K. Zadeck. Efficiently computing static single assignment form and the control dependence graph, ACM TOPLAS, 13(4): 451-490, 1991.
3. R. Reiter. A theory of diagnosis from first principles, AI, 32(1):57-59, 1987.

INTELLIGENT TECHNOLOGY FOR WELL LOGGING ANALYSIS

Zhongzhi Shi1   Ping Luo1   Yalei Hao2   Guohe Li3

Markus Stumptner2   Qing He1   Gerald Quirchmayr2 4
1 Institute of Computing Technology, Chinese Academy of Sciences, Beijing 100080, China

shizz@ics.ict.ac.cn, luop@ics.ict.ac.cn, heq@ics.ict.ac.cn

2 Advanced Computing Research Centre, University of South Australia, SA5095, Australia

Yalei.Hao@postgrads.unisa.edu.au, mst@cs.unisa.edu.au, Gerald.Quirchmayr@unisa.edu.au

3University of Petroleum,Beijing 100080,China

guoheli@ sina.com.cn

4 Institut für Informatik und Wirtschaftsinformatik, Universität Wien, Liebiggasse 4, A-1010 Wien, Austria

Abstract: Well logging analysis plays an essential role in petroleum exploration and exploitation. It is used to identify the pay zones of gas or oil in the reservoir formations. This paper applies intelligent technology for well logging analysis, particular combining data mining and expert system together, and proposes an intelligent system for well log analysis called IntWeL Analyzer in terms of data mining platform MSMiner and expert system tool OKPS. The architecture of IntWeL Analyzer and data mining algorithms, including Ripper algorithm and MOUCLAS algorithm are also presented. MOUCLAS is based on the concept of the fuzzy set membership function that gives the new approach a solid mathematical foundation and compact mathematical description of classifiers. The aim of the study is the use of intelligent technology to interpret the pay zones from well logging data for the purpose of reservoir characterization. This approach is better than conventional techniques for well logging interpretation that cannot discover the correct relation between the well logging data and the underlying property of interest.

Key words: Intelligent Technology, Well Log Analysis, Data Mining, MOUCLAS Algorithm

1.   INTRODUCTION

In the oil/gas exploration and exploitation well logging plays an essential role. Well logs record measurements of the rock's physical properties as well as the properties of the fluids contained in the rock. So-called well logging is a method of solving geological mission by means of physical principle. Since well logging detects the formation of a borehole from surface down to bottom, well logging data records all the formations' information about lithology, porosity, permeability, oil saturation and so on. According to the measurements of well logging there are three different kinds of data: electrical, nuclear and acoustic. Electrical logging is used to analyze oil saturation and water saturation of the formation. Nuclear logging is used to analyze the porosity and permeability. Acoustic logging is used to determine the amount of clay grain size.

Well logging interpretation includes qualitative and quantitative interpretation. Qualitative interpretation is done by interpreters traditionally. For example, when logging interpreters find the acoustic curve extent great which means porosity great, the neutron curve extent great which means hydrogen great, the gamma ray curve great which means amount of clay lower, they can determine this formation is a pay zone. After the qualitative interpretation, logging interpreters locate the pay zones and calculate the water saturation, oil saturation and amount of clay more accurately.

In order to make the well logging interpretation more efficient and automatic, intelligent technology is popularly adopted. The intelligent technique is fully using the nonlinear transformation to process information, and map the well logging data vectors to the formation features of lithology, porosity, permeability, oil saturation and so on.

Data mining based classification aims to build accurate and efficient classifiers not only on small data sets but more importantly also on large and high dimensional data sets, while the widely used traditional statistical data analysis techniques are not sufficiently powerful for this task. With the development of new data mining techniques on association rules, new classification approaches based on concepts from association rule mining are emerging. These include such classifiers as ARCS[1], CBA[2], LB[3], CAEP[4], etc., which are different from the classic decision tree based classifier C4.5[5] and k-nearest neighbor[6] in both the learning and testing phases. In this paper first we investigate inductive learning algorithm Ripper for well logging data analysis. Then according to the characteristic of well logging data we present a new approach to the classification over quantitative data in high dimensional databases, called MOUCLAS (MOUntain function based CLASsification), based on the concept of the fuzzy set membership function. It aims at integrating the advantages of classification, clustering and association rules mining to identify interesting patterns in selected sample data sets.

2.   BASIC WELL LOG CURVES

In this section we introduce some traditional well log curves and its physical significance.

Resistivity curve: Salt water will conduct electricity. However, Oil is an insulator and will not conduct electricity. An electrical curve measures the change in conductivity when tool is pulled up the well bore. Resistivity is the reciprocal of conductivity.

Gamma ray curve: The Gamma Ray device measures naturally occurring radiation given off by the rocks. Shale formations have more organic material so they emit more radiation. But sandstones, limestones, and salts have low organic materials. Thus, they have low Gamma Ray counts.

Neutron curve: The neutron log is radiation detector that measures the presence of hydrogen atoms in the formation. This indicates pore space by the assumption that the pores will be filled with water or hydrocarbons. The Neutron tool is more sensitive to statistical fluctuations and tends to be more "nervous" than other curves.

Acoustic curves: The sonic tool was the first tool developed to measure porosity. It consists of a transmitter that sends out a sound wave into the formation and a receiver, which detects that sound after a certain amount of time has passed. The transmitter and the receiver get out of synchronization with each other. This effect is called cycle skipping. Cycle skipping is a series of too early and too late arrivals back to the receiver, this causes a high to low zig-zag effect on the log. It is a sure indicator of gas in sandstones.

All the curves mentioned above and some other curves are the source of our conditional attributes data in the following experiments using intelligent data mining techniques.

3.   ARCHITECTURE OF INTWEL ANALYZER

It is useful to apply intelligent technology for well log data analysis. Intelligent well log analysis system called IntWeL Analyzer, which is shown in Figure 1, has been developed. IntWeL Analyzer consists of eight modules, including data warehouse, on line analysis processing (OLAP), data mining, knowledge acquisition, visualization, inference engine, knowledge base and interface.

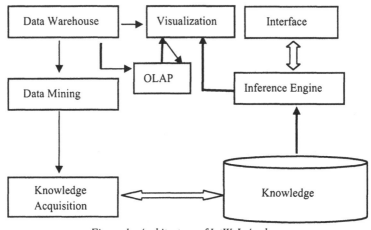

Figure 1. Architecture of IntWeL Analyzer

In IntWeL Analyzer first well log data is transferred into data warehouse, then it can be handled by on line analysis processing (OLAP module). Under data warehouse supporting, data mining module will extract knowledge from log data[8]. Knowledge acquisition module will convert data mining results into knowledge base. Inference engine module deploys knowledge to analyze well log data supported by knowledge base[9]. Users can interactive with the IntWeL Analyzer through interface.

We propose the object-oriented knowledge representation for the system. The knowledge will be represented in frame and semantic network based on object-oriented technology. This approach has all the features of an object-oriented mechanism, such as encapsulation, inheritance and message processing. The system puts all production rules into method slots.

In order to provide a powerful inference mechanism, as well as the maximum flexibility and convenience, the system proposes a high-level language, that is Inference Control Language (ICL), which can be used to describe knowledge and rules, and control the inference process.

4.   INDUCTIVE LEARNING

Inductive learning is an attractive research area in machine learning currently. The set of production rules generated by inductive learning is understandable to humans and this is one important reason we use it for the purpose of reservoir characterization. Among various inductive learning algorithms Ripper (Repeated Incremental Pruning to Producing Error Reduction) is one of the most effective and efficient. In this section we introduce Ripper algorithm first and then use it to analyze the well logging data in order to identify the pay zones of oil.

Ripper algorithm proposed by Cohen in 1995[10]. The underpinning of Cohen's algorithms is a descendant of REP (Reduced Error Pruning) which is a technique used in conjunction with a rule learning system in order to improve the accuracy of a generated rule set[11]. The whole algorithm of Ripper is consisted of two phases: the first is to determine the initial rule set and the second is post-process rule optimization.

1)   Generating the initial rule set

This sub-algorithm is described below:

```
procedure Rule_Generating(Pos,Neg)
begin
    Ruleset := {}
    while Pos   . {} do
        /* grow and prune a new rule */
        split (Pos,Neg) into (GrowPos,GrowNeg) and
    (PrunePos,PruneNeg)
        Rule := GrowRule(GrowPos,GrowNeg)
        Rule := PruneRule(Rule,PrunePos,PruneNeg)
        if the terminal conditions satisfy then
            return Ruleset
        else
            add Rule to Ruleset
            remove examples covered by Rule from (Pos,Neg)
        endif
    endwhile
    return Ruleset
end
```

The above is a separate-and-conquer rule-learning algorithm. First the training data are divided into a growing set and a pruning set. Then this algorithm generates a rule set in a greedy fashion, a rule at a time. While generating a rule Ripper searches the most valuable rule for the current growing set in rule space that can be defined in the form of BNF. Immediately after a rule is extracted on growing set, it is pruned on pruning set. After pruning, the corresponding examples covered by that rule in the training set (growing and pruning sets) are deleted. The remaining training data are re-partitioned after each rule is learned in order to help stabilize any problems caused by a "bad-split". This process is repeated until the terminal conditions satisfy.

After each rule is added into the rule set, the total description length, an integer value, of the rule set is computed. The description length gives a measure of the complexity and accuracy of a rule set. The terminal conditions satisfy when there are no positive examples left or the description length of the current rule set is more than the user-specified threshold.

2) Post-process rule optimization

Ripper uses some post-pruning techniques to optimize the rule set. This optimization is processed on the possible remaining positive examples. Re-optimizing the resultant rule set is called RIPPER2, and the general case of re-optimizing "k" times is called RIPPERk.

It is clear that the algorithm above is for the binary class attribute problem. Based on this Cohen used a technique called sequential covering to solve the multiple class attribute problem. After arranging the sequence of classes Ripper finds rules to separate $Class_1$ from $Class_2, \cdots, Class_n$, then rules to separate $Class_2$ from $Class_3, \cdots, Class_n$, and so on. The final class $Class_n$ will become the default. The sequence of the classes can be fixed by one of the followings: increasing frequency of class, decreasing frequency of class, optimal order using heuristic or the user-specified order. Consequently, the end result is that rules for a single class will always be grouped together. When predicting a sample if an example is covered by rules from two or more classes, then this conflict is resolved in favor of the class that comes first in the ordering.

Simplified oil/gas formation identification is a typical classification problem in data mining. It is used to identify the pay zones of gas or oil in the reservoir formation and helps to optimize production of oil/gas reservoir.

We analyze the data in petroleum database that contains three kinds of well logging quantitative data, including electrical, nuclear and acoustic data. The data in our application is from the boreholes in Xinjiang Province, China. There are 4 different layers under the ground: water, mixture of water and oil, oil and shale. They are the class labels of the record at certain depth.

Altogether, every 0.125 meters we get a record with 9 condition attributes and 1 class label. No depth information is used for training.

It is very important to mention that in oil/gas characterization problem the model extracted from the data in one area is not fit for the other area. Thus, we can't use the model from one area to predict the samples in another area. In addition, the training subset should cover the horizontal and vertical boreholes of producing wells. Thus, we combine all the records of different boreholes in one area into one data set and divide it into two parts: one is for training and the other is for testing. We divide the original whole data randomly in order to maintain the same proportion of different classes. The parameters of Ripper for training and the testing results are shown Table 1 and Table 2 respectively.

Table 1. Parameters description

No.	Parameter description
1	arranging the sequence of classes in increasing frequency of class
2	using the default rule searching space
3	each rule to cover at least 10 samples

Table 2. Testing results

No.	Proportion of records in training set	Proportion of records in testing set	Accuracy
1	2/3	1/3	93.10%
2	1/3	2/3	93.53%

Table 2 shows the testing accuracy is satisfactory. And we argue that Ripper really fits for the oil/gas identification application in well logging analysis.

5.   MOUCLAS ALGORITHM

The *MOUCLAS* algorithm, similar to ARCS, assumes that the initial association rules can be agglomerated into clustering regions, while obeying the anti-monotone rule constraint. Our proposed framework assumes that the training dataset D is a normal relational set, where transaction $d \in D$. Each transaction d is described by attributes $A_j, j = 1$ to l. The dimension of D is l, the number of attributes used in D. This allows us to describe a database in terms of volume and dimension. D can be classified into a set of known classes $Y, y \in Y$. The value of an attribute must be quantitative. In this work, we treat all the attributes uniformly. We can treat a transaction as a set of (attributes, value) pairs and a class label. We call each (attribute, value) pair an item. A set of items is simply called an itemset.

Since CBA indicates the feasibility of setting up a link between association rule and classification and ARCS proves that the idea of designing a classification pattern based on clustering can work effectively and efficiently, we design a *MOUCLAS* Pattern (so called *MP*) as an implication of the form:

$Cluster(D)_t \rightarrow y,$

where *Cluster(D)$_t$ is a cluster of D, t* = 1 to *m*, and *y* is a class label. The definitions of *frequency* and *accuracy* of *MOUCLAS* Patterns are defined as following: The *MP* satisfying minimum support is *frequent*, where *MP* has support s if s% of the transactions in *D* belong to *Cluster(D)$_t$* and are labeled with class *y*. The *MP* that satisfies a pre-specified minimum confidence is called *accurate*, where *MP* has confidence c if c% of the transactions belonging to *Cluster(D)$_t$* are labeled with class *y*.

Though framework of support – confidence is used in most of the applications of association rule mining, it may be misleading by identifying a rule A $\Rightarrow$ B as interesting, even though the occurrence of A may not imply the occurrence of B. This requires a complementary framework for finding interesting relations. Correlation is one of the most efficient interestingness measures other than support and confidence. Here we adopt the concept of reliability to describe the correlation. The measure of reliability of the association rule A $\Rightarrow$ B can be defined as:

$$\text{reliability} \quad R(A \Rightarrow B) = \left| \frac{P(A \wedge B)}{P(A)} - P(B) \right|$$

Since R is the difference between the conditional probability of B given A and the unconditional of B, it measures the effect of available information of A on the probability of the association rule. Correspondingly, the greater R is, the stronger *MOUCLAS* patterns are, which means the occurrence of *Cluster(D)$_t$* more strongly implies the occurrence of *y*. Therefore, we can utilize reliability to further prune the selected *frequent and accurate and reliable MOUCLAS* patterns (*MPs*) to identify the truly interesting *MPs* and make the discovered *MPs* more understandable. The *MP* satisfying minimum reliability is *reliable*, where *MP* has reliability defined by the above formula.

Given a set of transactions, *D*, the problems of *MOUCLAS* are to discover *MPs* that have support and confidence greater than the user-specified minimum support threshold (called *minsup*), and minimum confidence threshold (called *minconf*) and minimum reliability threshold (called *minR*) respectively, and to construct a classifier based upon *MPs*.

The classification technique, *MOUCLAS*, consists of two steps:
1.   Discovery of *frequent, accurate* and *reliable MPs*.
2.   Construction of a classifier, called *De-MP*, based on *MPs*.

The core of the first step in the *MOUCLAS* algorithm is to find all *cluster_rules* that have support above *minsup*. Let *C* denote the dataset *D* after dimensionality reduction processing. A *cluster_rule* represents a *MP*, namely a rule:

$$cluset \rightarrow y,$$

where *cluset* is a set of itemsets from a cluster *Cluster(C)_t*, *y* is a class label, $y \in Y$. The support count of the *cluset* (called *clusupCount*) is the number of transactions in *C* that belong to the *cluset*. The support count of the *cluster_rule* (called *cisupCount*) is the number of transactions in *D* that belong to the *cluset* and are labeled with class *y*. The *confidence* of a *cluster_rule* is (*cisupCount* / *clusupCount*) × 100%. The support count of the class *y* (called *clasupCount*) is the number of transactions in *C* that belong to the class *y*. The *support* of a *class* (called *clasup*) is (*clasupCount* / |*C*|) × 100%, where |*C*| is the size of the dataset *C*.

Given a *MP*, the *reliability* R can be defined as:

$$R(cluset \rightarrow y) = |\ (cisupCount / clusupCount) - (clasupCount / |C|)\ | \times 100\%$$

The traditional association rule mining only uses a single *minsup* in rule generation, which is inadequate for many practical datasets with uneven class frequency distributions. As a result, it may happen that the rules found for infrequent classes are insufficient and too many may be found for frequent classes, inducing useless or over-fitting rules, if the single *minsup* value is too high or too low. To overcome this drawback, we apply the theory of mining with multiple minimum supports in the step of discovering the frequent MPs as following.

Suppose the total support is *t-minsup*, the different minimum class support for each class *y*, denoted as *minsup_i* can be defined by the formula:

$$minsup_i = t\text{-}minsup \times \text{freqDistr}(y)$$

where, freqDistr(*y*) is the function of class distributions. *Cluster_rules* that satisfy *minsup_i* are called *frequent cluster_rules*, while the rest are called *infrequent cluster_rules*. If the *confidence* is greater than *minconf*, we say the *MP* is *accurate*.

The task of the second step in *MOUCLAS* algorithm is to use a heuristic method to generate a classifier, named *De-MP*, where the discovered *MPs* can cover *D* and are organized according to a decreasing precedence based on their confidence and support. Suppose *R* be the set of *frequent*, *accurate* and *reliable MPs* which are generated in the past step, and *MP_{default_class}* denotes the default class, which has the lowest precedence. We can then present the *De-MP* classifier in the form of

$$<MP_1, MP_2, \ldots, MP_n, MP_{default\_class}>,$$

where $MP_i \in R$, $i = 1$ to n, $MP_a > MP_b$ if $n \geq b > a \geq 1$ *and* $a, b \in i$, $C \subseteq \cup$ *cluset of* $MP_{i,}$.

6.   CONCLUSIONS

A novel architecture of IntWeL Analyzer for well logging data analysis is proposed in the paper. The IntWeL Analyzer integrates data mining and expert system together. An inductive learning algorithm called Ripper and a novel association rule classification algorithm called MOUCLAS are investigated in this paper for intelligent well logging data analysis.

For the future we will add more expert experiences and geophysical knowledge into the IntWeL Analyzer and attempt to establish a relationship between different well logs, such as seismic attributes, laboratory measurements and other reservoir properties.

7.   ACKNOWLEDGEMENT

This work was partially supported by the Australia-China Special Fund for Scientific and Technological Cooperation under grant CH030086, the joint China-Australia project under the bilateral scientific exchange agreement between The Chinese Academy of Sciences and Australia Academy of Science.

REFERENCES

1. B. Lent, A. Swami, and J. Widom. Clustering association rules. ICDE'97, (1997) 220-231
2. B. Liu, W.Hsu, and Y.Ma. Integrating classification and association rule mining. KDD'98. (1998) 80-86
3. Meretakis, D., & Wuthrich, B. Extending naive Bayes classifiers using long itemsets. Proc. of the Fifth ACM SIGKDD. ACM Press. (1999) 165-174
4. Dong, G., & Li, J. Efficient mining of emerging patterns: Discovering trends and differences. Proc. of the Fifth ACM SIGKDD. (1999)
5. Quinlan, J. R. C4.5: Programs for machine learning. San Mateo, CA: Morgan Kaufmann. (1993)
6. Cover, T. M., & Hart, P. E. Nearest neighbor pattern classification. IEEE Transactions on Information Theory, 13. (1967) 21-27
7. F. Aminzadeh, Future Geoscience Technology Trends in, Stratigraphic Analysis, Utilizing Advanced Geophysical, Wireline, and Borehole Technology For Petroleum Exploration and Production, GCSEPFM pp 1-6, (1996)
8. Zhongzhi Shi. MSMiner: Data Mining Platform, Keynote speech, ICMLC2002, 2002
9. Zhongzhi Shi. OKPS: Expert System Developing Tool, Technical Report, ICT of CAS, 2004
10. William W. Cohen. Fast Effective Rule Induction. In Machine Learning: Proceedings of the Twelfth International Conference, Lake Taho, California, 1995.
11. Clifford A. Brunk and Michael J. Pazzani. An investigation of noise-tolerant relational concept learning algorithms. In Proceedings of the 8th InternationalWorkshop on Machine Learning, pages 389–393, Evanston, Illinois, 1991.

SEDATALOG: A SET EXTENSION OF *DATALOG*

Qing Zhou
The Software Institute of Zhongshan University
Guangzhou, Guangdong 510275, P.R.China
lnszq@zsulink.zsu.edu.cn

Ligong Long
The Software Institute of Zhongshan University
Guangzhou, Guangdong 510275, P.R.China
longligong@tom.com

Abstract   In this paper we propose an extension, $SEDatalog$, of $Datalog$ so that sets can be naturally constructed in logic programming. In $SEDatalog$, sets can be defined by statements so it has a strong capability in creating sets. Three deductive rules are also introduced in this paper, which make $SEDatalog$ strong in deductions and programming even when sets are involved in deductions. The syntactical description and the semantical interpretation of $SEDatalog$ are comprehensively discussed in detail. The soundness and completeness theorem of $SEDatalog$ is proved, which provides a solid foundation of $SEDatalog$.

Keywords: The order of a set, The order of predicate, n-th order set

1.   Introduction

In this paper we propose an extension, $SEDatalog$, of $Datalog$ so that sets can be constructed in logic programming. As the extension is entirely based on what is common in every logic programming language, the extension could apply to Prolog and other logic programming languages almost without any modification.

In $SEDatalog$, we can define a set A such that $A = \{x : p(x)\}$ for every formula. By defining sets by statements we can not only construct finite sets but also infinite sets or more complicated sets such as a set of sets with certain properties. Also this is the way we define sets when we are working in mathematics, or in other areas. This definition, if without proper restrictions, would involve confusions among set construction levels and would lead to Russell's paradox. To avoid this, we restrict the elements to be contained in a set to only those which already exist, thus helping achieve clear indication of a set hierarchy to be constructed in $SEDatalog$. As hierarchies constructed this way are in line with the underlying principles of the axiomatic set theory i.e. ZF, avoidance of such paradoxes as "the set of all sets" or "a set containing itself" can be assured.

For this purpose we need an "order" for every set which indicates the level in which the set is constructed. Then statements in $Datalog$ can be used to define sets. We consider that these sets are of the first order. Using these sets and individuals in $Datalog$, which are of order 0, we can construct a group of statements, which are not in $Datalog$ in general, by which second order sets can be defined. Continuing by this way, we may have all the sets constructed. To ensure avoidance of any possible confusion in the construction, we have to give an order to every statement in $SEDatalog$, too. This means that every predicate in $SEDatalog$ can only allow those sets with order less than a constant integer (the order of the predicate) as its variables. So every predicate in $SEDatalog$ is a partial predicate, i.e. its domain can not contain any set which has the order larger than or equal to the order of the predicate. This takes care of the problem mentioned in the last paragraph.

2.   The Syntactical Description Of $SEDatalog$

The **alphabet** of $SEDatalog$ consists of variables, constants, predicates and connectives. Each constant, variable and predicate is assigned an unique integer to it. A n-th order term is a constant or variable which has been assigned n to it. The order of a predicate is n, if it is assigned n. We will use $o(t)$ to indicate the order of t if t is a variable, a constant or a predicate.

DEFINITION 1 *Formulas and their orders are defined as follows:*

(1) If p is a k-order n-ary predicate symbol, and for every i, $1 \leq i \leq n$, $t[i]$ is a term with $o(t[i]) < k$, then $p(t[1], \dots, t[n])$ is an atom formula and $o(p(t[1], \dots, t[n])) = k$;

(2) If $t[1]$ and $t[2]$ are terms, and $o(t[1]) < o(t[2])$, then $t[1] \in t[2]$ is an atom formula and $o(t[1] \in t[2]) = o(t[2]) + 1$;

(3) If $t[1]$ and $t[2]$ are terms, and $0 < o(t[1]) \leq o(t[2])$, then $t[1] \subseteq t[2]$ is an atom formula and $o(t[1] \subseteq t[2]) = o(t[2]) + 1$;

(4) If $t[1]$ and $t[2]$ are terms, and $o(t[1]) = o(t[2])$, then $t[1] = t[2]$ is an atom formula and $o(t[1] = t[2]) = o(t[2]) + 1$.

(5) If F, G are formulas, then $F \wedge G$, $F \vee G$ are formulas and $o(F \wedge G) = max(\{o(F), o(G)\})$, $o(F \vee G) = max(\{o(F), o(G)\})$.

*An atom with no free variables is called a **ground atom**. A **closed formula** is a formula with no free variables. An atom is called a literal in $SEDatalog$.*

Remark In the above definition, $F(x) \vee G(x)$ might not be well defined from Definition 1 for some x with order $o(F(x)) \leq o(x) < o(G(x))$ when

$o(F(x)) < o(G(x))$. To let the definition make sense, we consider it as $F'(x) \vee G(x)$, where $F'(x) \leftrightarrow F(x)$ and $o(F'(x)) = o(G(x))$, i.e. the domain of $F'(x)$ is extended to all terms with the order up to $o(G(x))$, although $F'(x) \leftrightarrow F(x)$. The same treatment is made for $F(x) \wedge G(x)$.

DEFINITION 2 *For each formula $F(x)$ with only one free variable x, the set defined by $F(x)$ is a constant $C_{F(x)} \in C_n$ with $n = o(F(x))$ such that for all t, $t \in C_{F(x)}$ if and only if $F(t)$.*

We often write $C_{F(x)} = \{t : F(t)\}$ to indicate the definition of $C_{F(x)}$.

Directly from our definitions, it is not hard to see that for every formula $F(x)$, $o(C_{F(x)})$ is a finite integer.

Then we turn to the deduction rules of $SEDatalog$. As an extension of $Datalog$, we first extend the deduction rule of $Datalog$ to be used on statements which contain sets as their variables. We call it "the ordinary rule". In addition to this ordinary rule, we add two more deduction rules, "the universal rule" and "the existential rule".

DEFINITION 3 *A **rule** of $SEDatalog$ is of the form $H : -A_1, \ldots, A_n$ where $n \geq 0$. The left hand side of : $-$ is a literal, called the **head** of the rule, while the right hand side is a conjunction of literals, called the **body** of the rule .*

*A **fact** is a special rule, whose head is a ground literal and whose body is empty.*

For convenience, we use the notation $vars(T)$ to indicate all variables occurring in T, where T is a term or a formula. Then $vars$ is a mapping from the set of terms and formulas to the power set of Var. We use $H(y)$ to represent a literal with variable y and $A(x)$ to represent a literal with variable x. Now we give the following three rules, which will be called **safe.** They are the basic deductive rules in $SEDatalog$:

(1) **Ordinary rule** is of the form

$$H : -_O A_1, \ldots, A_n$$

where $n > 0$, $vars(H) \subseteq vars(A_1 \wedge \ldots \wedge A_n)$ and $o(H) = o(A_1 \wedge \ldots \wedge A_n)$.

The informal semantics of this rule is to mean that "for every assignment to each variable, if $A_1, \ldots, A_n$ are true, then H is true"

(2) **Universal rule** is of the form

$$H(y) : -_U A_1(x), \ldots, A_m(x), A_{m+1}, \ldots, A_n$$

where $vars(H(y)) - \{y\} \subseteq vars(A_1(x) \wedge \ldots \wedge A_m(x) \wedge A_{m+1} \wedge \ldots \wedge A_n) - \{x\}$, $y \neq x$, $o(H(y)) > o(A_1(x) \wedge \ldots \wedge A_m(x) \wedge A_{m+1} \wedge \ldots \wedge A_n)$ and $y \subseteq \{x : A_1(x) \wedge \ldots \wedge A_m(x) \wedge A_{m+1} \wedge \ldots \wedge A_n\}$.

The informal semantics of this rule is to mean that "if every element x in y has properties $A_1(x), \dots, A_m(x)$, then y has the property H".

In this case, y is called **of the universal property** H.

(3) **Existential rule** is of the form

$$H(y) : -_E$$
$$A_1(x_1, \dots, x_k), \dots, A_m(x_1, \dots, x_k), A_{m+1}, \dots, A_n$$

where $vars(H(y)) - \{y\} \subseteq vars(A_1(x_1, \dots, x_k) \wedge \dots \wedge A_m(x_1, \dots, x_k) \wedge A_{m+1} \wedge \dots \wedge A_n) - \{x_1, \dots, x_k\}, y \neq x_1, \dots, y \neq x_k, o(H(y)) > o(A_1(x_1, \dots, x_k) \wedge \dots \wedge A_m(x_1, \dots, x_k) \wedge A_{m+1} \wedge \dots \wedge A_n)$ and $x_1 \in y, \dots, x_k \in y$.

The informal semantics of this rule is to mean that "if some elements $x_1, \dots, x_k$ in y have properties $A_1(x_1, \dots, x_k), \dots, A_m(x_1, \dots, x_k)$, then y has the property H".

In this case, y is called **of the existential property** H.

DEFINITION 4 *A SEDatalog **program** is a finite sequence of rules.*

DEFINITION 5 *A **substitution** θ is a finite set of the form $\{x_1/t_1, \dots, x_n/t_n\}$, where $x_1, \dots, x_n$ are distinct variables and each t_i is a term such that $x_i \neq t_i$, and $o(t_i) \leq o(x_i)$.*

*The set of variables $\{x_1, \dots, x_n\}$ is called the **domain** of θ.*

If T is a term, a literal or a rule then $T\theta$ denotes the corresponding item obtained from T by simultaneously replacing each x_i that occurs in T by the corresponding term t_i, if x_i/t_i is an element of θ.

*If each t_i is ground, then θ is a **ground substitution**.*

3.   The Semantical Interpretations of $SEDatalog$

Let $M_0 = \langle \mathcal{V}, \mathcal{P}_0, \mathcal{T}_0 \rangle$ be an interpretation of $Datalog$, where $\mathcal{V}$ is the universe of M_0; $\mathcal{P}_0$ is the set of the interpretations of predicate symbols of $Datalog$; $\mathcal{T}_0$ is the set of interpretations of those ground atoms of $Datalog$ which are interpreted as true; respectively. We define $\mathcal{U}_0 = \mathcal{V}$, and $\mathcal{U}_n = \mathcal{U}_{n-1} \cup \wp(\mathcal{U}_{n-1})$ where $\wp(\mathcal{U}_{n-1})$ is the power set of $\mathcal{U}_{n-1}$, i.e. $\wp(\mathcal{U}_{n-1}) = \{A : A \subseteq \mathcal{U}_{n-1}\}$. Then we give the full description of the interpretation of $SEDatalog$ as follows:

An interpretation M of $SEDatalog$ is a tuple: $M = \langle \mathcal{U}, \mathcal{P}, \mathcal{T} \rangle$, here $\mathcal{U} = \bigcup_{k=0}^{\infty} \mathcal{U}_k$ is the *universe* of M; $\mathcal{P}$ is the set of the interpretations of predicate symbols; $\mathcal{T}$ is the set of interpretations of those ground literals which are interpreted as true, respectively, such that:

(1) Each n-ary predicate symbol $q_{\langle k \rangle}$ is interpreted as a predicate $q_M \in \mathcal{P}$, i.e. $q_M \subseteq \mathcal{U}_k^n$, and $q_{\langle 1 \rangle}$ is interpreted as a predicate $q_M \in \mathcal{P}_0$;

Especially, $\in_{\langle m \rangle}$, $\subseteq_{\langle m \rangle}$ and $=_{\langle m \rangle}$ are interpreted as the usual meanings.

(2) Each constant c in C_n $(n > 0)$ is interpreted as an object (set) $M(c)$ of $\mathcal{U}_n$; and each constant c in C_0 is interpreted as same as in M_0, i.e. an object (individual) $M(c)$ of $\mathcal{U}_0$;

(3) A ground atom $q(t[1], ..., t[n])$ is interpreted as $M(q(t[1], ..., t[n])) \iff q_M(M(t[1]), ... , M(t[n]))$, for more complicated formulas such as $F(x) \vee G(x)$ and $F(x) \wedge G(x)$, their truth values are interpreted as usual;

(4) Now we define $\mathcal{T}$ as follows:

$\mathcal{T}_0$ is as same as the $\mathcal{T}_0$ in M_0;

$\mathcal{T}_k \subseteq \mathcal{T}_{k-1} \cup \{q_M(M(t[1]), ... , M(t[n])) : q_{<k>}(t[1], ... , t[n])$ is a ground literal$\}$ which satisfies $\mathcal{T}_{k-1} \subset \mathcal{T}_k$ and:

i) $M(c \in C_{A(x)})) \in \mathcal{T}_k$ if and only if $M(A(c)) \in \mathcal{T}_{k-1}$.

ii) $M(C_{F(x)} \subseteq C_{G(x)}) \in \mathcal{T}_k$ if and only if for all $x \in \mathcal{U}$, $M(F)(x) \in \mathcal{T}$ implies that $M(G)(x) \in \mathcal{T}_k$.

and finally, let $\mathcal{T} = \bigcup_{k=1}^{\infty} \mathcal{T}_k$.

With the interpretation of $SEDatalog$ described above, our next job is to give the description of the model of a $SEDatalog$ program:

Let P be a program. An interpretation $M = \langle \mathcal{U}, \mathcal{P}, \mathcal{T} \rangle$ is a *model* of P if and only if

(1) If A is a fact in P, then $M(A) \in \mathcal{T}$;

(2) If $r : H : -_O A_1, ... , A_n$ is an ordinary rule in P, then for each ground and legal substitution θ with $domain(\theta) \supseteq vars(r)$, if $M(A_1\theta) \in \mathcal{T}, ... , M(A_n\theta) \in \mathcal{T}$, then $M(H\theta) \in \mathcal{T}$;

(3) If $r : H(y) : -_U A_1(x), ... , A_m(x), A_{m+1}, ... , A_n$ is a universal rule in P, then for each ground and legal substitution θ with $domain(\theta) = vars(r) - \{x\}$, if $M(A_{m+1}\theta) \in \mathcal{T}, ... , M(A_n\theta) \in \mathcal{T}$, and $M(y\theta \subseteq C_{A_1(x)\theta}) \in \mathcal{T}, ... , M(y\theta \subseteq C_{A_m(x)\theta}) \in \mathcal{T}$, then $M(H(y)\theta) \in \mathcal{T}$, here $M(y\theta \subseteq C_{A_i(x)\theta}) \in \mathcal{T}$, $1 \leq i \leq m$;

(4) If $r : H(y) : -_E A_1(x_1, ... , x_k), ... , A_m(x_1, ... , x_k), A_{m+1}, ... , A_n$ is a existential rule in P, then for each ground and legal substitution θ with $domain(\theta) = vars(r)$, if $M(A_1(x_1, ... , x_k)\theta) \in \mathcal{T}, ... , M(A_m(x_1, ... , x_k)\theta) \in \mathcal{T}$, $M(A_{m+1}\theta) \in \mathcal{T}, ... , M(A_n\theta) \in \mathcal{T}$, and $M((x_1 \in y)\theta) \in \mathcal{T}, ... , M((x_k \in y)\theta) \in \mathcal{T}$ then $M(H(y)\theta) \in \mathcal{T}$.

DEFINITION 6 *Let A be a ground literal. An interpretation $M = \langle \mathcal{U}, \mathcal{P}, \mathcal{T} \rangle$ is a **model** of A if and only if $M(A) \in \mathcal{T}$.*

Now we are going to discuss the soundness and completeness theorem of $SEDatalog$. Before that let us introduce some related notions first.

DEFINITION 7 *A ground literal A is a **consequence** of a $SEDatalog$ program P (denoted by $P \models A$) if and only if each model M of P is also a model of A.*

DEFINITION 8 *A ground literal A is **inferred from** a $SEDatalog$ program P (denoted by $P \vdash A$) is defined as follows:*

(1) If $A = H$ and H is a fact in P, then $P \vdash A$;

(2) If there exists an ordinary rule $r : H : -_O A_1, \ldots, A_n$ in P and a ground and legal substitution θ, where $domain(\theta) = vars(r)$, such that $A = H\theta$ and $P \vdash A_1\theta, \ldots, P \vdash A_n\theta$, then $P \vdash A$;

(3) If there exists a universal rule $r : H(y) : -_U A_1(x), \ldots, A_m(x), A_{m+1}, \ldots, A_n$ in P and a ground and legal substitution θ, where $domain(\theta) = vars(r) - \{x\}$, such that $A = H(y)\theta$ and $P \vdash A_{m+1}\theta, \ldots, P \vdash A_n\theta$, and $P \vdash y\theta \subseteq C_{A_1(x)\theta}, \ldots, P \vdash y\theta \subseteq C_{A_m(x)\theta}$, then $P \vdash A$, here $P \vdash y\theta \subseteq C_{A_i(x)\theta}$, $1 \le i \le m$;

(4) If there exists an existential rule $r : H(y) : -_E A_1(x_1, \ldots, x_k), \ldots, A_m(x_1, \ldots, x_k), A_{m+1}, \ldots, A_n$ in P and a ground and legal substitution θ, where $domain(\theta) = vars(r)$, such that $A = H(y)\theta$ and $P \vdash A_1(x_1, \ldots, x_k)\theta, \ldots, P \vdash A_m(x_1, \ldots, x_k)\theta, P \vdash A_{m+1}\theta, \ldots, P \vdash A_n\theta, P \vdash x_1\theta \in y\theta, \ldots, P \vdash x_k\theta \in y\theta$, then $P \vdash A$.

Let $infer(P) = \{A : P \vdash A\}$ and $cons(P) = \{A : P \models A\}$. It is easy to show that, $cons(P) = \bigcap_M \{A : M = \langle \mathcal{U}, \mathcal{P}, \mathcal{T} \rangle$ is a model of P and $M(A) \in \mathcal{T}.\}$. Then we can prove The Soundness and Completeness Theorem:

THEOREM 9 $infer(P) = cons(P)$.

References

Abiteboul, S.,Grumbach, S.,: COL: A Logic-based Language for Complex Objects, ACM TODS, 16(1), *pp.*1-30, 1991.

Ceri, S., Gottlob, G.,Tanca, L.,: Logic Programming and Databases, Springer Verlag, 1990.

Chimenti, D.,Gamboa, R., Krishnamurthy, R., Naqvi, S., Tsur, S.,Zaniolo, C.,: The LDL System Prototype, IEEE Transactions on Knowledge and Data Engineering, 2(1), *pp.*76-90, 1990.

Dovier, A., Omodeo, E. G., Pontelli, E., Rossi, G.,: {log}: A Language for Programming in Logic with Finite Sets, J. of Logic Programming, 28(1), *pp.*1-44, 1996.

Jana, D.,: Semantics of Subset-Logic Languages, Ph.D. Dissertation, Department of Computer Science, SUNY-Buffalo, 1994.

Jayaraman, B.,: The SuRE Programming Framework, TR 91-011, Department of Computer Science, SUNY-Buffalo, August 1991.

Jayaraman, B.,Jana, D.,: Set Constructors, Finite Sets, and Logical Semantics, J. of Logic Programming, 38, *pp.*55-77, 1999.

Kuper, G. M.,: Logic Programming with Sets, J. of Computer and System Science, 41(1), *pp.*44-64, 1990.

Liu, M.,: Relationlog: A Typed Extension to *Datalog* with Sets and Tuples, J. of Logic Programming, 36, *pp.*271-299, 1998.

Lloyd, J. W.,: Foundations of Logic Programming, Springer Verlag, 1987.

Moon, K.,: Implementation of Subset Logic Languages, Ph.D. Dissertation, Department of Computer Science, SUNY-Buffalo, February 1995.

Osorio, M.,: Semantics of Logic Programs with Sets, Ph.D. Dissertation, Department of Computer Science, SUNY-Buffalo, 1995.

SESSION IDENTIFICATION BASED ON TIME INTERVAL IN WEB LOG MINING

Zhuang Like, Kou Zhongbao and Zhang Changshui
State Key Laboratory of Intelligent Technology and Systems,Department of Automation, Tsinghua University, Beijing 100084, P.R.China

Abstract: In this paper, we calculate the time intervals of page views, and analyze the time intervals to obtain a certain threshold, which is then used to break the web logs into sessions. Based on the time intervals, frequencies for each interval are counted and frequency vectors are obtained for each IP. Some IPs with special features of frequency distributions can be deemed as single users. For these IPs, we can define threshold for each individual IP, and separate sessions at the points of long access time intervals.

Key words: Web log mining, session identification, time interval

1.   INTRODUCTION

The World Wide Web continues to grow at an astonishing rate in both the volume of traffic and the size and complexity of Web sites. The technique of Web mining just tries to acquire useful information and knowledge from the huge amount of information in WWW. Web mining can be classified into three categories: content mining, structure mining, and usage mining [1]. Web usage mining focuses on providing efficient techniques to analyze and predict behaviors of users while users access the Web. The data used for usage mining is the web logs. Through usage mining, behaviors of users, such as access frequency and regularly visited web page etc., are analyzed and the corresponding rules are obtained. Furthermore, the rules are used to improve the design of web site. Some software tools for web log analysis have been designed and used for real-world applications. [2-4]

The first step for web log mining is the pre-processing of the raw log data, which is the most important step for its results will impact the subsequent steps of pattern discovery and pattern analysis directly [5].

Two typical methods for web log mining are proposed by Chen et.al. [6] and Han et.al.[7]. Chen et.al. [6] introduce the concept of using the maximal forward references in order to break down user sessions into transactions for the mining of traversal patterns. Han et.al. [7] have loaded Web server logs into a data cube structure in order to perform data mining as well as traditional On-Line Analytical Processing (OLAP). Both the methods include the tasks of user identification and session identification in pre-processing step.

Unique users must be identified for further session identification and analyses. While the existence of local caches, corporate firewalls and proxy servers make the task greatly complicated [8]. Many assistant techniques such as cookies and CGI scripts etc. are used to detect users. However if the users don't collaborate, the only thing to do is to deem the one individual IP as a user. In [9], if the agent log shows a change in browser software or operating system, each different agent type for an IP address are deemed as a different user. But there are still many users using the same browser and operating system visit the web site from the same IP address.

To do further pattern discovery and analyses, web logs need to be converted into user sessions. A session is a serial of page views of a single user when accessing the entire Web. The purpose of session identification is to separate the web logs of one user into individual sessions for further analysis. A simple method to identify sessions is to determine a threshold. If the time between page accessing exceeds the threshold, we assumed that the user starts a new session. On current research on this area, this threshold is determined from fifteen minutes to one hour based on experiences. Obviously, some users may browse a site hastily and others may spend more time when they begin a page view. Thus using the uniform threshold for all users is not proper and bring out imprecision.

In this paper, we calculate the time intervals of page views for each IP address, and then count the frequency for each interval and obtain the frequency vector, which is used as the feature of one IP. Some IPs with special features of frequency distributions can be deemed as single users. For these IPs, we can define threshold for each individual IP, and divide sessions at the point of long access time interval.

The reminder of this paper is organized as follows: In Section 2, we establish the frequency vectors of IPs. Section 3 details and discusses several typical frequency distributions. We propose a novel method to analyze the feature of access frequency and estimate the threshold of session in Section 4. The last section is our conclusion.

2.   FREQUENCY VECTORS OF IPS

The website of China National Tourism Administration (CNTA) [10] is a famous HTTP sever of China, which have large amounts access volume. The web logs from Oct 1st, 2001 to Oct 9th, 2001 of CNTA are adopted in our experiments. We delete some redundant information of the web logs, such as some assistant files with suffixes ``.gif", ``.swf", ``.css", ``.jpg", ``.cgi" etc.[5]. After preprocessing the raw data, we get 547,279 access records, all of which visited the sever from 21,438 IP addresses.

In Table 1, we show some access records of the data. For every record, it includes starting time of the access, URL, size, and so on. The starting time of a page view is key factor in our analysis of the session threshold. We define the time interval of page views as:

$$Diff\_T_k = T_{k+1} - T_k, \qquad k = 1, 2, \cdots, N-1, \tag{1}$$

where N is the amount of page views of one IP, T_k is the starting time of the k page view.

Table 1. A sample of server log

Date	Time	IP	Web page
10/02/2001	09:06:38	203.204.71.242	/26-zsyz/2j/dfly-12.asp
10/02/2001	09:07:41	203.204.71.242	/26-zsyz/2j/dfly-13.asp
10/02/2001	09:08:53	203.204.71.242	/26-zsyz/2j/dfly-14.asp
10/02/2001	09:09:58	203.204.71.242	/26-zsyz/2j/dfly-15.asp
10/02/2001	09:47:08	203.204.71.242	/12-gwcy/shopping/sichou.htm
10/02/2001	09:48:10	203.204.71.242	/12-gwcy/shopping/cixiu.htm
10/02/2001	09:49:38	203.204.71.242	/12-gwcy/shopping/china.htm
10/02/2001	09:49:57	203.204.71.242	/12-gwcy/shopping/tu/cixiou.jpg
10/02/2001	09:51:01	203.204.71.242	/12-gwcy/shopping/qiqi.htm

Figure 1 shows the time intervals of a serial of page views. In Figure 1, most of the time intervals converge from about 20 seconds to 140 seconds. We believe that in a normal session, the interval time of page views distribute in a range of value, the appearance of an extremely larger value may mean the beginning of another session. Then the 68th page views can be deemed as the beginning of a new session for the time interval between the 67th and the 68th page views is 2230 seconds, which is much larger than average value. The 68th page view just corresponds to the fifth access record showed in Table 1. For a special IP, the threshold to divide sessions can be obtained by the statistical analysis of the time intervals. This statistic is the frequency vector of the IP.

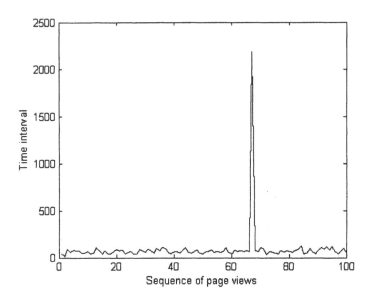

Figure 1. Time interval of a serial of page views

We define the frequency vector of an IP as

$$X^{(i)} = \{x_k^{(i)}, k = 1, 2, \cdots, M\}, \tag{2}$$

where i denotes the IP, k is the time interval between two adjacent page views, the unit is second. The value $x_k^{(i)}$ is the times that time interval k appears in the logs from IP i. M is the maximal time interval.

Since we think the very large value of time interval means the end of a session and starting of another one, these values don't express users' access behavior in one session. When take off 0.5% largest data in all access time intervals, the remaining data are with the maximal time interval of 897, which is just the M value we adopted. Thus, the frequency vectors of all IPs are established.

3.   FEATURES OF FREQUENCY VECTORS

Figure 2 shows the cumulated frequency distribution for all the data, the frequency S_n is acquired by summing up the frequency vectors of all IP addresses.

$$S_n = \sum_i^n X^{(i)} \tag{3}$$

The value n is the number of IPs in the data. The distribution of S_n exhibits a straight line in logarithm histograms, which shows power-law distribution. Power-law characteristics are shared by many nature and society system, such as computer systems and Internet. That is, the frequencies of events to their sizes are often exhibiting power-law distributions. [11,12]

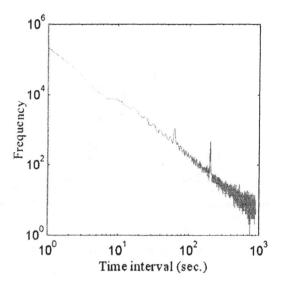

Figure 2. Frequency-time interval distribution for all IP addresses

For individual IPs, the frequency distribution can also be acquired. We observed these distributions of 25 IPs and get some interesting features. Two typical frequency distributions are showed in Figure 3.

The frequency distribution in Figure 3(a) also exhibits Power-law characteristics, just as the distribution of S_n showed in Figure 2. There are 101386 requests from this IP in 9 days, and from the figure, most of the accesses have very small time intervals, some requests are even occurred simultaneously. It seems that many users are accessing the web site according to the same IP, so it is probably a proxy server. We examined the IP and validated our supposition. For this kind of IP, session identification is extremely difficult, for they mixed with many users with different access features. Other techniques, such as using cookies or combining content/structure information can be used to deal with these kinds of complexity.

However, distribution in Figure 3(b) exhibits Gaussian Characteristic. We think it shows the browsing behavior of one unique user. For a frequenter of a web site, the feature of his access web pages reflects his/her psychologies, interests, reading style and reading speed etc., while has little thing to do with the content of the web pages. Then we can identify unique users according to the frequency distribution.

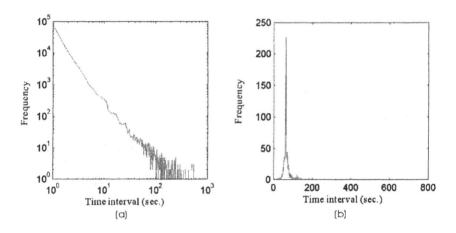

Figure 3. Two typical frequency distributions

4.   THRESHOLD OF SESSIONS FOR INDIVIDUAL IPS

From Figure 3(a), we can derive that there are many accesses with small value of time interval when IP serve as a proxy server, for concurrent accesses to the web site split the time interval to pieces. On the other hand, if there are not accesses with small value of time interval, we can deem the IP as a unique user. In Figure 3(b), stable behavior of unique user is acquired. For these cases, sessions can be divided at the threshold of time interval.

If we have determined that an IP is used by one special user, we can calculate the mean μ and standard variance σ according to the frequency distribution. Then the threshold to divide sessions can be defined as $\mu + 3\sigma$. The threshold of two IP whose frequency distribution are showed in Figure 3(b) are calculated as $453.8(65.9 + 3 \times 129.3)$.

Take the IP which shows the frequency distribution in Figure 3(b) as a example. Three are 1586 access records from this IP address. We do the session identification step to these logs using our proposed method together with traditional uniform threshold method.

For our time interval based methods, we separate sessions when time interval is larger than the threshold 453.8 seconds that calculated above. Then the access serial can be divided into 27 sessions. The duration of sessions varies from 60 seconds to 12361 seconds. In Table 2, we list part of the accesses in a span of time, the column of "#" is added by the author for convenience. Using our method, the session can be separated between record 2nd and 3rd, and between 112th and 113th, so this segment of logs can be separated into 3 sessions. It is proper in our intuition.

If the traditional uniform threshold are adopted, a fixed threshold are used to divide session, things may be different. For example, truncate sessions when 30 minutes arrived, all the logs from the IP are divided into 69 sessions. And the logs in Table 2 are divided into 6 sessions, the breakpoint are record 3rd, 30th, 61st, 86th and 113th respectively. Obviously, this separation is reasonless, one serial of access are interrupt into pieces.

Table 2. Sample of logs for session identification

#	Date	Time	IP	Web page
1	10/04/2001	12:05:11	66.77.74.212	/12-gwcy/index.asp
2	10/04/2001	12:06:47	66.77.74.212	/23-dfly/index.asp
3	10/04/2001	18:00:42	66.77.74.212	/ziliao/ztjj/lyuxcs-7.asp
4	10/04/2001	18:02:47	66.77.74.212	/23-dfly/2j/gd.asp
	...	...	...	...
29	10/04/2001	18:30:33	66.77.74.212	/22-zcfg/dfly.asp
30	10/04/2001	18:31:33	66.77.74.212	/21-wxzw/2j/zxq-1.asp
	...	...	...	...
60	10/04/2001	19:00:36	66.77.74.212	/ziliao/zlk/2000gn100q.asp
61	10/04/2001	19:01:35	66.77.74.212	/30-bkzz/jianjie.asp
	...	...	...	...
85	10/04/2001	19:30:54	66.77.74.212	/HTML/point/whyc.htm
86	10/04/2001	19:31:54	66.77.74.212	/23-dfly/2j/sh.asp
	...	...	...	...
111	10/04/2001	19:58:56	66.77.74.212	/ziliao/lyjjyj/50.asp
112	10/04/2001	19:59:59	66.77.74.212	/31-lysd/fs.asp
113	10/05/2001	2:16:17	66.77.74.212	/12-gwcy/shopping/m_hebei.htm
114	10/05/2001	2:17:36	66.77.74.212	/ziliao/zlk/lxcywnj7.asp

5.   CONCLUSION

In this paper, we propose a new method based on analysis of time intervals to do session identification. We separate sessions when the time interval is larger than a given threshold, which can be calculated by analyzing the features of accesses of individual IP addresses. It is different from traditional method that defines uniform threshold based on experiences.

We first calculate the time intervals of page views for each IP, and then count frequencies for each interval and obtained frequency vector for each IP. Some IPs show stable features in frequency distributions of time intervals, and they can be deemed as single users. On this condition, we can calculate threshold for each individual IP, and separate sessions at special points, where the access time interval is larger than the threshold.

For IPs used by many users, a large amount of accesses are often appeared simultaneously. The time intervals are spited into pieces. For these kinds of IP, assistant technologies are needed to identify users. The method proposed in this paper for session identification is not proper.

REFERENCES

1.   R.Kosala and H.Blockeel. Web mining research: a survey, *ACM, SIGKDD*, 2000.
2.   SoftwareInc. Webtrends. http://www.webtrends.com,1995.
3.   OpenMarketInc. OpenmarketWebreporter. http://www.openmarket.com,1996.
4.   NetGenesisCorp. Netanalysisdesktop. http://www.netgen.com,1996.
5.   J.Srivastava, R.Cooley, M.Dehpande, and P.N.Tan. Web usage mining: Discovery and applications of usage pattern from web data. *SIGKDD Explorations*, 1(2), 2000.
6.   M.S.Chen, J.S.Park, P.S.Yu. Data mining For Path traversal patterns in a Web environment. *In:Pro cof the16th Int'l Confon Distributed Computing Systems*, HongKong,1996.
7.   O.R.Zaiane, M.Xin, and J.Han. Discovering Web access patterns and trends by applying OLAP and datamining technology on Weblogs. *In:ProcofAdvances in Digital Libraries Conf. Santa Barbara*, CA,19-29,1998.
8.   R.Cooley, B.Mobasher, and J.Srivastava, Data preparation for mining world wide web browsing patterns. *Knowledge and Information Systems*, 1(1), 1999.
9.   P.Pirolli, J.Pitkow, and R.Rao. Silk from a sow's ear: Extracting usable structures from the Web. *In Proc. Of 1996 conference on Human Factors in Computing Systems (CHI-96)*, Vancouver, British Columbia, Canada, 1996.
10. http://www.cnta.com
11. Q.Chen, H.Chang, R.Govindan, etc. The Origin of Power Laws in Internet Topologies Revisited, *Proc. of IEEE Infocom*, 2002.
12. B.A.Huberman and L.A.Adamic, The nature of markets in the World Wide Web, *Quarterly Journal of Economic Commerce*, 1():5-12, 2000

EFFICIENTLY MINING FREQUENT ITEMSETS WITH COMPACT FP-TREE

QIN Liang-Xi [1, 2, 3], LUO Ping [1, 2] and SHI Zhong-Zhi [1]
[1] (Key Lab of Intelligent Information Processing, Institute of Computing Technology, Chinese Academy of Sciences, Beijing 100080)

[2] (Graduate School of Chinese Academy of Sciences, Beijing 100039)

[3] (College of Computer and Information Engineering, Guangxi University, Nanning 530004)

e-mail:{qinlx, luop, shizz}@ics.ict.ac.cn

Abstract: FP-growth algorithm is an efficient algorithm for mining frequent patterns. It scans database only twice and does not need to generate and test the candidate sets that is quite time consuming. The efficiency of the FP-growth algorithm outperforms previously developed algorithms. But, it must recursively generate huge number of conditional FP-trees that requires much more memory and costs more time.

In this paper, we present an algorithm, CFPmine, that is inspired by several previous works. CFPmine algorithm combines several advantages of existing techniques. One is using constrained subtrees of a compact FP-tree to mine frequent pattern, so that it is doesn't need to construct conditional FP-trees in the mining process. Second is using an array-based technique to reduce the traverse time to the CFP-tree. And an unified memeory management is also implemented in the algorithm. The experimental evaluation shows that CFPmine algorithm is a high performance algorithm. It outperforms Apriori, Eclat and FP-growth and requires less memory than FP-growth.

Key words: association rule; frequent patterns; compact FP-tree

1.   INTRODUCTION

Since the association rule mining problem was introduced in [2] by Agrawal et al., finding frequent patterns is always a crucial step in association rules mining. In addition to association rules, frequent pattern is also used in mining correlations, causality, sequential patterns, episodes, multidimensional patterns, maximal patterns, partial periodicity, emerging patterns and many other important data mining tasks. So, the efficiency of a frequent pattern mining approach has a great influence to the performance of the algorithms used in these data mining tasks. The following is a formal statement of frequent patterns (or itemsets) mining problem:

Let $I = \{i_1, i_2, ..., i_m\}$ be a set of literals, called items. Let database D be a set of transactions, where each transaction T is a set of items such that $T \subseteq I$. Each transaction has a unique identifier, TID. Let X be a set of items. A transaction T is said to contain X if and only if $X \subseteq T$. The support of a itemset X is the probability of transactions in database D that contain X. X is frequent if the support of X is no less than a user defined support threshold. We are interested in finding the complete frequent itemsets.

Agrawal, et al presented Apriori algorithm in [3], in which a prior knowledge about frequent itemsets was used. The prior knowledge is that if an itemset is not frequent, then all of its supersets can never be frequent. Most of previous studies adopted an Apriori-like candidate set generation-and-test approach, such as DHP algorithm[8], Partition algorithm[9], Sampling algorithm[10] and DIC algorithm[4]. The Apriori-like algorithms suffer two problems: (1) It is costly to generate huge number of candidate sets for long patterns. (2) It is quite time consuming to repeatedly scan the database to count the support of candidate itemsets to decide which one is a frequent pattern.

Zaki et al. presented Eclat Algorithm in [11], in which they use an itemset clustering technique, efficient lattice traverse technique and vertical database layout in the mining process. Agarwal et al. proposed TreeProjection algorithm in [1], in which they represent itemsets as nodes of a lexicographic tree and use matrices to count the support of frequent itemsets. Han, et al, developed the FP-growth algorithm [7] that is based on frequent pattern tree. This algorithm avoids time consuming operations such as repeated database scans and generation of candidate set. The efficiency of the FP-growth algorithm is about an order of magnitude faster than the Apriori algorithm and outperforms TreeProjection algorithm. But, there still exist some aspects in FP-growth algorithm that can be improved. For example, it needs to recursively generate huge number of conditional FP-trees that consumes much more memory and more time. It has appeared several improved FP-growth algorithms based on original one. Fan and Li [5] presented a constrained subtree based approach to avoid the generation of huge number of conditional FP-trees recursively in the mining process. They also reduced the fields in each FP-tree node. Their approach has better time and space scalability than FP-growth algorithm. Grahne and Zhu [6] proposed an array-based technique to reduce the time cost in FP-tree traverse. They also implemented their own memory management for allocating and deallocating tree nodes.

In this work, we adopts several advanced techniques which is inspired by [5] and [6]. One is using constrained subtrees of a compact FP-tree(CFP-tree) in the mining process, so that it doesn't need to construct conditional FP-trees. Second is using an array-based technique to reduce the traverse time to CFP-tree.

The remaining of the paper is organized as follows. The detailed description of CFP-tree based approach is given in Section 2. The CFP-tree mining algorithm is described in Section 3. In Section 4, we will give the experimental results. And in Section 5, we will give our conclusion and the idea about our future work.

2. COMPACT FP-TREE AND ITS CONSTRUCTION

The FP-growth algorithm [7] uses a data structure called the FP-tree. The FP-tree is a compact representation of frequency information in a transaction database. There are 6 fields in a FP-tree node. They are item-name, count, parent-link, child-link, sibling-link and next-link (a pointer to next node that has same item-name). However, child-link and sibling-link are only used in the FP-tree constructing process, parent-link and next-link are only used in the mining process. So we can reduce the number of fields by joining child-link with parent-link as cp-link which is first pointing to its child-node and after construction pointing to its parent node, and joining sibling-link with next-link as sn-link which is first pointing to its sibling-node and finally pointing to next node.

The compact FP-tree (CFP-tree) has similar structure as FP-tree. They also have several differences:

(1) Each node in CFP-tree has 4 fields, item-no (which is the sequential number of an item in frequent 1-itemsets according frequency descending order), count, cp-link and sn-link. Therefore, CFP-tree requires only 2/3 memory spaces of FP-tree.

(2) FP-tree is bi-directional, but CFP-tree is single directional. After the construction, CFP-tree only exists paths from leaves to the root.

The CFP-tree is constructed as follows.

Algorithm 1. (CFP-tree construction)

Input: A transaction database DB and support threshold minsup.

Output: Its CFP-tree.

Method: CFP-tree is constructed in following steps.

(1) Scan the transaction database DB once. Collect the set of frequent items F and their supports. Sort F in support descending order as L, the list of frequent items.

(2) Create the root of an FP-tree, T, and label it as "null". For each transaction in DB do the following.
Select the frequent items and replace them with their order in L, and sort them as Is. Let the sorted Is be [p|P], where p is the first element and P is the remaining list. Call insert tree([p|P], T).

The function of insert_tree(p|P, T) is performed as follows.

(1) If T has no child or can not find a child which its item-no=p, then create a new node N. N.item-no=p, N.count=1, N.cp-link=T; Insert N before the first node which item-no is greater than p.
If T has a child N such that N.item-no=p, then increment N.count by 1.

(2) If P is not empty, then call insert_tree(P, N) recursively.

After the construction of CFP-tree, we should change the sn-link from sibling-link to next-link and reverse the cp-link. The processing procedure is as follows: Traverse the tree from the root. Add current node CN to the link of header[CN.item-no] as the last node. If CN has no child or all of its children and siblings have been processed then let CN.cp-link=CN's parent, else process its children and its siblings recursively.

Figure 1 (a) shows an example of a database and Figure 1 (b) is the CFP-tree for that database.

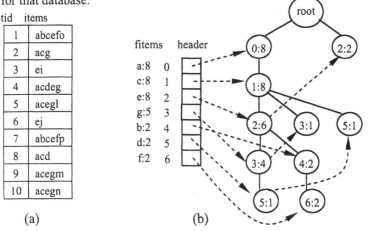

(a)   (b)

Figure 1.   An Example of CFP-tree (minsup=20%)

3.   CFP-TREE BASED MINING ALGORITHM

In the mining process, FP-growth algorithm must recursively generate huge number of conditional FP-trees that requires much more memory and costs more time. In [5], an approach that needn't to generate conditional FP-trees is proposed. It uses constrained subtrees to mine frequent pattern directly.

3.1   Constrained subtree

Definition 1. The semi-order relation "$\prec$" of two patterns (itemsets) is defined as follows: Let $\{a_1, a_2,..., a_m\}$ and $\{b_1, b_2,..., b_n\}$ be two patterns. $\{a_1, a_2,..., a_m\} \prec \{b_1, b_2,..., b_n\}$ if and only if exist $1 \leq i \leq \min(m,n)$, while $1 \leq j < i$, $a_j = b_j$, and $a_i \prec b_i$; or while $1 \leq j \leq m$, $a_j = b_j$, and $m < n$.

Definition 2. Let $i_1 \prec i_2 \prec ... \prec i_k$ be item orders. N is a node in the CFP-tree. P is a sub-path from root to N. We say P is constrained by the itemset $\{i_1, i_2,..., i_k\}$, if exist a N's descendant node M, such that $i_1, i_2,..., i_k$ appear in the sub-path from N to M, and i_1 is the item-no of N's child, i_k = M.item-no. N is called end node of sub-path P. Node M's count c is called the base count of constrained sub-path P.

Definition 3. In a CFP-tree, all of the sub-path constrained by itemset $\{i_1, i_2,..., i_k\}$ make up of a subtree, it is called a subtree constrained by $\{i_1, i_2,..., i_k\}$, nominated as ST($i_k,..., i_2, i_1$).

ST($i_k,..., i_2, i_1$) can be represented by an array, let it be EndArray, that every element of it has two fields: end-ptr (point to the end node) and base-count(store the base count of the constrained sub-path). The frequent items and count of ST($i_k,..., i_2, i_1$) can be represented by ST($i_k,..., i_2, i_1$).fitem[] and ST($i_k,..., i_2, i_1$).count[] respectively.

Figure 2 shows the constrained subtree ST(3) of the CFP-tree in Figure 1 (b).

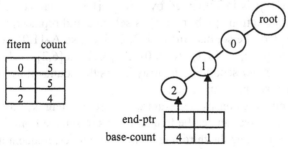

fitem	count
0	5
1	5
2	4

Figure 2. The constrained subtree ST(3)

3.2   An array technique

The main work done in the mining process of constrained subtree-based approach is recursively traversing a constrained subtree and generate a new subtree. For each frequent item k in constrained subtree ST(X), two traverses of ST(X) are needed for generate frequent items and counts of ST(X, k). Can the traversal time be reduced? In [6], an array-based technique was proposed to reduce the traversal time, this technique just supplies a gap of [5]. The following example will explain the idea. In Figure 3 (a), A_Φ is generated from database in Figure 1 (a) while building CFP-tree. Let the minimum support is 20%, after first scan of the database, we sort the frequent items as {a:8, c:8, e:8, g:5, b:2, d:2, f:2}. Let the itemset in support descending order be F1 (let the order of first item be 0).

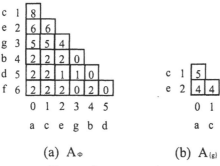

(a) A_Φ (b) $A_{\{g\}}$

Figure 3.   Two array examples

In A_Φ, each cell is a counter of a 2-itemset. Because c's order is 1, a's order is 0, cell $A_\Phi[1, 0]$ is the counter for itemset {c, a}, and so forth. During the second scan, the frequent items in each transaction are selected and replaced with their order in F1. Sort them as Is. When we insert Is into CFP-tree, at the same time $A_\Phi[i, j]$ is incremented by 1 if {i, j} is contained in Is. For example, the first transaction, {a, b, c, e, f} is selected and replaced with {0, 4, 1, 2, 6}. After sorted, the set becomes {0, 1, 2, 4, 6}, so $A_\Phi[1,0]$, $A_\Phi[2,0]$, $A_\Phi[2,1]$, $A_\Phi[4,0]$, $A_\Phi[4,1]$, $A_\Phi[4,2]$, $A_\Phi[6,0]$, $A_\Phi[6,1]$, $A_\Phi[6,2]$, $A_\Phi[6,4]$ are all incremented by 1. After second scan, array keeps the counts of all pairs of frequent items, as shown in Figure 2 (a).

While generating the constrained subtree of some item k, instead of traversing CFP-tree, now we can get the frequent items of subtree from the array A_Φ. For example, by checking the third line in the table for A_Φ, frequent items a, c, e and their counts can be obtained from g's constrained subtree ST(2).

It is just the same as CFP-tree, during the generation of a new constrained subtree ST(X, k), the array $A_{X \cup \{k\}}$ is filled. For example, the cells of array $A_{\{g\}}$ is shown in Figure 2 (b).

3.3   CFPmine Algorithm

From the analysis of above, we can give a new algorithm CFPmine based on constrained subtree and array-based technique. The following is the pseudocode of CFPmine. CFPmine is a main procedure, it output frequent 1-itemset and generate constrained subtree that has only one constraint item, then call mine procedure to generate frequent itemsets that have more than one item. The most work of mining is done by mine procedure.

Procedure CFPmine(T)
Input: A CFP-tree T
Output: The complete set of FI's corresponding to T
Method:
(1) patlen=1;
(2) for (k=flen-1; k>=0; k--) { // flen is the length of frequent itemset
(3)   pat[0]=fitem[k];
(4)   output { pat[0]} with support count[k];
(5)   generate ST(k).EndArray[];
(6)   mine(ST(k));
     }

Procedure mine(ST(i_k,...,i_2,i_1))
{
(1) generate ST(i_k,...,i_2,i_1).fitem[] and ST(i_k,...,i_2,i_1).count[], let the length be listlen;
(2) if (listlen==0) then return;
(3) if (listlen==1) then {pat[patlen]= ST(i_k,...,i_2,i_1).fitem[0];
          output pat with support ST(i_k,...,i_2,i_1).count[0]; return}
(4) if ST(i_k,...,i_2,i_1) has only single path then
        { output pat ∪ all the combination of ST(i_k,...,i_2,i_1).fitem[];
         return; }
(5) patlen++;
(6) for (k=listlen-1; k>=0; k--) {
(7)   generate array;
(8)   generate ST(i_k,...,i_2,i_1,k).EndArray[];
(9)   if ST(i_k,...,i_2,i_1,k).EndArray[] is not NULL then
            mine(ST(i_k,...,i_2,i_1,k));
(10)}
(11) patlen--;
}

In mine procedure, line 1 generate frequent itemset in the constrained subtree $ST(i_k,...,i_2,i_1)$. Line 2~3 process the condition while listlen is 0 or 1. Line 4 process the condition while constrained subtree has only single path. Line 6~10 generate new array and constrained subtree, then mine the new subtree.

Because the CFP-tree could have millions of nodes, thus, it takes plenty of time for allocating and deallocating the nodes. Just like [6], we also implement unified memory management for CFPmine algorithm. In the recursively mining process, the memory used in it is not frequently allocated and freed. It allocating a large chunk before the first recursion, and when a recursion ends, it doesn't really free the memory, only changes the available size of chunk. If the chunk is used up, it allocates more memory. And it frees the memory only when all the recursions have been finished.

4.   EXPERIMENTAL EVALUATION

In this section, we present a performance comparison of CFPmine algorithm with Apriori, Eclat and FP-growth. The experiments were done on 1Ghz Pentium III PC with 384MB main memery, running Windows 2000 professional.The source codes of Apriori and Eclat are provided by Christian Borgelt [12]. Thereinto, Apriori algorithm uses many optimizing techniques to improve the efficiency, such as it doesn't scan the database for many times and it uses a transaction tree to count the support of candidate sets. So, the Apiori here is much faster than the original one. The source code of FP-growth is provided by Bart Goethals [13]. All of these three algorithms are run in Cygwin environment. CFPmine algorithm is coded in Microsoft Visual C++ 6.0. All the times in the Figures refer to the running time from read data to the frequent patterns have been mined, but excluding the result writing time.

We ran all algorithms on two datasets. T25I20D100K, a synthetic dataset, is from IBM Almaden Research Center [14]. It has 100k transactions, 10k different items, and the average transaction length is 25. Connect-4 is a dense dataset. It is from UCI Machine Learning Repository [15]. It has 67557 transactions, 130 different items, and the average transaction length is 43. All of the algorithms get the same frequent itemsets for the same dataset under the same minimum support threshold.

Figure 4 gives the running time of the four algorithms on dataset T25I20D100K. It shows the performance is that CFPmine ≻ Apriori ≻ FP-growth ≻ Eclat. Thereinto, CFPmine is above five times faster than FP-growth. Figure 5 gives the running time of the four algorithms on dataset Connect-4 (The time plots in Figure 5 are on a logarithmic scale). It shows the performance is that CFPmine ≻ FP-growth ≻ Eclat ≻ Apriori (while support > 65%, Apriori ≻ Eclat). Thereinto, CFPmine is a magnitude faster than FP-growth.

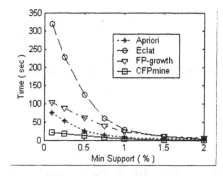
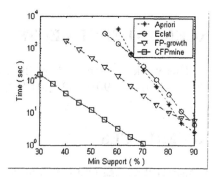

Figure 4. [Running time on T25I20D100K]   *Figure 5.* [Running time on Connect-4]

Discussion: From the figures, we can see that CFPmine is the most efficient algorithm in four algorithms. It also shows that the techniques used in CFPmine is effective. CFPmine algorithm has higher performance than FP-growth on the scale of either time or space. Apriori, Eclat and FP-growth have different efficiency on different dataset. It is because that: (1) The characters of two datasets is different. T25I20D100K is a sparse dataset, and Connect-4 is a dense dataset. (2) Each algorithm takes different data structure and mining strategy. The optimized Apriori is more efficient than FP-growth on sparse dataset, but FP-growth is more efficient than Apriori on dense dataset. It is because that Apriori uses a breadth-first strategy in the mining process, when the dataset is dense, the number of combinations grows fast makes it become less efficient. But the high compressed tree structure and the divide-and-conquer strategy make CFPmine and FP-growth efficient on dense datasets. Eclat uses a vertical representation of dataset. It is low performance on sparse dataset, and is relatively efficient only while the dataset is dense and has little items.

5.   CONCLUSIONS

We have introduced a new algorithm, CFPmine. It is inspired by several previous works. CFPmine algorithm combines several advantages of existing techniques. One is using constrained subtrees of a compact FP-tree to mine frequent pattern, so that it is doesn't need to construct conditional FP-trees in the mining process. Second is using an array-based technique to reduce the traverse time to the CFP-tree. And an unified memeory management is also implemented in the algorithm. The experimental evaluation shows that CFPmine algorithm is a high performance algorithm. It outperforms Apriori, Eclat and FP-growth and requires less memory than FP-growth.

ACKNOWLEDGEMENTS

This work is supported by the National Natural Science Foundation of China.(Grant No. 90104021,60173017)

REFERENCES

1. Agarwal R C, Aggarwal C C, and Prasad V V V. A Tree Projection Algorithm for Generation of Frequent Itemsets. Journal of Parallel and Distributed Computing, 2001.
2. Agrawal R, Imielinski T, Swami A. Mining association rules between sets of items in large database. In Proc of 1993 ACM SIGMOD Conf on Management of Data, 207~216, Washington DC, May 1993.
3. Agrawal R, Srikant R. Fast algorithms for mining association rules. In Proc of the 20th Int'l Conf on Very Large DataBases (VLDB'94). 487~499. Santiago, Chile, Sept. 1994.
4. Brin S, Motwani R, Ullman J D, and Tsur S. Dynamic itemset counting and implication rules for market basket data. In *SIGMOD Record (ACM Special Interest Group on Management of Data)*, 26(2):255, 1997
5. FAN Ming, LI Chuan. Mining frequent patterns in an FP-tree without conditional FP-tree generation(In Chinese). Journal of computer research and development, 40(8):1216~1222. 2003.
6. Grahne G, Zhu J. Efficiently using prefix-trees in mining frequent itemsets. In: First Workshop on Frequent Itemset Mining Implementation (FIMI'03). Melbourne, FL
7. Han J, Pei J, and Yin Y. Mining Frequent Patterns without Candidate Generation. In Proc of 2000 ACM-SIGMOD Int'l Conf on Management of Data (SIGMOD'00). 1~12. Dallas, TX, 2000.
8. Park J S, Chen M-S and Yu P S. An Effective Hash-based Algorithm for Mining Association Rules. In: Proc of 1995 ACM-SIGMOD int'l Conf on Management of Data (SIGMOD'95). San Jose, CA, 1995. 175~186.
9. Savasere A, Omiecinski E, Navathe S. An efficient Algorithm for Mining Association Rules in Large Databases, In Proc of 21st Int'l Conf on Very Large Databases (VLDB'95), pages 432~443. Zurich, Switzerland, Sept. 1995.
10. Toivonen H. Sampling Large Databases for Association Rules. In Proc of 22nd Int'l Conf on Very Large Databases (VLDB'96). pages134~145. Bombay, India, Sept. 1996.
11. Zaki M, Parthasarathy S, Ogihara M, and Li W. New algorithms for fast discovery of association rules. In Heckerman D, Mannila H, Pregibon D, and Uthurusamy R eds, Proc of the Third International Conference on Knowledge Discovery and Data Mining (KDD-97), page 283. AAAI Press, 1997. http://citeseer.ist.psu.edu/zaki97new.html
12. http://fuzzy.cs.uni-magdeburg.de/~borgelt/
13. http://www.cs.helsinki.fi/u/goethals/
14. http://www.almaden.ibm.com/software quest/Resources/datasets/syndata.html
15. http://www.ics.uci.edu/~mlearn/MLRepository.html

TOWARDS HUMAN ORIENTED WWW

Alex Abramovich

Hazionut 38/13, Haifa, 35312,Israel,10 Devikarumariamman second street, vijayanagar, velachery,chennai 600 042

Abstract: The ultimate aim of computer science is to assist humans with reasoning, decision-making and chores for their profession/living everyday complex problem solving. In other words, the target state of human-machine symbiosis is characterized by using a machine as a personal intellectual assistant. A principal impediment consists in the multi-disciplinary nature of the profession/living human activity. A customer, as a rule, is not a specialist in all related domains. This implies that an achievement of the posed problem is a providing a personal intellectual assistant with the multi-disciplinary knowledge. This paper deals with an approach to the problem via Web extension that contains Total Human Experience (THE Web).

Key words: Human experience, ontology, activity proposition, personal world, domain world

1.   INTRODUCTION

Without regard to the biochemical ground of human brain functioning note that human reasoning accompanies the physical/mental human activities and is an activity itself. Such as it provides an achievement of current activity as well as operates on the set of related activities and activities' states. In this connection human has to be aware of both his current activity and all related/influenced activities. Thereby he must operate of activities' knowledge.

Reasoning as human activity is executed in the following modes by a generation of executive directives or/and by calling the service providers:

- Recognition of an activity initialization's necessity (that is, a latchup of an activity as a component of cause-and-effect relations)
- Recognition of an activity initialization's availability (that is, a latchup of constituents of an activity initialization's conditions)
- An acquisition of missing data/knowledge including also a probability of the problems solution generation on basis of corresponding cause-and-effect relations
- A maintenance of an activity steps' execution
- A maintenance of an activity living conditions' protection. This implies an activity related KR standpoint, namely,
- It exists a knowledge, that is a system of socio/physical/mental causal relationships' representation, where every node is causality in a M.Bunge definition [15] (that is, a permanent and mono-semantic production) represented by generalized executive plan (Activity Proposition (see below))
- Semantics of causality as well as an activity component's is function of its position in causalities system or in Activity Proposition correspondingly
- Meaning of knowledge component is a representation of goal suitable available resource.

The present paper is based on the above-mentioned standpoint.

We will consider only verbalized experience. Verbalization practice, undoubtedly, is one of the most ancient human activities.

Multi-millennial endeavor of thought expression brought to beginnings of different languages under different grammars that, in turn, determine how the conceptual structures are linearized as strings of words in a sentence. In spite of all differences it exist 3 approach of the linearization [9], namely, SVO (English and Chinese, for example), VSO (Irish and Biblical Hebrew, for example) and SOV (Latin and Japanese, for example), where S is a subject, V is a verb, and O is an object.

Judging from this, *the basis human word usage's trend is an activity representation.* Generally speaking, an activity is a corresponding experience's knowledge utilization. Activities' execution is an origin of problems. Problems' solving generates a novel knowledge. A multifold physical or mental (both successful and failed) execution of activities constitutes a Total Human Experience (THE).

Thus, we dispose, at least, of one a proven THE representation approach (that is, a verbal approach). Note that THE is represented also by various materialized forms.

We hold an interest in Web representation of THE (THE Web).

It is naturally to assume that Web KR inherits from the existing forms of an experience representation. However, we don't see it in practice. Existing

Web knowledge-, ontology-, semantics-, reasoning-, decision-making-representation approaches are not related

directly with a verbal practice of activities representation. Existing Web KR approaches utilize the formal methods and languages that grounded by various world models, generative interoperability/reuse issues.

In lieu of formal methods THE Web applies a semantic marking of natural language sentences.

2.   ACTIVITY PROPOSITION

Note that man-Web symbiosis' interface aimed to both target setting in form of queries, requirements, situations' declarations, goal declarations as well as answers in form of quantitative/qualitative information. Thereby, the interface's lexicon is narrowed by framework of Web visitor's activities. To Sowa "The lexicon is the bridge between a language and the knowledge expressed in that language" [9]. We will take liberties with this formula. *The lexicon is the bridge between knowledge, expressed in the language, and the activity execution.* Lexicon consists of words and idioms. The words represent subjects, verbs, objects, auxiliary words, pronouns, interrogative words, etc. Part of lexicon is easy recognizable basic vocabulary (semantically lucid). A residuary (major) part depends on the context. We take an interest in the second part that represents a difficulty for the standard parsers.

Standard parsers are not context specified.

How is it possible an orienting of parser to the current context?

The current context's awareness gives rise to the binding words with meanings. Since semantics is, in general, the study of the relationship between words and meanings [10], the current context is utilized as input of the semantic analysis. The current context of communication is specified by the operating activities. So the target settings' as well as the answers' lexicon consists of activities related vocabulary (a contextual lexicon). As activities belong to the certain domains, the contextual lexicon belongs to the domain ontology.

On condition that, an intercourse's participants are the operating activities aware, it is possible to adequately interpret and to respond to input/output text.

Therefore THE Web intercourse must be anticipated by an agreement on all operating or desirable set of activities as well as about accompanying lexicon (that is, professional/living ontology).

3.   AN AGREEMENT OF ACTIVITIES

Granting requirement that THE Web must be available for everybody, it is necessary to keep in mind the following key features of system design by Everyman [11]:

- There is no a priori personal THE Web service to be built.
- Everyman ("end-user" who is not computer expert), as a rule, agrees at the most than to alter associations among participating components in the dynamic conditions and/or else to intercommunicate on the natural language.
- "The large majority of users cannot—and do not want to—be engaged in any kind of "programming" other than simple scripting. However, they *are* able to assemble components together by "wiring" them. This means that components should provide encapsulated chunks of behavior in the form of "probes" for structural coupling with other components, and the supporting environment should provide the means for "translating" the structural inter-component relationships to overall microworld behavior [12,13]".

THE Web agreement on activities is based on foregoing features, and lies in

- an assemblage by user and a fitting of separate actions for achievement of personal objectives
- an updating by user the existing service providing architectures by removing and/or insertion suitable functional components that are represented according to text or by sight
- a target setting by user in the form of what is given and of what is need or in the form of what is given only or in the form of what is need only
- an activity description by user as a context marking (in the network of a facilitating interface)

During an activity structure agreement THE Web engine must

- to submit a basis activity ontology to user approval (in that way THE Web engine learns user lexicon)
- to generate an activity description as a semantic marking sentence in IO-SV-TO form, where IO-SV-TO is an activity's Initial Objects (as a cause's conditions), Subject and Verbs (as a cause) and Target Objects (as an effect) accordingly
- to generate an activity's semantic assurance network, inclusive of cause-and-effect relations that join an activity's components.

4.   CONTEXT MARKING

Context marking of an activity's description sentence fixes the contribution of an activity's components to the activity's goals achievement. The marking is distributed into three groups, namely,

- Objectives
- Subject
- Verbs.
  THE Web allows denominating
- Objectives of place conditions, of time conditions, of facts presence, of actions presence, of goal conditions and other conditions under titles "On condition that" and "With the view of ".
- Subjects under titles "Main actor" and "Execute"
- Verbs under titles "Execute" and "programme".
  Current activity determination starts from a correlation the basis generic domain activity's proposition with private needs.

Example 1. Generic Activity proposition of *building construction*

On condition that:

Where : *place of the building according to the project documentation*

When : **period** : *contract period*

by direction of : *project documentation*

With the view of : *an achievement of a design statement*

Main actor: organization : *Building Contractor*

Execute : *building construction* :

Programme :

It's given : *project documentation*

Do :

[(*foundation, water-supply, power supply, sewerage system*),

For 1 **to** *the "number of floors according to the project documentation"* **by step** 1

Do : *floor, ceiling*],

Do : (*scavenging, finishing, planting of greenery*),

where "[]" holds a sequence of activities, and "()" holds activities that are executed at the same time.

First of all it inserts a name of Building Contractor and data from project documentation. After that it is necessary to correlate all included activities, namely, foundation building, water-supply building, power supply wiring, etc. A word's record under different context marks involves it different utilizations. Since a usage's context is determinate by an activity proposition, the chief task is a detection of operating activity. Discovered context launches the new perspectives in the

Nature Language Understanding area.

5.   TOWARDS A NATURAL LANGUAGE UNDERSTANDING BY MEANS OF CONTEXT MARKING

An orientation of European Commission and other interested parties to the Web personalized computing service for Everyman sets with a new force a problem of Natural Language Understanding (NLU).

Typographical method of text marking was served as conceptual model for Web mark-up languages' developers. But human intercourse doesn't reduce to an exchange of documents. Therefore existing mark-up languages are rough tools for maintenance of Web-user nature language interface. According to M. Polanyi [1], the components of an optimally organized system must not be further partible in the certain, defined for this system, ratio.

M. Polanyi made out of a system's components at a ratio of their contributions to the goal achievement. A component's position in the system's organization defines its semantics.

Its contribution defines a meaning of the component. NLU lies in the recognition of semantics and meaning of propositions.

Following M. Polanyi, it is necessary to be aware of interlocutors' goals or a reader's and text's goals or user's and software's goals.

This implies that NLU is characterized by a presence of two parties, and we must be acquainted with both parties of the NLU process.

In the focus of our attention is an establishment of an interaction between Web user and THE via AmI [2,3] technology .

"The concept of Ambient Intelligence (AmI) provides a vision of the Information Society where the emphasis is on greater userfriendliness, more efficient services support, user-empowerment, and support for human interactions. People are surrounded by intelligent intuitive interfaces that are embedded in all kinds of objects and an environment that is capable of recognizing and

responding to the presence of different individuals in a seamless, unobtrusive and often invisible way." Taken from the ISTAG scenarios document (see ftp://ftp.cordis.lu/pub/ist/docs/istagscenarios2010.pdf)

AmI-engine presupposes a presence of following features:

- A mobility and an ubiquity;
- An autonomic computing;
- An availability for Everyman;
- A personalization.

Realization of these features is possible on conditions that AmI-engine is aware of AmI's owner activities' models including these activities' domains of existence. At that *a personalization* for Everyman implies an intercourse on the natural language as well as

an autonomic computing implies a necessity of self-maintained information acquisition including from texts.

Thus, AmI-engine causes NLU parties awareness that grounds an opportunity of NLU carrying out. At that an opposition of two extremes on the semantics-based spectrum (that is, R. Montague's formalism and R. Schank's lack of a precise formalism [9]) is solved via Activity Propositions by a strict presentation of word usage context, on the one hand, and

by multiplicity of such presentations, on the other hand.

5.1   Semantics of Activity Proposition

From an infinite set of eventual word usage contexts it is necessary to find contexts that defined the generic words' semantics. Such contexts are both physical and mental generic activities' descriptions (activities propositions), where a generic activity is domain's constitutive activity.

A strict of generic activity proposition is caused by its an optimal organization that is verified by scientific (that is, by means formalisms) and by an experiment way.

Every name's semantics depends on its syntactic position in an operating generic activity's proposition, with inherits syntactic rules of a compound sentence.

Could say that Activity Proposition represents a semantic (in Polanyi sense) name space's sharing (Activity's Ontology (AO)).

For every AO it is fixed the name list that represents an activity's foundation_architecture. A presence of this, so called,

MinContext indicates an occurrence of a corresponding activity.

Word semantics' understanding comes to recognition in the ambient name space a MinContext of an operating domain generic activity's application (OPERA).

5.2   MinContexts' relatedness

Since a main problem consists in an acquisition of operating activities, MinContext's recognition is a simple FOL based procedure. It is possible utilizing of MinContext procedure both together with syntactic/morphological analysis and as detached mode. As result of the detached mode will be a resume about the text's semantic activity related content.

MinContext procedure, applied together with syntactic/morphological analysis, will results a semantically verified text translation.

MinContext procedure realizes also a lexical analysis, aimed for an acquisition of activity utilization specificity as well as level of executer proficiency and his personal identification.

OPERA detection implies both its formative activities and related activities, namely:

AmI related (*self-controlled*) activities and

External related activities.

AmI related activities (by THE Web notation) are the following:

Aexe(name) aimed to the achievement of OPERA's goals;

Repair(name) aimed to the restoration of lost functions and an overcoming of an operational problems as well as to the modernization of an operational structure;

Learning(name) aimed to the acquisition a new constructive knowledge for OPERA life support related;

Protection(name) aimed to protection OPERA from a destructive influence of both internal and external environment;

Provision(name) aimed to the maintenance of the no-break supply of OPERA execution by deliverables as well as by components and data;

Selling(name) aimed to the realization (or to the utilization) of OPERA results;

Direction(name) aimed to an organization of OPERA effective accomplishment,

where *name* is name of OPERA. This set of internal related activities is derived by AmI-engine from AmI's set of rooted activities (*AmI-root*). To THE Web notation AmI-root is invariant for customer support outside the dependence on the customer's type (that is, a government, an enterprise, professional and other communities, domain expert or Everyman).

Note that *AmI* related activities constitute an intelligence environment aimed to maintenance of OPERA's life cycle. THE Web builds an environment one as *a multi-agent system* (AmI-mas) under FIPA. AmI-mas based sharing of intellectual function together with AP representation standard as well as common AmI-root ontology ground systematization and regulating of FIPA

supported communicative acts [17]. External related activities are activities that input or output is based on the output or input of OPERA correspondingly. In other words, external related activities are activities that relate OPERA by cause-and-effect relations.

Furthermore, every state of the OPERA or OPERA related components, as a rule, are output of any activity that broadens MinContext's family.

Thereby, MinContexts of OPERA related activities pave an open-ended access to background knowledge (in Shank's sense [6]).

5.3   MinContext area

THE engine considers the following text origins: _
- Registered user (THE Web service owner, a person or organization, such as a business or an individual as well as *provider entity* (a person or organization) as well as a *requester entity* (a person or organization) [according to [16]]),
   - Unregistered user as a *requester entity* [16],
   - Software agent (*requester agent* and *provider agent* [16]),
   - Service provider as *provider entity* [16],
   - E-mail,
   - Web document.
Registered user's directives, replies, messages, queries and requirements are considered in a context of AmI run-unit and related activities. In this case MinContext area is known. Unregistered user's directives, replies, messages, queries or requirements are considered after recognition of his problem by means of namespace of *AmI-root propositions* (AmI ontology) and THE ontologybased browser (O'browser).

O'browser is aimed to the boosted THE Web's look-up. In this case discovered user's goal determines MinContext area.

An activity proposition's executor *Aexe* initiates software agents as well as service providers. Aexe is one of AmI-engine formative software agents. Its destination is an assembling of a process execution module according to the activity proposition.

With the purpose of the module filling by real meanings, Aexe invokes suitable software agents and service providers. In this case their output must fit the activity proposition context.

E-mail is considered by means of joint for a receiver and a sender activities' MinContexts.

Since Web document reading is initiated by Aexe or by AmI owner in the network of his activity performance, this implies MinContext is known.

Thus AmI-engine always deals with text that semantics belongs to known set of contexts. AmI-engine considers every current mined word as an opening or closing tag, and search a corresponding closing/opening tag in the ambient text space using initiated MinContexts as *semantic expectations* down to corroboration one of them.

Above-stated reasons indicate that THE NLU can be reduced to relatively simple rules that show what just categories of words may occur on the right or the left of a given word, and may be comparable with the Schankian expectations or the cancellation rules of categorial grammar [6].

Generic domain activity propositions causality- and AmI-related activity propositions as well as AP of domain world and AP of personal world (see below) define semantically specified ontology (Onto-surface) that grounded recognition of semantics and meaning of sentences by means utilization the ontology units as opening/closing semantic tags.

In other words, context marking of Activity Propositions (AP marking) represents both marking in the generally accepted sense (that is, by standard set of tags) and dynamic marking by AP owner's tags. Since AP operates with standard and specific sets of actions as well as with logic operations, every named AP component has its own marking, and so AP marking is n-dimensional one. Thus AP marking grounds searching of the OPERA and it's addressing.

6.   PERSONAL WORLD

Personal world (PW) is constituted by set of actual profession/living (p/l) activities as well as by knowledge of both personal and borrowed experience (that is, by knowledge of executing earlier p/l activities). Every p/l activity is correlated with others by time, by place, by power inputs and by cost. Space of correlated p/l activities is rank-ordered by AP of personal world (APpw) that

represents a scenario of parallel/sequential executable personal p/l activities, which are marked by a special set of tags. THE engine keeps *two AP special sets of AmI related semantic tags for* both enterprises and natural persons that define an activity's position in the personal world. APpw provides a semantic sharing of personal p/l activities as well as of personal p/l ontology.

Personal World Activity (PW Activity) represented by APpw is aimed to the achievement of p/l goals with cost minimization. A priority of APpw's performance produces a personal causal stipulation of person's behaviors as well as his responses to external occurrences (a personal logic). A corresponding APpw ontology has, therefore, personal semantic features.

A personal logic induces interoperability issue both on the profession and on the living level that must be considered as an operation problem both of PW management and of PWs interaction. In case that a response to an external occurrence is not contradict APpw performance it will meet expectation. If not, a response may be inadequate. In any case THE engine must model

APpw's performance subject to the response.

THE engine generates APpw on the ground both on information declared by customer and as response to his requirements.

APpw performance is achieved via personal Web portal

- By person as his p/l duties
- By person as his response to THE instructions/requirements
- By THE engine's reasonable exploitation of service providers as well as generic and personal activities (THE service).

7.   DOMAIN WORLD

Domain world is constituted by activities of professional communities, of enterprises and of specialists. THE Web engine keeps *AP special sets of AmI related semantic tags* that define a profession position of all domain world's participants. A corresponding domain world AP (APdw) provides a semantic sharing of domain activities as well as of domain ontology.

Domain world activity (DW Activity) represented by APdw is aimed to the achievement of domain socio-economic, sociopolitical and socio-productive goals with cost minimization. APdw performance is achieved via Web portal.

8.   ACTIVITY PPROPOSITION (AP) BASED SELF-OGANIZATION

Onto-surface constitutes the external level of human experience knowledge representation. Every Onto-surface's unit has a multisemantic position (AP-address) in the Activity Proposition net (AP-net) that represents set of triplets (APdwName, APName, OntoUnitName) and (APpw, APName, OntoUnitName). Recognition of MinContext in the current word's ambient determinates an actual word's AP-address.

On the other hand, every OntoUnitName relates to Web resource, containing its representation, namely, its *meaning* as well as modes of its *keeping* and its *initialization*. Note that AP represents the OntoUnit's *utilization*.

AP identification results from the text origins (see above) and from an analysis of Aexe's problems. Aexe problem indicates missing conditions for user activity support's continuation. In this case AmI-engine calls a dispatcher agent (Aforeman) that calls (depending on missing data type) one of AmI related APs. If it called Repair(name) agent, it considers the existing (an initial state) and required conditions (a goal state) as a target setting. A solution is a sequence of actions from initial state to a goal state.

As AP's internal form is represented by a causal triple (I,C,E) (where I is an initial activity's state, E is a goal state (that is, an effect), and C (cause) is a description of I's transformation to E),

A solution is a path from initial to goal nodes. The search tree starts with just the root node, which represents the initial state.

Nodes that are generated physically form a queue structure, composed of APs, that is AP too.

If Repair(name) returns a missing data, Aexe weighs anchor.

9.   THE P2P/GRID

"The term GRID refers to an emerging network based computing infrastructure providing security, resource access, information and other services that enable the controlled and coordinated sharing of resources among virtual organisations formed dynamically

by individuals and institutions with common interests " [14].

Since AP represents a scenario of an activity execution by means of activities and actions (realized by private applications, by software agents, by service providers and by other data handlers), it is a program of associated Web resource management. Thus THE Web involves AP based sharing of Web resources containing (and/or related to) the aforesaid tools. This implies an attaching of a corresponding computing infrastructure (THE GRID). Profession communities with common interests form THE GRID dynamically as well as individuals' and institutions' continuously supplement existing THE GRID by their AP nodes.

Obviously those THE GRID computers communicate directly with each other rather than via central THE servers (the opposite of client-server model) constituting THE P2P communication model.

An achievement of AmI owners' private goals is possible on basis of *load-carrying contacts* with a view a business, a scientific or/and cultural collaboration and transactions.

THE P2P computing is intended to complement existing client/server applications and to open up new opportunities to take advantage of the computing assets and resources of both individuals and organizations.

THE Grid/P2P should not be limited to the deployment of distributed computing on a known set of computers, of static topology and a stand-alone network of computer nodes. Furthermore it must take into account the dynamics of the computations. THE AmI nodes may join and leave the grid at any time.

10.   CONCLUSION

Just as a human behaviour is determinate by his knowledge, THE Web infrastructure unlike of other today's IT initiatives is produced from knowledge representation.

Majority of the software agent tools don't maintain the agents' development. Its objective is a providing the agents' interoperability in the networks or in the MASes. Software agents' development environments don't support a top-level total ontology creation.

THE Web initiative provides the knowledge engineering standard that grounds a functioning of split-level FIPA satisfying MAS (THE-mas). THE-mas levels are

- Knowledge formative level (an experience representation, an ontology mapping, Web resource mapping, private resources mapping)
- An activity formative level (an administration of knowledge level's resources)
- Domain world formative level (an administration of domain related knowledge resources)
- Private world (i.e. a person's-, an enterprise's-, a government's. world) formative level (an administration of a private world related knowledge resources).

In that way constituted system will obtain as a personal intellectual assistant for maintenance of customer's profession/living activities, decision making and generating irrefragable answers. At that a communication's issues are solved due to the total ontology and unitized agents' organization.

Since Web interoperability is a function of knowledge representation, THE Web is an approach of Web interoperability achievement.

Activity Propositions and derived THE Ontology, THE GRID, THE P2P ground a novel approach of private Web platforms creation (Personal and Domain Worlds) as well as of these platforms interaction. As a result of PWs' interaction will be a dynamical generation of e-business, e-learning, e-management, e-works and other Web services.

REFERENCE

1. M. Polanyi, Personal Knowledge, Harper & Row, New York, 1958
2. ftp://ftp.cordis.lu/pub/ist/docs/istagscenarios2010.pdf;
3. Mika Klemettinen, User Centric & Context AwareServices, AWSI Workshop, Tammsvik, Bro, Sweden,3.6.2003
4. Schank, Lebowitz, & Birnbaum, Integrated Partial Parser 1980

5. R. Schank and K. Colby, editors.*Computer Models of Thought and Language*. W. H. Freeman and Co., San Francisco, CA, 1973

6. R. C. Schank. *Conceptual Information Processing*. North-Holland, Amsterdam, 1975

7. R. Schank and R. Abelson. *Scripts, Plans, Goals, and Understanding.*Lawrence Erlbaum Associates, Hillsdale, NJ, 1977

8. R. Montague "English as a formal language", 1970

9. John   F.   Sowa,   Concepts   in   the   Lexicon,   Problems   and   Issues, http://www.jfsowa.com/ontology/lex1.htm

10. The Columbia Encyclopedia, Sixth Edition. 2001

11. E-Slate: a software architectural style for end-user programming George Birbilis, Manolis Koutlis, Kriton Kyrimis, George Tsironis, George Vasiliou Computer Technology Institute Riga Feraiou 61Patras 262 21, Greece {birbilis, koutlis, kyrimis, tsironis, vasiliou}@cti.gr

12. M. Koutlis, P. Kourouniotis, K. Kyrimis, N. Renieri, "Inter-component communication as a vehicle towards end-user modeling", *ICSE'98 Workshop on Component-Based Software Engineering*, Kyoto, Japan, April 26–27, 1998.Available at <(http://www.sei.cmu.edu/activities/cbs/icse98/papers/p7.html)>.

13. J. Roschelle, M. Koutlis, A. Reppening, et al.: "Developing Educational Software Components", *IEEE Computer 10,9, special issue on Web based* learning and collaboration, September 1999, pp. 50–58.

14. The Anatomy of the Grid: Enabling scalable virtual organizations, I. Foster, C. Kesselman and S. Tuecke, Int. J. Supercomputer Applic. 15, 3 (Fall 2001); see also www.globus.org/research/papers.html

15. *Mario Bunge. Causality. The place of the causal principle in modern science.* Cambridge: Harvard University Press 1959

16. W3C Working Group Note 11 February 2004. Web Services Architecture (http://www.w3.org/TR/2004/NOTE-ws-arch-20040211/)

17. FIPA   Communicative   Act   Library   Specification http://www.fipa.org/specs/fipa00037/XC00037H.htm

AN INTELLIGENT DIAGNOSIS SYSTEM
HANDLING MULTIPLE DISORDERS

Wenqi Shi
School of Computer Science, The University of Birmingham
Edgbaston, Birmingham, B15 2TT, United Kingdom
Tel: 0044-121-414-2884
W.Shi@cs.bham.ac.uk

John A. Barnden
School of Computer Science, The University of Birmingham
Edgbaston, Birmingham, B15 2TT, United Kingdom
J.A.Barnden@cs.bham.ac.uk

Martin Atzmueller
Department of Computer Science, University of Wuerzburg
97074 Wuerzburg, Germany
atzmueller@informatik.uni-wuerzburg.de

Joachim Baumeister
Department of Computer Science, University of Wuerzburg
97074 Wuerzburg, Germany
baumeister@informatik.uni-wuerzburg.de

Abstract   Although Case-based Reasoning has been applied successfully in medical domains, case-based diagnosis handling multiple disorders is often not sufficient while multiple disorders is a daily problem in medical diagnosis and treatment. In this paper, we present an approach which integrates two case-based reasoners for diagnosing multiple faults. This multiple case-based reasoning approach has been evaluated on a medical case base taken from real world application and demonstrated to be very promising.

Keywords: Intelligent Diagnosis System, Multiple Case-based Reasoning (Multiple CBR), Multiple Disorders

1.   Introduction

Medical Diagnosis problem has absorbed lots of AI researchers' attention since medical domain is not really well understood in some aspects by human being and Artificial Intelligence has potential to help diagnosis. Case-based Reasoning (CBR) employs existing experience to support problem solving without necessarily understanding the underlying principles of application domain. It takes a very different view from normal reasoning process which draws its conclusions by starting from scratch and chaining generalized rules. Case-based Reasoning has been demonstrated to be very suitable for weak theory domains, especially for medical domain.

Multiple disorders are a daily problem in medical diagnosis and treatment. However, case-based diagnosis handling multiple disorders is still a challenging task. Moreover, multiple disorder cases always occur with single disorder cases in real world applications which makes diagnosis more difficult.

In this paper, we present a multiple case-based reasoning approach (Multiple CBR) [1] which integrates naive case-based reasoning and compositional case-based reasoning to handle multiple disorder problem [2] . In the following section, we firstly describe Compositional Case-based Reasoning, then a multiple case-based reasoning system will be presented. This approach is evaluated on a medical case base in the subsequent section. We conclude the paper after a discussion of the presented work and related work, then give pointers to promising work in the future.

2.   Multiple Disorder Diagnostic Problem

Our context is a medical documentation and consultation system. In our application domain of sonography, the examination considers several partially disjunctive subdomains, eg., liver or kidney, which results in multiple disorders. To support diagnosis, we want to retrieve experiences such as explanations for a query case based on the presented similarity to former cases. We also want to retrieve additional information about therapy, complications, prognosis or the treating physician as contact person for special questions.

We use case-based reasoning to retrieve experiences and help diagnosis. However case-based diagnosis handling multiple disorders differs from handling single disorder. For instance, for a single disorder casebase dealing with 100 disorders, the chance of reusing a case is roughly one to one hundred. However, due to the combinatorial rules, the chance of reusing a case with 3 independent diagnoses from 100 alternatives is just one to one million. In a real world setting, our medical case base contained about 7 disorders per case on average, and have 221 disorders in total, thus the chance of reusing an entire previous case is very small. Moreover, naive case-based reasoning approach which performs good on single disorder casebase shows a poor performance. Naive case-based reasoning means to retrieve the most similar case to the query case and to adopt the solution of that similar case as the solution for the query case. This result indicates that we can not guarantee to retrieve a similar enough case and a desirable solution from a multiple disorder casebase.

In this paper, we argue that we can reuse portions of previous cases to construct disirable solution for a query case in the multiple disorder situation, although a similar enough entire case might be unreachable.

3. Intelligent Diagnostic System Using Multiple Case-based Reasoning

In this paper, we propose an integrated approach which aims at a real world application, where single disorder cases occured with multiple disorder cases when these cases or data were collected by hospitals.

Before we introduce our method, we define necessary notions concerning our knowledge representation schema as follows: Let Ω_D be the set of all diagnoses and Ω_A the set of all attributes. To each attribute $a \in \Omega_A$ a range $dom(a)$ of values is assigned. Further we assume Ω_F to be the (universal) set of findings $(a = v)$, where $a \in \Omega_A$ is an attribute and $v \in dom(a)$ is an assignable value. Let CB be the case base containing all available cases that have been solved previously. A case $c \in CB$ is defined as a tuple

$$c = (\mathcal{F}_c, \mathcal{D}_c, I_c),\qquad(1)$$

where $\mathcal{F}_c \subseteq \Omega_F$ is the set of findings observed in the case c. In CBR-problems these findings are commonly called *problem description*. The set $\mathcal{D}_c \subseteq \Omega_D$ is the set of diagnoses describing the *solution* for this case. I_c contains additional information like therapy advices or prognostic hints.

To compare the similarity of a query case c with another case $\acute{c}$, we apply Manhattan distance for continuous or scaled parameters

$$\mathrm{md}(x,y) = \frac{1}{k}\sum_{i=1}^{k} W_i \left| \frac{x - x_{max}}{x_{max} - x_{min}} - \frac{y - x_{min}}{x_{max} - x_{min}} \right| \qquad (2)$$

and Value Difference Metric (VDM) for discrete parameters (Wilson and Martinez, 1997).

$$\mathrm{vdm_a}(x,y) = \frac{1}{|\Omega_D|} \cdot \sum_{D \in \Omega_D} \left| \frac{N(a = x|d)}{N(a = x)} - \frac{N(a = y|d)}{N(a = y)} \right| \qquad (3)$$

where x and y are values of parameter a in case c and $\acute{c}$ respectively.

3.1   Compositional CBR on Multiple Disorder Casebase

Compositional adaptation was originally developed for configuration tasks. It decomposes problems into sub-problems and retrieves those sub-problems in the casebase, and then combines different parts of the solutions of similar cases (Wilke and Bergmann, 1998). However, in a multiple disorder situation, we can not perform decomposition because the findings cannot explicitly be divided automatically into different groups which are corresponding to different diagnoses without the help of experts.

We assume that in the multiple disorder situation, not all the diagnoses in the solutions of the k most similar cases will be suggested as the final diagnosis. Only the diagnoses with a high occurrence among the k most similar cases have a high probability to appear in the final solution of the query case. The underlying meaning of this assumption is that those findings in the k similar cases which are similar to the query case will contribute to those desired diagnoses with a high occurrence in the similar case solutions.

At the same time, we assume that the more similar the retrieved case is to the query case, the higher the probability that the diagnoses in this retrieved case will appear in the final solution. Thus, we add weights to the frequency of diagnoses in the set of retrieved cases.

Given a query case C_q, we retrieve the k most cases, and calculate the similarity-weighted frequency Fqc for each diagnosis D_j.

Definition 1 (Similarity-Weighted Frequency). *The similarity-weighted frequency of a diagnosis D is the weighted frequency of D within the k most similar cases.*

$$\mathrm{Fqc}(D_j) = \frac{\sum_{i=1}^{k} W_i \cdot \delta(C_i, D)}{\sum_{i=1}^{k} W_i}, \qquad (4)$$

where $D \in \Omega_D$ is a diagnosis; $C_i \in CB$ is the ith most similar case to the query case; $\delta(C_i, D)$ is 1, if D occurs in the i most similar case C_i, and 0 otherwise. W_i represents the associated weight, where we used the squared relative similarity between C_i and the query case C_q. Therefore, the weight is proportional to the similarity.

After we calculate the similarity-weighted frequency of the diagnoses appearing in the k most similar cases, we generate a candidate solution defined as follows:

Definition 2 (Candidate Solution). *A candidate solution*

$$CS = \{D \in \Omega_D : FQC(D) \geq \epsilon\}, \qquad (5)$$

is the set of diagnoses with a similarity-weighted frequency above a dynamic threshold $\epsilon = \alpha * \max_{D \in \Omega_D} FQC(D)$. This threshold has a linear relation-

ship with the mode of the frequency value of the diagnosis in the k *most similar cases and* α *is a coefficient.*

Thus, we only include a diagnosis into the candidate solution, if the similarity-weighted frequency of the diagnosis is greater or equal than the threshold defined by ϵ. The diagnoses that do not appear in the k most similar cases are not considered.

We summarize our Compositional CBR approach as follows, and evaluate it in the subsequent evaluation section, i.e. in section 4.

CompositionalCBR algorithm

```
{
    Given a query case Cq and casebase MCB,
    KMostSimiCase = Retrieve_kMostSimi (Cq, MCB);
    for( int j=0; j< Disorder_Number (MCB); j++ )
    {
        Fqc(Dj) = 0;
        Fqc(Dj) = Calculate_Fqc(Dj, KMostSimiCase);
        if (Fqc(Dj) >= ϵ)
        {
            Add Solution (Dj, solution);
        }
    }
    return solution;
}
```

3.2   Multiple Case-based Reasoning System

To deal with the real world situation in which single disorder cases occur together with multiple disorder, we separate the existing casebase into single disorder casebase (SDCB) [3] and multiple disorder casebase (MDCB) [4], and integrate compositional case-based reasoning and naive case-based reasoing.

Given a query case C_q, we use a ReasonerSelector component to find out which case-based reasoner should be applied for this case. According to the result from the ReasonerSelector component, naive CBR or compositional CBR will be applied. Compositional case-based reasoning retrieves a group of the most similar cases in multiple disorder casebase, then use compositional adaptation to get portions of the solutions of the most similar cases to get the final solution, while naive case-based reasoning retrieves the most similar case and adopts the solution of that retrieved case. After that, we combine this query case with the candidate solution and restore it either into the single or the multiple casebase according to the number of diagnoses in candidate solution.

Multiple Case-based Reasoning algorithm

```
{
    Given a query case C_q, casebase SDCB, casebase MDCB,
    selectSingle = ReasonerSelector (C_q, SDCB, MDCB);
    if ( selectSingle )
        {
            solution= TraditionalCBR (C_q, SDCB);
            blSingle=true;
        }
    else
        {   solution= CompositionalCBR (C_q, MDCB);}
    SolvedCase = Construct (C_q, solution);
    if ( blSingle==true )
        {   Restore (SolvedCase, SDCB); }
    else
        {   Restore (SolvedCase, MDCB); }
}
```

In the ReasonerSelector component, we retrieve the most similar case from both SDCB and MDCB respctively, and mark the corresponding similarity value as S_s and S_m. If S_s is greater than S_m, then we assume that the final solution for this query case has more potential to be a single disorder, thus we use naive CBR to retrieve the most similar case and adopt the solution for that most similar case. If S_s is smaller than S_m, then the solution comes up after compositional adaptation is applied. If S_s is equal with S_m, we prefer to use the single disorder casebase to get a single disorder solution, according to the Parsimiony goal (also referred as "Occam's razor", the goal of minimizing the complexity of explanation (Peng and Reggia, 1990)).

4.   Evaluation

For our evaluation we applied cases from the knowledge-based documentation and consultation system for sonography SONOCONSULT, an advanced and isolated part of HEPATOCONSULT (Huettig et al., 2004). Our evaluation case base consisted of 744 cases, among which there are 65 single disorder cases and 679 multiple disorder cases. The case base contains an overall number of 221 diagnoses and 556 symptoms, with a mean $M_D = 6.71 \pm 04.4$ of diagnoses per case and a mean $M_F = 48.93 \pm 17.9$ of relevant findings per case.

In the usual task of assigning an example to a single category, the accuracy is just the perecntage of cases which are correctly classified. But to quantitatively measure the accuracy of multiple disorder diagnosis, the simple accuracy measurement doesn't fit. Standard accuracy has also be demonstrated to be not very suitable for multiple disorder problem (Cynthia A and Mooney, 1994), which is defined as $(T^+ + T^-)/N$, where T^+(True Positives) is the number of disorders in the correct diagnosis that are also in the system diagnosis, T^-(True Negatives) is the number of disorders not in the correct diagnosis and not in the system diagnosis, and N is the total number of disorders.

We adopted the Intersection Accuracy (Cynthia A and Mooney, 1994), as a measure for multiple disorder problems. Intersection accuracy is derived by the two standard measures: *sensitivity* and *precision*.

Definition 3 (Intersection Accuracy). *The Intersection Accuracy $\mathcal{IA}(c, c')$ is defined as*

$$\mathcal{IA}(c, c') = \frac{1}{2} \cdot \left(\frac{|\mathcal{D}_c \cap \mathcal{D}_{c'}|}{|\mathcal{D}_c|} + \frac{|\mathcal{D}_c \cap \mathcal{D}_{c'}|}{|\mathcal{D}_{c'}|} \right) \tag{6}$$

where c and c' are two cases, $\mathcal{D}_c \subseteq \Omega_D$ is the set of diagnoses of case c, and $\mathcal{D}_{c'} \subseteq \Omega_D$ is the set of diagnoses contained in case c' likewise.

We used leave-one-out cross-validation which is a variation of k-fold cross validation, where each fold consists only of exactly one case.

We compare our method with Naive CBR, Set-Covering method (Baumeister et al., 2002) and Partition Class method (Atzmueller et al., 2003). These four methods were implemented respectively and evaluated using the same casebase. the set-covering approach combined case-based reasoning and set-covering models for diagnosis. The partition class method uses partitioning knowledge provided by the expert to split cases into several parts. Decomposed cases are retrieved and combined to get the candidate solution. The evaluation results are shown in the following table.

744 Cases from the SonoConsult Case Base		
Approach	*solved cases (percentage)*	*mean acc*
Naive CBR	20 (3%)	0.66
Set-Covering	502 (67%)	0.70
Multiple CBR	536 (72%)	0.70
Partition Class	624 (84%)	0.73

Table 1. Comparison of the approaches, using 744 cases

The results in the first line show, that the Naive CBR method performs poor with cases having multiple disorders. Naive CBR utilizing no adaptation and no additional background knowledge can only solve 3% of the cases in the case base, which is obviously insufficient. The Mulitple CBR method solves 536, i.e., 72% of the cases in the case base, with a mean accuracy of 0.70, which performs significantly better than naive CBR. This demonstrates the relevance of this method in the multiple disorder situation.

Multiple CBR is slightly better than the set-covering approach. This is probably due to two issues: The set-covering approach returns candidate cases in terms of cases with all their solutions and no sophisticated adaptation step is applied. The knowledge-intensive method using partition class knowledge performs best. However the multiple CBR method and the set-covering approach do not need background knowledge, and so can be applied in arbitrary situations when the partitioning knowledge is not available, while the partition class strategy needs aditional background knowledge.

Furthermore, we apply naive case-based reasoning and compositional case-based reasoning respectively on both the single disorder casebase(SDCB) and multiple disorder casebase (MDCB). This demonstrates the aptness of naive CBR on SDCB, and compositional CBR on MDCB, as shown in table 2.

65 cases in SDCB, 679 cases in MDCB		
Approach	solved cases (percentage)	mean acc
Naive CBR on SDCB	57 (88%)	0.68
Naive CBR on MDCB	125 (18%)	0.71
Compositional CBR on SDCB	19 (29%)	0.63
Compositional CBR on MDCB	561 (83%)	0.69

Table 2.   Aptness of Naive CBR on SDCB and Compositional CBR on MDCB

The results in the first two lines show, that the naive CBR method performs good for cases with single disorder while it performs relatively poor for cases with Multiple disorder. Compositinoal CBR shows more competence on handling multiple disorder cases, which solved 83% multiple disorder cases.

5.   Discussion

There are several points worth noting about our approach. Firstly, the case-based reasoning method itself corresponds to the diagnosing process that physicians always use. They recall former similar diagnostic case and compare the symptoms with those current patient have, make some adjustment based on the previous solution to adapt the current symptoms the patients have. The cognitive similarity between Case-based Reasoning and diagnosis makes it easy to get user acceptance.

Secondly our method involves two case-based reasoners working together for handling different casebases. This is different from most case-based reasoning systems using simplex reasoners. It evokes an idea of using multiple case-based reasoner, each of which may be suitable for different casebase or dataset.

Thirdly, our system deals with the problem of multiple disorder which hasn't been identified by most knowledge-based diagnostic systems (Gierl et al., 1998). This is due to the single disorder assumption, which assumes to use only one disorder to explain all the findings presented (Peng and Reggia, 1990).

Forthly, our approach uses flexible knowledge, and allows the automatic generation of the knowledge base from an existing database, which not only makes the CBR system easy to integrate into existing clinical information systems, but also, to some extent, avoids knowledge acquisition problem.

6.   Related Work on Multiple Dirorders

INTERNIST matches symptoms and diseases in general internal medicine based on forward and backward conditional probabilities (Miller et al., 1982). But it does not deal with interacting disorders properly because if the findings can be explained by a disorder, then these findings will be deleted immediately no matter how these findings could also lead to diagnosis of another disorder.

HYDI decomposes knowledge from the causal models into diagnosis units to prevent re-computation for similar problem to improve efficiency (Jang, 1993). But the diagnosis units in HYDI largely rely on the causal models which have been built in Heart Failure Program (HF) on heart disease. Only when all the causal models for other disorders are available, could HYDI's method be applied to diagnose other disorders.

HEPAR∏ (Onisko et al., 2000) extended the structure of Bayesian network and (Gaag and Wessels, 1995) use belief networks to diagnose multiple disorder, but they are both based on the medical literature and conversations with medical domain experts, which highlights knowledge acquisition problem.

7.   Conclusions and Outlook

In this paper, we introduce a multiple case-based reasoning approach to deal with multiple disorder problems. We apply compositional case-based reasoning to construct diagnostic solution from multiple disorder casebase and employ naive case-based reasoning to access single disorder casebase. Using real medical data, this method has been demonstrated to be promising.

There are many opportunities for future work. Firstly, our method has a potential source of error, the decision of which case-based reasoner should be choosen. We will investigate it in more detail in the future. Secondly, we believe that employing learning methodology to explore interactions between disorders will help to filter the candidate disorder or to add potential disorder during case adaption. Thirdly, experiments in other domains are desirable. Our work has the potential to be used to diagnose multiple faults in other diagnostic problem areas, such as diagnosis problems concerning machine faults.

Notes

1. Our Multiple Case-based Reasoning method is different from Multiple-Case-base reasoning (Leake and Sooriamurthi, 2003) which emphasizes case-based reasoning on multiple casebases, while our multiple case-based reasoning focuses on integrating multiple case-based reasoners together.

2. Here Multiple Disorders is in a broad sense, which includes single disorders and multiple disorders.

3. In a single disorder casebase, one disorder is ultimately used to explain all the findings for each case, although the single disorder casebase could have several disorders.

4. This multiple disorder is in a narrow sense, the multiple disorder casebase is a casebase with multiple diagnoses, we also call this multiple disorder only casebase.

References

Atzmueller, M., Baumeister, J., and Puppe, F. (2003). Evaluation of two strategies for case-based diagnosis handling multiple faults. In *Proceedings of the 2nd German Workshop on Experience Management(GWEM 2003)*, Luzern, Switzerland.

Baumeister, J., Atzmueller, M., and Puppe, F. (2002). Inductive learning for case-based diagnosis with multiple faults. In S.Craw and A.Preece, editors, *Advances in Case-based Reasoning (ECCBR2002)*, pages 28–42. Springer Verlag. Proceedings of the 6th European Conference on Case-based Reasoning.

Cynthia A, T. and Mooney, R. J. (1994). Inductive learning for abductive diagnosis. In *Proc. of the AAAI-94*, volume 1, pages 664–669. citeseer.nj.nec.com/thompson94inductive.html.

Gaag, L. and Wessels, M. (1995). Efficient multiple-disorder diagnosis by strategic focusing. In Gammerman, A., editor, *Probabilistic Reasoning and Bayesian Belief Networks*, pages 187–204, London. UCL Press.

Gierl, L., Bull, M., and Schmidt, R. (1998). Cbr in medicine. In Lenz, M., Bartsch-Sporl, B., Burkhard, D.-D., and Wess, S., editors, *Case-based Reasoning Technology:From Foundations to Applications*, pages 273–297. Springer-Verlag. ISBN 3-540-64572-1.

Huettig, M., Buscher, G., Menzel, T., Scheppach, W., Puppe, F., and Buscher, H.-P. (2004). A Diagnostic Expert System for Structured Reports, Quality Assessment, and Training of Residents in Sonography. *Medizinische Klinik*, 99(3):117–122.

Jang, Y. (1993). *HYDI: A Hybrid System with Feedback for Diagnosing Multiple Disorders*. PhD thesis, Massachusetts Institute of Technology.

Leake, D. B. and Sooriamurthi, R. (2003). Dispatching cases versus merging case-base: When mcbr matters. In *Proceedings of the Sixteenth International Florida Artificial Intelligence Research Society Conference (FLAIRS-2003)*, pages 129–133. AAAI Press.

Miller, R. A., Pople, H. E., and Myers, J. D. (1982). Internist-1:an experimental computer-based diagnostic consultant for general internal medicine. *New england Journal of Medicin*, 8(307):468–476.

Onisko, A., Druzdzel, M. J., and Wasyluk, H. (2000). Extension of the heparii model to multiple-disorder diagnosis. In Klopotek, M., Michalewicz, M., and Wierzchon, S. T., editors, *Intelligent Information Systems*, pages 303–313. Physica-Verlag.

Peng, Y. and Reggia, J. A. (1990). *Abductive Inference Models for Diagnostic Problem-Solving*. Springer-Verlag.

Wilke, W. and Bergmann, R. (1998). Techniques and knowledge used for adaptation during case-based problem solving. In *IEA/AIE (Vol. 2)*, pages 497–506.

Wilson, D. R. and Martinez, T. R. (1997). Improved heterogeneous distance functions. *Journal of Artificial Intelligence Research*.

AN INTELLIGENT KNOWLEDGE-BASED RECOMMENDATION SYSTEM

Xiaowei Shi
Philips Shanghai R&D Centre, P.R.C.,Email: nancy.shi@philips.com

Abstract: An intelligent knowledge-based recommendation system for multiple users in TV-Anytime environment is developed. The architecture of the multi-agent recommendation system is described. KQC (Keyword-query combination) user profile is proposed for information modeling. The priority filtering agent operates according to the similarity between the program and the KQC user profile. This knowledge-based recommendation system can provide personalized content to users based on their preferences more efficiently and more concisely.

Key words: Recommendation, User profile, Metadata, Knowledge Representation, Multi-agent

1. INTRODUCTION

With the rapid growth of communication technologies, there is an overabundance of DTV programs available. This precipitates a need for smart "recommender" to help people obtain personalized programs.

Existing recommendation system such as TV-Advisor and Personal TV [1,2,3] are based on basic EPG (Electronic Program Guide) metadata which includes program title, start time, and duration for each channel.

Today, metadata includes more detailed information such as genre, actors, directors, and so on. This provides a potential possibility for users to navigate and search the content more easily. In order to achieve this purpose, the metadata need to be standardized. The TV-Anytime Forum is working hard to set this standard [5].

In order to recommend the contents needed by users more efficiently, this paper proposes an intelligent program recommendation system based on KQC user profile and priority filtering method in the TV-Anytime environment.

2.   INTELLIGENT INFORMATION MODELLING

To minimize the requirements for memory and processing, a lightweight KQC(Keyword-query combination)   user profile is proposed for user modeling. The KQC user profile consists of two parts: 1) instant queries from users. The queries can be both explicit and implicit, such as a specific program or some specific types of information which user wants to look; 2) usual interest and dislike features. The following describes the structure of user profile in detail.

i> Part 1: instant query

Instant queries can be either explicit or implicit, such as a specific program or some specific types of information which user wants to look. Its priority is very high; but it will be updated for the next time. The part 1 is represented as:

$$P_1 = ((t_1, c_1), (t_2, c_2),..., (t_m, c_m)) \tag{1}$$

Where t_i represent a feature and c_i means the content of a feature t_i.

ii> Part 2: usual preference

For the usual interest and dislike features, to minimize the requirement for memory and processing, each feature is defined as a three-dimension vector (feature, weight, like-degree). If there are m different features in Part a of a profile, it is represented as:

$$P_2 = ((t_1, w_1, ld_1), (t_2, w_2, ld_2),...,(t_m, w_m, ld_m)) \tag{2}$$

where t_i is a feature; w_i is the weight of feature t_i; ld_i is the like-degree of feature t_i.

3.   MULTI-AGENT RECOMMENDATION SYSTEM

3.1   System Architecture

The recommendation system developed in this paper is based on multi-agent. Its structure is shown in Figure 1. The whole system includes three agents: the Priority Filtering Agent, the Adaptation Agent, and the User Agent. The User Agent consists of two subagents: the Feedback Report Agent and the Interactive Agent.

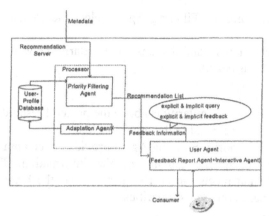

Figure 1. System architecture

The multi-agent recommendation system is flexible. It is easier to be modulated such as adding new agents for more function, or being divided into two parts (third party side, user side) to reduce the cost of the user side.

3.2   Priority Filtering Agent

The Priority Filtering Agent filters the information according to the similarity between the program and the user. Figure 2 shows the systematic framework of the Filtering Agent.

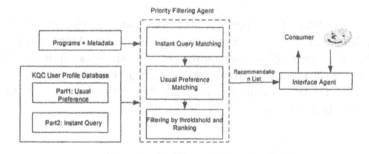

Figure 2. Filtering Agent systematic framework

When a piece of information metadata arrives, the Filtering Agent will evaluate it according to the priority. For each user, the recommended content is classified into two classes: content matching instant query and content matching usual interest. Different ways are used to deal with different part of the user profile (instant query, usual interest).

For matching instant query, if a query is a specific title, the Priority Filtering Agent directly select the content named by the title; If a query is a kinds of program, the Filtering Agent select the content that has the same properties.

For usual interests and dislikes, the similarity between the information C and profile P2 is calculated by:

$$sim(C, P_2) = \frac{C \times P_2}{\| C \| \times \| P_2 \|} \tag{3}$$

If the calculated similarity is above the preset threshold θ, the program is considered to be relevant to the user's preference.

Finally the Priority Filtering Agent provides a recommendation list to the user according to the ranking of the information. The recommended information that meets the user's querying has the highest priority. Others are ranked based on their similarities.

3.3   User Agent

The User Agent is Friendly and Secure. It consists of the Feedback Report Agent and the Interactive Agent. The Feedback Report Agent will report the program's interest degree to the Interactive Agent. The interest degree represents the user's viewing behavior.

The Interactive Agent provides the users a chance to modify the feedback report. In addition, the users can add their new interest, new need in this step. After that, feedback information is sent to the Adaptation Agent.

3.4   Adaptation Agent

The Adaptation Agent revises the user's profile based on feedback information. For the user queries, the Adaptation Agent will put it in Part 1(instant query) of the user profile directly and clear up the old Part 1. For other feedback information, the updating process only updates the features related to the content that the user has very different feeling from the similarity evaluation.

4.   APPLICATION SCENARIO

An application scenario is provided. Figure 3 shows the main user interface of the recommendation system. Functions are listed in the left column. A program recommendation list is on the topside of middle column. The description of a selected program is presented in the bottom of middle column. The interface contains a media player. For a selected program, three choices are provided to the user, which are "Display", "Delete", and "Skip".

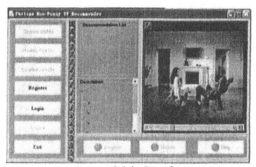

Figure1. Main Interface

5.   CONCLUSION

An intelligent multi-agent knowledge-based recommendation system is developed to provide personalized content for multiple users in TV-Anytime environment. The proposed KQC user profile can express the user's need clearly. During filtering, ranking and updating processes, the instant query part of the user profile has higher priority than the usual interest part, so the processes computation cost is reduced and the more reasonable recommendation list is gotten. The recommendation systems can be equipped in PDR or STB. From the application scenario, a friendly user interface is provided to help the user enjoy life more freely.

REFERENCES

1. Belkin, N.J. & Croft, W.B.. "Information filtering and information retrieval: two sides of the same coin". Communications of the ACM, 1994
2. P. W. Foltz and S. T. Dumais. "Personalized information delivery: An analysis of information filtering methods". Communications of the ACM, 1992
3. P W Foltz and S T Dumais. "Personalized information delivery: An analysis of information filtering methods". Communications of the ACM, 1992
4. Zheng Zhikai, Zhang Guangfan and Shao Huihe. Data Mining and Knowledge Discovery: An Overview and Prospect. Information and Control, 1999, 28(5): 357-365.
5. TV-Anytime Metadata Specifications Document, SP003v12 Part A AppendixB, TV-Anytime Forum, Jun. 2002.

A FORMAL CONCEPT ANALYSIS APPROACH FOR WEB USAGE MINING

Baoyao Zhou, Siu Cheung Hui and Kuiyu Chang
School of Computer Engineering, Nanyang Technological University, Singapore

Abstract: Formal Concept Analysis (FCA), which is based on ordered lattice theory, is applied to mine association rules from web logs. The discovered knowledge (association rules) can then be used for online applications such as web recommendation and personalization. Experiments showed that FCA generated 60% fewer rules than Apriori, and the rules are comparable in quality according to three objective measures.

Key words: web intelligence, knowledge discovery, data mining, knowledge-based systems, web usage mining, Formal Concept Analysis, association rules

1. INTRODUCTION

Web usage mining [1], also known as web log mining, aims to discover interesting and frequent user access patterns from web browsing data stored in the log files of web/proxy servers or browsers. The mined patterns can facilitate web recommendations, adaptive web sites, and personalized web search and surfing.

Various data mining techniques [2] such as statistical analysis, association rules, clustering, classification and sequential pattern mining have been used for mining web usage logs. Statistical techniques are the most prevalent; typical extracted statistics include the most frequently accessed pages, average page viewing time, and average navigational path length. Association rule mining can be used to find related pages that are most often accessed together in a single session. Clustering is commonly used to group users with similar browsing preferences or web pages with semantically related content. Classification is similar to clustering, except that a new user (page) is classified into a pre-existing class/category of users (pages) based on profile (content). Sequential pattern mining involves identifying access sequences that are frequently exhibited across different users. All of the aforementioned techniques have been successfully deployed in various web-mining applications such as web recommendation systems [3], whereby web pages likely to be visited by users in the near future are recommended or pre-fetched.

Formal Concept Analysis (FCA) [4] is a data analysis technique based on ordered lattice theory. It defines a formal context in the form of a concept lattice, which is a conceptual hierarchical structure representing relationships and attributes in a particular domain. Formal concepts can then be generated and interpreted from the concept lattice using FCA. FCA has been applied to a wide range of domains including conceptual clustering [5], information retrieval [6], and knowledge discovery [7].

A novel web usage mining approach using FCA is proposed. In particular, association rules are extracted from web logs using FCA, which can efficiently and accurately identify frequent patterns.

2.   FCA-BASED WEB USAGE MINING

Web usage data [2] can be extracted from the log files of web/proxy servers and browsers or any other data resulting from online interaction. Without loss of generality, only web server logs are considered here. Figure 1 gives an overview of the FCA-based web usage mining. The proposed approach consists of the following steps: (1) Preprocessing; (2) Web usage context construction; (3) Web usage lattice construction; and (4) Association rules mining.

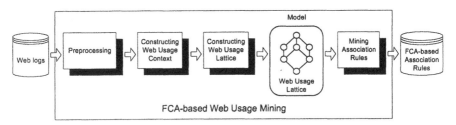

Figure 1. Overview of FCA-based web usage mining.

3.   PERFORMANCE EVALUATION

The performance of FCA mined rules is benchmarked against the Apriori-based algorithm [8] on a web recommendation dataset.

3.1   Web Recommendation

Association rules are well suited for web recommendations. The recommendation engine generates recommendation (links) by matching users' recent browsing history against the discovered association rules. Three measures are defined to objectively evaluate the performance of FCA versus Apriori.

Definition Let N be the total number of rules, N_c the number of correct rules (true for the page accessed immediately after the current page), N_s the number of satisfactory (fired) recommendation rules (for pages accessed later in the same session), N_n the number of all nonempty recommendation rules, then we define three measures: $precision = \dfrac{N_c}{N}$ $satisfaction = \dfrac{N_s}{N}$ $applicability = \dfrac{N_n}{N}$

Intuitively, precision measures how likely a user will access one of the recommended pages immediately. Satisfaction is a broader yet important measure that counts how likely a recommended page may be accessed in the future during the same session. That is because oftentimes the immediate following web page accessed by a user may be an interim navigational page instead of the target page. Applicability estimates how often recommendations will be generated.

3.2   Performance Results

Experiments were written in C++ and simulated on a 1.6 GHz machine. Two session datasets from Microsoft's Anonymous Web Data (http://kdd.ics.uci.edu) were used. This dataset records users' access in a one-week period during February 1998. To construct the web usage lattice, 2213 valid sessions out of 5000 were used, each with 2 to 35 page references (out of 294 pages). The test dataset contains 8,969 valid sessions (out of 32,711).

Figure 2(a) tallies the number of extracted association rules using a support of 10 and confidence values of 10% to 90% by AR and FCA. Clearly, FCA extracted far fewer rules (N_FCA) than Apriori (N_AR). Moreover, the precision, satisfaction, and applicability of FCA rules versus Apriori (AR) as shown in Figures 2 (b), (c), and (d) respectively are only marginally lower.

4.   CONCLUSIONS

A Formal Concept Analysis (FCA) approach for web usage mining was proposed and evaluated against the classical Apriori algorithm. FCA generated 60% fewer rules than Apriori with comparable quality according to three objective measures. The FCA approach is thus an effective and efficient tool for generating web recommendations. Another benefit of FCA is that mined association rules can be visualized directly from the FCA lattice (not shown here for brevity).

REFERENCES

1. R. Kosala, and H. Blockeel, "Web Mining Research: A Survey", ACM SIGKDD Explorations, Vol. 2, 2000.
2. J. Srivastava, R. Cooley, M. Deshpande, and P.-N. Tan, "Web Usage Mining: Discovery and Applications of Usage Patterns from Web Data", ACM SIGKDD Explorations, Vol. 1. No. 2, 2000, pp. 12 - 23.
3. Ş. Gündüz, and M. T. Özsu, "Recommendation Models for User Accesses to Web Pages", In Proc. of 13th Intl. Conf. Artificial Neural Networks (ICANN), Istanbul, Turkey, June 2003, pp. 1003-1010.
4. R. Wille, "Restructuring lattice theory: an approach based on hierarchies of concepts", In I. Rival. Editor, Ordered sets. Boston-Dordrecht: Reidel, 1982, pp. 455-470.
5. G. Stumme, R. Taouil, Y. Bastide, and L. Lakhal, "Conceptual Clustering with Iceberg Concept Lattices", In: Proc. of GI-Fachgruppentreffen Maschinelles Lernen'01, Universität Dortmund, vol. 763, October 2001.
6. C. Lindig, "Concept-Based Component Retrieval", In Working Notes of the IJCAI-95 Workshop: Formal Approaches to the Reuse of Plans, Proofs, and Programs, August 1995, pp. 21-25.
7. J. Hereth, G. Stumme, U. Wille, and R. Wille, "Conceptual Knowledge Discovery and Data Analysis", In Proc. of ICCS2000, 2000, pp. 421-437.
8. R. Agrawal, and R. Srikant, "Fast Algorithms for Mining Association Rules" In Proc. of VLDB Conference, 1994, pp. 478-499.

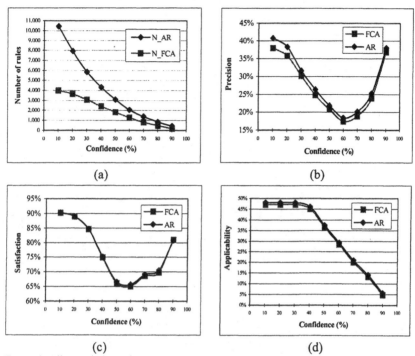

Figure 2. All association rules (AR) vs. FCA-mined rules (FCA) for web recommendation.

KNOWLEDGE-BASED DECISION SUPPORT IN OIL WELL DRILLING

Combining general and case-specific knowledge for problem solving

Pål Skalle1 and Agnar Aamodt2

Norwegian University of Science and Technology, NO-7491, Trondheim, Norway

1Department of Petroleum Engineering and Geophysics. pskalle@ipt.ntnu.no

2Department of Computer and Information Science. agnar.aamodt@idi.ntnu.no

Abstract: Oil well drilling is a complex process which frequently is leading to
               operational problems. The process generates huge amounts of data. In order to
               deal with the complexity of the problems addressed, and the large number of
               parameters involved, our approach extends a pure case-based reasoning
               method with reasoning within a model of general domain knowledge. The
               general knowledge makes the system less vulnerable for syntactical variations
               that do not reflect semantically differences, by serving as explanatory
               supportfor case retrieval and reuse. A tool, called TrollCreek, has been
               developed. It is shown how the combined reasoning method enables focused
               decision support for fault diagnosis and prediction of potential unwanted
               events in this domain.

Key words: Ontologies, Case-Based Reasoning, Model-Based Reasoning, Knowledge
               Engineering, Prediction, Petroleum Engineering,.

1.   INTRODUCTION

This paper presents a new level of active computerized support for information handling, decision-making, and on-the-job learning for drilling personnel in their daily working situations. We focus on the capturing of

useful experiences related to particular job tasks and situations, and on their
·reuse within future similar contexts. Recent innovations from the areas of
data analysis, knowledge modeling and casebased reasoning has been
combined and extended. The need for such a method was driven by the fact
that current state-of-the-art technology for intelligent experience reuse has
not been able to address the complexity of highly data-rich and information-
intensive operational environments. An operational environment, in the
context of this research, refers to a job setting where people's decisions
quickly lead to some operational action, which in turn produce results that
trigger decisions about new actions, and so on. The overall objective of this
work has been to increase the efficiency and safety of the drilling process.
Efficiency is reduced due to unproductive downtime. Most problems
(leading to downtime) need to be solved fast. Since most practical problems
have occurred before, the solution to a problem is often hidden in past
experience, experience which either is identical or just similar to the new
problem. The paper first gives an overview of our combined case-based and
model-based reasoning method. This is followed, in section 3, by an oil well
drilling scenario and an example from a problem solving session. This is
followed by a summary of related research (section 4), and a discussion with
future works in the final section.

2.   KNOWLEDGE-INTENSIVE CASE-BASED REASONING

Based on earlier results within our own group[1-4], as well as other related
activities, the method of case-based reasoning (CBR) has proven feasible
for capturing and reusing experience and best practice in industrial
operations[5-7]. CBR as a technology has now reached a certain degree of
maturity, but the current dominating methods are heavily syntax-based, i.e.
they rely on identical term matching. To extend the scope of case matching,
and make it more sensitive to the meaning of the terms described in the cases
- including their contextual interpretation - we suggest a method in which
general domain knowledge is used to support and strengthen the case-based
reasoning steps. The general domain knowledge serves as explanatory
support for the case retrieval and reuse processes, through a model-based
reasoning (MBR) method. That is, the general domain knowledge extends
the scope of each case in the case base by allowing a case to match a broader
range of new problem descriptions (queries) than what is possible under a
purely syntactic matching scheme. Integration of CBR and MBR is referred
to as "knowledge intensive case-based reasoning" (Ki-CBR). Ki-CBR allows
for the construction of explanations to justify the possible matching of

syntactically dissimilar – but semantically/pragmatically similar – case features, as well as the contextual (local) relevance of similar features. Earlier research reported from our group has also addressed this issue. However, the resulting architectures and implemented systems were basically CBR systems with a minor model-based addition, and tailored to specific problems. This has been taken further into a novel and flexible system architecture and tool – called TrollCreek - in which the model-based and case-based components may be combined in different ways.

2.1   The Model-Based Component

Methods for development of knowledge models for particular domains (e.g.drilling engineering) have over the last years improved due to contributions both from the knowledge-based systems field of artificial intelligence, and the knowledge management field of information systems. The knowledge models are often expressed in a standard language (XML-based). This facilitate that knowledge structures can end up in shared libraries, to become available for others. During the development of a knowledge modelling methodology for the petroleum technology domain, existing, more general, frameworks and methodologies, in particular CommonKADS, Components of Expertise, and CBR-related methodologies8-10 were adapted.

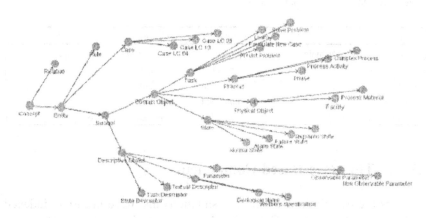

Figure 1. A part of the top-level ontology, showing concepts linked together with structural

relations of type "has subclass". Each relation has its inverse (here "subclass-of", not shown).

At the simplest level, the TrollCreek general domain model can be seen as a labeled, bi-directional graph. It consists of nodes, representing concepts, connected by links, representing relations. Relation types also have their semantic definition, i.e. they are concepts. The uppermost ontology of the TrollCreek model is illustrated in Figure 1. Different relations have different numerical strength, i.e. a value in the range 0-1, corresponding to a relation's default "explanatory power". For example, a "causes" relation has default strength 0.90, a "leads to" relation 0.80, and an "indicates" relation 0.50. All parameter values that the system reasons with are qualitative, and need to be transformed from quantitative values into qualitative concepts, as exemplified in Table 1. The entity "Weight On Bit" (WOB) is taken as an example. WOB is a subclass of Operational Parameter which is subclass of Observable Parameter in our ontology model. Currently, the oil drilling domain model contains about 1300 concepts related through 30 different relation types.

Table 1. Qualitative values and their definitions

Qualitative value	Quantitative value	Quantitative definition
Normal wob	wob-30	average value over last 30 m of drilling
High wob	wob-1 / wob-30 > 1.2	wob-1 = average value over last 1 m of drilling
Low wob	wob-1 / wob-30 < 0.8	

In Table 2 some relations between entities (other than subclass) are presented.

Table 2. Relations between some concepts.

Node 1	Relation	Target node
Background gas from shale	implies	Increasing pore pressure
Back reaming	leads to	Negative ecd
Balled bit	occurs in	Wbm
Blowout	enabled by	Kick
Bo through bop/annulus	caused by	Failed to close bop

2.2   The Case-Based Component

Cases are descriptions of specific situations that have occurred, indexed by their relevant features. Cases may be structured into subcases at several levels. They are indexed by direct, non-hierarchical indices, leaving indirect indexing mechanisms to be taken care of by the embedding of the indices within the general domain model. Initial case matching uses a standard weighted feature similarity measure. This is followed by a second step in which the initially matched set of cases are extended or reduced, based on explanations generated within the general domain model. Cases from the oil drilling domain have been structured in a manner which makes them suitable for finding the solution of a problem and/or search for missing knowledge. All cases therefore contain the following knowledge:

• characteristics that give the case a necessary, initial "fingerprint", like owner of problem (operator); Place/date; Formation/geology; installation/well section; depth/mud type

• definition of the searched data / recorded parameter values / specific errors or failures

• necessary procedures to solve the problem, normative cases, best practice, repair path consists normally of a row of events. An initial repair path is always tried out by the drilling engineer and usually he succeeds. If his initial attempts fail, then the situation turns into a new case, or a new problem.

• the final path, success ratio of solved case, lessons learned, frequently applied links From a case, pointers or links may go to corporate databases of different formats. Typical examples are logging and measurement databases, and textual "lessons learned" documents or formal drilling reports.

3. OIL WELL DRILLING SCENARIO

During oil well drilling the geological object may be as far as 10 km away from
the drilling rig, and must be reached through selecting proper equipment, material
and processes. Our work is addressing all phases of the drilling process; planning
(for planning purposes the TrollCreek tool is addressing the drilling engineer), plan
implementation (addressing the driller and the platform superintendent) and post
analyses (addressing the drilling engineer and management). Of all possible
problems during oil well drilling we have in this scenario selected one specific
failure mode; Gradual or sudden loss of drilling fluid into cracks in the underground.
This failure is referred to as Lost Circulation. Lost circulation (LC) occurs when the
geological formation has weaknesses like geological faults, cavernous formations or

weak layers. The risk of losses increases when the downhole drilling fluid pressure

becomes high, caused by i.e. restrictions in the flow path or by the drilling fluid

becoming more viscous.

3.1   An Example

Assume that we are in a situation where drilling fluid losses are observed, and the situation turns into a problem (Lost Circulation). See the case description to the left in Figure 2. TrollCreek produces first of all a list of similar cases for review of the user, see Figure 3, bottom row. Testing of Case LC 22 suggests that Case LC 40 is the best match, with case 25 as the second best. Inspecting case 25 shows a matching degree of 45%, and a display of directly matched, indirectly (partly) matched, and non-matched features. Examination of the best-matched cases reveals that Case LC 40 and 25 are both of the failure type Natural Fracture (an uncommon failure in our case base). By studying Case LC 40 and 25 the optimal treatment of the new problem is devised (the "has-solution" slot, see right part of figure 2), and the new case is stored in the case base. The user can choose to accept the delivered results, or construct a solution by combining several matched cases. The user may also trigger a new matching process, after having added (or deleted) information in the problem case. The user can also browse the case base, for example by asking for cases containing one specific or a combination of attributes.

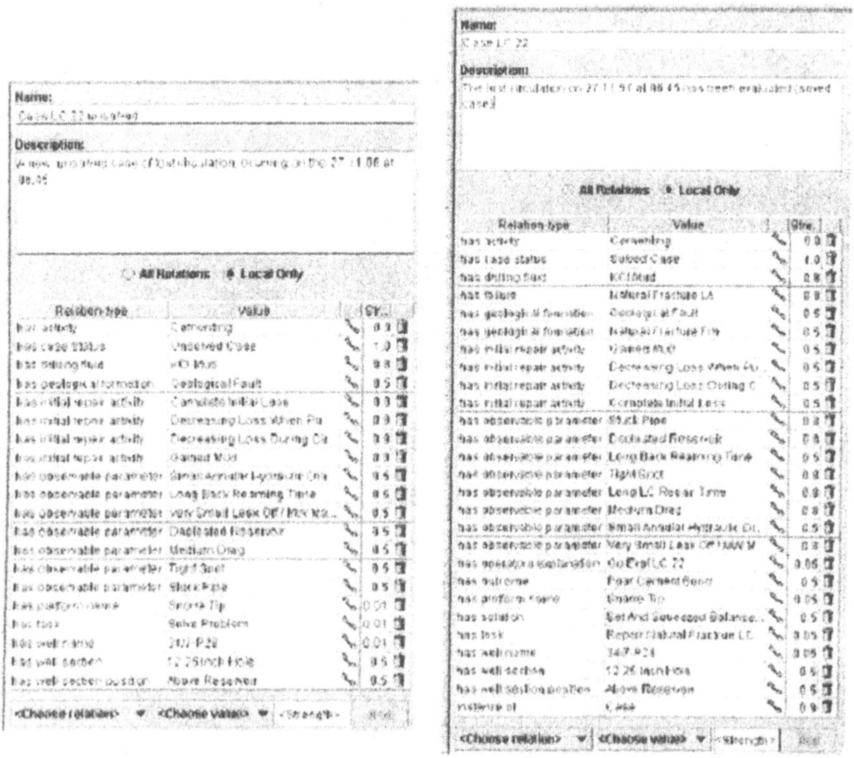

Figure 2. Unsolved case (left) and the corresponding solved case (right) of Case LC 22.

3.2 The role of general domain knowledge

A model of causal and other dependency relations between parameter states, linked within a set of taxonomical, part-subpart, and other structural relations, constitutes the core of the general domain model. This enables the system to provide a partial explanation for the reason of a failure. Figure 4 shows parts of the explanation structure explaining why Case LC 22 is a problem of the type Natural Fracture. An important notion in identifying a failure mode is the notion of a non-observable parameter, i.e. a parameter which is not directly measurable or observable, usually related to conditions down in the well. In Figure 4, examples of such parameters are Annular Flow Restrictions, Increasing Annular Pressure, Decreasing Fracture Pressure, Leaking Fm, Large LCD, Pressure Surge, High Annular Pressure. An important reasoning task is to relate failures to possible non-observable parameters, using the knowledge model, then relate these to other measured parameters until a set of possible failure modes are suggested.

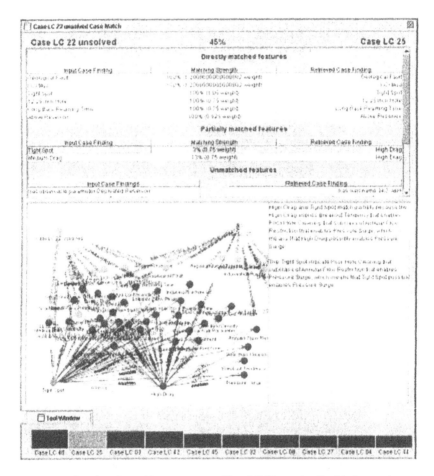

Figure 3. Results of matching a new case (Case LC 22 unsolved) with the case base

Indirect (partial) matching of case features is exemplified in Figure 3. The lower half of the display (hiding all but one of the unmatched features), shows a graphical display of concepts involved in the matching, and a textual description explaining the match. Identifying a failure and a repair for the failure are two types of tasks that the system can reason about. An explicit task-subtask structure is a submodel within the domain model, which is used in controlling the reasoning process. This is exemplified in Figure 5, which also shows (upper right) tasks linked to failure states. States are also interlinked within a state structure (not shown). By combining task and state models, with causal reasoning as illustrated in Figure 4, a solution may be found by model-based reasoning within the general domain model, even if a matching case is not found. If so, the system will – as shown before - store the problem solving session as a new case, hence transforming general domain knowledge, combined with case-specific data, into case-specific knowledge.

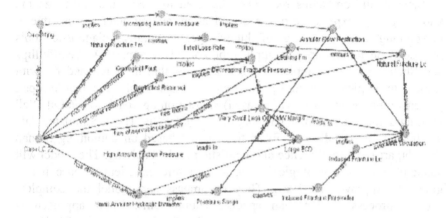

Figure 4. Some of the explanation paths behind the failure in Case LC 22

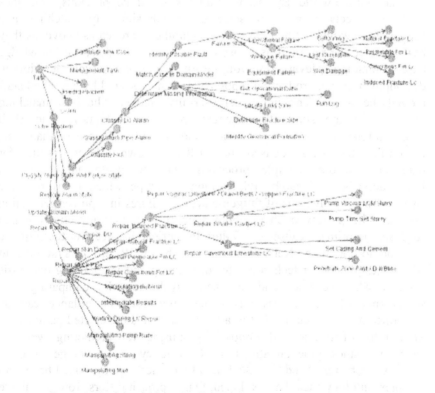

Figure 5. Partial task hierarchy, linked with parts of a failure hierarchy

4.   RELATED WORK

Several oil companies recognize the need to retain and centralize the knowledge and experience of the organization, among other reasons due to outsourcing and spreading of knowledge. Generally, diagnostic tools represent the largest area of application for AI systems[11]. Amoco/Phillips and Shell serve as examples of oil companies that have reached far with respect to implementation of experience transfer tools. Amoco/Phillips[12] presents a heuristic (experience based) simulation approach to the Oil Well Drilling domain, based on data sets of 22 actual wells. The accumulated data are treated statistically and fitted to a model based on combining human thought, artificial intelligence and heuristic problem solving. The model will adapt to a specific geological area, and capture experience, reuse it and gradually improve and learn. They encompass and model the complete drilling process, rather than specific subproblems. Their approach is therefore less focused than our approach. Parallel to this activity CIRIO[13] is leading a "Drilling club" in which all members contribute with well data from around the world. By means of a CBR technique, previous, analogous wells or aspects of well are selected through similarity matching, and adapted to new wells. Shell[14] has taken a similar approach as above, as they have selected the reservoir as a case entity. A common reservoir knowledge base, containing relevant reservoir information like reservoir description, development plans, production reports, etc., can be shared by any Shell staff around the world. The individual user may retrieve the best matching reservoir through similarity matching (reservoir analogues). The Shell approach represents, on the one hand, a more ambitious approach than ours, but on the other a less focused one. CBR are known to be well suited for maintenance of other complex processes, related to our domain. Mount and Liao[11] describe a research and learning prototype which helps find the answers and explanations of fatigue-cracking failures in a power generation process. The prototype covers both support in failure investigation and suggests the primary cause of a failure in a priory list, leaving the ultimate decision to the user. Netten[15] points out that CBR provides significant advantages over other techniques for developing and maintaining diagnosis systems, while accuracy and coverage may be low. By comparing with surveillance of the process this is certainly true. Surveillance can be performed at high accuracy but to a limited amounts of selected parameters. Monitoring of torque and drag[16] is promising for predicting wellbore cleaning / stuck pipe situations. High accuracy and coverage of CBR systems can be improved but comes at a high price. A large case library and complex ontology must be developed. Our approach differs from the above in the combination of case-specific and general domain knowledge. Further, the model-based reasoning module in TrollCreek assumes open and weak theory domains, i.e. domain domains characterized by uncertainty, incompletes, and change. Hence, our inference methods are abductive, rather than deductive, forming the basis for plausible reasoning by relational chaining[17].

5. CONCLUSION AND FUTURE WORK

As has been described, a new tool for handling knowledge-intensive case-based reasoning has been developed, and is now being tested. New cases are matching similar past cases with a high degree of user credibility, due to the ability of the system to justify its suggestions by explanations. Work related to failure diagnosis and repair is presented in this paper. Ongoing, parallel work includes prediction of unwanted events before they occur – also in the oil drilling domain, incorporating time-dependent cases and temporal reasoning[15]. Another challenge is how to automatically update the general domain model based on data, where we study probabilistic networks as a data mining method[2,18]. Additionally, work has been started to improve the knowledge acquisition and modeling methodology for both general and case-specific knowledge[10], automatically generate past case descriptions from text reports, and to facilitate this type of decision support in a mobile-computing environment. On the agenda for future research is extending the representational capacity of the system, e.g. to handle flexible forms of decision rules and conditionals on relationships. In the drilling industry the engineers tend to group problem related knowledge into decision trees. Decision trees are inherently instable, and alternative trees may produce different results[19]. A combination of the two may work well, our cases being the exceptions of the more rule based tree. Some frequently reoccurring problems may gradually (depending on failure rate) turn into a decision rule. Such problems will then enter the default best practice of the oil company. Best practice, or lessons learned, are notions of large interest in the oil drilling industry. Others have also investigated usefulness of case-based support tools for capturing lessons learned[20]. The approach presented in this paper is a contribution to a total strategy of retaining and putting useful knowledge and information to use when needed. We are currently discussing this issue, on a broader scale, with some oil companies. The challenges here are essentially twofold: One is to integrate a knowledge-based decision support tool smoothly into the other computer-based systems in an operational environment. The other, and not less challenging, is to integrate computerized decision support into the daily organizational and human communication structure on-board a platform or on shore.

ACKNOWLEDGEMENTS

Many people have contributed to the integrated system architecture, the TrollCreek tool, and the oil drilling knowledge base. Extensive contributions have particularly been made by Frode Sørmo, and additional parts have been designed and implemented by Ellen Lippe, Martha Dørum Jære, and people at Trollhetta AS. Financial funding of parts of the implementation has been provided by Trollhetta AS, through CEO, Ketil Bø, and – for an earlier version – by SINTEF, through Program Coordinator Jostein Sveen.

REFERENCES

1. Pål Skalle, Agnar Aamodt, Jostein Sveen: Case-based reasoning a method for gaining experience and giving advise on how to avoid and how to free stuck drill strings. Proceedings of IADC Middle East Drilling Conference, Dubai, Nov. 1998.
2. Agnar Aamodt, Helge A. Sandtorv, Ole M. Winnem : Combining Case Based Reasoning and Data Mining - A way of revealing and reusing RAMS experience. In Lydersen, Hansen, Sandtorv (eds.), Safety and Reliability; Proceedings of ESREL 98, Trondheim,June 16-19, 1998. Balkena, Rotterdam, 1998. ISBN 90-5410-966-1. pp 1345-1351.
3. Paal Skalle, Jostein Sveen, Agnar Aamodt: Improved efficiency of oil well drilling through case-based reasoning. Proceedings of PRICAI 2000, The Sixth Pacific Rim International Conference on Artificial Intellignece, Melbourne August-September 2000. Lecture Notes in Artificial Intelligence, Springer Verlag, 2000. pp 713-723.
4. Martha Dørum Jære, Agnar Aamodt, Pål Skalle: Representing temporal knowledge for case-based prediction. Advances in case-based reasoning; 6th European Conference, ECCBR 2002, Aberdeen, September 2002. Lecture Notes in Artificial Intelligence, LNAI 2416, Springer, pp. 174-188.
5. Irrgang, R. et al.: "A case-based system to cut drilling costs", SPE paper 56504, proc. At SPE Ann. Techn. Conf. & Exhib., Houston (3-6 Oct. 1999)
6. Bergmann, R., Bren, S., Göker, M., Manago, M., Wess, S. (Eds.), *Developing Industrial Case-Based Reasoning Applications – The INRECA Methodology.* Springer (1999)
7. Watson, I.:"Applying Case Based Reasoning", Morgan Kaufmann, 1997.
8. Schreiber, G., de Hoog, R Akkermans, H., Anjewierden, A., Shadbolt, N. and van de Velde, W.: *"Knowledge Engineering & Management", The CommonKADS Methodology.*The MIT Press, January, 2000
9. Steels , L. The componential framework and its role in reusability . In Jean-Marc David, J.-P. Krevine and R. Simmons, eds. *Second Generation Expert Systems.* 1993. Berlin:Springer Verlag.
10. Aamodt, A.: "Modeling the knowledge contents of CBR systems", Proceedings of the Workshop Program at the Fourth International Conference on Case-Based Reasoning , Vancouver, 2001. Naval Research Laboratory Technical Note AIC-01-003, pp. 32-37.
11. Mount, C. and Liao, W. Prototype of an Intellignet Failure Analysis System. ICCBR 2001, LNAI 2080, pp 716-730. Springer Verlag Berlin, Aha, D. and Watson,I. (Ads.).
12. Milheim, K.K. and Gaebler, T.: "Virtual experience simulation for drilling – the concept", paper SPE 52803 presented at *SPE/IADC Drilling Conf.*, Amsterdam (9-11 March, 1999) 317-328

13. Irrgang R. et al.: "Drilling parameters selection for well quality enhancement in deep water environments", SPE paper 77358, proc. at SPE Ann. Techn. Conf. & Exhib., San Antonio (29 Sept. – 2 Oct. 2002)

14. Bhushan, V. and Hopkins S.C.:"A novel approach to identify reservoir analogues", paper SPE 78 338 presented at 13th European Petrol. Comf., Aberdeen (29-31 Oct 2002)

15. Netten, B.D. Representation of Failure Context for Diagnosis of technical Applications. In Advances in Case _ Based Reasoning; B. Smyth and P. Cunningham (eds.), EWCBR-98, LNAI 1488, pp 239 – 250

16. Vos, B.E. and Reiber, F.:"The benefits of monitoring torque & drag in real time",IADC/SPE paper 62784, proc. at IADC/SPE Asia Pacific Drilling Techn., Kuala Lumpur (11-13 Sept. 2000).

17. Soermo F.: Plausible Inheritance; Semantic Network Inference for Case-Based Reasoning. MSc thesis, NTNU, Department of Computer and Information Science (2000).

18. Agnar Aamodt, Helge Langseth: Integrating Bayesian networks into knowledge-intensive CBR. In American Association for Artificial Intelligence, Case-based reasoning integrations;Papers from the AAAI workshop. David Aha, Jody J. Daniels (eds.). Technical Report WS-98-15. AAAI Press, Menlo Park, 1998. ISBN 1-57735-068-5. pp 1-6.

19. Cunningham, P., Doyle, D. and Longhrey, J. An Evaluation of the Usefulness of Case-Based Explanation. ICCBR 2003, LNAI 2689, pp 122-130. Springer Verlag, Berlin (K.D.Ashley and D.G.Bridge (Eds.)) 2003.

20. Wever, R., Ahn, D.W., Munoz-Avila, H. and Breslow, A. (2000). Active Delivery for Lessons Learned Systems. Paper from the EWCBR 2000, LNAI 1898, pp 322-334.Springer Verlag.

A NEW METHOD TO CONSTRUCT THE NON-DOMINATED SET IN MULTI-OBJECTIVE GENETIC ALGORITHMS

Jinhua Zheng [1], Zhongzhi Shi [2], Charles X. Ling[3] and Yong Xie [1]
1)College of Information Engeering, Xiangtan University, Hunan, China (411105)
2) Institute of Computing Technology, Chinese Academy of Sciences, Beijing, China (100080)
3) Department of Computer Science, University of Western Ontario, London, Canada (N6A 5B7)
jhzheng@xtu.edu.cn   shizz@ics.ict.ac.cn   cling@csd.uwo.ca

Abstract: There have been widespread applications for Multi Objective Genetic Algorithm (MOGA) on highly complicated optimization tasks in discontinuous, multi-modal, and noisy domains. Because the convergence of MOGA can be reached with the non-dominated set approximating the Pareto Optimal front, it is very important to construct the non-dominated set of MOGA efficiently. This paper proposes a new method called Dealer's Principle to construct non-dominated sets of MOGA, and the time complexity is analyzed. Then we design a new MOGA with the Dealer's Principle and a clustering algorithm based on the core distance of clusters to keep the diversity of solutions. We show that our algorithm is more efficient than the previous algorithms, and that it produces a wide variety of solutions. We also discuss the convergence and the diversity of our MOGA in experiments with benchmark optimization problems of three objectives.

Key words: Multi-objective Genetic Algorithm, Multi-objective Optimum, Dominated relationship, Non-dominated set

1.   INTRODUCTION

The Multi Objective Genetic Algorithm (MOGA), which is one of machine learning algorithms, is praised for its ability to solve high complex problems. Moreover, the real world tasks always involve simultaneous optimization of multiple objectives, and MOGA can find a wide spread of Pareto optimal solutions in a single simulation run. Hence, MOGA is getting very popularity in the recent years.

It is known that genetic algorithms can be used to solve single objective optimization, and the best solution is usually the global minimum or the global maximum in this case. However, multi objective optimization is very different from the optimization with only a single objective. There may not exist one solution that is best with respect to all objectives in multi objective optimization. There always exists a set of solutions that are superior to the rest of solutions in the search space when all objectives are considered, but are inferior to other solutions in one or more objectives. These solutions are called Pareto optimal solutions or non-dominated solutions. The rest of the solutions are known as dominated solutions. In MOGAs, the key problem is to construct a set of candidate solutions that are non-dominated for an evolutionary population. While the construction procedure is repeated, the set of candidate solutions is made go closer to the true Pareto optimal solutions continually, and reach the true Pareto optimal solutions in the end.

There exist several kinds of MOGAs with different approaches of constructing the non-dominated set. In this paper, we propose a new method called Dealer's Principle to construct non-dominated sets of MOGA (in section 3), and the time complexity of the new algorithm is analyzed (in section 3), which indicates that it is more efficient to use Dealer's Principle to construct a non-dominated set than the previous methods. To keep the diversity of the solutions, we discuss a clustering algorithm based on the core distance of clusters (in section 4). Then we design a new MOGA based on the clustering procedure, in which the Dealer's Principle is used to construct the non-dominated set (in section 5). We discuss the convergence and the diversity of MOGA, and we test our algorithm in the experiment with a benchmark optimization problem of three objectives (in section 6). It is shown that our algorithm is more efficient than previous algorithms, and that it produces a wide spread of solutions (in section 6).

2. A BRIEFLY REVIEW OF MOGAS

The popular MOGAs include Aggregating Function, Schaffer's VEGA, Fonseca and Fleming's MOGA, Horn and Nafpliotis's NPGA, Zitzler and Thiele's SPEA, and Srinivas and Deb's NSGA.

In Aggregating Function, multi objectives are fit together linearly into a single objective, and each sub-objective is assigned a coefficient. Thus, the optimization of multi objectives is transformed into the optimization of a single objective [1]. The main merit of this method is of high performing efficiency, but its disadvantages are also distinct. For example, the coefficient of each sub-objective must be changed continually in the evolution process, and it is difficult to find the Pareto optimal solutions no matter how to change the coefficients when the search space is concave [2].

In 1984, Schaffer proposed Vector Evaluated Genetic Algorithm (VEGA) in his doctor's dissertation. It seems that only the extreme points in Pareto optimal front can be found when applying VEGA to solve some problems [3], because it cannot be compromised in light of the attributes of each sub-objective. The VEGA has been improved by Ritzel, Wayland [2] and Surry [4], but it is difficult to find the Pareto optimal solutions when the search space is concave [5].

Fonseca and Fleming suggested another kind of MOGA [6]. Each individual is given a rank calculated respectively. The rank of all non-dominated individuals is 1, and the rank of the dominated individual is 1 plus the number of individuals that dominate it. The selection operation is implemented with the mechanism of the fitness function sharing. The main merits of the method are highly efficient and easy to implement [7]. Similar to the other MOGA with parameters, one of its disadvantages is that the method depends upon the choice of the parameters excessively. The other disadvantage is the premature convergence because of the selection pressure [8]. Moreover, the multi Pareto Optimal points cannot be found when different points correspond to the same function value [9].

Horn and Nafpliotis brought forward A Niched Pareto Genetic Algorithm for Multi objective Optimization (NPGA) based on Pareto dominated relationship [10,11]. At first, a comparison set called CS is selected randomly from the population, and then two individuals are also selected randomly. If one of the two individuals is dominated by CS, then the other is selected into the next evolutionary population; otherwise one of the two individuals is selected by the Niche shared methods into the future evolution [11,12]. The main merit of NPGA is highly efficient, and the Pareto Optimal front can be obtained by this method. Its disadvantage is that there is no general principle to select the sharing parameters and the size of comparison set.

In 1999, Zitzler and Thiele described Strength Pareto Evolutionary Algorithm (SPEA) [13]. The fitness of individual is called the strength. The strength of individuals in the non-dominated set is defined as the ratio of the individuals dominated by it over the population size. The strength of the others (dominated individual) is defined as 1 plus the number of individuals dominating it. Here, the low strength individuals have a high probability of reproduction. The time complexity is $O(n^3)$. Zitzler [14] improved SPEA, and advanced it to SPEA2 in which the time complexity is $O(n^2 \log n)$.

The Non-dominated Sorting in Genetic Algorithm (NSGA [15,16,17]) was proposed by Srinivas and Deb. First, for each individual two entities are calculated: (1) n_i, the number of individuals which dominate the individual i, and (2) s_i, a set of individuals which the individual i dominates. The individual i is non-dominated if $n_i = 0$; otherwise individual i is dominated. The non-dominated sorting procedure of NSGA has a computational complexity of $O(n^2)$.

The main merits of SPEA2 [14] and NSGA-II [17] are good performances in convergence and diversity. Moreover, MOGAs with no parameter (such as SPEA and NSGA) do not have the problems of selecting and adjusting parameters, so they have widespread applications. But their disadvantage is lower performing efficiency than MOGAs with parameters. To make MOGAs with no parameters more efficient, we propose a new MOGA in which the non-dominated set is constructed by using a new method called Dealer's Principle in this paper.

3.   DEALER'S PRINCIPLE TO CONSTRUCT A NON-DOMINATED SET

In the MOGAs based on Pareto optimum, it is very important to construct a non-dominated set efficiently because the speed of the construction affects convergent speed of an algorithm directly. Because the new method has no backtracking when constructing non-dominated sets, a new non-dominated individual needs not to be compared with non-dominated individuals that already exist. Firstly, a dealer, a reference individual, is selected from the candidate solutions in each round of comparison (the dealer is usually the first individual in the current evolutionary population). Then the dealer is compared with the other members of the current candidate solutions one by one. The individual dominated by the dealer must be removed immediately. After a round of comparison, the dealer is joined into the non-dominated set if it is not dominated by any other individuals; otherwise the dealer must be removed. This process is repeated until there is no candidate solution. Therefore, we call our new method the Dealer's Principle. Before we discuss our algorithm, some definitions are needed.

Definition 1: Assume the size of set P is n, every individual in P has r attributes, and $f_k()$ is an evaluation function ($k=1,2,...,r$). The relationship between individuals in P is defined as follows: (1) Dominated relationship: $\forall X, Y \in P$, if $f_k(X) \leq f_k(Y)$, ($k=1,2, ..., r$), and

$\exists l \in \{1,2,\cdots,r\}$ such that $f_i(X) < f_i(Y)$, then we have X dominates Y, or $X \succ Y$. Here "$\succ$" represents dominated relationship, and we say X is a non-dominated individual, and Y is a dominated individual. (2) Irrelevance: $\forall X, Y \in P$, if X and Y do not dominate each other, or there is no relations between X and Y, then we say that X and Y are irrelevant.

Definition 2: There exist $X \in P$, if not $\exists Y \in P$, $Y \succ X$, the X is a non-dominated individual of P. The set consisting of non-dominated individuals of P is called the non-dominated set of P.

Definition 3: Assume Nds is a non-dominated set of P, $Nds \subseteq P$. $\forall X \in P$, if X is a non-dominated individual of P, then $X \in Nds$. Nds is called the biggest non-dominated set of P.

Now we discuss the Dealer's Principle to construct the non-dominated set from a set of candidate solutions. Assume P is an evolutionary population, and Q is a set of candidate solutions. Starting with an empty Nds of the non-dominated set, let Q=P. One individual X is picked at random from Q (in fact, X is removed from Q in this case) and compared with other individuals in Q one by one, and then the individuals dominated by X are deleted. If X is not dominated by any other members of Q, then it is a non-dominated individual, and it is joined into Nds. We continue this process until Q is empty.

The Algorithm 1 shows how to implement the method to construct a non-dominated set of an evolutionary population.

Algorithm 1: Construct a non-dominated set with Dealer's Principle Function Nds (Pop: population) { Q=Pop; while $(Q \neq \phi)$ do { $X \in Q$, Q=Q-{ X }; x-is-non-dominated=.T.; for $(Y \in Q)$ { if $(X \succ Y)$ then Q=Q-{ Y } else if $(Y \succ X)$ then x-is-non-dominated=.F. } if (x-is-non-dominated) then Nds=Nds $\cup$ { X }; }}It can be proved that the Nds is a non-dominated set of P, and is the biggest non-dominated set of P. Now we analyze the computational complexity of the algorithm with the Dealer's Principle to construct a non-dominated set. Suppose that n is the size of set P, and there are m non-dominated individuals in P. Firstly we discuss three particular cases: (i) there exist (m-1) non-dominated individuals after (m-1) rounds of comparison, but (m-1) individuals do not remove any dominated individual from Q. After the mth round of comparison, the mth non-dominated individual removes (n-m) dominated individuals from Q. The computational complexity in this situation is: (n-1)+((n-2)+... +(n-m)=(2n-m-1)m/2<nm. (ii) While the early (n-m) rounds of comparison, all the (n-m) dealers are dominated individuals, and no other individual is removed from the current candidate solutions of Q by them, and the m non-dominated individuals are generated in the latter m rounds of comparison. This is the worst situation. The computational complexity under this situation is: (n-1)+ (n-2)+...+1=n(n-1)/2=$O(n^2)$. (iii) In the first round, there is an individual that is

not dominated by any members of Q, and this non-dominated individual removes (n-m) individuals dominated by it from Q. In the later (m-1) rounds of comparison, there are (m-1) non-dominated individuals generated. This is the best situation. The computational complexity is: $(n-1)+[(m-2)+ (m-3)+...+1]=(n-1)+(m-1)(m-2)/2=O(n+m^2)$.

As a general rule, there have been k rounds of comparison altogether, $m \leq k \leq n$. There are k individuals are removed naturally for k rounds of comparison, one at a time, here there are m non-dominated individuals and (k-m) dominated individuals. There are (n-k) dominated individuals removed from the set of candidate solutions Q for k rounds of comparison. Suppose that the probability of removing (n-k) dominated individuals is equal: (n-k)/k, the computational complexity of k rounds of comparison is: $(n-1)+ (n-2-(n-k)/k) +(n-3-2(n-k)/k) +...+(n-k-(k-1)(n-k)/k) =[(n-1)+ (n-2) +...+(n-k)]-[(n-k)/k+2(n-k)/k +...+k(n-k)/k]+k$ $(n-k)/k=[(n-1)+ (n-k)]k/2-[(n-k)/k+k(n-k)/k]k/2+ (n-k)=k(n-1)/2+ (n-k)/2= O(kn) <n^2$

From the analysis above, the time complexity of the algorithm to construct a non-dominated set with the Dealer's Principle is better than that in SPEA2 and NSGA-II. Especially in the early stage of algorithm execution, m is always much less than n (or m<<n), so the algorithm is more efficient.

4.   THE CLUSTERING METHOD BASED ON CORE DISTANCE

In the research of MOGAs, the diversity of solutions is one of the most important issues. MOGAs with parameters employ niche technique [11] and fitness sharing [12] to keep or maintain the diversity of solutions. MOGAs with no parameters employ a crowding procedure [16] or a clustering procedure [14,19] to maintain the diversity of solutions. It is shown from some studying [14,19] that the MOGAs that employ the clustering procedure have better diversity than these that employ the crowding procedure. While the early stage of a MOGA execution, a non-dominated set Nds is small, but it increases gradually. When |Nds|>n, how choose n individuals from Nds and keep the diversity of solutions at the same time? Therefore, a clustering procedure based on core distance is proposed in this paper.

The clustering procedure based on core distance employs a bottom-up approach to cluster individuals. Initially, we regard each of n individuals as a subclass and calculate the distance between their cores (centers), then combine two subclasses that they have the smallest core distance. The procedure of calculation and combination will be repeated until the stop condition is satisfied ($|Nds| \leq n$). The clustering procedure is depicted in algorithm 2.

Algorithm 2: clustering procedure based on core distance

(1) initialize cluster set C, let every subclass of C includes one individual in Nds: $C = \cup_p \{\{p\}\}$ $p \in Nds$ The core (o_i) of every subclass is the only individual in the subclass.

(2) if $|C| \leq$ bound, then goto (8). Here, bound is the maximal limit size of non-dominated set.

(3) calculate the core distance between any two subclasses: $d(o_i, o_j) = \| o_i - o_j \|$, $o_i, o_j \in C$ Where $\| o_i - o_j \|$ is distance between o_i and o_j.

(4) choose two new subclass c_i and c_j which have minimal distance between their cores: $c_i, c_j : \min\{d(o_i, o_j) | o_i, o_j \in C\}$ merge c_i and c_j into subclass c_k : $C = C \setminus \{c_i, c_j\} \cup \{c_i \cup c_j\}$

(5) calculate the core of subclass c_k , $d(p) = \min\{d(p,q) | p,q \in c_k, p \neq q\}$ $o_k = \min\{d(p) | p \in c_k\}$

(6) if $|C| \leq$ bound, then goto (8).

(7) calculate the distance from c_k to any other subclass of C between their cores. $d(o_k, o_l) = \| o_k - o_l \|$ where o_k , o_l is the core of c_k and c_l respectively, $c_k, c_l \in C$ and $c_k \neq c_l$. then goto (4).

(8) return $Nds = \cup \{ o_i \}$, o_i is the core of c_i, $c_i \in C$.

The time complexity of the clustering procedure is $O(n^2)$.

5.   MOGAS BASED ON CLUSTERING PROCEDURE

Assume that the size of the evolutionary population is n. Pop_t represents the population in t^{th} generation, Q_t denotes the new evolutionary population after the genetic operators (selection, crossover, and mutation) are applied to Pop_t, and the size of Q_t is also n. Set $R_t = Pop_t \cup Q_t$, and the size of R_t is 2n. By constructing the non-dominated set Nds of R_t continually, the individuals in Nds are going more and more close to Pareto optimal front in order to accomplish multi-objective optimization.

If $|Nds| < n$, by means of a clustering procedure or a randomization procedure, (n-|Nds|) individuals are generated and are combined with Nds to make a new population Pop_{t+1}. In this algorithm, the clustering procedure is evoked one time while the randomization procedure performing four times. This would achieve the best trade-off between the speed of the algorithm and the diversity of the solutions. If $|Nds| > n$, the clustering procedure is used to reduce the size of the non-dominated set. In this case, the clustering procedure is repeated until Nds include only n individuals or $|Nds| \leq n$. The

MOGA based on the clustering procedure, in which the Nds is constructed with the Dealer's Principle, is briefly described in Algorithm 3.

Algorithm 3: Multi-objective genetic algorithm based on the clustering procedure Multi-objective-GA(Pop$_0$) { $Q_t = \psi$ (Pop$_t$);   // ψ is a genetic operator including selection, crossover and mutation R_t=Pop$_t \cup Q_t$; //combine parent generation and new generation   Nds=Construct-Nds(R_t); //construct Nds with Dealer's Principle   if (|Nds|<n)   then if (count≤3) then { Pop$_{t+1}$=Nds $\cup$ {Random-procedure(n-|Nds|)};   //a randomization procedure is used to generated (n-|Nds|) individuals count=count+1 }   else {Pop$_{t+1}$= Nds $\cup$ Cluster (R_t-Nds, n-|Nds|); count=0 }   //the clustering procedure is used to generate (n-|Nds|) individuals   else if (| Nds|>n) then Pop$_{t+1}$ =Cluster(Nds, n);   //the clustering procedure is used to reduce the size of Nds   t=t+1; }

Here Cluster(P, m) is the clustering procedure, P is a population on which the clustering operator applies, and m is the size of the clustering result. Initially, count=0.

6.   EXPERIMENT

6.1   Convergence and Diversity

In this paper, we use a simple metric for evaluating convergence. A reference set is needed while evaluating convergence. A reference set P* is either a set of Pareto-optimal points (if known) or a non-dominated set of points in a combined pool of all generation-wise populations obtained from a MOGA run. This means P*=Non-dominated($\cup_{t=0}^{T} Nds^{(t)}$), where Nds(t) is the non-dominated set in the tth generation, (t=0, 1, …,T). From each individual i in the current non-dominated set, calculate the smallest normalized Euclidean distance to P* as follows [19]:

$$pd_i = \min_{j=1}^{|P^*|} \sqrt{\sum_{k=1}^{m} (\frac{f_k(i) - f_k(j)}{f_k^{max} - f_k^{min}})^2} \qquad (1)$$

Here, f_k^{max} and f_k^{min} are the maximum and the minimum function values of kth objective function in P*, and m is the number of the objective function.

Calculate the average of pd_i:

$$C(P^{(t)}) = \sum_{i=1}^{|Nds^{(t)}|} pd_i \Big/ |Nds^{(t)}|$$ (2)

In order to satisfy $C(P^{(t)}) \in [0,1]$, we normalize the $C(P^{(t)})$ values by its maximum value:

$$\overline{C}(P^{(t)}) = C(P^{(t)}) / C(P^{(0)})$$ (3)

Fig. 5 shows the convergence of three kind of MOGAs. It is clear that the $\overline{C}(P^{(t)})$ will become less and less when t increases. It also means that the set of candidate solutions will approach the Pareto optimal solutions gradually when $\overline{C}(P^{(t)})$ decreases continually.

Besides the convergence, we hope that the final solutions should have a good diversity. The obtained set of the first non-dominated solutions is compared with a uniform distribution and the deviation is computed as follows:

$$\Delta(d_i, \overline{d}) = \frac{1}{|Nds|} \sum_{i=1}^{|Nds|} (|d_i - \overline{d}|) \Big/ \overline{d}$$ (4)

$$\Delta_V = \sum_{i=1}^{10} \frac{(\Delta_i - \overline{\Delta})^2}{10}$$ (5)

Here, $d_i = Min\{s(i,j) \mid j \in Nds\}$, $s(i,j)$ is the Euclidean distance between individual i and j, $\overline{d}$ is the average of d_i, the deviation measure Δ_i is the value of $\Delta(d_i, \overline{d})$ in one run, the measure $\overline{\Delta}$ is the average of Δ_i for 10 runs, and _____ Nds _____ is _____ the _____ non-dominated _____ set. $\Delta(d_i, \overline{d})$ represents the variation degree of d_i. Thus, it is clear that an algorithm having a smaller Δ maintains better distribution of solutions. Here Δ_V is the variance of Δ in 10 runs, so the smaller the value of Δ_V, the better the consistency of the solutions. It is shown in Fig. 6 and in Table 1.

6.2   Simulation Results

The test problem DLTZ3 is identical to the problem described as follows:

Minimize $f_1(X) = (1 + g(X_K)) \cos(x_1 \pi / 2) \cos(x_2 \pi / 2) \cdots \cos(x_{m-2} \pi / 2) \cos(x_{m-1} \pi / 2),$

Minimize $f_2(X) = (1 + g(X_K)) \cos(x_1 \pi / 2) \cos(x_2 \pi / 2) \cdots \cos(x_{m-2} \pi / 2) \sin(x_{m-1} \pi / 2),$

Minimize $f_3(X) = (1 + g(X_K)) \cos(x_1 \pi / 2) \cos(x_2 \pi / 2) \cdots \sin(x_{m-2} \pi / 2),$

......

Minimize $f_{m-1}(X) = (1 + g(X_K))\cos(x_1\pi/2)\sin(x_2\pi/2),$

Minimize $f_m(X) = (1 + g(X_K))\sin(x_1\pi/2),$

$0 \le x_i \le 1,$ *for* $i = 1,2,\ldots,n$

    Where $g(X_K) = |X_K| + \sum_{i=m}^{n}((x_i - 0.5)^2 - \cos(20\pi(x_i - 0.5)), (x_m,\cdots,x_n) \in X_K$

    Here $|X_K|$ is   the   size   of X_K set,

$X = \{(x_1, x_2, \cdots, x_{m-1}, x_m, \cdots x_n)\}, X_K = \{(x_m, \cdots, x_n)\}$. The global Pareto-optimal front corresponds to $x_i = 0.5, (i = m, \cdots, n)$.

In experiment, the population size is 200, the crossover probability is 0.8, and the mutation probability is 1/len (where len is the number of variables). We use the binary coding and an equal length of genes in solving corresponding problems. We use FMOGA to denote our MOGA discussing in this paper.

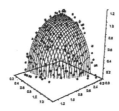

*Figure 1.*The NSGAII population on test problem DTLZ3

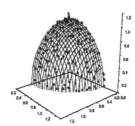

Figure 2. The FMOGA population on test problem DTLZ3

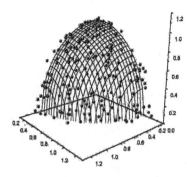

Figure 3. The SPEA2 population on test problem DTLZ3

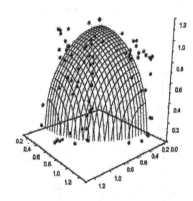

Figure 4. Fig 4. the NPGA population on test problem DTLZ3

We compare FMOGA with NSGA-II, SPEA2 and NPGA. Under the same environment, each algorithm runs for 500 generations. Figure 1 to Figure 4 show the distribution metrics for FMOGA, NSGA-II, SPEA2 and NPGA. In terms of the distribution of solutions, from the simulation results, it is shown that FMOGA, NSGA-II and SPEA2 do better than NPGA; furthermore, it is remarkable that FMOGA performs well than NSGA-II and SPEA2. Figure 6 shows the diversity at every generation of a MOEA run. The best performance is provided by FMOGA and the worst is NPGA. Figure 5 shows the convergence that FMOGA, NSGA-II and SPEA2 have reached closely to the true Pareto-optimal front, but NPGA cannot be shown in Figure 5 because $\overline{C}(P^{(t)}) > 0.3$.

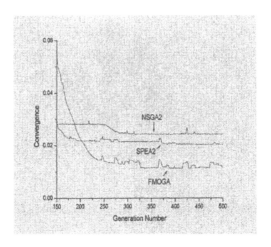

Figure 5. comparison of convergence metrics

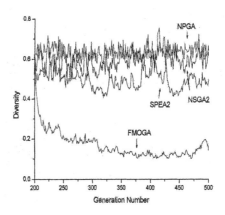

Figure 6. Fig 6. comparison of the diversity metrics

Table 1 shows the average value in 10 independent runs for FMOGA, NSGA-II, SPEA2 and NPGA. It is clear from Table 1 that NPGA is the fastest of all, and FMOGA is more efficient than NSGA-II and SPEA2. It is also shown in Table 1 that the FMOGA is more consistent than the other MOGA because its deviation Δ_V is the least of all.

Table 1.comparison of time, diversity and variance of diversity using four algorithms

Algorithm	FMOGA	NPGA	SPEA2	NSGA-II
Time	6.245	5.365	7.856	7.564

Diversity(Δ)	0.2306	0.6539	0.4093	0.6162
Variance of diversity(Δ_V)	0.0528	0.2642	0.0754	0.0862

7.   CONCLUSIONS

This paper proposes a new method to construct the non-dominated set of MOGA based on the Dealer's Principle. To keep the diversity of candidate solutions, a clustering procedure based on the core distance is discussed. To test the efficiency of the Dealer's Principle to construct the non-dominated set and the performance of the clustering procedure, we design a MOGA namely FMOGA. By the experimental results, it is shown that our new MOGA using the Dealer's Principle to construct non-dominated set and using clustering procedure to keep the diversity of solutions is of better performance on speed, convergence and diversity of solutions than previous approaches.

REFERENCES

1. Hisashi Tamaki. Generation of a set of Pareto-optimal solutions by genetic algorithm. T SICE, 1995, 31(8): 1185-1192.
2. Brian J. Ritzel, J. Wayland Eheart, and S. Ranjithan. Using genetic algorithms to solve a multiple objective groundwater pollution containment problem. Water Resources Research, 30(5): 1589-1603, may 1994.
3. Schaffer, J. D., Multi objective optimization with vector evaluated genetic algorithms. In J.Grefenstette, ed., Proceedings of an International Conference on Genetic Algorithms and their Applications, 93-100, 1985.
4. Patrick D. Surry, Nicholas J. Radcliffe, and Ian D. Boyd. A MultiObjective Approach to Constrained Optimisation of Gas Supply Networks : The COMOGA Method. In Terence C. Fogarty, editor, Evolutionary Computing. AISB Workshop. Selected Papers, Lecture Notes in Computer Science, pages 166--180. Springer-Verlag, Sheffield, U.K., 1995.
5. Richardson, J. T., Palmer, M. R., Liepins, G., & Hilliard, M. Some guidelines for genetic algorithms with penalty function. Proceeding of the third International Conference on Genetic Algorithms. Morgan-Kauffman, 191-197,1989.
6. Carlos M. Fonseca and Peter J. Fleming. Genetic Algorithms for Multiobjective Optimization: Formulation, discussion and Generalization, In Stephanie Forrest, editor, Proceedings of the Fifth International Conference on Genetic Algorithms, pages 416-423, San Mateo, California. University of Illinois at Urbana-Champaign, Morgan Kauffman Publishers, 1993.
7. Carlos Artemio Coello Coello. An Empirical Study of Evolutionary Techniques for Multiobjective Optimization in Engineering Design. PhD thesis, Department of Computer Science, Tulane University, New Orleans, LA, April 1996.

8. Goldberg, D. E. and Deb, K. A comparison of selection schemes used in genetic algorithms, Foundations of Genetic Algorithms, 69-93, 1991.

9. Kalyanmoy Deb. Evolutionary Algorithms for Multi-Criterion Optimization in Engineering Design, In Kaisa Miettinen, Marko M. Mäkelä, Pekka Neittaanmäki, and Jacques Periaux, editors, *Evolutionary Algorithms in Engineering and Computer Science*, chapter 8, pages 135-161. John Wiley & Sons, Ltd, Chichester, UK, 1999.

10. Jeffrey Horn and Nicholas Nafpliotis. Multiobjective Optimization using the Niched Pareto Genetic Algorithm, Technical Report IlliGAl Report 93005, University of Illinois at Urbana-Champaign, Urbana, Illinois, USA, 1993.

11. Horn J., Nafpliotis N., & Goldberg D. E. A Niched Pareto genetic Algorithm for Multiobjective Optimization. Proceeding of the first IEEE Conference on Evolutionary Computation, 82-87, 1994.

12. Goldberg, D. E., & Richardson, J. J. Genetic Algorithms with sharing for multi-modal function optimization. Genetic Algorithms and Their Applications: Proceedings of the second ICGA, Lawrence Erlbaum Associates, Hillsdale, NJ, 41-49, 1987.

13. Zitzler, E. and L. Thiele (1999). Multiobjective evolutionary algorithms: A comparative case study and the strength pareto approach. IEEE Transactions on Evolutionary Computation, 3(4): 257-271, November 1999.

14. E. Zitzler, M. Laumanns, and L. Thiele. SPEA2: Improving the Strength Pareto Evolutionary Algorithm for Multiobjective Optimization. EUROGEN 2001 - Evolutionary Methods for Design, Optimisation and Control with Applications to Industrial Problems, September 2001.

15. N. Srinivas and Kalyanmoy Deb. Multiobjective optimization using nondominated sorting in genetic algorithms. Technical report, Department of Mechanical Engineering, Indian Institute of Technology, Kanput, India, 1993.

16. Deb K., Agrawal S., Pratap A., & Meyarivan T. A Fast Elitist Non-Dominated Sorting Genetic Algorithm for Multi-Objective Optimization: NSGA-II. KanGAL Report No.200001, 2000.

17. Kalyanmoy Deb, Amrit Pratap, Sameer Agrawal and T. Meyrivan. A Fast and Elitist Multi-objective Genetic Algorithm : NSGA-II. IEEE Transactions on Evolutionary Computation, 6(2):182-197, April 2002.

18. Deb, K, Mohan, M. and Mishra, S. A Fast Multi-objective Evolutionary Algorithm for Finding Well-Spread Pareto-Optimal Solutions. KanGAL Report No. 2003002, February, 2003.

19. Deb, K and Jain, S. Running performance metrics for evolutionary multi-objective optimization. KanGAL Report No. 2002004, May 2002.

ENSEMBLES OF MULTI-INSTANCE NEURAL NETWORKS

Min-Ling Zhang, Zhi-Hua Zhou
National Laboratory for Novel Software Technology, Nanjing University,
Nanjing 210093, China
zhangml@lamda.nju.edu.cn zhouzh@nju.edu.cn

Abstract: Recently, multi-instance classification algorithm BP-MIP and multi-instance regression algorithm BP-MIR both based on neural networks have been proposed. In this paper, neural network ensemble techniques are introduced to solve multi-instance learning problems, where BP-MIP ensemble and BP-MIR ensemble are constructed respectively. Experiments on benchmark and artificial data sets show that ensembles of multi-instance neural networks are superior to single multi-instance neural networks in solving multi-instance problems.

Key words: machine learning; multi-instance learning; neural networks; neural network ensemble.

1.   INTRODUCTION

The notion of *multi-instance learning* was proposed by Dietterich et al. [2] in their investigation of drug activity prediction. In multi-instance learning, the training set is composed of many *bags* each containing many instances. If a bag contains at least one positive instance then it is labeled as a positive bag. Otherwise it is labeled as a negative bag. The labels of the training bags are known, but those of the training instances are unknown. The task is to learn something from the training set for correctly labeling unseen bags. Due to its unique characteristics and extensive applicability, multi-instance learning has been regarded as a new learning framework parallel to *supervised learning, unsupervised learning,* and *reinforcement learning* [4].

Recently, neural network based multi-instance classification algorithm BP-MIP [9] and regression algorithm BP-MIR [7] have been proposed, both of which are derived from the popular BP algorithm [6] with a global error function defined at the level of bags instead of at the level of instances. Considering that ensemble learning has been used to significantly improve the generalization ability of several multi-instance learners [10], this paper proposes to build ensembles of multi-instance neural networks to solve multi-instance problems, where BP-MIP ensemble and BP-MIR ensemble are constructed respectively. Experiments on benchmark and artificial data sets show that ensembles of multi-instance neural networks are superior to single multi-instance neural networks in solving multi-instance problems.

The rest of this paper is organized as follows. Section 2 proposes to build ensemble of BP-MIP. Section 3 proposes to build ensemble of BP-MIR. Finally, Section 4 concludes and indicates several issues for future work. Due to the page limitation, for more information about multi-instance learning, BP-MIP and BP-MIR, please refer to the literatures [7] and [8].

2.   BP-MIP ENSEMBLE

The *Musk* data is the only real-world benchmark test data for multi-instance learning at present. There are two data sets, both of which are publicly available from UCI Machine Learning Repository. Characteristics of those two data sets are summarized in Table 1.

Table 1. Some characteristics of the *Musk* data

Data set	Musk1	Musk2
Dimensionality	166	166
Number of bags	92	102
Number of positive bags	47	39
Number of negative bags	45	63
Number of instances	476	6,598
Average number of instance per bag	5.17	64.69
Maximal number of instances in a bag	40	1,044
Minimal number of instances in a bag	2	1

Leave-one-out test is performed on each *Musk* data set. In detail, for N bags, one bag is used to test while the others are used to train a BP-MIP ensemble in a loop of N iterations. In each iteration, bootstrap sampling [3] is used to generate four training sets from the original training set and four versions of BP-MIP neural network are trained respectively on each generated training set. Together with the BP-MIP neural network trained on the original training set, a BP-MIP ensemble containing five versions of BP-MIP neural network is constituted. The output of the BP-MIP ensemble under the test bag is determined by the outputs of its component BP-MIP neural networks via majority voting. The final predictive accuracy is calculated as the total number of correctly labeled test bags divided by N.

Table 2 compares the predictive accuracy of BP-MIP ensemble on the *Musk* data with those reported in the literatures. Configuration of component BP-MIP neural network is the same as that used in the literature [8].

Table 2. Comparison of the predictive accuracy on the *Musk* data

algorithm	Musk1 %correct	algorithm	Musk2 %correct
EM-DD	96.8	EM-DD	96.0
Iterated-discrim APR	92.4	Iterated-discrim APR	89.2
Citation-*k*NN	92.4	Relic	87.3
Diverse Density	88.9	Citation-*k*NN	86.3
RIPPER-MI	88.0	**BP-MIP ensemble**	**84.3**
BP-MIP ensemble	**87.0**	MULTINST	84.0
BP-MIP	83.7	Diverse Density	82.5
Relic	83.7	BP-MIP	80.4
MULTINST	76.7	RIPPER-MI	77.0

Table 2 shows that BP-MIP ensemble performs better than BP-MIP on both *Musk1* and *Musk2* data sets. Furthermore, the performance of BP-MIP ensemble, i.e. 87.0% on *Musk1* and 84.3% on *Musk2*, is comparable to 88.9% on *Musk1* and 82.5% on *Musk2*, i.e. the result achieved by Diverse Density [5], even though the architecture and parameters of component BP-MIP neural networks have not been finely tuned.

3.   BP-MIR ENSEMBLE

In 2001, Amar et al. [1] presented a method for creating artificial multi-instance data. The same as BP-MIP ensemble, leave-one-out test is performed on artificial data sets. The output of the BP-MIR ensemble under the test bag is determined by the outputs of its component BP-MIR neural networks via simple averaging. On the other hand, through rounding the real-valued outputs of component BP-MIR neural networks to 0 or 1, the predictive error of the BP-MIR ensemble can also be evaluated.

Due to the time limitation, we have only experimented on the data set LJ-80.166.1. Configuration of component BP-MIR neural network is the same as that used in the literature [7]. Experiments show that, compared with those of BP-MIR, the squared loss of BP-MIR ensemble reduces from 0.0487 to 0.0455 and the predictive error of BP-MIR ensemble reduces from 18.48% to 11.96%, even though the architecture and parameters of component BP-MIR neural networks have not been finely tuned.

4.   CONCLUSION

BP-MIP and BP-MIR are two neural network based multi-instance algorithms designed respectively for classification and regression tasks. In this paper, BP-MIP ensemble and BP-MIR ensemble are constructed correspondingly through employing neural network ensemble techniques. Experiments on benchmark and artificial data sets show that ensembles of multi-instance neural networks are superior to single multi-instance neural networks in solving multi-instance problems.

It is obvious that investigating better configurations of the component neural networks to further improve the generalization ability of BP-MIP ensemble and BP-MIR ensemble is an important issue to be explored in the near future. Furthermore, investigating other ensemble learning techniques to construct ensembles of multi-instance neural networks is another interesting issue for future work.

Acknowledgements

This work was supported by the National Outstanding Youth Foundation under the Grant No. 60325207 and the National Natural Science Foundation of China under the Grant No. 60105004.

References

[1]   Amar, R. A., Dooly, D. R., Goldman, D. R. and Zhang, Q.: Multiple-instance learning of real-valued data, In: *Proceedings of the 18th International Conference on Machine Learning*, pp. 3-10, Williamstown, MA, 2001.

[2]   Dietterich, T. G., Lathrop, R. H. and Lozano-Pérez, T.: Solving the multiple-instance problem with axis-parallel rectangles, *Artificial Intelligence*, 89(1-2) (1997), 31-71.

[3]   Efron, B. and Tibshirani, R.: *An Introduction to the Bootstrap*, Chapman & Hall, New York, 1993.

[4]   Maron, O.: Learning from Ambiguity, Ph.D. thesis, Department of Electrical Engineering and Computer Science, MIT, June 1998.

[5]   Maron, O. and Lozano-Pérez, T.: A framework for multiple-instance learning, In: M. I. Jordan and M. J. Kearns, (eds.), *Advances in Neural Information Processing Systems 10*, pp. 570-576, MIT Press, Cambridge, MA, 1998.

[6]   Rumelhart, D. E., Hinton, G. E. and Williams, R. J.: Learning internal representations by error propagation, *Nature*, 323(9) (1986), 533-536.

[7]   Zhang, M.-L. and Zhou, Z.-H.: A neural network based multi-instance regression algorithm, *Journal of Software*, 14(7) (2003), 1238-1242. (in Chinese)

[8]   Zhang, M.-L. and Zhou, Z.-H.: Improve multi-instance neural networks through feature selection, *Neural Processing Letters*, 19(1) (2004): 1-10.

[9]   Zhou, Z.-H. and Zhang, M.-L.: Neural networks for multi-instance learning. *Technical Report*, AI Lab, Computer Science & Technology Department, Nanjing University, Nanjing, China, Aug. 2002.

[10] Zhou, Z.-H. and Zhang, M.-L.: Ensembles of multi-instance learners. In: N. Lavrač, D. Gamberger, H. Blockeel and L. Todorovski, (eds.), *Lecture Notes in Artificial Intelligence 2837*, pp. 492-502, Springer-Verlag, Berlin, 2003.

A WORDNET-BASED APPROACH TO FEATURE SELECTION IN TEXT CATEGORIZATION

Kai Zhang, Jian Sun and Bin Wang
Insititue of Computing Technology, Chinese Academy of Sciences, Beijing, China 100080

Abstract: This paper proposes a new feature selection method for text categorization. In this method, word tendency, which takes related words into consideration, is used to select best terms. Our experiments on binary classification tasks show that our method achieves better than DF and IG when the classes are semantically discriminative. Furthermore, our best performance is usually achieved in fewer features.

Key words: Feature Selection, WordNet, Text Categorization

1. INTRODUCTION

Feature selection is a key step in text classification. There are many automatic feature selection methods such as Document Frequency, Information Gain and Mutual Information. They work well in many cases. [Sebastiani 02], [Aas 99] and [Yang 97] showed their formulas and gave comparisons. Most of them use frequency of words and disregard semantic information. Their methods assume that words are equal and isolated, but actually they are different and inter-connected in semantic. WordNet ([Miller 90]), one of the best lexical databases, would be helpful to feature selection.

There are a few studies in text classification using WordNet. Rodriguez's study ([Rodríguze 97]) using WordNet synonymy, involved a manual word sense disambiguation step, and took advantage of Reuters topical headings. Finally they got good results. Sam Scott's work ([Scott 98]) used hypernyms, and their representation works well for extended or unusual vocabulary like songs, but it is not likely to work well for texts that are concisely and efficiently written such as the texts in Reuters-21578. Word sense disambiguation is the bottleneck to his work, because it is difficult to select the correct meaning of a word in context. For feature selection, word sense disambiguation is not a sticking point. That's why we use WordNet to improve feature selection.

In this paper, we will study how to use WordNet to extract good features. The paper proceeds as follows. Section 2 discusses the usage of WordNet in feature selection. In section 3, we present the method of feature selection. Section 4 shows the experimental results and comparison. In section 5, we give comparisons with related work such as LSI and clustering of words. Finally section 6 presents the conclusions and future work.

2.   HOW TO USE WORDNET

In WordNet, English words have been organized into synonym sets (synsets), and each synset represents one underlying lexical concept. A word may have several meanings, corresponding to several synsets. There are different types of relations between synsets such as antonymy, meronymy and hyponymy. Nouns in WordNet are organized as a lexical inheritance system, hyponymy generates a hierarchical semantic organization, and meronymy is also implemented in the noun files. These relations are fundamental organizing principles for nouns, and useful for text mining.

Suppose we are trying to classify documents of two classes, for example, gold and livestock, given some samples for training. We do not know the topics of the classes. Without computer, which features can we choose from the training documents? It will be commonly observed that some similar words mostly occur in one set. These words are commonly good features. For figure 1, "gold", "silver", "mine", "beef", "hog" are usually good features. "Company" is not likely to be a good semantic feature, because his semantic neighbor "market" occurs frequently in both sets. Thus we can discover:

Good features tend to be gathered in semantics, especially the words that relate to the class topics. So similar words that mostly distribute in one training set would be good features.

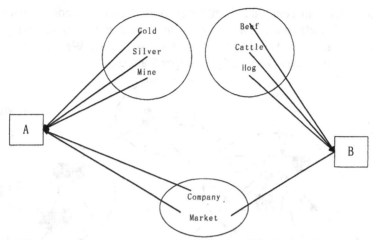

Figure 1: Two classes and the semantically clustered words.

Our method is to simulate this way. There are two semantically different classes: A and B. It is hard to find semantically related words directly, for there is no direct relation between words in WordNet. So we convert word frequencies to synset densities, which are the assumed frequencies of the synsets in training set.

Now we can interpret our method in another way. For each synset, it has two densities: density_A and density_B. If density_A is much greater than density_B, we can say the synset is tendentious to A. The formula *density_A/(density_A+density_B)* can be used to evaluate the tendency. However, as described above, a discriminative synset in semantics often has neighbors of the similar tendency. It would be better to take into account the neighbors of the synset. We cluster the synsets, and compute the total densities of the synsets in each cluster as the cluster densities of synsets in the cluster.

The formula *cluster_density_A/(cluster_density_A+cluster_density_B)* is more suitable to evaluate the tendency of synsets. Then the tendencies of synsets are converted to word tendencies. Finally DF is considered in the weight formula to remove infrequent words. All detailed formulas will be given in Section 3.

Figure 2 gives an example. The four words and their occurrences in both classes are shown at bottom. Synset and their relations are shown in the graph, types and directions of the relations are ignored. Densities are computed according to word occurrence. Black stands for synset density of A, while white stands for that of B. We notice that the only synset of Word3 has many black neighbors. Word3 would be a good feature. Word2 has 2 meanings: one is in a cluster of almost black, while the other is in that of half black. We can conclude Word3 has more semantic tendency than Word2, though Word2 does not occur in the training set of B and has more occurrences than Word3 in the training set of A. We can also conclude Word1 and Word4 are usually improper features.

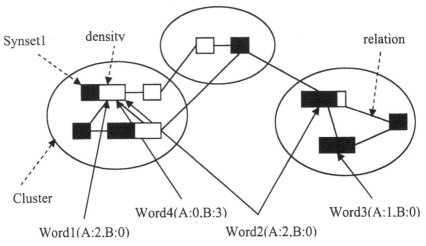

Figure 2:Clustering of synsets

3.   FEATURE SELECTION USING WORDNET

This section gives detailed algorithm of the feature selection method. First, we process the documents to get noun occurrences, which are the most useful information. Then as described in the previous section, we compute the density, cluster the synsets and give the weighting formula.

3.1   Preprocessing

In preprocessing, we use Eric Brill's part of speech tagger ([Brill 92]) to tag the training and test documents. It is a simple rule-based part of speech tagger. We only use nouns to select features. Verbs and other words are discarded, because they render less semantic information. The nouns are stemmed to their origin form. Finally, we remove the stop words and words that have more than 5 meanings. These words are commonly bad features.

3.2   Computing density

In WordNet, a word may have several meanings. Without word sense disambiguation, its frequency should be shared by its synsets equally. So the density of synset s should be summary of shares of several word frequencies. The "density" of a synset s corresponding to class c is given by:

$$density\,(s,c) = \sum_{w \in s} \frac{word\_frequency\,(c, w)}{Synset\_count\,(w)}$$

$$= \sum_{w \in s} \frac{times\,(c, w)}{synset\_count\,(w) \bullet word\_count\,(c)}$$

Times(c, w) denotes the occurrence of word w in the training documents of class c. Synset_count (w) is the count of synsets containing w in WordNet. Word_count(c) is the count of nouns in the training documents of class c. Synset density defined in this paper is similar to that of [Scott 98].

3.3   Clustering

Here we use one of the simplest clustering methods described as below. In the algorithm, the distance of two synsets is defined as the length of the shortest path between them in WordNet.

Input: The threshold T and N synsets
Output: Clusters of synsets
    1.   Arbitrarily choose a synset as a seed
    2.   Repeat
        Arbitrarily choose a synset (s) that is not clustered.
           Find the nearest seed (s') of s
           If the distance >T, let s be a seed
                Else s is put into the cluster of seed s'.
        Until all synsets are clustered.

We choose this method because it is simple. We don't think more complex methods will certainly get better result. It is difficult to achieve the most suitable method. This will be our future work to achieve more suitable methods.

3.4   Computing weights

After clustering, the density of a cluster r to class c is defined as:

$$cluster\_density\ (r,c) = \sum_{j\in r} density\ (j,c)$$

The cluster density can be regarded as the occurrence of some similar meaning in the cluster r in the training set of class c. Furthermore, we will have to compute word tendency to evaluate in which test set the word is likely to occur .The tendency should be decided by all the word meanings (synsets), but we use cluster density because of the hypothesis in Section 2.

The tendency of a word w to class A is defined as:

$$t(w) = \frac{\displaystyle\sum_{i\in Synset(w)} cluster\_density(cluster(i),A)}{\displaystyle\sum_{i\in Synset(w)} cluster\_density(clsuter(i),A) + cluster\_density(cluster(i),B)}$$

$$= \frac{\displaystyle\sum_{i\in Synset(w)} \sum_{j\in Cluster(i)} density(j,A)}{\displaystyle\sum_{i\in Synset(w)} \sum_{j\in Cluster(i)} density(j,A) + density(j,B)}$$

Where synset(w) denotes the synsets containing word w. Cluster(i) is the cluster of synset i. When $t(w)=1$, w is likely to semantically related to A. When $t(w)=0$, w is likely to semantically related to B. Words that have tendency of approximate 0 or 1 will be good choices for features.

For some reasons, some words have only one synset, and the synset is in the cluster of its own. They often gain good tendency, but they are not suitable for features.. To be a good feature, word frequency must be high .The final weight formula is given by:

$$WN(w) = |t(w) - 0.5| * \log(\min(DF(w),N) + 1)$$

Where DF (w) is the document frequency of the word w. N is the maximum document count of two classes. WN (w) is the final weight formula. Document Frequency would be a good parameter, and DF above N will be truncated to N. We use $log(DF+1)$ here, which is like the formula of TFIDF.

WN(w) can be the final formula. But to balance the features between A and B, interleaving can be done in feature sequence. Here is a sample of interleaving:

Original: A1,A2,A3,B1,B2,A4,B3,B4

Final: A1,B1,A2,B2,A3,B3,A4,B4

4.   EXPERIMENTS AND RESULTS

The classification tasks used in this study are drawn from three different pairs of classes in Reuters-21578. We do experiments using Rainbow, a good classifier with many options. We compared our method with IG and DF, which are regarded as two of the best feature selection methods. We use three pairs of classes ([gold/livestock], [crude/trade], [coffee/ship]), like that of Scott's experiments. For each pair of classes, we divide the documents for 20 times. For each division, we randomly choose 60 documents for training (30 for each class), and the others are documents for testing. We also have the option of feature count from 5 to 600 and DF threshold from 0 to 60. We use rainbow to get accuracy on different tasks and options.

First, table 1 gives the top 10 selected features in one classification in task of [gold/livestock], order by IG or WN (interleaved). We notice that features selected by WordNet are more semantically related to the class topics. "Company" perhaps is a proper feature for term frequency, but it is not directly related to the topics. From the relative small training sets, we can hardly draw the conclusion that "company" seldom occurs in the test set of livestock.

Table 1: Features selected by IG and WordNet

	IG	WN
1	Gold	Gold
2	Ounces	Beef
3	Ounce	Mine
4	Mine	Pork
5	Ton	Ounce
6	Cattle	Cattle
7	Lt	Ore
8	Company	Farm
9	Mining	Tons
10	Reserves	Hog

Second, Figure 3 gives the comparison between IG and WN in the task of [gold/ livestock]. The Y-coordinate is the average accuracy from 20 tests of different division, while the X-coordinate is the feature count. From the figure, we can see that WN get higher accuracy at fewer features. On the curve of WordNet, the vertex (99.46) is at the feature count of 10. The leftmost point shows the accuracy (99.04) at the feature count of 5. We can naturally draw the conclusion that our top 10 features are more discriminative than those of IG in this task. With the increment of feature count, the two curves almost converge like the curves in Yang's experiments ([Yang 97]).

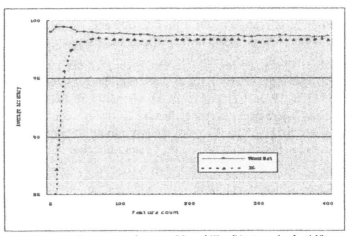

Figure 3: Comparison between IG and WordNet in task of gold/livestock

Table 2: The best error rates in different tasks

Tasks	Balance	IG	DF	WN
Gold/Livestock	134/113	1.52	0.69	0.53
Crude/Trade	626/543	2.66	3.07	4.33
Coffee/Ship	158/133	2.66	2.19	1.04

From Table 2,"Balance" refers number of examples in each class. "IG", "DF", "WN" show to the best error rates in different feature numbers. We can see that WordNet works well in task of [gold/livestock] and [coffee/ship]. While in Scott's experiments ([Scott 98]) WordNet does not improve the accuracy in task of [gold/livestock]. These classes are more specific, but for more general classes like crude and trade, it does not work well. The reason is that they have more semantic intersections, for example, the cargo may be oil and ore, which would be a little difficult for WordNet. It will be our future work to improve the accuracy of this kind of task.

5.   DISCUSSIONS

We achieve better results when using fewer features. Compared with other dimensionality-reduction methods such as LSI and cluster of words, it is worth noting that our feature space is still on English words. It is difficult to get higher accuracy in fewer word-features, because a feature in LSI or Cluster of words can be affected by a lot of words, a word-feature can be affected by only one word. Ten word-features perhaps do not occur in some test documents, but we get high accuracy in such risk.

Furthermore synset-feature is discussed in Sam Scott's papers ([Scott 98]). It is difficult to choose from synset-feature and word-feature. For synset-feature, it is important to get the right synset of words. However, the accuracy is not very high. For example, in Li's paper [Li.95], the accuracy is only about 72%. Without word sense disambiguation, experiments show that synset-feature is not found to produce significant performance. So word sense disambiguation will play an important role in text classification.

6.   CONCLUSIONS AND FUTURE WORK

Given the results from section 4, we can conclude that WordNet is a good resource for text classification. In this paper, we take the advantage of the related words using WordNet. Terms that have same tendencies as its neighbors will be good features. Based on this hypothesis, we use WordNet to extract more semantically related features. And this method can improve the accuracy in tasks that have semantically distinct classes.

However, as many people believed, significant advances must be made before NLP techniques can be used to improve text classification. Experiments shows that this method does not tend to perform well on classification tasks involving broadly defined or semantically related classes. This is a tentative and ongoing work. Clustering method and functions in this approach can be improved by using the WordNet hierarchy. And it would be helpful to incorporate other feature selection methods such as IG. For instance, formula based on WordNet can be given to tell which one is more suitable to certain classification task. And we will evaluate this method on more tasks to get more informative results. Multi-class tasks are also interesting.

Furthermore, we can also find latent features by using WordNet clusters. This perhaps works well for tasks that have smaller training sets.

REFERENCES

1. [Aas 99] Kjersti Aas, Line Eikvil.Text Categorisation: A Survey. Technical report,Norwegian Computing Center, June.
2. [Baker 98] L. Douglas Baker, Andrew Kachites McCallum. Distributional clustering of words for text classification. In Proc. SIGIR-98, Melbourne, Australia 1998.
3. [Blum 98] Avrim Blum and Tom Mitchell. Combining labeled and unlabeled data with co-training.In Proceedings of COLT'98,1998
4. [Brill 92] Eric Brill. A simple rule-based part of speech tagger. In proceedings of Third Conference on Applied Natural Language Processing, ACL, 1992
5. [Li.95] Xiaobin Li, Stan Szpakowicz and Stan Matwin. A WordNet-based Algorithm for Word Sense Disambiguation. In Proc. IJCAI_95, Montréal, Canada, 1995
6. [Miller 90] George A. Miller. WordNet: an On-line Lexical Database. International Journal of Lexicography 3(4), 1990
7. [Rodríguze et al.97] Manuel de Buenaga Rodríguze, Jos María Gómez-Hidalgo and Belén Díaz-Agudo. Using WordNet to Complement Training Information in Text Categorization. In Proc. RANLP-97, Stanford March 25-27,1997
8. [Scott 98] Sam Scott, Stan Matwin (1998). Text Classification Using WordNet Hypernyms. In S. Harabagiu & J. Yue Chai (Eds.) *Usage of WordNet in Natural Language Processing Systems: Proceedings of the Workshop*(pp. 45-52).
9. [Sebastiani 02] Fabrizio Sebastiani. Machine Learning in Automated Text Categorization. ACM Computing Surveys Vol. 34 ,No.1 March 2002 .
10. [Yang 95] Yiming Yang, Noise reduction in a statistical approach to text categorization. In Proc. SIGIR-95 (Seattle,WA,1995)
11. [Yang 97] Yiming Yang , Jan O.Pedersen. A comparative study on feature selection in text categorization. In Proc. ICML-97, Nashville, TN, 1997
12. [Yang 99] Yiming Yang , Xin Liu .A re-examination of text categorization methods. In Proc. SIGIR-99, Berkley, CA, 1999

A NEW SUPPORT VECTOR NEURAL NETWORK INFERENCE SYSTEM

Ling Wang and Zhi-Chun Mu
Information Engineering School, University of Science and Technology Beijing 100083,China

Abstract: In this paper, we present a new support vector neural network inference system (SVNNIS) for regression estimation. The structure of the proposed SVNNIS can be obtained similar to that in the support vector regression (SVR), while the output of the SVNNIS is unbiased compared with the SVR and the weights can be updated by the recursive least square method with forgetting factor. The advantage of this system is its good generalization capability. The simulation result illustrates the effectiveness of the proposed SVNNIS.

Key words: support vector machine(SVM); support vector regression(SVR); support vector neural network inference system (SVNNIS); regression estimation

1. INTRODUCTION

The Support vector machine (SVM) is derived from the Vapnik-Chervonenkis (VC) theory [1],[2]. Recently, SVM has also been applied to various fields such as classification, time prediction and regression. When SVM is employed to tackle the problems of function approximation and regression estimation, the approaches are often referred to as the support vector regression (SVR)[3]-[8].

The SVR type of function approximation is very effective, especially for solving the problems of multidimensional function regression estimation. Another important advantage for using SVR in function approximation is that the number of free parameters in the function approximation scheme is equal to the number of support vectors. Since the kernels of the SVR are similar to the basis functions of the RBF network, it is shown here that the

SVR can be reformulated as a RBF network with basis functions normalized. Jongcheol and Sangchul (2002)[9] proposed a new Support Vector Fuzzy inference system and used the SVM without bias. Nevertheless, the output of the SVR is biased, making it unsuitable for the neural network inference system. To overcome this limitation, we proposed a new support vector neural network inference system (SVNNIS). In contrast to the SVR, the output of the SVNNIS is unbiased. As the SVNNIS is a linear-in-weight network, the weights can be computed by the recursive least square method with forgetting factor.

This paper is organized as follows. Section 2 briefly introduced the fundamental ideas for SVM. In section 3, the new SVNNIS is proposed and its training process is described. Section 4 gives experimental results. Those results all showed the superiority of SVNNIS to the original SVR. Conclusions are given in Section 5.

2.   SUPPORT VECTOR MACHINES

The structure of the network and the training algorithm are important factors that affect the performance of the neural network. It is possible to reduce the modeling errors by increasing the complexity of the network. However, increasing the complexity of the network may overfit the data, leading to a degradation of its performance and reduced network transparency. between modeling errors and the complexity of the network. A principle generally adopted is to choose a network with the simplest structure, yet giving an acceptable precision. In [2] SVM are proposed with the network structure selected to satisfy a given precision. Suppose we have given data $\{(\vec{x}_1, y_1), (\vec{x}_2, y_2), \cdots, (\vec{x}_N, y_N)\}$ with $\vec{x}_i \in R^m$ and $y_i \in R$, where N is the number of training data, x_i is the ith input vector, and y_i is the desired output for the input $\vec{x}_i$. The SVM for estimating the nonlinear function $f(\cdot)$ is

$$f(\vec{x}) = \sum_{i=1}^{N} (\alpha_i^* - \alpha_i) K(\vec{x}_i, \vec{x}) + b \quad (1)$$

α_i^* and α_i are lagrange multipliers. The kernel function $K(x_i, x)$ is defined as a linear dot product of the nonlinear mapping,

$$K(\vec{x}_i, \vec{x}) = \phi(\vec{x}_i) \cdot \phi(\vec{x}) \quad (2)$$

The coefficients α_i^* and α_i of (1) are obtained by minimizing the following regularized risk functional $R_{eg}[f]$, which is a combination of the model complexity and the empirical risk, for given error bound ε,

$$R_{eg}[f] = \frac{1}{2}\|w\|^2 + C \cdot \sum_{i=1}^{l} L_\varepsilon(y) \quad (3)$$

Here, $\|w\|^2$ is a term which characterizes the model complexity, C is a constant determining the trade-off and the ε-insensitive loss function $L_\varepsilon(y)$ is given by

$$L_\varepsilon(y) = \begin{cases} 0 & for\, |f(\vec{x}) - y| < \varepsilon \\ |f(\vec{x}) - y| - \varepsilon & otherwise \end{cases} \qquad (4)$$

The minimization of regularized risk function in (3) can be converted to the following constrained optimization problem,

$$\left. \begin{aligned} \min_{\alpha,\alpha^*} w(\alpha,\alpha^*) = \min_{\alpha,\alpha^*} \frac{1}{2}\sum_{i=1}^{N}\sum_{j=1}^{N}(\alpha_i^* - \alpha_i)(\alpha_j^* - \alpha_j)K(\vec{x}_i,\vec{x}) - \sum_{i=1}^{N}(\alpha_i^* - \alpha_i)y_i + \varepsilon\sum_{i=1}^{N}(\alpha_i^* - \alpha_i) \\ subject\ to \sum_{i=1}^{N}(\alpha_i^* - \alpha_i) = 0 \\ \alpha,\alpha^* \in [0,c] \end{aligned} \right\} (5)$$

where the kernel function used is Gaussian and defined as

$$k(\vec{x}_i, \vec{x}) = \exp(-\frac{\|\vec{x} - \vec{x}_i\|^2}{2\sigma^2}) \qquad (6)$$

where σ is a constant. Note that only some of lagrange multipliers are not zeros and the corresponding vectors are called the support vectors.

3.   NEW SUPPORT VECTOR NEURAL NETWORK INFERENCE SYSTEM

In this section, the proposed SVNNIS is based on the multivariate nonlinear system, which is given by $y = f(x_1, x_2, \cdots, x_N)$. Now, we describe the learning algorithm adopted to train the SVNNIS, which is divided into two phases, the initial phase and the learning phase.

The initial phase is to determine the network inference system structure and the corresponding initial network weights through the SVR theory. When the cost function in (4) and the kernel functions in (6) are chosen, the initial weights and the structure of SVNNIS can be determined by the SVR theory as stated in the previous section. In this paper, After applying the SVR theory, an initial SVNNIS is obtained as

$$\hat{y} = \sum_{i=1}^{l} \beta_i K(\vec{x}, \vec{x}_i) + b \qquad (7)$$

where $\beta_i = \alpha_i^* - \alpha_i$, $\hat{y}$ is the output of the SVNNIS, $K(x, x_i)$ is a kernel function of the SVR theory, l is the number of kernel functions, which is equivalent to the number of support vectors, and $\beta = [\beta_1, \beta_2, \cdots, \beta_l]$ is the weight vector of the network. Since the SVR given by (8) can be considered as a two-layer neural network linear in its weights, it is intuitive to reformulate it as a RBF network using normalized basis functions. Now, Let's review the RBF network. First, the RBF network consists of m inputs with each input represented by n_i univariate basis functions, the number of weights is $n = \prod n_i$. Let the centers of the basis function can be chosen at the input data, $\vec{x}_i^l = [x_{i1}, \cdots, x_{im}]$, This is not restrictive, as the centers of the basis functions for this class of RBF networks can be chosen freely. Then the RBF network is given by

$$y = \frac{\sum_{i=1}^{n} \theta_i \mu_i(\vec{x}_i')}{\sum_{i=1}^{n} \mu_i(\vec{x}_i)} \tag{8}$$

where θ_i is the ith weight; and $\mu_i(\cdot)$ is the ith Gaussian basis function given by

$$\mu_i(\vec{x}_i) = \exp\left(-\frac{|\vec{x}_i - \vec{x}_i'|^2}{2\gamma^2}\right) \tag{9}$$

where γ and $\vec{x}'$ are, respectively the spread chosen to ensure a thorough coverage of the input space, and the center of the Gaussian function. The centers $\vec{x}'$ can also be considered as the fuzzy basis vector [10], since $\mu_i(\cdot)$ is the fuzzy membership function. The ith multivariate basis function is a product of the univariate basis functions obtained from the inputvariables, i.e.

$$\mu_i(\vec{x}_i) = \prod_{j=1}^{m} \mu_{i,j}(x_{ij}) \tag{10}$$

Where $\mu_{i,j}(x_{ij}) = \exp(-(x_{ij} - x_{ij}')^2 / 2\gamma^2)$. The centers $\vec{x}'$ are chosen from the input data $\vec{x}$. From (10), $\mu_i(\vec{x}') = 1$. It is assumed for simplicity that each input has the same number of basis functions, i.e.,

$$n = n_1 = \cdots = n_m \tag{11}$$

If (8) can be reformulated to the form of (9), the weights can also be estimated using linear least-squares method to overcome the biased problem of the SVR. For convenience, let the weights of the network be denoted by $[\theta_1', \cdots, \theta_{n+1}']^T$.

Then (8) can be rewritten as

$$y_i = \sum_{j=1}^{n} \theta'_j K_j(\vec{x}'_i) + \theta'_{n+1} \qquad (12)$$

Let

$$\lambda(\vec{x}_i) = \sum_{j=1}^{n} K_j(\vec{x}_i) \qquad (13)$$

$$\psi = \begin{bmatrix} K_1(\vec{x}_1) & \cdots & K_n(\vec{x}_N) \\ \vdots & & \vdots \\ K_1(\vec{x}_1) & \cdots & K_n(\vec{x}_N) \end{bmatrix} \qquad (14)$$

and

$$L = \lambda(\vec{x}_i) \qquad (15)$$

As the kernels in (13) are multivariate basis functions given by (9) and the SV are the respective centers, the two-layer neural network given by (13) can be rewritten as a RBF network. In matrix form, (13) becomes

$$Y = \psi \begin{bmatrix} \theta'_1 \\ \vdots \\ \theta'_n \end{bmatrix} + \begin{bmatrix} \theta'_{n+1} \\ \vdots \\ \theta'_{n+1} \end{bmatrix}, \qquad (16)$$

where $Y = [y_1, \cdots, y_N]^T$. Since $\sum_{j=1}^{n} K_j(\vec{x}_i)/\lambda(\vec{x}_i) = 1$, then

$$L^{-1}\psi \begin{bmatrix} 1 \\ \vdots \\ 1 \end{bmatrix} = \begin{bmatrix} 1 \\ \vdots \\ 1 \end{bmatrix}. \qquad (17)$$

Eq.(17) can be rewritten as

$$Y = \psi \begin{bmatrix} \theta'_1 \\ \vdots \\ \theta'_n \end{bmatrix} + L^{-1}\psi \begin{bmatrix} \theta'_{n+1} \\ \vdots \\ \theta'_{n+1} \end{bmatrix} = L^{-1}\psi \begin{bmatrix} \theta_1 \\ \vdots \\ \theta_n \end{bmatrix}, \qquad (18)$$

where $\{\theta_1, \cdots, \theta_n\}$ are the weights given by

$$
\psi \begin{bmatrix} \theta_1 \\ \vdots \\ \theta_n \end{bmatrix} = L\psi \begin{bmatrix} \theta_1' \\ \vdots \\ \theta_n' \end{bmatrix} + \psi \begin{bmatrix} \theta_{n+1}' \\ \vdots \\ \theta_{n+1}' \end{bmatrix}, \tag{19}
$$

Rearranging (20), the weights $\theta_1, \cdots, \theta_n$ can be expressed in terms of $\{\theta_1', \cdots, \theta_{n+1}'\}$ as

$$
\begin{bmatrix} \theta_1 \\ \vdots \\ \theta_n \end{bmatrix} = (\psi^T \psi)^{-1} \psi^T L\psi \begin{bmatrix} \theta_1' \\ \vdots \\ \theta_n' \end{bmatrix} + \begin{bmatrix} \theta_{n+1}' \\ \vdots \\ \theta_{n+1}' \end{bmatrix}, \tag{20}
$$

From (21), the following network is obtained.

$$
y_i = \frac{\sum_{j=1}^n \theta_j K_i(\vec{x}_i)}{\sum_{j=1}^n K_i(\vec{x}_i)} = \sum_{j=1}^n \theta_j N_j(\vec{x}_i), \tag{21}
$$

Where $N_j(\vec{x}_i) = K_j(\vec{x}_i) / \lambda(\vec{x}_i)$ is the normalized basis function. For convenience, the network given by (22) is referred to as the support vector neural network inference system (SVNNIS). The architecture of the SVNN is shown in Figure 1.

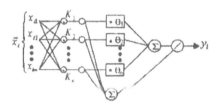

Figure 1. The architecture of the SVNNIS

In the second phase, the SV of the SVVNNIS are obtained by minimizing (5), the weights $\{\theta_1, \cdots, \theta_n\}$ are to be adjusted via the recursive least square method with forgetting factor algorithm. Rewriting (22) in matrix form gives

$$
y_i = B^T(\vec{x}_i)\theta \tag{22}
$$

where $B(\vec{x}_i) = [N_1(\vec{x}_i), \cdots, N_n(\vec{x}_i)]^T$ and $\theta = [\theta_1, \cdots, \theta_n]^T$. The cost function is

$$E(t) = \sum_{j=1}^{n} \alpha^{n-1}(y_i - \hat{y}_i(t))^2, \qquad (23)$$

$$\hat{y}_i(t) = B^T(\vec{x}_i)\hat{\theta} \qquad (24)$$

The linear least-squares estimate of the weights $\hat{\theta}$ is

$$\hat{\theta} = [\phi^T \phi]^{-1} \phi^T Y, \qquad (25)$$

Where

$$\phi = [N_1(\vec{x}_i), \cdots, N_n(\vec{x}_i)] \qquad (26)$$

and

$$Y = [y_1, \cdots, y_n]^T \qquad (27)$$

The learning algorithm is Where t is the epoch number, $\alpha \in (0,1)$ is a forgetting factor, $\hat{y}_i$ is the estimate of the y_i given by

$$\hat{\theta}(t+1) = \hat{\theta}(t) + \eta(t+1)\varepsilon^T(t+1), \qquad (28)$$

Where

$$\eta(t+1) = \frac{\alpha^{-1}P(t)\vec{x}_i(t+1)}{1 + \alpha^{-1}\vec{x}_i^T(t+1)P(t)\vec{x}_i(t+1)},$$

$$\varepsilon(t+1) = y_i - \hat{y}_i(t+1),$$

$$P(t+1) = \alpha^{-1}P(t) - \alpha^{-1}\eta(t+1)\vec{x}_i(t+1)P(t),$$

$$P(0) = I.$$

The SVNNIS learning algorithm is summarized as follows.

Step1) For a given set of training data $\{(\vec{x}_i, y_i), i = 1,2, \cdots, N\}, \vec{x}_i \in R^n, y_i \in R$; a set of testing data $\{(\vec{x}_k, y_k), k = 1,2, \cdots, N\}, \vec{x}_k \in R^n, y_k \in R$; .

Step 2) Initialize the SVNNIS structure with the given kernel function, the loss function, the threshold ε_R used for the determining the termination condition of the learning algorithm.

Step 3) The support vectors are obtained by the sequential minimal optimization (SMO) algorithm, so we can construct a SVNNIS.

Step 4) For each training pattern, compute the estimated result by (8) and its error.

Step 5) Update the weight vector $\hat{\theta}$ incrementally by (28).

Step 6) Compute the error defined by (23).

Step 7) If the termination conditions are not satisfied, then go to step 4; otherwise, termin ate the learning process.

4.   SIMULATION RESULTS

The simulations were conducted in the Matlab environment. The SVR toolbox provided by Gunn [11]. In this study, the results of various cases with different loss functions (the ε - insensitive function with 0, 0.01), different σ s, and different C s are presented for illustration. The forgetting factor α used in the simulation is 0.95. To analysis the performance of the proposed SVNNIS, the modeling error is defined by as Root Mean Square Error (RMSE):

$$E = \sqrt{\frac{\sum\limits_{k=1}^{N}(y_k - \hat{y}_k)}{N}} \qquad (29)$$

where N is the number of data, y_k and $\hat{y}_k$ are the system and the model output.

In this paper, the functions is defined as

$$y = x^{2/3} \quad with \quad x \in [-2,2]. \quad (30)$$

The test data sets with 200 patterns are also generated for both examples. The testing RMSEs of the SVR are obtained for various loss functions with different parameters sets $\{\sigma, C\}$. Detailed results are shown in [12]. From the simulations it can found that the parameter sets for the best performance in different loss functions are different. For example, in the case of using the ε -insensitive function with ε =0.1 as the loss function, when $\{\sigma, C\}$={0.5,5}, the performance is the best and the testing RMSE is 0.0743. For this case, after the SVNNIS learning, the RMSE becomes 0.0484. The testing RMSEs of SVR and of SVNNIS with ε =0.1

Table 1.

	C=0.5	C=1	C=5	C=10	C=50	C=100
$\tau = 0.5$	0.09153	0.08548	0.07438	0.09071	0.09478	0.09736
	0.03358	0.07348	0.0484	0.07546	0.09355	0.9668
$\tau = 0.7$	0.04112	0.02381	0.02582	0.02901	0.03919	0.04545
	0.01874	0.01475	0.01220	0.01603	0.02688	0.03334
$\tau = 1$	0.01801	0.01515	0.01513	0.01609	0.01842	0.01941
	0.00205	0.00300	0.00638	0.00793	0.01091	0.01207
$\tau = 2$	0.01506	0.01073	0.00779	0.00784	0.00892	0.00946
	0.00051	0.00078	0.00217	0.00301	0.00506	0.00579
$\tau = 3$	0.04518	0.02276	0.00986	0.00815	0.00675	0.00658
	0.01218	0.00804	0.00365	0.00278	0.00202	0.00189

The learned results of SVR and SVNNIS are respectively displayed in

Figure 2(a) and (b) for illustration. They are all the cases of using the ε - insensitive function with $\varepsilon =0$ and $\{\sigma, C\}=\{2,100\}$. These results match with the concept discussed in[13]. It can be found that the proposed SVNNIS can reduce the overfitting phenomena.

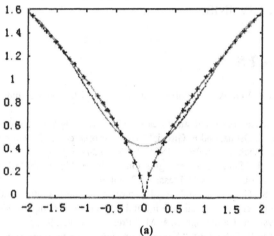

(a)

Figure 2. (a). Result obtained by SVR for function $y=x^{2/3}$

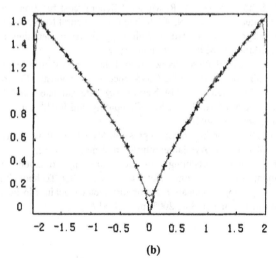

(b)

Figure 2. (b). Result obtained by SVNNIS for function $y=x^{2/3}$

5.   CONCLUSIONS

In this paper, a new support vector neural network inference system was proposed to enhance the generalization capability of the SVR approaches. The basis idea of the approach is to adopt the structure similar with that of the SVR, while the output of the SVNNIS is unbiased compared with the SVR, the weights can be updated by the recursive least square method with forgetting factor. The advantages of this system are their good generalization capabilities. The simulation result illustrates the effectiveness of the proposed SVNNIS.

REFERENCES

1. C. Cortes and V. Vapnik, "Support vector networks," Machine Learning, vol. 20, pp. 273–297, 1995.
2. V. Vapnik, The Nature of Statistical Learning Theory. New York: Springer-Verlag, 1995.
3. S. Mukherjee, E. Osuna, and F. Girosi, "Nonlinear prediction of chaotic time series using a support vector machine," in Proc. NNSP, 1997, pp.24–26.
4. H. Drucker et al., "Support vector regression machines," in Neural Information Processing Systems. Cambridge, MA: MIT Press, 1997, vol. 9.
5. V. Vapnik, S. Golowich, and A. J. Smola, "Support vector method for function approximation, regression estimation, and signal processing,"in Neural Information Processing Systems. Cambridge, MA: MIT Press, 1997, vol. 9.
6. A. J. Smola and B. Schölkopf, "A tutorial on support vector regression," Royal Holloway College, London, U.K., Neuro COLT Tech. Rep.TR-1998-030, 1998.
7. A. J. Smola, B. Schölkopf, and K. R. Müller, "General cost functions for support vector regression," presented at the ACNN, Australian Congr.Neural Networks, 1998.
8. A. J. Smola, "Regression estimation with support vector learning machines,"thesis, Technical Univ. Munchen, Munich, Germany,1998.
9. Jongcheol Kim*, sangchul Won* "New Fuzzy Inference System using a Support Vector Machine" Proceeding of the 41st IEEE Conference on Decision and Control,12 2002
10. Harris, C.J., Wu, Z.Q., Gan, Q., 1999. Neurofuzzy state estimators and their applications. In: Sinha, N.K., Gupta, M.M. (Eds.), Soft Computing and Intelligent Systems. Academic Press, New York, pp. 377 – 402.
11. S. R. Gunn. (1999) Support vector regression-Matlab toolbox. Univ. Southampton, Southampton, U.K.[Online]. Available: http://kernel-machines.org.
12. C.C. Chuang, "Robust modeling for function approximation under outliers," Ph.D.dissertation, Dept. Electr. Eng., Nat. Taiwan Univ. Sci. Technol., Taipei, 2000.
13. F. E. H. Tay and L. Cao, "Application of support vector machines in financial time series forecasting," in Int. J. Manage. Sci., 2001, pp.309–317.

AN IMPROVED VEHICLE CLASSIFICATION METHOD BASED ON GABOR FEATURES

Ying-nan Zhao, Zheng-dong Liu, Jing-yu Yang
Computer Department, Nanjing University of Science & Technology, Nanjing210094, China

Abstract: Vehicle classification is an important issue in the domain of ITS (Intelligent Transportation Systems). In this paper we presents an improved one based on Gabor features, which contains three consecutive stages: vehicle segmentation, Gabor features extraction and template matching. A novel non-even sampling of Gabor features is proposed. The experimental data show that this method can heavily reduce the computation and memory requirements, and illustrate good performance both in discrimination ability and robustness.

Key words: ITS, Gabor features, Template matching, Vehicle classification

1.   INTRODUCTION

Vehicle classification is an important issue in the domain of ITS. The conventional methods are mostly focused on the uncertainties associated with ground vehicle classification, for example vehicle orientation. Deformable template [1] is applied in this field. However, the uncertainties are comparatively minor in the application of park area, toll station, etc. In this context Gabor filtrer [2] is one good solution. To reduce heavy computation and memory requirements caused by Gabor features, we put forward a novel non-even sampling method on the basis of the edge features in vehicles as an improvement for vehicle classification.

The organization of this paper is as follows. Section 2 presents vehicle classification. Section 3 shows the performances of this method, and conclusions are drawn in Section 4.

2.   VEHICLE CLASSIFICATION

There are three stages in vehicle classification, i.e. vehicle segmentation, Gabor features extraction and template matching.

First, vehicle segmentation using background subtraction is applied in predefined area of the image. Logarithmic intensities are selected here to weaken the affection caused by illumination factor, as described in Ref. [3]. Then we do opening operation to smooth the vehicle edges. Next the vehicle at the optimal area will be clipped by calculating the cumulative histogram value for each possible existence of vehicle.

Second, we do Gabor features extraction. The Gabor wavelets can be defined as follows [4]:

$$\psi(x,y,\omega_0,\theta) = \frac{1}{2\pi\sigma^2} e^{-((x\cos\theta+y\sin\theta)^2+(-x\sin\theta+yx\cos\theta)^2)/2\sigma^2}$$
$$\times\left[e^{i(\omega_0 x\cos\theta+\omega_0 y\sin\theta)} - e^{-\omega_0^2\sigma^2/2}\right] \qquad (1)$$

where σ is the standard deviation of the Gaussian envelope along the x and y-dimensions (here $\sigma_x = \sigma_y$), ω_0 and θ are the radial center frequency, and orientation respectively. Let $I(x,y)$ denotes the image, then $C_{\psi l}(x,y,\omega_0,\theta)$, the convolution result corresponding to the Gabor wavelet at radial center frequency ω_0 and orientation θ, is defined as follows:

$$C_{\psi l}(x,y,\omega_0,\theta) = I(x,y) * \psi(x,y,\omega_0,\theta) \qquad (2)$$

where $*$ denotes the convolution operator. We select experimentally three center frequencies $(\pi/2, \sqrt{2}\,\pi/4, \pi/4)$ with a scale factor of $1/\sqrt{2}$, and 8 orientations as suggest in Ref. [3]. As for a specific point (X,Y), we thus get a set of filter responses for that point. They are denoted as a Gabor jet. A jet J is defined as the set $\{J_j\}$ of complex coefficients obtained from that point, and can be written as

$$J = \{J_i\} = \{a_j \exp(i\phi_j)\} \quad j = 1,2,\cdots,n \qquad (3)$$

where a_j is magnitude, ϕ_j is phase of Gabor features, and n is the number of sampling points.

To reduce the heavy computation and memory requirement caused by Gabor feature vectors and to maintain the recognition performance as well, we propose a non-even sampling scheme, which is described as follows:

(1) Detect edges in a sample image by Sobel operator. Open operation is done to remove the effect caused by some minor edges and isolated noises.

(2) Sort sampling windows descending by the number of edge pixels contained in each one.

(3) A certain percentage of the sampling windows are then selected backward as Key Sampling Windows (KSW). The remaining sampling windows are called Assistant Sampling Windows (ASW). If the sampling windows with edge pixels are inadequate to the selected percentage, the remaining without edge pixels, which are nearest to the center of the image, will be chosen as KSW to reach this percentage.

(4) We adopt different sampling interval on the KSW and ASW, as the points in these two kinds of sampling windows have different levels of importance for vehicle classification.

(5) A Gabor feature vector of lower dimension can therefore be generated. It can be concluded that most of the points in KSW appear near the important features in the sample image.

Finally, we use Gabor jet matching method to recognize vehicle type by the following equation:

$$\max_{\forall J'} S_a(J,J') = \frac{\sum_j a_j \cdot a_j'}{\sqrt{\sum_j a_j^2 \cdot \sum_j a_j'^2}} \tag{4}$$

where J is Gabor jet of the image and J' is Gabor jet of template image.

3.   EXPERIMENTAL RESULTS AND DISCUSSION

The proposed method is evaluated by recognition rate using 4 types of vehicles, i.e. sedan, truck, minibus and autobus. Table 1 shows the recognition rates with different sampling intervals in KSW and in ASW, and regular intervals in KSW only, where $n:m$ means that the sampling intervals for the points in KSW and in ASW are $n \times n$ and $m \times m$. The tested sample images are 30 unknown vehicles without disturbance. The results imply that the points in KSW contain the dominant discrimination information. Table 2 gives a comparison of classification rate using methods of Ref. [3] and the presented. 60 unknown vehicles are tested under four different circumstances, i.e. no disturbance, global blur, local glance and the highlighting, each of which is composed of 15 images. In the former, 4×4

sampling interval is selected, and in the latter, the portion of KSW is 2/3 and the different sampling interval is 4:6. The data show that the presented outperforms the conventional both in discrimination ability and robustness.

Table 1. The average recognition rates with two different sampling methods

Proportion of KSW	Sampling methods	Different sampling intervals			Sampling KSW only	
	Sampling interval	4:6	4:8	6:8	4×4	6×6
1/3	Recognition rate (%)	96.9	96.0	94.8	96.5	94.2
	Dimension (D)	4,352	3,456	2,176	2,304	1024
2/3	Recognition rate (%)	97.6	96.3	95.9	97.1	95.2
	Dimension (D)	5,632	5,184	2,624	4,608	2,048

Table 2. The comparison of average recognition rates (%) using different methods

Vehicle classification methods	Regular sampling			
	No disturbance	Global blur	Local glance	Highlighting
Ref. [3]	93.7	68.4	84.5	71.4
Presented	97.8	73.2	87.6	80.9

4. CONCLUSIONS

To lower the dimension of Gabor feature vector, we put forward a novel non-even sampling of Gabor features for an improved vehicle classification. The experimental results show that the presented method illustrates good performance both in discrimination ability and robustness. However, this method is only fit for the recognition of objects with apparent edge features. In fact, any features in an object do have different levels of importance for recognition. How to select key points and assistant points after the training of some samples for non-even sampling is our future work.

REFERENCES

[1] Jolly M.P.D., Lakshmanan S. and Jain A. K., Vehicle segmentation and classification using deformable templates, IEEE Transaction on Pattern Analysis and Intelligence, 1996, 18(3): 293-308

[2] Lim T.R and Guntoro A.T. Thiang, Car recognition using gabor filter feature extraction, Circuits and Systems, APCCAS'02, 2002, 2: 451-455

[3] Quen-Zong Wu and Bor-Shenn Jeng, Background subtraction based on logarithmic intensities, Pattern Recognition Letters, 2002, 23: 1529-1536

[4] Chui, C.K., An Introduction to Wavelets, Academic Press, 1992

AN INCREMENTAL ALGORITHM ABOUT THE AFFINITY-RULE BASED TRANSDUCTIVE LEARNING MACHINE FOR SEMI-SUPERVISED PROBLEM

Weijiang Long[1], Fengfeng Zhu[2] and Wenxiu Zhang[1]
[1] Institute of Information and Systems,Faculty of Sciences, Xi'an Jiaotong University,Xi'an 710049
[2] Department of Appled Mathematics, South China University of Technology,Guangzhou 510640

Abstract: One of the central problems in machine learning is how to effectively combine unlabelled and labelled data to infer the labels of unlabelled ones. In recent years, there has a growing interest on the transduction method. In this article, the transductive learning machines are described based on a so-called affinity rule which comes from the intuitive fact that if two objects are close in input space then their outputs should also be close, to obtain the solution of semi-supervised learning problem. By using the analytic solution for this problem, an incremental learning algorithm adapting to on-line data processing is derived.

Key words: Semi-supervised learning, Transductive learning machine, Support vector machines, Affinity measure, Incremental learning algorithm

1.   INTRODUCTION

One of the most important subjects in current data mining research is semi-supervised learning in which some of the observations have been labelled by the supervisor, while the labels of others are not obtained for various reasons. We respectively call these two kinds of observations the labelled data and unlabelled data. The main problem to study is how to infer the proper label of the unlabelled data using the observations including labelled and unlabelled data and relevant knowledge. The classical method for solving this problem is so-called induction-deduction method in which the labelled data are first analyzed to find a generalized rule and regard this rule to be justified for future observations (that is, from particularity to generality), and then this general rule is applied to the unlabelled data to infer their labels (that is, from generality to particularity).

In recent years, however, the transductive method, proposed by Vapnik(1998) has gained much concern. For semi-supervised learning, a general rule which is applied to both the unlabelled data and the possible other observations is indeed unnecessary in that only labeling those particular observations of unlabelled data is what we concern. The transduction method combined the labelled with the unlabelled data are used to derive the rule from particularity to particularity.

Up to now, there have been several examples of successful realization of transduction and experimentation on its superiority against traditional method. Chapell et al. (1999) implemented transductive inference by minimizing the leave-one-out error of ridge regression, and demonstrated that this transductive way for estimating values of the regression is more accurate than the traditional method. Bennettet et al.(1998) introduced semi-supervised support vector machines (S^3VM) by overall risk minimization, and demonstrated that S^3VM either make an improvement or show no significant difference in generalization compared to the usual structural risk minimization approach. Joachims (1999) suggested transductive support vector machines(TSVM) to deal with text classification. Furthermore, he presented a new transductive learning method in (Joachims, 2003) which can obtain the globally optimal solution by spectral methods. An algorithm was also proposed to robust achieve good generalization performance. Recently, Zhou et al.(2003a) studied semi-supervised learning problems by Hamilton method, and he latterly used objects programming involving norm in Zhou et al.(2003b) to derive the solution. However, it should be pointed out that is different from our paper. Zhou Guang-ya et al. (1993) gave many affinity-measures and applying rules which can be used in our discussing the machine learning problems.

In this paper, we deal with the semi-supervised learning transduction method based on affinity-rule by measuring the affinity of different objects in general space, and obtain an incremental learning algorithm. The principle comes from an intuitive fact that similar objects should have similar outputs. Because of the loose assumptions, this method has wider applications, more concise solution. We derive incremental learning algorithm adapting to on-line data processing. Its results are simple in expression and easy in calculation.

2.   METHODS AND PROPERTIES

Let X^* be the input space and Y^* be the output space. The obtained data set is

$$\{(\mathbf{x}_1, \mathbf{y}_1), (\mathbf{x}_2, \mathbf{y}_2), \cdots, (\mathbf{x}_l, \mathbf{y}_l), \mathbf{x}_{l+1}, \cdots, \mathbf{x}_{l+u}\},$$
$$\mathbf{x}_i \in X^*, 1 \leq i \leq l+u; \quad \mathbf{y}_i \in Y^*, 1 \leq i \leq l, n = l+u,$$

where $L^* = \{(\mathbf{x}_1, \mathbf{y}_1), (\mathbf{x}_2, \mathbf{y}_2), \cdots, (\mathbf{x}_l, \mathbf{y}_l)\}$ is labelled data set and $U^* = \{\mathbf{x}_{l+1}, \cdots, \mathbf{x}_{l+u}\}$ unlabelled data set. $\{\mathbf{x}_1, \mathbf{x}_2, \cdots, \mathbf{x}_l\}$ are labelled objects and $\mathbf{y}_i$ is the label of $\mathbf{x}_i$. We aim at inferring the labels of unlabelled data. For convenience, we assume that the labels stand for the different classes and discuss the classification problem. Let the number of the classes be c and $\mathbf{e}_i$ be the vector with the i-th element being 1 and others being 0. Therefore Y^* may be taken as $\{\mathbf{e}_1, \mathbf{e}_2, \cdots, \mathbf{e}_c\}$ in classification problem. In order to obtain the labels estimates of $\mathbf{x}_i$ for $i > l$, a general labelling variable $\mathbf{z}_i \in R^c$ is often considered, where $\mathbf{z}_i = (z_{i1}, z_{i2}, \cdots, z_{ic})^T$ is an auxiliary variable to simplify the complexity in solving this problem, and $\mathbf{z}_i$ is not necessary to hold the same form as $\mathbf{e}_j$. Then we use $\mathbf{y}_i = \mathbf{e}_{\arg\max\{z_{ik}; 1 \leq k \leq c\}}$ as the estimates of the labels. The following conditions are requested for $\mathbf{z}_i$. 1) If $\mathbf{x}_i$ is close to $\mathbf{x}_j$, then the general label $\mathbf{z}_i$ is also close to $\mathbf{z}_j$. 2) For the labelled data, the $\mathbf{z}_i$ and $\mathbf{y}_i$ are as close as possible. The measure of the closeness for two objects can be taken as various modes including the inclusion degree like that in Zhang et al.(1996), similarity (or dissimilarity, distance) etc.. The former measures have wider applications. For example, they can be used for the general symbolic data in the cases where even the symmetry does not hold. We use $s_{ij} = s(\mathbf{x}_i, \mathbf{x}_j)$ to measure the affinity between two input objects $\mathbf{x}_i$ and $\mathbf{x}_j$ where the matrix (s_{ij}) need not to be symmetric, but assume them to be positive. If the entries of (s_{ij}) are not all positive, we may consider $s_{ij}^* = s_{ij} + c$, $s > -\min\{s_{ij}; 1 \leq i, j \leq n\}$. Let $t_{ij} = t(\mathbf{z}_i, \mathbf{z}_j)$ be the affinity-measure between two outputs $\mathbf{z}_i$ and $\mathbf{z}_j$, and $f(v)$, $g(v)$, $h(v)$ be nonnegative increasing functions of v. The idea based on the affinity-rule is that the greater the affinity-measure between $\mathbf{x}_i$ and $\mathbf{x}_j$, the smaller the $-f(s_{ij})$ as the dis-affinity-measure between $\mathbf{x}_i$ and $\mathbf{x}_j$, and the smaller the $g(t_{ij})$ dis-affinity-measure between $\mathbf{z}_i$ and $\mathbf{z}_j$; $t(\mathbf{z}_i, \mathbf{y}_i)$ should be as small as possible for $1 \leq i \leq l$. Therefore, we obtain a general framework as follows

$$\max_{\mathbf{z}_1,\mathbf{z}_2,\cdots,\mathbf{z}_n,\xi} \quad -\sum_{i=1}^{n}\sum_{j=1}^{n}f(s(\mathbf{x}_i,\mathbf{x}_j))g(t(\mathbf{z}_i,\mathbf{z}_j))-Ch(\xi),$$

$$s.t. \quad \frac{1}{l}\sum_{i=1}^{l}r(t(\mathbf{z}_i,\mathbf{y}_i))\leq\xi, \quad \xi\geq 0,$$

where C is a penalty factor which takes a tradeoff role among the multi-objects functions.

As a concrete realization, we take the decreasing function of the squared distance between two objects as the affinity-measure, and $\|\mathbf{p}-\mathbf{q}\|^2$ as the dis-affinity-measure. Let $f(v)=h(v)=g(v)=r(v)=v$, $t(\mathbf{p},\mathbf{q})=\|\mathbf{p}-\mathbf{q}\|^2$, $\mathbf{z}_i=(z_{i1},z_{i2},\cdots,z_{ic})^T$, $Z=(\mathbf{z}_1^T,\mathbf{z}_2^T,\cdots,\mathbf{z}_n^T)^T=(\mathbf{z}_{(1)},\mathbf{z}_{(2)},\cdots,\mathbf{z}_{(c)})$, $\mathbf{y}_i=(y_{i1},y_{i2},\cdots,y_{ic})^T$, $1\leq i\leq l$; $\mathbf{y}_j=\mathbf{0}$, $j\geq l+1$, and $Y_0=(\mathbf{y}_1^T,\mathbf{y}_2^T,\cdots,\mathbf{y}_n^T)^T=(\mathbf{y}_{(1)},\mathbf{y}_{(2)},\cdots,\mathbf{y}_{(c)})$. We always suppose $s_{ij}>0$ without special declaration. Then we obtain the formal expression for semi-supervised transductive learning machine based on the affinity-rule as follows

$$\left.\begin{array}{cc}\min_{\mathbf{z}_1,\mathbf{z}_2,\cdots,\mathbf{z}_n,\xi} & \sum_{i=1}^{n}\sum_{j=1}^{n}s_{ij}\|\mathbf{z}_i-\mathbf{z}_j\|^2+C\xi, \\ s.t. & \frac{1}{l}\sum_{i=1}^{l}\|\mathbf{z}_i-\mathbf{y}_i\|^2\leq\xi, \quad \xi\geq 0,\end{array}\right\} \quad (P)$$

This is a convex programming and there is a globally optimal solution. Its Lagrangian function is

$$L=\sum_{i=1}^{n}\sum_{j=1}^{n}s_{ij}\|\mathbf{z}_i-\mathbf{z}_j\|^2+C\xi+\lambda\left(\frac{1}{l}\sum_{i=1}^{l}\|\mathbf{z}_i-\mathbf{y}_i\|^2-\xi\right)-\mu\xi,$$
$$\xi\geq 0,\mu\geq 0.$$

Note that

$$\sum_{i=1}^{n}\sum_{j=1}^{n}s_{ij}\|\mathbf{z}_i-\mathbf{z}_j\|^2=\sum_{i=1}^{n}\sum_{j=1}^{n}s_{ij}\sum_{k=1}^{c}(z_{ik}-z_{jk})^2$$
$$=\sum_{k=1}^{c}\left[\sum_{i=1}^{n}\sum_{j\neq i}(s_{ij}+s_{ji})z_{ik}^2-2\sum_{i=1}^{n}\sum_{j<i}(s_{ij}+s_{ji})z_{ik}z_{jk}\right].$$

Let

$$w_{ij} = \frac{1}{2}(s_{ij} + s_{ji}), \ j \neq i; \quad w_{ii} = 0; \quad W = (w_{ij})_{n \times n};$$

$$d_i = \sum_{j \neq i} w_{ij}, \ j \neq i; \ D = \mathrm{diag}(d_1, d_2, \cdots, d_n), \quad A = D - W;$$

$$I_l = \mathrm{diag}(1,1,\cdots,1,0,\cdots,0),$$

where there are l 1's in I_l, and A is a symmetric matrix. Therefore,

$$L_P = 2\sum_{k=1}^{c} \mathbf{z}_{(k)}^T A\mathbf{z}_{(k)} + \frac{\lambda}{l}\sum_{i=1}^{l}\| \mathbf{z}_i - \mathbf{y}_i \|^2 + (C - \lambda - \mu)\xi, \xi \geq 0, \mu \geq 0. \ (1)$$

To obtain the K-T points of (P), we calculate the derivative

$$\left. \begin{aligned} \frac{\partial L}{\partial \xi} &= C - \lambda - \mu \\ \frac{\partial L}{\partial \mathbf{z}_{(k)}} &= 4A\mathbf{z}_{(k)} + \frac{2\lambda}{l}I_l(\mathbf{z}_{(k)} - \mathbf{y}_{(k)}) \end{aligned} \right\}.$$

When Z is the K-T points of (P), then

$$\left. \begin{aligned} C - \lambda - \mu &= 0, \ \lambda \geq 0, \ \mu \geq 0, \\ (2lA + \lambda I_l)\mathbf{z}_{(k)} &= \lambda I_l \mathbf{y}_{(k)}. \end{aligned} \right\} \quad (2)$$

and the KKT conditions are hold

$$\lambda(\frac{1}{l}\sum_{l=1}^{l}\| \mathbf{z}_i - \mathbf{y}_i \|^2 - \xi) = 0, \quad \mu\xi = 0. \ (3)$$

In consideration of the limited space, we will omit the following some lemmas and theorems, and prove them in another article.

Lemma 1. The solutions of (P) with the condition (2) are constant values when $\lambda = 0$, which are trivial solutions. If the number of the labels for the labelled data is greater than one, then $\lambda > 0$.

Lemma 2. When $\lambda > 0$, we have
1) $(2lA + \lambda I_l)$ is invertible, and
2) $\rho(2l(2lD + \lambda I_l)^{-1}W) < 1$.

We deal with the dual problem of (P) now. Substituting the results of (2) into (1), and using (2), we obtain $0 \leq \lambda \leq C$ and

$$L_D = -\frac{1}{l}\sum_{k=1}^{c}\lambda\mathbf{y}_{(k)}^{T}I_{l}\mathbf{z}_{(k)} + \frac{1}{l}\sum_{k=1}^{c}\lambda\mathbf{y}_{(k)}^{T}I_{l}\mathbf{y}_{(k)} .$$

So, when $0 < \lambda \leq C$, by Lemma 2, the dual programming is

$$\left.\begin{array}{c}\max_{\lambda} -\frac{1}{l}\sum_{k=1}^{c}\lambda\mathbf{y}_{(k)}^{T}I_{l}(2lA + \lambda I_{l})^{-1}\lambda I_{l}\mathbf{y}_{(k)} + \frac{1}{l}\sum_{k=1}^{c}\lambda\mathbf{y}_{(k)}^{T}I_{l}\mathbf{y}_{(k)} \\ 0 < \lambda \leq C\end{array}\right\} . \quad (D) .$$

Lemma 3. For $0 < \lambda \leq C$, L_D reaches the maximum when $\lambda = C$.

Theorem 4. For the nontrivial solutions, $(Z, \xi, \lambda, \mu) = (\hat{Z}, \hat{\xi}, C, 0)$ are the Lagrangian saddle-point of (P), and $(\hat{Z}, \hat{\xi})$ are the globally optimal solution of (P), where

$$\hat{Z} = C(2lA + CI_{l})^{-1}Y_{0} \quad \text{and} \quad \hat{\xi} = \frac{1}{l}\sum_{i=1}^{l}\|\hat{\mathbf{z}}_{i} - \mathbf{y}_{i}\|^{2} .$$

3.   MAIN RESULTS

To discuss the problem with real-time constrain, we study the situations with information increment. Suppose that the given $n = l + u$ data have been expressed with the notations in Section 2. Let $s = 2l/C$ and denote respectively by $A_{n}, I_{l}(n), Y_{n}$, and U_{n} as the aforementioned A, I_{l}, Y_{0} and U in the case of n given data where $U_{n} = sA_{n} + I_{l}(n)$, $Z(n) = U_{n}^{-1}Y_{n} = (sA_{n} + I_{l}(n))^{-1}Y_{n}$, $I_{l}(n) = \text{diag}(1,1,\cdots1,0,\cdots,0)$, and rearrange these n data in such a way that the labelled data are in the front of the unlabelled data. We add a star to $Z(n+1)$ to stand for the rearranging version of $Z(n+1)$ with $n+1$ data.

Now, we study the semi-supervised learning problem with information increment for different cases respectively. In consideration of the limited space, we will only give an outline of some proofs as follows.

3.1) The $(n+1)$-th point is unlabelled. Let

$$Y_{n+1} = \begin{pmatrix} Y_n \\ 0 \end{pmatrix}, \quad Z(n+1) = \begin{pmatrix} Z_n \\ \mathbf{z}_{n+1}^T \end{pmatrix}, \quad I_l(n+1) = \begin{pmatrix} I_l(n) & 0 \\ 0 & 0 \end{pmatrix}_{(n+1)\times(n+1)},$$

and

$$A_{n+1} = \begin{pmatrix} A_n & A_{n,n+1} \\ A_{n+1,n} & d_{n+1} \end{pmatrix}.$$

where $A_{n,n+1}$ are an affinity vector between the $(n+1)$-th point and the n data given before, that is, $A_{n,n+1} = (a_{1,n+1}, a_{2,n+1}, \cdots, a_{n,n+1})^T$, $A_{n+1,n} = A_{n,n+1}^T$, and $d_{n+1} = \sum_{j \neq n+1} a_{n+1,j}$.

By the analytic solution of transductive learning machine based on the affinity-rule, we get

$$Z(n+1) = [sA_{n+1} + I_l(n+1)]^{-1} Y_{n+1}.$$

Then

$$sA_{n+1}Z(n+1) + I_l(n+1)[Z(n+1) - Y_{n+1}] = 0.$$

Therefore we have

$$\left. \begin{array}{l} sA_n Z_n + sA_{n,n+1}\mathbf{z}_{n+1}^T + I_l(n)(Z_n - Y_n) = 0 \\ sA_{n,n+1}^T Z_n + sd_{n+1}\mathbf{z}_{n+1}^T = 0 \end{array} \right\}.$$

Thus

$$\left. \begin{array}{l} Z_n = [sA_n + I_l(n) - \dfrac{s}{d_{n+1}} A_{n,n+1} A_{n,n+1}^T Z_n]^{-1} Y_n \\[2ex] \mathbf{z}_{n+1}^T = \dfrac{-A_{n,n+1}^T Z_n}{d_{n+1}} \end{array} \right\}.$$

By Sherman-Morrison-Woodbory formula

$$(M + BCD^T)^{-1} = M^{-1} - M^{-1}B(C^{-1} + D^T M^{-1}B)^{-1}D^T M^{-1},$$

we can write some simple expressions in Theorem 5.

3.2) The $(n+1)$-th point is labelled, and its label is $\mathbf{y}_{n+1}$. Define an elementary matrix as

$$P(i,j) = I - (\mathbf{e}_i - \mathbf{e}_j)(\mathbf{e}_i - \mathbf{e}_j)^T$$

Then $P(i,j) = P^{-1}(i,j)$. Let

$$P_{n+1} = P(n+1,n)P(n+1,n-1)\cdots P(n+1,l+2)P(n+1,l+1),$$

and $Y_{n+1} = (Y_n^T, y_{n+1})^T$. With the similar notations in subsection 3.1 and the method in Section 2, we have

$$P_{n+1}Z(n+1) = [sP_{n+1}A_{n+1}P_{n+1}^{-1} + I_I(n+1) + I_{(l+1)}]^{-1}P_{n+1}\begin{pmatrix} Y_n \\ y_{n+1}^Y \end{pmatrix},$$

where $I_{(i+1)} = \mathbf{e}_{i+1}\mathbf{e}_{i+1}^T$. Therefore we have

$$Z(n+1) = [sA_{n+1} + I_I(n+1) + I_{(n+1)}]^{-1}\begin{pmatrix} Y_n \\ y_{n+1}^Y \end{pmatrix}.$$

So,

$$\left. \begin{array}{l} sA_{n+1}Z_n + sA_{n,n+1}\mathbf{z}_{n+1}^T + I_I(n)(Z_n - Y_n) = 0 \\ sA_{n,n+1}^T Z_n + sd_{n+1}\mathbf{z}_{n+1}^T + \mathbf{z}_{n+1}^T - \mathbf{y}_{n+1}^T = 0 \end{array} \right\},$$

we obtain

$$\left. \begin{array}{l} Z_n = \left[sA_n + I_I(n) - \dfrac{s^2}{1+sd_{n+1}}A_{n,n+1}A_{n,n+1}^T \right]^{-1}[I_I(n)Y_n - \dfrac{s}{1+sd_{n+1}}A_{n,n+1}\mathbf{y}_{n+1}^T] \\ \mathbf{z}_{n+1}^T = -\dfrac{1}{1+sd_{n+1}}(\mathbf{y}_{n+1}^T - sA_{n,n+1}^T Z_n) \end{array} \right\}$$

Since

$$[U_n - \frac{s^2}{1+sd_{n+1}}A_{n,n+1}A_{n,n+1}^T]^{-1}$$

$$= U_n^{-1} - \frac{s^2}{1+sd_{n+1}}\left(1 - \frac{s^2}{1+sd_{n+1}}A_{n,n+1}^T U_n^{-1}A_{n,n+1} \right)^{-1} U_n^{-1}A_{n,n+1}A_{n,n+1}^T U_n^{-1}$$

$$= \left[I - \frac{s^2}{1+sd_{n+1}-s^2 A_{n,n+1}^T U_n^{-1}A_{n,n+1}}U_n^{-1}A_{n,n+1}A_{n,n+1}^T \right]U_n^{-1},$$

we may give some simple formulae in Theorem 5.

According to the analytic expression for transductive learning machine based on the affinity-rule, we can adjust the result in such a way that the labelled data are arranged in the front of the unlabelled data. Then

$$Z^*(n+1) = P_{n+1}Z(n+1).$$

We now sumarize the cases of 3.1)- 3.2) in the following theorem.

Theorem 5. Suppose that the solution of transductive learning machine based on the affinity-rule for the n data has been given as $Z(n) = U_n^{-1}Y_n = (sA_n + I_l(n))^{-1}Y_n$. Let P_{n+1} be the products of some elementary matrices defined as above. The incremental learning solution is that

1) if the incremental information is the $(n+1)$-th data which is an unlabelled point,then

$$\left. \begin{array}{l} Z_n = [I + \dfrac{1}{d_{n+1} - sA_{n,n+1}^T U_n^{-1} A_{n,n+1}} U_n^{-1} A_{n,n+1} A_{n,n+1}^T]Z(n) \\[4mm] \mathbf{z}_{n+1}^T = \dfrac{-A_{n,n+1}^T Z_n}{d_{n+1}} \end{array} \right\}.$$

and
$$Z^*(n+1) = Z(n+1) = (Z_n^T, \mathbf{z}_{n+1})^T$$
2)if the incremental information is the $(n+1)$-th data which is a labelled point and its label is $\mathbf{y}_{n+1}$,

$$\left. \begin{array}{l} Z_n = \left[I - \dfrac{s^2}{1 + sd_{n+1} - s^2 A_{n,n+1}^T U_n^{-1} A_{n,n+1}} U_n^{-1} A_{n,n+1} A_{n,n+1}^T \right] [Z(n) - \\[4mm] \qquad\qquad\qquad\qquad\qquad \dfrac{s}{1 + sd_{n+1}} U_n^{-1} A_{n,n+1} \mathbf{y}_{n+1}^T] \\[4mm] \mathbf{z}_{n+1}^T = -\dfrac{1}{1 + sd_{n+1}} (\mathbf{y}_{n+1}^T - sA_{n,n+1}^T Z_n) \end{array} \right\}.$$

When arranging the labelled data in the former part and the n abeled data in the latter part of the solution vector, we obtain
$$Z^*(n+1) = P_{n+1}Z(n+1) = P_{n+1}(Z_n^T, \mathbf{z}_{n+1})^T.$$

4.   CONCLUSION

We have described a semi-supervised learning problems by the transduction method in which both the labelled and the unlabelled data are used to derive the rule from particularity to particularity. Our transductive learning machine based on affinity has several advantages. It is adaptable to general input space objects and even can be extended to the situation with default values like those in Zhou et al. (1993). This method only requires a measure of affinity between the input objects and the input observation labels given by the supervisor to infer the proper labels on the other unlabelled objects. We have derived an incremental learning algorithm. Unlike other methods, when a new data comes, our method does not need to use both the original and the new data to solve the entire problem but uses the previous result and the new data to recurrence solution, and therefore is more adaptive to on-line processes.

REFERENCES

1. Ben-Hur, A. , Horn, D. , Siegelmann, H. T. & Vapnik V. (2001). Support vector clustering. *Journal of Machine Learning Research, 2*:125-137.
2. Bennett, K. , & Demiriz A. (1999). Semi-supervised support vector machines . In M. S. Kearns, S. A. Solla, & D. A. Cohn, (Eds.), *Advances in Neural Information Processing Systems 11* (pp.368-374), Cambridge: MIT Press.
3. Burges, C. J. C. (1998). A tutorial on support vector machines for pattern recognition. *Data Mining and Knowledge Discovery, 2*(2):121-167 .
4. Chapelle, O. , Vapnik, V. , & Weston J. (1999). Transductive inference for estimating values of functions. In Sara A. Solla, Todd K. Leen & Klaus-Robert M"'ller (Eds.), *Advances in Neural Information Processing Systems 12* (pp.421-427). Cambridge :MIT Press.
5. Chapelle, O. , Weston, J. , & Scholkopf, B. (2003). Cluster kernels for semi-supervised learning. In T. G. Diettrich, S. Becker, & Z. Ghahramani (Eds.), *Advances in Neural Information Processing Systems 14*. Cambridge: MIT Press(in press).
6. Joachims, T. (1999). Transductive inference for text classification using support vector machines. In *International Conferenceon Machine Learning(ICML)* (pp.200-209).
7. Joachims, T. (2003). Transductive learning via spectral graph partitioning, *Proceedings of the International Conference on Machine Learning (ICML)*.
8. Vapnik, V.(1998). *Statistical learning theory*. New York: Wiley.
9. Zhou, D. , Bousquet, O. , Lal, T. N. , Weston, J. , & Scholkopf B. (2003a). Learning with local and global consistency. (112), *Max Planck Institute for Biological Cybernetics, Tuebingen, Germany* (June 2003).
10. Zhou, D. , Bousquet, O. , Lal, T. N. , Weston, J. , & Scholkopf B. (2003b). Learning with local and global consistency. In S. Thrun, L. Saul & B. Scholkopf (Eds.), *Advances in Neural Information Processing Systems 16.*, Cambridge: MIT Press (in press).
11. Zhang, W.X., & Leung, Y. (1996). *The principle of uncertainty inference*. Xi'an: Xi'an Jiaotong University Press. (in Chinese).
12. Zhou, G. Y., & Xia, L. X. (1993). *Non-metric data analysis and its applications*. Beijing: Science Press. (in Chinese).

A SHORT TUTORIAL ON REINFORCEMENT LEARNING
Review and Applications

CHENGCHENG LI & LARRY PYEATT
Computer Scinece Department, Texas Tech University, Lubbock, Texas, 79401 USA

Abstract: Dynamic Programming (DP) has been widely used as an approach solving the Markov Decision Process problem. This paper takes a well-known gambler's problem as an example to compare different DP solutions to the problem, and uses a variety of parameters to explain the results in detail. Ten C++ programs were written to implement the algorithms. The numerical results from gamble's problem and graphical output from the tracking car problem support the conceptual definitions of RL methods.

Key words: Reinforcement Learning, Dynamic Programming, Monte Carlo method, Temporal Difference, Markov Decision Process

1.   INTRODUCTION

The three fundamental classes of RL methods are dynamic programming (DP), Monte Carlo (MC) and temporal difference (TD) methods. Almost all the RL methods are evolved from or from the combinations of these fundamental RL methods.

Dynamic Programming (DP) is one of the major methods used to solve MDP(Markov Decision Process) problems (Puterman, p.81). The policy iteration method is the straightforward way to apply DP to an MDP problem. A random policy or any non-optimal policy is evaluated by calculating the state values using the Bellman equation. A new policy replaces the old policy and is regarded as a more optimal policy than the old one, based on the calculated state values. The loop then keeps going on until either policy or state values converge and do not change. Value iteration is actually an improved version of policy iteration. It truncates the policy improvement process in policy improvement and still keeps a guaranteed convergence toward the optimal solution.

The basic idea of MC methods is based on averaging sample returns. If a state or state-action pair has been visited many times, the average value of the returns of these visits is supposed to converge to the true value of this state or state-action pair. Based on this assumption, MC methods only consider and use experience. MC methods do value evaluation and improvement simultaneously.

TD methods combine the advantages of both MC and DP methods. TD methods do not require a complete knowledge of the environment. However, TD methods use bootstrapping which is similar to DP methods. On the other hand, TD methods do not go through the whole episode. In stead, they use a number of steps in each episode. The most commonly used on-policy TD method is SARSA, and off-policy TD method, which evaluates one policy while following another, is Q-learning method.

2.   GAMBLER'S PROBLEM

A classic Gambler's problem is used to show a DP solution to a MDP problem. The description of the problem is as followings: "A gambler bets on the outcomes of coin flips. He either wins the same amount of money as his bet or loses his bet. Game stops when he reaches 100 dollars, or loses by running out of money." (Sutton and Barto, p.101)

Figures 1 and 2 show the value function and optimal policy when p=0.4, where p is the winning rate. The state value function is no longer linear. There are some local maximums when the capital reaches 25, 50, and 75. Fifty is the state with the most abnormally high state value. The policy is to reach the high value states before reaching the goal.

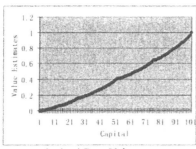

Figure 1. Optimal State Value Functions (p=0.4)

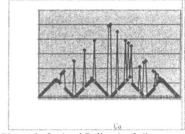

Figure 2. Optimal Policy (p=0.4)

There are many spikes in the graph shown in Figure 2, and they are considered noise. We found that it is caused by roundup errors of the floating point limitation of CPUs. Different errors are shown on AMD, Pentium, and

Sun CPUs. The computer makes the wrong decision due to the floating point limitation by truncating the number after the 16th digit. The solution to this problem is that an updated policy must increase the action value by at least the smallest decimal number which the CPU can handle, for example, 10^{-16} for double precision. By applying this concept, and changing the policy improvement rule from

" If (action_value > previous_max_value)

    Then choose this action"   to

" If (action_value > previous_max_value+10E-16)

    Then choose this action ," all the noise is eliminated. The optimal policy graphs for 0<p<0.5 are all the same. Another way to explain this is that because of the nonlinear property of the state value function, there is a certain amount of bet which can result in obtaining an optimal return for each state before betting all the capital. The exception to this is when current states are local maximums (25, 50, 75).

The local maximum is the smallest integer value divisible by a polynomial of two from the number of states. The reason is that the gambler problem is a discrete MDP problem, and every state has an integer value as capital. Keeping this in mind, let us further compare the results in Figures 3 and 4. Figure 3 has 1,024 states, which is a polynomial of two. So the local minimum is as small as 1. The result of this is that if a player sets a slightly different goal, for example, from 1,023 to 1,024, there may be completely different optimal policies for different goals, as can be seen in Figure 4, which has 1,023 states.

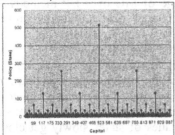

Figure 3. Optimal Policy (0<p<0.5), 1,024 States

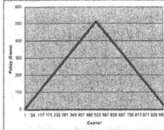

Figure 4. Optimal Policy (0<p<0.5), 1,023 States

3.   TRACKING CAR PROBLEM

The tracking car problem is very special which could be solved by using MC, DP, and TD methods. Thus, the tracking car problem can be used to compare the three methods. The specification of tracking car problem is as follows. "Find the best strategy to accelerate or decelerate a racing car at a turning track. The maximum velocity of the car is 5. A random accelerate on either vertical or horizontal direction may occur." (Sutton and Barto, p.127)

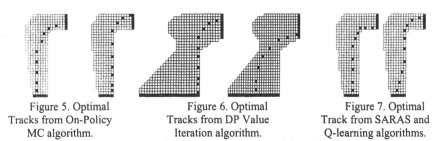

Figure 5. Optimal   Figure 6. Optimal   Figure 7. Optimal
Tracks from On-Policy   Tracks from DP Value   Track from SARAS and
MC algorithm.   Iteration algorithm.   Q-learning algorithms.

There are more states defined in DP algorithm for this tracking car problem because car positions on track with a particular vertical and horizontal speed are counted as factors of states. There are four horizontal and four vertical speed, and they can not both be zero. So, the number of states is calculated by

NumberOfStates=OnTrackPositions*(4*4-1)   (1)

4.   DISCUSSION ON RESULTS AND CONCLUSIONS

MC methods have a very close relationship to TD methods, which are also based on experience and sample episodes but bootstrap. If we increase the number of steps in the TD methods till the end of every episode, MC may be viewed as a special case of TD methods. MC methods are based on experience and sample episodes. They do not require a full definition of the environment, which is the major advantage of MC over DP methods. MC methods do not bootstrap and convergence of state or action values is guaranteed by a large number of visits on every state or action.

In practice, we found that correct setting of initial value of every state is critical for the correct convergence of state or action values. For example, we set that every state has been visited 45 times and every visit has a return of 1 before the loop starts. As a result, all states values are set much higher than their real values. The first several iterations of loop then would not set states to very low values. We then guarantee values of states slowly get close to their true values from only one side of their true values, so that large number of visits on every state are guaranteed.

Choosing greedy actions to update action values makes Q-learning an off-policy TD method, while SARSA is an on-policy TD method which uses e-greedy method. Figure 7 shows that SARSA intends to take a saver track and avoid being on the most left and the most top lanes of the track because the probability of being off the track is high on those lanes. Q-learning then chooses more greedy tracks than SARSA. If there is no or low-probability of random left and right accelerations, the results from Q-learning would be more close to the real optimal solution. If the probability of random accelerations is high, SARSA is the method to use. In most cases, greedy methods are more close to the real optimal solutions.

This study covers the major concepts of reinforcement learning and the Markov decision process. DP, MC, and TD methods are discussed and compared through solving problems. A noise reduction method and computer floating point limitations are also discussed. Ten C++ programs were written to implement the algorithms. The numerical results from gamble's problem and graphical output from the tracking car problem support the conceptual definitions of RL methods.

REFERENCES

1. Richard S. Sutton and Andrew G. Barto (1998), Reinforcement Learning: An Introduction, *MIT Press*, Cambridge, MA.
2. Martin L. Puterman (1994), Markov Decision Processes: Discrete Stochastic Dynamic Programming. *A Wiley-Interscience Publication*, New York.

HARDWARE DESIGN OF TWO WEIGHTED NEURAL NETWORK AND APPLICATION FOR OBJECT RECOGNITION

Wenming Cao , Fei Lu, Gang Xiao, Shoujue Wang
Institute of Intelligent Information System, ZheJiang University of Technology, Hangzhou 310014, China

Abstract: In this paper, the design methodology of neural network hardware has been discussed, and two weighted neural network implemented by this method been applied for object recognition. It was pointed out that the main problem of the two weighted neural network hardware implementation lies in three aspects. At final, two weighted neural network implemented by this method is applied for object recognition , and the algorithm were presented . We did experiments on recognition of omnidirectionally oriented rigid objects on the same level, using the two weighted neural networks. Many animal and vehicle models (even with rather similar shapes) were recognized omnidirectionally thousands of times. For total 8800 tests, the correct recognition rate is 98.75%, the error rate and the rejection rate are 0.5 and 1.25% respectively.

Key words: Pattern recognition, Two weighted Neural Networks, High dimensional Geometry

1.   INTRODUCTION

As a suitable calculation method for parallel computing, the two weighted neural networks have been widely used in application for control theory1, speaker recognition2 etc. But how to realize the two weighted neural network computing, there are various methods such as realizing it by software or by full curing special neural network chip. The purpose of this paper is to research the application realized by semiconductor hardware and the process of enlarging the application. In section 2, we described its structure. In section 3, it was pointed out that the main problem of the two weighted neural network hardware implementation lies in three aspects. Finally, two weighted neural network implemented by this method is applied for object recognition, and the algorithm were presented . We did experiments on recognition of omnidirectionally oriented rigid objects on the same level, using the neural networks. Many animal and vehicle models (even with rather similar shapes) were recognized omnidirectionally thousands of times. For total 8800 tests, the correct recognition rate is 98.75%, the error rate and the rejection rate are 0.5 and 1.25% respectively.

2.   STRUCTURE OF TWO WEIGHTED NEURAL NETWORKS

The model is

$$Y = f\left[\sum_{j=1}^{n}\left(\frac{W_j}{|W_j|}\right)^s \mid W_j\left(X_j - W_j'\right)\mid^P - \theta\right]$$

In which:
Y is the output of neuron ;
f(...) is the neuron activation function;
X_j is neuron jth input;
$W_j W_j'$ are direct weight and kernel weigh;
θ is the threshold;
n is the dimension of input.

We can easily get: if S=1,P=1 and all W are zero, then the above equation becomes the traditional BP neuron; if S=0,P=2 and all the W are one, then the neuron becomes RBF neuron; if S=0, change the value of W and P, and if the basis of function f (...) is zero, the track of input X becomes the following closing hypersurfaces. Figure 1, ts topography structure Figure 2.

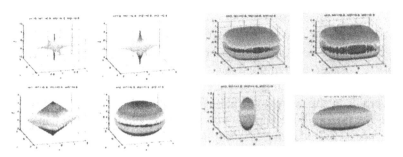

Figure 1. closing hypersurfaces

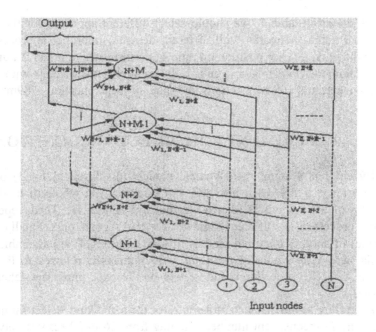

Figure 2. Structure of two weighted neural network

3.   ANALYSIS OF THE PROPERTY OF TWO WEIGHTED NEURAL NETWORKS HARDWARE

Artificial two weighted neural networks are a computing method and device with a large number of computing units specially connected to form complex computing functions.

Let's take the currency degree for example: in scientific research, without the demand for particular use and structure, the two weighted neural networks generally need more powerful currency but the two weighted neural networks used for engineering need less powerful currency. However for those trained two weighted neural networks with fixed uses, (even the weights are fixed), there is no demand for currency. So we can divide all the demands into three fuzzy grades, that is high (H), middle (M) and low (L). (H) means the demand is high, that is to say: high computing speed or high precision or large net scale or strong flexibility or low price or easy to use or quantity. (L) However means the demand is lower and (M) means the demand is between the above two. For different purpose and different realization, we get the mapping relationship shown in figure by dividing all factors into three grades.

As shown in table 1, we should select different approach for those two weighted neural networks with different demand. Improper approach may result the great inferior position on ratio of performance to price. A humor in Dan Hammerstrom[5] says: For a fully parallel network chip with 1 μ m interconnects and 109 connections, the spare of the connection is 89m^2.

4.   EXPERIMENT FOR OBJECT RECOGNITION

By circling 8 animal and vehicle models (displayed in Fig.3) by 360 degrees respectively, each provides 400 samples. The whole of total 3200 samples of the 8 kinds is referred to the first sample set. Then, repeat the above process at a different time to get the second one. Finally, 2400 samples of another 6 animal models (displayed in Fig.4) are assembled in a similar way. The whole of the total 2400 samples is referred to the third sample set. The procedures and results of the experiment are labeled as follows:

According to the distance of samples of the same kind, select samples of each kind in inconsistent numbers ranging from 26 to 50 respectively from the total 3200 samples of the first sample set to compose a training set, which consequently consists of 328 samples from all 8 kinds.

Construct 8 recognition networks corresponding to the 8 models under recognition , where the number of neurons is equal to that of the samples in the training set .

Take the total 6400 samples of the first and second sample sets for correct recognition rate test. Consequently, 6384 samples were recognized successfully while the rest 16 ones failed. However, the rest 16 samples are totally attributed to the case of rejection. Therefore, the correct rate and rejection rate are 99.75% and 0.25% respectively.

Figure 3. Testing Sample Set (1)

Figure 4. Training Sample Set (2)

REFERENCES

1. Wang ShouJue etc. "Discussion on the Basic Mathematical Models of Neurons in General Purpose Neurocomputer". ACTA ELECTRONICA SINICA, Vol.29 No.5, 2001
2. Wang Shoujue etc. The Sequential Learning Ahead Masking (SLAM) model of neural networks for pattern classification.Proceedings of JCIS98. Vol.IV. pp199-202. Oct. 1998. RTP. NC.. USA
3. Wang Shoujue. Priority Ordered Neural Networks with Better Similarity to Human knowledge Representation. Chinese Journal Of Electronics. Vol.8. No.1 ,pp. 1-4.1999,
4. Cao yu, Two weighted neural network approach, Master thesis, Institute of Semiconductors, CAS, 2002,

Table 1. Two weighted Neurocompouter Chip

Factors and Requests		Application				Implement Approach			
		ST	E	I	SP	S	DSP A	PS TWNN	OTON C
Computing Speed	H M L	H	L	H	H	L	H	H	H
Accuracy	H M L	H	M	H	M	H	H	H	L
Net Scale	H M L	H	M	M	M	H	H	H	L
Flexibility	H M L	H	M	M	M	H	H	H	L
Cost	H M L	L	H	M	L	H	L	M	H
Easy to Use	H M L	L	L	H	H	M	L	H	M
Quality	H M L	L	L	M	M	M	L	M	H

IMPROVEMENT OF WEB DATA CLUSTERING USING WEB PAGE CONTENTS

Yue Xu and Li-Tung Weng
School of Software Engineering and Data Communications
Queensland University of Technology
GPO Box 2434
Brisbane, QLD 4001, Australia
yue.xu@qut.edu.au, l.weng@student.qut.edu.au

Abstract   This paper presents an approach that discovers clusters of Web pages based on Web log data and Web page contents as well. Most existing Web log mining techniques are access-based approaches that statistically analyze the log data without paying much attention on the contents of the pages. The log data contains various kinds of noise which can significantly influence the performance of pure access-based web log mining. The method proposed in this paper not only considers the frequence of page co-occurrence in user access logs, but also takes into account the web page contents to cluster Web pages. We also present a method of using information entropy to prune away irrelevant papges which improves the performance of the web page clustering.

Keywords: Web log mining, clustering, Web contents, information entropy

1.   Introduction

Navigating through large web sites for finding desired information or some particular product to purchase can be tedious and frustrating as the WWW has grown to a huge size. Web agents that can consider users' own information needs and guide the users to their desired information are in great demand. This inspired the research on Web personalization. According to Mobasher [7], Web personalization can be described as any action that makes the Web experience of a user customized to the user's taste or preferences. In order to achieve Web personalization, we need to generate user profiles that characterize users' needs and interests. There are two major approaches used to generate user profiles. One approach is to take explicit rating information from users [6]. The user profiles consist of previous users' ratings and the current user's ratings as well. These ratings characterize the users' preferences for the items in the Web site. This approach relies heavily on human input and brings extra work. Recently, an increasing number of researchers have focused their study on applying data mining techniques to web server log analysis for automatically generating user profiles. Some proposed approaches analyze previous users web logs to discover user navigation patterns such as popular navigation sessions, item association rules, page clusters, and user clusters [2, 9]. These patterns form the user profiles that capture and model the behavioral characteristics of users interacting with a Web site. Obviously building user profiles based on Web usage mining will not bring any extra work to users and the coverage of the user profiles can be large if a great amount of logs are available. Moreover, the user profiles are dynamically generated from user navigation logs and not subjective ratings provided by user themselves, and thus the system performance does not degrade over time.

A variety of knowledge discovery techniques have been applied to obtain usage patterns. Clustering is one of the popular used techniques for grouping user navigation sessions or Web pages. The authors of [8] have proposed methods to classify users by clutering user navigation sessions. An algorithm called PageGather has been used to discover groups of pages based on page co-occurrence [9]. Mobasher research group has proposed several techniques based on clustering to extract usage knowledge for the purpose of Web personalization [7]. Web usage mining techniques are access-based approaches that statistically analyze Web server logs and do not pay attention on the content of the pages visited by users. However, solely relying on Web usage data for obtaining user profiles can be problematic since the Web usage logs contain noise such as missing page requests and containing irrelevant page requests made by users. These missing or irrelevant page requests can make great impact on the quality of user profiles obtained from the logs. For generating more accurate user profiles and thus providing more reliable recommendations, we should consider both Web usage data and Web content data in the generation of user profile.

In this paper, we will present an approach that generates groups of Web pages by using both Web logs and Web page contents. The page co-occurrence information and page topic information are considered at the same time when generating the user profile. The rest of the paper is organized as follows. Section 2 introduces briefly the data preprocessing. In section 3, we define some similarity measures to characterize Web pages and use fuzzy clustering method CARD [8] to obtain page clusters. Section 4 presents the use of information entropy to refine user navigation sessions. Finally, Section 5 summarizes the paper.

2.   Data Preparation

For any data mining application, the first step is to prepare a suitable data set to which data mining techniques are applied. The data set can be created by preprocessing some original data sources. The original data sources for generating the user profiles in our case include Web log data and Web contents. The essential tasks in log data preprocessing include data cleaning, user identification, and user session identification. The output of the preprocessing is a collection of user navigation sessions. A log file is an ordered set of requests made by users. A user's page request often results in several log entries in the log file since images and scripts are down-loaded in addition to the page HTML or JSP file itself. Actually only the page but the images or scripts is the real item interested by the user. Therefore, in order to capture the user's navigation intention, elimination of those irrelevant items from the Web log file becomes necessary. This is the task of data cleaning.

User requests are stored in the order that the server receives them. If multiple users are browsing the site concurrently, their requests are intermingled in the log file. The goal of session identification is to identify the page requests made by each user and construct the page accesses into sessions. Since a user may visit a web site more than once during a period of time, a user navigation session is usually defined as a sequence of pages visited by the same user such that no two consecutive pages are separated by more than, for example, 30 minutes [2]. Table 2.1 shows an example of a cleaned log segment that is obtained from the log data of the Web site of the Centre for Information Technology Innovation, Faculty of Information Technology at Queensland University of Technoloy. Table 2.2 shows the set of user navigation sessions obtained from the log segment.

3.   Web Page Clustering

The task we address in this section is to find clusters of related Web pages based on user access logs and Web contents. Data mining techniques have been widely applied to categorize Web objects such as Web pages. However, due to the ambiguity and imcompleteness in Web usage data, the categories in Web objects may not have crisp boundaries. This fuzzy nature in Web clustering makes the straightforward use of data mining techniques sometimes not very effective. A number of fuzzy clustering methods have been developed [5]. The most known method of fuzzy clustering is the Fuzzy c-Means (FCM) algorithm [1]. The FCM method is applicable only to object data that represents the objects by feature vectors. Hathaway's RFCM algorithm [4] extends the FCM to relational data that represents the objects by numerical values representing the degrees to which pairs of objects in the data set are related. However, both the FCM and the RFCM have a requirement that the number c of clusters

Item ID	Page Request
A1	127.0.0.1 - - [05/Sep/2003:10:27:55 10000] "GET /index.jsp HTTP/1.1" 200 8274
A2	127.0.0.1 - - [05/Sep/2003:10:28:33 10000] "GET /research/index.jsp HTTP/1.1" 302 -
A3	127.0.0.1 - - [05/Sep/2003:10:29:01 10000] "GET /research/sdl/index.jsp HTTP/1.1" 200 29217
A4	127.0.0.1 - - [05/Sep/2003:10:32:22 10000] "GET /research/sdl/projects/ HTTP/1.1" 404 -
A5	127.0.0.1 - - [05/Sep/2003:10:32:38 10000] "GET /research/sdl/robotsoccer.jsp HTTP/1" 200 40018
A2	127.0.0.1 - - [05/Sep/2003:11:29:33 10000] "GET /research/index.jsp HTTP/1.1" 302 -
A3	127.0.0.1 - - [05/Sep/2003:11:30:01 10000] "GET /research/sdl/index.jsp HTTP/1.1" 200 29217-
A4	127.0.0.1 - - [05/Sep/2003:11:32:42 10000] "GET /research/sdl/projects/ HTTP/1.1" 404 -
A6	127.0.0.1 - - [05/Sep/2003:11:32:48 10000] "GET /research/sdl/researchers.jsp HTTP/1.1" 200 21963
A7	127.0.0.1 - - [05/Sep/2003:12:09:06 10000] "GET /pubs/index.jsp HTTP/1.1" 200 19757
A8	127.0.0.1 - - [05/Sep/2003:12:09:19 10000] '"GET /pubs/2002.jsp HTTP/1.1" 200 43204
A9	127.0.0.1 - - [05/Sep/2003:12:10:46 10000] "GET /people/index.jsp HTTP/1.1" 200 18494
A10	127.0.0.1 - - [05/Sep/2003:12:10:49 10000] "GET /people/students.jsp HTTP/1.1" 200 47065

Table 2.2. An example set of user's sessions

Session Number	User Sessions
1	$A_1 \rightarrow A_2 \rightarrow A_3 \rightarrow A_4 \rightarrow A_5$
2	$A_2 \rightarrow A_3 \rightarrow A_4 \rightarrow A_6$
3	$A_7 \rightarrow A_8 \rightarrow A_9 \rightarrow A_{10}$

has to be specified prior to the clustering. Based on Frigui & Krishnapuram's Competitive Agglomeration (CA) [3], Nasraoui proposed the competitive Agglomeration algorithm for relational data (CARD) [8] that can cluster data into the optimal number of clusters without requiring a prior specified value for c. In this section, we first define the pairwise relational measurements to characterize the similarity beween Web pages in terms of user access frequency and page contents, we then present the use of the fuzzy clustering algorithm CARD to obtain Web pages clusters based on the page similarity.

3.1 Similarity Between Web Pages

3.1.1 Page Co-occurrence Measurement. If two pages frequently appear together in the same sessions, the two pages are considered related with each other in some aspect which may be interested by the user. Let N_s be the number of sessions, N_i be the number of sessions which contains page requests to page i, and N_i^j be the number of sessions in which page j is visited after page i has been already visited. The probability of a user requesting page i is defined as: $p(i) = \frac{N_i}{N_s}$. The probability of a user visiting page j after the user has already visited page i is defined as: $p(j/i) = \frac{N_i^j}{N_i}$. The joint probability of page i and page j given below is used to measure the co-occurrence frequency between page i and page j:

$$p(i,j) = \begin{cases} max\{p(i)p(j/i), p(j)p(i/j)\} & i \neq j \\ 1 & i = j \end{cases}$$

The $p(i,j)$ represens the probability that page i and page j are visited together in a session. We calculate the co-occurrence frequency of each pair of pages and create a matrix based on the frequency. Table 3.1 is the co-occurrence frequency matrix derived from the sessions given in Table 2.2.

Table 3.1. Co-occurrence frequency matrix obtained from the sessions in Table 2.2

	A1	A2	A3	A4	A5	A6	A7	A8	A9	A10
A1	1	0.11	0.11	0.11	0.11	0	0	0	0	0
A2	0.11	1	0.44	0.44	0.22	0.22	0	0	0	0
A3	0.11	0.44	1	0.44	0.22	0.22	0	0	0	0
A4	0.11	0.44	0.44	1	0.22	0.22	0	0	0	0
A5	0.11	0.22	0.22	0.22	1	0	0	0	0	0
A6	0	0.22	0.22	0.22	0	1	0	0	0	0
A7	0	0	0	0	0	0	1	0.11	0.11	0.11
A8	0	0	0	0	0	0	0.11	1	0.11	0.11
A9	0	0	0	0	0	0	0.11	0.11	1	0.11
A10	0	0	0	0	0	0	0.11	0.11	0.11	1

3.1.2   Page Content Similarity Measurement.   Web usage mining relies only on user access log data to discover useful patterns. However, the web logs may contain some data that does not really reflect user's navigation intention. One reason is that some data may be missing due to caching by the browser. Another reason is that the user may visited some irrelevant pages on their way to find the desired information. These irrelevant pages in the user's navigation sessions may make significant impact on the quality of the mining results. With a navigation goal in his/her mind, a user will visit the pages which should be content relevant. This suggests that the page contents can be used to eliminate or alleviate the impact caused by the missing data or the irrelevant pages.

In order to use page contents, the Web pages should be well characterized. One of the commonly used techniques for textual documents in Information Retrieval is to repreent each document as a feature vector. In this paper, the features are extracted from the meta data embedded in HTML files. We assume that associated with each page there is a specific tag in its HTML file that provides a list of topics and a weight for each topic. The list of topics is specified by the Web site designer and used as the feature vector or topic vector to measure the similarity among pages.

Suppose that there are totally n topics involved in a web site, and that associated with each page in the site there is an n-dimensional vector which characterizes the relevancy of each topic to the page. The ith element in the vector represents the relevancy assigned to the ith topic. Let H is the set of all pages in the site, $\forall h_i \in H$, there is a n-dimensional vector denoted as $T_i = < t_{i1}, \ldots, t_{in} >$, where t_{ij} represents the relevancy of the jth topic to the page h_i. The similarity between page h_i and page h_j can be measured by the *cosine* of the angle between their topic vectors which is calculated by:
$cosine(T_i, T_j) = \frac{T_i \cdot T_j}{\|T_i\|_2 \times \|T_j\|_2}$.

For the Web site of the Centre for Information Technology Innovation, there are 19 topics. For simplicity, we use 1 or 0 to weight the topics in the topic vectors involved. Table 3.2 gives the topic vectors of each page in the log segment shown in Table 2.1. A 10×10 similarity matrix, as given in Table 3.3, can be produced in terms of the pairwise *consine* value of each pair of pages. In this paper, we use a simple combination of the two measurements, as described below, to measure the similarity of two pages, where $0 \leq \alpha \leq 1$.

$$sim(i, j) = (1 - \alpha) * p(i, j) + \alpha * cosine(T_i, T_j) \qquad (3.1)$$

Table 3.2.   Topic Vectors of the pages requested in the log segment in Table 2.1

Page	Topic Vector
A1	1 1 1 1 1 1 1 1 1 1 1 1 1 1 1 1 1 1 1
A2	0 0 0 0 0 0 1 0 0 0 0 0 0 0 0 0 0 0 0
A3	0 0 0 0 0 1 0 1 0 0 0 0 0 0 0 0 0 0 0
A4	0 0 0 0 0 0 1 1 0 0 0 0 0 0 0 0 0 0 0
A5	0 0 0 0 0 0 0 1 0 0 0 0 0 1 0 0 0 0 0
A6	0 0 0 0 0 0 0 0 0 0 1 0 0 0 0 0 0 0 0
A7	0 0 0 0 0 0 0 0 0 0 0 0 0 0 1 0 0 0 0
A8	0 0 0 0 0 0 0 0 0 0 0 0 0 0 1 0 0 0 0
A9	0 0 0 0 0 0 0 0 0 0 1 0 0 0 0 0 0 0 0
A10	0 0 0 1 0 0 0 0 0 0 1 0 0 0 0 0 0 0 0

3.2   Fuzzy Clustering

Let $X = \{x_1, \ldots, x_n\}$ be a set of given data. For a given constant c, $2 \leq c \leq n$, the data set is to be partitioned into c clusters. Assume $U = [u_{ij}]$ is the membership degree with which the data point x_j belongs to the cluster i and

Table 3.3.   Content similarity matrix obtained from the log in Table 2.1

	A1	A2	A3	A4	A5	A6	A7	A8	A9	A10
A1	1	0.33	0.24	0.41	0.33	0.24	0.24	0.24	0.24	0.33
A2	0.33	1	0.71	0.41	0.5	0	0	0	0	0
A3	0.24	0.71	1	0	0.71	0	0	0	0	0
A4	0.41	0.41	0	1	0.41	0	0	0	0	0
A5	0.33	0.5	0.71	0.41	1	0	0	0	0	0
A6	0.24	0	0	0	0	1	0	0	1	0.71
A7	0.24	0	0	0	0	0	1	1	0	0
A8	0.24	0	0	0	0	0	1	1	0	0
A9	0.24	0	0	0	0	1	0	0	1	0.71
A10	0.33	0	0	0	0	0.71	0	0	0.71	1

$\mathbf{R} = [r_{ij}]$ is the relational data corresponding to pairwise distances between data points, where $r_{ij} = \|x_i - x_j\|^2$ and $\| \cdot \|$ is any inner product induced norm. Hathaway et al. [4] have proved that the squared Euclidean distance, $d_{ik}^2 = \|x_k - v_i\|^2$, from feature vector x_k to the center of the ith cluster, c_i, can be written in terms of the relation matrix $\mathbf{R}$ as $d_{ik}^2 = (\mathbf{R}v_i)_k - v_i\mathbf{R}v_i/2$, where v_i is the ith cluster center defined by $v_i = \frac{(u_{i1}^m,...,u_{in}^m)^t}{\sum_{j=1}^n u_{ij}^m}$. where $m > 1$. For a pre-defined relatively large value $c = c_{max}$, the CARD algorithm [8] starts by partitioning the data set into c clusters. As the algorithm progresses, in each iteration after the membership values u_{ik} is updated, the clusters whose cardinality N_i as defined below is less than a threshold whill be discarded, and thus the number of clusters is reduced.

The CARD algorithm is described as follows (see [8] for details).

1 Given relational data $\mathbf{R} = [r_{ij}]$. Choose a value for $\eta_0, \tau, \rho, \epsilon$, and c_{max}, generate randomly the membership matrix U^0 which determines a fuzzy c-partition, and set iteration number $t = 0$.

2 Calculate the cluster centers $v_i^{(t)}$ $(i = 1, \ldots, c)$ using $v_i = \frac{(u_{i1}^m,...,u_{in}^m)^t}{\sum_{j=1}^n u_{ij}^m}$.

3 Update the membership values $u_{ik}^{(t+1)}$ by $u_{ik}^{(t+1)} = u_{ik}^{FCM} + u_{ik}^{Bias}$, where, $u_{ik}^{FCM} = [\sum_{j=1}^c (\frac{d_{ik}}{d_{jk}})^2]^{-1}$, $u_{ik}^{Bias} = \frac{\eta(t)(N_i - \overline{N}_k)}{d_{ik}^2}$, $N_i = \sum_{j=1}^n u_{ij}$, $\overline{N}_k = \frac{\sum_{j=1}^c (1/d_{jk}^2)N_j}{\sum_{j=1}^c (1/d_{jk}^2)}$, $\eta(t) = \eta_0 e^{-t/\tau}$, and d_{ik} is calculated by $d_{ik}^2 = (\mathbf{R}v_i)_k - v_i\mathbf{R}v_i/2$.

4 Calculate N_i, $i = 1, \ldots, c$. If $N_i < \rho$, remove the ith row from both $U^{(t+1)}$ and $U^{(t)}$, update $c = c - 1$.

5 If $\|U^{(t+1)} - U^{(t)}\| \le \epsilon$ or a predefined number of iterations is reached, stop, otherwise set t=t+1 and return to step 2.

4.   Session Pruning

In information theory, Shannon's measure of entropy is used as a measure of the information contained in a piece of data. For a random variable X with a set of possible values $< x_1, \ldots, x_n >$, having probabilities $p(x_i)$, $i = 1, \ldots, n$, if we had no information at all about the value X would be, the possibility for each value should be the same, i.e. $1/n$. In this case, X is in its most uncertain situation. According to information theory, the entropy of X reaches its maximum in this situation. On the other hand, if the entropy of X is close to zero, the value of X has few uncertainties. In this case, there should be a small set of values with high probabilities and others with very low probabilities. Based on this theory, we propose to use the entropies of topics to prune the sessions.

$\forall h_i \in H$, its topic vector is $T_i =< t_{i1}, \ldots, t_{in} >$. Each topic can be treated as a random variable with two possible values: involved or not involved. The information entropy of topic t_j to page h_i can be estimated by $H(t_{ij}) = -(p(t_{ij})logp(t_{ij}) + (1 - p(t_{ij}))log(1 - p(t_{ij})))$, where $p(t_{ij})$ is the probability of t_j being involved in h_i. Let $s_i =< h_{i1}, \ldots, h_{ir} >$ be a session, $T_{ij} =< t_{ij_1}, \ldots, t_{ij_n} >$ be the topic vector of page h_{ij} with $1 \le j \le r$, $T_{s_i} =< t_{s_i1}, \ldots, t_{s_in} >$ be the topic vector of s_i, and $p(t_{ij_k})$ is the probability of the kth topic being involved in h_{ij}. The probability of the kth topic being involved in s_i denoted as $p(t_{s_ik})$ $(1 \le k \le n)$ can be calculated by $\frac{\Sigma_{j=1}^{j=r}p(t_{ij_k})}{r}$, and the information entropy of topic t_j to s_i can be estimated by $H(t_{s_ij}) = -(p(t_{s_ij})logp(t_{s_ij}) + (1 - p(t_{s_ij}))log(1 - p(t_{s_ij})))$.

The average entropy of all topics to the session can be calculated by the following equation:

$$H(s_i) = H(t_{s_i1}, \ldots, t_{s_in}) = (\Sigma_{k=1}^{k=n}H(t_{s_ik}))/n \qquad (4.1)$$

The entropy of a session estimates the certainty of the topics involved in the session. If the entropy is small, then there must be some topics with high probabilities and the others with very low probabilities. It means that the page contents in this session focus on a few topics which clearly exhibit the user's information needs. On the other hand, if the entropy is large, then the probabilities of the topics must be very close and low as well. In this case, it is hard to identify the user's information needs since the pages in this session involve many topics. In this paper, we use the average entropy calculated by Equation (4.1) to prune away sessions that have high entropy. Table 4.1 shows the entropies of the sessions in Table 2.2. The entropy of the first session in the table is higher than the other two sessions. The high entropy of the first session is caused by page A_1 which is the home page of the Web site. Because

A_1 involves many topics (see Table 3.2), it actually provides little information about the visitor's particular information needs. The sessions with high entropy value will be discarded, e.g. the first session in Table 4.1. Table 4.2 gives the clutering results to the original sessions in Table 2.2 and the set of pruned sessions as well. The results show that the entropy of the clusters of the pruned sessions is less than that of the original sessions. It also shows that the entropy is reduced when the page contents are used to evaluate the similarity among pages.

Table 4.1. Sessions and their entropies

User Sessions	Sesion Entropies
$A_1 \rightarrow A_2 \rightarrow A_3 \rightarrow A_4 \rightarrow A_5$	0.53
$A_2 \rightarrow A_3 \rightarrow A_4 \rightarrow A_6$	0.17
$A_7 \rightarrow A_8 \rightarrow A_9 \rightarrow A_{10}$	0.11

Table 4.2. Clustering results using ($\alpha = 0.5$) and without using ($\alpha = 0$) page contents

		$\alpha= 0$			$\alpha=0.5$	
		Clusters	Entropy		Clusters	Entropy
Original sessions	1	A_1: /index.jsp A_6: /research/sdl/researchers.jsp A_4: /research/sdl/projects/index.jsp A_2: /research/index.jsp A_3: /research/sdl/index.jsp A_5: /research/sdl/robotsoccer.jsp	0.24	1	A_1: /index.jsp A_4: /research/sdl/projects/index.jsp A_2: /research/index.jsp A_3: /research/sdl/index.jsp A_5: /research/sdl/robotsoccer.jsp	0.19
	2	A_9: /people/index.jsp A_{10}: /people/students.jsp A_7: /pubs/index.jsp A_8: /pubs/2002.jsp		2	A_9:/people/index.jsp A_6: /research/sdl/researchers.jsp A_{10}: /people/students.jsp	
				3	A_7: /pubs/index.jsp A_8: /pubs/2002.jsp	
Pruned sessions	1	A_6:/research/sdl/researchers.jsp A_4: /research/sdl/projects/index.jsp A_2: /research/index.jsp A_3: /research/sdl/index.jsp	0.14	1	A_4: /research/sdl/projects/index.jsp A_2: /research/index.jsp A_3:/research/sdl/index.jsp	0.06
	2	A_9: /people/index.jsp A_{10}: /people/students.jsp A_7:/pubs/index.jsp A_8: /pubs/2002.jsp		2	A_9: /people/index.jsp A_6: /research/sdl/researchers.jsp A_{10}: /people/students.jsp	
				3	A_7: /pubs/index.jsp A_8: /pubs/2002.jsp	

Some experiments have been conducted to test the improvement of Web page clustering by using page contents. In the experiments, a cluster was discarded if its cardinality (N_i) was less than $\rho = 3$. The experimental detail was omitted due to the space limit.

5.   Conclusion

Most existing web mining techniques for finding user navigation patterns are access-based approaches that statistically analyze the log data and do not pay much attention on the content of the pages. In this paper we have proposed an approach that takes the page contents into account to find out page clusters. The proposed method prunes away the sessions that involve irrelevant topics by using session entropy which is based on well-established Information Theory. After the pruning, the quality of the clustering is improved since the impact of irrelevant papges has been weakened. There are potentialities of using the user clusters in at least two contexts. On the one hand, the user clusters can be used to assist web users with navigating large web sites by recommending relevant pages that are classified in the category which the user belongs to. On the other hand, the user clusters provide information for the web site desinger to better understand the user needs and how the users visit the site. As a result, the contents or the organization of the web site can be improved to meet the user needs.

References

[1] J. Bezdek. *Pattern Recognition with Fuzzy Objective Function Algorithms*. Plenum Press, New York, 1981.

[2] J. Borges and M. Levene. Data mining of user navigation patterms. In *Proceedings of the Web Usage Analysis and User Profiling*, volume 1, pages 31–36, 1999.

[3] G. Frigui and R. Krishnapuram. Clustering by competivive agglomeration. *Pattern Recognition*, 30(7):1109–1119, 1997.

[4] R. J. Hathaway, J. W. Devenport, and J. C. Bezdek. Relational dual of the c-means clustering algorithms. *Pattern Recognition*, 22(2):205–212, 1989.

[5] R. Kruse, F. Hoppner, F. Klawonn, and T. Runkler. *Fuzzy Cluster Anallysis*. John Wiley and Sons, 1999.

[6] G. Linden, B. Smith, and J. York. Amazon.com recommendations: item-to-item collaborative filtering. *Internet Computing*, 7(1):76–80, 2003.

[7] B. Mobasher. *Web Usage Mining and Personalization (Chapter one in book Practical Handbook ofInternet Computing)*. CRC Press LLC, to appear in 2004.

[8] Nasraoui O., H. Frigui, A. Joshi, and R. Krishnapuram. Mining web access logs using relational competitive fuzzy clustering. In *Proceedings of the Eight International Fuzzy Systems Association World Congress*, volume 1, pages 195–204, 1999.

[9] M. Perkowitz and O. Etzioni. Towards adaptive web sites: Conceptual framework and case study. *Artificial Intelligence*, 118:245 – 275, 2000.

A PREDICTION APPROACH TO WELL LOGGING

Qing He[1], Ping Luo[1], Zhong-Zhi Shi[1], Yalei Hao[2] and Markus Stumptner[2]

1.The Key Laboratory of Intelligent Information Processing,Institute of Computing Technology, Chinese Academy of Sciences, Beijing, 100080)

2. Advanced Computing Research Centre, University of South Australia, SA5095, Australia

Abstract: How to provide a means or organize the information used in making exploration decisions in petroleum exploration is an important task. In this paper, a machine learning method is put forward to collect experiences and estimate or prediction the absent data. The well logging experiments show that the method is efficiently and accurately.

Key words: hyper surface, petroleum exploration，well logging

1.   INTRODUCTION

According to the Encyclopedia Britannica, around 547 billion barrels of petroleum remain undiscovered on Earth (plus known reserves of 1,119 billion barrels). Experts estimate we will run out of petroleum in 50 years at the current rate of consumption, around 60 million barrels per day. These facts drive the highly competitive oil companies to make their exploration more efficient.

How to provide a means or organize information used in making exploration decisions in petroleum exploration is an important task. An explorationist, who must recommend the wildcat well location and the payzone for the well, is making a decision which might cost a company millions of dollars. Thus, one who is able to assimilate and use the greatest amount of data is making a more informed decision.

Data about a potential petroleum-bearing area, i.e., a payzone, are obtained from various quantitative sources such as seismic instruments and well loggings and outcrop data, field notes, and maps. Large computer programs for analyzing numeric data already exist. The petroleum industry is today the largest industrial user of supercomputers. These programs provide the best quantitative data about the payzone. Those results, together with all of the other data collected about a payzone fill corporate database. Unfortunately, the amount of data is so great and diverse that it is not always accessible for the purpose of the payzone analysis in a reasonable amount of time. Before making a recommendation concerning the drilling target for oil or gas, the explorationist must "interpret" the data, i.e., making an analysis of its potential to produce oil or gas. At this point the experienced petroleum explorationist is at an advantage because he has interpreted other payzones. He draws very strongly upon his knowledge of other payzones, drawing as many as possible from his background. Moreover, these data has two inherent problems due to the amount and the nature of data available to the explorationst, leading to the difficulty in attempting to interpret a payzone. Firstly, data sets can easily reach 10 to 20 gigabytes and larger. Secondly, until recently, no one had a standard and comprehensive way to see the information. Therefore, no one could exploit the data's full value. For example, 3D seismic data reservoirs are characterized by 20 to 30 variables. It is very difficult to comprehend the data. For some payzones the corporate database overflow with data, and in others very little data are available. Sometimes data conflict and the explorationist must decide which data he believes to be of higher quality. Decisions are often made on the basis of incomplete and inaccurate data of dubious quality.

Classification method can be used for analysis well logging data. There are many classification methods have been studied in the past. Vapnik and his research group have studied machine learning based on finite samples since sixtieths in the last century. A complete theory, Statistical Learning Theory, has been established (see ref. 1-5). Moreover, a new universal learning algorithm SVM, Support Vector Machine, has been developed. It is an especially efficient classification algorithm for finite samples, nonlinear and high dimension data. The main idea of SVM is mapping the nonlinear data to a higher dimension linear space where the data can be linear classified by hyper plane. The mapping is a nonlinear mapping defined by inner product function. So a lot of repeat computations of inner product for m-matrices cannot be avoided, where m is the number of samples. It is almost impossible to classify large data more than 4000 samples by using PC (see ref. 6).

In fact, SVM maps the data into higher dimension linear space in which the data can be separated by a hyper plane. It is show that SVM is an indirectly method to solving nonlinear problem.

It is an important problem how to find a classification method, which has neither increasing dimension mapping nor computing a large matrix product. In paper (see ref. 7), a novel classification method based on hypersurface is put forward to solve the problem. Jordan Curve Theorem is the theoretic base of classification method based on hyper surface.

The next sections are arranged as following:

Section 2 introduces HSC i.e. classification method based on hypersurface, and put forward a prediction method. Section 3 put forward a method to display the petroleum data based hypersurface. Section 4 put forward a data prediction method and give some results of well logging experiments. Finally, section 4 contains the conclusions.

2.   THE PREDICTION METHOD

The Jordan Curve Theorem. Let X be a closed set in R^3. If X is homeomorphism to a sphere S^2, then its complement $R^3 \setminus X$ has two connected components, one bounded, the other unbounded. Any neighborhood of any point on X meets both of these components (see ref. 8).

The Jordan Curve Theorem shows that any 2D closed surface obtained from sphere by conscious transform separates three dimension space into two regions, one called inside, and the other is called outside. The surface can be used to classify data. This kind of surface is called hyper surface. For any given point, how to determine it is inside or outside about the hyper surface is the first important problem.

Classification Theorem. Let X be a closed set in R^3. If X is a homeomorphism to a sphere S^2, then its complement $R^3 \setminus X$ has two connected components, one called inside, the other called outside. For any $x \in R^3 \setminus X$, then the point x is inside of $X \Leftrightarrow$ the intersecting number between any radial from x and X is odd; x is outside of $X \Leftrightarrow$ the intersecting number between any radial from x and X is even.

Theorem   (Jordan Curve Theorem in High Dimension Space) .Suppose that $X \subset S^n$ is homeomorphism to a sphere S^m, then $m \leq n$, otherwise $X = S^n$ .If $m < n$, then the homology group of $S^n \setminus X$ is

$$H_k(S^n \setminus X)$$

$$\cong \begin{cases} Z \oplus Z, \text{ if } m = n - 1 \text{ and } k = 0, \\ Z, \text{ if } m < n - 1 \text{ and } k = 0, \\ 0, \text{ otherwise.} \end{cases}$$

Specially, if $m = n - 1$, then $S^n \setminus X$ composed by two connected components, and if $m < n - 1$, then there exists only one connected component.

Based on the Jordan Curve Theorem, space can be separated by a two-sided surface that is a homeomorphism to a sphere. The separating hyper surface may be consisting of many hyper surfaces. For any given point, how to decide whether it is inside of the separating or outside depend on that the intersecting number between the separating hyper surface and the radial from the point is odd or even. This classification method is a direct and convenient method. But how to construct the separating hyper surface is an important problem. Based on the Jordan Curve Theorem, we put forward HSC, i.e. classification method based on separating hyper surfaces in ref. 7.

Step1. Find a rectangle region that includes all samples.

Step2. Divide the region into some smaller regions, which only contain at most one sample.

Step3. Label each region according the inside sample's class. Then the frontier vectors and the class vector form a link.

Step4. Combine the same class connected region and obtain a separating hyper surface then saved it as a link.

Step5. Input a new sample and calculate the intersecting number of separating hyper surfaces for the sample. Draw a radial from the sample. Then according to whether the intersecting number between the radial and the separating hyper surface is even or odd, the class of the sample is decided.

Note: If there are different training samples in the same unit then divide the lattice again by unit lattices and do the same things as step 1 until all samples have been used. So a hyper surface formed and denoted by a string. This is called local elaborate strategy.

Suppose that there are d condition attributes and m values about some decision attribute given by the explorationist or obtained from experiment data such as well logging. To learn and collect the explorationist's experiences included in the data, we think that the data samples belong to m classes. The following training algorithm is put forward.

Step1. Input m classes' training samples. Let the training samples be distributed in the rectangle region.

Step2. Transform the region into unit region.

Step3. Divide the region into 10^d equal small regions.

Step4. Label the small regions by 1, 2......m according to the inside samples' class.

Step5. Remerge the frontiers of the same class regions in where is the same class then save it as a link table.

Step6. For any regions where there are training samples from different classes in the same unit, go to Step2.

Step7. Repeat the above until there is no region where there are different classes.

At the end, some separating hyper surfaces, which are described by the link tables, are obtained.

After learning from the training sample, the explorationist's classification experience is collected in the hyper surface, i.e. link table. Using hyper surface the absent data can be estimated or predicted from data such as well logging. The steps are as following.

Step1. Input a testing sample and make a radial from the sample.

Step2. Input all link tables of class k (k = 1,2,3......, m) obtained by the above training algorithm.

Step3. Count the intersecting number of the sample with the above link table.

Step4. If the intersecting number of the sample with the above link tables is odd then label the sample by k. It is mean that the prediction value is the th decision value, otherwise go to next step.

Step5. Input all link tables of class k +1 obtained by the above training algorithm. Do step3-4 until $k = m$.

Step6. Calculate the classifying accuracy rate.

This is a universal prediction method for large nonlinear data bases. In fact, For large data sets (10^7) (see Table 1 and Table 2), the speed of HSC is very fast. The reason is that the time of saving and extracting hyper surfaces is very short and the need for storage is very little, which is not the advantage of SVM. Another reason is that the decision process is very easy by using the Jordan Curve Theorem.

Table 1. Training results

Training Samples	Training Time	Recall Time	The Rate of Recall (%)
3,314	1s	2s	100.00
6,677	3s	4s	100.00
9,525	4s	7s	100.00
9,530	6s	7s	100.00
17,919	8s	12s	100.00
43,217	18s	31s	100.00
106,344	48s	1m 17s	100.00
1,053,125	9m 0s	12m 29s	100.00

Table 2. Testing results

Training Samples	Testing Samples	Testing Time	Precision of Prediction（%）
4,735	17,919	12s	99.29
9530	85189	1m	99.89
9,525	17,919	13s	100.00
9,525	43,217	30s	100.00
9,525	106,344	1m 14s	100.00
9,525	1,053,125	12m 19s	100.00

The experiment results in Table 2 of training on small scale samples and testing on large scale show that HSC has strong ability of generalization. If the scale of unit is too small then the hyper space may be separated into two parts. In a region with scattered samples, big unit is required, on the contrast at the region with highly sample density small unit is required. But the samples are not always uniformly distributed. So the locally decided elaborate division is an important strategy. The local division strategy improves the generalization ability and accuracy.

3.   DISPLAY AND PREDICT THE DISTRIBUTION OF OIL/GAS

After explorationists interpret the data from wildcat wells in a certain field, they may point out which well may be drilled out oil or gas and which well may not be drilled oil or gas. The critical problem is how to organize the decision information and apply the decision information to predict other point where no well has been drilled? HSC can help us do this.

HSC can solve the nonlinear classification problem which the samples distribute in any shape in a finite region. The method has nothing to do with the distribution of the data, even though the shape is interlock or crisscross. This advantage makes it useful for petroleum data. Figure 1 shows a slice of oil / gas distribution simulation data for a certain formation. Let isotropic homogeneity of the oil / gas field, it was created by our algorithm based on the wildcat data and regional petroleum geologic background. The domain marked blue represents domain where oil or gas may be drilled out. On the contrary, the domain marked red represents domain where no petroleum may be drilled out. HSC can obtain two hypersurface as shown in Figure 2. The hypersurface can be used to predict whether or not oil or gas exists at certain other points where no well exists.

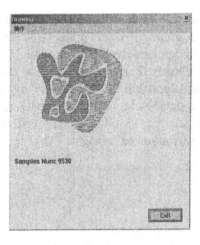

Figure 1. A Slice of Distribution of Petroleum

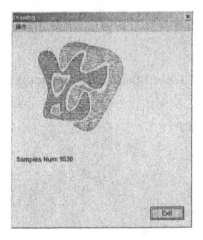

Figure 2. Hypersurface

4.   PREDICTION OF ABSENT DATA

Consider the sample data from Figure 3. They are described by $(x, y, z) =$ (DEPTH, GR, AC) and DEN which are four kinds of data from well logging. DEPTH is the well depth, GR is natural gamma, AC is acoustic wave time difference, and DEN is density. Now there are 4903 records or data samples about the above four attributes from one prospect, as shown in Figure 4. But only 4408 records are complete, the others lack DEN data. DEN is an important value in petroleum exploitation. DEN data range from $1.0g/cm^3$ to $3.5\ g/cm^3$. How to predict the absent DEN values is a problem. The problem can be solved by using HSC. The first, we divide the DEN values into 30 classes. The Second, training the above complete data by using the training algorithm. Obtaining the hypersurface as shown in Figure 4 the absent data's class can be predicted. So the DEN value corresponding to the class is decided. In this test correct rate is 94.80%. Figure 3 shows the distribution of samples.

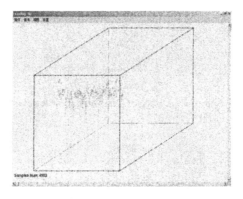

Figure 3. The Distribution of Samples

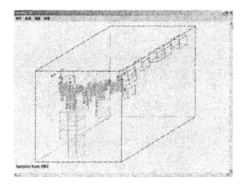

Figure 4. Prediction Hypersurface

5.   CONCLUSIONS

In this paper, a prediction method HSC is put forward to collect explorationist's experiences and estimate or prediction the absent data. The well logging experiments show that the new method is efficiently and accurately. The method has the following advantages.

1) High efficient and accuracy;

2) Strong ability of prediction;

3) Robustness, i.e. data noise can be controlled in a local region;

4) Independent on sample feature;

5) Multi-values prediction.

Because of these properties, HSC is useful for predicting the distribution of petroleum and absent data.

ACKNOWLEDGEMENTS

This work is supported by the National Science Foundation of China (No.60173017, 90104021), the 863 Project (No.2003AA115220) and China-Australia Special Fund for S&T Cooperation.

REFERENCES

1. Vapnik V. N. Support Vector Method for Function Approximation, Regression Estimation and Signal Processing. Neural Information Processing Systems, Vol.9. MIT Press, Cambridge, MA.
2. Vapnik V. N. The Nature of Statistical Learning Theory. New York: Springer-Verlag, 1995.
3. Vapnik V N.,Levin E,Le Cun Y.Mearsuring the VC-Dimension of learning machine. Neural Computation,1994,6:851-876.
4. Vapnik V. N. Statistical Learning Theory, J. Wiley, New York, 1998.
5. Burges C J C. A tutorial on support vector machines for pattern recognition. Data Mining and Knowledge Discovery, 1998, 2(2).
6. Schokopf,B.,Burges,J.C.,Smola,A.J. Advances in Kernel Methods Support Vector Learning. Cambridge, MA: MIT Press, 1999.
7. Qing He, Zhong-Zhi Shi, Li-An Ren, E. S. Lee. A Novel Classification Method Based on Hyper Surface. International Journal of Mathematical and Computer Modeling,38(2003),395-407
8. William Fulton, Algebraic Topology A First Course, Springer-Verlag 1995.

Author Index